HOLLAND PARK SCHOOL

A place of scholarship; determinedly academic with outstanding A level and GCSE results.

A place of ambition, endeavour, drive and creativity, with outstanding success in placing students in top flight universities.

A place of self-effacing confidence.

A place to find oneself and he

A place where the potency of   prowess embraces the human beating heart.

A place which believes that lives and futures can be altered and that chance can be marginalised.

An Ofsted outstanding and DfE designated teaching school.

HEAD: Colin Hall | ASSOCIATE HEAD: David Chappell

AIRLIE GARDENS, CAMPDEN HILL ROAD, LONDON W8 7AF
www.hollandparkschool.co.uk | admissions@hollandparkschool.co.uk

Need more info?
Visit us online...

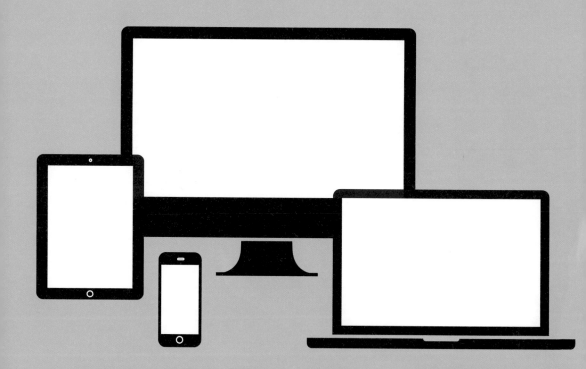

The Good Schools Guide website, now available on all digital devices. Access exam data, catchment area maps, special needs specifics and the latest news and opinion at home or on the go.

Visit **www.goodschoolsguide.co.uk** and try our interactive school search today

THE
GOOD
SCHOOLS
GUIDE

London South

www.goodschoolsguide.co.uk

The Good Schools Guide is a registered trademark

Second Edition published 2016 by Lucas Publishing Ltd
Address Good Schools Guide, 10 Greycoat Place, London SW1P 1SB
Website www.goodschoolsguide.co.uk
ISBN 978-1-909963-06-1 The Good Schools Guide London South 2nd edition
Copyright (c) 2016, Lucas Publications Ltd
Printed by Cambrian Printers Ltd

Acknowledgments

Writers

Beth Noakes
Carolyn Murphy
Carolyn Thomas
Charlotte Phillips
Emma Jones
Emma Vickers
Grace Moody-Stuart
Jackie Lixenberg
Janet Breeze
Janette Wallis
Judith French
Mary Langford
Melanie Bloxham
Ralph Lucas
Sandra Hutchinson
Sophie Irwin
Sue Fieldman
Susan Hamlyn

Design: David Preston, Harriet Plyler

Typesetting: Theresa Hare, Optima Information Design

Editorial review by Beth Noakes and team: Janita Clamp, Emma Lee-Potter, Charlotte Phillips, Kathryn Berger, Amanda Perkins

Advertising sales by Charlotte Hollingshead assisted by Jo Dodds, Publishing Matters

Web manager: Anthony Back

Project management: Katja Lips

Everything held together by: Shari Lord

Junior League of London for excerpts from *Living in London: A Practical Guide*

Photography: Thanks to all the schools who responded to our requests for photographs. Additional photography by Hannah Palmer and Laura Radford

Thanks to these schools for their cover photos:
Latchmere School
Putney High School
Haberdashers' Aske's Hatcham College
Broomwood Hall School (Nightingale Lane)
Reay Primary School
Cumnor House School For Girls
Sutton High Junior School

BROMLEY
HIGH
SCHOOL

EXCEPTIONAL EDUCATION FOR GIRLS
4-18 YEARS SINCE 1883

Fees assistance & Scholarships available in the Senior School

Tel: 020 8781 7000

admissions@bro.gdst.net **www.bromleyhigh.gdst.net**

Contents

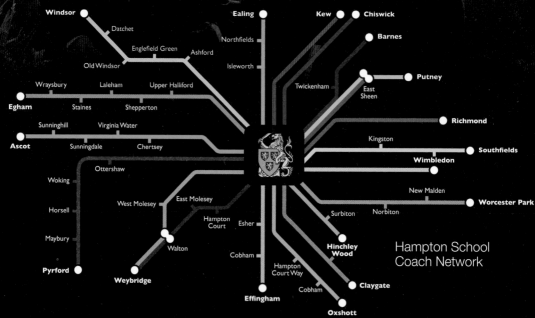

How to use this book

The age range of a school is indicated by the colour assigned to the title bar.

Junior School

Senior School

The circular symbols found within the title bars indicate the following school characterics:

 Girls' school

 Boys' school

 Co-ed school

 Boys' school with co-ed sixth form

 Girls' school with co-ed sixth form

 Co-ed pre-prep, then boys only

 Co-ed pre-prep, then girls only

 State school

 Independent school

 Boarding available

'Weekly boarding at Headington is the best of both worlds - you can spend the week at school with all your friends and take part in so many activities. Then you get to relax at the weekend with your family. I love it.'

Weekly boarder, aged 13

HEADINGTON
SCHOOL · OXFORD

'EXCELLENT' IN ALL CATEGORIES, ISI INSPECTION, MAY 2015

Successful day and boarding school for girls aged 3-18 set in 23 acres in the heart of Oxford

- Dance and Fitness Centre new for 2015

- 240-seat Theatre, Music School and Art School

- All weather sports pitches and swimming pool

- New Library and class room suite for 2016

Termly Open Days and Meet the Head events

www.headington.org/admissions

Headington School is a leading educational charity.
Registered Charity No. 309678 (1942)

London South map

Hertfordshire

For schools north of the river see
The Good Schools Guide: London North

SOUTHWARK

RICHMOND
UPON
THAMES

WANDSWORTH

LAMBETH

LEWISHAM

MERTON

KINGSTON
UPON THAMES

BROMLEY

SUTTON

CROYDON

Surrey

Essex

GREENWICH

BEXLEY

Kent

CENTRAL SOUTH 45

Lambeth
Southwark
Wandsworth

SOUTH WEST 171

Kingston-Upon-Thames
Merton
Richmond-Upon-Thames
Sutton

SOUTH EAST 289

Bexley
Bromley
Croydon
Greenwich
Lewisham

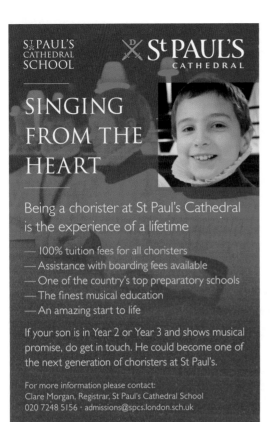

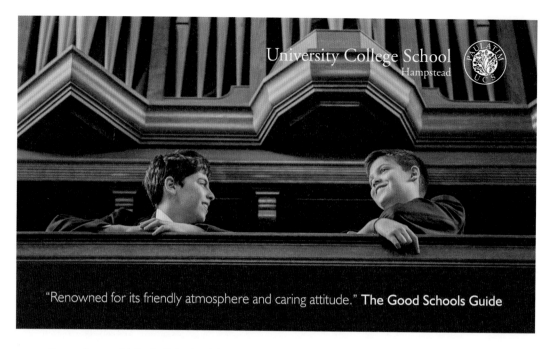

Introduction

Welcome to the second edition of the Good Schools Guide to London South. We offer you our knowledge, inside information, experience and opinions on what parents tell us are the capital's best schools north of the Thames.

In the first edition we reported on the shortage of primary school places that affects London probably more than anywhere else in Britain. This year the problem has spread to secondary schools, with fewer than seven in ten families getting their first choice throughout London, whilst some inner London authorities, such as Wandsworth offered first choice places to less than 60 per cent of applicants. In Bexley, on the other hand, nearly 78 per cent got their first choice.

One in four families is reported to have moved house or changed address to get a school place, with London parents paying a high premium for house near a favoured school, and many admitting to buying or renting a second home in a popular catchment area – to the chagrin of those who have lived there for years and find that their child has lost out on a place. Many south London authorities are tightening up on their admissions policies, but some inevitably slip through the net.

Certainly many free schools are springing up and new academies opening – but with local authorities being unable to open new schools, despite being responsible for providing places, the match between demand and supply is chequered at best. Less than 20 per cent of free secondary schools open in areas with severe shortages of school places, and overall a quarter of places in free schools are unfilled when they open. In London, particularly, some free schools are cancelled for lack of demand, or difficulty in finding a site: a proposed new school in Norbury was one of the latest to be scrapped. Others, such as the West London Free School, languish in 'temporary' accommodation for many years.

With the government promising 500 new free schools

over the next five years, evidently a vast proportion of education spending – which is liable to shrink in real terms – will be aimed in this direction, with £45 million spent on one central London sixth form. Whilst some free schools contribute a welcome diversity to the local education landscape – offering bi-lingual primary teaching, for example, or a sixth form specialising in maths and physics – others can best be described as niche.

Meanwhile, in the independent sector, four-fold fee rises in the last 20 years or so have resulted in some private schools becoming increasingly the preserve of children of hedge fund managers and the international super-rich. The doctors, accountants and solicitors who would once have sent their children to private school now tend to form queues outside the grammars and successful comprehensives.

The good news? London's schools – both state and independent – have never been so popular. London state schools are some of the best in the country, and although we can review only a small proportion, we give a rundown of the most successful primary and secondary state schools in each London borough.

The increasingly diverse London population is helping to raise standards in its schools, as aspirational parents pass on their ambitions to their children. Pupils who learn and play harmoniously together are a model for the wider world.

This guide celebrates the popularity and achievements of London schools. We describe local areas and their schools, and invite you to let us know about your own experiences. Join us in keeping up the pressure on authorities and educationalists to keep on raising standards, for the future of our children.

GSG Charter

No school can pay to be included in (or choose to be excluded from) The Good Schools Guide, and we do not charge schools for reviews.

In recent years we have helped to defray our costs by selling advertising space and licensing schools to reprint their own reviews for a fee. We make these offers only to schools that are already in the Guide on merit. Whether or not they choose to advertise has no bearing on their inclusion in the Guide nor on the content of their review. Schools we have not chosen for inclusion in the Guide are not allowed to advertise.

The Good Schools Guide Advice Service is a fee paying, personal consultancy service for parents. The Guide and our website also offer other advice on a vast range of education matters, free to subscribers. We receive no commission nor any other payment from any school for these services. We provide information on tutor companies on our website, and may charge these companies for carrying out a review, but they are only included after careful vetting.

We take our independence very seriously and the separation of commercial and editorial content is absolute. If you have any questions or concerns about our commercial policy, please write in the first instance to editor@ goodschoolsguide.co.uk.

· Our pupils are illuminated, inspired and independent ·

· We are proudly academic ·

· We believe Art, Music, Drama and Sport encourage our young people to flourish ·

· We are a community and family, not just a school that pursues results ·

· Our families love the full flexibility of our boarding ·

· Our stunning campus is just over an hour from London ·

The British education system

State schools

Many families head for London hoping for a place in a good local state school. There are huge advantages: at primary level in particular, your child's friends will almost all be local, you will soon feel part Tutors and tutoring in London page 415of the local community and you won't spend hours in a car trying to navigate London traffic or have to squeeze onto a rush hour tube or bus. Many London schools are used to young children arriving without fluent English and have systems in place to help. And of course they are free. At primary level you don't get the specialist teachers that many private preps employ, nor probably the level of facilities, but the quality of teaching at a good state school shouldn't be inferior (see Prep or primary? page 21). With a good comprehensive down the road, you are home and dry. However, state primaries don't prepare children for 11+ entrance exams, so if you are aiming at a selective secondary school you will probably have to rope in a tutor in year 5 or so (see Tutors and tutoring in London page 415).

Admissions

The tricky bit. Many families moving to London want to find a school before they commit to renting or buying a house. However, you won't be offered a state school place without proof of a local address.

Normal primary school admissions are at 3+ into the nursery or 4+ into the reception class (beware: getting a nursery place doesn't usually guarantee a reception class place; you will probably have to reapply). Some are divided into infant and junior schools, the latter starting at 7 years. Most secondary schools start at 11. For a normal application, you will need to apply – with a local address – by around mid-January for primary schools and the end of October of the year before entry for secondary schools, with some leeway for change

Secondary schools use various forms of selection, including ability, location or both

of address up till mid-December. Apply later, and you become a late applicant, probably joining the queue behind all those who applied on time (see Getting your child into a good state school page 29). NB selective grammar schools now set entrance tests in September, often with a closing date for applications in July of year 5 or even earlier.

Most state schools, primary and secondary, give preference to looked after children, those with specific medical or social needs, then siblings. Some schools have recently (and controversially) abandoned the priority given to siblings so this is something parents should double check. While no state primary school selects by ability or aptitude (except the London Oratory Junior House, which tests all applicants for general academic ability and musical aptitude), faith schools mostly give preference to regular church-goers. Secular primary schools give most of their places to those who live closest (which can, in many areas, mean more-or-less spitting distance).

Secondary schools are a mish-mash of various forms of selection, whether by ability, location or both. Secular comprehensives give most of their places to those who live closest. Academically selective grammar schools (NB many do not have 'grammar' in their name) range from those that offer places to the highest scorers in their entrance tests, regardless of where they live, to those that offer places only to local children. Some schools award a proportion of their places by 'aptitude'; some by church attendance; some use 'fair banding' to get a spread of ability. St Marylebone uses a combination of all three: 60 per cent of places are given to church-goers; it divides applicants into four ability bands, with equal offers to each band; and there are 12 'performing arts' places. For most, distance is the tie-breaker. The local authority will usually tell you how far the cut-off was for the previous year.

Independent schools

Many areas of London are well-equipped with prep schools. These are likely to have small classes, specialist teachers and a relatively biddable intake – if not the sports facilities you find in a country school. They also prepare your child for entrance exams to secondary schools, and advise on which are likely to be most suitable. Don't assume the teaching will be better than at a state school – both sectors include those who would be better off in a different profession. A prep school is judged at least partly by its leavers' destinations, so it will do its best to ensure your child moves on to a decent secondary school, even if it has to dampen down your expectations.

Prep schools generally don't care where you live, as long as you can pay the fees

A stand-alone pre-prep, that usually goes from age 3 to 7 years, may be a good bet if you are arriving in London at short notice. Some of the children who join at 3 may move on at 4 or 5, so places do come up. The disadvantage is that they are, inevitably, obliged to spend a significant part of the upper years preparing children for 7+ entrance exams.

Independent secondaries range from ferociously selective power-houses such as Westminster and St Paul's to those that provide a gentle haven from hothousing or social integration – with admissions policies to match. A glance at the league tables will give a clue as to the degree of selection they operate.

Admissions

Prep schools generally don't care where you live, as long as you can pay the fees. Many London preps give the illusion, at least, that if you don't sign your child up at birth you are too late. Some selective schools do close their waiting lists early, or have specific dates for registering; others operate on a first-come-first-served basis and do fill up on paper at least. However, it is always worth a phone call. London is a very mobile area and last-minute places come up at the most sought-after schools.

The thought of putting your 3 or 4 year old through a selection session or two may seem round the bend. Indeed, all-through schools (those with a senior school attached) that select this young rarely guarantee that a place at 4 will see you through into the senior school. Even those selected at 7 or 8 are sometimes weeded out at 11 or 13.

Nevertheless, your child may have to go through it. At 3, they may be asked to draw a picture, listen to a story and answer questions, cut out a circle, do a jigsaw, build a tower, match dominoes. Many schools send them out to play together, no doubt with an eye out to see who bites whom.

Selection at this age is not an exact science, and certainly does not mean your child is doomed to failure

Selection at this age is not an exact science, and certainly does not mean your child is doomed to failure because he didn't get a place at 3.

At 7, 8 and 11, most schools set maths and English exams, perhaps combined with reasoning tests. Many have previous papers on their websites. They will generally interview likely candidates and ask their previous school for a report, and may include some sort of group activity. Entry at 13 is getting more complicated, with increasing numbers of London schools setting pre-tests (generally maths, English and reasoning) in year 6 or 7. Those selected usually need to confirm their places by doing well in the Common Entrance exam (in a range of subjects) in year 8. This system is tricky to navigate if you are arriving with a child already in year 7 or 8, and you may need to track down one of the (dwindling number of) schools that don't use the pre-test system.

Many pupils change schools in the sixth form – whether

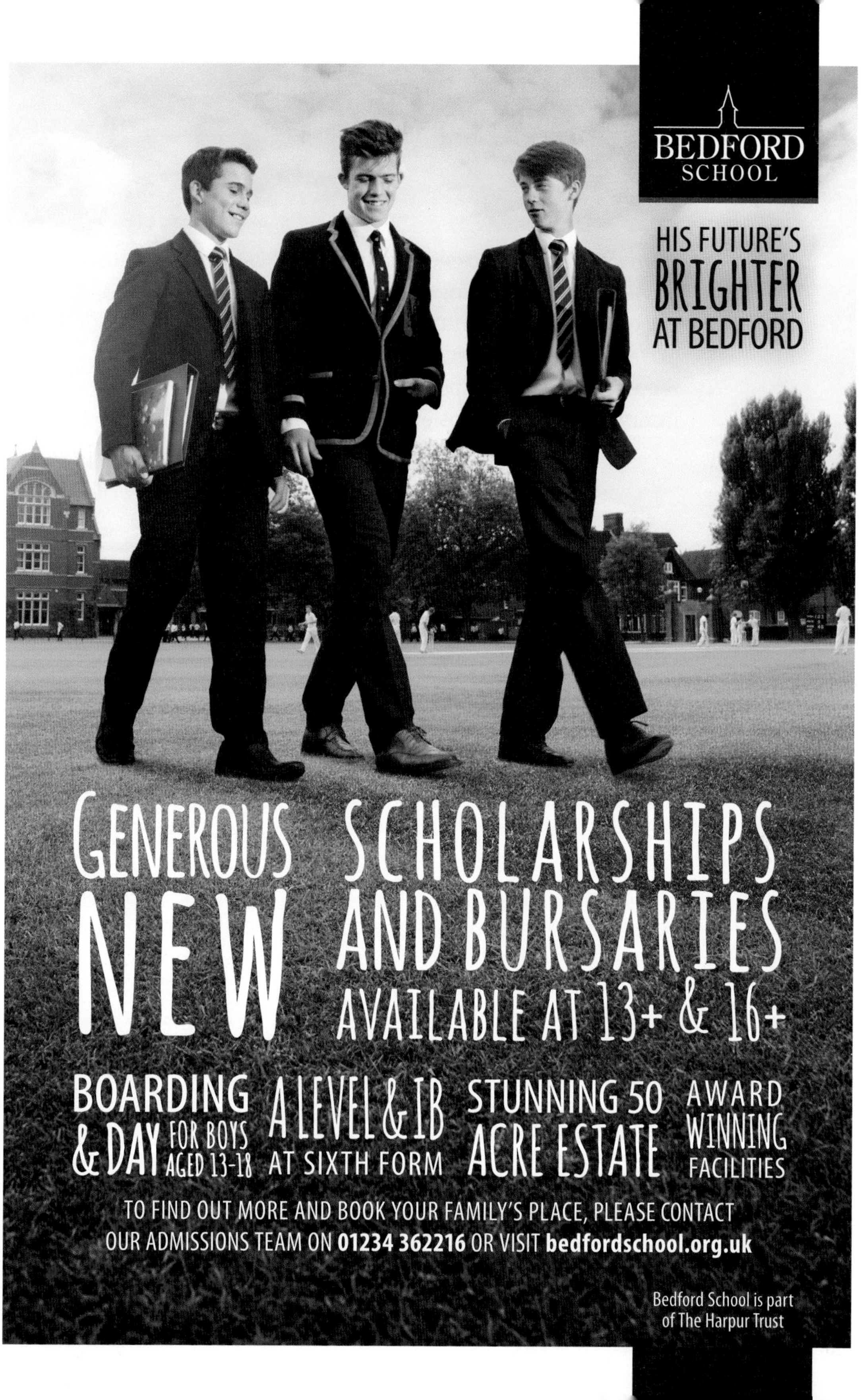
BEDFORD
SCHOOL
HIS FUTURE'S
BRIGHTER
AT BEDFORD
GENEROUS
NEW
SCHOLARSHIPS
AND BURSARIES
AVAILABLE AT 13+ & 16+
BOARDING
& DAY FOR BOYS AGED 13-18
A LEVEL & IB
AT SIXTH FORM
STUNNING 50
ACRE ESTATE
AWARD
WINNING
FACILITIES
TO FIND OUT MORE AND BOOK YOUR FAMILY'S PLACE, PLEASE CONTACT
OUR ADMISSIONS TEAM ON 01234 362216 OR VISIT bedfordschool.org.uk
Bedford School is part
of The Harpur Trust

from single sex to co-ed, boarding to day, state to private or vice versa. Some single sex schools admit pupils of the opposite gender into the sixth form. Both state and private schools almost always have some sort of entrance requirements at this point, generally involving GCSE grades, interviews and perhaps entrance exams.

Westminster Tutors

Est. 1934

A Level, GCSE and Retake courses

Oxbridge entrance and admissions tests

Top-flight tuition by highly qualified tutors

Very small groups or one-to-one

Average of 75% A*-B grades at A Level

Average of 50% progression to Russell Group

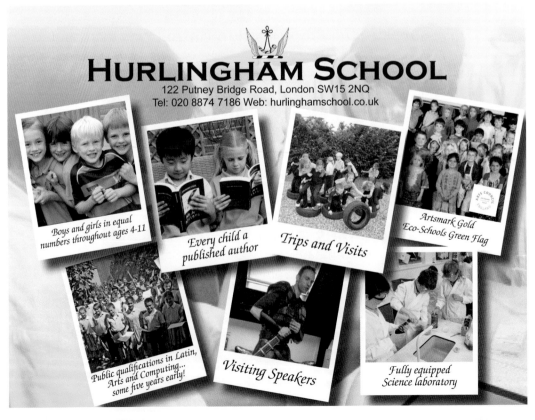

Prep or primary?

One of the questions most frequently asked of the Good Schools Guide Advice Service is, 'Should I send my child to a prep school or send him to the local primary and save the money for an independent senior school?'

This question is particular knotty for Londoners. While the standard of state schools in London is improving, the problems facing these schools are becoming more complex. Among them are shrinking budgets, growing pupil numbers and the fact that, increasingly, schools have to fund eg the needs of children with learning difficulties out of their existing budgets.

A primary school should be one to which all the children can walk so that your child's friends will be local

Primary

There are many excellent reasons for sending your child to the local primary – assuming, that it really is local. A primary school should be one to which all the children can walk so that your child's friends will be local – people to whose homes he can run round after school when he is old enough. You may find, if your children go to such a school, that your own circle of friends, well into later life, is still largely made up of those parents you met there. If your local school is well-run, the children are happy and the learning that goes on there is evident and interesting, then you are lucky and it would be hard to see why you would consider anything else.

However, not all state primaries offer such a start in life. Many are dilapidated, with transient populations of both pupils and staff. Discipline is lax, often because the parents do not back up the school, aspirations are low and energy levels – amongst the staff, the governors and the parent body – are insufficient to lift the school out of mediocrity. If that is your local school, you may, understandably, be looking for alternatives.

Prep

London prep schools are generally on the small side – though some have as many as 550 children. They always have smaller classes than city primaries and this is a particular draw for many families. They are exactly what they say they are, ie preparatory schools. Their reason for existing is to prepare children for senior schools – in most cases, for academically selective senior schools – and they stand or fall in a highly competitive market by their success in doing just that. A prep school which does not send its leavers in year 6 or year 8 to good selective schools will rapidly lose applicants.

Many people worry that if they don't get their child into a good prep at 4 or 7, they forfeit his chances of getting to a good academically selective – independent or state – senior school at 11 or 13. This is not the case.

The means by which senior schools assess children at 10, 11 or 13 have become very sophisticated. They are increasingly designed to identify children with natural innate ability. The modern computerised reasoning tests cannot be tutored for or even prepared for in any genuinely helpful way. Tutoring a child in English and maths is usually a good idea on educational grounds – all children improve if they have one-to-one time with good teacher – but even this, though it can help, cannot guarantee that a child of average ability will get through stringent entrance tests. Nor should it. Likewise, sending your child to a prep school from the age of 4, while he may have a lovely time in his small, orderly classes with good teaching and lots of sports, cannot guarantee that he will make it to a top London independent school.

Most London independent senior schools will take 50 per cent or more of their year 7 intake from the state sector. These academically selective schools are exactly what they

Most London independent senior schools will take 50 per cent or more of their year 7 intake from the state sector

say they are and it is the performance of your child in their subtly constructed tests which will, in the end, determine whether or not he gains a place.

Of course, tutoring or a prep school will help, but only in marginal cases will it tip the balance. And a child is done no favours by putting him into a fast-paced intellectual environment in which he will struggle from his first year and onwards – if he manages to stay. The schools are good at selecting those who will thrive in the academic atmosphere they offer, but we do get the occasional demoralised 13 or 14 year old who is struggling in a school where, through no fault of his own, he was always going to slip further and further behind. This can be demoralising and damaging for years to come.

Of course, tutoring or a prep school will help, but only in marginal cases will it tip the balance

State primary to independent senior

If your child is at a state primary he will not be prepared for entry to independent schools. That is not the job of state primaries – much though many parents wish it were. Consequently, it may well be that your child gets to year 5 or even 6 without ever having done a comprehension exercise to a time limit. To that extent, any state school child is at a disadvantage compared to a prep school child who will have been drilled and tested daily in order to give him the familiarity and practice he needs to tackle entrance tests.

This is when a tutor will help. A state primary child needs that little bit of extra help in doing maths and English tests to a time limit and having the support of an experienced and expert teacher will help to plug gaps, demystify problems and build confidence (see Tutors and tutoring in London page 415).

In general, a bright child from a state primary and with supportive parents like you (you must be or you wouldn't be reading this) has as much chance of gaining a place at an academically selective senior school – state or independent – as any child from a prep school and, quite possibly, more. Prep schools may vaunt the 'special relationships' they have as 'feeder' schools to the seniors, but no decent senior school would turn down the bright and naturally sparky veteran of a good state primary.

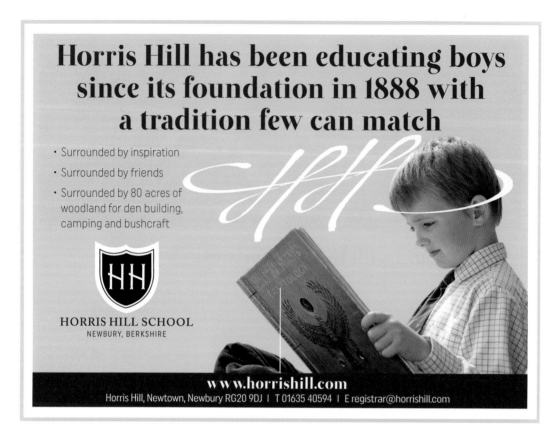
The
Good Schools Guide International

44 countries
50 cities
734 schools listed - the good, the bad and the ghastly
213 schools reviewed - only the good

Local knowledge
of schools around the world.
At your fingertips.

FINE ARTS
COLLEGE

WE OFFER A WIDE RANGE OF SUBJECTS AT A LEVEL AND GCSE

GRADED
OUTSTANDING
BY OFSTED

020 7586 0312   www.hampsteadfinearts.com

Getting your child into a good state school

If you are lucky enough to live in a part of London with flawless state schools that effortlessly accommodate all the local kids, you can skip this section. If not, here are some tactics to consider:

Get moving

Consider moving to a part of London with long-established state school excellence. Generally, but not always, suburbs trump inner city locations when it comes to good-for-ever schools. See our run throughs of the best state schools in each London borough. If you need to know which street to buy or rent in, the Good Schools Guide website features invaluable catchment area maps.

Get God

Failing that, get religion before the birth so your child can be baptised (before 6 months for many Catholic schools) and the family wholesomely engaged in weekly services and voluntary church activities. This will improve your chances of access to an excellent Catholic or Anglican faith school, something that enabled Tony Blair's children to complete their education in one part of London while living somewhere completely different.

Get stuck in

Your local schools may be going through a purple patch or you may be within range of the scattering of selective secondary state schools around London. They're so over-subscribed that getting in is a lottery, but your (bright) child has as much of a chance as anyone else's if you find a good tutor (see Tutors and tutoring in London page 415).

Some secondary schools also admit a small proportion of out-of-catchment pupils based on aptitude – language at Grey Coat Hospital, in Westminster, for instance, or music at

Camden School for Girls – while an increasing number use ballots to prevent parents gaming the system.

Get real

It may come down to helping your child do their best in a less than ideal school environment. This takes time and dedication and is a reason why thousands turn to home education.

Get the information

Research all the schools within your patch. Check to see which are reviewed in the Good Schools Guide. None will be perfect, so look at them from a range of viewpoints, and avoid being over-influenced by reputation and rumour (both can be substantially outdated).

Are the Ofsted reports confidence-inspiring? Are they reasonably up to date? Don't take them as gospel, though: a school may have got its outstanding rating by ticking the right boxes rather than by providing the sort of educational environment that will suit your child. Equally, it may have been rated 'requires improvement' for a failing that does not greatly concern you (and is anyway being dealt with). Do the able get stellar exam results? Do ordinary children do well, too? Do websites suggest a broad and fascinating as well as a successful education? Roughly what does their catchment area look like?

Even if secondary education is a long way off, research secondary schools in the area too. If they are poor, you could face more disruption when your child reaches 11. If good, do they give preference to children in named primaries and are your preferred choices amongst them?

Having arrived at a long list of potential schools, research the admissions process. Though increasingly complex, with every academy and free school entitled to set its own entry criteria, and faith schools providing various numbers of hoops to jump through, your local authority website should round up the lot.

Work your way through the admissions rules. The higher up, the more powerful they are. Find the one that best describes your child. Scrutinise cut-off criteria – often related to distance from the school but calculated in idiosyncratic ways. Note the preference given to siblings, which can benefit families whose younger children are admitted as a matter of right wherever they live, but scupper newcomers' chances in a year with a bumper crop of reception age brothers and sisters.

Don't take it as gospel though: a school may have got its outstanding rating by ticking the right boxes

Get practical

Once you know which good schools you like, might conceivably get into and are in areas you can afford to live in, go and check them out. Schools are individual places with their own styles and cultures. Though a comfortingly large number in London have come good over the last few years, reputation or results alone won't tell you whether they would suit your child. You need to find pupils who match your child in character and ability, and parents who share your outlook on education, and see the school through their eyes.

A visit is essential; being shown round by children during an ordinary school day is best, an open day less so, though it will give you a better chance to chat to teachers, and see everything that school is doing. Talk to locals. Drop into local watering holes and ask what the schools are like or – as a long term measure – consider volunteering to get a unique, in-depth insight.

Get going

At the end of all this work, you should know which schools you would like your children to attend and what you have to do to be sure of getting them there.

Nine times out of 10, at least in London, living in the catchment area is a non-negotiable. Move, live there for at least two years and don't cheat. The penalties if you do can range from cold-shouldering from other parents to the loss of a school place. Some boroughs may even disqualify you if you still own the home you lived in previously. What you do after serving your time is up to you – but you may want to check that siblings get priority over distance if you have younger children.

Move, live there for at least two years and don't cheat

If you need to change school later on, the rules may be different. Once the main process of entry is finished, some schools are individually responsible for filling any 'in year' spaces that may arise through pupils moving elsewhere (and, in London, people are always moving).

Although, nominally, the same entry rules apply, in practice things are much less clear. Schools, or the local authority, keep a waiting list, but the allocation of places can be hard to track. Sound out your favourite school: you are looking at a house nearby, might they have room for your children, if not immediately then over the next year or so? If you get a helpful response, visit them and make good friends. Persistence – and charm – can pay off.

How to judge a new school

There are many new and newish free schools in London and the Conservative government has promised many more. Whilst some are clearly flourishing, others lose heads and staff at an alarming rate, and sometimes promised premises fail to materialise.

Start a normal business and you can begin with baby footsteps, holding fire on major investment in resources and employees until you are confident you're on to a winner. Founders of new schools, however, don't have that luxury. In addition to substantial premises, other chunky overheads include a head, senior management team (possibly compatible, possibly not) a full pack of teachers (ditto), not to mention the pupils.

With such a potent cocktail, the scope for fast track failure even in an apparently well set up new school is almost limitless. So why should prospective parents be prepared to take the risk?

You, gov...

In an established school, all parents need know about the governors is that they are happy with the head – and vice versa. In a new school, however, the governing body's ability to choose a talented senior team, help get over inevitable initial difficulties and, most important of all, replace people fast if they have made the wrong choices, is vital.

You are looking for governors who are good as individuals and even stronger as a team, leading from the front and putting in the time to observe, listen (to you) and learn. Invisibility on open days or other school presentations is a serious warning sign that all is not well.

If your school has an academy sponsor, they will be involved in the governance. Some, like ARK, have stellar reputations. Others are close to disaster areas. Check out not just your school but the others they run. Their Ofsted reports may say more about them as a group than an individual prospectus ever can.

Heads up?
How confidence-inspiring is the head? With his or her massive extra workload and just one shot at getting things right, 'he'll do' or 'give her a try' just aren't enough. If you doubt the head's ability, give the school a miss.

Top marks for teachers?
Check out the teachers. Do they exude colleague appeal (a good new school will thrive on teamwork)? Do they radiate inspiration? And when you talk to them, do you wish you had been taught by them? Teachers in free schools and academies don't have to be qualified. Unqualified ones may be fabulous – of they may just be cheap to employ.

Parent power?
Observe the attitudes and behaviour of other parents or their children. As a group, you are all important in working together to set the school on the right course. It takes extra energy and commitment and you need to know that other parents will chip in. Do they have what it takes?

Premises
Many new free schools open in uninspiring 'temporary' buildings, with the promise of a move to a fabulous purpose built (but often unspecified) site in a year or two. If the year or two is stretching out indefinitely with no sign of building work finishing (or even starting), beware.

Do your homework
Read every line of the prospectus and then consider what's between those lines. How geared up is the school to deal

with 'a touch' of dyslexia? Do the less co-ordinated ever get picked for matches? Is this an 'all work and no play' school? What happens if it becomes successful and oversubscribed and its catchment area shrinks? Will your second child still qualify for a place or will you, and similar other pioneers, be penalised?

Now read on...

For the altruistic, the inner glow that comes with helping improve English education may be enough. For others, the hope that a brand new school will do your child proud is a more tangible benefit. Whatever your reason, good luck!

The Good Schools Guide Advice Service

The Good Schools Guide Advice Service (GSGAS) is a personal service for individual families covering every aspect of schools and education. The advisors are our most experienced and knowledgeable writers and most of them live and work in or near London. They have visited countless schools, quizzed innumerable parents, children, teachers and heads. This vast experience, coupled with the data, inside information and expertise of the entire team, is available to any parents who need assistance with their child's education. Perhaps most importantly, our advisors understand how challenging it can be to be a parent. We are sympathetic and will help in whatever way we can to set you and your child on the right track.

How can we help?
Because The Good Schools Guide Advice Service is a personal service, run on a one-to-one basis, we can help you in whatever way you need us to. You tell us what you require and we tell you how we can help, whether it's advice about places in London schools or something entirely different. Our website: www.gsgexpertschoolsconsultants.co.uk shows you all the services we offer. You can also see details about our advisors and how they can help you. All information is treated in the strictest confidence. Example fees quoted were correct at the time of publication.

London Service
In 2015, we launched our unique London Service, especially to meet the needs of families new to London who need guidance, not just on schools but on areas, family services, nurseries, playgroups, tutors etc in the capital. You will find all details on our website.

Shrewsbury House Preparatory School

Shrewsbury House School is an IAPS Preparatory School for boys aged 7-13

"This is a first class prep school where academic rigour is balanced by an equally strong offering in arts and sports."

The Good Schools Guide

"Rivals are green about Shrewsbury House's academic record"

The Tatler Schools Guide, 2016

"Extra-curricular activities contribute highly to school life."

ISI Inspection

107 Ditton Road, Surbiton, Surrey, KT6 6RL
Telephone: 020 8399 3066 Fax: 020 8339 9529
office@shspost.co.uk shrewsburyhouse.net

INSPIRATIONAL
Box Hill School
for girls and boys aged 11–18

BELIEVE IN YOURSELF

Box Hill School, Mickleham, Dorking, Surrey RH5 6EA
Telephone: +44 (0)1372 373382
Email: enquiries@boxhillschool.com

www.boxhillschool.com

State School Service

In order to meet the needs of increasing numbers of enquirers who are interested in the state sector only, The Good Schools Guide Advice Service now has a new service with its own expert in state school education.

Our aim to be as flexible as possible to meet whatever educational needs parents and children have. In order to keep the fees as low as possible, the State School Service offers parents a choice of consultation packages starting at £50.

Academic assessments

If you're not sure what academic level your child is at, we can undertake academic assessments; we also have a superb team of experts in SEN. Our advisors have professional links with leading experts in fields such as educational psychology and tutoring.

Scholarships and bursaries

The Good Schools Guide Advice Service has amassed information on scholarships and bursaries to create a unique central resource for parents. We now hold information on the fee assistance available at more than 500 schools and the number is growing daily. There is a cost for this service as the search can take some time but we keep our fees as low as possible. For example, if you want a list of ten top senior schools in London which offer, potentially, 100 per cent of fees for a bright child, we would charge around £150.

What should I do?

Phone us on +44 (0)203 286 6824 or send us a brief email to advice@goodschoolsguide.co.uk outlining what you need. Tell us the age of your child and where you live plus your contact details. We will contact you within 48 hours of your initial phone call or email and make sure that we match you with the right advisor. Consultations can be conducted over the phone or email but our advisors are happy to meet you face to face if you prefer. Urgent enquiries are dealt with urgently. We can find an advisor to speak with you within the hour if necessary.

How much?

We provide one of the most competitively priced tailor-made advice services in the UK. Check our website for current fees.

Uni in the USA

The British student's guide to great universities
in the USA from Harvard to Hopkins

Tells you how to choose, how to apply and how to pay

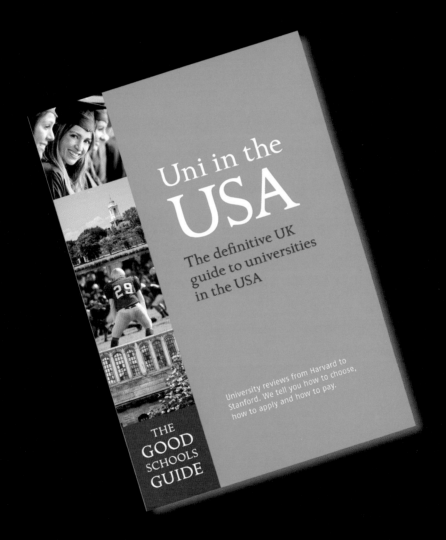

£18 for the book or 12-month subscription

www.uniintheusa.com

Central South

CENTRAL SOUTH

An introduction to Central South London and its state schools

Today London's state schools are amongst the best in England. This may come as a surprise to those who can remember back to the bad old days of the 1980s and '90s, when many parents were choosing to send children to independent secondary schools or to move out of London altogether to avoid the perils of the local comp.

This turnaround was largely due to the highly effective London Challenge, which operated between 2003 and 2011. This scheme saw strong heads mentoring those in weak schools, zero tolerance of low expectations and the smart use of data to track pupil progress. At its core was a commitment to breaking the link between deprivation and low attainment.

The injection of energetic, new graduates from top universities in the Teach First scheme contributed, as did the success of some of the early sponsored academies. The ethnic composition of London's schools is also important, with typically high pupil aspiration, ambition and engagement amongst recent migrants.

We can review only a small proportion of London's state schools, but here is a brief tour of the boroughs, their characteristics and a selection of notable state primary and secondary schools.

Lambeth

Lambeth is a skinny borough running from Vauxhall and Kennington in the north via Brixton and onto Herne Hill, the eastern parts of Clapham (more High Street than Common), then south to Streatham and West Norwood. Hard to believe in some parts, but not so in others, it is in the top 10 of London's most deprived boroughs.

At secondary stage, Catholic families are well-served with La Retraite for girls, and co-ed Bishop Thomas Grant in Streatham. Both are highly praised, but the seeming lack of choice for non-church goers causes some tearing of hair; we hear that children from Lambeth primaries often scatter to the four winds.

As a result the newly re-modelled Dunraven qv in Streatham, a dynamic, purposeful comprehensive, achieving well, is extremely sought after; this has led to the establishment of a new linked primary and an excellent sixth form. Admission is by entrance test, using ability banding. A relative newcomer, Elm Green in Tulse Hill, is the first 'parent promoted' school in the country, with GCSE and A level results that place the school in the top 10 per cent nationally.

Other options might be Platanos College Clapham, or the Lilian Baylis Technology School that partners with the South Bank University and the likes of Shell and IBM. Local parents advise taking a look with an open mind – there are some exceptional facilities, wide choice of options and strong leadership. Admissions for most are via a test co-ordinated by Lambeth and taken at the destination school closest to home.

Durand Academy qv in Stockwell is a large and exceptionally well-equipped state primary and middle school, and the visionary leadership has opened a fully funded boarding senior school in Sussex. Further south and less radically, the pick of the primaries is Paxton, which regularly makes national top 100 lists – hence admissions are oversubscribed seven to one. Also consider Elm Wood and Kingswood schools, part of the same federation, or the excellent Sudbourne. Catchment for all these is limited so you will need to live close by.

Rosendale, not to be confused with the nearby independent Rosemead, has a large intake, attractive location close to Dulwich village, and as its star rises, could be a savvy choice. The stylish renovation and expansion of Julian's School, both in the heart of West Norwood and on a dual site in Streatham, is causing stir in this upwardly mobile locale.

Also in the air are plans for a bi-lingual Spanish and English primary run by the group responsible for the over-subscribed free school in Brighton.

Catholic primaries are unusually thin on the ground, except for the celebrated Corpus Christi, though there's a fair share of good C of Es, led by St Jude's tucked away on the Brixton side of Herne Hill.

Southwark

Southwark comprises the picket fences, finger-posts and vast green spaces of Dulwich, trendy East Dulwich, bursting at the seams with young families on the run from south west London house prices, arty Camberwell, Peckham and on northwards to Borough and London Bridge. Shad Thames stretches east from Tower Bridge and has a high concentration of warehouse conversions (think A Fish Called Wanda) and new mixed use buildings of flats, shops and cafes.

Given the highly visible presence of the famous independent schools of Dulwich College qv, JAGS qv and Alleyn's School qv, it's somehow all the more galling that Southwark's state schools are very often under-performing. For the effortlessly academic, and those who may respond to tutoring, an Oyster card and a spirit of independence could bring the grammars of Kingston and Sutton within reach.

Closer to home, the most popular choice du jour is the re-invented Kingsdale in West Dulwich, a specialist music and sports academy. Academic results are still only average and Ofsted agrees there is work to be done but pupils are highly enthusiastic and the application process nail-biting. There are no distance criteria; places are allocated via ability banding, maths, music and sports scholarships available. Better exam results are to be had at the well-managed Charter School qv, a much fêted comprehensive with a no-nonsense attitude to discipline. The local Harris academies are working hard on their PR and results are definitely on the up, providing options for girls, boys and soon a new primary, on the site of the old East Dulwich police station. The recent news that the Haberdasher's Aske's Federation will open an East Dulwich College in September 2016 is welcome, as many travel all the way to the New Cross site. Secondary faith schools include St Saviour's and St Olave's C of E, and the star by far, Sacred Heart RC.

There are a few nicely performing primaries in the north towards the Thames including St Joseph's, Riverside and Boutcher C of E. Further south competition hots up considerably for places. The most sought after are Dulwich Village C of E Infants qv and Dulwich Hamlet Junior qv (no automatic transfer), where you either need a terrifically desirable address, good stamina for church-going or both. The icing on the organic cake could be Dulwich Hamlet's plans to open The Belham, a free primary in trendy Peckham.

Heber and Goodrich in the heart of East Dulwich remain popular despite an increasingly so-so reputation, while admissions rise at steadily improving Goose Green. In Camberwell, Lyndhurst School is their equal, and one to watch is Crawford Primary, newly outstanding after being taken under the wing of the Gypsy Hill Federation. No league-topping faith schools, but we know plenty of perfectly happy parents and children at St Anthony's Catholic primary and St John's and St Clements C of E.

Wandsworth

One of the largest boroughs, Wandsworth includes Putney and Southfields to the east and Earlsfield, Battersea, Clapham, Balham and Tooting to the west. Putney, along the south bank of the Thames, has a chain of attractive open spaces with extensive sporting grounds, especially rowing clubs – this is where the annual Boat Race (between Oxford and Cambridge) begins, packing the banks of the river and every possible pub and garden with cheering crowds. Battersea, dominated by Battersea Park and the formerly derelict Battersea Power Station, is now the location of the new American Embassy. The Thames frontage is the scene of incredible numbers of high rise blocks, finished and under construction, many sold as investments to absentee overseas buyers. 'Between the commons' and elsewhere in these villagey neighbourhoods are row upon row of Victorian and Edwardian houses primped to perfection, a heartland for affluent professional families.

Apart from proximity to central and west London and the choice of green spaces, a big draw is the excellent choice of good state primaries (see below). If one can successfully drop into the right street for the right primary, all well and good, but a word to the wise is that come 11+ it's a different story. Lack of suitable secondaries means many either look well outside the borough, or jump ship to independents or even grammars. Most parents consider a broad range of options, and as many applications as their offspring can stand.

There are two clear local winners in terms of popularity and performance at secondary level: Graveney qv and Chestnut Grove. Applications to Graveney most recently stood at 11 to one so back-up plans are advisable. Places for all secondaries are decided by the Wandsworth test, taken in November by all year 6 children and a source of much angst, with most schools looking at scores and distance. Chestnut Grove considers aptitude in art and languages for 40 per cent of its places.

Other options include St Cecilia's C of E with its music specialism and Ashcroft Technology College, which seems to divide opinion but is worth viewing.

Those wonderful primaries, a veritable crop of Ofsted 'outstandings' and impressive performances, include

Honeywell qv, Belleville qv, and Beatrix Potter qv in Clapham; Hotham qv and Brandlehow in Putney and Sheringdale in Southfields. Notable faith schools include Our Lady of Victories qv, St George's C of E qv, St Mary's C of E, St Boniface RC, St Anslem's and Our Lady of Heaven RC among many others.

Alleyn's Junior School

Linked school: Alleyn's School, 56

Townley Road, London SE22 8SU

Tel: 020 8557 1519

Independent • Pupils: 240 • Ages: 4–11 • C of E • Fees: up to £15,525 pa

Email: juniorschool@alleyns.org.uk
Website: www.alleyns.org.uk

10

Head: Since September 2015, Mr Simon Severino, previously head of St Andrew's Prep School, Eastbourne. He read geography at Oxford, started teaching at Culford Prep in Suffolk and then went to Dulwich Prep London as head of geography and deputy head. He joined St Andrew's in 2010. He is married with two young children.

Entrance: Tends to be very local – 'We try to be centred in the community'. At 4+, 18 places and some 220 applicants. No sibling policy – 'We could fill the place with siblings, and we like to encourage some diversity'. Intakes also at 7, 9 and 11 – 'If they don't get in the first time, we encourage them to see it as a postponement and to try again later'. Assessment 'looks for children who can participate in a very busy and structured timetable'. Allows for age: alongside raw scores, offers also made to those who come top in the month of their birth. Offers made to equal numbers of boys and girls. 'We try to take in children who have a lot to contribute. They may have lower academic scores but be brilliant at sport.'

Exit: All pupils have right of entry to senior school (one or two move elsewhere, often with scholarships) though everyone takes the 11+ exam and year 7 could be a probationary year for a child who is struggling to keep up. 'We value the real contribution of the child. A boy with dyslexia might have trouble with English but be brilliant at maths and go on to play for the school football team. We'd rather have a hard worker than someone who is bright but lazy.' The transfer exam 'is about celebrating hard work and achievement, not just about winning scholarships. Everyone gets a leaving certificate which includes details of what they have done for the life of the school.'

Remarks: A very busy, buzzy place tucked away in a quiet corner of the senior school site. Light, bright classrooms include a conservatory and a playground that doubles as an outdoor classroom. Magnificent IT suite; iPads integrated into lessons – 'We have embraced new technology'; giant iPad in art room. Science garden has wildlife pond, herb, flower and vegetable plots and ex-battery chickens.

English and maths taught in small groups from day one. Formal setting for maths from year 4 – 'For those in the B sets it's mostly about increasing their confidence and self-esteem'. Maths mentors come over from the senior school to help. Specialist teachers for French, music, art and PE from the beginning, and for every subject from year 4.

Support includes speech and language therapist, a literacy expert and learning support assistants – 'We've had children here with quite serious learning differences and we've done a great job with them. That's one of the things we're most proud of'. Pupils say: 'I like their attitude towards learning. The teachers help you to get better in a very calm way. The classes are very friendly.' Signs round the school during our visit proclaimed that it was anti-bullying week.

Excellent art in newly converted studio, set up to resemble a fish tank during our visit with strings of fish hanging down the windows. Pottery popular: 'Edward de Waal did a workshop recently and showed us how to make our own kiln and fire our own pottery'. Colourful artistic displays all round the school, and the Dulwich Picture Gallery is a regular destination.

Everyone learns a stringed instrument in years 2-4 and a brass or woodwind instrument in year 5, and many keep it up. Clubs include jazz band, choirs and L'Orchestre de la Grand Salle. Plenty of other music and drama – school tends to attract creative families so lots of talent/parental encouragement. The day of our visit was hip-hop day and year 6, in tee shirts they had designed themselves, were busy learning dance moves. Africa and India days also combine art, music and dance, and Alleyn's Junior Has Talent competition is a highlight of the year.

'A boy with dyslexia might be brilliant at maths and play for the school football team. We'd prefer a hard worker to someone who is bright but lazy'

Sport particularly strong, with the enviable senior school facilities including rolling green acres just next door. Large numbers of sports clubs include ballet and tae kwon do; A, B and often C teams play against other schools in sports ranging from girls' football to biathlon. Pupils we met were very enthusiastic – 'I do seven clubs a week, nearly all sport'; 'There's something that suits everyone'.

Congenial atmosphere. School aims to 'encourage respectfulness between adults and children. We're after more than good manners: we want our children to have the confidence to communicate with adults'. 'All the people here are very friendly,' say pupils. 'Even if you're not best friends with someone, you just get on with them.'

Alleyn's School

Linked school: Alleyn's Junior School, 55

Townley Road, London SE22 8SU

Tel: 020 8557 1500

11

Independent • Pupils: 983 • Ages: 4–18 • Sixth form pupils: 295 • C of E • Fees: £17,397 pa

Email: registrar@alleyns.org.uk
Website: www.alleyns.org.uk

Headmaster: Since 2010, Dr Gary Savage MA PhD Cantab (40s). Previously under-master at Westminster School, joining after 10 years' teaching at Eton, where his roles included head of history, community service coordinator and housemaster of the scholars' house. A historian of 18th century France, has a passion for watching sport (Ipswich Town supporter – he grew up in Suffolk and was state school educated) and for the arts. Has taught himself German, and he and his wife Natalie (a television and film producer) have a pied à terre in Berlin. Would like to encourage in his pupils his own appetite for learning.

'Imaginative....very charming...a good hand on the tiller,' say parents. Certainly a suspicion that he is more elitist in outlook than his predecessors, and parents fear that the school's liberal, creative ethos may be lost. Not so, he insists: 'I want our pupils to do very well in public exams – but emphatically not by turning Alleyn's into a hothouse. I want to expand horizons intellectually and socially without diluting or compromising the Alleyn's ethos. I want to work with not against the grain'.

Academic matters: Used to be the junior partner of the Dulwich triumvirate of schools in academic terms. No longer: the increasing popularity of co-education and a more selective entry has helped its rise up the league tables. 2015 saw 88 per cent A*-B and 68 per cent A*/A grades at A level; 90 per cent A*/A at GCSE. Maths much the most popular A level subject, as one would expect, but otherwise a good and broad spread of arts and sciences.

The head is 'passionate about non-examined academic enrichment'. He has instituted the Governor's research project prize, which is awarded for a piece of sixth form research – prize-winning subjects have ranged from an anthropological study on ape/human divergence to one on the mating habits of arachnids. He is encouraging a wider range of visiting speakers (A C Grayling and the Archbishop of Canterbury have been recent visitors), and has appointed a KS3 co-ordinator focussing on thinking skills – 'I want to celebrate the life of the mind without compromising our buzz, busyness and happiness'.

Everyone is screened during year 7 to help identify any learning difficulties. At the end of the year, staff get together to decide who is likely to need extra support or an ed psych assessment. Full-time learning support co-ordinator can give individual term-long learning skills courses to those who are struggling. 'They're very quick at picking up when things are not going right,' said a parent. 'We get detailed reports, and I really feel they're on the case.'

Part of the Southwark Schools Learning Partnership, which involves staff and students from 11 state and private schools sharing experiences and working together to improve teaching and learning. Now developing links with the state Sydenham and Forest Hill sixth form.

Games, options, the arts: Has always been viewed as the most liberal and arty of the local independent schools – and, of course, attracts many families from the creative professions. 'Fabulous' theatre (named after a post-war English master who set up the National Youth Theatre) hosts lower, middle and upper school plays as well as many sixth form and visiting productions each year. Full time stage manager, and students help with lighting and sound. 'The standard is amazing,' said a parent. 'They've really brought out my son's talents' – though inevitably it can be hard for lesser mortals to get parts in shows. 'But in the sixth form there's much more scope and they can put on their own performances,' said a student.

Headmaster has taught himself German, and he and his wife Natalie have a pied à terre in Berlin

Large numbers play instruments – flourishing orchestras, choirs and ensembles taking part in masterclasses and performing at 'astonishingly high standards'. Very impressive art, with many taking it to A level and a very high proportion of A* grades. Not a school that is sniffy about media studies, which has its own well-equipped studio with the latest high-tech editing equipment. Food tech is a GCSE option and there's a popular cookery club.

Enviable sports facilities include floodlit netball court in the centre of the quad and floodlit Astroturf, alongside sports hall, swimming pool, acres of playing fields. Sport for all but excellence too: whether the 1st XI footballers who recently reached the final of the Independent Schools Football Association cup, the girl who plays hockey for England, the extraordinary water polo teams (boys and girls have reached the national finals in every age group and the U14 girls were national champions for several years running), the fives enthusiasts or the cycling club which meets at the Herne Hill Velodrome. 'There's so much on offer that everyone finds something they want to do,' said a pupil.

Volunteering is important – 'They take it very seriously' – and houses raise funds for their own chosen charities. CCF very popular – opportunities to try gliding, go camping, do adventure training, learn radio communication – as is D of E, with large numbers at all levels. Huge numbers of overseas trips: eg football tour to Germany, geography society expedition to Iceland, religious studies trip to India.

Background and atmosphere: A direct descendent of the foundation Alleyn's College of God's Gift, set up in 1619 by Edward Alleyn, wealthy actor and proprietor of taverns, brothels and bear-baiting pits. Part of the foundation funded Dulwich College; in 1882, the upper and lower schools split, with the lower becoming Alleyn's Boys' School. It became a public school in 1919 and a direct grant grammar school from 1958, until that status was abolished in 1975. At that point it became independent and went co-ed. Other schools within the foundation include JAGS and several state schools.

Pleasant setting in between chic Dulwich village and trendy East Dulwich. Unpretentious red-brick facade of four-storey main building masks the main site, with its landscaped quads and acres of playing fields. A continuous development programme has, most recently, resulted in the dramatic

Edward Alleyn building with its theatre, lecture room, sixth form area and Costa coffee bar. Large sports hall, music school and excellent library.

Parents attracted by its reputation for a liberal, stimulating environment, with its history as a direct grant grammar school and perhaps less pretension than some more traditional public schools – 'We weren't interested in putting our children through a system that gave them an over-inflated view of their position in society,' said one parent. Generous bursaries help the social mix.

Pastoral care and discipline: A very happy place, say parents, with good pastoral care and good communications – 'Any questions get answered immediately'. The head concurs: 'When things go wrong we deal with it carefully, kindly and robustly. We have a strong pastoral set-up with many layers, and we all work together to ensure that any children with problems are helped. Everything else is secondary to this.'

Lower school – years 7 and 8 – has its own building, providing a sheltered introduction to the school and, say parents, particularly good individual pastoral care. Year 9 upwards join houses, which give a family feel and opportunities for those who don't make school teams/plays to compete in inter-house events, eg music, drama and sport.

Head reckons only a handful of bullying incidents a year – 'It is a remarkable testament to the ethos of the place' – and parents agree. 'We've never come across any bullying. It probably helps being co-ed, but it is a very well-balanced place'.

Very few exclusions – 'I've had to do a couple of suspensions – for low level disruptions and disengagement – but we can generally get them back on side. Sometimes children give you no room for manoeuvre and you have to say it's not working. But we tackle these things educationally and pastorally from the beginning, and generally the children buy into this'.

Pupils and parents: More bohemian than the other Dulwich independents – 'It's always attracted pupils of journalists, rock stars and theatre people,' commented a parent. The least multi-ethnic of the three schools, probably because high-achieving ethnic minority families tend to go for single-sex education. 'I'd love to see us reflect more broadly the south-east London community,' says the head, 'and I hope that a wider range of families will feel confident applying to us. I don't want us to be a bubble community.' Pupils tend to be 'charming, articulate, incredibly polite,' said a parent. Has produced an unusual number of well-known actors, musicians and writers.

Ex-pupils include actors Jude Law, Nancy Carroll, Jessie Ware, Simon Ward, Julian Glover and director Felix Barrett; musicians Florence Welch, Felix White, Gabriel Prokofiev and Ed

Simons; scientists Prof John Isaacs, Prof RV Jones and surgeon Prof Lord Kakkar; plus Air Marshall Sir Christopher Harper, writers CS Forester and VS Pritchett and former Sun editor, Kelvin MacKenzie.

Entrance: Main entry at 11, with 125 places and around 500 applicants. Reasoning, English and maths papers. Automatic entry for junior school pupils, but the occasional one who has been struggling may have a probationary year: 'We try very hard to make it work. We will see it through if we possibly can'. Generally a third of year 7 comes from the junior school, a third from local preps and a third from state primaries. 'We like to take as broad a range as possible, but they must be bright enough to flourish, to enjoy the pace and buzz of life here. We're looking for those who will have a fabulous time.' Around 15 places at 13, with science and language exams added in. Interview and school report important. Up to 20 places at 16 (but often fewer) – exams in three prospective A level subjects plus a critical thinking test.

Increasing popularity means that local families can no longer be confident of a place for all their children. Parents who went to Alleyn's themselves sometimes irked to find the academic bar has risen above their reach, with places going to those from all points east, west, south and even north of the river.

Exit: Few leave after GCSEs. Nearly all year 13 leavers to university, including Oxbridge (18 in 2015) and medical schools. Popular destinations are Bristol, Edinburgh, Leeds and Durham. Several to art foundation courses, one or two to drama school or music college, a few to American colleges, otherwise mostly to top UK universities to do a huge mix of subjects ranging from natural sciences to social anthropology.

Money matters: Enviably well-endowed with funds from the Dulwich Estate and from the Worshipful

Company of Saddlers, which pay for a generous staffing ratio and the ability to carry out a rolling programme of improvements. Some 30 pupils on 100 per cent bursaries and many more on 50 per cent upwards – school is fundraising to increase that number. Scholarships (maximum £3000 a year) for music, art and sporting as well as academic excellence.

Remarks: Traditionally a liberal and creative school, beloved of south London media families, which is increasing its academic clout. Parents like the fact the children are 'well-balanced kids with lots to do'. One commented: 'We really feel we landed on our feet – it's a superb school.'

Allfarthing Primary School

St Ann's Crescent, London SW18 2LR

Tel: 020 8874 1301

21

State • Pupils: 430 • Ages: 3–11

Email: info@allfarthing.wandsworth.sch.uk
Website: www.allfarthing.wandsworth.sch.uk/

Headteacher: Since September 2012, Ali Silke BA (40s); read geography at UCL. She started her career in publishing before deciding to train as a teacher. Married with two daughters at secondary school, she has been head of a beacon school in Tower Hamlets followed by Dulwich Village Infants, where she raised the Ofsted grading from good to outstanding. She has also spent time working as a trainer/consultant for the Ruth Miskin Literacy phonics programme, in primary, secondary and special schools. Fifth head in four years for Allfarthing, she assures us she is definitely staying put, much to parents' relief after an unsettled period. Committed and determined personality, always up with the lark; she is dedicated to pulling the school together and running the expansion project enabling the school to be three class entry. Her interests include cinema, reading, theatre, running and travel.

Parents say choir has developed over the past year and are impressed by numbers of boys who have joined. Encouraging setting for musical families, something of a rarity for a state primary

Entrance: At 3+ into the nursery or 4+ into reception. Priority goes to siblings and then those living closest to the school. Attending the nursery does not guarantee a place in the infant department. For occasional places in older age groups contact the school to check availability and put your name on their waiting list.

Exit: Popular state choices are Graveney, St Cecilia, Burntwood, Ricards Lodge, ARK Academy, odd one to Kingston or Surrey grammar schools. Around 30 per cent to independents, Emanuel, Ibstock Place, Wimbledon High School, Trinity and Whitgift.

Remarks: Situated on rather a busy corner, the tall 1920s building offers large, bright classrooms; eyes are immediately drawn to displays of children's work and art designed to capture imagination and interest. Standards are high and parents note a recent increase in monitoring and assessing progress across the age groups to ensure underachievement is picked up and addressed swiftly. Reception and nursery classes have indoor and outdoor classrooms, ample resources laid out thoughtfully. Early years classes follow the Read Write phonics programme offering a good grounding in literacy skills. Overall, school's results in English are impressive; lots of drama and speaking and listening activities are incorporated into the curriculum. Maths results not quite as high but catching up. Large inner-city mix; around 24 languages spoken in the school; everyone learns Spanish from year 3. Parents report good traditional teaching with interesting history and geography projects alongside whizzy IT; all classes can access iPads, MacBooks and trolleys of laptops. Graded outstanding, the school does very well in national assessments and has an above-average added value score. Curriculum is further extended with masterclasses provided by special partnerships with Graveney for ICT, Burntwood for sciences and Southfields for PE. Head feels SEN help should be delivered as required through small group or individual teaching, in addition to speech and occupational therapists visiting the school.

Two multi-purpose halls provide space for PE, assemblies and lunches cooked on site in the recently refurbished kitchens. On site sports include lacrosse, football, hockey and cricket; older pupils are bussed to Battersea Park School for swimming lessons. Sports days are held at Wimbledon Park where year 5 has a week of water sports, courtesy of the Friends Group.

Music features highly on the daily curriculum; super purpose-built accommodation with a dedicated music teacher. Opportunity for all from year 4 to learn an instrument, with many achieving grade 6 before moving to secondary school. Each child chooses a string or wind instrument for group lessons in year 3 and there is a budding choir that performs in the community. Parents say choir has really developed over the past year and are particularly impressed at the large number of boys who have joined in. Encouraging setting for musical families, currently something of a rarity for a state primary.

Remarkably good Friends of Allfarthing Group is an asset, raising money for all sorts of activities and equipment through traditional and creative ways. Friends contribute throughout the school, baking biscuits for meetings and fêtes and writing an introductory guide book for newcomers. Parent volunteers and staff recently collaborated to run a very successful lettuce planting project for the UNICEF Day for Change. Monthly book club lottery raises funds for the library and other book purchases. All tastes taken into consideration for after-school clubs, with parents and pupils suggesting some of the choices available.

Pupils are encouraged to voice their opinions through the school council and class reps, on school rules, sensible behaviour and other issues that benefit everyone's participation and enjoyment. A few rumbles from parents over staff changes and prospects of building works; most remain positive and feel the changes will be for the best. Overall a popular school, working hard to continually improve and develop provision, along with a number of little extras, or not so little, as the case may be.

Archbishop Tenison's School

55 Kennington Oval, London SE11 5SR

Tel: 020 7735 3771

State · Pupils: 525 · Ages: 11–19 · C of E

Email: school@ats.lambeth.sch.uk
Website: www.tenisons.com

Head Teacher: Since 2006, Mrs Elizabeth Sims, BEd MA. Initial degree in religious studies and English from Institute of Education, followed by MA in education management and administration. Previously deputy head at St Saviour's and St Olave's School. Passionate about young people's development and learning; has been involved in youth work since the age of 16. A member of the Tate Britain Advisory Council. Committed Christian. Loves reading.

Academic matters: At GCSE, 68 per cent scored five or more A*-C grades in 2015 including English and maths. Pupils generally take nine or 10 GCSEs, though some take as many as 13. BTec results strong. School is particularly proud of its excellent maths teaching.

The sixth form is a strength of the school and is improving rapidly year on year. Small numbers of girls in sixth form, though this looks set to grow as word spreads of the opportunities on offer. Girls typically come from schools that are less scholarly in order to pursue more academic A level options here. School works hard at arranging visits to universities and setting up diverse opportunities for work experience placements. Extended sixth form centre with study room and kitchen seen as a great success by pupils. Large proportion of sixth formers have own laptops, subsidised by school. A sixth form psychology class we sat in on was impressive – students fully engaged, lively, full of questions, keen to participate and enjoying their learning.

Class sizes quite small, averaging 26 or 27 but can be as few as six per class in the sixth form. Learning support department assesses each pupil in the school and sets up extra support if needed. Those with SEN are withdrawn for individual or small group support or are provided for in-class with learning support assistant or classroom assistant. Lower sets are offered additional literacy support while more able are offered Latin, philosophy and thinking skills. Enrichment programme targets gifted and talented pupils and school claims to be always on the look out for opportunities to extend learning for the most capable. For those with behavioural issues, workshops are arranged on anger management and social skills.

Games, options, the arts: Sport is taken seriously and school does its best to organise a rich diet of sport for all pupils. Football and basketball perennially popular and a number of alumni play football professionally. Lots of teams and matches regularly arranged. Sport is played at nearby Kennington Park or a train-ride away at Motspur playing fields, where pupils play rugby, tennis and athletics most days. Swimming takes place in Brixton. Pupils in the past have been offered American football training with teams from the NFL.

School choir performs at homes for the elderly and hospitals, as well as occasionally at Southwark Cathedral. There is an open invitation for boys to join the Pegasus Opera Singing Academy

Currently 25 students learn a musical instrument, including guitar, drum kit, saxophone and clarinet. Once a pupil has reached grade 2, the lessons are free. A very strong brass ensemble. Two choirs – gospel and traditional. School choir performs at homes for elderly and hospitals throughout the borough, as well as occasionally at Southwark Cathedral. There is an open invitation for boys to join the Pegasus Opera Singing Academy and currently about 10 boys are training to sing with this group. Samba band, piano club and rock school also on offer.

Around 20 boys take drama at GCSE and numerous theatre trips are on offer. Two school productions each year, 'though more likely to be a fun production than Chekhov,' says school. Strong art department housed in well-resourced sky-lit art studios at the top of the school. Outstanding artwork on display and frequent visits to art galleries encouraged.

Wide variety of clubs on offer, including philosophy, ICT, basketball and the very popular Debate Mate, which teaches debating to inner-city schools in areas of high child poverty. Easter holiday revision classes and Saturday school provision are funded by pupil premium payments for those who would benefit from extra structured support. Trips abroad arranged to Spain and France as well as a character-building trip to Herefordshire to foster teamwork. Boys who can't afford trips are helped financially by the school or by livery companies.

Pupils are encouraged to look beyond the school walls and some boys recently gave a presentation to TfL on safe and sustainable transport. Significant numbers of speakers visit the school each year, including authors, actors and CEO of Surrey Country Cricket Club. School goes out of its way to inspire the pupils to achieve through positive role models. Rapper Tinie Tempah made a lively addition to a recent school assembly when he presented a pupil with an award for his work against youth violence.

Background and atmosphere: School is very proud of its ancient origins. Founded in 1685 by Archbishop of Canterbury Thomas Tenison, who wanted to provide the first free education for boys in London. Its first home was in St Martin-in-the-Fields and the annual Founder's Day service still takes place in the church there. School moved to present site opposite the Oval cricket ground in 1928 and has an enviable view of the pitch on match days. Was a grammar school and this is still reflected in its ethos and outlook. The site remains a tight squeeze, particularly at break times, but no plans to look for another location.

Christian worship is an integral part of the school and religious assemblies are held twice a week. School has its own chaplain. At the heart of Tenison's are the values of 'justice, mercy and humility', which are combined with the school's core values of 'compassion, hard work, accountability, respect and trust'. School doesn't just pay lip service to these principles but takes them seriously and expects pupils to do the same.

Stable and contented staff – about 20 per cent have been here for more than 10 years. School states that 'when teachers do leave it is nearly always for positive reasons.' Roughly 50:50 male to female ratio. The teachers we met were enthusiastic, welcoming and dedicated to the school.

School now going fully co-ed; first intake of year 7 girls arrived in September 2015. 'We feel the time is right to offer our unique mix of Christian values, tradition and academic rigour to all young people, regardless of gender,' says the school.

Pastoral care and discipline: School prides itself on its pastoral care and there is a supportive, family feel to the school. Every pupil has a tutor keeping an eye out for them. On the morning we visited, one pupil was being looked after in a teacher's office while he let off steam before an incident escalated. The pupils know the staff are there for them at all times. Operates a zero tolerance policy on drugs, weapons and replica weapons but permanent exclusions are rare.

High standards expected regarding uniform; no baseball caps or trainers. Short hairstyles preferred on boys. Different coloured blazers for different age groups (younger boys in blue and older ones in black); house ties worn throughout. Sixth formers wear business uniform and the ones we saw generally looked immaculate, with only the odd rebel not toeing the line.

One boy, quite new to the school, rated Tenison's highly. 'It's good,' he told us. 'The teachers are nice and I enjoy the lessons. They show us respect. It's quite cramped but not too bad. It's much better than my old school, though I go home for lunch as I don't like the food.'

Pupils and parents: Majority of pupils come from local area, mostly Southwark and Lambeth. Fifty per cent black African; 15 per cent black Caribbean; a growing Latin American contingent; small numbers of Asians; roughly 10 per cent white. Excellent attendance record. Pupils are generally proud to be at Tenison's and deputy head commented that 'we have to remind some of them to go home at a certain stage in the evening. They don't want to leave. They trust us and feel safe here.' Large proportion has English as a second language though it's unusual not to be fluent on arrival at school. Those requiring EAL support are growing each year.

School says that the 'overwhelming majority of parents and carers are supportive'. Recent PTA pampering evening arranged for mothers and carers was a great success and saw the great hall converted into a beauty salon. Regular newsletters sent out and parents are encouraged to read pupils' homework diaries. Parents are expected to work with the school in their child's education and development and to support the school in what it is trying to do.

Entrance: Seventy per cent of places offered to those of Christian faith; 30 per cent open places. Not as over-subscribed as previously due to free schools and academies opening nearby, but still not short of applicants.

Exit: Vast majority of pupils go on to higher education (many being the first generation in their family to go to university); only a few head for the world of training or work. De Montfort, Greenwich, Kent and Kingston popular. One or two apply to Oxbridge most years. Huge spread of subjects studied at university, from physics to architecture and criminology.

Pupils are well supported with university applications including the writing of personal statements, through charitable organisation IntoUniversity, which supports young people from disadvantaged backgrounds to attain a university place or another chosen aspiration. As school deputy remarked: 'If they don't get an offer from a university, it won't be because of a poorly written personal statement.' A handful of students opt for art college (Camberwell, Chelsea or Central Saint Martin's) each year; others prefer to study fashion. Some to drama school – most recently to the competitive BRIT School in Croydon.

School has built up strong external links including with livery companies – The Worshipful Company of Cutlers provides bursaries for those studying medicine at university and The Worshipful Company of Dyers awards a university bursary to pupils who attend City University. Surrey County Cricket provides funding for students who study PE at university and often lends its facilities. Strong links also with St John's College, Cambridge and pupils also have opportunities to become involved in mentoring schemes with LSE.

Remarks: A small school which is going from strength to strength. Archbishop Tenison's remains a safe haven in this underprivileged part of south London and has increasingly high expectations of its pupils, taking every opportunity to celebrate individual and group success. The teachers believe in the pupils and students are rising to the challenge.

Beatrix Potter Primary School

Magdalen Road, London SW18 3ER

State • Pupils: 410 • Ages: 3–11

Tel: 020 8874 1482

22

Email: Info@beatrixpotter.wandsworth.sch.uk
Website: www.beatrixpotterschool.com

Headteacher: Since 1988, Stephen Neale MA Dip Ed Tech Dip Ed (late 50s). Growing older and wiser, he remains a popular hands-on head, described by parents as a real character, somewhat unconventional and very easy to get on with. Brave enough to make his own decisions and not a person to get tangled up in bureaucracy. Married to a Polish opera singer, with one grown-up son. His enthusiasm for travelling, links with other schools and exploring different cultures all over the globe influences many of the school's activities. Beatrix Potter has gained the British Council's Full International School's Award twice. A steam train enthusiast, Mr Neale also enjoys sailing and travelling.

Entrance: Admission to the school via the standard Wandsworth primary school admissions criteria. Looked after children and special needs pupils first, then those living closest to the school. Admission is usually oversubscribed, but if you are not lucky enough to get a place in reception, it's always worth calling the school for occasional places in the older age groups.

Exit: Pupils move onto a big mix of senior schools. Around 60 per cent to state sector: Burntwood, St Cecilia's, Southfields, Wilson's and Wallington Grammar. Forty per cent to independents, including Emanuel, Dulwich College, JAGS and Wimbledon High School.

Remarks: Good solid curriculum continues to be at the heart of this delightful primary school; all pupils are well grounded in literacy, numeracy and IT. Imaginative range of projects covering history, geography, sciences and international links are embedded into classroom work and the arts. Fab new technology suite and equipment, where pupils can contact children all over the world via Skype and Facetime. These links often turn into fantastic foreign adventures for pupils, and have led to the school being asked to host a European Link Project. The caretaker's house has been redeveloped so the school can offer accommodation to pupils and their teachers visiting from abroad.

It's not a pushy school, but everyone gets to where they want to go. School produces parents' booklets packed with information on how to support your child at home and get involved in their education. The ethos is all about being a happy, balanced person who is able to move on to senior school well equipped to cope in new settings. Head runs advice sessions for parents to assist them in selecting the right senior schools. Children with SEN are well cared for by full-time SENCo and her assistant, who run a variety of small groups for children with different additional needs. School is eager to work with parents and other therapists to help children

achieve to the best of their ability. Since the refurbishments, the building is now fully accessible for children with physical disabilities. Kids City runs on-site breakfast and after-school clubs.

Mr Neale and architects have worked hard over the last few years to redesign much of the school, and there are now two classes right through. Outdoor spaces have been improved with courtyard

---

Growing older and wiser, Mr Neale remains a popular hands-on head, somewhat unconventional and very easy to get on with, brave enough to make his own decisions and not a person to get tangled up in bureaucracy

---

areas, picnic tables and three outdoor courts and there's a large new sports hall. Sports coaches are brought in from local clubs for lacrosse, cricket, tennis, tag rugby and football. Parents say the arts are developing well, particularly now the school has separate spaces for art, dance and drama. Another bonus of the expansion is the new kitchen: the school can offer freshly cooked lunches every day. Initially the expansion process caused quite a few wobbles and rumbles from some parents. However, everyone is now in agreement that the school is able to offer more to its pupils while still maintaining its long-term reputation for being a warm, friendly community school. PTA and school governors are all very active and fundraise substantial amounts of money for both the school and various charities. Past and present pupils have many fond memories of the school. Some can't stay away, returning to do their teaching practice or even joining the teaching staff permanently.

Belleville Primary School

Webbs Road, London SW11 6PR

State · Pupils: 825 · Ages: 4–11

Tel: 020 7228 6727

Email: enquiries@bellevilleschool.org
Website: www.belleville-school.org.uk

23

Headteacher: Since 2001, Mr John Grove (50s) BEd MA, previously head at West Hill Primary School in Wandsworth. Two children, both at university; partner also works in education. A man consumed by his job, who found Belleville failing in 2001 and has worked uncompromisingly to make it the

most sought-after primary school in the area. In his rare moments off, admits to being a season ticket holder at Chelsea FC. A visionary, who still gets unexpected hugs from the youngest of his charges as he roams the corridors.

Entrance: At 4+, 120 places, in four forms of 30. Heavily over-subscribed. Usual local authority admissions criteria: special requirements, siblings and those living closest to the school (no more than around 270 metres away for a first offer). Popular on-site nursery takes 52 children each year, but nursery place does not guarantee entry to reception in main school.

Exit: Since Bolingbroke Academy opened up the road in 2012, approximately half to this new non-selective school, which local residents campaigned for. Others to a range of local state and private schools, including Alleyn's, Dulwich, Whitgift and Emmanuel. A few sit successfully for Graveney School, Tooting, which has a grammar stream. A steady trickle to the Lycée Kensington and the German School Richmond, reflecting the number of European families in the locality.

Remarks: Already large, Belleville is set to get larger. Glossy new site at Meteor Street houses a reception and a year 1 class, and will become a one-form entry campus for the school's full age-range as time goes by, complementing the existing three-form entry at Webbs Road. Head admits intake will probably have to stop at 900, but clearly frustrated by lack of space in this cosmopolitan neighbour-hood, where two-bed conversions go for £700k.

'My dream is to take one of these nearby private schools, turn it into a state school and expand,' he told us, his eyes gleaming behind their gold-rimmed specs. 'Only one?' we asked. He smiled.

> *'My dream is to take one of these nearby private schools, turn it into a state school and expand,' he told us, his eyes gleaming behind their gold-rimmed specs. 'Only one?' we asked*

As well as a penchant for the state sequestra-tion of private property, Mr Grove has a passion for doing things well. Housed in what was once a dark and gloomy Victorian maze, imaginative building work has turned Belleville into a really beautiful school, where old-time space and solidity meets modern light and technology. Walls have been knocked through, windows replaced, venetian blinds fitted in attractive colours, and everywhere painted to look bright and fresh. Intelligent, crea-tive use of ICT is integrated into the fabric of the school and is awesomely good: iPads and tablets are mounted in every corridor, displaying slide-shows of school events, offering information, etc. Classrooms have ICT projectors and interactive whiteboards, teachers use visualisers (for dino-saurs like this reviewer, that's a powerful digital camera that points downwards and projects onto the teacher's computer/projector screen, so that books, objects, etc can be magnified and displayed clearly to everyone in the room). We were gratified and impressed to see this head, at least, insisting that the children learn on both Macs and PCs, as well as on desktops, tablets, netbooks and smartphones, so that they can cope with whatever system a given environment has in place. But none of this has come at the price of old-fashioned excellence. Work on the walls showed both handwriting and content of a very high standard. Ofsted stated that 'pupils achieve exceptionally well', and everywhere we saw children working with a lively yet calm focus. 'The behaviour is excellent here,' asserts head, 'We have 800 children and I never have to raise my voice.' We believe him.

Specialist teachers are employed for art, music, PE, dance, French and computing, and the results are splendid. Wonderful artwork – inspired by, for instance, Van Gogh and Kandinsky – is everywhere, produced by the children from a modest-looking art room with love and skill. When we arrived, we were deafened by a terrific workshop on Sengalese drumming, which turned out to be a weekly event for all the classes. (One lad, so moved by the spirit that he couldn't sit still, suddenly left his djembe and did an impromptu breakdance, to fond applause). The children all learn French, and were keen to show us how much they knew.

SEN provision is strong and mostly integrated, with plenty of one-to-one support for individuals provided during regular lessons. 'We don't withdraw unless we have to,' confirms head. Parents report themselves satisfied: 'SEN support is really

Specialist teachers are employed for art, music, PE, dance, French and computing, with splendid results. We were deafened by a terrific workshop on Sengalese drumming. One lad, so moved by the spirit that he couldn't sit still, suddenly left his djembe and did an impromptu breakdance, to applause

good'; 'The school's been brilliant both at pushing my abler child and supporting my younger one.'

Belleville is one of only five primary schools in London to be awarded the status of National Teaching School, and professional development is inescapably at the heart of everything it does. In each year group there are teachers whose core job is to improve pedagogy and teaching, and the children certainly seem to enjoy their lessons. 'The teachers are really nice'; 'The teachers are fair'; 'They really try and make the lessons fun and they do succeed'; 'The teachers are very good people,' were just a few of the comments we heard. Parents agree: 'We've been impressed with the enthusiasm of all the teachers'; 'The classroom assistants have been an invaluable resource'; 'The staff are brilliant and the academics are brilliant'; 'My children have always had fantastic teachers.' There was also praise for the many clubs on offer, both in and out of school, with parents particularly grateful for the breakfast and after-school clubs: 'They cover long hours, which is very helpful for working parents.'

The school prides itself on its diverse community, although its location in the heart of Yummy Mummy Central (as Clapham Common is locally known) inevitably accounts for the very high proportion of articulate, well-mannered, middle-class children that we met there, most of them Caucasian. We heard murmurs from a few parents of different ethnic backgrounds, who, while remaining extremely positive about the school, felt that it could do more to acknowledge their children's needs. Belleville's motto, proclaimed in huge posters everywhere, is 'Relentless Drive For Excellence', and it's possible that this relentless drive has occasionally knocked a few obstacles out of its path. We couldn't help noticing the almost universal youth of the teaching staff, with its few older members hived off to the school's smaller Meteor Street site, where, presumably, fewer people could be offended by their wrinkles and grey hairs. (And in fact they too will soon be mostly replaced by younglings, head assures me, but will be redistributed at Webb's Road, where they can hide amongst the 20-somethings in plain sight.) But by any measurable standards, Belleville is an outstanding school. 'My children are thriving at Belleville, and are valued,' was a typical parental comment. 'My child has done as well as she could do,' was another. 'I can't imagine her doing better at a private school'. Which is just as well, really; if Belleville gets any more successful, there won't be any left.

Broomwood Hall (Garrads Road)

Linked schools: Broomwood Hall (Ramsden Road), 68; Broomwood Hall (Nightingale Lane), 69; Northcote Lodge, 139

3 Garrads Road, London SW16 1JZ

Independent • Pupils: 140 • Ages: 4–8 • Fees: £14,190 pa

Tel: 020 8682 8830

Email: admissions@northwoodschools.com
Website: www.broomwood.co.uk

Principal: Lady Katharine Colquhoun BEd (50s). Has a rather regal manner but her vision has seen this school mushroom from humble beginnings (handful of children in a local Methodist Church), to a thriving empire with over 600 pupils (as well as 200 boys at Northcote Lodge – the brother school down the road). 'She's remarkable,' one parent told us. 'Inflexible at times, and you have to toe the line with her, but she is seriously impressive.' Lady Colquhoun knows she has an able team behind her and believes the ability to delegate, which she learned as the eldest of five children, is her secret.

Lady Colquhoun has made the transition from headmistress to joint principal with her husband, Sir Malcolm. She still teaches literature to prep school girls, whilst he is in charge of administration and property. School has a board of directors which oversees both Broomwood Hall

and Northcote Lodge and comprises the principals, heads, bursar, director of admissions and Patrick Colquhoun (Malcolm's son).

Mrs Carole Jenkinson, head of the Upper School in Nightingale Lane, took over as headmistress of all Broomwood Hall in September 2015. Mrs Jenkinson is supported by Katie Paynter, who is responsible for the day to day matters at Garrads Road. Miss Paynter joined the school in January 2015, bringing with her a wealth of experience in teaching and learning from most recently Oakfield Prep and from the Shell International Schools.

Entrance: Hugely over-subscribed, non-selective and located in the heart of Nappy Valley. For reception class, parents must provisionally register their child in advance on the provisional list, and are invited to register formally and pay the £100 fee once they

have attended an open day or individual tour. This is followed by a 'readiness assessment' around the child's third birthday, a year prior to entry.

School says it looks for a wide variety of characters rather than a type and aims to have a good spread of birth dates throughout the year, as well as a 50:50 mix of boys and girls. Forty reception places here and 80 at Ramsdon Road. Priority to siblings.

A strict one-mile radius rule applies which ensures all children can walk, cycle or scoot to school. Head encourages parents to apply to a number of schools in the area, to avoid disappointment. Not a huge international contingent – still predominantly well-to-do British families with some Europeans and Americans. Small number with English as an additional language are given support if needed.

Exit: Most girls to Broomwood Hall Upper School in Nightingale Lane and the majority of boys transfer to Northcote Lodge. A few disappear at this stage to country preps (such as Cheam, Ludgrove, Farleigh and Cothill) and some opt for neighbouring day schools (Dulwich Prep, Dulwich College and King's Wimbledon among them).

Remarks: One of the two Broomwood Hall lower school sites, substantial arts and crafts style Edwardian mansion, a stone's throw from Tooting Common. Large, pretty garden with lots to keep children occupied – hopscotch, vegetable patch, climbing frame, sandpit and outside classroom for reading on summer afternoons.

School has a relaxed country feel; on the day we visited, pancake races were in full swing in the playground and children and teachers were having a ball. One mother we spoke to felt Garrad's Road was less academic than its Ramsden Road counterpart, but curriculum planning is done jointly and the same syllabus is followed. Good reports about the school's support for children with dyslexia and nurturing approach given to any pupils who are slower off the mark.

Smaller and cosier than the other Broomwood sites, with two classes per year group. Happy and friendly young staff. The parents we spoke to felt school gives a solid academic grounding as well as a joyful start to school life.

Talented head of music writes plays and composes scores for productions. Art and drama taken seriously. Substantial amount of sport on the weekly timetable. Full-size hard tennis court in the garden used for PE. Cricket, football and rugby pitches 10 minutes away on foot. One parent we spoke to felt this is 'possibly not the right school for a really sporty child,' though others disagreed and said there were plenty of matches going on. Wide range of after-school clubs, including karate.

Food considered to be excellent – 'probably better than they get at home,' said one parent. Children are expected to eat in silence for the main course and then chat over pudding, so they finish their plates and learn good table manners.

A welcoming, gentle school full of delightful children.

Broomwood Hall (Ramsden Road)

Linked schools: Broomwood Hall (Garrads Road), 67; Broomwood Hall School (Nightingale Lane), 69; Northcote Lodge School, 139

The Old Vicarage, 192 Ramsden Road, London SW12 8RQ

Independent • Pupils: 260 • Ages: 4–8 • C of E
• Fees: £14,190 pa

Tel: 020 8682 8830

Email: broomwood@northwoodschools.com
Website: www.broomwood.co.uk

24

Principal: Lady Katharine Colquhoun BEd (50s) (see Garrads Road entry).

Mrs Carole Jenkinson, previously head of the Upper School in Nightingale Lane, took over as headmistress of all the Broomwood Hall schools in September 2015.

Entrance: For details see Garrards Road entry.

Exit: For details see Garrards Road entry.

Remarks: This part of the lower school is located on two sites – The Old Vicarage, a rambling, red-brick former parsonage, for the first two years and 50 Nightingale Lane, around the corner, for the next two years. Both feel homely, with tartan carpets throughout, a fabulous mural of former pupils going up the stairs and attractive displays at every turn. Teachers engaging and inspiring; this is a lively place to work. Broomwood is a Christian school, children say prayers at break time and the

end of the day. There's also a weekly church service – 'but we don't bible-bash,' says head.

Reading is of paramount importance and the libraries are well-stocked and well-used. Classical music was being played in the background in one classroom on the day we visited, with calm, focused children enjoying their lesson. School rewards hard work in all areas: copious numbers of cups awarded to pupils (including for good manners and friendship). Head believes children have to learn that they will only win a cup when they have tried really hard and must learn to accept that they will not win every time.

Beautiful artwork. Music and drama seen as an important part of the timetable. Compulsory recorder at both lower schools from the off. A large number of individual music lessons take place each week, with every conceivable instrument on offer.

Head acknowledges that parents are more demanding than a decade ago, but understands 'that the significant financial output for school fees means they inevitably want to know they are getting value for money.' Cheerful, well-behaved children abound here.

Broomwood Hall School (Nightingale Lane)

Linked schools: Broomwood Hall (Garrads Road), 67; Broomwood Hall (Ramsden Road), 68; Northcote Lodge School, 139

68 – 74 Nightingale Lane, London SW12 8NR

Tel: 020 8682 8830

Independent • Pupils: 220 • Ages: 8–13 • Fees: £17,430 pa

Email: broomwood@northwoodschools.com
Website: www.broomwood.co.uk

25

Principal: Principal: Lady Katharine Colquhoun BEd (50s). For details see Garrards Road entry.

Headmistress: Since 2001, Mrs Carole Jenkinson BSc PGCE (50s). Varied career, including time as ski rep, with stints at International Tribune in Paris and British Council. Started her teaching career at Northcote Lodge. Universally respected

and admired by parents; everyone we spoke to described her in glowing terms. She exudes calm wisdom. Very knowledgeable about senior schools of every hue and spends a significant proportion of her time visiting potential schools up and down the country. Teaches maths to year 7 and verbal reasoning to year 4, so has a good grasp of each girl's abilities and character before recommending suitable senior schools. Now head of all three Broomwood Hall schools.

Entrance: Three forms per year, rising to four per year from year 7. Maximum 18 per class. Vast majority come up from lower schools. Those coming from elsewhere must register on the provisional list and provide a report from previous school. Parents have a tour and time with the headmistress, and prospective pupils spend a morning in the school where staff assess their academic ability in a classroom setting.

Girls come from as far afield as Fulham, Chelsea and Dulwich. A Fulham parent we spoke to felt that those who were not from the immediate area were made to feel like outsiders by parents – 'the Wandsworth brigade can be quite intimidating for non-locals as they stick together like glue.' The school itself bends over backwards to integrate the new recruits. Morning and evening minibus to Fulham and Chelsea. Places vacated by 11+ leavers are quickly snapped up.

Exit: About 20 per cent leave at 11, mostly to south London day schools (eg JAGS, Alleyn's, Streatham and Clapham High) or to boarding (Benenden, Downe House, Woldingham). More stay until 13 and then head to co-ed boarding eg (Bryanston, Marlborough, Wellington and Epsom College). A few to single-sex boarding (Benenden, Cheltenham Ladies', Heathfield, Tudor Hall) and local day schools. High number of academic, sport, art and music scholarships gained each year.

At time of writing, was awaiting the results of a planning appeal about converting adjacent Rayne

Principal is keen on instilling good manners in her pupils. Pretty uniform and girls are required to have a comb in their backpacks at all times; ear piercing strongly discouraged

House into a senior school for 13-16 year olds (max 120 pupils). Subject to approval the school will open with about 15 pupils in September 2015.

Remarks: A very well-run, flourishing school that knows where it is heading. For those who want a modern education underpinned by traditional values, there is arguably nowhere better south of the river. Wonderful garden, including an amphitheatre where girls perform plays. Tea is served at the end of lessons, followed by compulsory supervised homework at school. Viewed as a godsend by busy parents, and children say they like being able to relax (save for rote learning) once they get home. Some parents, admittedly, would prefer homework to be done at home so they can keep a closer eye on their child's progress. Clubs, including flower arranging and glass painting, finish at 6pm.

Good mix of long-serving and new staff, with some having chosen teaching as a second career. Biggest challenge is coping with teachers constantly going on maternity leave.

Principal is keen that girls learn that hard work pays off and girls certainly keep their heads down here, although there is also great fun to be

had along the way. Lots of lively young assistants, including Australian students and ex-pupils on gap years. School recommends tutoring for pupils who are having difficulties but is against tutoring just to get a girl into a certain school. Head believes it backfires once the tutoring stops and the child can't keep up at their next school. Setting in English and maths throughout school. Fantastic science labs.

Sixty pupils receive some form of SEN support. School feels able to support mild dyslexia and dyspraxia but wouldn't be the right place for anyone with severe difficulties. Currently 30 children with English as an additional language.

Principal believes old-fashioned values hold true and is keen on instilling good manners in her pupils. Children hold doors open for adults and look you in the eye when they talk to you. Pretty uniform and girls are required to have a comb in their backpacks at all times; ear piercing strongly discouraged. Pastoral care is a great strength of the school. A trained counsellor is at school regularly to help girls with eg potential eating disorders, exam phobia or bereavement. Pupils select their own tutor and are encouraged to talk to them about both academic and non-academic issues and the system works well. Resident matron deals with cuts, bruises and tummy aches.

The school is ahead of the pack when it comes to technology. Girls bring in their own iPads and older girls learn computer coding (which they love). Drama is a real strength, everyone is in two plays a year, one of which is biblical, 'so they know their Old and New Testament stories by the time they leave.' Flamboyant productions, including revues, well attended by parents. Bright art and DT studios, complete with impressive equipment. Art exhibitions include drawing, painting, carpentry, needlework and pottery. Eighty per cent play a musical instrument, with many girls reaching high grades. Four choirs, including a prestigious chamber choir for which there are auditions. Recent choir trip to the Vatican.

Good variety of sport on offer, including netball, lacrosse, hockey, rounders, tennis and sailing. Some sport played on-site but girls regularly bussed elsewhere for more space. Some pupils currently performing at pre-county level. 'We've definitely become a sportier school,' says head. Lots of teams, so the less talented can play in matches too. Currently winning or drawing three-quarters of matches; school excels at cross-country and netball.

Delicious food – 'my daughter thought the food was great and she's quite a fussy eater,' said one parent. Younger girls sit together and are supervised by a teacher; older girls eat canteen-style. Girls are encouraged to make conversation and to hold their knives and forks correctly. Leith's has written a bespoke cookery course for Broomwood.

All girls in year 7 have weekly cookery lessons in the sensational cookery department and during the summer term pupils put on their aprons and cook a three-course meal which they serve to their parents. Always a great success and highly anticipated.

Good communication between school and home. Parents are encouraged to get involved in school life, from providing costumes for plays and painting scenery to nit checks. Lots of social events, including leavers' dinner – a swish black tie affair for parents, pupils and teachers. Massive amounts of fundraising for a school it has built from scratch in Ethiopia. Parents are very supportive of the enterprise, though one or two grumbles about not enough money being given to local charities. Drop off and pick up times involve huge numbers of mothers, either in gym kit or walking the family labrador, though school notes that more and more mothers work. Some joint ventures with Northcote Lodge (debates, clubs and field trips) – but one mother we spoke to felt that in reality the girls and boys hardly mix and that this is a missed opportunity.

School turns out well-adjusted girls, fully prepared both academically and socially for the next stage. Broomwood celebrates success on all levels (cups are given for 'being a good egg' and for demonstrating originality) and parents emphasise what a great job it does in producing confident, happy and successful girls. As the school handbook firmly explains: 'We don't expect parents to become heavily involved in the minutiae of the learning process; we do expect you to leave your daughter's education to us and let us get on with it.' If you do that, your daughter will be in safe hands here.

Plans for further expansion include a newly acquired block of flats just behind the Nightingale Lane site, earmarked for Broomwood Hall Senior School, which will educate girls from 13-16, subject to planning appeals. Principal feels that 'some of our girls are not quite cooked when they leave us at 13.' She adds: 'If they can stay on here till 16, we will have done our job properly.' Current parents appear enthusiastic about the prospect of the school extending to GCSE level.

The Charter School

Red Post Hill, London SE24 9JH

Tel: 020 7346 6600

State • Pupils: 1,100 • Ages: 11–18 • Sixth form pupils: 250

Email: info@charter.southwark.sch.uk
Website: www.charter.southwark.sch.uk

Head Teacher: Since 2013, Mr Christian Hicks (40s) grew up in West Norwood and was educated at nearby Dulwich College, then collected a BA in German studies and European literature at Bristol, an MA in English and American literature at Newcastle and an MA in effective learning at the Institute of Education.

Very likeable, open and seemingly far less ego-bound than some heads. Mr Hicks lives in Beckenham with his teacher wife and three young children – two boys and girl. Out of school he thrives on learning new things, recently taking up magic and completing the Yorkshire Three Peaks Challenge. What could be more useful in a demanding headship than a head for heights, stamina and the ability to pull rabbits out of a hat?

Despite his own alma mater, he is committed to the principle of comprehensive, inclusive education. Previously deputy head of Blackfen girls' school in Bexley and before that deputy head of the Royal Docks Community School in Newham. His move was not without ambition. The Charter School is never far from the dazzle of the spotlight, its every move noted and often written about in national newspapers by the influential parental and local body. School's bid to create a new senior school of equal size half a mile away in East Dulwich has been approved by the DfE.

Head jokes about his tough remit of improving on the already vastly improved academic standards. Has high expectations of his pupils, aims to challenge, inspire and be highly visible: he isn't too grand for break duty and is on the door with his headship team every morning and afternoon to greet, send off and confiscate any attempts to flaunt the uniform. He sees one of the most vital parts of his role as 'getting the right people on the bus' – the hiring and firing of an exceptional team of teachers.

Academic matters: Unfazed by the ending of modular assessment at GCSE, 79 per cent of pupils gained 5+ A*-C including English and maths in 2015, with 64 per cent A*-B grades. At A level, 62 per cent of grades were A*-B and 29 per cent A*/A.

Standard-ish curriculum at GCSE, including French, Spanish and Latin plus Mandarin for those with an aptitude for languages at year 7. The school has been teaching Mandarin with some success and finds it accessible for those with dyslexia. GCSE English results have soared, maths is solid, and sciences are strong. History and art and design are both popular and successful. Weak spots most recently – media studies and RE.

Relatively few taking computer science, but the school is ahead of the curve in making the transition from ICT and is looking forward to pupils who have been coding at primary school joining in future years. A group of girls recently won a competition to design an app for a local business, whilst prizewinning games designers met the Duke of Cambridge at an enterprise event at BAFTA HQ.

A few less deskbound options such as catering, PE and performing arts and a handful of BTecs on offer – science, business, social care, engineering and ICT, with most success in business.

Head assured us that school will 'really push children who have been successful at primary school' – hence this school does well by the more able, with some 20 per cent of pupils generally achieving at least eight A*/As. Stand-out performances include lashings of A*s, but we noticed the school proudly trumpets the achievements of pupils gaining three Ds if this means that they have achieved well and are on track for their next step.

Head teacher thrives on learning new things, taking up magic and completing the Yorkshire Three Peaks Challenge

Best-performing subjects most recently at A level are: further maths and maths, biology, chemistry, fine art, English literature, history and a few -ologies. Languages seem a complete turn-off. Head says school is not alone in this. Aiming for an all-round academics, school will run subject even with a single pupil if necessary. Equal numbers of girls taking maths and a strong showing in sciences too.

Twenty-one teachers have more than 10 years' service – hard to believe as they appear extremely youthful. As one parent noted, 'teachers are mostly

young and cool.' In fact one was so young and cool that we witnessed the receptionist assuming he was a pupil. Head and parents point out the calibre of staff attracted here by the unusually leafy milieu for an inner city salary. Head is very clear about his expectations of staff: 'don't come here if you're not prepared to work hard for successful outcomes for the students.'

A thrilled father of three girls told us that 'science teaching at The Charter is fabulous; several staff have Oxbridge PhDs and the teaching is inspiring.' Others said: 'Our children are inspired by their teachers and are really motivated to learn' and 'the staff clearly work really hard and are extremely conscientious.' Average class size at key stage 4 is 20, with 30 the maximum and some as small as five for 'nurture groups.' In the sixth form the average is 18.

With regards to homework and pressure one parent said: 'There is a good balance of homework throughout the term and a very balanced approach to exams,' whilst another warned that 'it's very intensive.' Parents kept thoroughly in the loop. The school is quick to bring them in to discuss a student who is not attaining their individual target for each subject. Coasting is not permitted.

The school dazzles in its business and enterprise specialism, creating aspiration in thinking ahead to future careers – opening students' eyes to the wider world and maximising their situation in London is a real strength. The school has links with PwC, King and Woods Malleson, O2, King's College Hospital, the Worshipful Company of International Bankers, Shell UK and more than 100 business mentors.

One parent tells us that assistance given to her son included 'mock interviews, workshops on CV writing, presentation skills and financial awareness workshops.' The CEO of the Science Council recently spoke to year 10s about STEM careers and a doctor from King's College Hospital runs an annual seminar on applying to medical school. Students also sampled uni life at Lille, London South Bank and Brighton and large groups are taken to both Oxford and Cambridge to inspire.

Someone here is in possession of an amazingly A-list little black book – a truly top-notch class of the great and good drop in to inspire regularly. Imagine the thrill of a Romeo and Juliet masterclass with none other than Joseph Fiennes; Jo Brand speaking to celebrate International Women's Day; Professor Sir Michael Rutter talking about his latest research to psychology students; not to mention professional Bollywood dancers teaching the Samba. Nor are they short of invites: the day prior to our visit 30 pupils met Boris Johnson at City Hall at a reception to honour the contribution of African and Caribbean soldiers in the First World War.

Head emphasises the value of the growing D of E programme in fostering key learning aptitudes such as resilience. Around 300 day and residential trips every year, from Bletchley Park to Belgium, Berlin and Beijing. London theatres are made good use of with trips to the National, Unicorn and Young Vic this year. One parent said: 'The school also works closely with many charities and my son was lucky enough to take a charity trip to Kenya this summer.' The school is aware of hardship issues and helps with small bursaries where it can.

Quite high numbers of SEN: around 20 per cent of students across the school cope with varying degrees of learning difficulties, so everything from specific learning difficulties such as dyslexia or dyspraxia to physical disabilities, autistic spectrum disorder or ADHD. Large learning support team of 23 staff, including specialist SEN teachers, higher level teaching assistants and learning support assistants, support students in mainstream classes but may also be able to offer small group withdrawals, extra literacy and maths intervention sessions, touch-typing, handwriting and reading clubs and input from a range of external agencies.

Games, options, the arts: Sports are compulsory – and the only time girls and boys are taught separately. Footballers enjoy links with professional clubs such as Millwall and Fulham FC. Cricket and rugby are on the up: the MCC coach cricket and the RFU rugby. The coaching team includes national class coaches in table tennis and aquathon.

When the head was writing his mission statement, pupils asked him to add 'happiness' because that is how they feel

Students recently started play basketball competitively and are now enjoying BMX at Burgess Park.

Successes across the board, with pupils competing regionally and nationally, particularly the girls: the school boasts a national champion in rowing; under 13 girls' cricket team recently won the Lady Taverners' competition at the Oval; year 8 girls' rugby recently placed sixth in London; year 7 girls' netball team won the Southwark league. Over 500 pupils take part in after-school sports club every week.

The school appears rather boxed in by the neighbouring houses and plentiful sports ground of the neighbouring girls' school, but pupils use a playing field a five-minute walk away. Indoor sports hall is large and there is an on-site floodlit netball court, ball-court and Astroturf.

More than 200 learn a variety of 20 different musical instruments up to grade 8, with some lessons significantly subsidised and many trying an instrument for the first time. Two choirs and a jazz band, which may be led by teachers or pupils. Past students have gained places at the Royal Academy of Music. A favourite alumni is rising star Kwabs – The Guardian calls him 'the new Seal' and he has a recording contract with a major record label.

All pupils study drama once a week in years 7, 8 and 9, enjoying purpose-built drama studios and a flexible theatre space. A highlight of the dramatic year is the whole school theatre performance – most recently Guys and Dolls – featuring staff alongside pupils. A parent said of the art: 'I have been delighted with the art department. I feel the teachers really care about what they teach.' London galleries are frequented and facilities include a kiln, dark room, screen printing and Mac suite.

Lunchtime and after-school clubs include young historians, tennis, handball, track cycling, music theory, ukulele, African drumming and study skills. Pupils sign up on a first come first served basis. Most are free, with a small charge for tennis and swimming clubs.

Background and atmosphere: Smaller than most city comprehensives, The Charter squeezes into a plot a few strides from North Dulwich station and at the heart of Herne Hill. Built on the site of the defunct William Penn School, it opened in 2000 following a concerted campaign from parents in an area dominated by independent schools, but without a good state option.

Savvy parents realise that they have something of a find on their doorstep, but some nervousness persists locally around the legacy of the failed school, and the head is aware school has to work hard to ensure that no one child lets down the reputation of the whole amongst the local community. Ofsted has rated it outstanding twice since 2006.

Most of the buildings were remodelled rather than replaced. It is light and functional but now looking more than a little frayed at the edges, both inside and out. We wondered how a shy year 7 moving here from one of the cosy local primaries might make the transition. The head told us: 'This is a family school, a local school. When children move here they are often joining siblings or friends' – a third of every year group has school siblings. And everywhere in the mornings and afternoons one sees little gaggles of Charter pupils walking to and fro. Each year 180 new pupils join, but the school very often operates in year groups, with assemblies for each year. Lunchtime arrangements – a mix of indoor and outdoor seating under-cover – with year 7s heading to lunch 10 minutes earlier to avoid being overwhelmed.

Prior to lessons we noticed some boisterous boys in the corridor, but once lessons had commenced the atmosphere was exceptionally quiet and calm, with each lesson we viewed in both arts and sciences equally industrious.

Parents talk of happy children who are able to be who they want to be here. When the head was writing his mission statement, pupils asked him to add 'happiness' because that is how they feel.

Pastoral care and discipline: The relatively relaxed school uniform – polo-shirts and pullovers mostly, so no ties and without the blazers of the other nearby state seniors – is deceiving as to the school's culture of high expectations. Given the issues of the school in its previous incarnation, the school set out to be something of an innovator in managing behaviour and is known for its no-nonsense attitude to discipline, which it balances with care. Behaviour officers, not in evidence on our visit, have a remit to swoop into any classroom to remove a student who has overstepped the mark. The head says that 'any pupil who is disrupting the learning of others will be in school until 5 pm.'

More serious offences such as smoking will result in exclusion – gross misconducts are half what they were five years ago, although slightly up this year. The emphasis is on inclusion and working with pupils to find a way back to contributing positively. There is a whole raft of rewards including VIVO Miles – like air miles for good behaviour – extra school trips, presentations and a phone call to parents from the head or head of year.

Mobile phones are not allowed in school at all, except for sixth formers who must keep them out of sight. Any confiscated phones must be collected by a parent. No piercings other than one pair of ear studs; no hats, hoodies or outlandish hair colours.

Pupils should always have someone to talk to. There are strong relationships between staff and pupils, a tutor system, year 11 mentors for year 7s and a school counsellor. Even the staff get a buddy each.

Pupils and parents: A large part of the intake is from privileged Dulwich Village, Herne Hill and East Dulwich, but pupils encompass every kind of home life. More than 30 per cent of students are pupil premium students – the performance gap is significant but closing. On entrance, students demonstrate a wide range of ability but it is notable that by year 11, 56 per cent have risen to the two highest ability bands. A parent told us: 'This school is for children who want to learn, want to get somewhere in the world. It caters for all in that there is something for everyone.'

The school prides itself on its inclusivity and parents say it really 'celebrates diversity.' Forty-seven per cent of pupils describe themselves as white British, with black British African as the second largest group (11 per cent of pupils). Surprisingly few EAL students and whilst there are many bilingual pupils, 93 per cent have English as their first language.

Parents come from all walks of life. Very effective PTA has just bought a 16-seater minibus for inter-school sports matches.

Entrance: The hoo-ha over the school catchment area is in the past. Admissions criteria are looked after children, then siblings, then distance criteria using safest walking distance as a measure, which places the catchment currently at no more than 1,600 metres from the school. Parents in East Dulwich may want to get out their pedometers. No feeders as such but largest cohorts from Dulwich Hamlet Junior School, Dog Kennel Hill School, Heber and Goodrich local primaries.

The sixth form is more inclusive than many: pupils must have five A*-C grades including maths and English, with a minimum grade for subjects of study which varies.

Applications for places stand at seven to one. Crowded annual open days – often 2,000 attendees – are held in September for year 7 and November for the sixth form.

Exit: Virtually all achieve their guided first choice of university, with 51 per cent of pupils heading to top-ranking universities. Recent destinations include: Bristol, Durham, Birmingham, Edinburgh, Imperial College London and Leeds. One or two usually to Oxbridge (two in 2015).

Many pursuing other dreams have exited to equally prestigious destinations, such as RADA, major London art colleges and the Royal College of Music. Pupils have gained sought-after City apprenticeships with KPMG and investment company M&G, whilst the Queen recently presented one girl with a Southwark Council scholarship to pay all her university tuition fees.

Remarks: A truly local comprehensive and for those on the doorstep it may be the stepping stone to very good things. Well connected, with increasingly impressive academic results driven by a talented staff promising much for children who want to work hard and those who have previously found opportunities thin on the ground. For parents wondering whether there is life beyond school fees we recommend joining the open day throng.

DLD College

199 Westminster Bridge Road, London SE1 7FX

Tel: 020 7935 8411

Independent · Pupils: 500 · Ages: 14–21 · Sixth form
pupils: 400 · Fees: £19,000 pa

Email: dld@dld.org
Website: www.dldcollege.co.uk

3

Principal: Since September 2013, Rachel Borland, previously principal of Abbey College in Birmingham. She was principal of both DLD and Abbey College in London, until they integrated on a single, purpose-built site with student accommodation on Westminster Bridge Road in September 2015. She has previously been principal of an international boarding school in Nigeria, assistant director of studies at the British Council in both Hong Kong and Jordan, and worked at Bath University.

Academic matters: A small minority of pupils are there to do one-year GCSE courses, the rest one or two year A level courses. College offers a two-year GCSE programme geared for SEN students, also retake courses of varying length, up to one year. Maximum class size 10. Commendable results from a mixed ability intake. Most GCSE students take seven subjects, from a limited list that includes the basics plus French, religious studies, art, graphics and drama. Russian, Chinese, Spanish, Italian and German are available via individual tuition. In 2015, 16 per cent A*/A grades.

A level students get a choice of 35 subjects, including music technology, photography, film and media studies, sociology, psychology and languages, in more or less any combination. Art, economics, religious studies and philosophy are consistently popular, alongside English and maths; 60 per cent A*-B grades and 34 per cent A*/A in 2015. Will offer a greater variety of courses including BTecs and foundation courses in future.

Some students are disaffected when they arrive – 'but it is unusual for them to be anti-education after a few weeks. It's important to fit the right course to the right student. Because of the small class sizes they get lots of individual feedback and huge amounts of encouragement, and most start making progress very quickly'.

The college can cope with a wide range of special needs, generally picking up several previously undiagnosed cases each year. Most students need group support with study and essay writing skills; individual help is also available at extra cost. 'Our SEN students get more or less the same level of results as the others – due to getting the subjects right and plenty of support. Apart from English

for academic purposes, students can also have individual sessions with our SENCo.' Accredited by CReSTeD, whose most recent report speaks of it as a unique school.

No quarter is given academically – 'we will not accept scrappy work. We believe in raising standards and in helping students believe they can move up to the next level'. Many staff are from Oxbridge and some come from non-teaching backgrounds – the theatre, the City, the BBC. 'They work unbelievably hard,' said an insider. 'They put in a lot of effort for the students.' The most recent ISI report states that students like being at the college and are very happy with the personal support that they receive.

Games, options, the arts: A surprisingly arty college – A level art and photography are two of the most popular and successful subjects and several students are refugees from high-powered academic institutions where the creative side is less valued.

The main aim of most students is to pass their exams – extracurricular activities are not high on the agenda, except for those in plays and sports teams. A level students, in particular, often work long days. However, all GCSE students play curricular sport at local centres on Friday afternoons, including football, basketball, tennis, netball, dance, rock-climbing and aerobics – sports clubs and matches after school. The DLD youth theatre puts on two performances a year; the house band – organised by the drummer of Van der Graaf Generator, who is also the music technology teacher – plays well-attended gigs; film, Duke of Edinburgh Award, EPQ, debating and art clubs.

Background and atmosphere: Now one of 18 schools owned by the Alpha Plus Group, founded in 1931 to provide tutoring for Oxbridge and Colonial Service entrance exams. In 2004 it moved from Notting Hill to light, airy, refurbished premises in Marylebone; in August 2015 moved again, amalgamating with Abbey College in a new, purpose built site on Westminster Bridge Road.

Because of the small class sizes students get lots of feedback and huge amounts of encouragement

Informal atmosphere, closer to a college than a school, with staff and students on a first name basis. 'They're unfussy about clothes and about students in clinches on the stairs,' said an insider. 'But academically they're pretty tough. Students don't get away with things.'

Pastoral care and discipline: Strong pastoral system. 'Many students have had a shifting lifestyle and it's a real haven for them,' said an insider. 'There is a lot of respect because students know we care about them.' A register is taken in every lesson and parents are texted or emailed. Each student has a weekly meeting with their personal tutor to talk about progress and future plans. Tough sanctions for misusing drink and drugs – those under suspicion are sent for drugs tests, to general parental approval. 'There are a few troubled and troublesome students,' said a parent, 'but most buckle down eventually.'

'Occasionally there are students we don't manage to turn round. Then we'll often suggest to parents a gap year in the middle of the sixth form, preferably working in Waitrose. It concentrates their minds on the consequences of failing to work and the difference in maturity when they come back is often amazing.'

Sanctions include supervised study; also a system of verbal and written warnings based on employment law. Bullying is taken very seriously – 'They don't care about superficial things,' said an insider, 'but on work, drink, drugs and bullying they clamp down very quickly'.

Pupils and parents: Most students have come from private schools. Some have had enough of boarding; some have been ill; some have found their previous school too rigid or too stressful. Others come from peripatetic diplomatic families. Some lack confidence and need to learn good working habits. Most thrive in the informal but structured atmosphere.

Entrance: Those going into the sixth form need a minimum of five grade Cs at GCSE; if they haven't passed maths or English they will need to retake these. Everyone is interviewed and previous schools are asked for references. The college will not consider students who have been disruptive elsewhere.

Exit: A few GCSE students move on elsewhere – perhaps to state sixth form colleges – but most go through to the sixth form. Those aiming at Oxbridge are given an intensive course including lectures, seminars, mock interviews and individual tuition – one Oxbridge place in 2015. Extra help also for

potential vets, doctors and dentists, via a bespoke medical programme. Wide range of degree courses, with business, management and finance being the most popular, also art foundation, mechanical engineering, sports and exercise science.

Money matters: Several scholarships available, worth 10–100 per cent of fees, plus bursaries.

Remarks: Good at stimulating the very bright as well as re-motivating the disaffected. Informal atmosphere with strong staff/student relationships underly a structured regime where everyone is kept up to scratch.

DUCKS (Dulwich College Kindergarten and Infants School)

Linked schools: Dulwich College: The Junior School, 81; Dulwich College, 84

87 College Road, London SE21 7HH

Independent · Pupils: 167 · Ages: 3 m – 7 · C of E
· Fees: £7,170 – £13,605 pa

Tel: 020 8693 1538

Email: ducks@dulwich.org.uk
Website: www.dulwich.org.uk/ducks

13

Head: Since September 2015, Nicky Black, previously deputy head. A Durham graduate, she joined DUCKS from Hornsby House, where she was director of studies, head of lower school and head of maths. she is particularly interested in creative teaching and active learning.

Entrance: Into the kindergarten, six places for babies aged 6 to 18 months; 18 places for toddlers and up to 40 places for 'ducklings' of between 2 and 3 years. The infants' school comprises nursery from 3+ to year 2. There are usually five to 10 places available at the nursery, then 10 to 15 reception places, with places occasionally emerging higher up the school.

No assessment for entry into the kindergarten, but children entering at 3, 4, 5 and 6+ will have an assessment to ensure their learning at a stage where they can take advantage of everything the school has to offer. Priority throughout is given to the children of college staff and DUCKS siblings. We imagine the younger members of the college staff could keep the baby room next to filled. Given the small size, keen parents will want to register early.

Exit: Girls and some boys exit to a wide range of destinations – Alleyn's, JAPS, Sydenham High, Oakfield and Rosemead spreading to Streatham & Clapham High School and St Dunstan's College. The majority of boys move on to the junior school. There have been grumbles about the numbers being offered places. The school says in the last year 19 junior school places were offered and that the college may not be the right school for every child.

Remarks: The teaching staff is mostly female, some mothers with relatively young children themselves, hand-picked by the head based on 'qualifications and enthusiasm'. Parents seem to feel this a place where children can be themselves free from pressure. One said, 'It has impressed me that the staff are willing to work individually with children at a pace suitable for that child in that subject.' Another told us, 'My daughter is not interested in academic subjects but the teachers have awakened an interest in learning in her.' One felt that the head enables children 'to develop at the speed that they require, unlike the hothousing that is encountered at some prep schools.' This means 7+ time won't be overly-pressured, which won't suit all.

Teaching staff is mostly female, some are mothers, hand-picked by the head based on 'qualifications and enthusiasm'

Parents suggest that there is a good balance between the kind of learning through play where children are having so much fun they are oblivious to the learning and good, solid foundation skills teaching. 'Being taught how to count by jumping in puddles was a particular favourite of my sons,' said one mother. Another told us, 'My son rapidly caught up with his classmates in literacy skills, having moved to the UK from a country where phonics and literacy are started at a much older age.'

On our visit, the nursery children were busily and noisily involved in a variety of activities and play which only the trained eye would realise were carefully structured to deliver the early years curriculum – plenty of role play corners, freedom to go in and out, and excellent use made of glittery pasta. Their playground stretches up the grassy bank behind the school with Forest School elements newly introduced at the top. Reception classrooms are large.

Head of the kindergarten says modestly that the school is not unique but doing what they do well. She cites her staff as following the children's interests in their teaching – she points out the artwork on the wall where a child has painted what he wanted rather than following the given theme,

but it is still valued and appreciated. In the toddler room, currently decorated with a jungle theme, learning is very much child-initiated, with lots of sensory discovery.

No sightings of lunch, but pupils declared enthusiastically that the lunches are 'yummy' and 'tasty' – they are prepared on-site by DUCKS' own chef.

Achievements are celebrated in assembly, being invited to share a good piece of work with the head or with rewards including fruity tea. From year 1 the usual stickers, certificates, shields and trophies. Not a homework-free zone, but a parent said, 'just the right amount of homework and holiday work to keep the children ticking over.'

The school is committed to early identification of SEN – all pupils are carefully observed and assessed, if any SEN identified then work with the parents to establish the best support for the child. There are nine children with identified needs currently. The school recently admitted its first pupil communicating with British Sign Language – children, parents and staff have all received training with a BSL instructor.

Aims for PE set realistically for the age group, looking to develop spatial awareness, love of physical activity and play as well as social skills. Rather boy oriented, tag rugby, football and cricket on offer, and everyone learns to swim. A parent explained: 'The PE teacher is one of a kind, immensely talented and patient. The children have sports three times a week as well as extracurricular sports clubs if they choose. My son has at least five hours of organised sport a week.' Everyone learns to swim in the college pool.

Music is taught by specialists and all of year 2 learns the recorder. 'The music teacher pulls together amazing productions given the young age

'I love that my daughter has had the opportunity to start ballet with her friends at lunchtime,' says a mother

of the children.' Very able children are able to join groups at the junior school.

After-school activities every day of the week run until 4.30pm at a cost of around £4 per session offering an appealing mix of down-time or, for those with the energy, 3D modelling, swimming, ballet, football, netball and more. When there is always so much to fit into every day, lunchtime clubs can be useful: 'I love that my daughter has had the opportunity to start ballet with her friends at lunchtime', says a mother. So, clubs seem to offer redress the balance of the traditionally 'male' sport on offer for the girls.

DUCKS is so tucked away in Sydenham – one almost has to be in the know to venture in search of it when making the rounds of nurseries and pre-preps. If you are coming from Dulwich Village, Herne Hill or East Dulwich, it lies beyond a local curiosity, the Dulwich estate's antique toll-gate, which makes the road south of the college impassable to all but those willing to pay a pound a time to pass. Excitedly, we enquired as to whether DUCKS parents are given a toll-gate pass – not even staff are privileged with such a thing. Parents soon get the hang of the loop around.

A mere infant in terms of the almost 400 year old college, DUCKS recently celebrated its 20th anniversary. One might imagine that the school occupies only the large Victorian house fronting the road, but this is home only for the younger children: a good thing, as the rooms are slightly gloomy.

The majority of the classrooms are actually situated in a wooden-clad building looking over the playing fields and onwards to stunning views of the City and the glittering Shard. It looks very much like a cricket pavilion, echoing the actual pavilion used by the school until it burnt down in 1997 – the silver lining being the opportunity to create something which worked just for them.

The peace and quiet of the setting is a rare and unusual treat for any London family, and lends itself to numerous environmental themes, lots of muddy fun and gives rise to the names of the classes, all of wild birds. At the rear of the school are several soft surface playgrounds, segregated for various age groups, so plenty of space for letting off steam with no shortage of ride-on toys and a veranda ensuring children can play outside even on wet days.

The word used repeatedly by parents to describe the atmosphere here is nurturing. Parents told us, 'It is supportive of shy children but equally has the space and facilities for children who have boundless energy' and 'although not fiercely competitive, it does expect the children to stretch themselves.'

Whatever rumours of previous discord between staff and management have made their way to us, there have been key new appointments, teachers spoke of their happiness working here and much may now be set to change.

No concerns voiced with regards to pastoral care. One parent said, 'Outstanding pastoral care, and the school is good at communicating any concerns about our children with their parents'. 'They discuss bad behaviour in circle time in what appears to be a very meaningful way for the children.' Years 1 and 2 are all buddies to lower school pupils, whilst senior boys from the college visit as part of their community service.

Something about the building suggests a place more akin to a nursery than a school, but parents surprised us, saying it would suit 'a child

responsive to structure who is keen to learn' and 'those who prefer a more free and easy approach to learning would probably find things difficult.'

The school is proud of its pupils' cultural and linguistic backgrounds, celebrating them throughout the year. Currently 17 children in the kindergarten are at least bi-lingual and 29 children in the Infants' school are bi- or tri-lingual. Far fewer, just a handful, have EAL needs.

The school praises the parents, who embrace themes and initiatives keenly, even recently attempting to pry themselves from their phones and tablets for a 'screenless week'. One mother with an eye for telling detail said: 'This is not a school where working mothers and stay-at-home mothers compete, or where a parent can achieve kudos by the quality of party bags at their child's party.' Phew.

One summed it up with satisfaction: 'Outstanding. I have wanted for nothing.'

Dulwich College: The Junior School

Linked schools: DUCKS (Dulwich College Kindergarten and Infants School), 78; Dulwich College, 84

Dulwich Common, London SE21 7LD

Independent • Pupils: 225 • Ages: 7–11 • C of E • Fees: £18,231 pa

Tel: 020 8299 8432

Email: junioradmissions@dulwich.org.uk
Website: www.dulwich.org.uk

14

Head: Since 2013, Dr Toby Griffiths (40s). Educated at Whitgift School and the University of Edinburgh; completed a masters in educational psychology and

a doctorate in educational psychology at Oxford. Previously a six year stint as deputy headmaster at Lanesborough School in Guildford, where he was involved in the management and marketing of the school in a parent-facing role: a good precursor to being head. He has also taught at Colet Court, where boys are often on track to St Paul's, and eight years at The Dragon, where he was boarding housemaster and head of maths. Part of a teaching dynasty, his father taught at Whitgift for 38 years and his mother was a prep school head. He and his brother, also now a headmaster, were hockey blues together at Oxford. He considered teaching psychology, but from the moment he experienced the Dragon 'all bets were off' – he loves the junior school age group: 'their energy and enthusiasm, they seem so alive'.

Parents enthuse: 'he is approachable and responsive' and 'very much involved in every aspect of the college and knows the boys well'. Determined and no doubt extremely competitive: 'bring it on!' he said (with regards to a forthcoming school inspection).

The green spaces of Dulwich made moving to London easier. He lives nearby with his wife, Vicky, now working in the City. Their son is at the top of the junior school and daughter at nearby Sydenham High.

Entrance: Approximately 45 places available at age 7+, many taken by boys coming up from DUCKS, six to eight places in years 4 and 5. Register in the autumn preceding the desired year of entry. Tours most Friday mornings for prospective parents and autumn open days. Assessments during January in maths, English, verbal and non-verbal reasoning. Not looking for perfection, understanding of differing educational experience, but all round ability. Successful applicants invited for an interview and an activity morning.

Dr Griffiths says the junior school has gone from being popular to very popular, with now over

This is the time for experimentation. 'We want boys to be and to try everything by the time they leave here – a rugby player, actor, musician, chess player, mathematician and writer'

three applicants per place, and is increasingly seen as the 'start of the college'. Boys come from as far away as Greenwich, Orpington and Fulham, up to a 40 minute commute. The school lists an eclectic list of feeders at 7+ in addition to DUCKS: Herne Hill, Bertrum House, Broomwood Hall, The Villa Pre-Prep, River House Montessori and Babington House, seemingly not many of the nearby state primaries.

Exit: Almost all (95 per cent) go on to the college. The head says that those who don't go on from the lower school are very rare, and only after extensive dialogue over several years regarding where they would thrive best, and then it is the parents' decision. We asked a parent if they felt their son was well-prepared for the next stage; they replied, 'absolutely. And if we didn't, we would feel comfortable raising any issues with the teachers and headmaster.'

Remarks: Once more sporty than academic, the balance has been redressed, and it is now much more of an all-round school. Dr Griffiths says, 'It had always been a through school, but at one time the boys from the junior school had taken their foot off the pedal whilst everyone else worked hard to get there [the college], so four to five years ago the bar was really raised to ensure primacy of the classroom'. It does mean that there is no need for exam pressure to dominate. Focus is on 'doing their best, not pass or fail'. Boys we spoke to were quite nervous about the forthcoming 11+ tests despite in reality the certainty of a place – all carefully designed to ensure they arrive in the college confident in exam technique and on a level playing field.

Dr Griffiths is enjoying the best ever set of academic results this year, with half of the top 10 11+ entrants to the college coming from the junior school. Teaching time has been increased by 40 minutes per day and all children now have two periods of French per week. No gripes about teaching reached our ears, quite the opposite: 'The boys seem fired up by what they learn. There has been a practical element to subjects which fires the imagination and creates interest.'

Curriculum is delivered by form tutors with specialist staff initially for French, art, DT, music and games, with additional specialists in later years.

Parents pretty united on homework, saying, 'We don't feel it is intensive at all. Obviously there is homework, but we feel that it is suited to our sons' capabilities. There is extension homework for those boys who are more academic and help for those who perhaps find it takes longer to grasp certain things.' No holiday homework – other than when preparing for the 11+ exam. 'Doesn't feel too pressured re exams or testing'.

Improved rewards system – commendation certificates, bronze, silver and gold, are presented in assembly. Reports for parents show effort and attainment, which is appreciated by parents who conclude, 'it will likely do much to encourage the children.' 'Very little pressure on the lead up to exams. In general, we haven't known when the boys are due to have any sort of assessment. And while there is homework every day, it is rare that it will take more than 30 minutes'.

Surprisingly low levels of SEN. All children are screened for dyslexia on entry to year 3. Some may be referred for further testing and diagnosis. There are four full-time learning support teachers shared between the junior and senior schools. In the junior school, teachers work with individuals and small groups to provide extra support where needed, perhaps in terms of how their working memory affects spelling, organisation, numeracy, creative writing or comprehension. Less than two per cent receive EAL support, but many from multilingual families.

This is the time for experimentation. The headmaster tells us, 'We want boys to be and to try everything by the time they leave here – a rugby player, actor, musician, chess player, mathematician and writer'. Should not have to choose between a swimming gala and orchestra practice – the sporty head says he won't let fixtures take over.

'With 70 acres of fields there is no shortage of sport and it is all first class,' cried a delighted parent. All boys play rugby, football, hockey and cricket, everyone has the opportunity to play a competitive fixture, whether extra or intra school. Aim is for boys to represent the school in every sport – 'everyone gets to go on the coach and shake hands with the opposition', so far managed it for football. 'Our sons are not in the A or B teams for sports, but they always get to play matches and be involved in the sporting community'. Fitness should be a given with gymnastics, swimming, rackets and athletics in addition. Stars include a year 6 national breaststroke champion and several county representatives in cricket and chess. A highlight for many is the trip to the college's outdoor centre in the Brecon Beacons.

Everyone performs in the year 3 and 6 plays. The recent Bugsy Malone performed in the Edward Alleyn Theatre looked enormous fun.

Music department seen as first rate. All the boys in the junior school learn a stringed instrument in year 3 and a wind instrument in year 4, and perform in two major productions. Some 40 per cent then have individual lessons. 'Our younger son has decided to have extra violin and guitar lessons and we are not a musical family,' said a surprised parent. A year 5 pupil recently won the prestigious Bach piano competition, open to the whole college. There are opportunities to play in ensembles and orchestras and sing in the choir. Boys have performed at London venues including Southwark Cathedral, the Cadogan Hall and St John's Smith Square. Pupils benefit from the wider college co-curricular activities, recently taking part in Dulwich Creative by designing their own graffiti t-shirts.

These boys are readers – the library has 8,000 books and a full-time enthusiastically chatty librarian who insists that books are not just for book week, that she never tells everyone to 'shhh!' and that 'life's too short to finish a book you're not enjoying'. The Roald Dahl day is an annual fixture where everyone dresses up as their favourite character. Art projects line the walls, currently takes on Mark Rothko and work inspired by a trip to Tate Modern to study Henry Moore.

Just the swim squad and chamber group up and at it early. At lunchtime a couple of by invitation clubs such as madrigal and chapel choir, but also each year has choices such as karate, tennis, book club, chess, sewing and various music ensembles. After-school clubs have been extended and now run until 5pm. Boys can do their prep in the homework club or try Russian, dance, cycling, magazine club or French aviation.

The location on the southerly edge of the college campus in a peaceful backwater just a stone's throw from the useful South Circular, and station makes drop-offs and collections pleasant. The building itself is modern and handily adjacent to the lower school, with a pitched roof, wide corridors upstairs and quite spacious classrooms. The library tucks under the roof, giving cosy reading nooks. Year 3s have their own playground.

We were impressed that year 6 boys were entrusted to lead us solo on our tour of the school, with only a little assistance from Dr Griffiths on time-keeping – not every school entrusts its pupils, of whatever age, to speak as they see fit with a visitor wielding a pen. It speaks volumes. Parents, too, speak of this level of trust between boys and teachers. One said of their son, 'He truly looks forward to being at school. He has had very supportive form teachers – strict, but fair, so there is an obvious level of trust.'

Boys seem to feel listened to and have seen their ideas put forward to the school council come to fruition, such as more play equipment for the playground.

A parent told us, 'This school excels in its pastoral care. We couldn't ask for better.' Others agree, 'They know the students very well and truly try to understand not just individual students, but the different dynamics amongst various groups of boys.' And in the case of a problem with peers raised with the school, 'The boys were supported, but given opportunities to address the issues themselves.' Teachers are seen as responsive – known to answer emails out of school hours.

Competitiveness abounds – house allegiances start here – but there is room for inclusiveness: all year 6 boys are prefects, rather than an elite group. And every year 6 child has a buddy in the lower years – our guides introduced them to us with grins as we went around: we might have thought they were siblings.

Parents say, 'The boys feel like they belong in the school and with each other.' And, 'The atmosphere is one of feeling included. It is not an exclusive school.' Parents themselves sound unpretentious and appealing, describing each other as 'friendly, relaxed, supportive of their children', 'from all walks of life', 'welcoming, fun, and interesting.'

As for the college as a whole, appearances can be deceptive and there is a rich social mix. Many say there is no type for whom the school particularly caters, 'it's tough to see what kind of child the school wouldn't be suitable for.' Several say: 'He can't wait to leave the house in the morning.'

A few academic scholarships at 10 per cent of the tuition fees, plus means-tested bursaries may be available for the very able whose families fulfil the financial criteria.

Dulwich College

Linked schools: DUCKS (Dulwich College Kindergarten and Infants School), 78; Dulwich College: The Junior School, 81

Dulwich Common, London SE21 7LD

Tel: 020 8693 3601

Independent • Pupils: 1,525; 130 full and weekly boarders • Ages: 11–18 • Sixth form pupils: 450 • Fees: Day £18,231; Boarding up to £38,052 pa

Email: info@dulwich.org.uk
Website: www.dulwich.org.uk

15

Master: Since 2009, Dr Joseph (Joe) Spence BA PhD (mid-50s), a graduate in modern history and politics; the Irish histories and literature of his postgrad line his study walls. Previously headmaster of Oakham School and for 10 years until 2002 held the prestigious position of master in college at Eton, housemaster to the King's scholars 'surrounded by the brightest'; it was here he found his vocation. His first decade at Dulwich College will coincide with the college's 400th anniversary, entwining their legacies.

Grammar school educated, he describes his career path as the 'story of accident', a happy one.

The turning point was a friend's encouragement that one 'no longer has to be behind a desk as headmaster'. Immensely warm and charming, putting one at ease, the embodiment of the oft repeated 'Dulwich boys can talk to anyone'. He brings a sense of fun to those around him, appearing to wear his responsibilities lightly, preparing to ad lib a speech to a grand assembly as he says goodbye.

He is married to a lawyer, with two sons and daughter. He still finds time to write, recently penning a new libretto for a concert at King's College Cambridge, turning a poem written by PG Wodehouse's brother into a song. He wants these

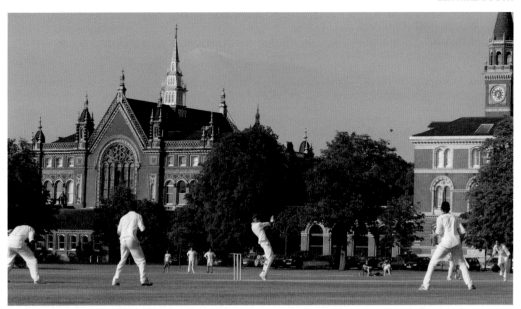

sustaining passions for the boys: 'my duty is to make sure that every Alleynian leaves with something intellectual... a passion which will be with him for the rest of his life'.

Parents, seeming to have adopted the Ofsted phraseology, unanimously declare him to be outstanding. They enthuse: 'a good orator, a great listener'; 'as fiercely passionate about the arts as academics'; 'a great presence and a motivational leader'; 'excellent, effective and innovative'.

His vision for the transformations in progress – physical and philosophical – start with 'get the classroom right, then everything else', but quickly go beyond with the desire to create a generation of original thinkers. You don't have to be a scientist or an artist here – 'learning that is free from the syllabus', allows boys to take risks in a dazzling (we've rarely seen such a weighty catalogue of riches) programme of challenges, national and international competitions, symposia, external prizes, performances and physical adventures.

Academic matters: It's well known that improving the academics was top of the agenda. The college is now in the top eight per cent for value added nationally and the master is confident that the best is still to come, just around the corner, given the way the current GCSE cohort is flourishing.

In 2015, 85.2 per cent of I/GCSE grades were A*/A. Plenty of A*s in sciences, English literature, maths, French and Spanish. At A level/Pre-U, 62.3 per cent A*/A, and 89.4 per cent A*-B. Maths is most popular by far, followed by physics, history, economics and chemistry. High percentage of A*/As in physics, plus history of art, English, further maths, history and art. A levels remain as the core

upper school offer but individual heads of subject have the flexibility to offer Pre-U.

Academic teaching is described by parents as solid lower down the college but inspirational higher up. Thirty-five per cent of teachers in residence for over 10 years. The master says candidly that now only a handful are perhaps not on message, and he won't see boys stuck with them, which chimes with parents, who say, 'very good standard of teaching, noticeable improvement' and 'incompetence would not be tolerated'. They also describe staff as 'hugely committed'; 'they understand a boy's potential'; 'they set the bar high academically' and 'the daily report system is excellent'.

The master drives innovation. A key appointment is the director of science, formerly at lauded Brighton College. Turning things on their head, 'flip' lessons might give boys homework first, then the boys come in and discuss how they found it, or mini-whiteboards may enable a teacher to see at a glance whether boys have 'got it'. Boys were initially consulted on their view of assessments, and came back saying they actually felt there was grade inflation – pupil voice has been used in every key decision since. Staff share with each other a 'speciality dish' ie what is working for them in the classroom.

Curriculum is largely as one might expect; choosing options is quite complex. Languages have a particularly strong focus throughout. French, Spanish, Chinese and Latin are taught in the lower school, later on there is the addition of German, Italian and Greek. Appealing language trips: year 9s to Salamanca, year 11s to Florence. The boys describe them as holistic, taking in both language and culture, raising their passion for the subject up a notch. Exchanges take place too, but with boys considerably settled in host families in pairs.

The only setting is for maths. All pupils study separate sciences up to IGCSE and the college doesn't necessarily encourage the collection of an excessive number. Intellectual boys wishing to stretch themselves further between years 7 and 11 can enrol on the scholars' programme, described by one as 'the highlight of my week'.

Quirkier A level options include critical and contextual studies and ancient history. Liberal studies in the upper sixth in conjunction with the girls at JAGS allows boys to try something new: modern poetry, yoga, book-binding, Italian cinema and even ballroom dancing.

Also for sixth formers, the Dulwich Diploma, which looks to offer the depth of A level with the breadth of the IB: the three components comprise academic study, at least four AS levels and three A2s, an extended essay or research topic of their choice – recent examples Who Killed Sylvia Plath? and Is Medical Research the New Imperialism? – engagement beyond the classroom and preparation for life after Dulwich.

Whilst all of this adds up to a very full plate, parents say there are 'high expectations with excellent support through study skills sessions' and 'it's pretty intensive in terms of workload but not too high pressure'.

Dr Spence brings a sense of fun, appearing to wear his responsibilities lightly, preparing to ad lib a speech to a grand assembly as he says goodbye

A team of four well-qualified learning support teachers are shared with the junior school, and provide support to individual boys with a diagnosed learning difficulty – 20 per cent. Eight per cent of middle and upper school boys receive EAL support.

Games, options, the arts: In year 7, whilst skills are built and some sports tried for the first time, rugby, football, hockey and cricket are all compulsory. By year 8 choices emerge, one being dropping rugby for fencing. Tennis currently squeezed for space with only three courts. No single sport is compulsory in the middle school but a plethora of teams make it tempting to get involved – skiing, rowing, fives, squash, cross-country and basketball, to name but a few. Years 10 and 11 may try golf, rock-climbing, self-defence, taekwondo and rugby 7s, whilst upper school choices aim to involve boys in sport however that may be, perhaps officiating

Our curiosity was piqued as to what goes on at the Gentlemen's Club (no-one seemed to know); presumably no cigars

or coaching as well as trying gentlemanly pursuits such as croquet, horse-riding and sailing. The school has responded to the national appetite for competitive cycling and boys are able to use the superb facilities at nearby Herne Hill velodrome.

Seventy acres of playing fields recently re-seeded, and rugby is the triumphant sport with 1st XV recently winning the NatWest Schools cup for the third consecutive year. Success, too, for the under 14s rowers, who are national champions, and the school supplies four members of the under 15 GB water-polo team. Boys we had lunch with laughingly said the only thing they didn't like was swimming as there was no point trying to keep up with the Olympic swimmers and water-polo players.

Dr Spence continues to ponder how one achieves balance amidst such rich opportunities: '50 boys will have played at Twickenham, that's a once in a lifetime experience', but are there 'boys who might have done better academically if they had not done so much?'

'Arts, music and co-curricular are outstanding'. We arrived just in time to be treated to a sensitive rendition of W H Auden's Stop All of The Clocks as part of that day's house poetry competition. The school has a rich theatrical tradition, a flexible theatre space, Chewetel Ejiofor and Rupert Penry-Jones are OAs, makes the very most of the London theatre scene, and each year produces three drama festivals and 24 performance pieces.

A parent said, 'What I really like is the drive to go beyond the curriculum and inspire'. This term's Dulwich Creative week was produced with all of the finesse and confidence of a national arts organisation gone guerrillan and saw art hijacks where every pupil – astonishingly even the babies in the kindergarten – produce a clay self-portrait, which then came together into one installation. A surreal note remains overlooking the cricket pitches, giant polyurethane mushrooms by international street artist Christian Nagel. A new 'found' space, The Store, chills to the bone, but provides an edgy, white-washed, informal rehearsal space which boys can call their own, which also houses art exhibits.

Art and DT facilities are light and bright, and where we found some of the most exuberant classes in full flow. We admired Grayson Perry-ish vases produced in ceramics classes, and groovy dog kennels in DT.

Numbers learning instruments peak in the lower school at 45 per cent of boys, falling naturally enough to 25 per cent by the upper school. Standard of musicianship varies from enthusiastic beginners to boys who are leaders of section in the National Youth Orchestra or principals at Glyndebourne and the ENO. The music department is in the process of upgrading: there is a shiny new Mac suite for music technology, a new acoustic percussion suite, and small and large practice areas. Another funky new facility is the electric 'shed', fully sound-insulated, a great place to let rip with the electric guitar.

Formidable debating team, who recently trounced the competition at the Oxford and Cambridge Unions. Where next for the boy currently ranked number one in the world?

Long lunch hours ensure even the senior boys feel they have time for clubs and societies, which continue after school. For the lower school these might include fencing, card games, woodwork and Scouts. For the middle and upper school a sophisticated list offers Japanese culture, alternative thinking, finance, Norse and Germanic, ultimate frisbee and rocketry. Poultry society boasts its own hens; whether they are ever eaten is set to be a college myth. Our curiosity was piqued as to what goes on at the Gentlemen's Club (no-one seemed to know); presumably no cigars.

The careers office has a 2,000 strong network of former parents and corporate contacts: a recent event invited 40 such to the Dulwich Picture Gallery. Boys were instructed to read up on everyone's biographies then were sent off to network fiercely.

Background and atmosphere: Founded in 1619 by the wealthy actor and businessman, Edward Alleyn. He set up and endowed the Foundation, which distributes its surplus profits to a group of schools including Dulwich College, JAGS and Alleyn's. The college moved to its present site in the 1870s. The main buildings are stunning Italianate red brick designed by the son of the architect of the Houses of Parliament. Inside, the panelled Great Hall lined with the names of Oxford and Cambridge scholars – up until the wall space ran out in the 1960s – has featured in a Hollywood film or two, more often the site of Old Alleynian dinners, the master's library and the Wodehouse library (PG is an Old Alleynian), with a significant theatrical archive including a Shakespeare First Folio.

Sitting amidst vast manicured pitches, the college is a gracious and intriguing south London landmark. Closer up, the collection of modern buildings forming a large part of the teaching spaces, particularly in the lower school, are plain and nothing more than functional, quite possibly a bit depressing. The buildings housing the upper school feel fresher – Ed's place looks like

a commercial café, and there is a huge common room, whilst a second one was sacrificed to create a popular 'work room' with banks of computers. Ironically for a school that appears so stunning to the passer-by, it's the fabric of the school which could currently disappoint parents if not boys.

However, much of that is set to change – we donned hard hat and work boots to inspect the almost complete Laboratory, costing over £21m, which will put the college's science offer ever more firmly on the map. The first phase opened in April 2015, the second is due to be completed for summer 2016. Led by prestigious Grimshaw Architects – Cutty Sark, The Eden Project – It literally removes the divide between arts and sciences, including a 240 seat auditorium, as well as five IT suites and 18 glassy labs looking over the beautiful trees of Dulwich.

At its centre is displayed Shackleton's boat, a treasured college possession previously residing appropriately enough with a stuffed penguin in a chilly cloister. Conrad Shawcross RA, with a committed team of 10 boys, worked on an installation. Naturally it leads the way environmentally too. The finishing touch, which may transform the feel of the college as much as anything, is the bright idea of removing the central car park, replacing it with landscaped recreational and thinking spaces.

The Dulwich College partnership schools overseas thrive, the latest in Singapore, but the master is clear that Dulwich is his absolute focus: he has delegated all but top level sign-off. Similarly, although he has championed outreach and partnership with a London academy group, a pie-chart of time devoted would see this account for only 10 per cent.

Sartorial traditions define the college – 'colours' blazers are boldly striped affairs awarded in recognition of achievement. 'Buy a big size,' advises the school captain – they will be de rigueur come

OA reunions. You need a spotters' guide to identify old school ties, there are so many for every society and event. The master sees the Christmas fair attracting 3,000 local residents as a way to prove that the school isn't 'stuck up'. He is aware that the uniform gives off mixed messages, but wants the boys to wear it with pride. Believes the school is and should be 'class, creed and colour-blind'.

School lunches seem due for a make-over, but boys won't starve. Students we spoke to in the lower school were amusing, boisterous; those higher up articulate, but not at all arrogant, and all with different interests. A regular visitor to the school said, 'The boys appear relaxed and happy, there's always plenty of banter and camaraderie in evidence'.

Pastoral care and discipline: A senior prefect told us he's a rarity, having been at the school all the way from year 1, but has relished meeting new boys – 'each intake year interests and friends shift' – and although the school is large, boys feel they know each other within their year. The transition points are handled thoughtfully, ensuring boys get to bond with each other, for instance on a Welsh adventure when joining the lower school.

Houses are named after great Englishmen, and wooden boards throughout the school see Drake, Spenser et al jostling for position – house competitions facilitate new friendships as well as much rivalry.

We were on the look-out for indifferent pastoral care, but found no evidence for it whatsoever, instead much praise. A parent – 'Boys know where they stand with the master, and whilst he's friendly and approachable, boys know he won't tolerate certain misdemeanours...hard line on bullying'. Another, 'He strikes the right note on being nurturing but also seeing that the boys get on with

The master sees the Christmas fair attracting 3,000 local residents as a way to prove the school isn't 'stuck up'

being independent'. 'A caring atmosphere which celebrates the individual,' said a parent of a child diagnosed with ASD. One noted realistically that 'pastoral care is good, but the biggest problem is to get the boys to overcome male pride and admit they need help.' Gross misconducts such as possession of drugs or bullying would result in consideration for exclusion, whether fixed term or permanent, rather than an automatic exclusion.

Pupils and parents: The college is academically selective and socially inclusive, with a very culturally and ethnically diverse population, augmented by the boarders mostly from China or Hong Kong. Lots of multi-lingual children who might speak Chinese, Russian, Spanish or French at home. Boys mentioned pupil-led assemblies: recent topics include homosexuality and discrimination. The school captain said: 'There is no Dulwich way. You don't have to conform.'

A parent: 'It takes boys who are sporty, academic, musical, artistic and a mixture of all those things. If your child is gifted in one area, they will soar here. If they are a good all-rounder they will be encouraged to be a great all-rounder.' And it may come as a surprise to find that parents describe each other typically as 'a good bunch of mixed, non-stuffy parents', 'un-snobbish and not cliquey.'

Entrance: Not the ultra-elite intake of a few London schools, but still a top 15 per cent ability profile. At 11+, half of the 75 boys arrive from Dulwich College Junior School and half from a variety of local primary and prep schools including Hornsby House, Blackheath Prep, Rosemead, Dolphin School, Oakfield, Honeywell, Belleville, Corpus Christi, Dulwich Hamlet, St John's and St Clements. Parents are asked to send a letter from a registered professional regarding SEN needs to ensure appropriate assistance with the entrance exam. At 13 + the main feeders are Dulwich Prep London, Northcote Lodge and Fulham Prep. Non-refundable registration fee of £100 for Brits and £200 for overseas candidates.

A good number come from the immediate vicinity of Dulwich, but Foundation coaches brings pupils from as far away as Notting Hill, Canary Wharf, Wimbledon and Chislehurst.

Exit: Pupils recently exited to 52 universities, a list headed by Manchester, but closely followed by UCL,

Durham, Bristol, Exeter and Warwick. Oxbridge places are consistently around 10 per cent of places, (17 in 2015). There will be an increasing focus on global destinations, particularly Ivy League. Currently around a dozen each year exit to overseas universities – often the Chinese University of Hong Kong, a couple to Harvard, Dutch universities in the slip-stream but the list has also included MIT and UCLA.

Money matters: Currently 411 boys in receipt of financial assistance of various kinds – 145 have means-tested bursaries ranging in value from five to 100 per cent and 266 have scholarships, ranging in value from 10 per cent to one-third of tuition fees. 'Superb value for money,' said one parent of three privately educated children. 'Quite simply, Dulwich College far outstrips the rest in terms of communication, professionalism and results'.

Perhaps most exciting of all in terms of evolution is the college returning to its early 20th century past in launching a New Dulwich Experiment, championed by the master, which will see up to 50 per cent of pupils coming from families who cannot afford to pay full fees, opening up admissions to some of the brightest pupils from all backgrounds. In some ways it is a protective measure against becoming a school for the global super-rich, and the master freely admits it is 'enlightened self-interest', but partly funded by OAs keen to give something back, it sits very well in this already socially enlightened place.

Remarks: A school with a long tradition, with all of the prestige that comes with it, but now with a thrilling new dynamism which is raising the academic ante in every way, creating glittering new learning spaces and delivering a stunning co-curricular vision. Far more inclusive than one might imagine, the new bursary scheme needs to be trumpeted far and wide to ensure the school is on the radar of the brightest from all backgrounds.

Dulwich Hamlet Junior School

Dulwich Village, London SE21 7AL

State • Pupils: 390 • Ages: 7–11

Tel: 020 7525 9188

Email: office@dulwichhamletjuniorschool.org.uk
Website: www.dulwichhamlet.southwark.sch.uk

16

Headteacher: Since 2007, Mrs Sonia Case BA PGCE (50s). Previously deputy head of Greenstreet Green Primary, she has had a number of years' experience teaching in Bromley schools. Married with two grown-up daughters and with her broad artistic background, ideally placed to helm this primary school. Originally trained in theatre, she worked in performing arts and marketing, before turning her attention to education and leading this unique school with its truly enhanced curriculum. She is supported in her work by a diverse and committed team of teachers and specialists. Her enthusiasm and cheerful personality are much appreciated by staff and parents, who feel children just love being at the Hamlet. Mrs Case appears to be something of a wizard when it comes to the school budget.

Has now also taken on the headship of the new Belham Primary School in Peckham.

Entrance: At 7+, 90 places; entry is via the Southwark admissions policy. Pupils come from many local primaries, particularly Dulwich Village Infants. Always oversubscribed, but don't let that put you off applying.

Exit: At 11+, majority to The Charter School; others to eg St Dunstan's, Dulwich College, Sydenham, Alleyn's, Grey Coat Hospital, Kingsdale. Pupils regularly win scholarships and awards for music and academics.

Remarks: Probably Southwark's most sought-after primary school. The Hamlet continuously develops and updates its spacious site, which consists of several Victorian and modern buildings skillfully blended and connected. Most recently, a fabulous space has been redesigned to create a multi-purpose hall, dining room, design and technology suite and children's cookery area. Adventurous and inspiring curriculum has ensured the school remains a top performer both academically and artistically. Classrooms are attractive and well-resourced, with traditional equipment alongside all the latest technology. Classes are mixed ability and large, usually about 30 pupils; setting for all year groups in maths.

School continuously updates its spacious site. A fabulous space has been redesigned to create a multi-purpose hall, dining room, design and technology suite and children's cookery area

Undoubtedly the most distinguishing feature is the arts curriculum, particularly music, which is almost unheard-of today in the state sector. Nearly all pupils learn an instrument and structured music lessons are part of every child's education. Impressive range of instruments, anything from euphoniums to Gamelan gongs. Choirs, woodwind, strings and brass groups and ensembles regularly entertain parents, and the children are invited to many public performances and festivals. A variety of dance and drama projects run and children have 100 per cent pass rate for LAMDA exams. Several art exhibitions in-house and in local galleries and school is involved in community art projects. Musicians, actors, artists and writers regularly invited to the school to talk to the children and run workshops.

Music lessons are part of every child's education. Choirs, woodwind, strings and brass groups regularly entertain parents, and the children are invited to public performances and festivals

Technology is embedded across the curriculum – everyone has the opportunity to learn touch-typing, Apple Macs for animation, art projects and of course music technology. French is thriving – year 5s are taken on annual residential trip to France. Sports Active Mark – pupils take advantage of the local sports facilities, a number of sports specialists visit the school to coach gymnastics, netball, cricket and football. Young athletes represent Dulwich in swimming and athletics competitions. Enrichment afternoons run during the summer term, giving children the opportunity to explore all kinds of activities and discover new interests. Around 15 after-school clubs to choose from – amongst the most popular are cookery, magic and table tennis. A full-time inclusion manager is responsible for running additional support programmes, and specially-trained teachers for those requiring SEN provision. Speech and occupational therapists work with the school as necessary. ESOL can also be arranged.

Pastoral care is organised through the PSHCE curriculum, producing confident, articulate and responsible pupils who come from a wide variety of backgrounds. Healthy eating is important here – lunchtime is a social event in the new dining room or outdoor picnic area. Monthly menus are on the website and all food is freshly made. The Hamlet Herald keeps the school community up to date with all the current happenings; also an excellent user-friendly website. Parents are asked to make a small voluntary contribution each term to school activities and an enthusiastic PTA and governors run a variety of social and fundraising events.

As you might imagine, judged outstanding by Ofsted in all areas. The school continues to play an important role in supporting trainee teachers working with Southbank and Goldsmith's Universities. An educational treat.

Dulwich Prep London

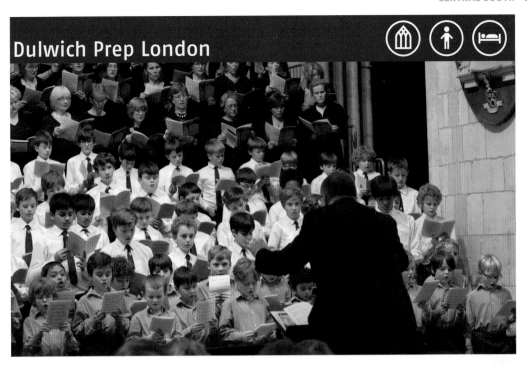

42 Alleyn Park, London SE21 8AT

Independent • Pupils: 850; 20 weekly boarders
• Ages: Boys 3–13, girls 2.5–4 • C of E • Fees: Day up to
£16,185 pa; Boarding up to £20,961 pa

Tel: 020 8670 3217

Email: registrar@dulwichpreplondon.org
Website: www.dulwichpreplondon.org

17

Headmaster: Since 2009, Michael Roulston MBE MEd (50s). Married with three children, educated in Ulster, he is warm and friendly, zipping about and offering to 'play mother' with the Darjeeling on our visit. First impressions aside, one senses his combination of vision, drive and no nonsense was forged during his first headship in the 1980s at The Model School – an informally religiously integrated school in Northern Ireland. His contribution to conflict resolution in the field of education was recognised by the BP Gulbenkian Citizenship Award in 1994.

After a stint in Japan as headmaster of The British School in Tokyo, earning him an MBE for services to education, he returned to the UK as head of Cranleigh Prep in Surrey. This is a man who clearly thrives on challenge and change, with his eye on the prizes – his and the boys'. We see him as a definite moderniser, sprucing up the old traditions, delivering a slickly presented school with a few fashionable nods – boules, allotments – without straying from his brief of happy parents and pupils at common entrance. Prior to our visit we had heard him described by parents as being 'rather like a successful CEO'. We found him to be

business-like certainly, but not stiffly corporate. Yes, very 'on message', but sincere too.

He says of the school, 'It's fun, full of energy from the earliest years all the way though...every day you cannot but be inspired by what the boys do. They are valued, recognised and well-loved'.

Head of the Pre-Prep Early Years since 2011, Mrs Ruth Burtonshaw BSc Phd PGCE Dip dyslexia and learning, is an early years specialist, appointed by Michael Roulston.

Entrance: Admission is selective. Multiple points of entry but majority start in the nursery at 3+ (girls and boys), at 4+ (boys only) or at 7+ (boys only). Limited number of means-tested bursaries to new applicants in years 3 and 4, determined by academic assessment.

Exit: Don't think that entrance to DPL is a do-not-pass-go ticket straight to Dulwich College, but a large proportion of pupils do gain entrance – with others heading in a variety of directions, foremost Westminster, Alleyn's and Tonbridge. Recent leavers exited to 28 different schools. Conversation regarding choice of senior school starts as early as year 4, and headmaster claims that every boy achieves his first (guided) choice of destination. Good tally of academic, sport, art and all-rounder scholarships or exhibitions, with many scholarships offered to Dulwich College. Only two or three boys a year choose to leave at 11+.

Remarks: The main curriculum is fairly traditional. French from year 1 and everyone tries their hand at Latin. Spanish offered as alternative to French. We found the lack of fashionable forward-thinking options such as Chinese or Russian surprising when even the local state primaries are giving them a go. The Head says Mandarin has been offered as a club in the past, but there was little interest.

Setting in maths from year 4, extended to all examined subjects by year 7. This really works, with parents confirming there is sufficient flexibility for boys to move within the year to find the right level for them, and to be encouraged by their ability in different subjects. In each of the classes we visited, young male teachers were particularly noticeable, in amongst the boys or sitting on desks, easily relating to the boys in lessons ranging from European history, via maths to music technology. Energy fairly resounds and parents of pupils at the lower school, particularly, describe it as 'buzzing'.

Almost 20 per cent of boys are identified with a learning difference, mainly mild to moderate dyslexia. The head says that the school will do its best by all, but any with significant difficulties may find themselves guided to a more specialist school such as Fairley House. Highly-trained specialists lead a good number of staff in the learning support department. We saw great learning integration in the older years with dyslexic boys using laptops alongside their peers; parents confirm that boys don't feel singled out in any way if they need extra

help. Nonetheless, some comment with feeling on just how tough it can be and wish for a little more two-way communication with teachers.

Headmaster is warm and friendly, zipping about and offering to 'play mother' with the Darjeeling

Sport is well resourced, with fixtures both after school and on Saturdays. Seven full-time PE teachers, specialist coaching from year 4, more than 70 teams, and achievements at national level, particularly in rugby and swimming. Every boy has an opportunity to play. Parents say coaching is less good at the lower levels, and whilst clubs offer exciting opportunities from rock-climbing to kayaking, 'alternatives to the obvious sporting options are very limited in the younger years'.

Homework is as ever controversial. One mother comments that whilst the boys love the varied topic work, parents find it 'never-ending' at weekends.

Drama varies from year to year. There is a year 6 play and an upper school play each year. Year 7 classes have drama and each year 8 class is off time-table for two weeks to produce an original production. Art continues to year 8 with clearly inspiring teaching, new facilities and technologies. We were wowed by the boys' 3D acrylic sculpture after Jackson Pollock, and the excitement in the room as the boys made sophisticated digital animations.

Music is rich, appealing and widely pursued, with over 20 ensembles and choirs, concerts of every type at venues in and out of the school, such as the Royal Hospital, Chelsea and Southwark Cathedral. Ninety per cent of the boys from year 2 upwards study an instrument, many achieving grade 8 before they leave.

Clubs (only a few additional charges) and activities run at lunch-time for boys from years 1-4, but also 4-5 pm from year 5. Current options include Lego, Warhammer, movie-making, bee-keeping, street dance, juggling, Greek, golf and gymnastics. Wide array of trips – no stone unturned on the London museum circuit – further afield during school holidays (often built into the fees) eg Pompeii and Normandy. All this plus a thought-provoking lecture series – featuring recently a holocaust survivor, notable writers, broadcasters and adventurers.

The school was founded as Dulwich College Prep School (DCPS) in 1885. Despite the confusion arising from its name, the school is completely independent from Dulwich College and is an educational trust with its own governing body. This has recently been clarified with the school now styled as Dulwich Prep London (DPL). Situated in a wide, quiet West Dulwich street a few minutes from the

train station, the buildings, mostly fairly modern, crowd around the playground.

With just over 800 pupils the school is large, but we saw how the division of the school into four distinct sections, each with its own library and classrooms, really works – 'the boys are quite protected from feeling lost in a huge place, and they're fully prepared for moving on,' says a parent.

Parents from the nursery year to higher up the school all comment on the benefit of a single sex school where teachers are free to focus on knights, dinosaurs, bloody battles etc. If there's one thing this school seems to do brilliantly it's the ability to really 'get' boys and how they learn and put this into practice. There is wiggle time (dancing around between lessons), marble parties or even a pool table as a whole class reward – 'the motivation and excitement are huge'.

The school motto is 'one for all and all for one' and the houses are named after North American Indian tribes from Chippeway to Objiwas. The winning tribe raises their flag weekly up the pole in the playground and if this is all sounds incredibly macho, we hear the boys sometimes choose to sing ABBA as their victory song! Meanwhile others, who choose the calmer activities from book club to weaving and needlework, do so without fear of ridicule. Some parents transfer from a co-ed environment for exactly this reason.

While the head's emphasis on character and kindness rings true – right on cue we witnessed children relating the story of the Good Samaritan to their day – a couple of parents commented that it can take a good while to find your niche. 'If you're not good at sport, you're not popular in the playground.' This is a school which aims to develop 'resilience'. When asked which kinds of boys would be happiest here, parents suggest: 'the bright and the best', 'a self-starter, bright and athletic', 'you've got to be robust'.

No surprises that the majority of parents are highly affluent, most living within an expanding 10 mile radius of the school. However, we hear that there is a healthy mix from the scarily ambitious to the more laid back, so there is a good chance of finding like-minded souls.

School has one boarding house called (not so aptly in our opinion) Brightlands; this can accommodate 25 weekly or flexi-boarders from year 4. Rather a sombre looking house with a garden next to the pre-prep, it's been recently redecorated, and though the housemaster and his family are young and welcoming and boys rush around busily, we spied scary paint colours downstairs and 1950s style curtains in the dining hall. We wondered how this rated as a home from home compared to the boys' weekend surroundings. Definite fun, though, is one week a year when years 5, 6 and 7 stay from Sunday to Thursday; they experiment with life away from home and gain the Tomahawk Award for life skills such as button-sewing and bed-making.

The Pre-Prep Early Years department is a stunningly designed new-build – all wide open flowing spaces, blending indoor/outdoor, the classrooms give way to a huge covered sand-pit for wet days. It has a delightfully green outlook surrounded only by playing fields, woodland and the grounds of Dulwich Picture Gallery. Nothing locally compares to the rural feel of this setting, a great comfort for any parent who didn't expect to raise their children in one of the world's biggest cities.

Girls are the minority but are carefully selected and more than hold their own. Parents of girls have little need for concern – except getting them in: applications are over-subscribed. Rainbow Club, staffed by regular teaching staff, offers care and activities pre and post, from 8am to 4.45pm.

The head assists in girls' applications to local private and state schools. Almost all the boys exit to the prep.

Dunraven School

94–98 Leigham Court Road, London SW16 2QB

State • Pupils: 1,300 (plus 168 in linked primary)
• Ages: 11–18 (plus linked primary 4+) • Sixth form pupils: 250

Tel: 020 8696 5600

Email: info@dunraven.org.uk
Website: www.dunraven.org.uk

Principal: Since September 2003, David Boyle (40s), BA NPQH FRSA. Married with a young daughter. A north Londoner by birth, 10 years at Dunraven have made him a thoroughly naturalised Streatham man, and proud of the success he's done so much

to create. 'My main interest is work,' he explains (although he concedes a liking for literature and cinema) 'and after work, my family.' Under his energetic leadership, the school has achieved creditable results, and acquired a bewildering array of designations: High Performing Status, Beacon Status, Advanced Healthy School Status, Investors In People status – and on it goes. Along the way, it's become the most popular school in Lambeth with seven applicants for every place. Parents describe him as an excellent manager and highly effective communicator. The secret of his success? 'I love what I do,' he shrugs. 'And I like working with people who enjoy what they do.'

Head of secondary phase is Jessica West.

Academic matters: Results are a testament, says head, to the commitment of 'a fantastically creative and hardworking staff team.' At GCSE, 70 per cent of students achieved 5 A*-C including English and maths in 2015. Expectations are high. 'We start from the premise that the children will do well, and might do even better than we think.' Younger pupils are kept aware of how well the older ones are doing, and the benchmark is set higher each year. 'We're aiming for "astounding",' says head, with a modest smile. Recently rated outstanding by Ofsted.

The curriculum in key stages 3 and 4 is broad and balanced, thanks to what's called the Dunraven Baccalaureate: English, maths, science, humanities, languages, and all the arts, because 'the kind of learning opportunity you get through the arts is invaluable.' Other subjects are also offered, notably DT, ICT and PE/dance. Visiting teacher from Westminster comes in every week to teach Latin, which is proving a popular option at GCSE and A level, but we thought the language provision could have been broader. French and Spanish are offered, with the G&T students given the chance to do both; but there used to be Mandarin. The impressive

The children agree. 'The teachers are good and you learn stuff,' said a cheerful year 7 boy. 'You make friends, you learn, every class is suited to you,' added a strikingly poised year 10 girl

sixth form (230 students), housed in its own new purpose-built centre, is the most successful in Lambeth, and offers a wide range of academic and vocational courses – A Levels, BTecs, GCE applied and the AQA baccalaureate. It was rated 'outstanding' by Ofsted; 23 per cent A*/A grades at A level in 2015. All Dunraven year 11s can apply to study there and most do, but places are sought after and are not guaranteed. Strong enrichment programme, includes theatre and opera visits, excursions, exchanges, competitions, and residential trips abroad.

SEN provision is excellent and enlightened. The school has its own on-site speech therapist, and parents were full of praise for the SENCo, who was described as 'fantastic', 'works like a Trojan', 'highly empathetic'. 'We felt that our child was properly supported throughout her time here,' was a typical remark. Hosts a specialist centre for children with speech, language and communication needs.

There were parental murmurs about their child being unable to study all his/her preferred subjects

at GCSE due to timetabling issues (a problem not unique to Dunraven), but the majority of feedback was overwhelmingly positive. 'My child left with a love of all his subjects, based on great teaching,' was one comment. 'There is rigour in all that Dunraven does,' was another, and everyone we spoke to praised the 'constantly rising level of academic achievement.' The children agree: 'The teachers are good and you learn stuff,' said a cheerful year 7 boy, who'd been temporarily sent out for being cheeky. 'You make friends, you learn, every class is suited to you,' added a strikingly poised year 10 girl.

Games, options, the arts: You can do almost any sports here: in addition to football, rugby, cricket and basketball, there are opportunities for badminton, fencing, swimming, diving, the martial arts, boxercise, trampolining and ice-skating (using facilities at Crystal Palace). Engagement with games remains good throughout KS4. Drama, dance, art and photography are all popular, and the Soul Choir enlivens many a local church concert. Music is also strong, and the excellent Play It Live initiative, part-funded by the local authority, enables the children to work regularly with professional musicians.

Background and atmosphere: The school is approaching its 100th anniversary. Originally founded with a bequest from the Earl of Dunraven, it expanded onto its present site in 1950, moved into the Philippa Fawcett College in the 1970s, became grant-maintained in 1993 ('A very important decision for the school'), and became an academy in 2011. £20 million mixture of rebuild and refurb (under the last government's Building Schools for the Future initiative) now complete, including new sixth form centre. Some very inventive touches, including the use of recycled shipping containers for new buildings, which look incredibly smart and cost half of what was originally planned. Now has an attached primary school – the first reception children started in 2013 and moved into their permanent £5 million home in September 2014.

Smart blue and grey uniforms, own clothes for sixth form (with a requirement to be 'respectable'). Students work purposefully, and – during our visit, at least – an air of orderly quiet prevails. The pupils we met were polite and helpful. Even the malefactors hanging around outside the classroom who'd refused to go in, for reasons they were unable to articulate, knew what was expected of them. After chatting to us about how much they liked their school really – 'It's fun here...there are nice trips... a good after-school club, something to do every day' – they filed in equally to begin geography.

Pastoral care and discipline: Considering the size and diversity of this school community, we were impressed at how calm and purposeful the

students were. The emphasis everywhere is on courtesy and consideration, and the pupils confirm this: 'The people are nice. The teachers are good and you learn stuff.' Parents praise the staff as 'incredibly supportive', and any bullying is dealt with swiftly and effectively with 'restorative justice' sessions and behaviour contracts. Very low turnover of staff tells its own successful story.

Pupils and parents: An inclusive, socially and ethnically mixed intake that reflects the diversity of the area.

Entrance: Entrance tests put children into one of five ability bands; the school, which is heavily oversubscribed, then takes 20 per cent from each band, allocating places in line with its (non-academically selective) admissions policy.

Children from the new primary phase will have an automatic right of entry to Dunraven Senior The head positively radiates excitement: 'This provision will eliminate the trauma of secondary transfer. Everyone will benefit. We'll be able to offer expertise and opportunities to enrich the primary experience, and their approach will increasingly influence us.' Heady times indeed.

Exit: At 16, the majority (65 per cent) progress to Dunraven sixth form; a few move to local sixth form colleges, training etc. At 18, nearly all leavers go on to university, with an increasing number of top university successes every year, including

Oxbridge, Imperial, Bristol, Sussex and Queen Mary. The rest take a gap year, or have a lead into work of some kind. Head says, 'The aim is to get to the end of Y13 with a choice.'

Money matters: EFA-funded academy since August 2011, and in receipt of many grants and awards in recognition of its academic success and work for the community.

Remarks: A dynamic, exciting, successful school community. Proof that you can have a comprehensive school that works for everybody.

Durand Academy

Hackford Road, London SW9 0RD

State · Pupils: 1,059 · Ages: 3–14

Tel: 020 7735 8348

Email: headteacher@durandprimary.com
Website: www.durandacademy.com

5

Interim Executive Head: Since September 2015 Mr Mark McLaughlin. Previously head teacher, Mr McLaughlin was appointed at very short notice after Mr Greg Martin, who had been at the school since 1986, stepped down from the post in the last week of the summer holidays, though will stay on as a governor for the 2015-2016 academic year.

Entrance: At 3 into the nursery (60 places) or at 4 into reception (125 places). NB Nursery children must reapply for reception, but get guaranteed places. Otherwise by distance.

Exit: Durand children won't have to leave until they are 16 – a middle school for 11–13 year olds opened on the same site in September 2012 and a weekly boarding school in Sussex, for 13-16 year olds, opened in September 2014.

Remarks: Calling this a state primary (and now middle) school is rather like calling St Paul's Cathedral a church. It is one of the largest and best-equipped in the country, and not content with opening a middle school on the same site, has made history by starting its own country boarding secondary school, which is entirely free of charge (unlike other state boarding schools, which charge for board and lodging, though not for tuition).

Controversy has dogged the school, from planning and funding difficulties with new boarding school (irate locals included a Tory councillor who resigned after a racist outburst in the Mail on Sunday) to persistent criticism of Mr Martin's salary arrangements (he has a financial stake the in leisure centre that operates on the school site).

From the front the junior school looks innocently like a larger than average Victorian primary school building. Round the back, however, is a sports centre with swimming pool, fitness room and café, five-a-side Astroturf and accommodation blocks, which are the key to the school's achievements and ambitions. Parents can pay £30 a year to use the swimming pool, the Astroturf is available for hire in the evenings, and language students and key workers (including NQTs working at the school) rent the flats. The latter brings in a tidy sum – some £400,000 a year – which has facilitated the expansion (the government has chipped in some £17 million to refurbish the West Sussex country pile, once a private school, for boarding secondary pupils) and helps pay for small classes. It also funds mostly organic school meals and ergonomi-

---

School philosophy is that 'SEN can be blown out of all proportion. Most is due to poor teaching and parenting'

cally designed chairs and tables for the children. The nursery and infants' section, down the road at the Mostyn site (once a failing primary school), also boasts its own swimming pool.

Pupils do not come from the four-square, yellow-brick, Victorian homes just round the corner but mostly from the local authority flats across the busy Clapham and Brixton Roads. Some 96 per cent are black Caribbean or African, around half are eligible for free school meals, depending on the cohort, and a significant proportion live in overcrowded accommodation. Many come from single parent households. The 35 or so per cent with some sort of SEN are rarely granted statements (and thus extra support) by Lambeth. But the Durand philosophy is that 'SEN can be blown out of all proportion. Most of it is due to poor teaching and poor parenting – not an inherent intellectual problem'. So Durand gets parents involved early and keeps closely in touch.

Many of the children come from challenging backgrounds and join the school with well below average skills. The school's first job is to teach them to sit still, concentrate and follow directions, hence a system that prioritises order, ritual and structure and gives them a sense of security. All classrooms have the same layout, lessons have the same structure, and a common marking system. Each child's performance is regularly monitored and tracked. By the time they join the junior school, nearly all can read fluently and write neatly.

At this point they are divided into forms by ability, with perhaps 12 children in the least able classes and 20 in the most able, and at least one teaching assistant in each class. 'Those who find English difficult generally have trouble with maths too, because it is often about language – they must be able to understand the words. But it doesn't really matter which group they are in because each child has a personalised learning programme. The teachers have time to sit down with each child and go through their work with them.'

Prefers to grow its own teachers and a large proportion is newly qualified – 'Many new teachers have a wonderful naivety of spirit and excitement. They tend to be very positive, receptive to learning and accepting of our structures and expectations. It is harder to get experienced teachers to fit into our ways of doing things. These may not be the only ways that work, but they're the only ways that work here.' (Most of the management team started out as NQTs here.) 'We're very clear about what we expect. We never shout and we never fight for control. The adults are the role models, and we must behave the way we like the children to behave.' The school decries the current fashion for insisting that all of every lesson must be exciting – 'We like to make work challenging and interesting, but some bits, like handwriting, spelling and times tables, are boring, and children need to learn that that's the nature of life'.

The classes we visited were characterised by calm, quiet children seated round tables getting on with their work – which was beautifully presented. Each blackboard listed the objectives of the lesson and key words. Handwriting, spelling and grammar are important here. So are targets: these are reviewed with parents three times a year, and constant feedback means that any problems are picked up very quickly. As a result, at least 90 per cent achieve level 4 in year 6 Sats, the level that shows they are ready for secondary school, and around half get to level 5, well above average.

Everyone learns to swim in the school pools. This also helps them to learn to dress and undress – a skill many lack when they first join the school – and to listen to instructions. They start swimming at 3 years old, 'and we'll be disappointed if we don't have any children heading for the Olympics eventually'. They play sport on the Astro pitch, have PE and dance sessions in the gym and climb on the fabulous climbing frame. Parents welcome the subsidised after-school club, which runs from 3.30–6pm, with a huge range of activities from sports to languages.

Successor will undoubtedly need similar drive and ambition to keep such a very different school on track. Critics will be eagerly following developments, as will parents and supporters

In the past these bright, motivated, well-educated youngsters have moved on to a huge variety of secondary schools and many – particularly boys – have sunk without trace in more chaotic environments where working hard is not seen as cool – 'They're swamped by ill-prepared children and our children get dragged to the bottom'. No longer – to parents' huge relief, the Durand middle school for 11–13 year olds opened in 2012. In 1999 Durand took over Mostyn, a local failing primary school, turning it round within months. The site was eventually refurbished to house the Durand early years section, leaving space for the middle school in the main site. This extension enables the school to employ specialist teachers, who can teach the younger children as well. It also enables more flexibility – 'Age won't matter nearly as much, as we'll have more time with them, and we may be able to teach different ages who work at the same level together'.

In 2014 the first children moved on to the Durand upper school, a weekly boarding school in the Sussex countryside. Eventually Durand all-through academy should include some 1,800 children aged 3–16 (the current plan does not include a sixth form), and staff are beginning to plan a 13 year approach to learning. Controversial he may have been, but successor will undoubtedly need similar drive and ambition to keep such a very different school on track. Critics (and there are many) will be eagerly following developments, as will the school's parents and supporters. Boarding, says the school, provides, 'space and time for them to do plenty of sport, music, art and drama ...to be competing in teams and to be proud of it'. The children arrive from London on Monday mornings and return on Fridays. 'School has an immense and lasting influence. [We] want them to be able to say, "I went to Durand and it saved my life".'

Eaton House The Manor Girls' School

Linked schools: Eaton House the Manor Preparatory and Pre-Preparatory Schools, 99; Eaton House the Vale and Eaton House Belgravia see *The Good Schools Guide: London North*

58 Clapham Common Northside, London SW4 9RU

Independent • Pupils: 145 • Ages: 4–11 • Fees: £14,244 pa

Tel: 020 7924 6000

Email: admin@eatonhouseschools.com
Website: www.eatonhouseschools.com

Headmistress: Since 2010, Mrs Sarah Segrave (40s) BA Ed MA, educated at Cranbrook and Durham University, where she studied education and history. Married, with two small children. Previously taught at and became head of the pre-prep in 2001, until she crossed the playground to become head of the new girls' school. She teaches general studies to all age groups and enjoys organising quizzes and history in action events for the girls. Cheery and practical, parents tell us it really helps that she has young children herself and is able to relate to hopes and fears.

Entrance: At 4+ non-selective – put your name down early as a waiting list operates on a first come first served basis. Occasional places in older age groups, entrance exam and a visit to the school for an assessment day.

Exit: Streatham & Clapham High most popular London next step, with a couple to each of Alleyn's and Francis Holland and others to eg JAGS, Queen's College, Putney High. The Cheltenham Ladies'

College and Woldingham most popular boarding schools; others to St Mary's (Ascot and Calne), Benenden, Downe House etc.

Remarks: New, stylish, bright, architect-designed building next to the boys' school. Three floors of classrooms with a huge basement activity hall/gym and ICT room; pupils share some of the boys' school facilities. The school opened in 2008 and has space for 140 children – one class of approximately 20 pupils in academic year group, so much smaller than the boys' school. Well-balanced academic curriculum; the girls are continuously assessed and 5 and 6-year-olds are screened to identify any specific learning difficulties. Part-time specialist SEN teacher and visiting occupational and speech therapists can be arranged when necessary.

Specialist subject teachers for the arts, French, science and sports. Forward thinking and gentle pastoral care, mentoring 'big sister' scheme to encourage older girls to look after younger and new pupils. Good selection of sports including all year round swimming lessons, dance classes for budding ballerinas. Lots of lively drama and music; tuition on any instrument is available and girls produce two dramatic productions every year. Wonderful art studios accommodated in the main building give the opportunity to work with a range of different media. Every term sees a selection of

extracurricular clubs, along with an after-school homework club.

Staff, led by Mrs Segrave, have created a charming, traditional girls' school in a nurturing and relaxed atmosphere. Superb asset to the Eaton House group of schools.

Eaton House the Manor Preparatory and Pre-Preparatory Schools

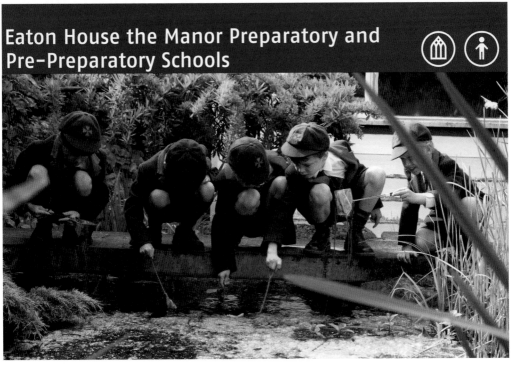

Linked schools: Eaton House The Manor Girls' School, 98; Eaton House the Vale and Eaton House Belgravia see *The Good Schools Guide: London North*

The Manor House, 58 Clapham Common Northside, London SW4 9RU

Independent • Pupils: 188 prep; 215 pre-prep • Ages: 3–13 • Fees: up to £17,424 pa

Tel: 020 7924 6000

Email: admin@eatonhouseschools.com
Website: www.eatonhouseschools.com

27

Headmaster: Since 2010, Mr Jeremy Edwards BA MA (50s) has been head of the prep school. Previously head of Westminster Under and deputy head at Emanuel School, Battersea. Married to Alexa, who is managing director of her own medical public relations company. They have three children, two at senior school and the eldest at university. Head has an MA in education management and his specialist subject is English. Polite and unassuming character, always readily available to give advice and share his knowledge of educating boys with parents. Many moons ago Mr Edwards was an international oarsman and rowing coach – he remains a

keen supporter of all the school's sporting events. He was a considerable catch for Eaton House.

Pre-prep head: Since September 2013, Mr Huw May, previously head of Sydenham High Junior School. Has also headed Roedean Junior School and St Aubyns Pre-Prep. A professional singer for several years before taking up teaching, he is also an ISI inspector.

Nursery head: Since 2004, Mrs Roosha Sue (30s).

Entrance: Non-selective at 3+ and 4+ for the nursery (co-ed) and pre-prep – first come first served waiting list operates. At 8+ for the prep school internal candidates are continually assessed to ensure their suitability for the prep. External candidates sit an 8+ entry examination; academic, music, sport, art and design and all-rounder scholarships for 8-year-olds.

Exit: At 8+ small number of boys opt for country boarding schools. At 11+ a few move to London day schools – Dulwich College, City of London. Majority sit 13+ for a good mixture of traditional public schools – Eton, Marlborough, Winchester, Harrow, Radley, Stowe and Charterhouse – or day schools like Westminster, St Paul's, King's College School (Wimbledon) and Dulwich.

Remarks: The school opened in 1993 as a boys' pre-prep. Today The Manor hosts a co-ed nursery, boys' pre-prep and prep school and the most recent addition is a girls' school (see separate entry). All accommodated in an attractive Georgian manor house and its grounds in Clapham. Fortunately, the school sits on the edge of Clapham Common, which provides the ideal location for sports lessons as on-site outdoor space is limited.

The cheerful purpose-built nursery is the starting point and then onto the pre-prep. The same successful teaching methods are used as in its brother school across the Thames. Children are taught in small ability related groups within their classes. Pre-prep children also benefit from magic touches, which include structured creative writing classes and the all-important but often forgotten skill of handwriting.

Most boys go on to the prep school, where they are divided into two parallel classes per year group.

Headmaster is a polite and unassuming character, always readily available to give advice and share his knowledge of educating boys with parents

Latin and French are introduced in the first year of the prep; most classes are taught by subject specialists and setting for English and maths.

School can support children with mild dyslexia/dyspraxia and ASD, an area that is being developed. Full-time SENCo makes referrals as necessary and runs a small team of teachers, most of whom have specialist training.

Bright airy classrooms, decorated with delightful art displays. Exciting range of art and design classes to suit all tastes and talents, wonderful top floor studio overlooking the London skyline. Music has been developing steadily – a good orchestra, string quartets, two choirs and frequent musical assemblies. Drama classes throughout the age groups, boys perform lively plays and sketches and a musical play each summer.

Parents are invited to help with stage designs for plays, hanging art displays and listening to children read. They are also active fundraisers for the school's charity of the year and annual fête. Supervised homework club, great choice of extracurricular activities and a holiday club. Overall a strong all-round school. Parents say the approach is fairly formal but, thankfully, less stuffy than it used to be.

Emanuel School

Battersea Rise, London SW11 1HS

Independent · Pupils: 835 · Ages: 10–18 · Sixth form pupils: 180 · C of E · Fees: £17,019 pa

Tel: 020 8870 4171

28

Email: enquiries@emanuel.org.uk
Website: www.emanuel.org.uk

Headmaster: Since 2004, Mr Mark Hanley-Browne MA (50s). Educated St George's College, Weybridge, BA in natural sciences at Oxford then PGCE at Cambridge. Previously, taught at Sevenoaks for five years, assistant master at Charterhouse for nine years and deputy head (pastoral) at Highgate for seven years. Enthusiastic and ambitious, has led the school forward and academically upward, making some 'dramatic changes' along the way. Particularly proud of three new computer suites named after old boy, Sir Tim Berners-Lee, creator of the World Wide Web.

Is 100 per cent pro the A level system and has no intention of introducing the IB. 'Specialising at 17/18 is the right timing, four subjects is enough. After all, they will have to specialise even more at university. And we do quite a lot of the extras the IB offers, more self-motivated research and involvement in charities and community support.' Believes that all children should be doers and really want to participate; 'the child who is quite good at everything but not excellent at something' would not really fit. All prospective pupils interviewed, which

he believes is the most important part of the entry procedure; woe betide anyone lacking a focal interest, no matter how bright he/she may be. Parental views seem to vary. Some say he is 'a bit aloof', others say 'affable', 'approachable' and 'often seen about the place'. Married to Rachael, who works for an American business school. They live locally.

Academic matters: Seems to be steadily pulling its socks back up again. In 2015, 64 per cent A*/A grades at GCSE and 45 per cent at A level, with 69 per cent A*/B. Head 'not in the least interested in league tables' and has withdrawn from them. He feels that he is giving his pupils a far broader, all-round education than exam results alone can show.

Parents certainly happy with the experience their children are getting. 'The teaching quality is good', and the staff 'dedicated and supportive', particularly the heads of year, although they also spoke about some finding it difficult to keep control over classes. The head says, 'Getting good staff has been my top priority.' Pupils feel that, on the whole, teachers are 'brilliant and inspiring' and several new ones in the last few years who are 'great'. The majority of children in the first year (6) come from local primary schools and parents feel are probably disadvantaged where maths and French are concerned, but they seem to catch up quickly enough.

Certainly the facilities are all here – science, language and design technology labs plus computer rooms all spankingly up to date. We saw children working with wood and metal, experimenting with science, heads down solving mathematical problems; they all looked happy,

positive and intent, with relaxed looking teachers keeping them absorbed. Classrooms are well equipped with the latest technological aids.

Headmaster feels that he is giving his pupils a broader, all-round education than exam results alone can possibly show

An active, imaginative learning support department has its own room with computers and other important aids, alongside a team of specialists who also have their own area of teaching, so are also fully involved in school life. Open door policy when possible but chaplain always around to act as counsellor as well. Pupils are assessed and continuously monitored with constant parental consultation. Tries to keep one-to-one sessions out of lesson time – head doesn't really like children being withdrawn from classes. Also runs a homework club after school for those who need help. Between 12 and 15 per cent have mild learning difficulties.

Games, options, the arts: Fantastic sport, music, art and drama – this is where the school really wins hands down. Rugby, netball, rowing and cricket their major sports – the teams compete at all levels both at home and abroad with many successes.

On-site games fields, access via a private gate to the facilities on Wandsworth Common plus 14 further acres of sports ground at Blagdons, near

Raynes Park; own fantastic sports hall which includes a climbing wall, exercise rooms, ergometers, as well as a PE classroom; large swimming pool which pupils say is 'great' with recently refurbished changing facilities. Huge boathouse at Barnes housing 70 boats – no wonder so many Emanuel pupils win sporting awards at all levels, from local to international, and some girls and boys even go on to represent the country in their chosen field. All do pretty well in (what they deem) minor sports as well – athletics, swimming, fives, rounders, dance and tennis.

Several orchestras, bands and choirs – something for everyone. Pupils we talked to particularly keen on number and variety of bands. Children sing in the National Youth Choir and play in the National Youth Orchestra. Plenty of chances to learn individual instruments – we were told 250 music lessons given weekly. Concerts and recitations regular events, have recently put on Haydn's Creation.

Great excitement when we visited about current production of Oliver! – plenty of parts for everyone. Pupils said drama department 'very brave', presumably for putting on ambitious productions – certainly they have the facilities. We would agree that to put on Tom Stoppard's Arcadia was pretty brave, but they did, and it was a great success. Enlarged theatre opened in 2013 by Ralph Fiennes and Mike Leigh.

Art studios amazing – recent project on 'passions and obsessions' produced fascinating results. Enthusiastic teacher with equally eager pupils. Head is a great art fan and views the school as a showcase – certainly everywhere we went pictures hung on walls, and apparently lots more also stacked in storage rooms: some really wild and wonderful. Says he commissions pictures from students every year. Lots of trips, home and abroad, to expand their horizons – singing in Venice a recent highlight. Work underway on a £9 million art and humanities block.

Pupils say school seems to recognize what each child is good at, promote it and create confidence. Out of the mouths of babes. Must be good. Whole place feels happy and welcoming

Background and atmosphere: Originally richly endowed by the Dacre legacy in 1594, there's a courtyard in the middle of the main building dedicated to three Queen Elizabeths. The first on the throne at their foundation; the second who planted the central tree, Queen Elizabeth, later the Queen Mother, in 1951; the third, her daughter who made a royal visit in 1994. Surrounded by glass, this is typical of the traditional/modern mix in this school. Old buildings house modern facilities and new buildings grow up out of old ground. The library, which could be said to be the hub of the school, is a good illustration. With silent areas behind glass and a circular staircase leading up to an archive room full of school history, it is a great place for pupils to gather for meetings, research or quiet study. A good learning resource centre. Librarian relaxed and welcoming, pupils often stay to do homework there; which would explain why one parent said her daughter never seems to bring much home. Its renovation one of the head's decided successes.

Main building originally a Crimean war orphanage, taken over by Emanuel in 1883. Although, internally, it has been through many changes, the chapel, on the first floor, remains and assemblies held there daily. This is still a Christian school bearing Christian values and commitment to the community outside as well as within. Pupils are polite, open and, according to those we talked to, have good relationships with their teachers. Also spoke positively about their headmaster. Year 9s talked about team building, peer mentoring and the way older years interact well with the younger ones. School council seems to help this, as does the house system. They say school seems to recognize what each child is good at, really promote it and thus create confidence. Out of the mouths of babes. Must be good. Whole place feels happy, friendly and welcoming. Parents say school good at making sure course work is done on time otherwise 'big trouble'.

Split of school day seems to work well with two classes before a short break, then two more

before half an hour's assembly and two more before lunch at 1.15pm. Excellent food, say pupils, good choice, but queuing system not good if you are late. Lovely to have tables outside in summer. Sixth form thrilled with their common room and café (only open at certain times and not for lunch), very grown up. Whole sixth form area with all its own facilities is brill. Parents say very friendly and lots of activities and involvement for them as well.

Pastoral care and discipline: Tutor system combined with house system and easy access to head of year ensures that any problems that arise should be spotted and dealt with quickly. We asked pupils where they would go if they needed to talk to someone sympathetic and they agreed that it would probably be the head of year first and then the chaplain. Chaplain also has sixth form team to help him when necessary. Christian ethos is important and responsibility for others would seem to be endemic. Big emphasis on being part of community and charitability. Natural interaction and mutual respect between teachers, pupils and year groups does appear to be working.

All pupils carry conduct cards recording homework timetables, commendations and misconduct records – five commendations and you get a chocolate, but get a misconduct signature and you have to start again. Beware of getting five misconduct records: Saturday morning detention looms.

Separate, comprehensive policies on bullying addressed to parents, teachers and pupils. This is something almost bound to occur, in some form or other, in a school full of alpha boys and girls. The majority of parents we talked to were not worried and felt that school handled problems well. However, some think there should be zero tolerance and, at the moment, don't feel this is happening. Most praise the pastoral care whole heartedly but a few doubts remain over the handling of difficult or sensitive cases.

Pupils and parents: Mainly local, but many from anywhere that is a train or bus ride from Clapham Junction. Typical London mix. Many working to make sure their children get a good education.

Ex-pupils include Sir Tim Berners-Lee (founder of the World Wide Web), Michael Aspel, Andi Peters, Michel Roux Jr, Naveen Andrews and Peter Hain MP. Also Max Fowler (Wolf Hall), Emma Healey (winner of the Costa First Novel Award 2014), Ben Wilkins (Oscar winner for sound mixing in Whiplash).

Entrance: Competitive at 10+, 11+, 13+ and 16+. Must get at least 60 per cent in entrance test and show special aptitude somewhere. Good command of English, both written and spoken, essential. Priority for siblings as long as performance report from previous school OK. Popularity has surged;

now caps 11+ registrations at 600 and 13+ at 150; two-form entry at 10+. Everyone gets an interview. Must have special interest but need not be academic. They are looking beyond pure academia. Sibling policy – get one child in and any subsequent children only have to get over the minimum academic hurdle of 55 per cent. Same hurdle applies to those offered a scholarship in art, drama, music or sport.

Exit: Around 90 per cent stay for A levels. Most popular universities are Durham, Exeter, Leeds, Manchester, Newcastle and Bristol. Some to art, music or drama school. Several each year to Oxbridge: four in 2015.

Money matters: Lots of scholarships (which can be topped up by bursaries), not only academic but also music, sport, art and drama. Varying degrees of financial support. Strong bursary fund, constantly growing, aiming for self-perpetuation. Big fundraising drive with ex-parents. Governor of the school, James Wates, created special fund; six children benefit from his bursaries at the moment.

Remarks: An amazing campus to find in an urban area close to Clapham Junction. For parents who can scrape the fees together, in a borough sadly lacking in good secondary schools, it is ideal. For sporty, arty, musical children, the opportunities to expand their talents and their horizons are all here.

Finton House School

171 Trinity Road, London SW17 7HL

Independent • Pupils: 320 • Ages: 4–11 • Fees: up to £14,325 pa

Tel: 020 8682 0921

Email: admissions@fintonhouse.org.uk
Website: www.fintonhouse.org.uk

29

Interim Head: Curriculum deputy head, Karol-An Kirkman, is taking the reins, assisted by the senior leadership team, until a new head is appointed.

Entrance: If you want the certainty of a place, get on the phone as soon as your child is born. Apart from siblings, who have priority, it is very much first come, first served. Two entrance lists – once opened in September, one in March, to give spring/ summer born children a chance. Occasional vacancies higher up when the prospective pupil will be invited to spend a day at the school to see if he/she will fit. At least three places each year for special needs children, who will be assessed to verify that the school can meet their requirements; and the head will meet the parents. Places then offered to those whose needs can be met, on a first come, first served basis. Some state funding for statemented children. One means-tested place per year available via Sally Walker Bursary, funded by relations of the much loved ex-headmistress, as well as past and present parents.

Exit: Mostly after 11+, to a wide range of schools, mostly London day schools but a few to boarding. Current choices include Streatham & Clapham High School, Broomhead, Alleyn's, Francis Holland, Whitgift, Royal Russell, JAGS, Wimbledon High and Tudor Hall. A handful, mainly boys, move on at 8. Several scholarships and exhibitions each year.

Remarks: Happy, informal, inclusive, buzzes with enthusiasm. A strong community-based school, very supportive and particularly good for those families with challenged children. Every parent we talked to was full of praise, several saying that their shy, unconfident children had blossomed beyond belief. A local school which, we were told, is reflected in the friendly feel of the playground at the beginning and the end of the day: 'It is full of relaxed, chatty parents, and we go on chatting even after the children have all gone into school.' Emphasis on inclusion, individuality and results without pressure make this a very special school.

The teaching staff are a great strength. Loyal and imaginative, some have been at the school since it started, in the mid-80s, and some have been away, had children and come back. Others are ex-pupils returning to relive happy memories. The rest just love the school. 'The ethos is wonderful.' 'I intend to teach here as long as I possibly can.' With half of the full-time staff over 40 and a third of them having been at the school for over 10 years, experience and continuity prevail. One parent talked about 'the same old projects, there's not enough change'. Sometimes the proven old is better than the new. Certainly these teachers seem to know and understand their pupils. From one parent of a special needs child: 'I can't describe how amazing they are; the care and support they give is unrivalled'. Another said, 'They quickly picked up on my child's shyness with adults; she is now much more confident'.

The teaching staff are a great strength. Loyal and imaginative, some have been at the school since it started, in the mid–80s, and some have been away, had children and come back

The teaching standard is high and the curriculum broad. We've been told that there's something special about the way Finton teachers operate, through relaxed, informal, but focused, learning. It does seem to work: we didn't see an unhappy child anywhere. Less homework than at most other schools yet all 11 year olds seem to get into their first choice of senior school. The children said: 'Everyone's kind and if you get something wrong, no-one laughs', 'Teachers are your friends', 'No matter who you are you are never treated differently'.

Four articulate, happy, enthusiastic year 6 pupils took us proudly round their school, across the playground to the reception block where three mixed classes experience 'fun learning'. 'We love reading stories to them'. There certainly seemed to be a lot going on. They pointed out the lift, 'which is only used sometimes', and embarked upon a straightforward and informed discussion about how some of their friends needed extra help. Then back across to the classrooms, in the main building. Two staircases, well decorated with projects and pictures, led to smallish classrooms, containing happy-looking children sitting round tables (in year 1) and at desks (in years 2-6). Interactive whiteboards, used imaginatively, everywhere. We saw everything: the well-stocked library which they are all taught to use properly in weekly lessons, the DT room full of fascinating projects, the lovely, light art room, the rather warm ICT room, the science room; it would appear they have all they need and creations abound. Eager children pointed out their favourites. Back on the ground floor, lunch is prepared in their on-site kitchen – suitable choices for all and staff on hand to make sure everyone eats a balanced meal. 'There's always something I like,' said one of our guides and the others nodded in agreement.

'This is our fantastic music block,' one of them announced as we crossed the playground again. A third of pupils in years 3-6 learn an instrument (brass, woodwind, piano). Lessons are timetabled on a rotational basis during the school day and there are special sessions for choirs and music groups. Individual practice is done at home. Most children take part in a number of concerts, in school and externally. Art and drama also hit a high note. Not long ago, nine pupils had their pictures selected for the Royal College of Art's Young Artist competition and their work was put on public display. Small plays are put on in the school hall, larger productions down the road in the nearby church hall, or at a local theatre. We were lucky enough to see a year 1 play, specially written with lots of songs. What fun they all had, and how well they performed. Brand new specialist teaching rooms for music, DT and science in an innovative basement unit under the playground, plus new learning support building, enlarged classrooms and new playground.

Lots of sport, both compulsory and in after-school clubs. Matches played against all the local schools – appear to win pretty often, which says a lot for a small school. Currently the local swimming champions. A wide range of after-school clubs, sporting and creative, in which children are encouraged to take part. Wide choice which varies from term to term. 'We even have an early morning running club. The reward is hot chocolate back at school!'

Not an SEN school, but some places reserved for a wide range of educationally-challenged children: Finton House is committed to making sure that pupils of all abilities have their individual needs addressed. All children monitored from the start to see if extra help needed. Deputy head also head of special needs; her team includes a SENCo, a learning support co-ordinator, a speech and language therapist, an occupational therapist and seven learning support teachers. So there is plenty of help on hand for one-to-one support when necessary. Many opportunities for children to be taught individually or in small groups as 20 teaching assistants also on hand. 'The key is flexibility and the full classroom integration of all children.' Special one-to-one sessions charged extra but otherwise all is included.

Graveney School

Welham Road, London SW17 9BU

Tel: 020 8682 7000

State • Pupils: 1,955 • Ages: 11–18 • Sixth form pupils: 700

Email: info@graveney.wandsworth.sch.uk
Website: www.graveney.org

30

Principal: Since 1989, Mr Graham Stapleton MA (60s). Read history at Cambridge and started teaching at the school 40 years ago when it was Battersea Grammar School. Married with two grown-up children, his hobbies include reading (20th century American novels) and listening to soul and jazz. He has the air of a history professor about him. No immediate plans to retire as he wants to stay and oversee the new Tooting Primary School and the building of a new sixth form block. 'Fantastic and inspiring', declared one parent. 'He really cares about each and every student'.

Academic matters: School is regarded as one of the top 200 state schools in the country. In 2015, 63 per cent A*/B grades at A level, with 34.2 per cent A*/A.

. Thirty-five subjects available at A level – English literature the most popular and film studies recently added to the list. In 2015, 84 per cent of pupils obtained five or more A*-C grades including maths and English at GCSE, with 43 per cent A*/A grades. Focus is on the academic subjects. Some 85 per cent of students take triple sciences. RE is a compulsory GCSE. All students study a foreign language – French, Spanish or German (with Latin and Mandarin available as twilight subjects – before or after school).

Pupils are divided into ability bands as soon as they enter the school in year 7. They are banded largely by English scores and then set for maths from year 8 onwards. Extension programme for those nominated by teachers (includes PE, music

We met a student being mentored by the principal. 'Are you making sure your homework is handed in on time?' he enquired. 'Mostly,' mumbled the student

and art as well as English, maths and science). Some concern from potential parents about what school is like for those who don't get into the top band (extension group), but anecdotes from current parents say that the next band (upper) is also very high achieving. 'Whichever band your child is in, the teachers will push them to achieve their best', said one mother. 'They seem to have a knack of finding out what motivates your child and then encouraging them'. There is movement between the bands so no need to panic if your child is not in the extension group. However, some parents complain about the high number of students in the extension classes – up to 33 in some cases.

Large number of students with special needs (55 with statements) – 'because we have such a good reputation', explains the principal. SENCo and various learning mentors look after these students.

Games, options, the arts: Everyone is encouraged to take part in team sport and play for their form or house. Sports include rugby, football, volleyball, netball, cricket, tennis, athletics and basketball. One parent complained that there is only one timetabled session of games per week but principal stresses that all students are encouraged to take part in one extracurricular sports club after school. Even PE classes are streamed, so students get chance to play with others of similar ability.

School puts a special emphasis on music. All children eligible for free school meals get free music tuition. Around 350 learn an instrument at school (taught by peripatetic teaching staff) and more learn outside school. Each year around five students are members of the London Schools Symphony Orchestra and some students go on to study music at university or music college. School orchestra has 40 students, and choir has 70. All encouraged to take part in a musical event or production. When we visited, rehearsals were in full swing for annual sixth form production – Annie Get your Gun (with 200 students taking part).

Background and atmosphere: School is spread out over two campuses so despite its size (around 2,000 students) it doesn't feel overcrowded. Formerly a teacher training college, the original Georgian building (now rather scruffy) houses the art department. Other buildings have been added on over the years. School was due for refurbishment before government budget cuts so now looks rather tired.

When we visited at break time, students were orderly and well behaved. Pupils all stood up when principal entered class – emphasis on good old-fashioned manners. No lockers, so pupils have to carry everything round with them, complained one parent.

School meals fantastic – delicious food and good selection, though some grumbles about the lengths of the queues. New lavatories for boys and girls (replacing the 'rather ghastly' previous ones) were built during 2014.

Pastoral care and discipline: Teachers really do seem to care about each and every student. When we visited we came across the head of art berating an A level student for not completing his coursework. Afterwards she confided, 'he'll get an A* but he needs to understand that he has to put in the work.' This attention to detail is followed through at all levels. We also met a year 11 student being mentored by the principal to ensure that he gains the all-important five A*-C grades at GCSE. 'Are you making sure your homework is handed in on time?' he enquired. 'Mostly', mumbled the student.

Pastoral care is very good and students with difficulties are mentored by students higher

up the school who have been through the same experiences.

Pupils and parents: Parents include middle class arty types and a good cross-section of the local community. Pupils in the extension group (those selected by ability) travel from further afield whereas others live locally and walk to school. Pupils are proud to belong to the school. 'Now I'm at Graveney I believe I can do anything', a year 9 student told us proudly.

Alumni include Naga Munchetty, BBC newsreader, and Amol Rajan, editor of The Independent.

Entrance: For year 7 entry all applicants take the Wandsworth year 6 test. This selects top 25 per cent (63 pupils out of 2,000 who sit the exam), and then 75 per cent selected on proximity to school. Sibling policy now applies to all pupils, including ability places (although it does not guarantee a place in the extension group: pupils still have to take the test to see which class they go into).

Students need five GCSE A*-Cs (including maths and English) to stay on into the sixth form. Most do and are joined by an extra 150 (over 1,000 apply for these open places). Sixth form popular with pupils from the private sector, especially from single-sex schools. 'I think they want a more culturally diverse environment', says the head, 'and of course at that age they want to meet the opposite sex'.

Exit: Some 20 per cent leave after GCSEs, perhaps because they haven't achieved the crucial 5+ A* – C grades. Those with poor AS level results are also advised to find alternative courses. Around half to Russell Group universities (including nine to Oxbridge) in 2015. Some to music, art or drama colleges.

Remarks: Pupils who manage to get in are assured of a top class education in a socially mixed environment. Local parents often turn down places at schools like Alleyn's and Dulwich if their children manage to get places here.

Hall School Wimbledon, Junior School

Linked school: Hall School Wimbledon, Senior School, 111

Stroud Crescent, London SW15 3EQ

Independent • Pupils: 205 • Ages: 4–11 • Fees: up to £13,740 pa

Tel: 020 8788 2370

Email: enquiries@hsw.co.uk
Website: www.hsw.co.uk

 31

Headmaster: Since 1990, Mr Timothy J Hobbs MA (50s), educated at Eastbourne College and St Andrews, where he read medieval and modern history. He founded the school in 1990 (see senior school entry) and as numbers grew and the school developed a senior and junior section, his brother Jonathan joined as principal of the junior school in 1999.

TJH remains head, oversees operations and devotes massive amounts of energy to preserving the original spirit of the place. Entirely child-focused and delighted to leave the detail and day-to-day running of the school to Jonathan. He's based on the senior school site, but visits almost every day and takes assembly once a week. 'Children are very at ease with him,' said one mother. 'Of course there's respect and formality, but they like him and aren't afraid of him.'

Jonathan M Hobbs MA (education management from OU) was also educated at Eastbourne College and then at the British School of Osteopathy. He is married with children; his wife also works at the

school. Ably assisted by deputy Susan Harding, who is more parent-facing – his brief is largely finance and management.

Entrance: First come, first served for the 44 reception places, with priority for siblings. Holds assessments and interviews for occasional places in years 1 to 6 and requests report from previous school. Parents from wide socio-economic spread, a chunk – about 20 per cent – from overseas.

Exit: About two-thirds to HSW Senior School – entry is automatic, but the children sit the same exam as the external senior school candidates to give an idea of where they are. Others to a range of mostly London schools, eg Kingston Grammar, Surbiton High, Reed's, King's College Wimbledon, Ibstock Place, Emanuel.

Remarks: Like the senior school, a very free-thinking place, all about celebrating the individual. The current site is a former state school – it's been

improved and landscaped, TJH himself doing lots of planting. An American garden was added after 9/11 and serves as a place of reflection. Also incorporates a library in a colourful caravan. School backs on to Wimbledon Common and staff take full advantage of this with plenty of expeditions.

Mixed ability classes, each about 15-20 strong, within which children may be set different work, so treated according to their ability without feeling singled out for special treatment. 'We don't like to take the weaker pupils out and teach them separately because it's hugely important that they gain from hearing what their brighter friends say,' explains Mrs Harding. Huge focus on reading in the early years – they have to 'get it' and school won't rest until they do. Unique homework and monitoring system of senior school called Flints begins from year 3 – it's based on a theory of 'little and often' testing to reinforce what's been taught in school. Most of the schemes of work, methods and innovations of the senior school begin here. Hence it follows components of the common entrance and national curriculum, with its own HSW-stamp on it all.

About 30 children need EAL or special needs support. Two special needs support teachers and a new enhanced learning unit. School is happy to take on children with mild learning difficulties, visual impairment, dyslexia and dyspraxia. As with senior school, some perception amongst outsiders that the place includes a high proportion of special needs pupils; such views strongly denied by school and dismissed by a parent as 'coffee-morning tittle-tattle – it's not a special school: most of the children are just regular kids'. Within the school grounds is Ann Margaret House (named after T and J Hobbs'

mother), which caters for children with severe autism. Managed by the school but really a separate entity, although sometimes the main school children will come in to play with the AMH children.

The children are taught the joys of using books. 'They need to know that a sparkling new book may yield them very little of use, whereas a tattered old thing may be packed with good stuff'

Parents told us how much their children's confidence had increased – like the senior school, a huge focus on encouraging the children to think for themselves. 'We want to rein back from too much guidance, noise and teachers' voices,' says TJH. 'Thinking needs time. We want to challenge their minds.' Plenty of opportunities for the children to have a go at everything – and the academic are valued as much as the artistic or the sporty. The message is: do as well as you can, whatever your strength.

Very strong sport here. Like the senior school, the day begins with 30 minutes of circuit training – even in the drizzle – followed by tons of sporting activities, changing each week, rather than each term, the idea being everyone will do something they enjoy – if gym is not your thing, what about rugby? Hockey is currently flavour of the month and

109

the school is sponsoring Wimbledon hockey club. Children apparently get used to all the running about. No swimming, though – no pool nearby, so travelling and changing times involved make it hardly worthwhile. If your child is not into sport would it be a living nightmare? We asked one of our year 6 tour guides what would happen if you didn't enjoy all the outdoor activity. 'Tough luck,' he replied grimly. School has recently bought some nearby playing fields and a farm/field centre in Wales.

Major music and drama productions each term, plus children prepared for external LAMDA exams. From year 4 children can join school choir and orchestra and get lots of performance opportunities. School provides a solid foundation in art – lots of inspiration surrounds the children in the classrooms and corridors – and they complete varied craft and design projects, everything from basic architectural concepts to costume and set design, bookbinding and mosaics.

Their ICT experience will not be so wide – as in the senior school, it will not be studied for its own sake. The children are taught the joys and frustrations of using books as a resource – 'They need to know that a sparkling new book may yield them very little of use, whereas a tattered old thing may be packed with good stuff,' says TJH. No interactive whiteboards in classrooms nor so much as a whiff of an ICT suite.

Longish day – from 8.50am to 3pm for youngest, and from 8.30am to 4pm for years 3 to 6: a lot to pack in. Outside lesson time the children play beautifully, with all ages mixing together. Particular praise for 'fantastic' field trips – 'I know I'm verging on hyperbole, but they are nothing short of magical,' said one mother: educational, but also full of great experiences and treats of the kind normally only available to a scout or guide these days, as not many parents are prepared to sit in the garden while their children fry bacon over a campfire or abseil down the walls.

Pupils' birthdays are celebrated on a major scale, with the child in question entertaining their parents and a few chosen friends at their class table for lunch. Then he/she stands on their chair while everyone sings Happy Birthday before they cut and share their Hobbs-baked cake. Even the most retiring soul basks in the spotlight for a few minutes. 'It's a wonderful ritual and the children love it so much,' said one parent. 'Those with summer birthdays spend inordinate amounts of time planning for the school celebration once they get back in September.' And as well as the cake, every child gets a present from school's own Father Christmas – again to show that they are valued as individuals.

Lunchtimes are said to be 'special' – lunch is served in a family way; from years 3 to 6 the children say grace and are encouraged to develop good table manners. 'I think children take the lunchtime ritual for granted while they are here, but after they have left they say it's one of the main things they miss,' said one mother.

The place is boy heavy (60/40, like the seniors), but mothers of girls don't seem to find this a problem – 'Teaches them an early and necessary lesson in how to hold their own in the world,' says one mother. Behaviour is good – no real need for punishments: 'The children quickly get to understand what is expected of them and rise to it,' says the school. Parents are generally delighted that all their children learn good manners, strong morals and simple courtesies almost by osmosis here. Writing thank you letters, standing back for others, saying 'Good morning' as you pass somebody in the corridor – all de rigueur.

Real mix of parents from all walks – bankers, lawyers, media-types, fewer working mothers than at senior school. A bit more sociable, too, with organised coffee mornings for everybody to get to know each other. Parents also help on trips and come into school to share any expertise they may have – recently a Japanese parent delighted with a demonstration of origami. 'I like the fact that the school offers all the best bits of a traditional education, while rejecting the silly stuff that goes on elsewhere,' said one mother. HSW school life won't be for everyone, but definitely worth a look.

Hall School Wimbledon, Senior School

Linked school: Hall School Wimbledon, Junior School, 108

17 The Downs, London SW20 8HF

Independent · Pupils: 250 · Ages: 11–16 · Fees: £15,750 pa

Tel: 020 8879 9200

Email: enquiries@hsw.co.uk
Website: www.hsw.co.uk

32

Headmaster: Since 1990, Mr Timothy J Hobbs MA (50s), educated at Eastbourne College and St Andrews, where he read medieval and modern history. Abandoned accountancy training in favour of a teaching post at Hill House International Junior School, which he left six years later, encouraged by parents, to set up his own school – the original Hall School Wimbledon Junior School. (In 1999 his brother Jonathan joined as principal of the junior school.)

Unmarried – except to the school, which TJH (as he likes to be known) hates us saying, but no better way to describe his passion and dedication to the place. An avuncular figure with quite old-fashioned (in the nicest possible way) sensibilities. He's a stickler for good manners, a strong advocate of books over computers and likes the children to be outdoors in the fresh air as often as possible. Alongside such Blyton-esque objectives, he espouses a rigorous and thorough approach to teaching, tested weekly in his personally devised homework system.

Works tirelessly at the sharp end and consequently gets to know every child very well. Does some teaching but, more pertinently, personally leads the many school expeditions – basically count him out for the summer term: he's 'on tour'. Traditionally has baked every pupil a cake for their birthday – 'a great way to focus on that child for half an hour and think about their needs in the coming year,' he says. But less keen on thinking about their parents – he's not interested really: he's all about the children. 'I've never met him,' said one mother who has been at the school a couple of years. 'He's very nice,' thought another, rather vaguely. 'But you'll never see him glad-handing at the gates.' TJH happily defends his position, 'I can't know and run the school properly if I'm seeing parents all the time: I have some excellent staff who do that. I am keen that parents speak to the right person to deal with their questions/concerns. If that person is me, then I will meet with them.'

Opinionated on occasion, one gets the impression that it is his way or the highway – you either buy into his ethos of the school or go elsewhere. Admits he dislikes detail and dealing with the minutiae of running a school – 'He does tend to wander off,' agrees the school secretary – but he's absolutely your man for some blue-sky thinking, pushing the envelope, outside the box type of approach. Cutting something of a maverick figure, he and his school have a local reputation as being quirky; although actually he and the whole set up are much more traditional than reputation would have it. Outside school, he is interested in culture, particularly art, which he collects and hangs at the school.

Academic matters: For a largely non-selective, mixed-ability school, does extremely well. The ethos is that learning should be a pleasure, not a chore, and that exams are not the be all and end all – as the prospectus says, 'Thought is the most important activity taking place at our school'. So no teaching to the test, other than, obviously, complying with the requirements of the GCSE and common entrance syllabuses. A nod to the 'spirit and content' of the national curriculum, all combined in school's own Work Programmes.

Pre-GCSE the core curriculum includes English, maths, French, German, science, history, geography, religious studies (including a chunk of philosophy), art, DT, music and drama. At GCSE the timetable will be written around that year's cohort. No ICT GCSE (see below) or PSHE, which is covered 'more naturally' during conversations on school trips, lunchtime and as part of the RS syllabus.

The ethos is that learning should be a pleasure, not a chore, and that exams are not the be all and end all

Children are encouraged to believe that all subjects are equal – poetry as valuable as science – with no more praise given to a mathematician than to a pianist than to an athlete. 'It sounds ridiculously clichéd, but we do faithfully honour the individual,' says TJH. Forget the league tables and think about the value-added. 'Some of our children will leave with a full set of A*s, while for others a collection of B and C grades will be a personal triumph and just as worthy of celebration.'

IGCSE is preferred in science – largely because they are, in school's view, 'more child-friendly – we are an international school after all'. Certainly the language used is simpler, making them more boy-friendly perhaps. In 2015, 45 per cent of GCSE grades were A*/A.

Homework is relevant, contained and limited to 45 minutes a night, all designed to reinforce what has been taught in the classroom. It's a system of the school's own devising called Flints. Based on a 'little and often' philosophy, the pupils get bite-sized exercises in four or five different subjects every night and are then tested at school on Friday morning in what is called a 'Flint Wall'. Some parental feeling that CE children pushed a little harder than the rest – which would be unsurprising. Hard to over-emphasise the importance of Flints, which are an enormous part of the school – 'My child is quite obsessed with them,' says one mother. Certainly parents can see exactly what is going on (particularly valued by those overseas). 'It gives trust and comfort that their children are being prepared at the highest level,' says TJH.

One area where children may not be so highly skilled is in ICT – TJH is not a fan but, bowing to the modern world, such technology is tolerated and available, with laptops permitted where it helps a dyslexic child. School dropped the ICT GCSE because it felt the syllabus did not deliver and was genuinely not useful. Computers available in classrooms, two dedicated ICT suites. TJH prefers that children are trained to use books as a resource. But it is worth noting that the Flint system is a highly sophisticated computer-based one, so although anti-ICT for its own sake, the school isn't exactly advocating chalk and slate – it's more of a philosophical position. DT is also not strong – really only facilities for woodwork and the subject falls off the curriculum after year 8.

The school says it has average numbers of special needs children for a private school. Lots of dyslexia, so surprising to hear from one parent that her child's dyslexia was neither picked up nor sympathetically handled – don't assume school has it covered. TJH says, 'HSW is diligent about not labelling children, hence possible explanation for this comment. Every child is assessed annually.' SENCo (praised by a parent) who tries to meet most needs within the classroom – inclusivity is everything here. Nearby Kingston upon Thames and New Malden have large Korean and Japanese communities and a third Hobbs brother has links in the Far East – reflected in school numbers. Predominantly female staff with several long-standing members steeped in Hobbsism.

System of deputies and senior tutors aims to devolve power down from the head. For the future, a sixth form is on the cards – parents would welcome it and school is similarly keen to get stuck into A levels, but space limitations make it no-go at the moment.

Games, options, the arts: Lazybones and other such slackers need not apply. Get your children used to the great outdoors – they will be thoroughly aired here with lots of sport and all sorts of clubs. Every day begins with a wake-up call of 30 minutes' circuit training from 8.30am and loads of sport is timetabled throughout the week – some each day, bad weather rarely stops play. Rugby, hockey and netball feature large – no swimming facilities, though, and no playing fields on site, but extensive playing fields and sports facilities nearby. More chances for girls to play in the teams as fewer of them in the school. Fantastic place for netball – borough champion, long established tour to New Zealand extremely popular. Boys' rugby tour to NZ recently added. TJH admits to feeling 'rather galled that Epsom, Cranleigh and Millfield get credit for having international players who are actually former HSW pupils who got their first touch of a ball with us'. The Levels, new play/sports facility at the junior school, used for PE programme and training ground for strong climbing tradition – lower circuit level provides two parallel obstacle courses and upper climbing level includes a traversing wall.

Drama in its many different forms runs through the timetable for all years. Every child has a role to play in his or her year group's annual performances and learns that production, lighting, costume and make-up are just as important as starring roles and comic cameos. Also dance laid on for girls. Well-equipped music studios and peripatetic teachers offer vocal, guitar, piano, woodwind, percussion, music theory and music technology lessons, plus an orchestra, choir and various ensembles. A long day school day helps the children fit it all in.

Hard to overstate the importance of field trips at this school – usually in the summer term and always led by TJH. They are educational – picking up on the history and geography of whatever location, eg Northern France and D-Day landings – but

also provide an opportunity to talk through PSHE-type issues, undertake physical challenges and bond as a group.

Background and atmosphere: All very civilised. Original Victorian building has nice features including a 'country house-style' library filled with giant bean bags, although as one parent pointed out, the bean bags are more in evidence than the books. And no librarian – all a bit strange for a school that claims to value books so much. Not a glamorous place, and some of the newer parts (from 1980s and '90s) are a bit dismal (the school tells us that they have been recently redecorated), although all floors are carpeted and windows curtained to minimise nasty ambient noises. Walls are decorated with original artwork, including TJH's own collection. Not much of the children's work around the place – although we did visit early in a new term. Classrooms are of different sizes, but space is well used and no feeling of crush and cramp. Unusually for a secondary school, years 7, 8 and 9 stay put and the teachers come to them; from year 10 the more traditional set-up of children moving around.

The place is boy-heavy – school says 60/40, but perception is more 70/30 as you walk around; it varies throughout the school, some years more boy-dominated than others. Although school says it desires equal numbers and a new campaign recently launched to increase numbers of girls to 50:50 by 2020, lots of very good girls' schools in the area make for strong competition. TJH says he is very mindful – and keen to change the fact – that some girls might not come to the school because of male feel to the environment. But no nasty role-modelling – children will see TJH gardening, cleaning and even hanging curtains.

An active place – outdoor pursuits-style uniforms say it all. Nice to see children (admittedly year 7s) actually playing at break time rather than skulking around trying to looking cool. Balls allowed – or rather encouraged – and we can't believe this place would have any truck with conker-bans and the like. 'They really celebrate childhood here,' said a parent. 'When it snows they are told to get sledging.' Similarly, where many schools would have a ban on running, here running outside is good.

We can't believe school would have any truck with conker bans. 'They celebrate childhood here,' said a parent. 'When it snows they get sledging'

Forty-five minute break mid-morning and a similarly decent break in the afternoon – on both occasions your child will be encouraged to get fresh air. Freshly cooked food for lunch. As well as a birthday cake large enough to share with their class and take a piece home, every child is given a Christmas present by TJH – 'They are simple acts of kindness to show each child that they matter to us'.

TJH conscious that some wariness exists over family owned schools and is keen to stress that the place is not a 'Tim Hobbs' production – 'There's a proper structure here, with Jonathan (TJH's brother and head of junior school) and I each supported by a very able deputy and a system of senior tutors'. We feel it would be some deputy that made much headway against a Hobbs brother – though TJH disagrees.

Pastoral care and discipline: TJH extremely strict on all interaction at the school, proud of the fact it is 'a very safe place', and of course its small size makes it reasonably easy to monitor. 'I've found that the school watches the children very closely, particularly as they get older,' said one mother. Few rules, mainly common sense. The fact that TJH displays his own art collection around the place speaks volumes – obviously no vandalism. 'We spend a lot of money on making the school nice and comfortable; they wouldn't write on their parents' walls and we don't expect it here either,' he says.

Little call for punishments as children quickly understand what's expected of them – 'We try not to create pointless barriers and rules'. But action will be taken if necessary – a child was expelled a few years ago for bullying, which the school 'loathes' and is the ultimate no-no here, widely defined to include even ignoring somebody: this place is very inclusive. Parents all mentioned how their children grew in confidence at the school. If somebody does do wrong, staff are 'shocked and upset' rather than angry. No detentions – school would not want to send a message that break-time activities were not important and could be dispensed with at will. Ever evolving, at one stage considered providing make-up lessons for the girls – in reality, probably no better way to put girls off the whole idea.

Pupils and parents: Sixty per cent from the rather prosperous local area – which is roughly mid-way between Raynes Park and rather grander Wimbledon. Others from Kingston, New Malden, Dulwich and Clapham, with a couple from Kensington, Knightsbridge, Barnes and the like, so a fairly up-market clientèle, including the odd famous name. Children of all shapes, sizes, nationalities and abilities – parents similarly mixed bunch. No PTA or sports days (by design) so not the easiest place to get to know other parents, particularly if you haven't been at the junior school – though the school doesn't accept this comment.

Entrance: By assessment at 11+ – applicants spend a day at the school: interview with deputy, English and maths assessment and they take part in drama, music and games activities. 'We're watching for behaviour too – it's quite an elaborate process,' says TJH. Prides itself on seeing the good in all. Consequently this can involve two or three meetings with parents – all handled by long-serving deputy. 'While there is no such thing as a HSW child, we are looking for a good match.' Regular 11+ open mornings (four Tuesdays each term).

Exit: About 10 per cent fall out at 13 as the common entrance group leave. Pupils go all over the place – locally to King's Wimbledon, Lady Eleanor Holles and Westminster, alongside further afield Winchester, Cranleigh and Millfield and St John's Leatherhead. All out at 16, eg to Epsom College, but not to one particular school/sixth form.

Remarks: A happy school, brave enough to take on children that other London schools might well turn down. Children who are a bit eccentric will be comfortable and accepted here. A humane place that concentrates on all-round development (not just academia – so not for league table obsessed parents) and turns out confident, personable, polite and physically fit teenagers.

Herne Hill School

The Old Vicarage, 127 Herne Hill, , London SE24 9LY

Independent • Pupils: 280 • Ages: 3–7 • Fees: up to £13,305 pa

Tel: 020 7274 6336

Email: enquiries@hernehillschool.co.uk
Website: www.hernehillschool.co.uk

18

Headteacher: Since 2007, Jane Beales BEd Cantab (50s); first came to Herne Hill to teach in 1991 and has never looked back. She gained solid experience in her very first post after qualifying at nearby Dulwich College Prep School for boys, now DPL.

After a two-year stay in Brussels, accompanying her Bank of England husband and supply teaching at the British and European Schools, she became both a Herne Hill teacher and parent, enrolling her two young daughters – now a lawyer and an accountant – at the school. And hence, why she and her deputy Ngaire (pronounced ny-ree) Telford, mother of no less than four Herne Hill children, some now teenagers, have a real commitment to make their school work for working parents: 'It matters we get that right'. When not at school, she'll be found dog walking or enjoying time in Norfolk.

We found Mrs Beales to be open, highly motivated and absolutely clear in her vision for the school. It seems her attitude to any challenge is how to exceed, not meet expectations. One parent comments with considered admiration, 'she's tough but delivers,' and another, 'Mrs Beales is a firm hand on the Herne Hill ship'. And, if the going gets tough at 7+ application time, she would undoubtedly be a great person to have in your child's corner.

Entrance: Three points of entry: into the nursery at 3+, with a split autumn/spring/summer intake dependent on age within year; into the kindergarten at 4+ or into reception at 5+. Each entry point has its own registration deadline and assessment month, with some sibling priority given. Early registration is key, as this is the dominant factor in the allocation of places, hence there are elements of a mixed ability intake here.

There are approximately 40 nursery places. These children are then joined in the kindergarten by others, mostly from local Dulwich and Herne Hill nurseries, to make a total of 70. The array of parked scooters testifies to the proximity of the families who come here, but there are children from more distant parts of South London: Peckham Rye, Brixton, Clapham, and Crystal Palace.

Exit: All children exit at 7+, a few to the sought-after maintained Dulwich Hamlet school, the majority to the six independent schools in the area that top most parents' wish lists. Three-quarters of girls exit to James Allen's Prep School, Rosemead, Alleyn's or Sydenham High. Dulwich College heads the list for boys, followed closely by Alleyn's, then DPL and a few to Sydenham, Rosemead and others.

Remarks: The school began as a private nursery in 1976 and became an independent day school 10 years later. The meticulously planned spaces, including solar tiles on the roof, are carefully chosen by the school's director since 2005, Dominik Magyar, a Swiss businessman with an eye for detail and high standards. Surprisingly hands-on – during our visit, he phoned to consult on choice of chocolates for staff thank-yous.

There are three classes in each year from kindergarten to year 2. The parents we spoke to describe their children as 'always happy to go' and 'always loved it.'

Children certainly appeared very happy in every classroom, enthusiastically involved with their activities: making a potion of 'yukky' words, completing jigsaws of the organs of the human body, sequencing numbers to 20 by ordering themselves into a line, or working intently on laptops under the watchful eye of a specialist technician. Carefully differentiated learning was in evidence, allowing children to tackle the same topic within a single lesson at their own pace.

English teaching is definitely a strength – the co-ordinator we met on our visit was extremely impressive in her passion and attention to detail: one parent noted of her child that 'he learned to read at lightning speed'. The school is also very good at 'teaching' parents, with curriculum

Children enthusiastically involved: making a potion of 'yukky' words, completing jigsaws of the organs of the human body or sequencing numbers by ordering themselves into a line

evenings every term and English hand-outs from Herne Hill known to be begged and borrowed by parents at other local independents.

There are some quirks – reading books are given, not chosen, until year 2; no pens for handwriting by year 2 (only for display work) – but we noted the careful thinking behind every decision.

Maths has been a bit of a weak spot, which the head is addressing with a new curriculum, training, and some setting of years 1 and 2. She points out that children score well in their Sats, with 80 per cent recently achieving level 3. Homework consists of just reading and spellings until year 2, when there is a maximum of 20 minutes to get children into the swing of it for middle school.

French lessons are with a native French speaker, and there are the usual cross-curricular science, French and book weeks. Comforting for the less competitive, the school considers what parents may be able to whizz up of an evening, in terms of costumes, and reflecting their sensitive pastoral care, provides something for any child whose busy parent has forgotten.

We've heard that pupils work very hard here and we don't doubt it, but in the reception classes there is still space for play with role-play corners. Every classroom bursts with cheerful artwork of a high standard and plenty of glitter.

A distinctive feature of the school is the high staffing ratios – up to four in a class of 20 pupils in the kindergarten, although plenty of young faces, as some of these are newly qualified or gap students. Some 25 per cent of the 50 staff has been there 10 years, and there are currently two male teachers. The head ensures that teachers across the year groups don't spend time on playground duty or hymn practice, but rather spend an afternoon each week lesson planning, pooling ideas. Parents are largely very happy with staff – 'they're totally committed' – but mention some highs and lows around teaching experience.

Currently less than 10 per cent of pupils receive learning support, mostly for mild learning differences. Many children with EAL but none needing extra support, as they are bilingual. Learning support teaching has been boosted with full-time staffing, and is sensitively handled – all children may have some lessons with these specialist teachers, so that it becomes the norm.

Music and drama top the list of parental satisfactions. As one says, 'amazing concerts, like a professional choir at year 1 and year 2'. Years 1 and 2 learn the recorder and specialists visit for individual music tuition, which parents are invited to listen in on if they wish. Space on-site is limited for PE – though enhanced by new hall – but the high quality of the coaching is a real plus – the school uses a well-qualified outside team coach and makes use of the various local playing fields, whilst swimming is a mini-bus ride away at Crystal Palace.

Tucked just behind an imposing church, a short (steep) walk from the useful Herne Hill station, the school is housed partly in the well-maintained, large vicarage, together with a new building comprising the nursery to year 1 classes. This building really works, with some automatic doors and large, light classrooms with ensuite loos. New nursery classroom means 3-year-olds can now stay all day, new hall provides space for drama, PE and assemblies, and new kitchen provides hot lunches.

The nearby residential streets are lined with cars, making parking almost impossible, so that many parents switch to arriving on foot. Once through the doors, the open space behind both buildings is an unexpected delight, providing a large, soft-surface playground, and areas for den-making and gardening beneath the trees of a small copse.

Complete on-site wrap-around care, from 8am to 6pm and provided by Herne Hill staff, keeps things simple for working parents. It could stack up financially for full-time working parents: we calculate £1,000 per term per child for 8am to 6pm, but only a handful use it so consistently. There are a few club activities after school too: gardening, drama and, sure to be popular, a new cycling club teaming up with the nearby Herne Hill velodrome.

What kind of child will thrive here? A parent comments: 'I think the school is great for developing confident, outgoing children, but suitable for all types of children – outgoing kids, quieter kids, studious kids and triers'.

Parents are perhaps a little younger than average, mostly busy professionals, but not too busy to be involved in the PTA, as the head says, 'just as much or as a little as they want'. One says of her experience: 'Parents are very friendly and supportive. We have made some great friends through Herne Hill.'

The fact that children arriving at 4+ have only a short time here before parents must think again about the choice of middle schools and more assessments is an undeniable downside of Herne Hill School. However, in our view, the quality of care, the pleasant environment and the high standards of early years teaching, particularly in English, make Herne Hill a definite contender for first choice of school up to 7 years.

One parent confides regarding her daughter's time here, 'a great start to her schooling, which I wouldn't change (even with hindsight of the year 2 assessment process). The children seem mostly unaffected – the pressure is on the parents.'

Honeywell Infant School

Linked school: Honeywell Junior School, 119

Honeywell Road, London SW11 6EF

State • Pupils: 335 • Ages: 3–7

Tel: 020 7228 6811

Email: office@honeywell.wandsworth.sch.uk
Website: www.honeywellschools.org

33

Head Teacher: Since 2004, Ms Jane Neal BEd NPQH. Previously deputy head, she has been at the school for 23 years in total. Two children – one at secondary and one at Honeywell. Softly spoken and reflective. Proud of her school and devoted to those in her care – 'a very safe pair of hands,' one parent told us. 'She's seen it all over the years and not much ruffles her feathers,' said another. Passionate about early years learning and keen on reading, walking, cooking and children's theatre.

Entrance: At 3 to nursery, although there's no automatic transfer to infant school at 4. Nursery offers 50 part time places, plus 14 full time places (39 maximum in a class). From reception, three parallel classes, with 30 per class. Usually one assistant per class from reception. A handful leave at the end of nursery. All must reapply to get from nursery into reception. Criteria for offers to infant school – looked after children, siblings, those with exceptional medical or special need, proximity to the school (as the crow flies). Once through to the infant school, each child is allocated a place in the junior school, though it's still necessary to reapply via the borough.

Exit: All to junior school. Transfer over to juniors is generally smooth, thanks to system of reading partners (pupils) and induction sessions (parents). As one parent put it: 'There's just enough mixing of the two schools for the move to the big school to seem like a natural progression.'

Remarks: School is housed in an imposing Victorian building, a stone's throw from Wandsworth Common. Infants on the same site as the juniors, though each has its own head, both of whom specialise in their own age group. Schools share a governing body, staff room and some facilities. Infants get to see the highlights of junior school, but lead separate existence day to day. As the head says, 'we get the best of both worlds.'

A total of 40 SEN children offered group and individual support. A small number of children with statements. Nurturing environment, especially in the early years. Forensic attention to detail when assessing the needs of each child – the school isn't just paying lip-service to treating each child as an individual. Excellent results at each stage. Head is aware that the middle achievers deserve special consideration too, not just the high flyers and the ones who are struggling. School is currently focusing on how to make maths more 'girl friendly.'

Loads of outside space and vast amounts of equipment for the pupils. The head told us: 'The children can do all the things here that they can't do at home.' Pupils have their own playground as well as the shared playground garden, complete with tepees, toadstools and enchanted forest – inspiring, imaginative and the envy of other schools. All-weather surfacing means that it's now used come rain or shine. . Jolly ICT suite, just for infants, complete with multi-coloured keyboards.

Head is proud of her school and devoted to those in her care – 'a very safe pair of hands,' one parent told us. 'She's seen it all and not much ruffles her feathers,' said another

Good manners are high on the agenda and behaviour is very good. Head stresses that school wants Honeywell pupils to be decent citizens, as well as achieving academically. No uniform, after lengthy consultation with the school community, and some pupils could do with smartening up.

A very welcoming school. Happy staff and happy children, who are having an exciting time. Bright classrooms, with huge windows and colourful displays at every turn. Learning is made fun at Honeywell. The school produces articulate, confident children who are capable of working independently from early on. One parent told us: 'Honeywell's strength is that there is a feeling of community about the school. Everybody is looking out for each other.' As ever, the school is hugely popular but isn't resting on its laurels. Children get off to a flying start here and parents are willing to move heaven and earth to get their offspring a place.

Honeywell Junior School

Linked school: Honeywell Infant School, 117

Honeywell Road, London SW11 6EF

State • Pupils: 360 • Ages: 7–11

Tel: 020 7223 5185

Email: office@honeywell.wandsworth.sch.uk
Website: www.honeywellschools.org

Head Teacher: Since 2001, Mr Duncan Roberts BEd NPQH (50s). Previously deputy head. Inspiring and popular head who is well respected by teachers, parents and pupils. Good sense of humour. Keen sportsman who enjoys swimming, football and playing water polo and instils in the children 'the importance of both winning and losing with dignity'. One parent described him as 'a born leader, but also a team player,' while another told us that 'he gets on with everybody.' Has two young children.

Entrance: Once at the infant school, each child is allocated a place in the junior school, though it's still necessary to reapply via the borough. Places do become available further up the school, so it's worth persevering. Incredibly popular – no problem filling vacancies.

Exit: At 11, roughly half to the state sector, including Bolingbroke Academy, Graveney, Burntwood, Grey Coat, Tiffin and Lady Margaret's. Those going to independent schools head for Alleyn's, Dulwich, Whitgift, JAGS, Emanuel, Wimbledon High, Streatham and Clapham High.

Much support and guidance given to parents when selecting a secondary school. Head knows that a lot of tutoring goes on at top of school and concedes that the right tutor can help with fine-tuning. As one parent told us: 'It can get pretty competitive around here at the start of year 6, though I think it's more the parents getting stressed than the children. The school manages to keep the kids pretty grounded but it can be fairly tense at times.'

Remarks: School is situated in a prosperous, middle-class area and the intake mostly reflects this. Head observes that a good proportion are 'advantaged children.' Thirty pupils per class. Around 17 per cent have English as an additional language but bilingual children catch up quickly, with weekly sessions for those who need extra support.

Excellent Sats results, with a number of pupils gaining level 6 (head isn't complacent, though). The progress of each child in the school is monitored very closely and immediate action is taken if anyone is seen to be treading water. The current focus is on improving the standard of reading comprehension. Low turnover of staff. One assistant for each year group from year 3. French taught to all pupils. Well-resourced school.

Huge orchestra with 60 members. Individual tuition on a variety of instruments (recorder, violin, flute, cello), with regular concerts and performances for parents. Head's attitude is 'now you've got your grade 1, let's all enjoy it'

A total of 75 SEN children in the school and support is given both inside and outside the classroom – in groups and individually. Playground can be a noisy affair in this large school. Lego club has been set up for quieter souls who find the hustle and bustle of break-time too much, as well as a cordoned off quieter zone, but some parents still say 'it's a bit of a jungle out there.' School council's requests listened to and acted upon.

Sport is a major strength of the school and is taken very seriously from year 3. Inter-class competitions recently introduced (including tug of war) so 'everyone can take part.' Welcomed by parents, as some felt that previously only the sportiest were given the chance to play. School takes part in every tournament going – often with great success. Huge number of trophies on display to prove it. Swimming from years 3 to 5. Not just predictable sports here – cross-country and orienteering offered and lacrosse played at the highest level. Before and after-school clubs are very popular. All tastes catered for – tennis, Mandarin, gym, maypole dancing, knitting and baking. Early morning running club on the nearby common for pupils, parents ('mostly mums') and teachers. House system recently introduced and house points hard fought for. No uniform (apart from PE kit), after consultation with entire school community.

Gold Artsmark awarded to school for high level of provision in the arts. Huge orchestra with 60 members, as well as string orchestra. Individual tuition on a variety of instruments (recorder, violin, flute, cello), with regular concerts and performances for parents. The head's attitude is 'now you've got your grade 1, let's all enjoy it.' Recorder compulsory for year 3. Two choirs, so something for everyone, including one dedicated to popular music (scores from West End musicals). School hires drama facilities from nearby Alleyn's to put on a year 5 and 6 production involving all 180 children. Recent productions include Bugsy Malone and We will Rock You.

This is a school which makes the most of being in the capital – lots of trips, visiting speakers and workshops. Year 6 outdoor pursuits residential trip to the Isle of Wight is a high point in the final year and everyone is encouraged to go.

Supportive, vociferous PTFA. Whether they're hearing readers, producing a snappy school magazine, fundraising or coming in to talk about their experiences, they're a force to be reckoned with. Excellent wrap-around care on offer, including holidays. Communication between parents and staff has improved recently with the sharing of teachers' email addresses.

School has strong links with the community and actively supports local charities. The importance of being a good citizen and of giving back to society – 'either in time, effort or finances' – is instilled in the pupils.

Honeywell is a first-rate state primary that offers the lot. School produces independent, confident children ready to cope with the next stage of their education. Old pupils are always coming back to visit. As one parent told us: 'My girls loved Honeywell. I genuinely believe that it gave them the best possible start.'

Hornsby House School

Hearnville Road, London SW12 8RS

Independent • Pupils: 412 • Ages: 4–11 • Fees: up to £13,815 pa

Tel: 020 8673 7573

Email: school@hornsbyhouse.org.uk
Website: www.hornsbyhouse.org.uk

35

Headmaster: Since September 2012, Edward Rees BA (40s). Previously deputy head at Dulwich College Junior School, also an ISI inspector for the past 10 years. He grew up in Hampshire and became a keen cricketer while attending Charterhouse, playing in the past for the MCC. Today he lives in south east London and is married with a son and a daughter who currently attend Hornsby House. Parents say

he is a sociable and hands on head, always willing to talk, and quick to respond to issues or concerns they may have. The school was founded in 1988 by educational psychologist Bevé Hornsby, best known for her pioneering work in the field of dyslexia.

Entrance: At 4+ into reception. Non-selective, places are offered on a first-come first-served basis from a waiting list, in order of the age of the child at the date of registration. Priority is given to siblings. Thereafter occasional places; prospective pupils sit assessment tests in English, maths and reasoning. Not as many places as there used to be at 8 as the majority of boys and girls stay though to 11+. At 8+, the school offers a few means-tested bursaries. Always worth applying for as it is not overwhelmed with applications.

Exit: At 11+ pupils move mostly to London day schools; popular destinations include Dulwich College, Alleyn's, JAGS, Whitgift, Emanuel and Streatham & Clapham High. A few choose the weekly boarding schools such as Royal Russell and Woldingham, with one or two transferring to boarding prep schools to sit 13+ common entrance.

Remarks: Over the last decade, Hornsby House has earned itself a good local reputation for offering a lively all-round education to pupils of varying abilities. A wide and carefully planned curriculum runs through this inclusive school, enabling children to develop at their own pace. All subjects are taught to mixed ability classes, with setting in mathematics for older age groups. Modern foreign languages are taught via a range of exciting topics and projects, French for reception to year 4, then Spanish

for years 5 and 6. Parents feel teachers provide plenty of back-up work when needed plus extension activities for the more able pupils. Full-time SENCo with part-time specialists can offer support to children with milder specific learning difficulties, either individually or through small group work. There is an additional charge for one-to-one specialist teaching. The buildings are wheelchair accessible and staff are always willing to work with speech and occupational therapists as necessary. The school prides itself on developing potential in sports and the arts as well as academics, alongside helping parents to choose the right secondary school for their child. Proof is in the pudding: around a third of pupils are offered awards for music, art, sport or academics each year.

Good mix of male and female, teachers predominantly youngish, although there are some long servers. High staff ratio: two deputies, subject specialists, and all year groups have assistant teachers; reception classes have two each. A number of gappers add bounce to the sports and arts staff team. Many of these popular jobs go to past pupils; the gap year mentor remembers most of them from when they were in reception themselves.

Fairly compact site, cleverly designed by architects: it boasts lovely, light modern classrooms which sit side by side with the original Edwardian buildings. Whiteboards have disappeared in favour of the latest interactive technologies, all looked after by full-time technicians. Computing is very much on the curriculum. Minecraft, a newish club, helps with coding skills; pupils also use visual programming software. Art, drama, music and science have their own specialist rooms and teachers. Abundant arts and crafts on offer; Hornsby has been rewarded for all its hard work in art, DT and drama with Artsmark Gold. Pupils commemorated the 25th anniversary of the school by designing and constructing a fabulous mosaic in conjunction with artist in residence Tamara Froud. Drama teacher supported by an assistant puts on a variety of productions throughout the year across the age groups so everyone gets a chance to perform. Much looked forward to annually are the major year 4 and 6 productions. Music provision has developed in leaps and bounds since our last visit: two open choirs, chamber choir by audition and a small orchestra. Music room packed with instruments, mouth organs to African drums; pupils also benefit from workshops run by visiting musicians. Everyone learns the recorder and ukulele in class and individual tuition is available on some 11 other instruments. Considering the facilities and staff enthusiasm, some parents feel the orchestra is not particularly well supported.

Despite a lack of on-site space, sport is one of the jewels in Hornsby's crown; pupils use all the local facilities and are taken on sports tours. Main sports football, hockey, rugby and netball; all have successful teams, some impressive winning streaks and are always striving to improve. Cricket for all in the summer, proving very popular with the girls: definitely a few old girls who say they wish it had been on the agenda in their day. Anyone with physical difficulties or injuries can join in at their own level with the help of one of the stalwart sport assistants. Large underground kitchens and dining hall, which doubles up as extra space for gymnastics and dance. Parents and children like the open kitchens and serving hatch; children can see food cooking and what they're eating. 'Absolutely yum,' said two little ones.

All is brought together by the school community's positive, can-do attitude, and the house system which sees children of all ages working together on different projects. There is also a good choice of lunchtime and after-school clubs. Year 3 upwards get the opportunity to go on residential trips around the UK and France. Most families live locally; many are part of the strong Parents' Association, with some going on to become school governors. Parents we spoke to all commented on the friendliness of the children and the pleasant character of the school. In the final year pupils work towards the leaver's qualification the Hornsby House Certificate. This involves achievements including taking on leadership roles, displaying resilience during the year 6 trip to a Scottish activity centre, taking part in a charity event and speaking confidently in public: an ideal finale to the junior school years.

Hotham Primary School

Charlwood Road, London SW15 1PN

Tel: 020 8788 6468

36

State • Pupils: 420 • Ages: 3–11

Email: info@hotham.wandsworth.sch.uk
Website: www.hothamprimaryschool.org.uk

Headteacher: Since January 1998, Miss Pam Young BA. Graduated from Otago University in New Zealand with a degree in early years education.

Came to the UK in 1987 and was previously the deputy head of a school in Camden. Still teaches, taking year 6 one day a week and offering other classes and booster lessons where needed. Serious and quiet on first acquaintance, but underestimate her at your peril. She is fiercely proud of her school, of its pupils, teachers and parents, and will brook no criticism. She knows the name of every child, enjoys the support of her governors, her 'great critical friends', and relishes the cultural diversity of the intake. Running marathons as a hobby might give a clue to her tenacity.

Entrance: The nursery class admits 36 full and part time children each year. Reception class of 60, including bilingual class.

Waiting list for places in most year groups, which is an indication that someone is doing something right, considering four state primary schools in very close proximity, one of which is virtually next door. Admissions policy is administered by Wandsworth local authority so out of head's hands.

Exit: To a range of 15 different secondary schools. Maybe two or three a year go into the private sector but the majority are state school bound. Ashcroft (formerly ADT) is popular, but some also to Shene School, Burntwood, St Cecilia's.

Remarks: At first glance this looks like a typical Victorian primary school. It even has the original boys' and girls' entrances. The classrooms have high, light, draughty windows and are accessed by corridors and stairwells decorated with those funereal tiles so beloved of that era. The whole place cries out for a lick of paint and some TLC. Outside, the obligatory grey, hard playground is surrounded by a high wall.

Look further still and you come across a secret garden containing wood piles to provide homes for dozens of creepy crawlies, and an amazing human sundial

However, what lies within tells a very different story. Take a closer look at that playground, for example – well-tended, well-planted flower beds all around the edge, each one the responsibility of one year group. Look further still and you come across a hidden, secret garden containing bird boxes, trees and plants to represent the four seasons, wood piles to provide homes for dozens of creepy crawlies and a quite amazing human sundial which looks very like a mini Stonehenge. All this surrounds a small classroom usually inhabited by the man affectionately known as 'Mr Hotham'. Retired, he then

In the bilingual class, around 15 per cent of the week is spent speaking French, increasing by year group. Four French speakers on the staff and years 5 and 6 go on school trips to France. There's a link with a school in Paris

returned part time to give extra help to those in need and seems to embody the spirit of the school.

The classes are large (26-30 on average) but all supported by TAs. Twenty per cent of the pupils need EAL help, with full support on offer. Special needs pupils include those on the autistic spectrum, some dyslexic, some have cerebral palsy, some with language delay, some have ADHD. All are supported within the classroom as the head can see 'no point in doing anything else'. She sees the school as a 'place where we all learn from one another' and her greatest wish is to see her pupils become 'independent learners, to use their initiative and solve problems by using their fantastic, inquisitive minds'.

A bilingual stream has been introduced into the reception class and is making its way up through the school. In the bilingual class, around 15 per cent of the week is spent speaking French, and this proportion increases by year group so that by the last year the children will spend about 50 per cent of their time using French. Four French speakers on the staff and years 5 and 6 go on school trips to France. There's a link with a school in Paris.

Music is very strong, with choirs performing in Wandsworth events. All year 4s learn the clarinet. Swimming is taken seriously in KS2 when all children are taught in four ability groups over a six month period. Teams in football, cricket, netball, cross-country, swimming. After-school clubs in gym, yoga, photography, art, French. Very active PTA – recently completely refurbished the library. Polite, happy children in smart red, white and blue uniforms. Excellent handwriting throughout (would put many a private school to shame). As one parent remarked, 'Despite the presence of two excellent faith schools in the vicinity, Hotham gives a brilliant start to its kids. Its multicultural mix seems to work well.' Has won the Green School of the Year Bike-It award and two of the staff were finalists in the annual Teaching Awards.

This is a solid primary school offering a solid education to its local community from the nursery ('the best in the borough', according to one parent) to the final year, where discussion groups in the class are animated and passionate. One book which should not be judged by its cover.

Hurlingham School

122 Putney Bridge Road, London SW15 2NQ

Tel: 020 8874 7186

Independent · Pupils: 325 · Ages: 4–11 · Fees: up to £15,030 pa

Email: admissions@hurlinghamschool.co.uk
Website: www.hurlinghamschool.co.uk

Headmaster: Since 2010, Jonathan Brough BEd (Cantab) NPQH (40s). Mr Brough (rhymes with ruff) was head of English at two boys' preps, deputy head of Bute House and finally head of City of London Girls' Prep before taking over at Hurlingham. Married to Harry, a leading ICT lawyer; they live in north London. Amicable, upbeat personality, he knows all the children by name and places a huge emphasis on happiness being central to everything that goes on in the school. Very popular with parents, staff and pupils, he teaches Latin and extension classes and is a much-appreciated supply teacher for all age groups when the class teachers are away.

One of those heads who takes an interest in everything going on around the school, be it new seeds for the garden or scholarship papers. He's recently enhanced house competitions with a rewards system and excellence book, and parents get sent surprise postcards informing them of their child's special achievements. An avid reader and writer since childhood, he particularly enjoys writing stories for children. He arranges for a good number of authors to visit the school, run workshops and book-themed events. Growing up in Devon, the son of two teachers, he has been surrounded by educational and literary influences all his life. When he awards himself some free time, he enjoys travelling and cooking, especially baking, which he hopes one day might make an appearance on the extracurricular calendar.

Entrance: At 4+ non-selective on a first come, first served basis, with priority to siblings and those living closest to school.

Exit: Feeds a number of senior schools. Popular choices for girls are Godolphin & Latymer, St Paul's Girls, Surbiton High, Francis Holland, Wimbledon High, or boarding schools Woldingham and Benenden. Boys go to King's Wimbledon, Hampton, Emanuel, Kingston Grammar or Reeds. Odd one or two to the state sector, Lady Margaret or Tiffin.

Remarks: Proudly mixed ability and does extremely well by its pupils. Reception class children are divided into three classes by date of birth. As children move through the school they are split into ability-related sets – maths from year 1 and English

from year 5. The school is structured to ensure that everyone achieves success at their own pace to the best of their ability. Core subjects maths, English and science are all very strong and taught by subject specialists. No formal exams until they start practising for the 11+ tests. French is introduced in reception and Latin in year 4. By the age of 11 all the children take and pass an OCR 16+ entry level Latin qualification, demonstrating their skills in translating, comprehension and Latin coursework. The school is very keen to emphasise how the early Latin programme helps develop English and spelling skills. Children can try out other languages, including Greek, in after-school clubs.

EAL is available as necessary. SEN is catered for case by case depending on individual needs. There is a qualified head of learning support and three assistant teachers for small group work, one-to-one sessions and advising staff on differentiation within class. Homework is a serious matter and everybody is expected to complete it; lots of help available for anyone who is not sure what to do, along with a free after-school homework club. During year 5 parents have a meeting with the head and class teachers to discuss suitable secondary school choices.

Music and drama well embedded into the curriculum; a good variety of different types of theatre and concerts. There's a full-time dedicated music teacher and good proportion of pupils learn instruments.The corridors are well decorated with the children's art and designs; specialist art teacher from year 4 and the school boasts its own kiln. Well-planned traditional sports options, all taught by specialist coaching staff. Good choice of clubs each term, ballet in the elegant mirrored studio and karate being extremely popular. Particularly impressive karate, one of the largest school programmes to run in the UK, with about a third of the school taking part. This year they broke their own records with 100 per cent success in karate exam gradings.

Pastoral care is sensitively run; older children can become playground and reading buddies. There are five straightforward golden rules to follow and

He is one of those heads who takes an interest in everything going on around the school, be it new seeds for the garden or scholarship papers. Parents get sent surprise postcards informing them of their child's special achievements

everyone knows there are consequences if they fail to stay within the boundaries. House competitions and activities enable children to mix and get to know other age groups. Lunch times look incredibly civilised for a junior school: youngsters sit in house groups, about eight children to a table, and tuck into tasty meals cooked on the premises. Tea is also provided for those who stay at school until 5:30pm.

The school is on a cleverly-designed compact site with a reasonable sized playground and bronze award eco-garden on the first-floor terrace. Lots to occupy children at playtimes: table tennis, climbing wall, giant games of Connect Four and chess, and a nature garden with a water feature for those who just want to chill. Recently graded outstanding in all areas and awarded Excellence in Education status by the ISI. Continues to go from strength to strength; parents comment that it's such a reliable school, and whatever happens your child's welfare and education will be looked after. The energetic Mr Brough is one of the safest pairs of hands for miles.

Ibstock Place School, Preparatory and Kindergarten

Linked school: Ibstock Place School, 127

Clarence Lane, London SW15 5PY

Independent • Pupils: 312 • Ages: 3–11 • Fees: up to £14,745 pa

Tel: 020 8876 9991

38

Email: office@ibstockplaceschool.co.uk
Website: www.ibstockplaceschool.co.uk

Headmistress: Mrs Anna Sylvester-Johnson is overall head (see senior school).

Head of prep school is Miss Diana Wynter – warm, enthusiastic and much-loved. 'She reads us things out of classic books and organises lots of fun trips for us,' say pupils.

Entrance: First come, first served at Priestman House (nursery), with priority to siblings. Now massively oversubscribed so names down as early as poss. Occasional occasional places on account of relocating families. At 6+, entry to Macleod House (prep), by individual assessment. At 7+ and 8+ papers in English and maths. At 9+ and 10+ English, maths and reasoning. Everyone is interviewed.

Exit: Up to 90 per cent go up to the senior school, having taken the entry exam in year 6. However, Mrs S-J tells us, 'there is some humpiness that not all Macleod House children go up to the senior school. The two languages can be a barrier (everyone has to take two at GCSE). But we give them lots and lots of warning and we do help to find an appropriate school for them.'

Remarks: Three buildings situated in the gardens opposite the rear of the elegant main house accommodate the tinies. They start in Priestman House, a delightful nursery with lots to do, lots of attention and an open door through which they run to the activities outside in their own safe and enclosed space. A good mix of free and structured play and happy, relaxed tots. A great sense of having fun while learning everywhere in Priestman – we wanted to eat the yummy sausage rolls they were cooking and we loved the wheelbarrows they fill with plants each term. PCs in each classroom used wisely and they grow their own veg. Froebel-inspired learning principles,

A good mix of free and structured play and happy, relaxed tots. A great sense of having fun while learning – we wanted to eat the yummy sausage rolls they were cooking and we loved the wheelbarrows they fill with plants each term

though later educational thinkers also influence the sound and sensible curriculum. Macleod House houses the 6-10s – again, an attractive child-sized building. We were impressed by the number of books everywhere – a relatively rare sight. Orderly classrooms with very stimulating displays – we like the artwork inspired by Kandinsky and van Gogh, the clever Roman mosaics and the 'wow word of the week' palm tree. Good light art studio, and DT workshops with lively work. Year 6 pupils have their own building – Roberts House – which also houses good drama studio with retractable seating and gives them a useful transition between junior and senior schools. Those with more than mild SEN probably wise to look elsewhere. Some extra help at an extra charge. Delightfully forthcoming and friendly children. Overall, the kindergarten and preparatory schools are carefully organised, well-structured and offer a happy, healthy and stimulating start for your bright child.

Ibstock Place School

Linked school: Ibstock Place School, Preparatory and Kindergarten, 125

Clarence Lane, London SW15 5PY

Independent • Pupils: 658 • Ages: 11–18 • Sixth form pupils: 138 • Fees: up to £18,390 pa

Tel: 020 8876 9991

Email: registrar@ibstockplaceschool.co.uk
Website: www.ibstockplaceschool.co.uk

39

Headmistress: Since 2000, Mrs Anna Sylvester-Johnson BA PGCE – known to all as 'Mrs SJ' (50s). Previously head of The Arts Educational School in Turnham Green, prior to which she taught at The Lycée and before that she was head of English at The Green School for Girls in Isleworth. An interesting and eclectic mix. Chic, svelte and very much in control, she is a mix of smiley and steely. That she has made the school the success it is today is beyond doubt. The splendid new-build that has transformed the school and the elegance and taste with which no visitor could fail to be impressed will be a lasting monument to her drive and commitment.

Academic matters: IGCSEs in all core subjects now. A distinctive feature – and one of which we approve – is the insistence that all take two languages at IGCSE. German, Spanish, Mandarin, Italian, Latin and Greek all on offer, which we applaud. French the most popular and the most successful and the vast majority take this plus Spanish. Eng lit results outstanding, as are the results for those who take individual sciences, though dual award candidates'

results weaker and parents report problems in the science dept which, school tells us, are now resolved. Physics and history among the top achieving subjects. Overall, an impressive 79 per cent of I/GCSEs A*/A grades in 2015.

Ibstock's sixth form is a relatively late bird – it began in 2006 – and its size now reflects its growing reputation and success. Philosophy, psychology and economics offered alongside the more trad subjects at A level – biology, English, psychology and maths being the most popular. All sixth formers now take the extended project qualification. In 2015, 55 per cent A*/A grades and 81 per cent A*/B. Small sixth form means, mostly, small classes – a definite plus.

Parents praise school's flexibility in moving pupils between sets when appropriate. No specific learning support unit but school supports mild dyslexics, dyspraxics and Asperger's children. Learning support – at an extra charge – given to 69 pupils at time of our visit. This school is assuredly not a haven for those who would struggle elsewhere and anyone who applies with this is mind 'is under an illusion from the distant past when the school was hippy-dippy!' One-to-one EAL support given to a few.

127

The site overall would be tricky for a wheelchair user but the corridors – especially in 'new school' – are wide and easily navigable.

Games, options, the arts: 'We believe in competition – children are inherently competitive,' says Mrs S-J and plenty of opportunity to compete – in sports, debates, drama, you name it – both in and out of school. Good cross-curricular initiatives, much public speaking and sensible trips to worthwhile places. Usual range of sports supplemented by good range of extracurricular opportunities. Notable individual successes in many competitions and sports – representatives in several national squads. Music, art and drama all thrive (new performing arts centre). 'The teachers put a lot of time into the arts side,' parents told us. There's a warm sense of encouragement to try things out – witness the lively art and DT we enjoyed.

Background and atmosphere: In a nook on the edge of Richmond Park, between plush Sheen and the louring Roehampton modernist blocks of the late 1950s, sits the quite lovely Ibstock Place House, built in 1913 by Frank Chesterton (cousin of the more famous GK) and home of the Duchess of Sutherland until 1920, during which time she was Mistress of the Robes to Queen Mary and indulged her considerable taste in decorating the house. Between 1925 and 45 it was owned by the Paget family who brought in many mod cons eg a telephone system and a swimming pool. After three

Generously proportioned, elegantly decorated, embellished with grand mirrors, vases of opulent flowers and country house elegance – this must exert a civilising influence on young minds

years of being requisitioned by the Ministry of Supply for scientists engaged in top secret work in radar development, the house was, in 1945, bought by the Froebel Educational Institute as accommodation for its 'demonstration school' – to practise the principles of the pioneering educationalist, Friedrich Froebel, whose fearsome bust still supervises the school gardens.

Rapid growth led to the building of the kindergarten and prep school buildings and various other add-ons until the quite magnificent extension to the main building – 'new school' – in 2011. The main building gave the new one something to live up to. Generously proportioned, elegantly decorated, now embellished with grand mirrors, large vases of opulent flowers, rugs, sofas and general country house elegance – all this must exert a civilising influence on young minds and spirits. New school, housing classrooms, labs and staff workrooms, is similarly appointed – ceramic tiled, spacious, with civilised loos and ample locker room, energy-saving lights etc. Well thought-out, tasteful and inviting. A sense of pride pervades the place and rightly so.

Good, two-floor library with up-to-date stock, big chairs and a view of the school's 'woods'. Woods, orchard, 'bike city', two all-weather surface pitches and little garden make up main site's 10 acres of attractive outside space. 'Over the road' reached by a bridge is school's new performing arts centre, sports hall, drama studio, art room and two large pitches. Not the easiest place to get to – school runs pro bono minibuses for senior pupils from Barnes Common station in the morning and after school from 4 to 6pm. Several public buses stop on Roehampton Lane, a short walk through the university campus. The popularity of 'bike city' is testament to the number of senior school pupils who cycle to school. Otherwise, you'll need a school run partner or three.

Pastoral care and discipline: Universal praise for the pastoral care and parents largely reported 'very happy children'. House system is key to the school and all appreciate the vertical groups in houses which make for a family feel. No drink incidents in anyone's memory, likewise few other discipline problems and bullying 'instantly dealt with – our investigations are always very thorough'. Some parental grumbles about high staff turnover – to the seeming mystification of Mrs S-J and definitely not seen as a current problem. Immensely sensible 'no bag' policy. You take your bag to your locker, take out what you need and can't go back for the next two hours. Result – no-one bashes you with a rucksack in a corridor, no heaps of bags at entrances and everyone has to think ahead. Hooray! Very attractive and sensible uniform worn, by most, with style and decorum.

Pupils and parents: The vast majority from the Putney, Roehampton, Richmond, Sheen areas. However, school contained children from over 250 junior schools when we visited, the most coming from Sheen Mount, East Sheen Primary, The Roche and Putney Park – after the school's own prep, that is. Active PTA and parents praise home-school communication. Parents a mix of professional, artistic, City and everything else. Notable former pupils include Emily Blunt, Nigella Lawson, Frieda and Nicholas Hughes and, head girl in the then top year, at the age of 13, Iris Murdoch.

Entrance: Register asap. Everyone interviewed for 11+ and all sit papers in English, maths and reasoning. Hugely oversubscribed. Some 500 children try for 90 places at 11+. At 13+, a few places for which there are 40+ candidates. At 16+, around 30 apply for around 10 places. A minimum of 57 GCSE points required plus As in A level subjects.

Exit: Just over a fifth leave after GCSEs. Bristol a popular university destination, followed by Bath and Oxford Brookes. Four to USA in 2015; two to Oxbridge. Lots off to study languages including Chinese and Japanese, others to a range from mechanical engineering to art history. Generally several to art foundation courses.

Money matters: Music, drama and sports scholarships at 13+ (no longer at 11+). Up to 10 academic, creative arts and sports scholarships at 16+. Bursaries means-tested here as everywhere.

Remarks: Attractive school offering all-through education in a London suburb. Improving academics. Turns out thoroughly nice young people.

James Allen's Preparatory School (JAPS)

Linked school: James Allen's Girls' School (JAGS), 132

East Dulwich Grove, London SE22 8TE	Tel: 020 8693 0374
Independent • Pupils: 300 • Ages: 4–11 • Fees: £14,385 pa	Email: Japsadmissions@jags.org.uk Website: www.jags.org.uk/japs

19

Headteacher: Since 2007, Ms Finola Stack BA PGCE Mont Dip. Currently working towards an MA. Co-founded Finton House School in 1987, before moving on to Cameron House as head in 1994. ISI inspector. Highly articulate, Miss Stack goes to great lengths to express herself as unambiguously as possible. One parent we spoke to described her manner as being 'quite restrained, which can seem chilly, though she is probably just being careful.' Revered by the girls. Parents describe her as 'kind' and 'sensitive,' and appreciate her professionalism. Finds time to boost those girls with low self-esteem. The consensus among parents seems to be that she is 'fair, reasonable and at pains to do her best for the girls and for the school...but she won't be bullied by parents'. Not a head that hides herself away in her study. 'Very visible,' commented one parent. Leads running club on Thursdays and regularly sports a tracksuit at galas and inter-house matches.

Teaches RE. Three grown up sons. Her main interests are 'family, theatre and exercise.'

Head of pre-prep, JAPPS, is Mrs Sue Saunders, Cert Ed MA. Taught in the state sector, at Dulwich College and was deputy of DUCKS before arriving here. Friendly, straightforward and warm. Greatly loved by the pupils. On the day we visited, the older girls mobbed her in the playground. Two adult daughters. Likes to travel and socialise, though currently free time is spent working on her PhD.

Entrance: Entry at 4+ and 7+ in December and January each year. Highly competitive at both stages. Over 100 apply for 36 places at 4+. Open morning in October and school tours offered on Wednesdays. Reception teachers carry out assessments for 4+ entry through varied pre-reading, writing and number activities. 'Nothing to worry about,' reports one parent. 'The girls think they are just playing.' Written report from nursery requested. 'We're looking for academic potential. We're not looking for a specific type of girl. We offer places to a wide cross-section of girls with different dispositions and from a wide cultural base too,' comments Mrs Saunders. School does not recommend tutoring as it creates a false impression of child's ability. 'We're not looking for the facts they know. We're interested in their thinking process. It is spottable,' she says.

Maths, English and reasoning papers sat by prospective 7+ candidates. If girls meet the academic criteria, they are invited back for a reading test and interview with head. Report from current school requested. No sibling policy at any stage. Ms Stack comments, 'I do feel bad that sometimes sisters aren't accepted but we are entirely transparent in this. If we start muddying the waters, people will become confused about what we're doing.' All occasional places filled in double quick time.

Exit: Up to 90 per cent moves on to senior school (JAGS), often with around seven academic, music provided that girls are up to scratch in maths and English in years 5 and 6. If not suited to the highly academic environment of the senior school they are encouraged to look elsewhere. Head takes great care with those who are moving on: 'If a girl has received good support at home and at school but is still not making the progress we anticipated and it looks as though she will struggle at the senior school, then I'll work with the family to find the right school for her. It's a sensitive process'. All JAPS girls heading for JAGS must sit the entry exam on same day and in same circumstances as external candidates so they have access to scholarships and bursaries. 'This in line with us being transparent.

Beautiful garden with immaculate lawn, trees and a summer house. Heaven on earth for children. Plenty of time is spent outside just being little girls

It also helps the senior school to see the nature of the cohort they are getting,' explains head.

Remarks: Prep-prep runs from 4-7 and is housed in a converted Edwardian mansion in Dulwich Village. Two parallel classes per year, with 18 per class, rising to 24 in middle school. 'A wonderful start on the educational journey,' remarked one parent. 'I can't criticise the school,' said another. 'It's a lovely, gentle, happy place,' said a third. Beautiful garden with immaculate lawn, pear trees, lavender and a summer house. Heaven on earth for children. Plenty of time is spent outside just being little girls, pottering about, playing and riding up and down the path on wheeled toys. Sensory garden includes a house for a hedgehog and instructions written by the girls on the gate to 'Look out for thorns!' As Mrs Saunders says, 'A 4 year old is a 4 year old, however bright. Emotionally they are still very young.' No one is forced to grown up too fast here. How refreshing.

Praise and encouragement readily given. Girls are rewarded with gold leaves which they place on the gold leaf tree. On the day we visited, the tree was weighed down with leaves. One leaf celebrated

a girl's ability to concentrate well, another was awarded for impressive show and tell presentations.

Even from early days, girls are given responsibilities and are listened to. They are taught to analyse problems and find solutions for themselves. Pupils from key stage 1 onwards have a school council. Girls recently suggested a 'Fun Friday' when they can let their hair down. Everywhere we looked at the pre-prep, the girls were busy but not frantic. One father summed the atmosphere up as being 'comfortably dynamic.' A winning combination.

No worksheet-driven teaching here. Girls are competitive and lively and there was a distinct buzz in the air on the day we visited. For bright, sparky girls, it's hard to imagine a more exciting environment. Possibly a little harder for those who are less academically whizzy. French teaching singled out by parents as being exceptional – French, PE and music lessons taught totally in French as part of the immersion programme. Accents apparently spot-on by the time they leave. Plenty of differentiation but not rigid setting anywhere.

Teaching considered very strong throughout. We hear reports of some outstanding teachers and certainly witnessed a couple on the day we visited, including a dedicated science teacher busy preparing equipment for the imminent solar eclipse. By year 5, all lessons are taught by specialist teachers.

This school is constantly looking to ways to improve what it delivers. Recently introduced reading sessions after lunch break to encourage girls to read more avidly. Makes the most of its links with the senior school. Older girls come over to help with projects and to give extra mathematical support to the very gifted as well to run language clubs.

Currently 17 on SEND register, mostly for dyslexia, dyscalculia and dyspraxia – no global learning difficulties here. SENCo and her team provide academic and pastoral support, free of charge. Pastoral care taken seriously with a successful buddy system in place to reinforce this. Librarians also provide a sympathetic ear for pupils who want to share worries with a non-teacher. The girls feel well nurtured here. Plentiful opportunities for enrichment offered.

Huge amount of extracurricular activities on offer as school 'wants to work out what engages a girl.' Clubs currently include sessions on climbing wall, portraiture, gardening and coding. Mostly free of charge. Shares sport facilities with JAGS, including swimming pool, pitches, courts and athletics track. Plenty of matches against other schools. Good variety of sport offered including football, hockey and rounders. Everyone makes a team and sport here is inclusive, C and D teams fielded when possible. JAPS hosts a netball festival in the autumn which is specifically designed for schools that cannot get matches organised for lower performing teams.

Head of music considered exceptional. Parents are transfixed by his enthusiastic conducting at carol concerts. Utterly dedicated – he attends everything from pre-prep children timidly playing Three Blind Mice to the year 6 play where he performs the incidental music. Huge variety of instrumental lessons and three-quarters play something right up to grade 7. Girls encouraged to perform as often as possible. Numerous choirs, ensembles, string and wind groups as well as orchestras. Music set to feature even more prominently with a community music centre planned. Parents report on the high standard of drama. Year 4 and year 6 put on annual productions, the latter performed in the senior school's theatre.

Impressive design technology and art department. On the day we visited, one class was trying to work out how thermoplastic is like chocolate. Girls were enthusiastic, engaged and enjoying themselves. Art studio jam-packed with animal masks, lino prints and still life drawings. Beautiful displays adorn the walls at both pre-prep and prep.

School makes good use of its London location. On the day we visited, the youngest children were preparing for a trip to the local fire station. The excitement, though contained, was palpable as these bright-eyed and articulate girls discussed the visit. Further afield, year 2 heads for Lille for a day, year 4 to Swanage, year 5 to Cornwall on an outdoor pursuits adventure and year 6 to Paris. When classes are mixed up at the start of year 5, three days of bonding on a bushcraft course occur. Pretty primitive – no running water and the girls have to cook their own food. 'Some of our girls would never normally do something like that!' comments head.

Multi-ethnic families from all over central and south London send their girls here. Coaches dart back and forth to Alleyn's, Dulwich College and JAGS daily. Every class has bi-lingual children and EAL support given to those who need it. Extra French conversation classes for bi-lingual girls. 'Lots of smart mummies with multiple children dashing about on the school run. Some fairly glamorous types with shiny black four-by-fours and sunglasses, as well as a smattering of tiger mothers,' commented one parent, though school feels this is an 'unrepresentative appraisal.' Increasing number of families where both parents work. After-school care on offer is activity-based rather than glorified babysitting.

Parents remark on the sense of community here and participate in the life of school. 'It's important that the girls see we're a community, with teachers and parents all working together,' says head. Many come in to give presentations in assembly such as at Chinese New Year and Passover. Parents fundraise for projects, such as for a pond in the sensory garden. Head feels majority of parents is supportive and positive about the school but alert to the fact that 'some parents have strong views.'

Though some locals claim this is an elitist school that produces sharp-elbowed girls, school feels this is not the case. Head believes that 'above all, it's important all children here should be challenged, engaged and learn to give back. Given the advantages they have had, they need to ask themselves what they can then do to benefit others'. This ethos runs throughout the school.

JAPS deserves its outstanding reputation. With its enviable facilities, energetic teaching and dedicated leadership, it's unrivalled in this part of town. These charming, articulate and happy girls seem ready to take on the world by the time they leave.

James Allen's Girls' School (JAGS)

Linked school: James Allen's Preparatory School (JAPS), 129

144 East Dulwich Grove, London SE22 8TE

Tel: 020 8693 1181

Independent • Pupils: 785 • Ages: 11–18 • Sixth form pupils: 203 • C of E • Fees: £15,885 pa

Email: henrietta.kiezun@jags.org.uk
Website: www.jags.org.uk

20

Headmistress: Since September 2015, Mrs Sally-Anne Huang MA MSc PGCE, previously headmistress of Kent College, Pembury. Educated at Bolton School for Girls and Lady Margaret Hall, Oxford, where she read classics and English, then PGCE at King's College, London. Married to Alexis, a management consultant whom she met at Oxford; two young sons. Spent six years at Sevenoaks School, where she taught English and classics and was latterly a housemistress. Moved to Roedean as sixth form housemistress, then senior housemistress and spent four years as deputy head before moving to Kent College.

She has two sons. Her interests include cinema, the life and works of Mary Shelley, and looking after the family's various pets, including a dog and four cats.

Academic matters: Teaches Pre-U English literature – 'It allows the girls to read more widely and really develop their critical skills' – and some subjects, eg English and maths, have moved to IGCSE for a

better course; otherwise the school is still committed to A levels and GCSE – JAGS girls like to choose their own subject combinations so the IB is not for them. A strong showing, with 77 per cent A*/A, 95 per cent A*/B at A level in 2015 and 93 per cent A*/A at GCSE. A wide range of languages offered to GCSE and A level, including Italian, Russian, Spanish, German and Japanese, with a good take-up at A level. Maths, biology and chemistry are other popular A level subjects, alongside English and history. 'Our daughter has learned to work hard without pressure from us,' said a parent. 'She's had some fantastic, enthusiastic teachers who have really inspired her.'

A few girls have mild dyslexia/dyspraxia and the school has also accommodated children with sight/hearing problems. It does not provide one-to-one help, except for those with a statement of education need/EHC plan, but the SENCo liaises with staff and parents to ensure that girls are coping within normal classes, are provided with,

Six art rooms, with students most years going on to foundation courses. 'The art department really pushes you,' said a pupil. 'You learn such a lot'

eg, laptops where necessary and get extra time in exams if they are entitled to it.

Part of the Southwark Schools Learning Partnership, which includes five state and three independent schools working together on a huge range of projects. 'A real partnership is organic. It develops out of shared interests. We all have something to learn from one another. If we're having a theatre company or a speaker in, or a training session, we'll invite other schools over, or we may go to them.'

Games, options, the arts: Several pupils said they had chosen the school for its music – indeed, a huge variety of orchestras, choirs, ensembles and groups to choose from, playing in over 30 concerts each year. 'There's something for everyone, whatever you play,' said a pupil. Ralph Vaughan Williams and then Gustav Holst were the school's first two music teachers. Planning permission has been granted for a community music centre (active fundraising in progress), to be open to the community after school and at weekends as well as for school use during the day. Art also very strong, including fabric and textiles, with six art rooms

and several students most years going on to art foundation courses. 'The art department really pushes you,' said a pupil. 'You learn such a lot.' Drama is 'exceptional,' said a parent, including joint productions with Dulwich College and trips to perform at the Edinburgh Festival.

A very sporty school – plays an extensive and generally successful programme of inter-school matches, with house competitions giving the less physically-talented a chance to shine. One pupil commented: 'You have to be really good to play for the school.' PE GCSE and A level options. Facilities include a sports hall with squash courts, multi-gym and 3D climbing wall, a dance studio – 'we do everything, from flamenco to Bollywood to street dance' – and an elegant swimming pool with a large spectator area, plus extensive playing fields, artificial turf and courts. A wide range of sporting opportunities in the upper school, including ice skating and dry slope skiing.

Background and atmosphere: Part of a foundation established by talented Elizabethan actor Edward Alleyn, which includes Dulwich College and Alleyn's School. The school was founded in 1741 by James Allen, a Master of Dulwich College, as a free reading school for local poor children. He died five years later, leaving a bequest to secure his school's future. It has been girls only since 1845 and moved to its present site in 1886.

Much development since, culminating (so far) in rather swish dining room and Deep End café in what used to be the swimming pool. Grammar-schoolish dark wood stairways and window frames in the older parts contrast with light and airy glass,

white paint and pale wood in the newer areas. Fabulous library, dance and drama studios, 200 seat theatre, labs and DT rooms, walls lined with notice boards crammed with photos, lists, cuttings and posters.

But best of all are the 22 acre grounds, where girls are free to wander at will during break times, which, alongside sports pitches and courts, include botanical gardens (originally planted over 100 years ago by pioneer ecologist and head of science Dr Lilian Clarke), engagingly shaggy woodland and wetland areas and even a tree-lined country walk. Also a bridge over the railway line which runs through the grounds, with views down the line to North Dulwich station. The school has its own environmental manager who runs a biology club, welcomes children from nearby state primary and special schools for nature trails and pond-dipping and spreads the ecological word to other schools in the area.

The school is keen for the girls to share their privileges with the wider community. 'You need to get in the habit of giving something back. We're training them to roll up their sleeves and do something'. So, as well as sharing their sports and other facilities with other schools and local people, girls are encouraged to visit the nearby Cheshire Home, work with Romanian children with special needs and help with the Saturday literacy scheme for local children.

Pastoral care and discipline: Unashamedly old-fashioned over behaviour: no bad language, no graffiti, no chewing gum. Best suited to girls with no great inclination to rock the boat. Has excluded permanently for bringing drugs to school and temporarily for physical violence and being caught smoking more than once. 'If there's any chance of pupils misbehaving outside school, they'll be down like a ton of bricks,' commented a parent. However, the school says that sanctions are rare. 'We're tough, but we don't have a lot of discipline issues'.

A many-tiered pastoral system which includes

Best of all are the grounds, where girls are free to wander at will during break times, which include botanical gardens, engagingly shaggy woodland and even a tree-lined country walk

---

form tutors, heads of year and the two school nurses, who are also trained counsellors. Girls say they like having a range of people they can go to for help but report most people rub along well together. However, some felt that occasionally, stressed students are not noticed and that the pastoral net does have the odd hole. The school says it has worked very hard to improve pastoral care over the last few years and keeps a look out for stress and anorexia. 'But they do mostly enjoy their food. When we banned sweets and cakes from the tuck shop, they came up with charity cake sales'.

In the main school girls are usually allocated forms according to their houses, with staff and students getting together in fundraising events such as sponsored space hopper race, teacher karaoke, film-and-cake club. Sixth formers have vertical tutor groups, including year 12s and year 13s, so the younger girls can learn from the older ones' experiences of going through the UCAS process.

Pupils and parents: Diverse ethnically and socially, with plenty of girls on bursaries and some 50 home languages. Girls are bright, buzzy, focused. 'They come out very confident, streetwise kids,' said a parent. 'They're used to standing up for themselves and arguing their point.' They travel in from a wide area by train or bus, mostly from south of the river but increasing numbers from the north (12 minutes by train from London Bridge). OGs include Anita Brookner, Lisa St Aubin de Terain, Dharshini David and Sally Hawkins.

Entrance: Hot competition. Everyone is interviewed in the autumn term; maths, English and verbal reasoning exams in the spring term. Around a third comes up from the junior school and some 40 per cent of new entrants are from state primaries. Sixth form entry for outsiders depends on entrance exam, GCSE results, school reference and interview. Generally 10 or so join at this stage.

Exit: Around 10 per cent a year leave after GCSEs, mostly for co-ed sixth forms. A level leavers virtually all go to university: five Oxbridge places in 2015, Edinburgh, Exeter, Bristol, Imperial and Leeds also popular.

Money matters: The last part of James Allen's bequest was used to establish a Scholars' Fund to replace the abolished government assisted places in 1997. Twenty-six James Allen's Bursary places, which can pay for up to full fees plus help with uniform, lunches and school trips, awarded each year. School also gets an annual grant from the Dulwich Estate, which pays for more scholarships and bursaries. More than a third of pupils are on some sort of financial assistance. Up to 20 scholarships at 11+, including music, art and sports awards. Major scholarships of £1000 pa and minor scholarships of £500 pa can be means-tested up to full fees. A few 16+ scholarships of £1,000 awarded on the basis of GCSE results.

Remarks: High-achieving school at work and play, with a strong social conscience. Suits bright, well-ordered girls who are keen to get involved. 'You feel really proud that your daughter is at JAGS,' said a parent. 'You know she's set up for life.'

Merlin School

4 Carlton Drive, London SW15 2BZ

Independent • Pupils: 220 • Ages: 4–8 • Fees: £12,981 pa

Tel: 020 8788 2769

Email: secretary@merlinschool.net
Website: www.merlinschool.net

40

Headmistress: Since 2003, Mrs Kate Prest BA Music/ Ed PGCE (40s). Studied at Oxford Brookes. Formerly head of pre-prep at The Harrodian, and before that, teacher and music specialist at Oratory Primary, Chelsea. Welcoming, lively and overflowing with enthusiasm, she treasures the school's unique, homely feel. 'We work very much as a team, which extends through staff, pupils, parents and even grandparents,' she told us.

Believes in the importance of communication and keeping children aware of the world they live in. Operates a complete open door policy, which parents told us works a treat. Prefers verbal communication and does not do email. She hurriedly assured us, however, that the school secretary does. Always there to help and advise parents on the next stage. Lives locally and is married with three children, all of whom have attended the Merlin (daughter still there). Husband works in the City, so has no plans to move on. 'I'm not going anywhere,' she says. 'This is good. I love this school.'

Entrance: Non-selective. Parents attend an early afternoon talk and tour of the school. Places are then offered on receipt of registration – priority given to siblings, then it's first come first served. Advisable to view early. There are occasionally places higher up the school.

Exit: Some leave at 7 and the rest at 8. They go to schools all over and, apart from a high number to The Harrodian at 8 (no feeding but a link, whereby they are interviewed in November rather than examined in January), there is no particular pattern. Other destinations include Bute House, Putney High, King's College Junior School, Colet Court, Shrewsbury, Milbourne Lodge, Rokeby, Westminster Under, Broomwood House, Glendower Prep, King's House Richmond, Fulham Prep and various boarding schools.

Remarks: Located in a large, converted Victorian house in a leafy Putney street, the school is homely, welcoming and cosy and initially appears quite old-fashioned in approach and look. We were shown round by three articulate, enthusiastic pupils – luckily they knew where they were going because we got completely confused. Good sized and light classrooms, well decorated with children's work. Very little evidence of IT influence. One interactive whiteboard – head says, 'I want teachers in front of my children.' They have an ICT room, where all years have a lesson every week. Each classroom has a computer – used by the children in rotation. Separate science and art rooms. 'We dissect in year 3,' one enthusiastic pupil told us.

Class sizes are small (average 17). All classes are mixed ability. Some subjects are classroom-based, while others follow the teacher. Divisions according to ability in maths and English. Never a really competitive feel, apart from in an advanced maths class. Children seemed happy, relaxed and attentive – and eager to tell us what they were doing.

Drama and musical productions are an important part of the school year. Lots of music, vocal, instrumental and theoretical (not surprising with a music-trained head). Head still takes all the children for weekly classes. About a third learn violin, piano or guitar as an extra, with lessons rotated in school hours and practice done at home.

A spacious playground with Astroturf – plenty of room for outdoor play and sports practice. On the far side, purpose-built classrooms are occupied by year 2 classes. Well designed for indoor and outdoor use. Popular and experienced sports master ensures that everyone can try everything. Two training sessions a week in the playground (or inside if necessary), to build up co-ordination. Off-site practice once a week at a local sports venue. Fixtures against similar schools in football, hockey, cricket and rugby, but other sports on offer too. 'My bright, but not at all sporty, child gets to try everything and never feels that he's not excelling,' a parent told us. Chess is popular too – it's one of a host after-school clubs.

Dining hall in basement, and our young guides said the food, on the whole, is excellent. Sensibly, there isn't a great deal of choice. 'We have to try everything, but if we really, really don't like it, we are allowed to scrape it into a bowl,' they told us. All cooked in-house, with nutritionist's supervision. Catering staff have a list of all children with specific dietary requirements. School is very hot on manners too.

Warm, caring and fully-trained head of SEN, with two sympathetic assistants to make sure

> *Food, on the whole, is excellent, say pupils. 'We have to try everything, but if we really don't like it, we are allowed to scrape it into a bowl'*

every contingency is covered. Good at identifying and dealing with problems. School says it is important to find each child's particular strengths. Early dyslexia screening for the youngest and full screening if suspected in older children. Parents always informed first. Continual staff meetings to discuss children and identify any possible problem areas. School runs own phonics, maths and spelling programmes and tries to give extra help in groups; if one-to-one is necessary, that is charged for. Always enough help in class, from gap year students and parent volunteers. An extra reading clinic in year 1. Occasional EAL pupils given extra support as necessary.

A happy, friendly school that builds children's confidence and prepares them well for the next step. One parent told us: 'My child has had an amazing experience. He has learned and grown and is ready to move on.' Another said: 'We have been really happy with the quality of education and care our son has received. They really find out what children are good at and make it happen.' Not for those who want acres of outside space, but a real home from home.

Newton Prep

149 Battersea Park Road, London SW8 4BX

Tel: 020 7720 4091

Independent · Pupils: 620 · Ages: 3–13 · Fees: up to £17,625 pa

Email: registrar@newtonprep.co.uk
Website: www.newtonprepschool.co.uk

41

Headmistress: Since September 2013, Mrs Alison Fleming BA MA(Ed) PGCE (40s), a grammar school girl and theology graduate. Previously head of Dulwich College Junior School for four years, prior to which she was deputy head at Highgate Junior School. A team inspector for the ISI and a governor of a local school. And, far more importantly, an ace head.

Forthright, articulate, warm and confident, Mrs Fleming inherited a large prep in good heart, good nick and with a massive new-build. She spent her first year listening, looking, learning and thinking. And now, subtly but decisively, change (all for

the good, as far as we can judge) is on the way. This is summed up by Mrs Fleming's hope of relocating her own study away from the admin corridor to, ideally, somewhere at the core of her capacious school. Her aims are to maintain the school's 'academically ambitious' ethos while developing its community links, parental involvement and partnership with eg Kids' Company. In these aspirations, she appears to carry her own eclectic and inclusive school community with her. But there is far more of sound educational value afoot too.

Warm praise, especially from seasoned parents who have been part of the school under the

last three regimes and who value the increased headmagisterial presence around the school. 'She is always smiling and approachable,' we were told. 'She is independent-minded and has lots of ideas,' another enthused. A third said, 'She is fabulous. Really enthusiastic and has a really good combination of strength, warmth, leadership and vision.'

Entrance: Oversubscribed at nursery stage when they have 48 places. Application process ensures an even balance of i) boys and girls and ii) of autumn, spring and summer birthdays. There's a waiting list and those who don't get in can reapply for reception. Sibling policy.

Informal assessment the autumn term before entry into reception. 'A gentle process'. Staff observe the children to see how they relate to adults, their peers and the world around them. 'Occasional places' happen occasionally. Year 1 or 2 candidates spend a day in class and take tests in reading, English and maths. Admission at year 3 and above by competitive testing. Any applicant for year 3 is considered for a scholarship (currently worth £250 per term) or a place backed up by a means-tested, top-up bursary. For a school only in its third decade, a surprising amount of financial help available. Most of those admitted at nursery or reception move smoothly up but this isn't guaranteed.

Exit: Leavers' lists are encouraging largely because there is clearly no stereotyped Newton product and they go to a wide spread of schools at both 11 and 13. Good range of scholarships – art, sports, dance and academic – won too (11 in 2015). Year 6s to eg Alleyn's, JAGS, Emanuel, Dulwich College, City of London Girls, Sevenoaks, St Paul's Girls and the local GDSTs. Year 8s to similar plus impressive boarding schools (Wycombe Abbey, Wellington, Eton, Harrow, Bedales), Westminster and KCS. New role on the senior management team for a deputy head with responsibility for senior school transfer – a rare, if not unique position amongst prep schools. Watch the others scampering to follow suit!

Remarks: This part of London – behind the power station, which, along with a wide area round about was being comprehensively rebuilt and regenerated at time of our visit – is not generally appealing. To find an enormous, sought-after prep school housed, partly in an Edwardian block of debatable attractiveness and partly in impressive and extensive new build is unexpected. However, one only has to enter the somewhat alarming steel wire cage that encloses the school to be transported into a very different and disarming world.

Warm praise, especially from parents who have been part of the school under the last three regimes and value the increased headmagisterial presence

First impressions are formed by the children. They are happy, confident, relaxed, articulate, polite and eager to share their school with a visitor. They inhabit delightful spaces. Second impressions come from the place itself. From nursery, through lower school and up to the subject specific classrooms and studios of the top two years, each learning area is well-structured, full of colourful, stimulating and thoughtful displays and staffed by smiley, interesting teachers. We longed to linger – the language rooms ('souriez et entrez!') invite learning, the art rooms are full of creativity and a vast array of creative opportunities, the science labs and IT suites are sleek and the library is simply the best we've seen in a prep anywhere. Worth lingering especially here – exceptionally well-stocked, each child's reading is guided and encouraged and the children find that they have everything they need for research. A real understanding here that books can provide complementary riches, in so many ways, to the internet – which is equally well-used. Sofas, carpets, bean bags and cushions and hundreds of lovely books. Learning and inventiveness hums. We ventured into the RS room and were instantly involved in a fascinating discussion about the compatibility or complementarity of religion and science.

The old building, seamlessly now melded to the new, is old school standard eg green and brown tiles, sensible corridors, parquet. The new build is high, broad, confident with big spaces of the kind you'd expect from a sizeable and prosperous high school. The newest bits are breathtaking for a prep. A splendid auditorium and equally impressive,

acoustically perfect, recital hall. Many senior schools would drool. Vast airy dining room with seriously inviting food, eaten by all. Scooter and bike park: 'they really encourage us to bike or walk to school – you get a special badge for it,' we were told. Sports hall, gym and other spaces for muscle stretching. Two art studios full of lovely stuff. We liked especially the monster sculptures – custombuilt in some cases ('our librarian really wants a dragon to hang in the library'), the earth-colour tribal shields, the batik, the ceramics, the marionettes.

Best is the collaborative ethos and sense of community. Inclusiveness is key and eccentricity relished – the history teacher gives WW1 bullet shells as rewards rather than house points

Outside space is equally enviable – there is so much of it! A huge all-weather pitch and various other good-sized safe-surface areas, well-equipped and colourful – for the different age groups. So sports thrive and, as parents crow 'it's not exclusive – they have a C team and everyone has a chance'. Most delightful is the 'garden' – tucked away between car park and road but a rus in urbe idyll once you're in, with shady leafy nooks, fruit trees (one was a blackberry tree, we were solemnly informed) plots and beds, all well used by keen gardeners and for lessons of all sorts.

Around eight per cent have some sort of SEN – vast majority mild dyslexia, small numbers with eg ADHD or some speech and language delay in early years. Support is given either on an individual or small group basis by the director of learning development and teaching assistants in classrooms but head acknowledges that there is work to be done on the SEN side which will be welcome to parents current and future. Music too, now, under sparky new head of dept rising to match the stunning new facilities. We anticipate the Newton's impressive lists of art scholarships might well be matched by music similar in coming years.

About 20 to a class except for two nursery classes of 24. Pupils from all over south west and central London; locals walk or scoot to school. All speak good English though around 50 (9 per cent) are bilingual eg French, Spanish, Italian, Urdu, Arabic, Russian spoken at home. Small group EAL sessions for those who need them.

Best is the creative and collaborative ethos and the sense of community. Inclusiveness is key as parents testify – 'my children are totally different characters and it's been great for all of them'

– and eccentricity is relished. (The history teacher gives WW1 bullet shells as rewards rather than house points.) There is little of the preciousness and snobbery one can occasionally encounter in other preps and the pupils feel part of something bigger than themselves. As they told us: 'Our teachers are so approachable. You can always ask for help'. 'You're not babied by the teachers.' 'There's no fear between the year groups. Year 3s often come and chat to us in year 8.'

A parent summed it up, 'We're going to be really sad to leave.'

Northcote Lodge School

Linked schools: Broomwood Hall School (Garrards Road), 67; Broomwood Hall (Ramsden Road), 68; Broomwood Hall (Nightingale Lane), 69

26 Bolingbroke Grove, London SW11 6EL

Tel: 020 8682 8888

Independent • Pupils: 220 • Ages: 8–13 • Fees: £17,430 pa

Email: northcote@northwoodschools.com
Website: www.northcotelodge.co.uk

Headmaster: Since September 2015, Mark Smith, previously deputy head, and before that head of maths, at Caldicott School. Prior to Caldicott, he spent 20 years at Millfield, as housemaster and head of year 9. He is a keen sportsman, qualified to coach cricket, football and rugby and fond of the odd round of golf.

Entrance: At 8. At least two-thirds from Broomwood Hall, the sister school, round the corner. The others mostly local, although school minibuses bring in some from across the river. Parents and families attend an open day and meet the headmaster. If they all like each other, zap, they are on the waiting list. A year before entry it's assessment time. A couple of hours at the school include tests in English, maths, verbal reasoning and ball skills, an interview with the head and some carefully observed playtime, including a snack. If your son is offered a place, you have to cough up half a term's fees immediately. Fifty per cent will be refunded on first term's bill, rest will be kept until boy moves on. They feel this encourages only those really serious about the school.

Exit: Mainly to board at a wide range of public schools, including Marlborough, Wellington, Bradfield, Eton, Radley, Harrow and Sherborne.

Most of those continuing to day school have gone to Dulwich College. Recent scholarships include academic, music, sports and all-rounder. Inevitably some find the transition, from small protected school to large busy one, difficult at first, but school feels they are doing as much as possible to ease the path for them.

Remarks: A day school with the ethos of a boarding prep. 'A boarding school – but pupils don't bring pyjamas.' Boys arrive immediately after breakfast and go home late afternoon having already done their homework. Parents like this as it takes off a lot of pressure. Plenty of after-school clubs as well – quite a full-on day.

Small classes, never more than 16, and enthusiastic teachers, average age mid-30s, approximately half/half male and female, create a good learning environment. All mixed ability, but setting in maths and English starts in year 4 and increases through other subjects as pupils move up the school. Plenty of playground space for kicking balls around or net practice at break time. Boys appeared relaxed, open and polite, quite happy to talk about what they were doing. School thinks they should be 'confident but not cocky; polite and affable; ready for next stage at 13'. Feels appearance important too and clean shoes essential – much used polish and brushes kept on bench in playground, just outside matron's room. Full-time matron, very jolly and welcoming – boys happy to take problems to her, a fully qualified nurse and a key figure on the pastoral care side.

Up to date science laboratories – apparently imaginative teacher recently bought a shark from Billingsgate for boys to dissect: Jaws, how exciting

The large, grade 2 listed Victorian building has been a school (first for blind children, then disadvantaged girls) for the last 100 years. Several new additions have helped bring it bang up to date and you have to get to know your way around – we walked up and down different staircases and in and out of the main building, but, we were assured it was all totally logical. Probably a good thing that the younger boys stay put in their classrooms and it's only the top three years that move about.

Good art and DT studios, busy busy, lots of different things going on. Up to date science laboratories – apparently imaginative teacher recently bought a shark from Billingsgate for boys to dissect: Jaws, how exciting! Well equipped IT room, used by the younger groups for computer studies and as lesson extensions by the older ones. Music timetabled for all and about half also play an individual instrument, at the moment trumpet is most popular. A variety of musical groups and an active chapel choir, which has toured in Europe. Well-equipped gym can also be transformed into fully functioning theatre for the complete dramatic experience. Drama lessons part of the curriculum, about a third take the LAMDA exam. Several productions a year, hopefully something for everyone. Public speaking also encouraged – could be reciting a poem, taking part in a debate or reading out a match report in assembly: 'We want them to be seen and heard'.

Sport is big and played every day. Karate part of the curriculum, compulsory for first two years – 'it's good for confidence, concentration and self-esteem'. Masses of black belts. Main outdoor sports football, rugby and cricket, either across the road on Wandsworth Common or at Trinity Fields, 10 minutes' walk away. Plays matches against other schools, sometimes at weekends, but, parents say, possibly not competitive enough. No dedicated, specialist sports teachers, which can mean boys not properly prepared. Lots more to try in after-school clubs, including cross-country, golf and shooting – definitely modelling itself on a country prep.

Regular residential trips for all, ranging from PGL in year 5 to outdoor pursuits in year 8 – good formative stuff. The usual French trips, rugby and cricket tours and, less common, yearly exchange with a South African school. Also plenty of excursions in and around London, making the most of what it has to offer. All trips and excursions compulsory and included in fees.

EAL not an issue as only accepts fluent English speakers. Caters for mild learning difficulties – one-to-one help available, but nothing too severe and definitely no disruption. Parents say teachers good at communicating and problems quickly identified and dealt with. School says as far as possible everything is in place to counteract any problems or if a boy is unhappy. All boys have prep diaries, containing school rules and all contact details – parents use these for important notes. A Christian school and, though other faiths are welcome, they must join in with daily assemblies and attend the weekly church service.

Our Lady of Victories Catholic Primary School

1 Clarendon Drive, London SW15 1AW

State • Pupils: 200 • Ages: 4–11 • RC

Tel: 020 8788 7957

Email: info@ourladyofvictories.
wandsworth.sch.uk
Website: www.ourladyofvictories.wandsworth.sch.uk

43

Headteacher: Since 2011, Mrs Deirdre McDonald BA PGCE NQPH (40s). After studying English at university, Mrs McDonald worked in publishing, then decided to train as a teacher. She has a long association with the school – she was a governor and taught year 6 for eight years before becoming deputy head and more recently head. Her own children are now at university but attended Our Lady of Victories. Forward thinking and inclusive – parents say she is a caring and committed head who's available to all families as and when they need her assistance. Her background in publishing and interest in literature and language has inspired and influenced many school activities. Definitely an artsy type, she enjoys cinema, theatre, reading and travel.

Entrance: Priority to Catholics in all categories; siblings only get preference if parents still regular worshippers. Ballot allocation decides places in inevitable event of oversubscription. Places sometimes come up in the older age groups (usually due to families moving away from London), so it's worth contacting the school for occasional vacancies.

Exit: At 11+, just over half of pupils move to popular Catholic secondary schools like Cardinal Vaughan, The London Oratory, Sacred Heart, Ursuline High School, Wimbledon College, Gumley House. The rest go to local independents (Emanuel, Ibstock Place, Latymer, Hampton) or to Catholic boarding schools (Worth, The Oratory School, Reading and the IBVM convents).

Remarks: A first-rate primary school tucked into the residential streets of Putney, in the parish of Our Lady of Pity and St Simon Stock. Originally run by the Sisters of the Poor Servants of the Mother of God, the school was handed over to the Diocese of Southwark in 1978. Housed in the former convent (there are several modern extensions), its compact site is well kept and decorated with an array of colourful artwork by the children.

School is exceptionally well accomplished in all areas. The majority of children achieve level 5 by year 6, with everyone's progress assessed each half term. A well-balanced curriculum is delivered throughout and children achieve particularly well in maths and English. French classes from year 1. The school has won silver and gold awards in junior maths challenges. Creative writing is strong and pupils do variety of science, history and geography projects each term. Older children practise verbal and non-verbal reasoning for the Wandsworth 11+ tests and are taught how to write timed essays.

The school has strong links with the parish – it celebrates a number of religious festivals and the local priest visits the school regularly. At Holy Communion, children process from school to church, a day rounded off with a visit to the ice cream van. The choir sings in the church and at local care centres. Music, led by a dedicated music

> *School has strong links with the parish. At Holy Communion, children process from school to church, a day rounded off with a visit to the ice cream van*

teacher, is very strong. Lots of music lessons in school, concerts and the school's recorder group and choir attends annual Music for Youth festival. Pupils take part in the National Theatre's Primary Programme (workshops held in school and theatre visits), alongside trips to concerts and the ballet.

Impressive PE programme offers a range of sporting activities at Dover House Road playing fields and swimming at the nearby Putney Leisure Centre pool. Good range of clubs includes fencing, zumba and Latin. SENCo and visiting speech and occupational therapists supervise learning support. Head is keen to ensure awareness of SEN throughout the school. Regular in-house training days and some teachers attend training courses run by a school specialising in specific learning difficulties and differences.

Lots of fundraising for charity organised by the school and parents, with many of the events run by the children themselves.

Prospect House School

75 Putney Hill, London SW15 3NT

Independent • Pupils: 290 • Ages: 3–11 • Fees: up to £16,785 pa

Tel: 020 8780 0456

Email: info@prospecths.org.uk
Website: www.prospecths.org.uk

44

Headmistress: Since April 2004, Mrs Dianne Barratt BEd MEd (50s); vast experience and knowledge of young children, having taught across the spectrum in UK and USA, from large challenging state primaries and specialist schools to selective independent preps. Previously deputy head at Croydon High Junior School and acting deputy head of JAPS. Her specialist subjects are psychology and language and literacy teaching. Her management has transformed a once rather shaky Prospect House into a thriving school with a number of outstanding features. Parents say she is a mine of information and does her best to help with a problem, big or small. Her smiling face and enthusiasm for developing the school and children's potential are appreciated by

staff and parents. Married with two grown-up daughters who were educated in London day schools, she enjoys running and holidaying in Turkey.

Entrance: Mainly at 3+ nursery and a few places at 4+ reception, waiting list first come first served, non-selective, sibling policy. Thereafter telephone to inquire about occasional vacancies in older age groups. Some scholarships available for children from state schools from age 8.

Exit: At 11+, some to boarding schools, mostly to London day schools. Mrs Barratt and her staff take time with parents to ensure appropriate secondary school choices. Popular destinations include Kew

House, King's College Wimbledon, St Paul's Girls', Hampton, Latymer, Godolphin & Latymer, Kingston Grammar, Ibstock Place, Putney High, Surbiton High and Emanuel. Pupils are significantly successful in gaining scholarships at 11+.

Remarks: Highly organised and well planned, achieves great things for its pupils without being pushy. Considering the intake is non-selective, this is impressive. Pupils do well across the curriculum, particularly in core subjects, with around 90 per cent achieving level 5 in year 6. All progress is tracked – personal development as well as academic; extra support is available for strugglers and streaming for maths and English from year 3. ICT is outstanding, embedded into all subjects, thus adding new dimensions to classroom-based learning. Modern server-based network of Apple Mac equipment, interactive whiteboards throughout, and wireless laptops. First independent school in the country to be awarded an ICT Mark of Excellence by BECTA – has gone on to win best school in the UK for primary ICT. Staff:pupil ratio is very high, as is the number of subject specialist teachers.

Good choice of games on offer, with a 'sport for all' policy leading to many successful fixtures and tournaments. Large purpose-built hall for dance, drama and gymnastics; all-weather sports pitch and local sports grounds are used for team sports. Musical opportunities are outstanding for a small school – inspiring class music for all taught by a specialist teacher. Traditional methods alongside Suzuki teaching; pupils can choose to play instruments with one of a number of specialist instrumental teachers who visit school. Award-winning choir, several ensembles and school orchestra. Terrific variety of clubs to choose from each term; old favourites – tag rugby and handicrafts – run along with the more unusual archery, wii fit and animation.

Head's management has transformed a once rather shaky Prospect House into a thriving school with outstanding features

SEN is forward thinking. Qualified and experienced SENCo with three specialist visiting teachers run a well-resourced learning support department. Good links with local speech and occupational therapists, who visit the school as required. Some support and screening is included in the fees; an additional charge is made for one-to-one sessions.

Pupils' well-being and pastoral care are thought to be outstanding. 'Getting home-school contact right is not always easy – this school really tries,' say parents. Active PTA works with the head to organise social and fundraising events. Volunteer parents help to run the school's library. Occupies a compact site at the top of Putney Hill which has been cleverly designed and extended to offer just about everything; however no on-site kitchens, so everyone brings a packed lunch. Has just added another building a few minutes' walk away and is now two-form entry.

A thriving school for the 21st century doing a great job, with added bonuses of fantastic ICT provision and excellent senior management.

Putney High Junior School

Linked school: Putney High School, 146

35 Putney Hill, London SW15 6BH

Tel: 020 8788 6523

Independent • Pupils: 320 • Ages: 4–11 • Fees: £13,785 pa

Email: putneyhigh@put.gdst.net
Website: www.putneyhigh.gdst.net

Head: Since 2011, Mrs Joanna Wallace BMUS MA PGCE. Previously head of the pre-prep at Shrewsbury High School, another GDST school (she attended one herself). She views Putney as a school about challenge – whether academically, artistically or on the sports field – and creativity. Believes everyone learns best when they are happy and a cross-curricular approach should mean that lessons are great fun. Spends holidays in Scotland, visiting the Edinburgh Festival or climbing munros. Still plays the cello and has performed in chamber music festivals in Germany and Italy.

Entrance: Selective at 4+ and 7+. Expansion (from one to two form entry since our last review) has gone well. School says it's hard to put a finger on a 'Putney girl' – 'there are many different types here, all individuals'; 'My team worked out the other day that between us we have 250 years of experience in selecting 4-year-olds – that's got to count for something'. Parents feel that the Putney team knows exactly what it's looking for; almost an X factor, with no priority for siblings. 'I don't know how they get it right, but they do,' says one

mother whose youngest was rejected several times and now totally supports the decision. 'It wasn't the right place for her – they saw it before I did.' Assessments, described as 'friendly and informal', last one and a half hours for 4-year-olds and twice as long at 7+, where new applicants will complete papers in English, mathematics and non-verbal reasoning. (At 7+ junior classes increase from 22 to 24, thus a minimum of four extra places). Existing pupils do not need to sit this test. Girls come from a wide area of south-west London, but most are local, say a five-mile radius.

Exit: Vast majority (75 per cent in 2015) to linked senior school where they 'qualify' rather than 'compete' for a place. As the girls are monitored so closely from day one, no horrible surprises for parents when the time comes to move to senior school – year 5 is the latest you'll hear if your daughter is failing to cut the senior mustard. Small exit elsewhere at 11+, though the school probably does not advertise this. An undoubted expectation to go on to the senior school and although applications elsewhere are not encouraged and other entrance exams are not particularly prepared for odd one to St Paul's, Lady Eleanor Holles, Wycombe Abbey and other top of the pile destinations.

Remarks: A punchy place full of very confident little girls. Fairly structured from the off – classic girls' prep. Teachers are (mainly) highly regarded by parents – 'absolutely fantastic,' says one – and well supported and managed, thus minimising the high staff turnover levels that can plague London schools. High standards throughout for everything from handwriting to gym squads. Handwriting taken terribly seriously. Everything taught very thoroughly and then tested and retested (though much of it without the girls realising they are being scrutinised).

'My team worked out the other day that between us we have 250 years of experience in selecting 4-year-olds – that's got to count for something'

School is now a 'tablet academy' with iPads in use throughout (year 4 to 6 pupils have their own). Two language lessons a week taught by specialist staff from reception upwards. Specialist staff also teach music and PE from reception. Quite unpushy on homework – feels enough is packed in during school day. Class sizes are the (large-ish) GDST norm – 22 at KS1 and 24 at KS2.

A learning support teacher and SEN coordinator. 'Learning support offered as required,' says school. No SEN testing on entry. Extra-curricular activities for the gifted and talented.

Music is great – 90-strong school choir was runner-up in BBC Songs of Praise School Choir of the Year in 2008, 2010 and 2013. Parents delighted to spot their daughters on TV. Huge percentage learn a musical instrument – many learn two – and it's not uncommon for them to have reached grade 6 by year 6. Orchestra of over 50. Lots of performance opportunities; universal praise for first ever junior gala concert in 2009. Performing arts centre opening in September 2015, complete with professional sound and lighting.

Sport majors around netball, tennis (Surrey under-11 champions) and gymnastics (second place in UK national floor and vault competition), with addition of swimming from Year 1. A 'sport for all' policy to encourage everyone to have a go. Overall feel is that sport has improved since our last visit. Girls are kept busy after hours, too, with good selection of clubs, plus rehearsals and games practice, and lots of trips, both day and residential.

Generally life moves along in a happy fashion. Despite its thorough approach to education, it's not stuffy and regimented. The working environment is fresh and smart, with some new building to cope with recent increase in numbers. And what a sensible idea – new classrooms for the littlies have been designed to include loos inside them. Junior school shares small but pretty site with senior school but has its own playground, one of the nicest we've seen, including a stage and benches, pirate ship, Wendy house, giant chess board and even tables with games board tops – lots to keep them busy at break.

Junior school is divided into two – Garden House is reception to year 2, Lytton House years 3 to 6. Each has a 'secret safe' where the girls can post notes detailing any worries or concerns. Robust house system – great participation in hustings. Parental involvement encouraged and school advertises a very open-door policy, though some complaints that persistence is needed to get past the school secretary. Parents say fees provide value for money – but expect to write cheques for FOPHS, the parents' association. It's something of a social whirl – Putney parents know how to party while whipping up support for the place. Generally parents are a worthy selection of the great and good of south west London.

Overall school comes very well recommended by parents as a safe choice. Rather a prescriptive place – it's not particularly exciting or off the wall creative – but it does know exactly what it's about and undoubtedly delivers the goods.

Putney High School

Linked school: Putney High Junior School, 144

35 Putney Hill, London SW15 6BH

Independent • Pupils: 600 • Ages: 11–18 • Sixth form pupils: 150 • Fees: £16,740 pa

Tel: 020 8788 4886

Email: putneyhigh@put.gdst.net
Website: www.putneyhigh.gdst.net

46

Headmistress: Since September 2015, Mrs Suzie Longstaff, following a year as acting head after predecessor Dr Denise Lodge took a sabbatical to care for her sick husband. Before joining the teaching profession, Mrs Longstaff had a successful rowing career. Highlights including coxing the GB Women's VIII at the Atlanta Olympics in 1996.

After joining the school in 2009 as head of sixth form, was promoted to deputy head (academic). An economics graduate (Durham), she has a 'passion' for lifelong learning, something she has put into practice with acquisition of diploma (in computing) from the University of Oxford and MA (in education) from the University of Bath.

Academic matters: Very academic place – some seriously bright girls here, working very hard, but not too pressured. Excellent results – at GCSE in 2015, an impressive 87 per cent A*/A grades. Good

performances in sciences, English and music. At A level 72.5 per cent A*/A grades. Fantastic to see in a girls' school that maths is the most popular choice at A level, by a long way. Parents say it is a happy school that holds its own against St Paul's and Godolphin and Latymer, though the feeling on the outside is that St Paul's is still a jump ahead.

In year 7, when girls are mainly taught in form groups, they average (a large) 28. School is quick to defend the numbers. 'One third of lessons in year 7 are taught in groups of 21/22 – maths, art and science. Furthermore, DT/ textiles is taught in half classes of 14. By year 9 only PHSE (life skills) is taught as a group of 28.' For sixth formers, the average class size is eight.

Good to see that girls are not over-burdened with lots of homework – theory is that they work hard enough during school day. No setting in year 7, but in year 8 they are set for maths. It's more a

Site is something of an oasis off uninspiring Putney Hill. A few steps from this busy London road and you are in a far more rarefied atmosphere – parallels with Narnia and Mr Benn abound

matter of pace than ability – all can still aim for A grades by the end. Studies all based around a considerably developed national curriculum which is pleasingly broad and flexible. Sciences all taught separately from year 8, when Latin also makes an appearance. School happily retains minority subjects. Nice to see Mandarin on the list of modern foreign languages – now available as a GCSE and A level subject. Writer in residence conducts workshops and classes promoting qualities such as independent thinking and learning.

No testing for SEN, but specialists on the staff, though the impression from the school is that it is not a huge specialist area, so not a first choice school for a girl with SEN problems. Extracurricular activities for the exceptionally gifted and talented.

Games, options, the arts: A great place for all-rounders as games and music are very well done here. 'Would be a shame to come here as a pure academic – you would miss out on so much,' sums up one parent. Storming sports results lately. School has produced GDST champions in netball, lacrosse and tennis. Playing fields are off-site (but close by) – the downside of London location. Rowing increasingly popular and successful, more than 100 Putney girls take to the river with a rowing club which runs seven days a week. School now leases boathouse at one of the most prestigious locations on the Thames.

Great music – choir tours are legendary and colossal, orchestras and ensembles abound. 'I just cannot get over the music here,' says one mother to a chorus of agreement. A mixture of planning and fortune has seen the music department refurbished, with all the toys necessary for GCSE and A level composition. Lovely to see 16 girls a year take music GCSE – higher than the average elsewhere. New performing arts centre opened in 2015. Art also very good – average of 20 go on to A level, with eight or nine then to art school. Tons of extracurricular stuff on offer – over 200 clubs, from barbershop to zumba. Almost everyone does Duke of Edinburgh.

Background and atmosphere: Set up in 1893 with 54 pupils in five scattered houses, coming together as one on its present site in 1918. Typically of London

schools, the site is relatively small, but it really makes the most of what it has, with some beautiful gardens, and is something of an oasis off uninspiring Putney Hill. Just a few steps from this busy London road and you are in a far more rarefied atmosphere – parallels with Narnia and Mr Benn abound. And of course the upside to this urban location is fab transport links – short walk from tube and BR trains and streams of buses stop right outside.

Inside some super-smart facilities – spectacular library, swish new drama studio and language lab, but overall facilities won't blow you away with glitz and glamour. Doesn't matter, though, as everything underpinned with great teaching and wide-ranging opportunities.

Pastoral care and discipline: Parental praise for pastoral care – knows the girls well and understands all the ages and stages they go through. Worthwhile life skills programme is used to discuss bullying, eating disorders et al. 'We pride ourselves on spotting problems early on,' says the school. 'Obviously there are occasional issues, but we address them fast and in a supportive way.' Happy, well-motivated girls with things to do and places to go to are unlikely to spend much time in detention. The usual system of praise and punishment in place as and when necessary – house points, detentions, that sort of thing – but overall a happy ship. Good

teacher/pupil relationships make formal sanction the exception rather than the rule. 'When a school is working well like this you can afford to be a bit relaxed,' says the school.

Tough rather than tender, no nonsense rather than nurturing – but the bright and robust will thrive. Can be rather rigid about rules and regulations – parents complain about a lack of a personal touch with standardised responses to their queries and of secretarial/admin staff at times not being as helpful as parents would wish.

Pupils and parents: The hard-working middle classes abound and are really supportive of the school. Perhaps not surprisingly, as they are discussing their own daughters and her friends, most parents describe the girls as 'down to earth' and the place as 'not snobby or élitist'. Pupils are largely a full-on bunch, full of attitude and ideas – and might overwhelm those who don't shine in anything in particular, so not the obvious place for the shy or unconfident. School is proud of its girls and their 'can do' attitude – when confronted with a minor inconvenience, they just get on with it. Pupils are a reasonably smart, normal bunch with no wacky hairstyles, jewellery etc.

Parents very welcome to contribute – preferably via parents' association rather than helping within the school itself: 'They prefer to keep us out of the

Putney is after the top 10 per cent. Don't coach to get your daughter here – school knows exactly the girls it wants and you either fit or you don't

way a bit,' says one mother. The parents' association is thriving, seemingly a great place for a night out and one of the few we've come across who make special mention of welcoming single parents who might otherwise find some school events a little daunting. Newcomers will be swept up and supported. Generally the school is big on fundraising.

OGs bear witness to the wide range of talents encouraged at the school, eg newsreader Sophie Raworth, fashion designer Edina Ronay, gardening broadcaster Pippa Greenwood, author Sophie Kinsella, politicians Virginia Bottomley and Baroness Elizabeth Symons, journalist Melanie Phillips, sculptor Emily Young, Sandie Okoro, president of International Lawyers of Africa and entrepreneur Calypso Rose, a London young business person of the year.

Entrance: Selective, at 11+, described by the school as 'by competitive examination (papers in English and maths, each one hour 15 minutes) and friendly interview'. If an average selective school is looking for the top 25 per cent, Putney is after the top 10. Don't struggle and coach to get your daughter here – school knows exactly the girls it wants and you either fit or you don't. 'They'll need to have been well-taught,' is the only hint we could glean for you. Competitive, lots of interest – 2,000+ at open day, 400 will sit entrance exam, and bear in mind that every other year almost 50 per cent of the places will go to the about 44 possible arrivals from linked juniors (less than a handful of the junior school brigade won't qualify). The school alternates between a three and four-form entry (three in 2015). Register by November the year before admission. Lots of locals, but as girls are older and travel independently, net cast slightly wider than for juniors.

At 16+, girls need six GCSEs at A*/A, with A*/As in subjects they want to study at A level. Used to have a reputation for weeding out at this stage, ie booting out those of their own who do not make the grades, but we're told that this is no more – a major relief for parents. Newcomers will need references and informal interviews with Putney staff.

Exit: Majority move up to the sixth form, though some head off to co-ed or boarding elsewhere. At 18+ most to redbrick universities of their choice, eg Bristol, Edinburgh, Exeter; six to Oxbridge in 2015.

Subjects range from neuroscience to anthropology. US universities coordinator supports girls applying for American colleges.

Money matters: Academic scholarships awarded on merit – all 11+ candidates automatically considered. Music scholarships via audition at 11+ and 13+. At 16+, academic, music, art, drama, design and sport scholarships. Travel scholarships in modern languages and science for internal candidates only. Means-tested bursaries available.

Remarks: Super school best for very bright and diligent all-rounders who enjoy a busy life. An impressive and substantial offering.

Reay Primary School

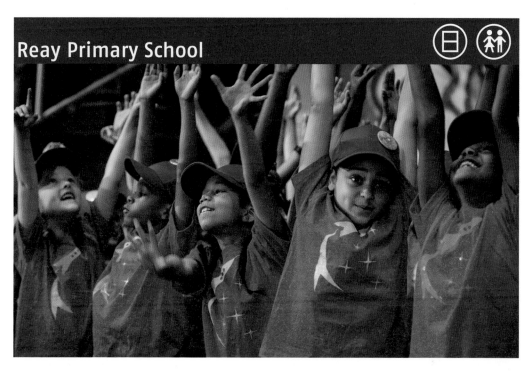

Hackford Road, London SW9 0EN

Tel: 020 7735 2978

State • Pupils: 250 • Ages: 3–11

Email: admin@reay.lambeth.sch.uk
Website: www.reay.lambeth.sch.uk

6

Headteacher: Since 2014, Caroline Andrews, previously co-head of Wix Primary School.

Entrance: At 3+ to the nursery, 4+ reception class, thereafter occasional vacancies only. Standard Lambeth admissions policy – pupils with special requirements, siblings, then distance from the school.

Exit: At 11+ pupils are successful in gaining places to the independent and maintained sector. Most choose to go on to Wandsworth and Lambeth secondary schools.

Remarks: A welcoming and friendly primary school which caters for a wide range of abilities and provides an outstanding quality of education to all. Higher than average numbers of the staff have advanced skills teacher status; quality marks for both literacy and numeracy. Everyone, from the nursery upwards, learns French. An annual trip to Paris for 8 to 9 year olds. Artsmark Gold – has its own art and dance studios; children are offered excellent choice of artistic and dramatic activities; several teachers have art degrees. An enterprising barter system is run with artists, dance and drama groups exchanging use of the studios for workshops and teaching services. All age groups are taught music by a specialist part-time teacher and children can have individual lessons on the flute, violin or brass instruments.

School is dedicated to developing a really good awareness among pupils about environmental issues and has been awarded, for the second time, the green flag for eco-friendly schools. Sport is popular: own Astroturf for football and netball matches, pupils keen to compete in local tournaments and mini leagues. A good playground area and small garden with a frog pond. Governors and parents give much support to the school and also organise fundraising events and charity collections. Reay aims to look after the whole child and has its own learning mentor and school counselling service.

Do not be put off by first appearances. The exterior of the school is somewhat austere, particularly in comparison with the imaginative and well-run interior. Reay is a little gem in the heart of Stockwell.

The Roche School

11 Frogmore, London SW18 1HW

Tel: 020 8877 0823

Independent • Pupils: 280 • Ages: 2.5–11 • Fees: up to £13,050 pa

Email: gcac@therocheschool.co.uk
Website: www.therocheschool.com

Principal: Since 1989, Dr James Roche BSc PhD (60s). Educated at St Paul's, read physics at Bristol and has a PhD in general relativity from Manchester. Taught for two years in a London state school then spent 19 years teaching A level physics and maths at London tutorial colleges, latterly as principal of Collingham College, Kensington, where his wife Carmen taught languages. She set up the Roche School and they are joint principals, but he insists that she is the 'principal principal, the éminence grise', and that he has been 'happily demoted'. Head teacher since 2010 is Vania Adams ('I have to obey not only my wife but her too'); she was busy rehearsing the very confident year 6 cast of the forthcoming West Side Story production when we visited.

Dr Roche reveals that he was 'very scared' of changing from GCSEs and A levels to primary teaching when he joined the school, 'but it was just the same. You just have to explain things so children can understand them. He still runs scholarship classes in mathematics for years 5 and 6 plus any younger ones who are preparing for 7+ and 8+ exams. He has a weekly meeting with a boy in year 4 'who is interested in science – we talk about the photoelectric effect and e=mc squared and tectonic plates and all these amazing theories'. He also teaches some year 6 science. 'I'm just interested in the theory, because if I try an experiment it goes wrong...happily the other year 6 science teacher is very good at experiments.' He has the air of a loquacious, slightly eccentric uncle, and we can see why he is 'particularly well thought of' and 'marvellous with slightly off-beat children'.

If the school has a particular aim, it is to make learning fun. 'It's our business to encourage children who want to know things – to encourage their enthusiasms.'

Entrance: Most join one of the two nurseries, or the reception class. Non-selective, and first-come-first served at this level; those after a place higher up 'come in for a morning or a day. We hear them read, and talk about it, see what their writing is like, if they know anything about how numbers work. We're not looking for technical skills but for a basic understanding.' Some very bright children, but also happy to take children with learning difficulties 'as long as they can benefit from what we offer. If they don't have any enthusiasms, if they're not interested in stories, that's difficult.' Can cater for dyslexia, dyspraxia, Asperger's, Down's syndrome, speech and language difficulties, ASD, ADD and those with EFL needs as long as they have the ability to catch up with their year group.

Quite a through-put, particularly of international families, so worth trying for a place higher up. Some bursaries available, both to incomers and those already at the school.

Exit: A few leave at 7+ or 8+ ('we're happy to prepare children at any age'), but most at 11+ to eg Ibstock Place, Kingston Grammar, Tiffin Girls and Boys, Putney High, More House, JAGs, Wimbledon High, Dulwich College, King's Wimbledon and Latymer Upper. A few to boarding school eg Bedales.

Remarks: Carmen Roche set up Mrs Roche's Coaching Establishment in her West Kensington basement in 1983, largely to prepare children for 11+ and 13+ exams. In 1988, she bought the office block of a Wandsworth laundry in a quiet back street between the A3 and the suburban railway line, and, after some refurbishment, The Roche School moved in. Classrooms mostly compact. Building work has added a library (in concept stage when we visited), increased the size of the assembly

Dr Roche was 'very scared' of changing from GCSEs and A levels to primary teaching when he joined, 'but it was just the same. You just have to explain things so children understand them'

hall and added some bright top floor rooms 'where you can see the weather approaching right across London.'

Teaching arrangements are 'adaptable to the needs of pupils across a wide range. Children learn at very different rates.' Three ability groups for maths and English from year 2 upwards. Specialist French, music, PE and art teachers.

Plenty of practice for 11+ exams. 'The biggest step we have to ask year 5s and 6s to make is to learn to read the question in detail and use the information they are given. They need to get the habit of precision, of engaging their intelligence.' With his tutoring background, Dr Roche finds preparing children for exams 'exhilarating'. 'Anything that's worth learning is going to be more or less difficult. If we can help children to be patient with themselves we do them a favour.'

High flyers encouraged to fly, whilst 'if you're in year 5 and you've forgotten something you learned in year 2, we're happy to explain it again. A child should feel no shame at not understanding something'. Not a competitive ethos: 'I hope that the slower ones feel just as pleased with their progress as the faster ones.' Great praise from parents of dyslexic children for the care taken in helping them progress. One-to-one tuition, for special needs or EAL, at extra cost.

When we visited, some of year 4 were learning about meditation and Buddhism – 'next week we're going to bring in candles and make a proper temple for a meditation class' – while others were off for games in Wandsworth Park. A year 1 class was having a practical lesson about perspective, whilst some reception children were painting clay pots they had made (school has a kiln). Year 2 were studying the ancient Greeks – 'such fantastic stories'.

Reasonable sized playground behind the school, which also contains the art room (art taken seriously; specialist art teacher) and some sheds about to be replaced by music practice rooms. All the usual sports played in Wandsworth Park, and many inter-school fixtures; after-school clubs (some at extra cost) include cricket, football, judo, netball, swimming, chess, drama and dance.

Lots of chances to act in plays, speak in public, play in the orchestra and in concerts. Children come out 'confident and caring', say parents, tend to 'interview really well', and 'are very proud of their school'. Cosy, nurturing atmosphere; children encouraged to look out for and care for each other.

Bullying 'does sometimes happen: we talk carefully to both sides'. Has never asked anyone to leave on academic grounds, 'though it could happen if a child was interrupting the education of other people, or really had no chance of understanding their work.'

Not a typical London prep. Parents talk of slightly disorganised admin, a great tolerance for eccentricities; a school that really does treat everyone as individuals. 'My two children – one dyslexic and one very academic – both loved it here.'

Rosemead Preparatory School

70 Thurlow Park Road, London SE21 8HZ

Independent • Pupils: 360 • Ages: 3–11 • Fees: up to £11,286 pa

Tel: 020 8670 5865

Email: admin@rosemeadprepschool.org.uk
Website: www.rosemeadprepschool.org.uk

Headmaster: Since 2012, Arthur Bray, CertEd from Bristol University (50s). Highly experienced; prior to Rosemead, he was headmaster of GEMS Hampshire in central London, for 26 years. Previously, at Millfield Junior, he and his wife were both senior houseparents for 10 years. Also formerly chairman of the Independent Schools Association and director of the Independent Schools Council.

Father of two grown-up children whose childhood portraits line the walls of his study – a daughter who is now in a senior post at a London prep school and a son who is a director of a City firm. We found him to be easy to talk to and animated when sharing his knowledge of the nuances of how individual children learn. Perhaps the polished antiques suggest an 'old school' headmaster, but his door was deliberately open onto the corridor, where children milled about chattering between lessons.

There is clearly work ahead, with changes already begun with a view to both academic results and 'preparation for life', but avoiding babies and bathwater. The headmaster tells us he has been very aware of listening first and then implementing, 'evolution not revolution'. One parent commented: 'He is very committed to making Rosemead the best that it can be. He is energetic and determined.'

Head's door was deliberately open onto the corridor, where children milled about chattering between lessons

Head of the pre-prep: Since 2005, Mary-Elizabeth Everitt, BEd (Hons) Goldsmiths College (40s). She started in the state sector, before teaching for 14 years at Dulwich Prep London. She has a grown-up daughter at university. Friendly and quietly spoken, she is focused and clearly made of steely stuff.

Entrance: Describes itself as 'mixed ability'; the majority of children enter the prep via the pre-prep. Children may enter the nursery during the term of their 3rd birthday; at 4+ into reception or at 7+ into year 3. Whilst the nursery is almost fully subscribed, there are sometimes a few places available at the prep. Assessments begin the November prior to entry, with a 45-minute play session for the nursery or reception entry and language and maths exercises for years 1-6.

Means-tested bursary scheme with no limit on numbers. No scholarships. Maximum class size is 22 in the pre-prep and 20 in the prep. No strict sibling policy, but will be taken into account. Unless your family is of Von Trapp proportions, the discount for four or more siblings is unlikely to assist you.

Exit: Pupils exit at 11+, with the school aiming to leave choices 'wide open'. We sense determined parents, as children make three applications on average, for which they are prepared with one-on-one interviews as well as practice papers. Most recently, places were offered to all pupils who sat entrance exams to St Dunstan's College, over 90 per cent to Sydenham High School, just under 60 per cent to James Allen's Girls School, 50 per cent to Dulwich College and 30 per cent to Alleyn's – it's a strong, but by no means guaranteed show of tickets to good and premier destinations. Since Mr Bray's arrival, there has been a rise in both places offered and a higher ratio of awards, particularly academic.

Remarks: A traditional curriculum ticks all boxes, but there is modernising afoot, which is going down well. The head cites updating the texts used in English, and in maths a new online tutor sets tasks at an appropriate level for each child, 30 minutes in class and 30 minutes at home each week, with parents able to dip in any time online to see how they are doing.

A carefully thought through decision to switch from the traditional French to the more globally relevant Spanish has been pretty universally accepted and lessons have been doubled to twice a week. Spanish commences in the pre-prep with singing, stories and movement. The school might have offered Mandarin, but a Mandarin club proved short-lived in popularity.

Next in line for overhaul will be history, geography and science, including an eagerly-awaited science lab. New ICT facilities have arrived. Humanities are supported by a wide array of trips, and highlights of the year are cross-curricular theme days and celebrations.

One of the first things the headmaster instigated is a new means of assessment, and reporting which looks at core skills such as concentration and organisation skills, as well as subject-specific scoring, all of which can be far more useful than a paragraph of commentary.

Staff mix – 18 per cent of staff in place for more than 10 years. Not a high turnover, but the headmaster has made appointments since arriving, ensuring there is now one male teacher per year group at the prep. Reports from some parents are not spotless – but others impress upon us the warm atmosphere between staff and pupils: one mentioned the 'strong emotions shown by all of the year 6 children as they leave the teachers they have grown fond of'.

Decision to switch from traditional French to more globally relevant Spanish has been pretty universally accepted

With three classes per year in the prep, the class groupings sometimes change after year 3, once teachers have been able to assess how children work together. this can be a tad unpopular, as it isn't necessarily about friendship groups. However, classes are fixed by year 5. Setting for maths from year 3.

The anti-bullying policy has been carefully reviewed, with a buddy scheme throughout the school and year 6 visiting to read to the younger ones, and sharing special assemblies such as that for Chinese New Year.

The prep looks like a tall, red-brick Victorian school building, but was a rehearsal space for the Old Vic theatre, hence the school hall resembling a proper theatre with fixed stage

Learning support, termed Enrichment, has four staff, one of them full time, with one-to-one support for just under 10 per cent of the school. Very small number with EAL.

The fenced playground, high up above the street, is the venue for learning a variety of ball skills. Years 3 to 6 have a weekly PE lesson, a swimming lesson and a full games afternoon. There are two male PE teachers, and a female director of PE. With children taken to nearby Dulwich sports club and Rosendale playing fields for football, hockey, netball, rugby, tennis, cricket and athletics by coach, using the Astroturf pitches at nearby newly refurbished Elmgreen School, and making use of Crystal Palace's national training facilities for swimming from year 2, one parent commented, 'It's a small school with minimum on-site sports facilities, but they seem to offer a lot and children don't know or care that the sports grounds aren't owned by the school.' Rosemead regularly has children taking part at the ISA finals, both as individuals and in teams, and recently at competed at national level in football.

How high pressure is it? A parent who has had three children through the school reported: 'I think Rosemead gets the balance right – one of the reasons we chose it... the amount of homework is about right, more than your average state primary, but not as much as some of the more high pressure private schools in the area.'

Parents commented to us in no uncertain terms that art has been a real weak spot in the past, but we visited the large, new dedicated art studio and saw the specialist teacher in action – a highly talented former assistant from the pre-prep praised by staff and parents. It may have been early in the term when we visited, but there are a lot of blank walls to fill.

The prep has more than its fair share of violinists, as all year 1 at the pre-prep learn violin in groups. Some 150 children have individual instrumental tuition, with several reaching grade 5 by year 6. There is a large school orchestra and two school choirs; ensemble clubs for cello, brass, strings and recorder; and an 'electric fusion band' which plays at the annual Dulwich Festival. A musical highlight is the major concert at the end of the spring term. One parent commented on the 'superb Christmas carol concert in local church... very impressive'.

Clubs – morning, lunch-time and after-school – offer mainly sporty and musical options, with a good show of language clubs for Spanish, French and Russian. Increasingly, this is a school for working parents and the school is well set up to offer a full day from 8am to 6pm. Clubs start in year 1, most end at 4.30pm, and these can combine with after-school care for all, provided by a third-party, Kids City, with staff chaperoning children between sites and taking any parental emergencies in their stride.

This is a school in transition which, as anyone who has had the builders in knows, can be painful and disruptive but well worth the effort. When we visited the façade was covered in scaffolding, with smart new year 6 classrooms just revealed, together with a new library, bigger dining hall and ICT suites. Meanwhile, downstairs everything looked a bit shabby and utilitarian.

What will hold the school together as well as the headmaster are the parents – due to its strong sense of community as well as unique governing structure. Already established as an independent school for 70 years, in 1974 a group of parents took over the managing of the school and it became a limited company with an all-parent management team. It is now a non-profit making charitable trust. All but one of the governing body are parents of current pupils.

Notable and somewhat off-putting is the location on the edge of Dulwich – a bit of a no-man's land on the traffic-heavy South Circular road – however, we did note that once inside we could not hear the traffic and the location between two overground stations is convenient for commuting quickly into town. The prep looks rather like a tall, red-brick Victorian London school building, but was actually a rehearsal space for the Old Vic theatre, hence the school hall resembling a proper theatre complete with fixed stage.

Parents say, 'Children work hard, concentrate and give of their best.' And our visit backs this up. The atmosphere was calm and industrious, perhaps particularly due to year 6 exams looming. One parent described it as 'a down-to-earth, happy school that will offer an all-round education and ensure a good secondary transfer without putting children under huge pressure in the early years.'

Two-thirds of families live close by, often walking to school; the rest come from all over south London, some from as far as Bromley and Elephant and Castle. This is a school for active parents who want to get involved – fundraising isn't just for external charitable projects but for valuable extras around the school. Talking of active, the previous term, a team of Rosemead mothers rowed the Channel!

The heads report being bowled over by the response to their appeals for help: turning a piece of wasteground into a sunny little allotment for the pre-prep over the weekend, or creating a rota of volunteer librarians for the new prep library. All of which builds a real sense of community. Parents are a mixed and reportedly friendly crowd – we certainly saw gaggles lingering post drop-off – but particularly evidenced by the Easter family ski trip, which is not just for pupils but unusually everyone: parents, siblings, grandparents, old boys and girls and their families too.

The pretty purple uniforms are a delight, but the stand-out feature of the pre-prep is the charming church building, sympathetically developed to create high ceilinged classrooms, with beautiful arches and bits of stained glass – a lovely space in which to work.

The pre-prep has assistants in every class and high staff ratios in the nursery. School commences in earnest at reception with some parents wishing for a greater emphasis on play: 'hardly any toys in the classroom, much like year 1'. Reception is very different in feel to the boisterous fun we saw in the nursery, but the head points out the gentle start with just 20 minutes of phonics a day compared with an hour in year 1.

It seems to be different things to different families – the pre-prep's church building brings back fond memories for some parents of what a first school should be like; more pragmatically, it could well be a port in a storm when faced with the ultra-competitive local options at 4+.

St George's CofE Primary School

Corunna Road, Battersea, , London SW8 4JS

State • Pupils: 222 • Ages: 3–11 • C of E

Tel: 020 7622 1870

Email: admin@st-georges.wandsworth.sch.uk
Website: www.st-georges.wandsworth.sch.uk

48

Head: Since 2015, Sarah Collymore (mid 30s); BA in primary education from Northumbria University. Went straight into teaching at 21 at a school local to her in Newcastle, but then decided to come to London with a friend and never looked back: 'We visited at Easter to view some schools – St George's being one of them. I rocked up one day and 12 years later, I'm still here.' Hired initially as a teacher in early years, at the same time as her predecessor Janet Hilary (former head) – this in-suppressible duo took the school from special measures and on the verge of closure to Ofsted outstanding.

A Geordie lass who oozes warmth and likeability – the kind-natured, sincere head that every school should have. Dedication for 'her' children is tangible, and she is clearly popular with both parents and pupils alike – a few of whom came up to her in the playground (whilst we were there) to congratulate her on her new post as head. If one great head was going to leave, she was the only other person for the job and the only one with enough experience to drive the school forward. And this is where she plans to stay; 'If you have the will and desire to serve a community that is where you stay. There is no question that my work is where what I do will make a difference.'

Mrs Collymore has been described as 'an outstanding teacher' in all the phases of primary education she has worked – from early years through to key stage 2, then to deputy head prior to becoming head. One parent told us: 'I feel very confident in Mrs Collymore's ability to lead the school.' Married with one step daughter (her husband runs an exclusion unit in a large secondary comprehensive), she laughed when asked what she does in her 'spare' time.

The passion and pure dogged determination that former head Janet Hilary put into the school cannot be overlooked. She clearly left an indelible mark on both the pupils and parents who we spoke to. One parent told us: 'I chose this school because I was aware of Mrs Hilary's work before becoming head of St George's, and I knew how she worked. Her skill was that she pulled parents and teachers together.' However, after 12 years in the post, Mrs Hilary felt it was time to move on and embrace other challenges. She was appointed executive principle for Floreat Wandsworth and Floreat Brentford, 'an opportunity I couldn't turn down.' But she does very much plan to stay in touch with St George's and maintain a close partnership with Mrs Collymore: 'We are the No.1 Ladies' Leadership Team after all!'

Entrance: After the customary priority for looked-after children, 50 per cent of the school places are offered for church attendance, mostly from the local St George's Church, although some have come from further afield. One parent told us she travels in from Brixton. 'I wanted my child to go to this school, so I drive him there every day.' The

This small one form primary school could be easily overlooked. Indeed we almost walked past it, which would've been a shame, as this wholly unpretentious school is quite a hidden gem

remaining half of the school's intake are siblings followed by distance, although alarmingly we were told that being on the same road doesn't guarantee a place: 'Because there are so many tall blocks, some of those residents won't get a place.' Cohort is predominantly Eastern European/Russian, Caribbean, West African, South Asian, and an increasing proportion of South American pupils. A large majority comes from single parent families: 'Diversity is very healthy for us. It enriches us all.'

Exit: The largest share goes to the local comprehensive St Cecilia's CE, followed by St John Bosco RC, a new voluntary aided college. Other local comprehensives include Ark Putney Academy, Southfields Academy and Lambeth Academy. If you have a girl, Lady Margaret – 'virtually impossible to get in to' as well as Grey Coat Hospital ('if it's good enough for the Prime Minister..') – are the schools of choice. One parent did say that she worries about the lack of decent secondary school education in the area, 'but try not to worry about it yet.' However, the head remains positive about the regeneration of the area and the new demographic buying into these properties. She says: 'I believe that in two years we'll have a secondary school of choice on the patch.' Last year, for the first time in the school's history, one of their students was awarded a scholarship to Dulwich College, and has since become something of a legend in the school – a source of huge aspiration for the other pupils. The head told us: 'Nothing can come close to the feeling you get when a child from the Patmore Estate in South London tells you that they are going to Dulwich College and will study to become a heart surgeon.'

Remarks: Set amidst the Patmore and the Savona estates in Battersea, dwarfed by the numerous regeneration projects in the area (most notably Battersea Power Station and Nine Elms construction, which is right next door) and tucked away at the end of a residential street, this small one form primary school could be easily overlooked. Indeed we almost walked past it, which would've been a shame, as this wholly unpretentious school is quite a hidden gem.

Over the past four years, standards of attainment achieved by the school have been among the highest in the country, and its progress measures puts it in the top five per cent of schools. This year alone the school received two ministerial congratulations: for the phonics results (100 per cent) and for being one of the highest achieving schools in the country in terms of attainment and progress.

For any primary school this would be a major achievement, but for a school where the proportion of pupils eligible for free school meals is well above average, and nearly 60 per cent of the intake comes from homes where English is not a first language (32 languages spoken at the school), the sheer ambition cannot be underestimated.

The school's motto, 'The best we can be', is not a useless platitude, but something that they really aspire to for every child. As the head told us, 'We teach our children dignity and respect and teach them to come to school ready to learn'. No time is wasted in helping and encouraging children who speak other languages at home to begin to speak standard English; 'language is our bedrock because of where the different parents come from.' In reception, children are 'spellbound during phonic sessions by the teacher's funny hat, the silly songs they sing to keep them all on task and by the praise they are constantly given for their hard work. Phonics lessons are consequently a joy, and filled with giggling, gleeful responses.' Ofsted.

The school's motto, 'The best we can be', is not a platitude, but something they really aspire to

Teaching generally very impressive and children we saw were well behaved and enthralled in what they were being taught. Innovative use of of teaching staff to create small focused teaching groups in years 5 and 6 has been highly successful, and means that no pupil is left behind, and all are able enjoy high levels of challenge in English and maths. Each class has one teacher and one designated teaching assistant, in order to free up one of them to give individual help to any struggling pupils. 'It's important to spend time with a pupil if they don't get it, before they become disengaged.' Fairly high turnover of staff because of promotion elsewhere. 'Being a one form entry, it is hard to promote staff at St George's, but as we're diligent with our funding, we never have a shortfall.'

Those with special educational needs progress exceptionally well because the assessment and understanding of their needs is finely tuned. Former head said: 'I find it difficult to believe that when I started here, apparently 72 per cent of pupils had special needs. Now there are 12 per cent. I believe too often children are labelled as special needs if they are under-achieving.'

Statistics and academia aside, the first thing that struck us on entering the school was how very serene it was. Nobody spoke in loud voices and staff almost glided to their various destinations – we could virtually hear a pin drop outside the classrooms we visited. Evidently, much thought has been given into making this school a calm, inviting and safe haven for pupils – the antithesis to many of their lives. The small, but stunningly immaculate and colourful garden which acts as a centrepiece for the school ('there are around 15 goldfinches in the gardens and we grow our own rhubarb and strawberries') offers pupils the opportunity to sit and read or reflect – and the dinner hall has been designed to overlook these gardens. This is all part of the 'Calm School Code' ethos, which everyone is expected to adhere to.

The second thing that struck (as we too glided from classroom to classroom on account of the very shiny floors), is how immaculate the classrooms were and how pupils demonstrated such pride in all aspects of their schooling, from their beautifully laminated workbooks (with some exceptional examples of joined up handwriting from the lower year groups), to their pristinely turned out selves in their smart navy uniforms with tied back or braided hair. As one parent said, 'The school is pretty strict on uniform, but that is because they don't want anyone to stick out.'

Much thought has been given to making this school a calm, safe haven – the antithesis to many pupils' lives

Very little wall space seems to be taken up by specific topic work but instead by an assortment of learning aids – phonics, maths, famous quotes, charts etc. One wall was virtually made up of aspirational charts. Pupils can belong to the 144 Club (children need to know all their times tables up to 12 and recall them quickly), the 20-20 Club for years 1, 2 and 3 etc etc. Perhaps the most prestigious of all of these is the Superstar award. It is the responsibility of each class team to encourage as many children as possible to become Superstars. All classrooms must have the 'HAPPY' chart (an acronym for homework, attitude, punctuality, participation, yourself)) on display and must demonstrate all aspects of 'HAPPY' to receive their badge. Teachers are responsible for talking to parents about how they can support with any of these areas. At the end

of each term the children who have been awarded their Superstar badge receive a reward. Autumn term – Christmas movie at the local cinema. Spring term – party and disco. Summer term – trip to Chessington.

Aspiration seeps through the very foundations of this school, from the extremely well stocked and well looked after library, to weekly maths assemblies (where certificates are awarded to pupils who have completed maths challenges) – through to enrichment days at local Independent schools such as Newton Prep, where years 4 and 5 get to use the facilities and are taught art, music, sport, science etc by specialist teachers. Some lucky pupils have enjoyed a trip to nearby Chelsea Football Club where strong links have been forged, whilst others will sit in amongst the musicians of the Orchestra Vitae later on in the year. One parent told us: 'Credit to the leadership team at this school for encouraging our children so much that they want to achieve, and then achieve more.'

Breakfast club on offer from 8.15am and after-school care offered until 6pm. A wide range of after-school clubs including dance, cooking, zumba, football, karate, tennis, choir and gardening. Participation in sporting competitions including athletics, cricket, golf, netball and basketball, and swimming lessons offered from year 4.

This is a proactive school in every conceivable way – no opportunity is left untapped. Instead of being bah humbug about the extensive building work in the area, the school has seized the opportunity to work with the architects, designers and builders on the Nine Elms Regeneration Project – and even managed to secure a substantial donation from its developers for a brand new all-weather sports pitch and art classroom.

If this wasn't enough, the school has set up a programme of motivational speakers for the older children and thus far the likes of Baroness Scotland, Sir William Atkinson and broadcaster Julie Etchingham have all come to speak at St George's. The head says: 'We want our pupils to have ambition and aspiration and this programme really helps them to think about careers and life choices.' Generous donations and sponsorship have also provided many rich opportunities for the pupils, including seaside trips (many pupils never having been to the seaside), theatre trips and funding for the new school uniform.

Unspoilt and wonderfully refreshing, the pupils we spoke to talked of becoming chartered accountants, vets, footballers and comedians. What came through were spirited, happy children with big personalities and a real sense of ambition. One particular pupil who was touchingly wise beyond his years, just seemingly so grateful for being at this school: 'I just wish there was a St George's secondary school for us to go to.'

Streatham & Clapham High Junior School

Linked school: Streatham & Clapham High School GDST, 158

Wavertree Road, London SW2 3SR

Independent • Pupils: 242 (32 in nursery including 3 boys) • Ages: 3–11 • Fees: up to £12,255 pa

Tel: 020 8674 6912

Email: junior@schs.gdst.net
Website: www.schs.gdst.net

Head: Since January 2015, Thomas Mylne (40s), previously deputy head of the Gatehouse School in east London. BA from the University of Brighton and PGCE from the Institute of Education; he has also taught at an east London primary school and been deputy head (curriculum) at Wimbledon High Junior School. Interests include cinema, travel, music and cycling; he is married (his wife works in publishing) with two daughters.

Entrance: Applications for co-ed nursery can be made from birth to 2+. Children join at 3 and spend morning with nursery teacher in term prior to entry. School 'is looking for happy, inquisitive children'. Girls then move into reception (more places become available) in September following their 4th birthday. Informal one-to-one assessment with foundation stage co-ordinator.

Further intake at 7+ when girls are assessed by head or deputy head and take tests in maths, English and verbal reasoning. Written report from previous school also needed at this stage.

Exit: More than 80 per cent to the senior school. Not automatic – they all sit assessment test in year 5. Girls whom teachers feel will thrive are offered guaranteed places. All those wishing to move to senior school take an exam in year 6.

Remarks: School's unattractive building belies exceptionally light, large classrooms and happy atmosphere inside. Building benefits from the fact that it was once a senior school in terms of the facilities and space it provides. Enormous sports hall, where girls can play hockey, and excellent outdoor area with adventure playground and enough space for rounders and tennis, guarantee plenty of fun, games and team training.

We were shown round by enthusiastic, confident girls who led us from the well-equipped nursery (with own outdoor play area) to busy reception classes and virtually every corner of the school. 'Do you want to see the loos?' they chirped. Huge library contains vast range of books and specific reading lists for each year. We also spotted shoes created out of recycled material and models of school areas (our guides proudly pointed out their own creations). Light art room with terrific views over London – 'whenever we do art, we know we're going to do something really messy', said our guides. 'It's such fun'. Science room was locked (health and safety) but they showed us well-equipped computer room and music room. Interactive white boards and computers in all classrooms.

Two classes throughout KS2, with potential for growth in KS1. Girls happy, relaxed and proud to show us their work and talk about what they were doing.

Good learning support. All children assessed on arrival at school, targets set each term and parents involved early if problems arise. Head meets all teachers once a term to ascertain that children have reached the expected levels. Parents told us: 'Communications are very good. All the staff are positive and professional.' The only thing they felt could be improved was sport. There's always something.

Streatham & Clapham High School GDST

Linked school: Streatham & Clapham High Junior School, 157

42 Abbotswood Road, London SW16 1AW

Independent • Pupils: 441 • Ages: 11–18 • Sixth form pupils: 74 • Fees: up to £17,355 pa

Tel: 020 8677 8400

Email: enquiry@shc.gdst.net
Website: www.schs.gdst.net

9

Head Master: Since 2012, Dr Millan Sachania MA (Cantab) MPhil PhD (40s). Former comprehensive student who gained a double first and a doctorate in musicology at Cambridge and then stayed on as a music tutor for five years. After (shock, horror) reading an undergraduate's paper on Beethoven's Ninth Symphony, he decided to train as a schoolteacher and acquired a PGCE at Kingston University. Was impressed with GDST experience at Croydon High while following the course, and after stints as head of music at a girls' school in Windsor and

deputy head at a co-ed HMC school in north London, was delighted to accept this post. 'Are you married?' we asked. 'Yes, to my piano'.

Parents praise his 'phenomenal attention to detail'. One told us he was 'not an obvious choice, but perfect', while another reckoned 'we are lucky to have him'. Other parental comments include, 'definitely an individual', 'quirky', 'incomparable' and 'probably just what we needed but not everyone's cup of tea'. The girls seem to love him – 'even though he uses words we've never heard before'.

After (shock, horror) reading an undergraduate's paper on Beethoven's Ninth, head decided to train as a schoolteacher

Has a 'rescued' Bechstein grand piano in his study, which they are definitely allowed to tinker on.

Dr Sachania is amazed by the energy of both the school and the girls, which he feels derives from their cultural diversity. Impressed with their intelligence and really wants them to broaden their horizons and achieve beyond their potential 'across the width of endeavour'. Says he has an holistic approach and doesn't believe that pupils should obsess about being competitive with each other. He wants each girl to find her own forte and achieve her own personal best.

Has already made a few changes – some popular, some less so – and there are more to come. Lessons have been shortened. Head says that 'shorter equals sharper and if necessary lessons can become double'. The sixth form, which is in a separate building, now has its own popular café area while a small lecture theatre is used for a variety of activities, from musical recitals to the once-a-week head master's lecture period.

Academic matters: 'The school has really pulled its socks up' – that's the view of one parent we talked to. It offers a broad curriculum covering all the core subjects, and a wide variety of co-curricular activities to ensure pupils can learn and discover in depth. Economics A level and English IGCSE (to replace GCSE) recently introduced. In 2015, 48.9 per cent A*/A at A level, and 71.5 per cent A*/A grades at GCSE. Setting in maths, sciences, modern languages and, occasionally, English. Class sizes are maximum of 26, many groups in the sixth form in single figures. All staff friendly and enthusiastic – average age 42. About a quarter have been at the school for more than 10 years, giving stability and a sense of continuity to a school that is growing and changing. Plenty of men on the team – four out of five of the senior leadership team are male. All pupils are expected to take four additional subjects alongside the core at GCSE; a selection of 12 on offer to which they can add ancient Greek and astronomy if they wish. Parents say science and humanities are now particularly strong. Head sees each year 11 girl individually with her parents to discuss A level choices.

One of the first things the head did was to introduce Kinza, a compulsory enrichment programme offering a range of over 30 topics which the girls study one afternoon each week in the Michaelmas and Lent terms. Staff run courses in subjects they don't teach (including forensic science, bee-keeping and Arabic) and mixed age groups work together. He says the course is 'emblematic of my educational philosophy'. His aim is to create 'civilised human beings equipped with a philosophy for living'.

Bubbly and enthusiastic head of learning support in school three-and-a-half days each week. School has inclusive policy, as long as girl passes entrance test. Statemented children have individual teaching assistants who produce strategies to help them deal with problems. Otherwise school provides help in small groups for 20 minutes once a fortnight from year 7 to year 9, and before school, after school or at lunchtime for years 10 and 11. One-to-one help has to be resourced externally.

Games, options, the arts: Surprising to find a girls' school in a leafy London suburb with its own sports

grounds and an enormous, all singing, all dancing sports hall, plus a dance studio and fitness centre. Plenty of cups to indicate sporting success. Football, hockey, tennis, athletics and lots of indoor sports – something for everybody. National gymnastic champions recently and notable successes in acrobatics, fencing, tennis and netball. The only criticisms from parents are that the school 'needs to offer more for C teams to improve their skills' and 'the sports department needs better organisation and more staff'. Needless to say, this is being addressed. One mother told us: 'The school is truly inclusive – my non-sporty child loves sport'.

Music strong (as you would expect with a musically talented head master), with lessons compulsory up to GCSE. Several choirs, orchestras and ensembles. Roomful of keyboards specifically for compositions. Parents say art facilities are 'brilliant' and we were impressed too. Large art room, smaller one specifically for the sixth form and separate pottery room with its own kiln. Drama also right up to standard; new creative arts building under construction. When we visited the whole school was involved in A Midsummer Night's Dream, with non-performers making costumes and painting scenery.

D of E taken pretty seriously – girls go trekking in Morocco's Atlas Mountains and have reached base camp of Everest. Most participants reach at least silver level.

Background and atmosphere: School was founded as Brixton Hill High School for Girls in 1887 and was one of the earliest GDST member schools. It later became Streatham Hill High School, housed in the building now occupied by the junior school. Current building was originally Battersea Grammar School. This merged with Rosa Bassett School to form a comprehensive in Tooting, allowing Streatham &

Clapham High School to move to bigger premises in 1993. Large, light classrooms are a good legacy and the new buildings have created a spacious, well-equipped school, with facilities suitable for the 21st century, with more major building work under way. The four-and-a-half acres of ground they stand in are miraculous in this busy area of London.

Take one newish headmaster, add a handful of enthusiasm, pep up the curriculum, add ambition and belief, introduce Kinza, tune a piano and – eureka – numbers rise. Something is working

School dining hall has relaxed atmosphere and offers reasonable selection of food, which girls said was always pretty good. Plenty of staff around to make sure everyone eating properly. School lunches are compulsory up until year 11. Sixth form café is popular and older girls like having their own area to meet and chat.

Pupils' general feeling is that this is a happy, focused school. Parents say the support given to pupils is second to none. Although the school says the expectations are definitely there for girls to achieve and do their best, parents are adamant that it's 'not a hothouse'. Comments included 'there's no excessive pressure', 'they are allowed to be individuals and gain confidence', 'they mix across the year groups and get to know each other better that way'. One told us: 'At parents' evenings, they really do seem to know and understand our two very different daughters'. Another, with an exceptionally bright daughter, said that the way classes are divided, sometimes by ability, sometimes mixed, works a treat. 'My daughter is never bored', she said. 'The expectations of each girl are relevant to the goals she has been set'.

Pastoral care and discipline: Deputy head mistress is in overall charge of pastoral care and system is in force for identifying problems early. Parents say communication is exceptional – emails are answered immediately and problems dealt with sympathetically. A parent told us of 'some unpleasantness... handled and dealt with properly and quickly'. Another talked about 'problematic disorder' in a particular class, which was 'completely sorted out by the head of department within a week'.

House system ensures girls work together as teams, across year groups, competing to gain house points at all levels. Each form has a representative on the school council, alongside form captain, so

ample chances to raise welfare problems. PHSCE programme deals with topics such as relationships, moral issues and citizenship in a sensitive and informed way.

Deputy head mistress says that school aims to deal with problems promptly. It acts positively in rare bullying-type incidents, normally resolving quickly and amicably. Sixth form mentor teams are invaluable – girls often prefer to talk to them rather than a member of staff. Year 9 form mentors help girls transferring from the junior school.

Pupils and parents: Mainly from the surrounding areas of south London and from variety of backgrounds – moneyed professional classes and entrepreneurs to local shopkeepers. Typical GDST range of ethnic and racial diversity.

Around 85 per cent arrive from the junior school and others join from state and private schools. Parents of girls in state primaries said they like the smaller size classes, which gives all girls a chance to be involved. Ex-pupils include June Whitfield, Angela Carter, broadcasters Maryam and Nazanine Moshiri, soprano Elizabeth Llewellyn and V&A curator Susannah Brown.

Entrance: Competitive – interview and exam at 11+ and 13+. Those coming up from the junior school at 11 have to pass a test in year 5 and also sit the 11+ exam. Prospective pupils are interviewed in groups at 11+ and individually at 13+. At 16+ minimum of six GCSEs required, with A*/A grades in subjects to be studied at AS level, letter from previous head and interview with SCHS head master and sixth form head. Early registration for all levels suggested as waiting list is limited. Occasional places crop up at other stages, subject to relevant testing.

Exit: Some leave at 16 for local comps, sixth form colleges or boarding but this is decreasing – around 60 per cent stay on. Majority progress to good universities.

Money matters: Typical GDST school fees, so more reasonable than elsewhere. Several non-means tested academic scholarships available and number of means tested, subject based scholarships/bursaries at 11+ and 16+. All curriculum-related non-residential trips included in fees.

Remarks: Streatham & Clapham High is on the up. Take one newish head master, add a good handful of enthusiasm, pep up the curriculum, add ambition and belief, introduce Kinza, tune a grand piano and – eureka – numbers rise. It would certainly appear that something is working. There is now a consistent waiting list for places and numbers staying on for A levels have rocketed from 36 per cent to over 60 per cent. As one parent told us, 'the new head master is having an amazing effect'.

Thames Christian College

Wye Street, London SW11 2HB

Independent • Pupils: 125 • Ages: 11–16 • Fees: £13,560 pa

Tel: 020 7228 3933

49

Email: info@thameschristiancollege.org.uk
Website: www.thameschristiancollege.org.uk

Executive Head: Since September 2006, Stephen Holsgrove (50s) PhD. Studied engineering and ICT; before setting up Thames Christian College he worked as a development director of a software engineering company. Married to Catherine; three daughters, who all attended the school, two are now pursuing their own careers, the youngest is studying performing arts. Catherine is the school registrar and runs all the administration. Head and governors are all committed to making a difference to future generation's education and lives. They hope that in the future Thames will be a model for further similar establishments.

Academic matters: A non-selective school doing extremely well by its pupils, who mostly outperform their predicted grades. In 2015, 50 per cent of GCSE grades were A*/A, with 85 per cent of pupils gaining 5 A*-C grades including maths and English. The school commits to ensuring that, wherever possible, everyone achieves at least a C grade in English and maths. The ethos is to bring out the best in each individual and encourage pupils to find and develop their strengths. All pupils are monitored, small classes, setting for some subjects, as well as small group teaching for those who need it. Head of English is a bestselling author of English curriculum materials for 11 to 16-year-olds, so ideally placed to help everybody achieve the highest results. Good range of GCSE and IGCSE subjects to choose from; the options are tailored to each year group's preferences. Alongside maths, all study personal finance to prepare for running their own budgets, be it financing university or setting up a business. Everyone studies Spanish and there is an annual trip to Spain for a mixture of sightseeing and intensive Spanish lessons.

Lunchtime and after-school enrichment classes offer the opportunity to study in more depth. The school strives to broaden young minds with a variety of cross-curricular activities, eg medieval murder mysteries to solve, design a Tudor king's football kit, and film making. Whilst doing very well for its brightest pupils, it is also able to bring on pupils with specific learning differences: dyslexia, dyspraxia, mild Aspergers and those who have not fared well in much larger establishments. CreSTeD listed, the school has a dedicated team of learning support teachers. It prides itself on attracting well-qualified teachers, some of whom also work in their own industries, giving pupils an insight into the world of work and how certain skills and qualifications can translate into careers. Parents feel they are prepared to go the extra mile to assist pupils in their learning.

Games, options, the arts: Excellent art department nurtures much budding talent and achieves outstanding results. Art curriculum has recently been redesigned to give pupils the option of taking two art GCSEs, graphic communications and fine art. The graphics element includes a brief designed by a creative director of an advertising agency, who is a visiting lecturer at the school. Part of this course involves pupils having to pitch their ideas for client presentations. Design and technology curriculum introduces pupils to ceramics, woodwork, sculpture

Aim, to provide suitable education in a safe environment, has paid off: the school generally expands year-on-year

and textiles. PE teacher and various specialist coaches offer a range of different sporting activities and team games. The school uses local sports centre facilities and the various courts and pitches at Wandsworth common. Strong drama, led by a working actress; pupils study the LAMDA Bronze Certificate and other LAMDA qualifications. New keyboards and mixing desks are part of the update to the music department, there is a band and choir, and two professional singers amongst the staff. Tuition on any instrument can be arranged and many pupils choose to have individual instrumental lessons. The school has links with a primary school to give pupils the opportunity to work with children in the community. Community projects involve drama, music, art, sewing and a mentoring scheme. Friday afternoons are dedicated to clubs. Each term a selection of clubs and societies: eg inventions club, textiles, debating, current affairs and creative writing.

Background and atmosphere: Founded by executive head and his wife, Thames Christian College opened its doors in 2000 with 12 pupils; today it accommodates over 120. Having viewed secondary school choices in London for their own children, the Holsgroves decided there was room

for something a little different, and decided to set up their own school. The underlying principles of the school involve individuals and values alongside top service delivery. Their aim, to provide suitable education in a safe environment, has paid off: the school generally expands year-on-year. The atmosphere is about hard work and caring for each other rather than flashy facilities.

Pastoral care and discipline: As a Christian foundation, the school's ethos centres on mutual respect, Christian values and understanding others' opinions. Pupils of all faiths and backgrounds who share these values are welcome. School rules are very clear and non-negotiable, expectations are high: behave sensibly, work to the best of your ability and be considerate to others at all times. Teachers need to be able to channel their energies into teaching rather than having to deal with discipline issues. 'We do have strict rules here,' say pupils, 'and things like bullying or any type of unkindness are not tolerated.'

Pupils and parents: Wide catchment area: families come from all over London and Surrey – the school is located a few minutes' walk from Clapham Junction. Pupils come from a variety of backgrounds; ethnic and social mix typical of the surrounding areas. Parents are encouraged to be involved and work collaboratively with the school, particularly with fundraising and religious festivals and celebrations. Thought to be a committed bunch, with shared values and hopes for their children's futures.

Entrance: 11+ test to assess potential and ability. Non-selective.

Exit: At 16+ most continue to A level or (occasionally) IB at London day schools – in 2015, one pupil each to Dulwich College, City of London and Southend

High School for Boys. Also Royal Russell School, Esher College and Graveney School. Some go on to study vocational qualifications at eg the BRIT school.

Money matters: A not-for-profit organisation; fees are inclusive, making them very competitive in comparison with other independent schools. Small number of bursaries available at the head's discretion.

Remarks: Small is beautiful. A unique school set up to meet the needs of individuals. Able children are stretched, and for those who find school more of a challenge there is plenty of support.

Thomas's Battersea

Linked schools: Thomas's Clapham, 166; for Thomas's Fulham and Thomas's Kensington see *The Good Schools Guide London North*

28–40 Battersea High Street, London SW11 3JB

Independent · Pupils: 540 · Ages: 4–13 · C of E · Fees: up to £18,330 pa

Tel: 020 7978 0900

Email: battersea@thomas-s.co.uk
Website: www.thomas-s.co.uk

50

Headmaster: Mr Ben Thomas MA (40s). Educated Eton, Durham and ultimately at the Institute of Education. First teaching job, aged 26, head of

Thomas's Kensington, a bit of baptism by fire. After four years took over headship of Battersea and parents now say 'outstanding' and 'really has his finger on the pulse'. Says that this definitely affected his style of headship and believes that it makes him less didactic. Vice principal of the group, Jill Kelham, based at Battersea, has, apparently, been a huge help to him. Has built up excellent teaching team, including well respected heads of year, and now believes his main function, as far as parents are concerned, is advising on senior schools at 13+. Visits several of these each term and feels he really does know the heads. Parents praise his 'excellent advice'. Says that the school should be about 'enjoyment for the lower school, learning for the middle school and achievement for the upper school,' and is a big believer in the most important school rule, 'be kind'. One of the four principals of the whole group of Thomas's London Day Schools, originally founded by his parents, David and Joanna Thomas in 1971, describes himself as the headmaster, 'doing the fun stuff', and his brother Tobyn as the administrator controlling finance, buildings etc. It is a huge business and would appear to be extremely profitable, though some parents feel that the fees are increasing a little too fast. 'Four to five per cent is a bit steep in the current financial climate.' Married to Katie, a full time mum, with three children all at the school and totally satisfied with his current existence. 'I love being head. It's great for family life'.

Entrance: Mainly at 4. Competitive and oversubscribed. Register as soon as possible, preferably at birth. Assessments in November prior to entry in September the following year. Three applicants for each place offered. Up to six boys and girls per hour's session. Looking for children who 'have a measure of confidence, are responsive, sociable,

School should be about 'enjoyment for the lower school, learning for the middle school and achievement for the upper school.' Head is a believer in the most important school rule, 'be kind'

with a light in their eyes.' Sibling priority but not absolutely guaranteed. Occasional places further up the school when candidates are assessed while spending half a day with their peer group. Written report from previous school also necessary. More places at 11+ but majority of these tend to be taken by children from Thomas's, Kensington.

Exit: Very few leave at age 7 or 8 as no preparation for these exams although, inevitably, the odd trickle whose parents are scared they may not make it later. At 11+ to St Paul's, Godolphin & Latymer, GDST schools, Francis Holland SW1, Downe House, Wycombe Abbey, St Swithun's. At 13+ to, Eton, St Paul's, King's College Wimbledon, Westminster, Winchester, Dulwich College, Alleyn's, Charterhouse, Bryanston, Marlborough and Wellington. Impressive range of destinations at both levels with some scholarships (11, including one for music, in 2014).

Remarks: A big, busy, slightly chaotic school for cosmopolitan parents who want their children to have the best English education money can buy.

That is what they want and, to a large degree, that is what they get. Plenty of opportunities for pupils to excel but withdrawn types might find it all somewhat overwhelming.

Occupies an attractive, listed ex-grammar school building, with many modern additions and plenty of playground space. This last is easily transformed into a car park at the beginning and end of each day as public transport not particularly convenient. Has own fleet of buses which convey children from Kensington and ferry the whole school to sports venues etc. All the facilities for a broad curriculum. Great science labs – 'we do chemistry, physics and biology here,' said our youthful guides – computer suites and all the modern aids to a tip top education. New music centre, with 245 individual lessons taking place each week on instruments that range from piano to cornet; an orchestra, various bands and ensembles, choirs at all levels (recent concert had the school orchestra playing alongside the Southbank Sinfonia) and their own choral society where they are joined by parents from the other schools and members of the local community. Two great art studios and two pottery rooms with their own kiln. Imaginative creations displayed all over the school. We particularly liked the charcoal drawings lining one staircase alongside a written request to please not rub against them. And, of course, being a Thomas's school, the drama is outstanding with huge productions by each year group being put on over the year. 'Only drawback', said one parent, 'is that they are always musicals. Not much use if your child can't sing'. School assures us there's always something for everyone. Great Hall where they perform is pretty splendid.

Probably most cosmopolitan of the Thomas's schools, with a mix of international parents and 19 different foreign languages spoken at home. About 25 per cent of children on the EAL register

Lots of sport, say it takes up about 20 per cent of the timetable from year 3 onwards. All the usuals with sculling added in the summer term at the top of the school. Matches inter-house, inter-Thomas's and against other schools. Great gym and school playground excellent place for organised and unorganised games. Also use facilities at Battersea Park, Barns Elms and the Wandle Centre. Youngest children, reception to year 2, have fantastic and imaginative rooftop playground on high.

Academically, teaching deemed pretty good, though lots of coaching still occurring in the last years. 'Just as insurance,' say the parents. We did feel that this was definitely more about anxious and ambitious parents than inadequately taught children. As in all the schools, some specialist teaching from the beginning. Mixed ability classes, with setting in maths and English only, until they reach the upper school when they are divided into those doing 11+ and those staying on and academia becomes the be all and end all, with all classrooms subject-based and a tutor system coming into operation. Not a wide choice of languages, although 11+ leavers have the option of German, Spanish or Italian after their exams. French from Reception, Latin compulsory from year 5.

Enthusiastic, experienced head of learning support who also teaches maths in the lower and middle schools and study skills to years 7 and 8. Determined to catch children early so that they can let go of support by year 6 or 7. Works closely with class teachers, showing them how to help pupils. Mainly milder end of the spectrum but one-to-one teaching available for more serious problems and laptop training when absolutely necessary. Parents always involved and communication apparently good.

Probably most cosmopolitan of all the Thomas's schools, with a wide ranging mix of international parents and 19 different foreign languages spoken at home. About 25 per cent of children on the EAL register. A few of these need extra support which is well provided. School celebrates and appears to make the most of this range of different cultures.

Thomas's Clapham

Linked schools: Thomas's Battersea, 163; for Thomas's Fulham and Thomas's Kensington see *The Good Schools Guide London North*

Broomwood Road, London SW11 6JZ

Tel: 020 7326 9300

Independent • Pupils: 650 • Ages: 4–13 • C of E • Fees: up to £17,145 pa

Email: clapham@thomas-s.co.uk
Website: www.thomas-s.co.uk

51

Headmaster: Since 2012, Mr Philip Ward BEd (50s). One of two new heads to the Thomas's group of London schools, the first ones to be appointed from outside of the Thomas family dynasty, in person Mr Ward is the very image of Hugh Bonneville as the Earl of Grantham. Perhaps it's his winning charm as head of the Clapham family, bonhomie, liberal sprinklings of the word 'chap', not to mention the labrador behind his desk. Any similarity ends there, however, as we found him to be a highly astute, strategically minded leader. Very persuasive; anyone wishing to challenge his point of view could need considerable determination not to be swept along with him.

Educated at Reigate Grammar School, he read history and PE at Exeter University, thence straight to Uppingham where he became director of PE and chair of the games committee, ascending through the ranks finally to headship of Feltonfleet prep in Surrey.

As he talks he often refers to 'we': part of a husband and wife teaching double-act. His wife Sue now teaches year 5 here. The move seems something of a surprise but they are enjoying being in London, able to nip into town for an evening. It also went down well with their two grown up children. Milly, the chocolate lab, comes to school every day and has been known to get lucky with the odd cupcake or two not meant for her. They like to get out to the Surrey Hills at the weekends for long walks if they can. During the week, there are a lot of late nights, and missed dog walks.

We were impressed by Mr Ward's delightful manner with the children as we went around the school. He knew the name of every child we met. Some parents are sagely reserving judgement just yet, but others are bursting with 'excellent!' already. One parent told us, 'The children love him' – we could see why.

Having taught at a senior school, he knows what's in store for children later in terms of pressure, and for now wants them to have fun, a childhood.

Entrance: The school advises that successful applicants register their children before 18 months, but if we're correct in seeing Thomas's Clapham as very much in the ascendancy, together with much more of an eye on marketing, then 'register at birth' is still our advice. Pupils are selected at an informal assessment day at 3+, most recently seeing 180 children for 80-ish places. And with no 7+ entrance, this is pretty much it.

This is a neighbourhood school in the main: children arrive from more than 30 different local nurseries. Those at the Thomas's kindergartens in Battersea and Pimlico are guaranteed an assessment, but not a place. Strong sibling priority, but no guarantees. Sibling discounts for up to four children. They look for children who will 'have a go' and are genuinely keen as well as sociable and co-operative within a group.

Very occasionally places available higher up the school. Fifteen to 20 Thomas's Fulham pupils move over to Clapham at 11+, their transition now given much greater care and consideration.

New-style show rounds every few weeks, for groups of six or eight prospective parents to meet the head and see the school – more intimate than previous hall talks, very deliberately sending out a new, more personal and welcoming message from the off.

Exit: The word from parents and pupils is that they have 'absolute confidence' in the school enabling them to reach their guided first choice (more than 40 scholarships in 2015). Girls exit at 11+ to a list headed by James Allen's Girls' School and Wimbledon High but also co-ed destinations such as Alleyn's. Less than a handful of boys leaving at 11+ to Dulwich College, Whitgift and Trinity.

Head is the image of Hugh Bonneville as the Earl of Grantham. Perhaps it's his charm, sprinklings of the word 'chap', and labrador behind his desk

Destinations at 13+ headed by Wellington College, Dulwich College and King's College School, with clusters of pupils heading to Tonbridge, Whitgift, Alleyn's, Emmanuel, Marlborough and St Mary's Ascot. Around two-thirds to boarding school.

Remarks: The school opened in 1993, and is housed in a huge four-storey Victorian red-brick, typical of many London schools of the time, this one formerly a girls' grammar school in the centre of prime, residential Clapham. Inside, shining maroon tiled corridors, very London tube like, multiply the children's voices at every change of lessons – it's

reassuringly loud and exuberant. Reception classes are housed in groovy-looking pods with an in and out space – fun, but quite compact, and perhaps a bit warm in summer – with so much vibrant work hanging from the ceilings, it's like being inside a mobile.

The dining room needs some reinvention, currently high windows and too small, so that pupils eat in shifts. The food seemed no better than 'school dinner-ish' to our eyes, and it was Friday, but plenty of fried food as well as more healthy options. Large rear playground for breaks and games, with roped-off picnic tables for those who don't want to run around.

Specialist teaching introduced gradually up the school. Year 6 splits between those going for 11+ and 13+, with former getting much special preparation with past papers. Latter get exam technique and revision strategies in year 8, with a creative post-exam programme of extension subjects. The staff is a stable one, with 15 teachers having been at the school for more than 10 years. In his bid to make the school less autocratic, head introduced a new senior leadership team. Small changes have included greatly reduced homework and a less intimidating approach to school exams.

Parental praise for the teaching: 'Our children have enjoyed a multitude of inspirational teachers who go the extra mile'. 'Very supportive and nurturing whilst at the same time instilling the need for self-discipline and effort.' 'Apart from the French department, which needs a serious overhaul, the standard of teaching is superb. They manage to engage the children with original and inspiring teaching whilst also ensuring that the essential rote-learning/repetition aspects are in place.'

New director of computing and much investment in hardware. French is taught from day one by a native French speaker, but there is work to do for the new head of modern languages, who is expected to 'revitalise the department'. Latin from year 5, Mandarin now taught in year 4, Spanish a possibility in future.

Around 10 per cent of children have SEN, mainly dyslexia. Emphasis on differentiated learning and in-class support, but some withdrawal for one-to-one lessons. Strong learning support team assists some 150 pupils with a spread of learning differences, including a more able group. Refreshing for a London prep to be so proud of its efforts in this regard.

Great art facilities in a modern, light and bright separate block and an experienced newish head of art (formerly from Feltonfleet) is sensitively designing projects for each year group. Exciting to see a whole row of potter's wheels, and we were wowed by the impressive group of sculptures children had made by wrapping themselves in foil, inspired by Kader Attia's Ghost installation. Cookery a new addition. A film-maker in residence, a former head of art, is no doubt ensuring every moment is captured for the sharpening marketing act, as well as helping children to record and

A film-maker in residence is no doubt ensuring every moment is captured for the sharpening marketing act, as well as helping children to record and present multi-media projects

present multi-media projects across the curriculum. New DT specialist.

Sports fixtures list expanded with the aim of enabling everyone to play for a team. For the high achievers some glamorous tours such as South Africa too. Girls play netball, hockey, rounders and athletics. One parent told us: 'The head of sport gets the most amazing results out of the children, training and praising in just the right measure, and always there with a cuddle if they hurt themselves. The kids would throw themselves under a bus for her. The girls hold their own very well against schools with a far bigger pool of pupils and better facilities and the trophy cabinet is weighed down with the evidence of that.'

Boys play football, rugby and cricket. In part to keep the boys beyond 11, the head has beefed things up. We saw two current and former professional rugby players coaching the boys at the cricket nets, using an iPad to compare each boy's batting with that of a famous player. Further thoughts are hockey for the boys and lacrosse for the girls. Weekly swimming off site for years 1 to 4. Ballet part of the curriculum from reception – cue a class of tinies performing to parents and their iPhones on our visit. Mostly girls latterly; the boys who continue are often talented.

Performing arts are an outstanding feature – highlights from the current year include a performance at the Albert Hall in celebration of childhood. A parent commented: 'There seems to be something on every week! It is quite astounding that children are so confident and unfazed by the opportunities to perform, either in sport or on the stage.'

Some 350 children have individual music lessons, currently beginner level to grade 8. A wide range of groups and ensembles, and frequent recitals, soirées and concerts. Those with gifted voices may be invited to sing in the chapel choir, whilst 'new voices' and senior choir provide opportunities for all to perform.

More than 60 before and after school clubs include fencing, debating, golf, computer coding, newspaper publishing, running and Airfix modelling (run by the head).

Special days for everything, with plenty of outside expertise brought in to deliver workshops. 'Make a difference day' caught our eyes, with children heading off in mini task forces to spend time in genuinely helpful projects across the community, such as making decorations for their local hospice, visiting a Christian Aid centre and sending cards to sick children. Pupils seem to get out and about, get stuck in and see things for themselves. 'Woodland Adventure' on Wimbledon Common is 'by far the most popular day of term'.

Strong focus on PSHE. A new 'Inspiring Living' course is a philosophy of the school as well as a taught subject. A key component is a new focus on mindfulness, and Mr Ward is at the forefront of the curve. 'We're going to do mindfulness together... more thinking time, more time for reflection,' he says with enthusiasm. We applaud him, but wonder how he will stop his mind spinning with ideas and objectives during his allotted four minutes.

Head and team have set out to reinvent school's pastoral care systems. The head has been known to drop external meetings and return from conferences to pick up immediately on anything that arises. A parent confirmed: 'They take issues such as bullying seriously and take measures to address it instantly.' Parents describe the atmosphere as 'Very caring, and competitive in the right way, ie set out to win, but it doesn't matter if you don't, as long as you try your best'; 'Positive, determined yet caring and fun' and 'Nurturing'.

The head says, 'Every child wants a bit of metal on their shirt' and so there are now myriad opportunities to lead and take responsibility: as well as the usual heads of houses and games there are prefects for subjects or for eco and charities, even flag captains.

Parents are not first time buyers in the main: many boarding school educated, and an impressive bunch of achievers. One parent described them as 'Vocal! Very involved in all levels of school life.'

South West

Kingston-Upon-Thames
Merton
Richmond-Upon-Thames
Sutton

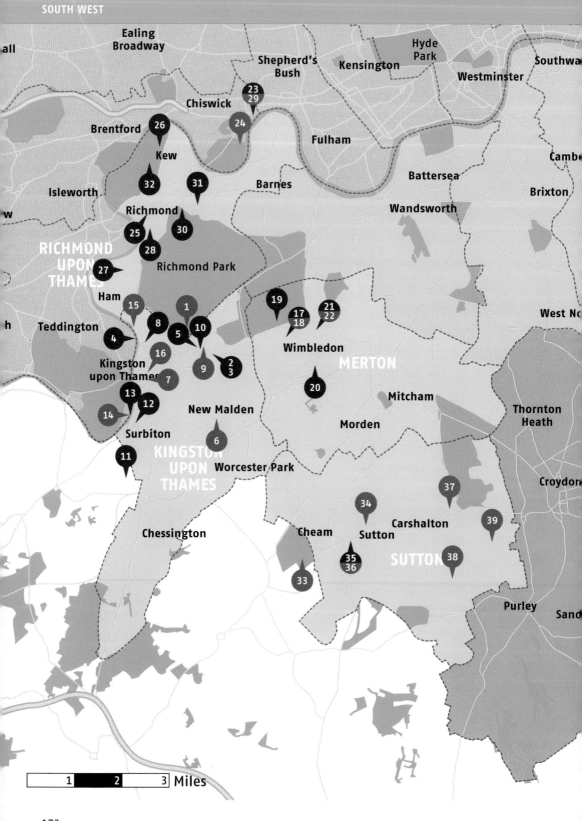

SOUTH WEST

An introduction to South West London and its state schools

Kingston-upon-Thames

Like neighbouring Richmond, Kingston has finally bitten the bullet, accepted the reality of a rapidly growing primary school population and recently announced plans to create new reception places (210 extra this year alone) with the help of almost £5 million in government funding. Two new free schools (one primary, one secondary) added in 2015, with a second primary due in 2016.

Educationally, the borough has a lot going for it. According to Ofsted, 87 per cent of primary age pupils attend a good or outstanding school and rising.

Its schools, 11 senior and just under 40 primaries from this autumn (still not enough, say locals) perform well above average, though there's considerable variation, not to mention disparity between inspection ratings and results: King Athelstan Primary, for example, currently rated 'good' despite pretty dismal attendance and KS2 results.

Though 100 per cent of pupils in Kingston's two surviving grammars, the Tiffin School (boys) and Tiffin Girls' School, achieve five A*-C GCSEs, including English and maths, they attract pupils from miles away, and thus can't, if you're being picky, be said to represent purely local attainment levels.

Locals whose children don't secure a place there (which will be around 90 per cent of those who attempt the exercise) shouldn't despair as most of the borough's other secondaries turn in results that are a least respectable and often much better, with borough-wide focus on singling out high achievers for special attention.

There's borough-wide buddying up, Coombe girls (very successful) with Coombe Boys (slightly less so); Hollyfield, currently more down than up, now shares head and teaching expertise with Grey Court School – an outstanding National Teaching School in neighbouring Richmond. Girls at the Holy Cross School (not to be confused with nearby independent girls' prep of same name) and boys Richard Challoner (also known for fab SEN provision) have long-standing and successful sixth form partnership – and consistently good exam results.

You don't even have to be a believer to do well. Borough's only community school Chessington, formerly below average in exam and inspection results, now shooting up in both, while Southborough School heads the innovation list, going all-through this autumn with on-site primary school and fully co-ed from 2017. Big focus there on most able who are singled out for an accelerated programme of study with the expectation that they'll deliver top GCSE results. Steady (if not stellar) rise in percentage achieving five GCSEs with English and maths suggest it's a sensible move – and it's happening in other Kingston senior schools as well.

As elsewhere, there's muttering about shortage of places, though growing links with Richmond, evident also when it comes to shared resources for special needs, also see many Kingston children moving on to Richmond comprehensives. A more permanent solution will be new co-ed secondary school, The Kingston Academy, opening September 2016 in the north of the borough, run by a three-way partnership that includes Kingston University and Kingston College and with a 180 pupil intake in its first year 7 cohort.

Creation of two new primaries – Kingston Community School opening this September and Surbiton Primary School next year – should also help, as will recent decision to turn St Paul's, currently an outstanding junior school into an all-through primary, and do the same for its current feeder school Alexandra Infants, split site commute the only downside.

Many local primaries, particularly those in more affluent parts of the borough, are highly desirable. Coombe Hill Junior School, a fixture in the GSG together with Latchmere and Fern Hill could, arguably, be joined by 10 or so other high performers.

Faith schools almost all brilliant. While most prioritise the godly, one – St Luke's – is breaking ranks to ditch church attendance as entry requirement from 2016 (to mixed media reception). St Andrew's and St Mark's C of E Junior School is outstanding. Christ Church Primary CE in Surbiton is currently down a notch to good, though notable for hard working staff, in reassuringly early and staying late at night, as well as 'lovely' head, though 'wish parents would stop children running through residents' gardens,' says disgruntled local.

Catholic schools range from outstanding (pace St Agatha's, near Richmond Park, popular with Norbiton's arty-crafty set) to Corpus Christi Catholic Primary School (good) though St Joseph's, despite positive inspection, currently out of favour with chattering classes.

Grand Avenue Primary and Nursery School a good alternative for those failing to meet religious criteria, achieving terrific results in English (shame about the maths) despite numbers – has almost 500 pupils on the roll.

In further reaches of borough less pricy housing meets decent education at Ellingham in Chessington which scores a 'good' with decent Sats results, ditto Green Lane Primary and Nursery, a community school on Epsom borders which scores on staff retention, says local parent. Tolworth Junior school (also good) once renowned for 'tough parents and tough children,' according to local, wears gritty location with pride, progress made by pupils source of great pride.

Merton

At primary level not quite as successful as more urban neighbours, in bottom five of London boroughs for proportion of pupils in good or outstanding schools, though a lot more successful with secondary schools. Also notable for elusive small-scale parent partnership (recently renamed to reflect focus on SEN) whose one-strong team, based at local primary school where it (allegedly) borrows a room, attempts to dole out impartial advice to parents across the borough.

Despite the territory – fair chunk of Merton is God's own banker's bonus land – parents at state schools 'aren't arrogant – arrogance tends to go private,' reckoned local. A few are boomerang returners – left for dream life in rural(ish) Surrey, struggled with the daily commute and moved back to enjoy Wimbledon Common's 1,200 acres, used by riders, walkers and picnickers.

Noah's Ark like, schools here come in pairs, Catholicism is your best option. First class attendance at local church is the result. Ursuline (girls) in particular is 'excellent,' says local, while pointing out that though tip top for those who want to learn, 'you can shrink away if you don't.' Unofficially looks to Wimbledon High qv as natural competitor when it comes to exam results (with close to 90 per cent achieving GCSE A*-C grades, few nearby state schools provide much of a challenge). Co-ed sixth form, twinned with Wimbledon College, the boys' equivalent, has seen effective pooling of resources and excellent range of subject choices as a result – philosophy and ethics, for example. As with any Catholic school, entrance, eye of needle etc, is depending on faith, with rumours of entrants being quizzed not just on church attendance but even subject of Sunday sermon.

Occasional difficulties – 'had bad press when rivalry with another school resulted in the occasional fight,' but bar inevitable ups and downs of different year group temperaments, it's all plain sailing. 'Had an amazing time there,' says former pupil.

Not the end of the road if you don't make it there, with Ricards Lodge (girls), Rutlish (boys) and joint sixth form both shooting up the reputation league, around 70 per cent of pupils in both getting five good GCSEs in including maths and English. Both well-rated, re-invigorated leadership at Rutlish presiding over better academic tracking (one of top 100 schools in country for pupil progression last year, with good support for gifted and talented. 'Got rid of a lot of kids,' says local rumour mill (though vague about exactly how accomplished). 'Don't despair if your child gets a place there,' says local.

Work in progress at St Mark's Academy (60 of 180 places allocated to Christian/other faiths) makes it another to watch (from a distance: GCSE results need a bit more oomph, ditto attendance, though also has substantial numbers with learning needs and on free school meals). Harris Academy, labouring under similar disadvantages, also viewed with caution.

To south west, there's Raynes Park School. Not an Ofsted darling, it is getting peer support from other, stronger schools. Well regarded for support for learning needs (we hear it's good with high functioning ASD, for example) it remains default choice for many local parents. While performance, feels locals, marred by chunk of pupils whose thirst for learning is somewhat modest, exam results have showed modest climb, just above national average in 2014. Justifies view, feel locals that as more on the ball pupils feed through, their motivation and ambition will rub off. You have to hope.

Most of official attention in recent years has focused on primaries which have 'really pushed themselves on' thinks local, following ending of middle school system, something of a rarity in these parts.

It's resulted, say locals, in widespread pushing up of standards. West Wimbledon Primary (houses nearby aren't accelerating way to mansion tax values quite as fast as in rest of borough) recently gained Ofsted outstanding. Remains popular and in demand – too early to say if shock disappearance of head at end of 2014 will have an impact.

Garfield another rapid riser – head big on parent involvement (previous regime saw all school events, including fairs, held on weekdays – 'hopeless for working parents') while Dundonald Park similarly strong on appeal to middle class professionals, traditional family model much in evidence with working father who is 'something in the City' but possibly, given slightly lower property prices here (relative, we know, in this area) with a slightly less expensive BMW, Audi or Land Rover to go with it.

Many of primaries notable for setting, including popular Bishop Gilpin, with own fields and flanked by pricey housing close to pretty Wimbledon Village. Wimbledon Chase Primary (a Good Schools Guide old-timer) also 'stunning' says local, thanks to own, beautiful grounds of former manor house, fields front and back and 'masses' of green space. Academics were a bit dim a few years ago but with recent, terrific head, formerly the deputy, has been a marked improvement in results. While not the smallest of schools, isn't the most massive either. 'They've got a good team there who have done a great job,' thinks local. Property prices, though again on the up, that bit more reasonable than elsewhere.

Plenty of primary appeal elsewhere, too, Merton Park, St Matthew's CE, Holy Trinity CE, Sacred Heart Catholic, Hatfeild (sic), Merton Abbey, Pelham and Cranmer all well-regarded.

Hollymount also a huge favourite with parents – 'Regarded as the best because of its location,' (in plushville Wimbledon, though in process of expansion). Now has results – and inspection – to justify local view that previous dip in both was temporary and caused by wayward intake.

Richmond-upon-Thames

Straddling both sides of the Thames, Richmond's borough limits can confuse even locals (just as well they don't go in for drumming strangers out of town: they'd probably never leave).

South of the river and west of Putney lies Barnes, is lined with leafy roads, river front mansion flats and low terraced

Edwardian and Victorian houses. Old reservoirs, once the source of most of London's drinking water supply, now make up the London Wetland and rather secret but public Leg O' Mutton reservoir near the Hammersmith Bridge – along the route of The Boat Race. Barn Elm – historically discreet site for duels as a means of dispute resolution – is now the Barnes sporting grounds, and local shops line the high street ending at the village duck pond.

South west of Barnes, Richmond village is a suburban one with bustling high street, steep hills with views over London that dip down to the river, large houses and extensive gardens behind old brick walls. From leafy to nearly rural, home to Kew Gardens and the 2000 acre former royal hunting grounds of Richmond Park, it's still just a quick tube, train or bus ride from the centre of London.

The Richmond comprehensives, with the notable exception of Waldegrave on the north bank of the Thames, have until recently been no better than they should be and, in many parents' eyes, rather worse, given excellence of primary school performance that should give pupils a substantial head start.

Not that you'll get many to admit their doubts openly. Indeed, more militant members of liberal-leaning book clubs have been known to cold-shoulder those who give up on the state system post 11, though some are to be found hiding behind pillars at independent establishment open days a few years later...

That said, most Richmond senior schools are starting to perk up, with GCSE results rising (able children particularly well catered for), vast majority of schools now scoring an Ofsted 'good'. Some extenuating factors, too. As the only single sex senior school in the borough, Waldegrave plunders the area's girls, boys currently accounting for approaching 60 per cent of pupil roll almost everywhere else.

As for ones to watch south of the Thames – we'd put money on Grey Court School and Richmond Park Academy, both boy-heavy and with higher than average numbers with English as additional language but with GCSE results showing year on year improvements.

Primary schools throughout the borough suffer from the same overcrowding problem which, as elsewhere, is seeing school numbers rise, stories of place-less reception children an annual headline grabber in local press. The LA is tackling the problem, tacking on classrooms and building two new schools from scratch. Meanwhile, living as close as you can to the desired school (dustbin in playground ideal if has own postcode) has never been a better idea. So is downloading a copy of the council's admissions policy and read it till your eyes bleed to make sense of the myriad of admissions criteria.

Worth the effort, however, because Richmond primaries are borough's jewel in the educational crown, with 90 per cent of pupils educated in a school that's either good or outstanding and Sats results regularly putting them amongst top ten in the country.

Four south of the river are currently included in Good Schools Guide: St Elizabeth's Catholic Primary School (weeny and wonderful, doing its bit for population bulge by taking an extra class on rota basis with two other Catholic schools); Sheen Mount Primary School (cracking results, highly motivated parents – with all that suggests); Russell Primary School (child-centred, separate SEN unit and – an area feature – highly motivated parents) and The Queen's School, Kew (all-round excellence – some pupils go on to independents including Lady Eleanor Holles qv and the like).

Plenty of other stars in the firmament, too. Good new additions include Kew Riverside and Marshgate which similarly pushes the pace with action-packed days that verge on frenetic, says local. Masses of older favourites, including St

Mary Magdelen's Catholic School.

Downsides headed by danger of low-flying helicopter parents (as well as flight path noise). If not ubiquitous, they're definitely a feature of Richmond's schoolgate life, with Vineyard, says one local 'operating like an independent school because of its location and the kind of parents it attracts.' Reasonably typical though not universal, East Sheen, something of a rarity with 'council estate pupils giving it less stolidly middle class feel,' says insider.

Following amalgamation of formerly separate infants and juniors departments, Stanley School, with head count of 700 plus, though worlds apart from quaint little village school, academically very much on the up.

New kid on the block, Deer Park School, opened in 2015 in a temporary location on a busy road with no obvious green space, let alone freely roaming Bambis. Plans to move to permanent site on Lower Mortlake Road in 2017.

Sutton

What it lacks in character, Sutton makes up for in academic desirability – and popularity. It's currently in the process of adding a whopping 1,314 new school places in 2015 – 2016, 875 secondary, 360 primary and 80 for SEN. Plans for a new free secondary school to open in 2017, taking specialisation from location – will be European life sciences centre – are well on the way.

Its grammar schools remain its brightest beacon of desirability, attracting candidates from miles around (two hour journeys aren't uncommon). All are highly selective and produce top class results with such ferocious competition that this is admissions as an extreme sport.

Even this microclimate has its own best of the best, however, with a bit of jostling for top slot – Wallington County School, with ambitious new head, recently nudged just ahead of Wilson's. Not that the others, including Sutton Grammar and Wallington High for Girls, are to be sniffed at, though they have their (slight) ups and downs, Nonsuch academically on the up after a few slightly below par years [turnover of heads also above average – which probably hasn't helped].

If your child doesn't make the cut (and with that weight of numbers, many very bright children won't) but is a) a girl and b) Catholic, St Philomena's Catholic High School for Girls, one of the top 100 non-selective schools in the country (they've got the letter from the minister on their website to prove it), is a more than acceptable alternative. Heavily oversubscribed in year 7 (too many Catholic applicants, let alone other faiths) it does offer more hope post 16, when a number of non-Catholics are admitted. John Fisher does well – if not quite so well – for Catholic boys.

Pick of the also rans is probably Glenthorne High School. Bad old days when known, says local, for 'louder, rowdier, fighting teens,' now firmly consigned to the past. Instead, it's an arts specialist, also outstanding and partially selective, offering 25 performing arts places, candidates attending a competitive workshop though more, as with grammars, will pass than can be offered places. Super range of clubs for all (ukulele orchestra and songwriting amongst them), gifted and talented programme also strong, with some sitting early GCSEs in English, maths, science, drama and RS.

There's lots of goodness in the area at primary school level too, with 92 per cent of pupils attending good or better schools (down slightly over the previous year) and 87 per cent attaining at least level 4 in reading, writing and maths combined – second best result in the country.

Westbourne Primary School, rated outstanding and substantially improved inside and out, with netball and tennis court, two football pitches, as well as outdoor adventure playground for younger pupils. Slight deficit on leafiness of surroundings (close to busy A 217 and Tesco), lower property prices the upside.

No shortage of other ultra desirables, from Nonsuch Primary, so good that government website is at a loss to find a better performing similar school within 75 mile radius, to St Mary's Catholic Junior School ('God is at centre of everything we do' they say – and they're not joking – baptismal certificate required with application; even looked after children have to be Catholic, or living with one. St Elphege's Catholic School, currently being expanded, and St Cecilia's RC Primary both outstanding and similarly stringent.

Definitely a case of 'O, come all ye faithful' in C of E schools, too, with St Dunstan's C of E Primary, All Saints Carshalton C of E Primary and All Saints Benhilton C of E Primary (also all rated good) allocating most of reception to regular worshippers (you'll need to take a pew twice a month for two years).

Cheam School Infants is doing rather better as are many others in the area, with Avenue Primary School also scoring highly for location in desirable South Sutton/Belmont, Beddington Park Primary (largish community school, on the up) and Cheam Park Farm Junior (now an academy, strong Sats results). Manor Park Primary, Robin Hood Junior, Stanley Park Junior also rate honourable mentions.

Worth noting one spectacular fall from grace; Cheam Common Junior School has dropped from outstanding to inadequate in just five years and is now being helped back to health with new governors and coaching from more successful neighbours. As elsewhere in London, however, many of the good tend to stay that way or get even better. With even special schools in Sutton doing well – Limes College, a unit for excluded pupils, has just risen from inspection 'good' to 'outstanding' – it's good to know that it's not just the high flyers who can soar.

Canbury School

Kingston Hill, Kingston Upon Thames, Surrey KT2 7LN

Tel: 020 8549 8622

Independent • Pupils: 60 • Ages: 11–16 • Fees: £15,660 pa

Email: enquiries@canburyschool.co.uk
Website: www.canburyschool.co.uk

Head: Since September 2014, Ms Louise Clancy BEd, formerly deputy head of Greenacre School in Surrey. She previously taught in Middlesex and Nottinghamshire. She has two daughters and spends her free time walking the family dog, playing badminton, life drawing and generally 'being very busy.'

Academic matters: Small, inclusive school catering for children who would not necessarily thrive in large comprehensives. Good range of subjects on offer; the majority of pupils take around nine GCSEs. Considering it is non-selective, results are commendable, especially for maths and English. Options at 14+ now wider with additional GCSE subjects. In 2015, 33 per cent of students achieved 5+ A*-C grades. Small class sizes enable teachers to provide that ever-important individual attention – staff pupil is ratio 1:7. Sensible amount of homework with clear guidelines for each year and an optional homework club.

A number of children with SEN, mostly dyspraxia, dyslexia and mild Asperger's/ASD. One-to-one support with specialist teachers in house to ensure individual needs are meet. Local speech therapists and occupational therapist work with the school as required. English as a foreign language tuition is also provided on a one-to-one basis or small group, depending on the needs of pupils.

Games, options, the arts: Excellent range of sporting activities for a smaller establishment, so something to suit everyone's tastes. Takes advantage of the numerous local sporting facilities in Richmond Park, Kingston and on the Thames for sailing, canoeing and rowing. Cross-country running is a major sport in which pupils compete successfully and everybody gets the opportunity to learn to swim.

Has the advantage of backing onto Richmond Park, where many sporting activities take place

Visual arts are strength – colourful, expressive art displays and many different media are used; parents say three-dimensional design, ceramics and collage are particularly popular. Class music is taught for the first three years and some children have individual instrumental tuition and enjoy performing in informal concerts. Drama taught mainly through small group work with an emphasis on developing communication skills and building confidence. Younger pupils tend to be the actors, with older ones taking on technical roles and directing the productions.

A variety of clubs run at lunchtimes and after school, table tennis, karate and arts being popular. Good variety of excursions and field trips arranged each term for all to help pupils develop new interests – prides itself on taking the children out and about.

Background and atmosphere: Founded in 1982 by John Wyatt, accommodated in a large Edwardian house on Kingston Hill. Whilst the site is compact, it has the advantage of backing onto Richmond Park, where many of their sporting activities take place. Facilities include a modern ICT room, a smart science lab, impressive art and design & technology rooms. Fully accessible – able to consider applications from children with physical disabilities. An educational charity administered by a board of governors whose aim is create a genuine community where individuals can be happy and motivated to achieve their maximum potential. Despite pupils being hard at work, calm and less formal atmosphere in comparison with many other schools.

Pastoral care and discipline: Pastoral care is high on the agenda to ensure well-being and self-esteem. Caring – everyone treated as an individual and taught to feel good about themselves and their abilities. Form tutors are always available to deal with any day-to-day problems, homework diaries are used to convey messages between home and school. A member of staff is a trained counsellor and pupils have a school council. Clear set of school rules are presented in a booklet, The Canbury Code.

Pupils and parents: Mostly professional parents from all walks of life and a range of backgrounds, both international and UK based. Families tend to be fairly local, from within a five mile radius from Richmond to Weybridge, handful come from central London. A school council is run by pupils (overseen by staff) to raise funds for the chosen charity of the year.

Entrance: At 11+ pupils spend an assessment morning at the school. Places are offered following a meeting with the head and satisfactory reports from previous schools.

Exit: At 16+ most choose to go to further education colleges, Epsom, Esher and Guildford. A few opt for sixth forms at local schools, eg Coombe Girls.

Money matters: Both current and prospective pupils can apply for means-tested bursaries.

Remarks: A good choice for children who require a sympathetic approach to their education. Definitely fills a gap in the education market, comment parents. A positive and warm atmosphere, where everyone is made to feel welcome.

Colet Court

Linked school: St Paul's School, 231

Lonsdale Road, London SW13 9JT

Independent · Pupils: 435 · Ages: 7–13 · C of E
· Fees: £18,102 pa

Tel: 020 8748 3461

Email: ccschoolsec@stpaulsschool.org.uk
Website: www.coletcourt.org.uk

23

Headmaster: Since 2007, Mr Tim Meunier MA (Cantab) CChem FRSC PGCE (Cantab). Educated at Forest School and Trinity College Cambridge, where he read natural sciences. Married to Sarah, whom he met at Cambridge when they sang in the same choir, and has two grown-up sons and one new grandson. Began his career at senior level teaching science at Clifton College and Felsted, but was persuaded to take up a post at The Dragon School as head of science in 1994. He returned to Clifton in 1998, this time as director of studies and, subsequently, deputy head; but the chance of the headship at Colet Court brought him back to the prep school world, because 'this is a wonderful school, and a fantastically stimulating place to be.' Began his tenure here by abolishing the scholarship form, 'because it was hothouse and over-competitive and I didn't like it.'

A keen musician, he sings baritone for various choirs, and can also be found playing Real Tennis whenever he gets the chance. A quiet, thoughtful man, passionate about the school's history, who knows all his young charges individually and is praised by pupils and parents alike for his blend

of kindness and professionalism. 'He's very good, very concerned, takes the time to know students individually, the boys like him,' was a typical comment. Boys say, 'When you get to know him, he's really down to earth. And he likes to get to know us. He's not looking to be a pain or scary, he's a nice person and a great teacher.' High praise, we thought.

Entrance: Has 38 places at 7+ and a further 38 at 8+, in classes of 19 boys each. In the January of the proposed entry year, applicants sit the school's bespoke entrance tests in maths, English (combined comprehension, reading and spelling), verbal and non-verbal reasoning. Always sought-after, competition for places increasing sharply, with applicants from 'literally hundreds of schools'.

If 7+ and 8+ are no pushover, entry at 11+, which guarantees a place at St Paul's, starts to resemble the Krypton Factor. Around 400 applicants try for just 20 places. Up to 10 of these are reserved for candidates from state primaries, who apply in year 5 for deferred entry in Y7 (or the Fourth, as it's known here). In this way, explains head, state-educated boys are given a level playing-field: instead of competing against heavily-prepped boys from the top independents, they're only up against boys from other state schools. If they don't succeed, they're free to try again in their year 6 for the remaining places, along with all the independent school applicants (who can only apply at this time).

Because of the very large number of boys applying, the school has devised a 'filter test' which is sat online in December of candidates' Y6. This consists mainly of verbal reasoning questions, and the top 100 scorers are invited to Colet Court to take the entrance tests (English and maths). Finally, the 30 best of these are called for interview. All of those 30 boys will be very bright, so what's the school looking for at this stage? 'A boy who's going to enjoy himself here,' says head, 'Someone intellectually curious who wants to learn, and with good talents – he's likely to have something going for him outside school.' Insists that 'we're not looking for a particular character type.' NB There's no filter test at 7+ and 8+; all such applicants come to Colet Court to sit the entrance papers.

Exit: Boys are expected to transfer to St Paul's at the end of year 8 (Fifth), and parents sign a form confirming that it'll be their first choice of senior school, 'but in reality we can't hold them to that,' says head. Typically, out of 90-odd leavers, a maximum of half a dozen might go elsewhere, almost always to boarding schools such as Eton and Winchester. For boys who join Colet Court at 11+ the place at St Paul's is unconditionally theirs – 'If it's a mistake, it's our mistake.' For those who joined at 7+ or 8+, the places are conditional, and very rarely – 'in fewer than one case per year group' – there'll be one for whom St Paul's isn't right ('if they're struggling academically on more than one front'). Head insists that in such cases the school always works with the child to bring him up to scratch, and all parents confirmed the tirelessness of the teachers in this regard. When asked if any 'weeding out' took place, Mr Meunier didn't initially understand the phrase, and then looked shocked when he did. 'Our aim is completely to get

187

100 per cent of Colet Court boys to St Paul's. And that's what usually happens.'

Remarks: A huge and splendid map of London hangs on one of the main walls, dotted with pins that mark where each individual Colet pupil travels from in the mornings. We commented on what a very wide geographical area it was, and the head agreed, but added, 'You have to be a bit careful of the map, though, because the boys like to pick out the pins and put them back in Heathrow Airport.'

In many ways, this enjoyable little quirk sums up the Colet Court ethos: learned, rooted in tradition, intellectually elitist, yet still a very boysie boys' school where boys have a great deal of fun. The school has had its detractors down the years, who have blamed it for being uncaring and inflexible, but hand on heart, we found no evidence of such things when we visited. Quite the contrary.

'An enormous amount of looking after went on in the first two years,' commented a mother whose son had been four years at Colet Court, starting aged 7. 'He couldn't have been more gently brought into the school. The staff were amazing.' Another, who has had multiple sons go through the school, confirmed, 'We have not had the sense that it's the pressure-cooker that it's reputed to be. The teachers are friendly, accessible and attentive, and the pastoral care is very good.' 'It's a kind place,' stated a

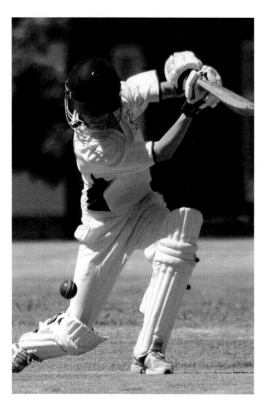

third. One of the Y8 boys we spoke to said that he would miss his teachers when he went up to St Paul's, because 'they get to know you very well, and they're like friends.'

A vast amount to do here outside lessons, ranging from a quiet little club for Four in a Row to a full scale production of Guys and Dolls

Colet Court's fees are not quite so friendly, and ensure that the school is more culturally than socially diverse. Only 5-10 per cent of boys are on any kind of bursary assistance (although for those few the subsidy can be up to 100 per cent), but there are sibling discounts of a kind: if you have three or more sons at the school, you get a whopping five per cent off the bill. Yay!

Founded in 1881 by Samuel Bewsher to secure numbers for St Paul's, our impression was that Colet Court still finds itself pushed off the sofa now and then by its big brother, which seems consistently to grab the biggest share of the financial pie and the nicest spaces on the site. St Paul's is having a multi-million pound makeover, but it was impossible to find out if any of it was coming Colet's way. 'I'm pretty confident that there'll be something,' said Mr Meunier loyally. Meanwhile, the Colet buildings remain drab and ugly – on the outside, at least – and it's hard to find anything positive to say about them, except that 'they're not about to fall down'. The entrance hall is underwhelming, there's a nasty little garden courtyard, and the reference section of the library was recently bagged by St Paul's for its expanded boarding provision. (These older brothers, eh?) Nonetheless, life here is simply buzzing and Colet Court has plenty of reasons to be proud, not least because its pupils love it here. Every parent who contacted us – and there were many – confirmed that their son was having a whale of a time. And the boys – animated, enthusiastic, well-mannered and full of fun – were proof of it.

Colet Court is about excellence, and absolutely all parents and boys praised the teaching here. 'Exciting, challenging, and very intellectually stimulating,' was how one parent described the atmosphere, and others agreed. 'The teachers have inspired him to work hard'; 'The academic pressure and demands are very high, but the atmosphere is cheerful and there's a sense of community'; 'The teaching is superb'; 'The teaching is excellent, and always keeps the boys interested'; 'The teachers are fantastic, and really great at making things seem easy' were typical comments. Standards and expectations are extremely high, and the work we saw bore this out. Writing in particular was accurate, lively, witty, informed and a pleasure to read. Maths is exceptionally strong, with the best of Colet's young mathematicians regularly winning national challenges, but all boys are encouraged to achieve; again, many parents told us of how supportive the teachers had been ('they all love their maths teachers'). The learning support room looked a little bare to us, but the very experienced SENCo got a huge vote of confidence from everyone, boys and parents alike. There are, acknowledged the head, no present Coletines with dyscalculia – which is unsurprising, given the demands of the entrance tests – but there are pupils with dyslexia, dyspraxia and 'shades of autism and Aspergers', and the head disputed my suggestion that only mild cases would flourish here. 'We have to assess every case that comes to us, but if we thought a boy was suitable for Colet Court, we'd put our backs out to accommodate him.' Several parents praised the languages here, although there are actually very few on offer: the only modern language studied is French, at which many pupils excel, with Latin and Greek also taught. The boys we spoke to said they would like to learn Spanish: school please note.

Is there too much homework? Some said yes, others said no. Some parents lamented that homework dominated evenings and weekends and could take their child hours to complete. But all agreed that the homeworks were enjoyable, and the head defended the school's policy. 'We think a lot about homework and we're pretty sure that we don't overload: we did a survey recently with comparable schools and found we weren't setting the most. We do sometimes say to them that there's no need to do so much, but our boys are very competitive as well as bright and conscientious and they often go beyond the tasks set.' He also hinted that Colet parents were not wholly without the competitive gene themselves, which might account for some of the more spectacular assignments handed in. The Good Schools Guide, of course, is written by parents for parents, so we couldn't possibly comment; but we were impressed by how very articulate and assertive this parent body was, particularly the mother who told us that her son hadn't been offered a place at CC first time around 'because of oversubscription'.

There is a vast amount to do here outside of lessons, ranging from a quiet little club for Four In A Row to a full-scale production of Guys and Dolls, one of no fewer than eight drama productions mounted every year. Music is outstanding – boys can learn anything, even the organ in the school hall – and the school fields any number of orchestras, ensembles and choirs. 'I cannot say enough positive things about the music department,' cried one parent. 'It manages to foster and encourage the talents of both beginners and accomplished players. The breadth of offerings is staggering. The boys

are tremendously lucky to have such a committed music department at their disposal.' On the head's wish list is a bit more light in the art room, but the quality of the artwork on the walls is astounding, so something's clearly going right.

Undeniably, life at Colet Court is not a walk in the park but an eagerly-contested run

Perhaps the most popular and successful extra-curricular activities here, however, are the sports, which feature very prominently in what the school offers. The facilities, many of which are shared with St Paul's, are superb, and the boys can do rugby, football, cricket, tennis, volleyball, fencing, athletics, aikido – the list goes on. All the boys we spoke to adored this part of their life here; which is as well, because they're expected to be highly committed in their chosen sports, and weekends are often dominated by training and fixtures. 'Demanding, but worthwhile,' was one mother's verdict. Another's praise was more ambivalent, and seemed to refer to more than just the sport: 'You have to be willing to live with a certain amount of stress if your son goes to Colet Court. The whole family has to make sacrifices.' The head agreed with this last statement, but was unapologetic. 'Parents do have to get behind the school,' he said firmly.

Undeniably, life at Colet Court is not a walk in the park but an eagerly-contested run. The boys who get here – and the school does seem to know how to choose them – clearly find it exhilarating. As one engaging young man put it to us, 'I love it immensely here. I can't think of any faults.' Parents are pretty much convinced too. We heard disquiets about a lack of parent-school communication ('compared to my other children's schools, it's dreadful'); that parents were too often shut out of the picture ('they're not interested in the parents now that they have the raw materials needed to manufacture the next generation of Paulines'); that boys sometimes formed into cliques based on sporting ability, leaving others alienated. But for each of these concerns there was a parent who told us the opposite, and even the most critical added, 'my son loves Colet Court and everything he does

there, so all my criticisms are pretty much irrelevant.' Interestingly, a phrase that came up again and again amongst parents was 'This is the right school for him.' The school knows a Coletine when it sees one, it appears.

So don't worry if your extremely bright son isn't offered a place here. There are many ways in which to be brilliant, and this one won't suit every clever boy. But for those for whom this is the right place, Colet Court is very, very impressive, balancing superb academic provision with genuine kindness and care. Top of its class.

St Paul's and Colet Court are currently under investigation following recent allegations of historic child abuse, said to have taken place between the 1960s and 1980s. In separate incidents, two Colet Court teachers resigned in 2013 after being arrested for alleged impropriety.

Coombe Hill Infant School

Linked school: Coombe Hill Junior School, 191

Coombe Lane West, Kingston upon Thames KT2 7DD

Tel: 020 8942 9481

State • Pupils: 330 • Ages: 4–7

Email: admin@chi.rbksch.org
Website: www.coombehillinfants.com

Headteacher: Since 2013, Mrs Janet Berry. SENCo and senior assistant head for three years prior to taking over the headship and a member of the senior leadership team. Has been at the school for 13 years, starting part time when her children were pupils and progressing through the ranks as they got older.

Entrance: Much sought after local school. The closer you live the better, although it may still prove difficult to get in. More than 550 first choice applications for 90 places; over half go to siblings. Admission policy strictly adhered to – medical or social needs get priority. Occasional bulge years add an extra class.

Exit: Almost without fail to the junior school next door. One or two to local independent schools, of which there are plenty.

Remarks: From the moment you walk into it, through the art gallery entrance, you realise that this is a lively school bursting with happy, interested children. A vast ethnic mix – about 60 per cent need some EAL support, mainly in class except in extreme cases. No attached nursery, so some

children arrive speaking no English at all while others speak two or three different languages. The resulting mix is 'demanding but fascinating to work with.' All classes – five or more of up to 30 children in each age group – mixed ability. One full time teacher for each, plus a teacher's aide for at least half of the day and other extra staff who help wherever needed. All are highly trained and experienced, often current or ex-parents. 'The school has a really family feel,' we were told.

Fantastic semi open-plan layout, all on one floor, loads of natural light. Corridors of well-equipped classrooms, all with interactive whiteboards, computers and educational displays. Children's creations abound. Pupils enjoy themselves, eagerly joining in all activities. When we visited all of them were absorbed, participating and learning, and eager to show us what they were doing. Three excited year 2 pupils were delighted to take us round their school and point out their favourite places and activities.

Fantastic IT suite, good lending library with videos, games, reading and maths schemes. Great art on display everywhere.

One of the special things about this school (and the junior school next door) is the massive amount of outdoor space. Plenty of room to run, climb and explore. Children certainly make the most of it – log cabin for special projects and areas for planting and learning. Imaginations soar. Pupils have the use of a heated swimming pool (in the junior school's section of the shared open land) in the summer term. Each class has weekly sessions, weather permitting.

Mix of nationalities means cultural activities from all over. Most festivals are celebrated and any excuse for dressing up is grabbed. Knowledge of the world is part of the learning process – every child and every country is important. Music and art are an essential part of the school day.

Lots of after-school clubs that change termly. Sport, drama, music, art, computers and other themes – all good fun, all for a minimum charge.

This is a popular school and houses in the area are very sought after. They are very lucky, too, to have active, involved parents who raise a fortune and provide funds for the school's continuing excellence.

Coombe Hill Junior School

Linked school: Coombe Hill Infant School, 190

Coombe Lane West, Kingston Upon Thames KT2 7DD

State • Pupils: 390 • Ages: 7–11

Tel: 020 8949 1743

Email: admin@chj.rbksch.org
Website: www.coombehillj.kingston.sch.uk/

Headteacher: Since September 2014, Mr Mark Clutterbuck, previously deputy principal at Chessington Community College.

Entrance: Some 99 per cent automatically from the infant school. Others all local, round the corner.

Exit: Majority to local state schools, impressive number to the highly selective Kingston state grammars Tiffin Boys and Girls, more to Coombe Girls and Boys, others all over. With the improvement that has taken place in the current local state schools, very few pupils now move into the private system.

Remarks: A brilliant, buzzing, exciting state school more than ever holding its own against the many local private sector schools. Very much an upmarket area; the pupils are a huge ethnic mix from a variety of backgrounds, with parents who help, encourage and enjoy the multinational involvement.

We were taken round by some senior pupils eager to show us everything that was going on. We didn't miss a nook or a cranny and were suitably impressed. Everywhere was clean, bright and full of happy, thoroughly involved children. Classrooms overflowing with interesting displays. Technology everywhere. Parents told us 'excellent teaching', 'fantastic, exuberant teachers', 'great facilities' and 'really like the way they make learning fun and incorporate different subjects in one lesson'. We were delighted to see a good number of male teachers, two of whom are heads of year. Classrooms a bit squashed but that didn't appear to matter; flexibility is the name of the game. All mixed ability but the brightest separated into four groups for maths and literacy. We were told, 'the teaching is something special, a real collaboration between teacher and pupil, teacher and teacher, and pupil and pupil, they all help each other'. 'No cramming, the education is broad and full, they are taught to debate and to question and to discover for themselves'.

Lots of music, singing and playing different instruments. Private lessons available for those who want to learn a particular instrument. Everyone learns the recorder in year 4. Our guides proudly showed us the range available for them to try. Great art on display in the atrium and, when we were there, models of Andersen shelters – 'very difficult to make!' For a state primary, the sport is exceptional. A brand new games area provides for cricket, netball, basketball, football, rugby and other sports, some of which they play competitively against other schools. Not enough, some parents think, but it is a privilege not there for all primary school children, so they are lucky. And they have their own heated swimming pool – two sessions a week for each class. Added to that PE and dance form an important part of the curriculum.

A large variety of after-school clubs which are extremely popular and introduce children to new skills and ideas. An hour a day, all taught by their

There are wild life areas, including a pond and a 'hotel' for insects, a vegetable garden – 'some we eat, some we sell' – and, really exciting, a pen for chickens

regular teachers with a minimal charge to cover materials.

Our guides led us proudly round their extensive grounds. Every class has an outdoor learning day once a year. As well as the usual play areas, there are wild life areas, including a pond and a 'hotel' for insects, a vegetable garden – 'some we eat, some we sell' – and, really exciting, a pen for chickens whose eggs, of course, also get eaten.

Sympathetic SENCo who seems to really care for the children, making sure no needy child slips through the net. Several groups, run by learning support teachers, take pupils out of class where necessary, but never during a core subject. Non-stop records kept and a provision map for every child in the school. Those with behavioural problems get one-to-one support but they do try to make sure that they are given enough individual space. SENCo works closely with both the behavioural team and the class teachers, trying to tackle problems before they go too far. Says it's important to try and preempt difficult situations before they get out of hand. 'I really love my job'. Parents say, 'Children respected and nurtured. Bad behaviour not tolerated'. 'Quick to deal with problems'.

Parents rave about every aspect, haven't got a single criticism. Only worry, will they be able to maintain this high achievement level?

All in all a tip-top school that has managed and absorbed the necessary expansion it has seen over the last few years and the broad ethnic diversity that is Greater London today.

Fern Hill Primary School

Richmond Road, Kingston Upon Thames, Surrey KT2 5PE

State • Pupils: 670 • Ages: 3–11

Tel: 020 8247 0300

Email: office@fernhill.rbksch.org
Website: www.fernhill.kingston.sch.uk

4

Headteacher: Since April 2015, Adam Scott, previously deputy head, who has been at the school for over 15 years.

Entrance: Very popular, very oversubscribed, move very close. Usual local authority admissions criteria apply, which essentially means siblings and distance. Obviously catchment varies, but always tight

– anecdotally an 800m radius most recently. Due to population bulge, Kingston has had a problem with reception place numbers and the school is expanding. Worth staying on the waiting list as odd spaces do come up.

Exit: Be aware that although packed with good primaries, North Kingston is short of secondary school places – though the new Kingston Academy should ease matters, and some leavers are moving on there. Many pupils progress to Grey Court in Ham, which is actually in the neighbouring borough of Richmond. Others feed elsewhere into the Kingston and Richmond secondary systems. Handfuls to the much sought after places at very nearby selective Tiffin Grammar schools (NB almost everyone in North Kingston uses private tutoring to try and get to these schools) Some plunge into the private pool (some always planned to), including Kingston Grammar (co-ed), Hampton (boys) and Surbiton High (girls).

Remarks: A top-notch school – regularly vies with neighbouring Latchmere for unofficial 'best in borough' award. Sets high standards, has high expectations and unsurprisingly attracts high numbers of the white middle classes who abound in this area. A real community school – just be aware that the community is North Kingston, swarming with young professionals hell-bent on achieving a first class state education for their brood. After the white middle classes, largest ethnic group is Asian. School says not all is leafy and lovely in Kingston and there is some social housing around, but this accounts for a minority of the cohort.

Ofsted rates Fern Hill as 'outstanding and providing an excellent all-round education', praising pupils' achievements both academically and in terms of their personal development.

Academic standards are good – generally around half the year group achieves at least level 5 in maths and science Sats. School acknowledges that many of its pupils enter the school with above average skills but, even so, these results are sparkling and seemingly achieved without too much pressure – 'The parents are probably pushier than the school', comments one mother.

There's a distinct private school feel to the place – and not just because the children are beautifully turned out in smart uniform. Everything is orderly and fairly calm, but not sterile, children all appear engaged and on-task, overall a quite traditional feel to things. Children sit in groups around tables, but for year 6 move to rows to support the sense that year 6 is a special year and to ready them for their more formal secondary schools. Lots of praise for teaching staff – stable and nice mix of youth and experience, few men (but including deputy head with high parental approval rating). When staff do leave it is rarely to work at another local school. Teaching assistants everywhere (more assistants than teachers) some class-based, others working with individual children, more senior TAs leading activities such as PSHE, ICT etc.

School packs it all in via a tight timetable and has made real efforts to introduce more creative ways of learning, for example using drama to help pupils empathise with historical characters. Lots of cross-curriculum and project work helps to free up the day – eg non-fiction literacy as part of history,

writing for a purpose. Teachers add breadth to the national curriculum diktats introducing supplementary topics of their choice. 'We are always looking at the curriculum and trying to find links'. 'Obviously some subjects need to be directly taught, but in other areas we can pull things together to make things less prosaic and more interesting for the children'. Homework manageable, about half an hour a week for years 3 and 4, rising to half an hour a day by year 6. School adamant that young children need a life and to have time to do other things outside school. 'Homework is not a central part of the school'. Tutoring for entrance to the Tiffin schools is huge in this area and school is reasonably relaxed about it but admits to some concern for any child who is hauled around to take lots of different entry exams.

Specialist French teacher; all pupils learn from nursery with every class having a short French lesson each week, with some language and vocabulary incorporated into the children's learning during the rest of the week. Several other teachers are confident French speakers and the long term aim is for all teachers to be able to teach French to their own classes. Also a specialist music teacher now comes in two days a week which, together with links to Kingston Music (and Arts) Service, has seen some improvements in this area – previously a little weak for this school. There is now a school choir and orchestra in which a few parents play too. Around 45 pupils learn an instrument and each year 3 has an opportunity to learn strings.

Gold award for art, kite mark for PE – school takes this side of the curriculum just as seriously as the academic work.

School has had a good reputation for picking up problems or learning difficulties early

The school has a special needs/inclusion coordinator with a team of teaching assistants and a dedicated resource, the Rainbow room. Some 60 odd pupils are on the SEN register, six with statements. These children are taught with their class as much as possible, with one-to-one or small group sessions used to support this as necessary. EAL support is available but, although some 180 pupils have English as a second language, their English is usually good. Flexible ability grouping within each class, and there is plenty of room to take small groups out for focused teaching as necessary. School has had a good reputation for picking up any problems or learning difficulties early – some parental concern over whether staff will be able to maintain this focus as school expands.

School is very keen on good manners, politeness and respect. Overall pupil behaviour and attitude is great – for the most part these children are on-side and eager to learn. They abide by 'golden rules', the breaking of which results in the loss of 'golden minutes' from playtimes. (But other times they gain – we passed children returning from the playground after a five-minute, mid-lesson 'brain break'.) All the children understand the school's focus on the 6Rs – resourcefulness, resilience, reflection, responsibility, reasoning and respect – promoted around the place by Winnie the Pooh and his friends. 'We are generally very lucky that our children are well-behaved. But there are some little pickles that we need to manage, as well as looking out for the quiet ones so that they don't disappear'.

Be aware that the community is North Kingston, swarming with young professionals

School environment enjoys all the advantages that come with having been purpose-built (co-incidentally in response to a shortfall in school places back in 1994) including wide doors and corridors and specialist toilet facilities for disabled children. Use of space is very good throughout. Classrooms are all a reasonable size, lots of outdoor activities for the tinies and separate playgrounds for nursery, infants and juniors (though again playground space at a premium as school size increases). Full-time social skills assistant on hand to encourage play and mediate where necessary. External facilities also include an environmental area and inner courtyard with amphitheatre feature.

New buildings include a sports hall, small hall and music room on the back of the school, together with alterations to the existing hall to make seven new classrooms, an art room, new special needs room and additional multi-purpose small group rooms. The field at the back of the school landscaped to include an all-weather surface, new football pitch and other playtime activities. Part of the school has become two-storey.

Great displays are all around; a lot goes on here and it is all written up, drawn, photographed, modelled, reviewed or rewarded in pen, pencil, paint, clay, crayon – you name it and it's probably up on a wall somewhere. It's not an especially tidy place, but nor is it sloppy – it's just a reflection of a busy school life.

Strong and competitive house system, busy school council with some powers and facilities all help promote positive peer groups. (Recent pupil decision was to swap the older girls' and boys' loos as it was felt that the boys would benefit from having an open window in their facilities. Pupil power in action.) Lots of after-school clubs, till 4.30pm. No other on site before or after-school care facilities, but the school does have a close association with the nearby YMCA Hawker Centre which provides breakfast and teatime clubs and will take and collect the children to and from school.

Parents feel involved, lots help and home/ school communication is good. Colonised by the middle classes who are willing (and encouraged) to get fully involved in school life, the PTA is, as you would imagine, very active and well-supported. 'It's

a very special place,' said a parent, 'and we all want to do our bit'. It's a secure, happy place with lots going on. Plenty of trips and visitors – everything from theatre groups to fire engines and animals. 'There's nothing boring,' said one dream pupil, 'We're always doing something fun'.

To our question, 'Any notable former pupils?' school answers positively, 'Not yet' – but you come away feeling that there certainly will be in 20 years' time. You would be delighted to have this state offering on your doorstep – which is indeed where it will need to be for your child to attend.

The Harrodian School

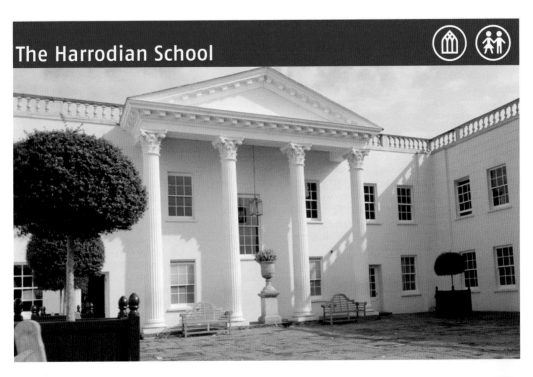

Lonsdale Road, London SW13 9QN

Independent • Pupils: 982 • Ages: 4–18 • Sixth form pupils: 163 • Fees: up to £20,298 pa

Tel: 020 8748 6117

Email: admin@harrodian.com
Website: www.harrodian.com

24

Headmaster: Since 1999, Mr James Hooke BSc PGCE (50s). Educated up the road at Hampton, read geography at Leeds and then straight to the City as a banker. Soon became bored and took off to Latin America, where he taught at St John's School in Buenos Aires. Impressed the former head, when he arrived here in 1995, with his knowledge of languages and very soon became deputy head. His youthful appearance belies a steady, practical and considered approach. He loves the job and is totally committed to the pioneering ethos that is being achieved here. His daughter and son are both at

the senior school. One parent commented that he seems to float around the place – no one is very sure what he is doing to steer the ship. His subtle touch seems to be effective, though – as soon as the slightest problem is brought to him, it's swiftly and decisively resolved.

The head of the prep school is Mr Matteo Rossetti (30s), an Oxford classicist (Balliol), passionate, with a rounded, highbrow approach. He injects still more of an international flavour to the school while being determined to increase its academic profile.

Mrs Horan, calm, capable and homely, has been running the pre-prep since 2004. Her previous experience has been in the state sector – Our Lady of Victories in Putney and deputy head at the Oratory in Chelsea.

Another key player in the management of the whole school is the principal, Mr Peter Thomson. Formerly the surmaster at St Paul's, he ran The Harrodian for a short period until he 'retired' in 1999. A colourfully eccentric individual, he is thoroughly committed to the school but describes his role as largely 'advisory and supportive'. He will do anything that is thrown at him, whether it be showing parents round or jumping on his bike on an errand, but what he clearly loves is leading the tinies in their singing and music assembly on a Friday afternoon. His grandchildren are in the pre-prep and all the children here seem to regard him as a kindly elderly relative.

Academic matters: High standards without undue pressure is the consistent message. 'Children can learn at their own pace and grow in confidence,' was the observation of more than one parent. Streaming in English, maths and languages. As it becomes more academically selective at every entrance point, and the image that this is a school for the clotted cream of society starts to fade, the results continue to make dramatic improvements. Eighty per cent A*-B at A level (43 per cent A*/A) in 2015 and 60 per cent A*/A at GCSE – impressive stuff.

He will do anything that is thrown at him, whether showing parents round or jumping on his bike on an errand, but he loves leading the tinies in their singing

Those with SEN, so long as they have mild to moderate needs, are well looked after. A team of 10 support staff, run by the experienced and highly praised SENCo, work closely with mainstream staff. Pupils are taken out of sport or Latin to the appealing suite of rooms tucked away at the top of the main building for mostly one-to-one attention. No formal programme for the gifted and talented – this is not pegged onto learning support. 'We don't like the implications of branding a child as gifted and talented – it sends the wrong message to others.' High proportion of EAL; a lot of language support is available. Those identified as being gifted and talented are given extra challenges in the classroom and a mini chess club for years 1 and reception.

Maverick and colourful members of staff from all walks of life who, unsurprisingly, thrive in such a civilised environment. Muttering among some parents about the high turnover of antipodeans, but Mr Hooke is keen to point out the cultural diversity and energy young Australians bring. Average age of staff is young – 35 to 40 – and 20 have been there for more than 10 years.

The curriculum is mainstream with a heavy emphasis on modern languages – key to a civilised life; how refreshing. All learn French to a more or less bilingual level, taught wholly by native speakers. They can also do Italian, Spanish and German; Japanese, Chinese etc are available by arrangement. Latin and religious studies survive – can offer Greek for those who want to do it. Media and business studies are popular. Graphic design recently introduced as an A level option.

ICT is well provided for in three dedicated spacious rooms as well as in various key rooms around the school. Everyone has a lesson a week and is encouraged to use it in other academic areas. Interactive whiteboards making slow progress – some but not many. We speculated that the founder's penchant for York stone took precedence but were told firmly that his resistance to teaching technology is based on educational principles – children get enough screens at it is; he wants to avoid any interference in the teacher/pupil oral interaction.

Overall good, and promising to become better and better – 'Academic bar is being raised each year,' says head.

Games, options, the arts: One pupil remarked that she contemplated going to boarding school but realised she didn't need to – she could go to the Harrodian. The sense of space (25 acres of pitches, courts, play areas and gardens) and the emphasis on getting plenty of exercise and fresh air (they carry on even in torrential rain) are central to the Harrodian experience. Winning isn't, however: lots of fixtures in traditional sports, as you would expect, but competition isn't the main focus – 'It would be wrong to thump a team 12-0,' says head, and one parent remarked that sports day was a bit of a joke: plenty of races but no one with really any idea of what's going on. 'It's more about happy kids enjoying themselves.' Mr Hooke is keen to counter that while they have an inclusive approach – A, B, C and D teams – the A team is competitive. Plus a highly-qualified team of sports coaches, high tech equipment that can record a match so you can replay it MOTD style to comment on technique, as well as the best sports equipment.

Swanky sports hall will provide a gym as well as fencing salle and dance studios. In true Harrodian style it's not just the conventional that is on offer either – a smattering of glamorous options, eg a racing ski team will compete in France and attend a three day training camp; golf is being developed at Dukes Meadows; yoga, karate and self-defence as well as boxercise and volleyball. Small but heated outdoor pool in attractive colonnaded courtyard – open April to October.

Lots of dynamic and bubbly music – from opera (The Magic Flute recently performed by the prep school) and musicals to the hugely popular Battle of the Bands judged by a celeb from the music industry. Bands allowed to record CDs on site and make their own photographed cover. Intimate recital/theatre studio with fixed raked seating and individual practice rooms housed in the music school, which bursts with activity of all kinds – three senior choirs, orchestra and smaller groups. A less-than-confident guitarist may be called upon to accompany a singer in assembly – while excellence is recognised and valued, it's not over-lauded.

His elderly mother can be spotted eating lunch in the dining room with the children

Drama is dynamic and innovative. Pupils here are confident about getting up on stage and often take the initiative themselves to write and perform, eg comedy sketches. One boy in the prep school took a few terms out to perform in the film of Peter Pan. Artistic endeavour is encouraged, opportunities valued. Art happens in three different rooms

around the site – all equally pleasantly cluttered; 20 per cent take art at GCSE, impressive photography and graphics studio – we saw haunting models of WW1 soldiers recreating the carnage of the trenches. An A level student's sculpture is displayed online in the Royal Academy A Level Art Exhibition. Very little cookery, textiles club popular with girls in the prep school but not much evidence of it in the senior school. DT markedly absent – surprising in such a creative school.

Background and atmosphere: As eccentric as you would expect. In a previous incarnation it was the country club for Harrods employees. Sir Alford and Lady Houstoun-Boswall – a couple with a vision – bought it in 1993 (pipping The Lycée and St Paul's Boys' at the post), he the eighth baronet, she an American multi-lingual teacher, headmistress and restorer of historical buildings (who went off to set up Hampton Court House), and proceeded to create a dream – a co-ed school run according to civilised values in a civilised environment to produce relaxed, happy children. The original intention was to create a prep school but two-way expansion occurred and now it runs from 4 to 18. Strong sense of family ownership and involvement – Sir Alford's sister, Mrs Moore, lives in a flat in the school and has a pastoral role, he has an office and comes into the school most days and his elderly mother can be spotted eating lunch in the dining room with the children.

The dream appears to have been realised – this is one of the least institutional schools we have visited: no sign of industrial carpets and concrete here. York stone courtyards embellished tastefully with inessential but elegant and stylish jeux d'esprit – little fountains and stone vases, olive trees, loggias and parterres. Spacious reception areas with sweeping staircases, three piece suites nestled on landings and in comfortable corners. No signs, no bells, no uniform, and no common rooms for staff or pupils ('Reduces the chance of any whispering behind doors,' says head). Real three course lunches eaten on tablecloths in a dining room that could seamlessly become a ballroom. A coffee shop, complete with open fire and floor to ceiling plush curtains (no crisps, no coke). And yes, the children are relaxed and are happy and seem surprisingly unspoilt by the privileges they enjoy here. We heard tales of some children returning, having left, and others ecstatic when they didn't get into another school.

Real three course lunches eaten on tablecloths in a dining room that could seamlessly become a ballroom. A coffee shop, complete with open fire

Although this is very much one large school with many of the buildings and facilities used by all age groups, the pre-prep is self-contained in a separate building surrounding a small paved courtyard. Huge classrooms with large bright windows. No one ever feels cramped here. A conservatory at the back where small group work can take place opens up onto Astroturf, where reception can play with fluid access between the classroom and the outdoors. A charming allotment complete with scarecrows and dung, as well as the French Garden for quiet contemplation.

The prep school is more integrated into the senior school, but cleverly arranged so that its pupils don't seem to get swallowed up by lanky long haired teenagers.

Pastoral care and discipline: We were fully prepared to witness a level of chaos – not a bit of it. One parent described the discipline here as 'contained liberalism but certainly not lax'. Boundaries are clearly defined and pupils respect that, while enjoying an unusually equal and positive relationship with staff. If you miss homework you will be given a detention; these can take place on a Saturday morning (when no school) but the number of detainees is small – a reflection, we were told, of how well the system works. Zero tolerance on drugs – 'I have

expelled children for drugs and wouldn't hesitate to do so again,' says head. Pupils have a mature self-regulating approach but it's not the place for someone who persists in pushing the boundaries – 'They wouldn't fit in,' says head.

Unlike the senior school where no uniform, the prep school has a (pretty relaxed) dress code. This includes collared shirts, but boys can wear the Harrodian hoodie with their collared shirt underneath. The pre-prep wear simple navy uniforms. Discipline is discreet. Children here are given responsibility and respect and are largely self-regulating. No bells; parents are welcomed and can get as involved as they wish to be.

Pupils and parents: Increasingly trendy media and fashion types from central London, with a fair helping of celebrities, but the core group of middle class professionals from affluent Barnes are still here too. A few first time buyers who are coming to grips with what is meant by a Russell Group university. Plenty of money, though – not many families here are scraping to find the fees and this is reflected in the lavish activities and trips that your child will want to attend. Children less bothered than their parents by this – thank goodness – and are confident, relaxed but polite, and relishing the space and the stimulation of the place.

Entrance: Huge waiting lists for the pre-prep – 'It's getting to the stage that you may wish to plan your caesarean at the beginning of the month,' we were told, with only a slight hint of irony. Non-selective. Strong sibling policy. Competitive at 8+ and 11+ and for occasionals. 11+ applications from a huge range – local state primaries as well as local preps; 'Girls' schools are less sniffy now,' head said. Becoming increasingly competitive – 250 applicants for 20 places. Two-thirds of candidates are interviewed, in some cases on the strength of an excellent school report notwithstanding a poor exam result. Despite evident delight at the quality and calibre of applicants in recent years, head keen to preserve the ethos of not creaming and cramming.

Takes a few more (around 5-10 from 70 or so applicants) at 13+. Entry to the sixth requires six or more Bs with As in the subjects chosen for A level. Standards less stringent for internal applicants.

Exit: A decreasing few at CE to trad boarding schools (Eton, Harrow, Charterhouse, Marlborough, Wellington etc) and the odd one or two to single sex London day schools (St Paul's Girls', King's College School etc). Be ready to put in a lot of extra help if you want your child to go to one of the more academic establishments. Loses a few after GCSEs to, eg, tutorial colleges and boarding. Most leave for good universities – Edinburgh, Oxford Brookes, Exeter and Leeds all popular – to read a well-balanced mix of arts and sciences, creative and practical courses.

Money matters: Fees pretty average for location and what's on offer, but very little help available to pay them – limited bursaries (the funds are kept for a crisis emergency) and no entrance scholarships. Academic awards are offered at 13+ and 16+.

Remarks: The secret of this unique place is undoubtedly out, as the gap continues to narrow between its local reputation – a country club for kids – and the experience of those on the inside – it's possible to achieve high standards without being tense and worried about doing it. The challenge will be how the school manages to maintain that ethos, as competition to experience such a delightful way to learn and grow becomes ever more fierce.

Holy Cross Preparatory School

George Road, Kingston-upon-Thames, Surrey KT2 7NU

Tel: 020 8942 0729

Independent • Pupils: 285 • Ages: 4–11 • RC • Fees: £11,979 pa

Email: admissions@holycrossprep.com
Website: www.holycrossprepschool.co.uk

Headteacher: Since 2011 Sarah Hair BEd (40s). Joined the school in 2004; 'knows the school inside out,' say parents. She has spent time as a class teacher, maths and English coordinator at a previous school then director of learning at Holy Cross. Passionate about education and IT; she was one of the first teachers in the 80s to have a computer in her classroom. Teaches year 5 computing: amongst her many interests in new technologies is how IT can be used to support education today and in the future.

Married with three teenagers, one son and two daughters, she comes from a family of educationalists, a tradition she is keen to continue. Parents say she has a lively approach to school life and learning

and they all appreciate her bright and cheerful personality.

Entrance: Non-selective at 4+; priority to siblings and Roman Catholics, although the school welcomes all faiths. Prospective pupils attend an introductory morning. At 7+ children are invited to visit for the day where they are assessed for their suitability for the school. Admissions staff are friendly and helpful, occasional places do arise and a waiting list is kept for interested families.

Exit: Girls move onto a wide variety of secondary schools eg Lady Eleanor Holles, Wimbledon High, Surbiton High, Kingston Grammar or top girls boarding schools eg St Mary's, Ascot, Benenden,

Wycombe Abbey and Woldingham. A few to local state grammars and Holy Cross Senior.

Remarks: Whilst Holy Cross is not overly selective they achieve excellent results for all pupils. Well planned and thoughtful curriculum ensures high standards, so giving pupils the chance to cherry pick when it comes to choosing a secondary school. Reasoning is part of the core curriculum from year 3. Maximum class size is 22 and all classes have fully trained, high-level assistant teachers. Fantastic grounding in maths, English and IT, say parents. Specially structured English scheme used across the age groups, with a big emphasis on developing good essay writing techniques mixed with lots of speaking and listening tasks. This starts early, with even the youngest members developing the confidence to be able to stand up and address their classmates on a number of topics and share any special skills they may have.

There are four separate small teaching rooms for pupils needing individual support from the SENCo, and EAL is available as required. Drama and IT are linked to other subjects, helping to keep learning relevant and to encourage creativity. Well-resourced art and design rooms where pupils can engage with all types of media, much of which is elegantly displayed around the school. Impressive collections of pottery; the girls also benefit from having DT days, enabling them to plan, design and complete their projects as a whole. Science room full of active little girls in their goggles, with interesting experiments taking place and a specially designed area for baking and cookery clubs.

The old coach house is now the IT suite where pupils build websites and learn programming skills. The school has designed its own app for communicating with parents, and parents can contact teachers at any time.

Science room full of active little girls in their goggles, with interesting experiments taking place and a specially designed area for baking and cookery clubs

Music is a serious subject with a full-time teacher coordinating and 13 visiting teachers, Early years classes learn recorder, then in year 3 everyone learns a brass instrument. Pupils are taught to read and compose their own music, and many go on to do exceptionally well, joining national youth orchestras and choirs.

The huge outdoor spaces offer lots of different play areas and all sports take place on site.

Sister Ursula, the last remaining nun, has had a long influence, teaching pottery and running the Welcome Room where parents and children drink her tasty cocoa

Ample courts, three rounders pitches and own athletics track. Sports facilities are also used by other schools, for community activities and charity events. Pupils are keen participants in Surrey schools sports tournaments. Younger children have their own outdoor classroom and garden where they grow vegetables, harvest them and then learn how to turn them into soup.

Lovely Victorian buildings nestle comfortably next to modern additions; the new multi-function halls are cleverly built into the hillside so as not to lose any of the gardens. Unique setting for a school bordering London: eight glorious acres of well-tended grounds with views out to Epsom Downs, situated in a historical estate that once belonged to the crown and is now part of the pricey Coombe Estate. The house was once occupied by John Galsworthy, author of the Forsyte Saga; in 1971 the sisters of Holy Cross purchased the buildings for a school. Still retains many original features including beautiful stained-glass windows and a wood panelled library.

Warmth and the quality of relationships remain at the heart of the school and the well-established pastoral care system. Sister Ursula, the last remaining nun, has had a long influence on the school, teaching pottery and running the Welcome Room where parents and children come to drink her tasty cocoa and chat. New school council has recently evolved to give the girls a voice in the day-to-day running of the school and discuss the all-important issues of new play equipment and lunch menus. Girls are elected as officers, with each class providing two representatives; all very democratic. School council chooses charities to support, the girls run a number of enterprising fundraising events themselves, and they have an ongoing link with Build Africa. Parents are unanimous about the positive effects of the school's pastoral ethos. One parent told of the kindness shown to her daughter when she first arrived, making the transition to a new school so comfortable. Wednesdays are homework free to ensure that girls have time to visit friends and pursue outside interests.

A school that shines for its holistic, inclusive and caring approach mixed with academic rigour. Continues to be a fine example of 21st century education, and provides a wonderful start in life.

The Holy Cross School

25 Sandal Road, New Malden, Surrey KT3 5AR

State • Pupils: 940 • Ages: 11–18 • Sixth form pupils: 200 of 410 (federated with Richard Challoner) • RC

Tel: 020 8395 4225

Email: hxs@holycross.kingston.sch.uk
Website: www.holycross.kingston.sch.uk

6

Headteacher: Since 2001, Mr Tom Gibson MEd NPQH BSc DipEd (40s). Educated Wimbledon College, read physical education and sports science at Loughborough University. Previously taught at St Joseph's, Beulah Hill, Glyn ADT and St Gregory's, Kenton. Married to a fellow teacher, four children. Well-experienced in different areas of education, a pleasant, unassuming gentleman who has brightened all horizons.

Academic matters: A mostly long-serving, committed staff of all age groups delivers an 'innovative curriculum' and the 'quality of teaching and learning is outstanding' (Ofsted). Class sizes are around 30. A level results improving (54 per cent A*-B in 2015; 22 per cent A*/A) and with a high level of value-added. At GCCE in 2015, 85 per cent of pupils got 5+ A*-C grades including English and maths, and 43 per cent of GCSEs were A*/A. Specialist science status has enabled the school to develop its provision in science, maths and ICT. Independent working habits are encouraged. A £5.4 million building project has provided excellent facilities for drama, music, science and IT. New-ish sports hall and dance studio. The sixth form is in partnership with a local boys' school, enabling them to offer a wider choice of subjects – much appreciated by pupils and parents. SEN and EAL are catered for by specialist teachers throughout the school.

Games, options, the arts: Two garret-style studios provide an inspiring setting for art and DT. A hard-working music teacher is making new waves with the orchestra in an impressive music suite, and individual instrumental tuition on most instruments can be arranged. The school trains year 10 as Wimbledon ball girls. Creative drama department in purpose-built drama facilities is growing – many do GCSE. Duke of Edinburgh Award Scheme along with an extensive selection of after-school clubs, including astronomy and young engineers.

Foreign language exchanges to France and Spain plus opportunities such as working in orphanage in Thailand, trips to Lourdes, skiing, year 7 camping trip and a music tour to Europe.

Background and atmosphere: The Sisters of the Holy Cross founded the school in 1931. It became grant maintained in 1993 and in 1999 became a voluntary aided school within the diocese of Southwark. The original buildings have been much added to and updated. Caring and moral values help deliver a smooth, organised atmosphere. Whilst Roman Catholicism predominates, all other faiths are welcomed. Pupils are encouraged to be involved in the community through voluntary work.

Pastoral care and discipline: Sensible school rules – girls are expected to be mature and aware of others' needs; all have form tutors. Strict uniform code – girls ticked off if not properly dressed. Sixth form pupils expected to be self-disciplined and present themselves well.

Pupils and parents: Good ethnic mix; 90 per cent are Catholics. 'We are from all walks of life here, professionals to refugees; most are somewhere in the middle.' The common interest is a well-balanced and Christian education. Serious PFA.

Entrance: Pupils come from a wide catchment area. First preference to practising Catholics. Applications from girls of other faiths are welcomed, as well as from any girls whose families are in sympathy with the school's Catholic ethos. From September 2016, 150 year 7 places. Year 6 girls with accepted offers are tested to determine streaming.

Exit: Currently 85 per cent of students move on to the federated sixth form, with 15 per cent moving to local colleges and a small number to the world of work.

Remarks: With a young and dedicated head, a school for parents to watch develop. Ofsted stated that Holy Cross 'is an outstanding school. Christian values and concern for others are at the heart of its work.'

King's College Junior School (Wimbledon)

Linked school: King's College School (Wimbledon), 203

Southside, Wimbledon Common, , London SW19 4TT

Independent • Pupils: 465 • Ages: 7–13 • C of E • Fees: up to £17,850 pa

Tel: 020 8255 5335

Email: jsadmissions@kcs.org.uk
Website: www.kcs.org.uk

17

Headmaster: Since 2006, Dr Gerard Silverlock (50s), affable, articulate and clever; despite having spent most of his career as a senior historian in senior schools (Millfield et al), a natural prep school head. Did his PhD on European disarmament 1918-25. Previously head of Aberdour in Banstead. Has four children of his own and is clearly held in much affection by his charges, who follow him about, demanding he sign their commended work, and seem determined that they – and not we, on our visit – are what matters. With which we entirely agree. Parents say he's 'approachable and easy to get on with'.

Entrance: English, maths and reasoning tests and all 7+ and 8+ candidates are interviewed. Beyond that, those 'whose performance in the written papers suggests that they could benefit from the education which we offer' are seen. 'Our boys are bright. We are highly selective,' says Dr Silverlock – anything up to 10 applicants per place at 11+ (this is being phased out in 2016), with entries also at 7+, 8+, 9+ and 10+ – 'but we are not a hothouse.' With this level of aptitude, they would have no need to be. No automatic acceptance of brothers. The school also maintains two local pre-preps – The

Squirrels and the Rowans – though entrance to the KCJS is not automatic from these. Scholarships on offer from 11+, awarded to those who excel in the entrance tests. Means-tested bursaries up to 100 per cent of fees if the boy is outstanding and the parents are broke. Home visits, of course.

Exit: Mostly to the senior school via The King's transfer exam in year 8 – around 90 boys go up. A few who would not thrive there are given plenty of warning and helped to find a nook elsewhere. Four in the last 13 years, which isn't much. 'When a boy is offered a place at any age, our expectation is that he will be here until he is 18'.

Remarks: Physically attached to the main school, though also with a building or two of its own, the junior school shares facilities with the senior school and is integral to it. The two main buildings – one for the youngest boys, Rushmere, and Priory for the older boys – are in themselves worthy of note. Rushmere, formerly the home of sculptor, David Wynne, is a beautiful Georgian house with lovely decorative features and makes a surprisingly appropriate school for small boys. The younger boys are taught,14 to a class, in the former bedrooms en

Held in much affection by his charges, who follow him about, demanding he sign their commended work

haut and the older ones, 22 to a class, in the drawing and dining rooms en bas. Thence to Priory in classes of 18-24. All rooms are well-lit, well-aired and have good displays. We liked the junior forum board which asked 'have you got ideas for improving life at KCJS?' and felt this was typical of a school which encourages its denizens to think, express themselves and enjoy school. And the achievements here are notable, among them winning for the three years prior to our visit the prestigious Townsend-Warner History Prize.

The boys we saw were smiling, bright-faced and relaxed with, seemingly, an easy relationship with their attendant adults. Clearly, much satisfaction derived from a special relationship with the primary school they support in Obera, Kenya, and we were moved by a modest description of just what that means in practice – both ways. This, plus the 1st XI cricket team's raising of over £50,000 for the Nelson Mandela Children's Fund, as a part of their South African touring activities, and the outreach programme, Junior Aspirations, involving teaching support for able boys and girls from state primaries, makes for a healthy interaction with the real world outside, which can only be good.

Junior school parents are grateful and unanimous. 'It's fabulous'; 'Almost without exception the teachers are amazingly inspirational'; 'I wish I'd had this sort of education'; 'The sports are good, but my two boys are very different and it doesn't matter if you're not sporty – a lot of attention is given to music: boys are encouraged to develop their own groups'; 'It's been fantastic'.

King's College School (Wimbledon)

Linked school: King's College Junior School (Wimbledon), 202

Southside, London SW19 4TT

Tel: 020 8255 5300

18

Independent • Pupils: 859
• Ages: 13–18 (will admit 11 year olds from 2016) • Sixth form pupils: 397 (96 girls) • Fees: £19,830 pa

Email: admissions@kcs.org.uk
Website: www.kcs.org.uk

Head Master: Since 2008, Mr Andrew Halls MA (50s), previously head of Magdalen College School, Oxford, prior to which he was deputy at Trinity in Croydon and head of English at Bristol Grammar School. An impeccable trajectory. All preceded by a Cambridge double first in English, which is always encouraging. When you meet him you can see how well it fits him. Spare and fine-featured, quietly-spoken, assiduous and gently donnish without any of the waspishness that can accompany the brilliance – he is 'the compleat headmaster'. He is driven by the soundest of educational values. Hence his preparedness to modernise and innovate, even if the owners of tender toes squeal a bit, and hence his willingness to fight on behalf of pupils if he thinks any injustice has been done to them in public exams. A man of high principle and warm enthusiasms, especially for the partnership programmes undertaken by his school, real partnerships with local, national and international communities. You sense that the initiatives all schools need to take to maintain their charitable status are undertaken here from genuine conviction and principle, not just expediency.

Married to a fellow teacher, Mr Halls has two daughters. He is deeply proud of the school he inherited and to which he is devoted, and he pays tribute especially to his 'generous' staff and the generosity of spirit he finds in the school as a whole. He was a precociously young head when appointed to his first headship, to which he brought energy, vision and courage. Now, he is a wise and experienced leader – one who, seemingly, leads discreetly rather than with PR as his priority. The only parental criticism we heard of him was that they didn't know him or see him much. But one suspects he is discreetly everywhere. No questioning his quiet, dedicated authority and the clear assuredness of his vision. An exemplary head.

Academic matters: King's – or KCS as it is as often known – used to offer only the International Baccalaureate, but reintroduced A levels in 2013, citing the A* grade as a way of recognising exceptional performance. Mr Halls takes a balanced view and, though convinced of the IB's worth and breadth, is no blinkered zealot. Consistently excellent IB results. In 2015, the co-ed sixth form pupils averaged 41 points out of 45. At A level in 2015, 76 per cent A*/A (39 per cent A*).

League tables of results can be read any number of ways, but the Daily Telegraph – when gauging success in A level, IB and pre-U results all together placed King's as the third highest ranking sixth form in the UK in 2014. The IB has been seen as a great draw for those who enter at 16 but as a mixed blessing by others. One long-serving parent – who was full of praise for the school – said: 'I sent my boys there despite the IB rather than because of it.' Another told us: 'We think it's fantastic and most can manage it, but it isn't for everyone'. However if you take it on, you can be assured that you will be taught it here as well as it can be taught, it will flex to support your weaker areas and challenge your strengths as they should be challenged. 'The IB is so much work – I don't dare tell my friends at my old school – but I do even more extracurricular stuff because we are all so busy all the time. I didn't know I could do so much,' enthused one girl.

At GCSE – most now take IGCSEs – 97 per cent of grades were A*/A in 2015. A number take 10 or more, often adding a new language in year 11 – Russian or Italian. Most also take additional maths GCSE. No weak areas. Penny numbers of B grades in most subjects and virtually no Cs in anything. At all levels, the range of options is impressive. At IGCSE, pupils have choice of six mainstream languages; individuals also catered for – around 80 have English as an EAL. We enjoyed the notices on language room doors – eg 'Chiudere la porta!' Parents and pupils full of praise – 'The teaching is fantastic and the classes are very small. My sons have an

excellent bantering, relationship with their teachers – it gets even better as they go up the school'. Excellent academic library with displays changed

---

Vast, classic Great Hall with organ, WWII commemorative tablet, gothic window and splendid beamed ceiling – all as Hogwarts as you could wish

weekly plus private study reading room.

Around 10 per cent have some kind of SEN, though none with statements – mild dyslexics/dyspraxics by no means in the majority in this cohort: motor skills difficulties, emotional and communication problems and the more severe dyses all taken on and supported individually in class or via withdrawal, as needed.

Games, options, the arts: Powerful and impressive on all fronts and the advent of sixth form girls has given them an extra edge. A bit of a sporting breeding ground – in team and individual achievement they figure prominently in many activities, most notably perhaps in tennis, rowing, rugby, athletics and football. New sports pavilion; on-site sports hall, pool, courts (recently refurbished) and pitches and additional 'fantastic' facilities in West Barnes Lane. Opportunities for travel include D of E, endless sports camps, languages trips and exchanges, history, geography and classics visits – nothing

obviously OTT and unnecessarily spoiling for the over-privileged. Excellent list of outside speakers/visitors brings the great outside and its challenges into school, eg Prof Sir Lawrence Freedman (think war studies and the Chilcot Commission), Mike Atherton, Simon Russell Beale, Carol Ann Duffy and Andrew (Churchill) Roberts all popping in.

Music, art and drama really exceptional. We found the art unusually expressive and free – especially rare in what is predominantly a boys' school – and felt quite exhilarated by the wit and life in what we saw in many media. We quite liked the fact that it was a bit messy too. Drama is legendary. The school takes shows to Edinburgh and sells out. Beautifully staged shows in the main theatre and little ones in the drama studio. Music likewise – housed, as so often, in less than shiny accommodation, but producing outstanding performances and performers in many genres. Chamber orchestra tour to Spain, concerts in St John's Smith Square and St James Piccadilly, The Cadogan Hall and St Paul's Cathedral. Debating and many other activities offer far more than your average teenager could do in twice the number of school years he has.

Much made of the school's partnerships with local state primaries and seniors. Sixth formers teach Latin at one and football at another; lively participation in the 'aspirations' programme, designed to help less privileged children raise their sights.

Background and atmosphere: Founded in 1829 as a junior branch of King's College, London – hence various ties still extant, eg the shared school and College colours. The move to Wimbledon was made to accommodate more boys – just over 200 – and 1911 saw the school being granted its independence. Junior school opened in 1912 and since then the school has grown and flourished abundantly. Its history – we visited in its anniversary year – is proudly, though not in-yer-facedly, celebrated in displays around the school, and most interesting it is too. Controversially, the sixth form has admitted girls since 2010 – not controversially inside the school (it seems an unqualified good thing) but clearly, the hard-working local and less local girls' schools are less than thrilled. The boys are converts. 'We were very excited at the idea of the girls coming – it was a bit awkward at first but everyone has come together now'.

The school faces a quiet corner of Wimbledon Common; the main building is solid, Victorian red-brick. We often describe a school's setting as 'leafy' – this is about as leafy as a top London senior school can get. Its neighbours are the imposing detached houses of the very prosperous and the more modest 18th century terraces and pub which still evoke a villagey feel. Behind the main building, the extent of the school surprises. Many later buildings – mostly functional rather than architecturally glorious,

but the site overall is a pleasure to encounter. Vast, classic Great Hall with organ, WWII commemorative tablet, gothic window and splendid beamed ceiling – all as Hogwarts as you could wish. One-storey wooden music practice block – 'It arrived on a lorry and they just planted it there – quite surprising!' Most subjects in their own blocks or corridors. Good displays in most areas – we liked the maxims, eg 'Forgetfulness is the parent of poverty', which stimulate thinking, though we were told that some displays hang about rather too long. Wind turbine and solar panels contribute some power. Courtyards, much attractive brick paving, sculpture – notably that which marks the school's adoption of the IB with all its internationalism (Japanese stone lantern, African stone and wood pieces, Chinese lions etc) – and clever and well-tended planting make for a relaxed and pleasant place.

First stage of a major development and refurbishment programme has been completed with the renovation of the Great Hall entrance. Work now under way on a classroom block, quad, music school and additional sporting provision.

Pastoral care and discipline: House system valued and relished by most. Also tutor groups, in which a pupil remains for his entire school life. System makes for a sense of security and consistency and ensures that you are known – valuable when it comes to UCAS forms. Parents praise the supportive atmosphere. 'It's been very good for my boys, who are all very different,' we were told. Although 'the success of the system depends entirely on the tutor – we've been very lucky, but it's not been so for everyone'. Some parents of boys who enter at 13 feel more could have been done to integrate their sons and help them make friends, but this has now been addressed by the appointment of a 'brilliant' head of middle school, a long-serving head of house who has 'transformed' their integration. Much parental praise for general school organisation, home-school communications and school's skill in picking up problems. `They're usually onto it before you are,' we were told. 'If you get there early – at 7am – the car park is full of staff cars. They put in a huge amount of extra effort.'

School officers chosen via application, election and interview – the positions are coveted and hugely prized. Counselling service and chaplain to pick up birds with broken wings, but it seldom gets that far. Separate faith assemblies once a week. Smart plain suits and shirts for the sixth allow for some individual expression and no-one looks like a clone. Vast sixth form common room with TV, all-day coffee bar and a range of seating from the upright, austere I'm-here-to-work kind to the flop-on-a-sofa-just-leave-me-for-a-bit kind. Large dining room serves wide choice highly appetising food which almost all eat – staff and pupils ensemble.

The girls we spoke to were incredibly happy and none seemed to regret their move. 'We're much more modern – we feel more grown-up here,' was the consensus, but then of course, they didn't stay at their previous schools to experience the sixth

> *None seemed to regret their move. 'We're much more modern – we feel more grown-up here,' was the consensus*

form there, did they? They positively relish the house system – 'It was a joke in my old school' – and are wowed by the 'team spirit'. Perhaps a lesson for the girls' schools here, many of which cling to the idea that houses and team spirit are somehow olde worlde and passé (as indeed, they once were).

Pupils and parents: A real mix, as you'd expect: academic and professional parents alongside first generation immigrants with bright offspring on bursaries. Common denominator is brains and enthusiasm and they come from a very wide area. Good range of bus services means you don't have to grind through the traffic. Impressively eclectic list of former pupils (OKs) includes Sabine Baring-Gould (wrote Onward Christian Soldiers), Dante Gabriel Rossetti, philologists Sweet and Skeat, Robert Graves, composer Robin Holloway, traitor William Joyce, the Beeb's Alvar Liddell, Roy Plomley and Mark Urban, actor Ben Barnes, musician Marcus Mumford and no fewer than five VCs.

Entrance: Now has entry points at 11 and 13 (though junior school still goes up to 13). Registration deadline end of September of year 6 for 13+ and mid-November for 11+. Same tests in maths, English and reasoning in January for both, with best performers interviewed. Those offered 11+ places (around 40-44) do not take any further entrance exams; 13+ places (about 35) are subject to CE results or King's own scholarship exam. Most 13+ entrants – around 80 – come up from the junior school.

At 16+ they admit girls – 'very, very clever girls,' an admiring mother of boys told us – from a range of girls' schools, though predominantly Putney and Wimbledon HSs, usually attracted by the IB, or from Godolphin & Latymer, which does the IB but for a far smaller cohort. All 16+ applicants take tests in English, maths and a general paper and then have four interviews. The vast majority taken at this stage are girls, reflecting the greater number of applicants as well as their performance in the assessments. Roughly four applicants per place.

Exit: A few leave post-GCSE, often in pursuit of A levels (likely to become even fewer in future). The rest stay on and leave for the top universities – 53 Oxbridge offers in 2015; the rest to London University colleges or heavyweight provincials, eg Durham and Bristol, to do traditional subjects. Increasing numbers heading across the pond.

Money matters: Good range of scholarships and bursaries considering that, unlike the ancient foundations not so far away, this is not an endowed school. Increasingly, here as elsewhere, money being diverted into means-tested bursaries to attract the bright but broke. Well worth enquiring

– up to 100 per cent fee remission possible in certain cases.

Remarks: It makes every kind of sense to get in early – the competition for places at 13+ and now 11+ being so tight. By any standards a top school offering an exceptional education under a notable head.

King's House School

68 King's Road, Richmond, Surrey TW10 6ES

Independent • Pupils: 450 • Ages: 3–13 • Fees: up to £14,910 pa

Tel: 020 8940 1878

Email: schooloffice@kingshouseschool.org
Website: www.kingshouseschool.org

25

Headmaster: Since 2011, Mark Turner BA PGCE NPQH (40s). Studied French and Spanish at Bristol before training at Sandhurst with six years in the army. After leaving, taught at Merchant Taylors' before joining Durston House, Ealing where he was deputy head for nine years. Married with four children, two of whom are at the school. Feels he is lucky to have taken over such a good, friendly, and mainly local school. Says it has a strong sense of community and provides a broad education. Parents like the fact that he teaches French to year 4, thereby getting to know the senior boys and say he's 'very approachable' and 'a classic boys' prep school headmaster'. Feel that he has made the school gentler. One of his aims is to unite the three

sections of the school: at the moment they feel like separate entities. To that end, he spends more time in the junior section than his predecessor, which can't be a bad thing.

Entrance: From the term they turn 3, boys and girls at nursery level. Then reception, boys only, September after 4th birthday. No testing, places offered a year before entry in order of registration. Siblings take priority. A few more places at 7+ and 8+ subject to passing entrance test. Occasionally places occur at other times, each individually assessed. Mainly families from surrounding areas including Roehampton, Kingston and Barnes. Buses run from Chiswick and Putney.

Exit: A handful at 11+, trying to beat the rush, but the school does not give this much support. About two-thirds to boys' only London day schools at 13+ with St Paul's, King's College Wimbledon and Hampton all high on the list. Big range of boarding schools, with Bradfield, Charterhouse, Epsom, Eton, Winchester and Harrow amongst the current favourites. Several scholarships, both music and academic, most years.

Remarks: On three sites in leafy Richmond. Seems a happy, hard-working school. We were taken round by two delightful, polite and enthusiastic senior boys under the eagle eye of the school's marketing manager – we were certainly given the spiel!

Large nursery building on two floors. Huge, bright rooms with different areas for learning and play. Plenty of constructive fun to be had by eager under-4s, both boys and girls. Parents love it – one even said 'flawless'. Two outdoor playgrounds, one for physical play, one for creative/imaginative play. They think of everything these days. Send your children here and your sons get automatic entry to the junior school. Your daughters? They seem mainly to head off to the Old Vicarage.

The junior school – reception to year 3 – is just across the road from the senior. Two reception classrooms on the ground floor have their own outdoor play areas where all is still reasonably relaxed. It may only be the beginning of learning but they are definitely being prepared for the next stage; homework starts straight away. Writing practice first, then, when they are ready, reading. Only 10 minutes at a time but it's still homework for 4 year olds.

The rest of this rather rambling house contains two year 1 classes and three each for years 2 and 3. Average class size about 20. All have a classroom assistant as well as a fully trained teacher. It is at

It may be only the beginning of learning but they are definitely being prepared for the next stage; homework starts straight away

this point that the serious learning begins. More work, less play. Classrooms are not enormous but they are bright and buzzing. All the boys appeared happy and attentive. Space is at a premium, the library fills in a corridor and a piano lesson seemed to be going on in a passageway. The IT room contained a lot of slightly restless boys learning computer basics. But, no worry, there is plenty of room for burning energy outside in the big playground which, cleverly, has a partially covered area. Parents full of praise for Mr Gower, head of juniors, who they say is extremely approachable and quick to answer emails. He's usually there to welcome boys in the morning. Also, we were told, all children love Nurse Jo who cures all their woes.

In year 4 they move across to the senior school where they can take advantage of some bang up-to-do date facilities, of which our guides were rightly proud, and the real pressure goes on. Initially all classes are mixed ability and, apart from those subjects needing special equipment, are classroom based. In year 5 they begin to build up towards the common entrance syllabus and are setted in English and maths. Two science labs; DT and art rooms; two computer rooms including a suite of Macs for composing and design; a music room; a theatre where, our young guides boasted, amazing productions are put on; and a well-equipped music room. Parents say 'music used to be one of their weaknesses but is now one of their greatest strengths'. These are lucky boys.

There's plenty of outdoor playing space as well, for organised and free play, that area having been completely re-vamped recently. Parents say it's a 'shame there's not wider extracurricular'; 'there could be more broader based after school clubs'. We got the feeling that the emphasis is mainly on the curriculum, with the pressure to succeed being the be all and end all. A 21st century London problem? Or just a lack of understanding that there is more to life than passing exams? The head comments: 'We believe the breadth and balance of our curriculum is a strength and is far from being too focused on the academic. We also feel that while some schools reduce art, DT, drama and ICT to carousel lessons, we still give them regular lesson time up to year 8.'

We didn't see the 35 acre sports ground as it is a coach ride away in Chiswick, but we have seen a DVD and it looks pretty impressive. Senior boys go there twice a week and junior boys once. Rugby, football and cricket all played competitively – 25 rugby, 34 football and 20 cricket teams. Wow! And they have silverware to prove their prowess (including Prep Schools Rugby Nationals U13 winners). Tennis, swimming and athletics also figure. Astroturf area within the senior school grounds and a well-equipped gymnasium ensure plenty of PE.

Inevitably, in a non-selective school, there is a wide variation in ability but, parents tell us, lots of help in the junior school who are 'quick to pick up struggling children and help them so they don't get left behind'. Continual monitoring, boys needing specific help are given it free of charge – 'we give them the building blocks' – being taken out of class for an hour at a time. Free, individualised education programmes provided.

Strict code of behaviour both in and out of the classroom, weekly PHSE sessions and a pupil teacher ratio of approximately 12:1 ensure that the majority of problems are caught quickly. House and tutor systems also provide continuous monitoring. Parents say, 'communication lines excellent and emails responded to quickly'; 'quick to pick up on problems and good at keeping on top of them'.

Communication certainly seems to be a great strength; no parent could say they are not kept fully up to date. From the headmaster's termly letter to the weekly school newsletters, everything is covered. Information on matches, charities and school trips, contributions from teachers, prizes and praises – it's all there. An active and busy school.

Kingston Grammar School

London Road, Kingston Upon Thames, Surrey KT2 6PY

Independent • Pupils: 815 • Ages: 11–18 • Sixth form pupils: 230 • Fees: £17,430 pa

Tel: 020 8546 5875

Email: registrar@kgs.org.uk
Website: www.kgs.org.uk

Head Master: Since September 2014, Mr Stephen Lehec, previously head of Aylesbury Grammar School. He joined Aylesbury as deputy head from Maidstone Grammar in 2006, becoming head in 2008. He has a history and English degree from Southampton and a PGCE from Oxford. He is a keen football, cricket and tennis player, and has coached teams up to county level.

Academic matters: Now does IGCSEs in maths, English, sciences and languages. No Pre-U yet,

though under consideration as an alternative to A levels. Maths is popular at both levels and results are outstanding – pupils praise the brilliant teaching, and even those who say they aren't mathematical find it hard to resist. Eng lit, physics, biology and history also star. Smaller take-up in langs despite good teaching. Department currently musters 14 languages. Greek taught in collaboration with Tiffin Boys. In 2015, 58 per cent A*/A grades and 88 per cent A*/B at A level across the subjects; 78 per cent A*/A grades at GCSE. No great surprises in the curriculum, though sports studies and theatre studies offered at A level. A few pupils yearn for cookery. IT seen as a tool, not an end in itself – all sixth formers take the European Driving Licence.

Learning support department helps those on the dys strata, mostly mild, a few moderate. Learner profile compiled for all children seen by ed psych or specialist teacher – school a great believer in constant monitoring and tracking to ensure progress. Site pretty accessible and school will put itself out to support mobility if needed. Lots of laptop users and open to those with aural/visual impairment – 'so long as they can cope with the site'.

Impressively stocked library, actually called 'the library', not 'the resources centre'. And books actually used – most reassuring. Pupils praise their teachers and librarian unreservedly – 'They will always run extension classes if you ask'; 'They'll order anything in for us'. Parents praise the academic ethos – 'It's not pushy, but they do get the results'; 'They really encourage them to think for themselves'; 'They're quick to pick up on people's talents and nurture them – even talents the children didn't know they had'.

Games, options, the arts: The extracurricular opportunities here are seemingly limitless or, at any rate, fill a 40-page booklet. In an area full of good schools – and some of them are free – this is what gives Kingston the edge and makes it the first choice even for those whose children are super-bright and might well gain a place at a local grammar. Half a dozen activities pre-school, a dozen or more in the lunch break and a further dozen after school make for a busy, busy life.

Pupils we spoke to said they stay after school every day – though this, of course, not true of everyone. Loads of trips (local, national and

international), an excellent programme of outside speakers and an expanding sports programme ('one of our newish teachers, an ex-army officer, thinks anything is possible') which includes girls' football, now countering erstwhile grumbles of sport being only for the best. Netball no longer a poor relation but zooming. Boathouse on the Thames provides rowing option – 'It's huge!' we were told. CCF very popular with the first year's cohort, tails off thereafter, though masses of opportunities for RAF flying, summer camps (very popular) and some get scholarships to Sandhurst at the end.

Expanding sports programme ('one of our newish teachers, an ex-army officer, thinks anything is possible') which includes girls' football

The Cage (two on site courts with soft surfaces) due for upgrade, but most sport takes place on the Fairfield – a field behind the main site – or off-site at Ditton Fields, a bus ride away. New stress on community service to people, locally and beyond, less fortunate than themselves. Older pupils admit 'it's a bit of an eye-opener' for those who had, hitherto, looked inwards rather than outwards.

Music acknowledged to be outstanding. Music tech new and burgeoning – already growing out of space – but trad music also supported, though small academic uptake. 'We want music that will appeal to everyone but which has a high class end.' Drama, well-housed in excellent, flexible and well-equipped performing arts centre, produces classy shows, including annual Shakespeare festival and real plays – good to see something other than High School Musical and Grease for once. House drama, Ad Lib and annual dance fest much enthused over, even by boys.

Art and DT are exceptional – masses of workshop/studio space and we drooled over brilliantly conceived and executed mini-dresses made from sweet papers or exquisitely embroidered canvas. Professional quality furniture made by GCSE class, perspex clocks and clever ceramics make you want to get your hands gummy. Previously blank walls now acting as showcases for pupil work – a welcome and humanising change. The list of national awards, prizes and achievements across the extracurricular spectrum fills several pages.

Background and atmosphere: In the midst of Kingston's tarmac tangle, it's fine if you know your way but, if you don't, leave an hour or so to locate it and then park – no parking on site and even the staff have an efficient system of sharing lifts and spaces. The school itself looks like a real old-fashioned grammar on the outside – solid, brick-built and purposeful –though, once you get inside, the modernisation and bright, light spaces change one's initial impression. The trad grammar style persists in the school hall from your parents' childhood, with honours boards, memorial tablets to those who fell in the two wars and faint echoes of 'Praise my soul the King of heaven' lurking in the curtains. Space is certainly not lavish here, though the school is less cramped than some of its central London peers.

Pupils wear white shirts and black or grey uniforms – they look sensible and tidy. 'They have really cracked down on very short skirts – they want everyone to look smart. It's made a huge difference,' we were told by one rather elegant sixth former. About half the school eats school lunches, acknowledged to be much improved and gaining support (it looked good to us) and lots of choice. The place feels relaxed and welcoming. Pupils like the house system, which enables friendships between the years – 'we feel far more like a real community now'. Good café for sixth form – into which staff also pop ('It's OK – they don't come in in large numbers') – with TV, stereo system, drinks and snacks. Good home/school IT links. Email used all the time now, we were told. The most appallingly ear-lacerating school bell we have ever heard.

Pastoral care and discipline: Good system of heads of year and form tutors – 'they get to know you really well' – but discipline scarcely an issue here. 'They're really hot on bullying,' we were told; 'they've always got time to talk to you if you've got something you need to sort out'. Misconduct marks, summons to head of year, rare Saturday detentions generally all that's needed. No smoking, drink or drugs problems that anyone can recall. 'The pastoral care is extremely good,' a parent told

us. 'They're quick to pick up problems and keep parents in touch. It's in the culture of the place.'

Pupils and parents: From only around a three mile radius, so they probably know how to navigate Kingston's surreal road system. From over 150 primaries – some 65 per cent from state schools.

Notable former pupils include Edward Gibbon (The Roman Empire one), Michael Frayn, Jonathan Kenworthy, James Cracknell, Neil Fox, Andy Sturgeon (imaginatively roped in to help with the reshaping of the school's landscape) and 2012 Olympic gold medal rower Sophie Hosking.

Entrance: The main entry points are 11+ and 16+ with some spaces available for 13+ entry. An option to sit a 10+ deferred entry examination in year 5 to secure a place in year 7. More or less equal number of boys and girls arrived at through merit, not engineering. Interview seen as important, 'We are not academically exclusive in our selection – we look for potential'. School works closely with the feeder schools – especially at 13+ so as to not to encourage unrealistic applications. 'We don't believe in disappointing people'.

Exit: They spread over the country. Destinations include Nottingham, Bristol, Birmingham, Exeter, Manchester, London, Warwick – and a few to art school. Annual sprinkling to Oxbridge – seven in 2015. Biggest range of courses you could imagine.

Money matters: Scholarships worth 10 or 20 per cent of fees available at all entry points and awarded on results of tests. Bursaries worth up to 100 per cent of fees also at all entry points and means-tested. Worth a serious look if you are local, clever and strapped.

Remarks: Great school, great future.

Latchmere School

Latchmere Road, Kingston Upon Thames, Surrey KT2 5TT

State • Pupils: 879 • Ages: 3–11

Tel: 020 8546 7181

Email: office@latchmereschool.org
Website: latchmereschool.org

8

Headteacher: Since 2008, Mrs Julie Ritchie, CertEd BPhilEd MSI SIP (Special) (50s). Previously at St Matthew's C of E Primary School, where she was shortlisted for head of the year award. Qualifications (bucket-loads of them) include degree in multi-sensory impairment, a souvenir of decade-long post

in the 1990s as deputy headteacher at Dysart, a Surbiton-based special school.

Grew up in Grimsby, drawn to teaching from an early age – something of a family thing as a brother is also a head, though neither of her two grown up children has so far been bitten by the bug. Inspects for Ofsted, a heart-gladdening experience, though never fails to feel thrill of returning 'home' afterwards. Though she doesn't teach – she's at her desk by at 6.30am as it is, notching up 12-hour days – she's available to parents first and last thing and regularly consulted by staff too. 'I've got a lot of experience and they know that,' she says.

Gets to know pupils well – no mean feat given numbers – and parents are duly impressed. 'She made a point of saying how well my child had acquitted herself in a school production. I was quite taken aback as she is someone who could very easily be missed', comments one.

Smiley and effortlessly calm, head rarely raises her voice. 'This is a no-shouting school', she says, and indeed it's as quiet as they come. Short, sharp blasts of the school bell that periodically lash the air are the only sound to puncture the serenity (not to everyone's taste but necessary to minimise euphemistically termed 'time drift').

Makes no bones about need for exceptional staff to deliver the goods, tough old selection process identifying those who, like able pupils, enjoy being stretched and 'have the potential to be outstanding'. With many taking on load-bearing roles, they need to be. School's best practice managers, one to a year group, carry the can for quality of teaching and learning, and 'could be heads in their own right'. Within the next post or so, they often are. Numbers likely to be augmented as fast track trainees, appointed under government Schools Direct scheme, start to make their mark.

Professional to her fingertips, caring too, head sees parents as the ultimate experts. 'We know what the child presents in school but it's at home where they pour their hearts out. If we feel they're not functioning, parents are the ones who know'. Her biggest buzz comes from seeing 'children achieve what you wanted for them'. 'Pupils love her and have unbounded respect,' confirms a parent. And so they should.

Entrance: Very oversubscribed, with 500 applying for 120 reception places and not a hope for anyone living more than a kilometre away. Solid core of 'aspirational' parents, some Forces families (there's a nearby army base). All year round wraparound care a boon to working parents.

Looked after children have precedence, siblings (up to 50 a year) get second dibs. Only exception is eight-pupil Topaz unit where pupils may come from further away.

Virtual school tour will, hopes head, ensure that non-starters are gently discouraged online rather that getting taste of paradise during a face to face visit, only to have it whisked away again when logistics are explained.

Exit: Some to local independents eg Hampton, Surbiton High, with scholarships. A very few to Tiffin grammars (rarity down to ever increasing levels of competition, so over-subscribed that place hunting has become an extreme sport).

Majority to Grey Court School, Coombe Girls and Coombe Boys. Potentially all change with new secondary school opened September 2014 just a few hundred yards away.

Remarks: Author Jacqueline Wilson's primary (and much changed for the better, she reckoned,

What really rocks parents' boats is success with non-standard issue pupils. 'What counts is how good they are with the off the peg kids,' reckoned one mother

when she revisited). Opened in 1936, just in time for Second World War (nearby aircraft factory was regular bombing target). Infant school added a year later – dividing wall in place until 2007.

Large site with playgrounds generously bestowed means most year groups have a space they can call their own in addition to larger shared areas for infants and juniors. Substantial on-site asphalt legacy is greened up with trees and bushes, plus veg garden in small courtyard, together with reception-only delightful green run between knee-high rows of plants (like nursery, have own secure play area). Tactical introduction of soft surfaces underneath sturdy and attractive play equipment for older children also helps, while nearby shared playing fields are used for some clubs, junior games and sports day, now back to traditional competition-driven format and considered all the better for it.

Inside, plenty of space with large classrooms for all. Spares too, as though school is geared up for expansion to four-class entry, will take time to permeate every year group. Two schools into one means inevitable layout quirks, corridor-heavy design putting well-stocked library on the through route. Potential dinginess offset by lots of colour, particularly in nursery and reception areas where primary colours rule and some toilets have gone green (paint rather than eco flush). Assumes more monochrome hues as you go up through the school, though brightened with lots of little extras including giant paintbrushes strung across art room ceiling and boards, inside and out, crammed with enigmatic clay masks.

Reigning delight is flashy new building housing year 6 classrooms upstairs, lunch/sports hall on ground floor. Also used for Monday morning whole school assemblies, smaller hall taking year groups two by two on other days, and notable for impressive red and blue light up buttons (disappointingly measure air quality rather than summoning International Rescue).

Though fab new buildings help, what really rocks parents' boats is success with non-standard issue pupils. 'Schools can all do the straightforward ones', reckoned one mother. 'What counts is how good they are with the off the peg kids'. Latchmere aims (learning, local community, laughter, loyalty, love and leadership) are oft recited, children 'accepted for who they are' and inclusion, very dear to head's heart, a big, well resourced, thing.

Despite leafy setting (Richmond Park within easy reach), pupil make up has a grittier, urban feel than you might expect, with challenges to match, including a few with difficult home lives and nearly one in five with English as a second language.

Staff, average age 40, around a third male (average pupil to teacher ratio of just over 21 to one) are expected to get on together, and get on they do. No coasting, either. Jaw-droppingly efficient systems still have enough give for teaching talent to flourish outside the box. One teaching assistant, a professional actor, has leave of absence to go on tour in term time, in return lending talents to sky's the limit school productions.

Mantra is constant improvement. 'Whatever we do, I ask staff how we can do it better next time', says head. 'And because they're bright, I only have to ask them once'. Accolades roll in, Artsmark award in head's sights adding to quiverful that already includes Sing Up and Sportsmark awards (both pure gold).

Most recent success is designation as Teaching School (an eat your heart out award bestowed only on the whizziest of establishments). Confers membership of six-strong alliance who pool ideas and resources, a boon when it comes, amongst other things, to pitching for extra funds.

Range of needs includes specific learning difficulties, speech and language and behavioural,

emotional and social difficulties (BESD), while Topaz unit accommodates eight pupils with Asperger's, currently all KS2 but will extend to KS1, who join peers for some lessons, often with one-to-one support, but have separate base with own play area (small, nicely green, enclosed by no-nonsense fencing). Once identified (here, as elsewhere, some parents call in their own experts to speed up the diagnosis) support is unstinting, with nth degree differentiation in class taken as read. Pupil with memory and processing issues had checklist of stages to tick off on wipe clean board. 'Personalised it beautifully', thought mum.

Inspires 'very warm and fuzzy feelings' towards the school, said a parent, with size a plus point rather than drawback. Thirty-strong classes, bolstered with teaching assistant while nursery sessions (25 children in each) have two nursery nurses plus teacher. 'More people means more friends', felt a year 5 pupil, though in troubled times, 'there's a room you can go to if you're sad or lonely.' Felt, however, that some peer to peer disagreements are best resolved without teacher input. 'They can make it worse'.

Parents too, favour school over other highly regarded and smaller alternatives because of what one terms 'lack of prissiness'. Whereas artwork on display elsewhere was 'incredibly beautifully framed on the wall', only the best examples had made the final cut. Here, in contrast, it was 'messy, in a good

Popular blue room, shoe-free, carpet rich and decorated with skyscapes

way, with pictures from even the kids who couldn't draw'.

Resulting confidence is unmissable, pupils a winningly well mannered bunch, helped to become so by oft-stressed emphasis on social skills. Lunch for reception children is part of the curriculum, with big teacher input, emphasis on eye contact and handshaking, stressed through the school, ensuring the conversational niceties are a (nicely) observed feature of school life. 'Are you having a lovely day?' head was recently asked by pupil. Impressively, words 'self-control' were all it took to calm large group of pupils: here, it's viewed as innate rather than a skill to be learned and children live up to expectations.

Equally true of trips (year 5s just back from up to the neck mud in Ashdown Forest) and school clubs (including astrophysics and Techo DJ, both catering for the starry-eyed). School stresses that 'only exemplary behaviour will be tolerated' and sanctions are well understood. 'We have a consequences list. If we're too out of control, we get sent to the head', said a pupil.

Much more, however, in the way of encouragement, explanation and reflection, from popular blue room, shoe-free, carpet rich and decorated with skyscapes, to peer mediation and circle time. Very youngest join the debate, too, with 'brilliant' nursery head encouraging exploration of moral dilemmas, in one instance through medium of glove puppets.

Parents are also expected to do their bit – recent newsletter noting rise in pupil absences the week before half term. With current 'outstanding' status at risk if attendance plummets, nudge psychology designed to keep families onside seems to be working, thinks head.

Pupils tackle everything with gusto. Top perks include later lunch sittings and joy of second helpings for top two years (Portuguese chef's creative ways with assorted healthy options much admired, though occasional pizza and hot dogs days remain top favourites).

Responsibility also enjoyed from the off. Nursery children check themselves in online ('no need to be afraid of technology', reassures prospectus), while covetable posts for year 5 and 6 pupils include monitor who hands out free break-time snacks baked on the premises. Lessons are regarded with equal enthusiasm, consistency a big strength with two deputy heads stepping into the breach to cover staff absences. Teachers' approval counts. 'Oh, no, they'll be so disappointed in me', said reception pupil after mother threatened to expose mild cheekiness at drop off.

Relationships are excellent. 'I love all the teachers,' said year 5 girl. 'They're really kind and make lessons fun'. Even more so now, following introduction of creative curriculum, many months in the making and all the school's own work. Substantial ring-bound master plan so full of fizzing ideas that it probably glows in the dark.

Core subjects taught by class teachers, topped up by specialists for art, some sport, music and French (rapid progress made courtesy of native speaker means 'pupils are probably bored out of their minds when they get to secondary school', thought insider). Resulting variety is relished – diplomatically. 'Nice to have a change; not that you ever get bored with your teacher', said year 5 pupil.

Spritely lessons big on group or paired activity. 'Means you can share ideas or ask if you don't understand', said pupil. Recent highlights include 'Victorian' maths (everything in imperial measurements, dunce's cap for wrong answers); hands-on science, year 5s adding bicarbonate of soda to vinegar and inflating balloons ('we weren't meant to shake it but we did, anyway',) and drama-packed history lesson, with army trenches improvised from desks and teacher 'shouting' commands (though we're sure it wasn't very loudly).

Buzz, frequently mentioned, could well be down to synapses sparking merrily away in the background as staff respond to latest gauntlet thrown down by the head. School has many laurels but you'll never find anyone resting on them. Instead, there's a ceaseless quest for improvement, anywhere and everywhere.

Some setting (maths from year 2), high achievers treated to once a week sessions in small groups, one-to-one support scooping up small numbers at risk of Sats underperformance. Though results aren't the highest in the local borough, pupil progress puts them almost at the very top. 'They may not always get it right first time, but they don't give up and keep on trying,' says a mum. Latest innovations include recruitment of weaker readers to mentor younger pupils, some improving by more than a complete Sats level in the process. School has also introduced pupil challenges to up the excitement factor, reception recently wowing head with enormous sheets of paper covered with 'the biggest numbers they could think of'.

But though competitive instincts once more considered acceptable, children know when to rein them in. Unsuccessful year 6 candidate in election for one of four team captain posts was gracious in defeat. 'I am delighted and he has my full support', he said. Politicians take note.

Fundraising clout is substantial. A jolly crowd, forging friendships that often endure well beyond the school, parents are big on purposeful socialising, coffee mornings and cake-making featuring heavily in weekly school newsletters. Have their own choir, adding to pupils' very well regarded three, plus orchestra (healthy numbers boosted by local authority-subsidised taster lessons). Take school duties extremely seriously, finding the wherewithal to equip Apple suite not once, but twice as new technology succeeds the old. Also fund and manage school's own swimming pool which 'wouldn't exist without them', says insider, in constant use from April to October. Children adore it, two even asking for donations towards running costs instead of birthday presents (surely a first).

Not the school for anyone in search of 00 gauge miniature education. This is a scaled up version that works, thanks to a head who expects non-stop excellence, staff who buy in to the challenge and pupils who benefit from constant quest to do everything that bit better every time. 'It's such a lottery', said one mum. 'You buy the house and hope for the best. I just couldn't believe my luck'.

Marymount International School

George Road, Kingston upon Thames, Surrey KT2 7PE

Independent • Pupils: 260; 85 full, 14 weekly boarders • Ages: 11–18 • Sixth form pupils: 100 • RC • Fees: Tuition up to £21,340; boarding supplement up to £14,770 pa

Tel: 020 8949 0571

Email: admissions@marymountlondon.com
Website: www.marymountlondon.com

9

Headmistress: Since 2010, Sarah Gallagher MA (40s). Educated at a convent school, she studied for her degrees at University College Galway. Previous teaching and leadership posts at boarding and day schools including Queen's Gate, Lord Wandsworth College, most recently St Leonards-Mayfield School, taught in Rome. Dips in to teach Latin at Marymount from time to time.

Attractive, stylish and poised, she is articulate and empathetic in her interactions with others, strategic in her approach. The girls say she is 'busy and important' but also approachable. 'Ms Gallagher is so intelligent that you just think to yourself you could not possibly have a conversation with her, but when you do she is lovely.' Can picture this head on Mastermind or in the finals of a schools' edition of 'Strictly'. Husband also a teacher, two daughters at university. 'I want to build on the strength already here, a tremendous appreciation for learning and its significance in the school and its application outside school. The girls are learning for life; building character and community is integral to this. It's an exciting place to work, parents and students are committed, the philosophy of the IB and RHSM and Marymount London are all compatible.'

Academic matters: Marymount is a Catholic secondary girls school offering the IB Middle Years (MYP) and IB to an international community. The first (1979) girls' school in the UK to take up the IB in Britain, Marymount's grade 6-10 curriculum is built on solid institutional foundations. In 2015 pupils scored an average of 36, with 25 per cent earning 40+ points; one candidate achieved a perfect score (45), a result attained by fewer than 0.2 per cent of students worldwide; several other Marymount girls have achieved similar results in previous years.

No resting on laurels, they've been reviewing the MYP to align it with IGCSE content, ensuring all topics are covered in the IBMYP context by end of grade 9. Head wants parents to be assured of MYP rigour, the priority is to be learning-driven, not taught to the test. Range of IB subjects and results is excellent. Lots of sciences, 'and we do lots of field trips', say the girls. The school is offering a relatively new IB course, environmental systems and societies, which satisfies either the IB science or IB humanities requirement. 'My sister likes geography and science so it's perfect for her.' Marymount's MYP covers the broad spectrum of disciplines, with the interesting addition of philosophy to introduce the girls to 'the language of philosophy' before they embark on theory of knowledge at diploma level. As would be expected, religious education is also a key part of the programme.

'Ms Gallagher is so intelligent that you think you could not possibly have a conversation with her, but when you do she is lovely'

School prides itself on the wide range of languages offered. Extra mother tongue support in German and French in grades 6-8 dependent on enrolment. Parents warn that languages are sometimes subject to demand and in a small school it's not always possible to satisfy all requests for second language. It seems that there are mixed messages here and prospective parents are advised to discuss this at the early stages to clarify. The school does its best to support girls in working out alternative options – as one pupil explained, 'a friend who speaks Thai is taking IB Thai mother tongue; she's self-taught with the help of a tutor'.

The school is wireless throughout; iPads now in grades 6-9 and will move up the grades as pupils

progress; girls were excited to show off the first new Mac TVs, there are more to come. The library has undergone a complete refurbishment – it has 9,000 volumes and membership of London Library enhances the collection.

Classes never more than 16 and many, particularly at diploma level, only four to six, fewer still for languages. Some classrooms are designed with small seminar-style groups in mind.

The teaching faculty is an international bunch, average age forties. Pupil-teacher ratio is six to one and staff seem to know most of the girls, affirming parent comments about supportive and nurturing environment with a caring individualised approach. Low turnover and enough long-termers to provide a cohesive core. Plenty of support staff and school nurse on site.

Mild/moderate learning difficulties and other issues managed collaboratively by the learning resource coordinator, teachers, parents and students themselves. Lots of individualised support throughout the school and the girls themselves were quick to talk about peer tutoring offered during free periods or after school.

The enrichment programme for able students has about 40 on the register. These students are invited to apply to programmes sponsored by Ivy Leagues (Stanford, Yale, Princeton, Johns Hopkins) and top tier UK universities. Additional provision includes extracurricular activities as well as resources which are made available to students for independent study and wider reading.

Games, options, the arts: Mix of competitive and non-competitive sporting activities available for all grades on and off site. If the school does not offer a particular sport they will help connect with local teams. Marymount is part of the International School Sports Association and they have produced an impressive record of results in soccer, badminton and tennis at championship tournaments hosted by member schools in different parts of Europe. One pupil training with the Chelsea ladies' development squad and several play with the Richmond Volleyball Club. When girls were asked why they chose Marymount, one replied that she came for the sport and when you hear that one of their football trainers is with Chelsea, no prizes for guessing which team Marymount girls support.

Musicians have plenty of opportunities to play in ensembles and chamber groups. About 20 per cent take private instrumental or singing lessons; school boasts a 100 per cent pass rate in grade exams. Entry to the choir is by audition and choristers participate in school concerts and annual tours to European cities, performing in major churches and cathedrals. Teachers encourage girls to perform in local festivals and competitions.

Drama is inclusive and the entire community builds up to a major production each year; in true girls' school tradition male roles are played by the girls. Keen thespians can participate in ISTA (International School Theatre Association) festivals and when we visited girls were buzzing about their weekend ISTA trip to Stratford upon Avon. LAMDA examinations offered. Visual arts seem focused on painting and photography – the girls tell us that the art teacher is an inspiring photographer. Framed art by generations of pupils displayed throughout the school.

Consensus is that the most fun of all is the 'international day', when everyone shares their culture and cuisine.'The Japanese do the best, and the [boarding] girls are already planning even though it's still months away'! Zumbathon – a fundraising activity involving the whole community beeping and bopping, swinging and swaying to music, was also highly popular and yielded no casualties.

As a Catholic IB school, community service involves everyone at Marymount. Middle school do environmental projects that include cleaning along the bank of the Thames. Older girls volunteer in local activities including soup kitchens and schools and further afield join other RHSM students in projects working with children in places such as Zambia. All students take part in the spiritual life of the school and attend an annual retreat. Girls of all faiths come to Marymount and this provides opportunities for students to learn about other beliefs and traditions; care is taken to ensure that everyone feels comfortable at mass and prayer. We visited on a Hindu feast day and the girls said they had started the day with a Hindu prayer; Muslim girls wear their headscarves with confidence.

Background and atmosphere: Established in Kingston in 1955 by ten nuns from the Religious of the Sacred Heart of Mary (RSHM), sent by the Eastern American Province. Mid-19th century French founder of RSHM aspired to provide charity for all classes through schools, homes and orphanages that worked interactively across socio-economic barriers. Schools opened in France, Ireland, Portugal, England, the US and later Latin America and the rest of the world. The first sisters who came to Kingston started a 'year abroad' programme for US university women, then a school offering the US secondary school curriculum. Early 70s saw the arrival of Sister Anne Marie Hill, a determined Irish mover-and-shaker, well known in international education circles and now executive director of the network of schools. She introduced the IB making the school more relevant to its growing international student body and reflecting RSHM's original ethos. During the noughties Marymount had a series of heads as RSHM grappled with transition to lay leadership and during that time the board of governors was created.

In Ms Gallagher the sisters seem to have found the ideal head who brings continuity at the top, leading the school from strength to strength thanks to the partnership forged with the RSHM sisters and the board she describes as 'independent and experienced'. Enrolments are at an all-time high and it's all-systems-go for development plans aimed at enhancing programmes and facilities. School works closely with the other Marymount partners under Sister Anne Marie's guidance, meeting every six to eight weeks to discuss areas such as strategic planning and communication. Increasingly involvement with the international network of RSHM schools – 19 worldwide – is now bringing more opportunities to the pupils.

Everyone, including day parents, feels that the day girls and the boarders are pretty integrated

The school is based in an affluent part of Surrey occupying a large Edwardian house plus various more recent additions connected by walkways. Elegant grounds with lawns, manicured flowerbeds and sculpted hedges. 'The teddy bear topiary sold me', says one dad, 'How can you not love a school that has teddy bear topiary?' (We presume he had

---

Consensus is that the most fun of all is the 'international day', when everyone shares their culture and cuisine. 'The Japanese do the best, and the girls are already planning'

already consulted the GSG about minor details such as teaching and pastoral care.) Main house with original wood panelling and stained glass, is head office and reception. The nuns are loved by the girls and parents appreciate their presence. Small school chapel is used by boarders and local community alike and plans to re-develop and open the ceiling to the rafters and heavens above are underway.

Modern blocks house multi-purpose classrooms, the library and university and careers counselling rooms. Another block has the gym (floor replaced recently), music rooms and auditorium for assemblies, all-school mass, drama. Yet another has more dorms, cafeteria (food is 'so-so', particularly at weekends), classrooms, infirmary, student lounges. A new quasi-Scandinavian wooden structure houses more small tutorial rooms just right for the many language classes and designed with IB language examination conditions in mind. Most of the buildings surround the garden and have big windows that bring the outdoors in and give a refreshing sense of space and light.

Pastoral care and discipline: Spiritual values underpin the ethos of Marymount, rooted in the mission of the RSHM, 'that all may have life'. These values are made explicit on the website, even the most casual browser will see them on every page, running alongside photos. School welcomes girls from all faiths but we think it might not be a comfortable environment for the girl who has none.

Plenty of support available at the school: academic, social, emotional and personal; more expertise called upon if necessary. The headmistress is well briefed and aware of anyone who may be feeling overwhelmed, unhappy, unsettled. Girls say she shows genuine interest.

Parents Association hosts a welcome back family barbecue during the first weekend of the school year when boarding parents are there dropping off daughters so they are able to meet day families. One parent said the school went out of its way, allowing their daughter to board temporarily so she could start at the beginning of the year, before the family transfer to London took place. Another described how the teachers made an effort to encourage her daughter to join the orchestra for a big performance, even though her late arrival meant she had missed several rehearsals.

Clear procedures allow boarders off-campus freedoms to visit friends and family while ensuring their safety. One guardian who has long looked after boarders during half-term breaks told us that some older girls feel the school is too strict. She helps them, and their far-off parents who hear the grumbles, appreciate that the school is being understandably cautious and not at all unreasonable. Two exclusions in the last three years of boarders who, after several warnings, broke the rules about leaving campus.

Pupils and parents: Marymount girls are internationally diverse, cheerful, articulate, academically motivated, quietly confident and as a bunch, quite enchanting. More aspirational then ambitious, they love their school and really enjoy having peers from all over the world. They look out for each other, especially new ones, and although one day girl says she wishes there were more ways to get closer to the boarders, everyone, including day parents, feels that the day girls and boarders are pretty integrated.

The girls are reflective about the realities of being in a single-sex environment. They feel they are able to focus more on learning, but they would like to find a 'partner' boys' school and the student council have made some moves in this direction. Trouble is that 'all the boys' (schools) seem to be taken', but they have not given up. Head is a big advocate of the girls' school advantage, having also worked in mixed schools. 'When adolescent girls become interested in boys, it can be frustrating to see how much they measure themselves against the approval of the boys in the group. Without that distraction they can develop as intellectually rigorous learners, they are their own people.'

The families that choose the school value the ethos of school, its Catholicism and internationalism, but are equally attracted to the IB. There are 40 nationalities in the school, British representing just over half. Other significant groups are German, Spanish, Japanese, Chinese, US, Australian, Korean and Italian. The numbers within these groups are balanced very carefully to facilitate integration. The school bus service extends into London to Sloane Square and more routes are under consideration.

Parents association organises events including outings for parents which are appreciated by newly-arrived expats.

Entrance: Local families are urged to attend one of the open days. Inbound expats on 'look-see' trips to London may book appointments. Girls' admissions based on availability and a review of school reports and teacher references. The headmistress interviews all girls prior to offering a place. English language fluency is required with exceptions made for younger students for whom English is a second language. Most classes have waiting lists so best to apply a year in advance though there is some turnover so you could be lucky.

Local feeder schools include Holy Cross, The Study, Fulham Prep, St. Agatha's, The Grove, The Old Vicarage, The German School (Deutsche Schule London), Putney Park, Garden House, Unicorn School, Cameron House, Ursuline School. Day girls come from most SW London postcodes including Richmond, Wimbledon, Putney, Chelsea, South Kensington.

Exit: Small number leave to do A levels elsewhere. Most head to university and the chart we saw on the college counsellor's wall listing every 12th grader's destinations confirms that they are applying to many countries. Counsellor stays in close contact with parents, especially boarder parents, about each girl's plan and the process they must follow depending on the country of their destination. PSAT and SATs also offered.

Occasional one to Oxbridge with the rest going to Bristol, Durham, Exeter, Imperial, King's, Queen Mary, UCL, Warwick, York, Bath, St Andrews, Royal Northern College of Music as well as universities in the USA, Japan, Hong Kong, Spain and Germany.

Money matters: School has no endowment so financial stability is maintained by tuition and fundraising initiatives. 'Being an international school and in the current economic climate, we need to be sure we are guarded and forward looking – we

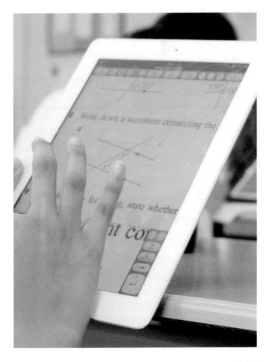

can't rest on our laurels.' The PA also fundraise for activities that support the school and pupils.

Scholarships (academic, art, music, drama, sport, community service) for grade 6 and 8 students. Some offered for grades 10, 11 and 12. Some financial aid available for means-tested students. About 20 per cent of the pupils benefit from this.

Remarks: Successfully serves a niche market of internationally-minded families seeking a girls' school with a Catholic ethos. In the words of one parent, 'We've been over-the-top-happy. The school provides excellent support and people from all over the world fit in and are welcome there.'

Nonsuch High School for Girls

Ewell Road, Cheam, , Sutton, Surrey SM3 8AB

State • Pupils: 1,220 • Ages: 11–18 • Sixth form pupils: 340

Tel: 020 8394 1308

Email: office@nonsuch.sutton.sch.uk
Website: www.nonsuchhigh.co.uk

33

Interim head: Deputy head Tracey Hartley has been holding the reins, after Peter Gale was sacked in April 2015 for 'unprofessional and inappropriate conduct'.

Jane Burton is the executive headteacher of the Nonsuch and Wallington Education Trust which was formed on 1 September 2015.

Academic matters: Anything these girls do, they do not just well, but very well indeed. Exam results – 81 per cent A*/A grades at GCSE and 80 per cent A*-B (21 per cent A*) at A level in 2015 – put them towards the top end of grammar school performance and well into the rarified heights of super-boffin territory. A small number of children (just over one per cent) have learning difficulties, currently spanning physical disabilities and mild dyslexia.

There's some setting (maths from year 8, for example) but many subjects are tutor group based up to the start of GCSEs (girls take a minimum of 10.5). A generous handful will get 12 or 13 straight A*s, many going on to five AS and four A levels. Some complete GCSE maths in year 10.

A science and languages specialist, the school does both proud. Demanding GCSE triple science is taken by nearly all, taught in 11 well-equipped labs with adjacent prep rooms, and vast numbers carry on to A level, 85 doing chemistry alone. Girls study one language in year 7 and then choose two from French, German, Spanish or Latin and, from year 10, GCSE ancient Greek. There's even Mandarin, run as an after-school club for the linguistically adventurous. Lessons can be good fun – European Day of Languages was marked in year

7 by a Eurovision-style contest including 'Baby, hit me one more time' in German – and there are extensive study/work experience opportunities, currently European-based but no reason why, thanks to Skype and well-equipped language labs, girls shouldn't soon be at least chatting on-line to peers in China and elsewhere, believes the school. Arts are also on the up, with drama GCSE performances singled out for praise by exam board.

It's good to see a range of less traditional GCSEs on offer, photography among them (some stunning images in school magazine) and, unusually, astronomy. School has its very own dome, open to local societies, in a secure, passworded building, where budding Sir Patrick Moores troop for their own Sky at Night sessions. Not all the girls are alive to the magic of the constellations, though. 'It's just a telescope in a white dome,' said one, prosaically, when asked if a tour could be arranged.

Inevitably, pupils with a broad range of interests have to make tough decisions at A level, especially would-be scientists and medics. At A level critical thinking and the EPQ are offered. Judged solely by the results, the teaching clearly delivers the goods, and, for sixth formers especially, can be inspirational. 'You really see the passion in the teachers, you've got a different relationship... (The teachers) leave you to do the mundane stuff on your own, then use the lessons to explore the subject,' says one. Staff regularly go on to greater things elsewhere – one of deputy heads promoted to headship at Wallington High School, for example. However, the school is also committed to developing wider skills and is beginning to introduce a curriculum which develops independent learning, teamwork, communications skills and resilience. The culture of the school is shifting to encourage risk taking and to ensure students are prepared for the test of life rather than a life of tests.

Games, options, the arts: Monthly school newsletters invariably feature pupil sporting successes in school and out and there's huge enthusiasm for fiercely-contested inter-house competitions and even (a surprise) a burgeoning cheerleading team. Clubs abound; some, like judo, pilates and aerobics, run by outside firms and paid for, others, like lunchtime cycle club, exploring Nonsuch Park grounds, run by motivated staff (average age early 40s) and all done for love.

Facilities, including tennis/netball courts, playing fields, 400m grass track and floodlit artificial turf pitch, are good, while a deal with a private fitness firm has added a cavernous sports hall, small(ish) changing rooms and, in some parents' eyes, rather limited access (morning lesson time only) to a jewel of an indoor pool. Parents, though realistic about inevitable bias towards academics, feel sport becomes somewhat perfunctory higher up the school. 'If you have a very sporty child, you end up getting your fix elsewhere,' says one, though school fields respectable number of sports alumni.

Arts meanwhile are buzzing (possibly humming, too), with several children selected for national drama and music groups and so many learning instruments (650 and rising) in and out of school that you could staff a symphony orchestra several times over, with spares. With lots of highly regarded productions, recently My Fair Lady and Lawfully (sic) Blonde, house talent shows and a range of ensembles – some, like the flourishing Indian music group, are set up by the pupils – all nine practice rooms are usually busy at break time (forward booking, somewhat inevitably in these highly organised surroundings, is essential).

Add an excellent range of trips to Sorrento, Large Hadron Collider in Cerne, China and Costa Rica together with extensive community service options, and it's almost impossible not to acquire a CV bulging with career-enhancing goodies. Even year 7s compete to design and sell their own fundraising product, while sixth formers run a huge range of clubs and societies in school and at local primaries. CCF is optional (for year 9s upwards) and DofE (all levels) is run in conjuction with local authority.

Background and atmosphere: So quiet that the only thing a visitor hears is the clicking of the friendly PA's heels as she escorts you down grey corridors offset with lots of colourful photography and artwork to the staff loos (and waits outside to escort you back again).

Motion-detecting lights, which take a while to come on, give winter evening forays up dark staircases an adventurous quality

The redbrick buildings, mainly three-storey and geometrically straightforward (though feeling anything but to the first-time visitor) date back to 1938, when the school, named for the next door palace built by Henry VIII, first opened. They're in generally good shape with lots of nice, bright rooms, many refurbished – art is especially appealing with vibrant-looking masks and wire sculptures.

From the plasma TVs giving regular updates on school events to smart card technology allowing girls timed access to buildings and fingerprint payment for meals, everything resonates with efficiency, though the motion-detecting lights, which can take a while to come on, give winter evening forays up dark staircases a certain adventurous quality. Even the loos have useful notices on the inside of the doors – 'I suppose it gives us something to read,' says a pupil.

At time of writing, was consulting about forming a multi academy trust with Wallington High.

Pastoral care and discipline: Behaviour is generally excellent – lapses are so rare that there's a pause while girls struggle to remember what happens, the only recent incident of note being a brief on-line teacher-baiting episode in 2010, swiftly sorted with suspensions and detentions, and reinforced by new cyber mentors (girls, not robots) trained by CEOP, the on-line protection body, to keep everyone on the straight and narrow virtual road.

As for the rare underachiever – a relative term as they'd be a big success anywhere else – there's lots of help. Form tutors are the first point of contact for most issues and keep a watching brief on academic performance, working with the child and parents to resolve any underlying problems and organise a bit of extra support if required.

Most importantly, girls are extremely supportive of each other, often working and revising together informally, with younger pupils readily approaching older ones for assistance through the house system.

The girls are a nice, modest bunch – braggadocio must be one of the least-used words in extensive vocabulary

'There's the feeling that everyone wants to help,' says one girl, who agreed, as did others, that knowing their friends were looking out for them takes the edge off the anxiety that all accept as an inevitable, if occasional, fact of life. '"Serve God and be cheerful" is our school motto,' points out a sixth former, 'and that is our ethos.'

Pupils and parents: Parents 'very supportive', thinks school. Come across as a hard to impress bunch – 'ambitious, focused and driven families pushing to get their children in there,' says one mother – who expect the school to deliver against stiff competition from neighbouring girls' grammars, Tiffin Girls in next door Kingston in particular, and are quick to note any slippage in results. Does it matter? To this bunch, very much indeed. Having delivered their side of the bargain – producing bright, motivated daughters – it's up to the school to ensure they fly through exams and straight into Russell Group universities. Some have Oxbridge in their sights when their daughters first arrive. Not that they necessarily leave it up to the school, and novices assuming tutor traumas are behind them once their daughters start here are in for a shock. What one mother describes as a 'significant percentage' carry on having them tutored all the way through, not because they're struggling but to keep them at the top.

The girls, meanwhile, are a nice, modest bunch – braggadocio must be one of the least-used words in extensive vocabulary – and have a genuine and touching pride in each other's achievements. They're delightfully enthusiastic, too, writing reviews in the school newsletter that describe everything from competing in the local music festival and even 'a short geography trip in Cheam Village' as 'exciting,' 'great' and 'fantastic'.

And while they may be lacking in spontaneity, perhaps it's no bad thing, given their likely careers, madcap impetuosity being low on the list of desirable qualities for any budding brain surgeon or atom-splitting scientist.

Ex-pupil Joanna Rowsell won gold in the track cycling in the 2012 Olympics.

Entrance: Hugely over-subscribed (around 1,650 sit the exam) and highly competitive – numerous on-line/local press tutor ads say it all. Early deadlines, so essential to keep track. Selective Eligibility Registration Form, from school, must be in by early Sept; Common Application Form (CAF), from candidate's LA, submitted Oct (both can be completed online). Pass/fail results in October, but as more candidates pass than there are places, agony continues untl March when offer letters sent out. Up to ten places available on basis of score to children who have triggered pupil premium, 85 places awarded regardless of location (unless a tie for final place, when proximity is the deciding factor): remaining places go to top-scoring local candidates within catchment area, with 15 places ring-fenced for children who are residents of the London Borough of Sutton. No sibling priority. Waiting list for runners up runs to end of the academic year, then deleted unless parents advise otherwise; very occasional vacancies in other years determined by science, English and maths exams. Unsuccessful 11 plus or mid-term candidates will not be considered again until sixth form.

Limited intake in sixth form requires minimum GCSE average points score of 50, places offered on the basis of predicted grades.

Exit: Around 95 per cent to higher education; sends more girls off to read science subjects than almost any other school in the country. Sixteen to Oxbridge in 2015, lots of medics, dentists, vets and linguists, plus a broad range elsewhere, from psychology, sociology and economics to editorial photography, management and art foundation, and one off to start a brand new degree course in paramedic practice.

Remarks: Does well by its seriously bright, highly motivated and caring girls. 'Unus pro omnibus, omnes pro uno' could be its alternative motto. While not necessarily a natural home for the seriously zany, its strengths in performing arts add a welcome swirl of colour to its more sober, science-based accomplishments. There's no getting away from it, however. Elsewhere, girls may just wanna have fun. Here, first and foremost, they wanna do well.

The Queen's Church of England Primary School

Cumberland Road, Kew, Richmond, Surrey TW9 3HJ

Tel: 020 8940 3580

State · Pupils: 405 · Ages: 4–11 · C of E

Email: info@queens.richmond.sch.uk
Website: www.queens.richmond.sch.uk

26

Headteacher: Since 2011, Miss Katie Bentham (30s). Trained at Bishop Grosseteste College in Lincoln, part of the University of Hull. Began her career in London, at St Mary Magdalene C of E Primary in Westminster and Newbury Park Primary in Redbridge, where she also gained a masters in science education. Relocated to Scotland for her next job at Westfield Primary in Cumbernauld, then back to London and Marshgate Primary in Richmond, where she was the SENCo and part of senior management. Queen's is her first headship, and she was parachuted in after what appears to have been a bit of a hiccup with the previous incumbent. Our impression is of a pleasant and energetic lady who is working with steely determination towards that coveted Ofsted 'Outstanding'. The parents we spoke to hadn't met her in person, but, said one mother, 'The children feel they know her, and when they're at home they even refer to her as Katie!' (Head adamant that this doesn't happen in school.) 'Not afraid to make changes,' was one parent's verdict. 'Miss Bentham's great!' pupils confirmed to us, eagerly.

Entrance: Two-form entry, so 60 reception places each year. Usual admissions criteria: looked after children, medical needs, siblings. Thereafter, at least one parent must be a 'committed and regular worshipper' at one of the three Kew Anglican churches (St Anne's, St Philip & All Saints', St Luke's); after that, it's down to proximity. Rather convoluted – if in doubt, contact the school office. School is oversubscribed, but not dishearteningly so. Also worth applying further up, as much of the Kew community is professional and mobile, and occasional places do become available.

Exit: As you'd expect in this locality, a high number of private and grammar school places every year:

Latymer Upper, Hampton, Lady Eleanor Holles, Tiffin, Kingston. Popular non-selective state school destinations include Christ's, Waldegrave and Richmond Park Academy. As with other state primaries, school doesn't prepare for 11 plus, and parents report that a fair degree of private tutoring goes on in the upper year groups. The children, however, were inclined to attribute their success to the school. 'It's really, really helped me get into the school I'm into,' said one engaging year 6 lad, who could have passed for Benedict Cumberbatch in his young days.

Remarks: Queen's is sited a stone's-throw from Kew Village, which inevitably accounts for some of the school's character. As far as we could tell, this was a London-accent-free zone, and all the pupils we met were chirpy, well-spoken, well-mannered and quite delightful. We suspect that there isn't huge social diversity, and we saw very little cultural diversity as we looked round the lunch-time crowds. (School says that it has above the national average number of pupils from ethnic minority groups.) But that said, the school works tirelessly to give the best school experience possible to its students, and clearly succeeds. Parents were incredibly warm in their praise, with the school's kind and friendly ethos mentioned again and again: 'A very positive culture of caring'; 'My two children love it there, they go happily every day'; 'The outstanding thing has been the care from all the staff'; 'The great strengths of the school are the atmosphere and the teachers, who are of a high quality and very dedicated'; 'A very friendly, inclusive environment'; 'Gentle and positive'; 'All the staff care about every child'. The children unanimously confirmed this. 'Is it friendly here?' we asked as we moved about the school, and group after group gave us an instant and emphatic 'YES!'

The Anglican faith is central to the school's ethos, and plays a greater part here than we've seen in any other C of E primary school. Fathers Nigel and Peter from St Anne's and St Luke's take assemblies every week, there's a Passion Play every year complete with crucifixion scene, and attendance at church services is regular and frequent: when we visited, for instance, the whole school had just returned from Ascension Day service. Even competitions can be devotional in nature, with the winning entries in the Easter Crosses competition making a colourful display on the school's website. But there was nothing dour about any of it, and the children impressed us with their cheerful and confident benevolence towards life, the universe and everything. There was also a happy awareness of other faiths, and visits to a synagogue and a mosque had been followed up with some lovely work.

The standard of writing and maths that we saw was very high, and Queen's academic record is sterling: in 2013, the Daily Telegraph placed it 10th in the country for its Sats results, and most children here achieve well above the national average, with a number of them successfully taking the level 6 tests (a pass at level 6 is expected of the average 14-year-old). Robust systems of monitoring are in place to make sure that children's performance is being tracked. One parent criticised the 'large and ill-defined projects' set for homework and felt that the school didn't do enough to push the children to do as well as they possibly could; whilst another, conversely, felt that the school put too much emphasis on getting the children to perform 'excessively' well in their Sats. The majority, however, said they were contented with the academic provision. 'Very good academic results achieved without extra pressure on the students', and 'an excellent academic environment' were typical comments. There are bang-up-to-date interactive whiteboards in every classroom, an attractive library and excellent, well-thumbed resources. SEN provision was 'not in the best place when I joined' according to the head, but both she and the SENCo have worked hard to bring it up to scratch, and we liked what we saw of the provision in this area.

Popular breakfast and after-school clubs are welcomed by working parents, and there's a lively programme of extracurricular activities, with music being a particular strength. Despite its small size, the school fields two orchestras and two choirs, and a wide variety of instrumental lessons are offered. 'The concerts are brilliant!' enthused one parent. 'Every time you go into school your hear children singing or playing music!' Views on the sports provision were a little cooler, with many parents and pupils (boys in particular) wishing there were more, but everyone agreed that it was getting better, and there was much praise for a recent cricket tournament. The head insists that the amount of sport at Queen's has 'dramatically increased' over the past year, and two swimming trophies in her office bore testimony to sport's being 'one of our vision priorities.'

Queen's is the only school in the country to change its name according to the gender of the reigning monarch – it was The King's School until 1953 – and is held in warm regard locally. A recent alumni evening was well attended and produced some misty-eyed comments in the visitors' book. But there's no question of things standing still.

School is being rebuilt under the Priority School Building Programme. Building work underway iand new school will be ready in September 2016, with improvements to the grounds evolving throughout the autumn term. These are clearly exciting times for a school that has much to be proud of.

Rokeby School

George Road, Kingston upon Thames, Surrey KT2 7PB

Tel: 020 8942 2247

10

Independent • Pupils: 373 • Ages: 3–13 • Fees: up to £15,513 pa

Email: admissions@rokeby.org.uk
Website: www.rokebyschool.co.uk

Headmaster: Since 2007, Mr Jason Peck BEd. Joined school in 1996 as a year 4 and science teacher, becoming deputy head in 2004. Long term association – also has two sons at the school – 'means parents know what they're dealing with,' he thinks. 'He knows the school, how it needs to be run and the traditions,' agreed mother.

Despite influence of several inspirational teachers as he grew up (together with deeply scary cane-wielding head), was initially keen to train as a vet, only to realise during work experience that was thoroughly squeamish, not helped by cow-averse mentor. Absence of James Herriot moments led him instead to a spell travelling and running own

business, arriving at Kingston University in mid-20s better versed in ways of world, he feels, than some younger out of the egg fellow students. Didn't necessarily agree with modish teaching theory but was able to rustle up sufficient veneer of enthusiasm to please tutors and perk was instant pupil rapport during classroom experience where proved himself to be an inspirational teacher.

First and only previous post was in tough middle school in Merton. Was surprised, 'perhaps naively so,' at depth of opposition when announced plans to turn to the dark side, aka independent education. Stunned by opportunities, educational and otherwise, and, bar briefly considering more senior science role elsewhere before management beckoned, hasn't looked back since.

Personable, interesting, open, has retained sense of humour despite very considerable challenges, and definitely needs it. After spending first year taking stock, has made several far-reaching changes, broadening curriculum so doesn't operate exclusively on work/sport axis with little in the middle. In addition to making much more of arts, has also encouraged specialist staff to teach all the way down to pre-prep (not right for all, he says; 'those used to teaching senior school pupils aren't always going to be able to cope with very young children').

School has long had first class reputation for securing year in, year out places at KCS and St Paul's, the competitive parents' most wanted establishments, and 'we have to make sure we hit them,' he says. Remains singularly successful even now with record competition, as demonstrated by school's waiting lists (knee deep in every year group).

You wouldn't guess it, however, from levels of parental sniping, which are considerable and take in everything from regular easing out of those deemed not to be making the grade to bullies being rewarded rather than punished, to staff disaffection and defection, and even parents being frightened to speak out in case results in repercussions.

Was initially keen to train as a vet, only to realise during work experience that was thoroughly squeamish

In the far corner, however, are Mr Peck's enthusiasts, equally firm in their praise of his leadership, dismissive of any tales of Flashman-style antics in the ascendance and baffled by them, too. One, with several children at the school, was 'surprised' to hear about negative feedback. 'I love it. I think it does just what it says on tin and tries hard to make nice boys.' Unusual, in fact, to find parental opinion so polarised. Recent school inspectors, we're told, were equally bemused, encountering ferocious criticism in feedback forms, yet unable to substantiate any of points made during their visit.

Only areas that both sides agree on is that some of admin team can be fairly robust to deal with (not unusual, in our experience), and that when it comes to teaching science, Mr Peck is the best in the business (and, fortunately for lucky pupils, who also think he's pretty fab, it's something he still finds time to do, though not as much as he'd like).

Mr Peck accepts that 'as a head, some will like my style, some won't', but points to efforts to improve school communications – regular parent rep forums, often free and frank in style, cover gamut of issues, and complaints procedure is being reviewed. As to pupils being asked to leave, yes, 'if a boy is struggling, we will help him find a better school,' but tiny numbers involved – three in past seven years, isn't, to his mind, a big issue.

School insider wondered if turbulence might be linked to structure of board of governors which could appear to be something of a closed shop – not easy to put yourself forward for election. In the meantime, Mr Peck is keen to get all dissenters to identify themselves and talk to him. 'Much better if they're inside the tent,' he says. We tend to agree.

Entrance: Catchment tends towards Wimbledon and Putney rather than Kingston and up into Teddington/ Richmond. Other parents almost incestuously local, with the neighbouring homes on what amounts to a mini-me St George's Hill, Weybridge estate (barrier-only entry to the private roads that surround it – school issues passes to non-residents). Some go further afield. But with the added convenience of next door Holy Cross, a similarly high-performing prep for the sisters, why would you bother?

At 4, start in reception, now non-selective: 'You'd end up testing at 2 – just not possible,' says head. A very few leave at end of year 2 to go either to King's College Junior or Colet Court, paper queues forming to snap up spaces – recently had 80 applications for just four slots. Rest carry on through the school, regular assessments tracking progress based on initial maths and cognitive ability assessments in year 1.

What is it with schools and porthole windows? Nautical imagery? All at sea? 'Friendly underwater feel,' thinks delightful guide, a year 8 veteran of countless school tours

Exit: Doing the business with KCS, St Paul's, Eton, Harrow, Epsom, Dulwich College and Hampton amongst desirable destinations. Head working overtime to ensure that out of many worthy candidates deserving of places, school gets its fair share (and ideally a few more as well). Ups and downs come with the territory (change in senior school admissions teams means entire getting to know you process has to start again from scratch) but evens out over the years. No doubt that it's getting tougher, leading to ever closer bonds with out-of-town schools from Epsom College to Charterhouse. Mr Peck admits to pressure to talk up candidates, but 'relationships with senior schools can only work on trust,' so isn't about to give in to it any time soon.

Remarks: What is it with schools and porthole windows? Nautical imagery? All at sea? 'Friendly underwater feel,' thinks delightful guide, a year 8 veteran of countless school tours ('I've done around 20') who shows us round and whose choicest oft-repeated phrases show every sign of being breathed on and rubbed with a shirtsleeve to bring back the shine.

Not till we reach newest building, recently opened by royalty, featuring said porthole windows, does world-weariness disappear. Can't blame him – place is gorgeous, a new home for lucky pre-preppers, all beautifully behaved; reception children, now liberated from shackles of prescriptive EYFS curriculum, quietly immersed in directed play (teachers and TAs also eat with them to create family atmosphere); year 1 pupils having a terrific time matching (and sampling) food with regions that produce them: potato farls from Ireland and, according to worksheet, fairy cakes from Kingston.

Older pupils get to use gorgeous new performing arts theatre with colossal screen, teachers bravely attempting live link with National Archive, chap dressed as slave intermittently beaming in, hoots and cheers from (otherwise immaculately behaved) year 8 boys marking the frequent occasions when computer said 'no'.

With exception of two science labs (neat collection of animal skulls – real – and Henri the skeleton – plastic), sports hall (clean and white, like the song says, with pitched, pine-lined roof that makes it airier than the norm) and assorted music rooms (tuneful violin solo wafting from windows – standard here is high), most classrooms run length of main building, newer addition running into sober, solid Victorian original. Gradual revamping is subtracting old-style slam lid desks (atmospheric but heavy to move owing to volume of stuff stashed by boys) and adding floor to ceiling wooden units – very swish – either side and over the top of whiteboards, not unlike show home bedroom makeover.

What won't change, however, are the classroom names, each brass plate proudly announcing name of historic figure or – more rarely – veteran member of staff. Renaming opportunities vanishingly rare, accorded only to chosen ones – normally Mr or Ms Chips types combining longevity with universal outpouring of love. Lessons delivered in commendably low-stress style by cheerful-looking teachers 'who just want you to feel OK,' thought pupil and are homily-light, preferring, he thought, to encourage older pupils to realisation of any gaps to be filled.

Class sizes reduced with recent division of year 5 upwards into three forms (was two until year 7), maths and English both set, smaller teaching groups the norm in music, head's goal to do something similar with other subjects including science.

Lots of staff enthusiasm, including evangelical DT enthusiast honing latest batch of scholarship hopefuls, charismatic drama specialist encouraging boys to create living poster show as part of term-long project to save fictional circus from closure and art teacher presiding over series of excellent, if sinister, screaming faces (inspired by Messerschmitt – artist rather than German plane).

Few complaints from pupils. Latin 'a bit of a Marmite subject – though I love it.' Otherwise, science loved for 'experiments and interactive games in last five minutes of lesson' and, unusually, pupil praise for teachers' awareness of different learner types – auditory, visual and kinaesthetic.

Many highlights, reckoned parent. 'English and maths are good and the history is inspirational,' said one. Not everyone felt the same, some sensing staff disaffection. If so, were certainly hiding it well. One, with child in pre-prep, was thoroughly enjoying the experience. Another wished 'I'd known about school – wasn't on my radar. If it had been, would definitely have sent him here.' Website, apparently constructed for those already in the know, wouldn't currently help. Though it's

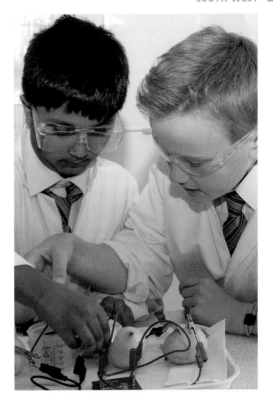

not a place lacking confidence – 'the first 125 years' is the title of recent school history – its online parent comms currently needs, and is shortly about to get, an update.

In the flesh, however, plenty of non-airy-fairy robustness, not least when it comes to sanctions and rewards. The aim, says head, is 'to find one thing every boy can do well and help him do it even better.' There's leadership training for years 6 to 8 and masses of good work incentives, from house points to red books (not actually red... or a book) rarer than hens' teeth (once every three years, reckoned one pupil). Presentation by Mr Peck about as big as it gets, only disappointment the disappearance of sweets. Big on detentions, too, or at least the threat of them for range of transgressions. Pays to double check teacher's written homework instructions against what's written on the board and transcribe correct version into homework diary as 'can differ slightly,' thinks pupil.

Pastoral care 'excellent', thinks parent, with head quick to respond to queries, masses of notes all round school commending virtues of good manners (classes and individuals painstaking about standing for visitors) as well as clearly very committed and caring staff. Cheerful learning support teacher runs popular sessions, while library, despite top heavy fact over fiction title weighting, is clearly something of a sanctuary. There's little chatting space and year 8s plan to campaign for old pre-prep classroom to be converted into common room.

Pupils adamant that school won't tolerate bullying which rarely goes beyond 'boys' banter', said one. On rare occasions it happens, it's a call to the parents and 'immediate' after school detention. Former transgressors might have conduct explained to them, be punished but then, later, be rehabilitated. Though some parents aren't keen, head felt second chances important. 'Who would want a child to feel that their life had already been written off?'

Plenty of opportunities for redemption, sport a major feature, though less dominant now than

it used to be. Many more and different sports and far more emphasis on arts now than used to be the case. Teams go all the way down to F in lower years (less so further up the school, but 'everyone still gets games,' said pupil).

Could so easily be swamped by pressure and riven with nerves. And that's just the parents. Despite substantial gripes from some parents, results and atmosphere give it undeniable cachet as prep whose top leavers continue to have the entrée to some of south west London's most sought after senior schools. Currently, worth doing a spot of fact, and faction, checking before you sign up. Under which king, Bezonian, could well apply here.

The Russell Primary School

Petersham Road, Petersham, Richmond, Surrey TW10 7AH

State • Pupils: 280 (plus 52 in nursery) • Ages: 3–11

Tel: 020 8940 1446

Email: info@russell.richmond.sch.uk
Website: www.russell.richmond.sch.uk

Headteacher: Since 2011, Samantha Leir, previously deputy at the school. Her first teaching job was at Russell in 1994. From there she went to work for the local authority as a lead literacy teacher. Returned to Russell as deputy in 2003. 'She's always been a huge part of the school,' said one parent.

Two sons (6 and 12) who both attend schools in Surrey. Grew up in Wales, the only girl with four brothers, so rugby is a big part of her life. Supports the Ospreys (Swansea). Her sons and husband also play rugby. She enjoys reading, cooking and swimming.

Entrance: Moved to two-class reception entry in September 2015. For nursery places apply direct to nursery and for school through local authority.

Exit: Most go on to Grey Court in Ham, a couple to local grammars (Tiffin Girls' and Tiffin School), a handful to independent or church schools (Christ's, The Green School, Gumley), or to Waldegrave School for Girls if they live in Twickenham.

Remarks: Set in four acres of grounds, feels more like a campus university than a primary school. While we were being shown round by the head we bumped into students with a teacher doing orienteering! 'We have more square footage of land per child than any other school in Richmond,' the head told us proudly.

A large single storey 1950s block houses the nursery. The building is rather tired looking, but

colourful wall displays and mobiles brighten up the space. Nearby is the unit for children with severe learning difficulties. The school has specialist provision for up to five children at key stage 1 (aged 4 to 7) on the autistic spectrum. The unit is staffed by specialist teachers.

It feels like a village school and it's amazing to have such space on the outskirts of London

Originally two schools (Petersham and Orchard Junior) built in the 1950s, they joined together to form the Russell School in 1980. The original buildings are therefore a bit scruffy but the outdoor space more than makes up for them. There is a nature area with ponds, an outdoor classroom, an allotment. They even have their own orchard and keep chickens. Hot school dinners are cooked fresh on the premises.

There are Gifted and Talented groups for maths and writing. A Battle of the Books competition is available for gifted readers in year 2 and year 4.

Music is important here. A specialist music teacher is at the school for half of the week. She is also responsible for the school choir and orchestra. Children can learn recorder, flute, guitar, violin and even the harp. There are trips to the Royal Festival Hall and each year the school takes part in the O2 Young Voices competition. 'My son was so proud to be representing the school at the O2 centre,' explained one parent.

Drama is also strong, and as well as a big Christmas production and a year 6 performance (last year it was based around the theme of Pompeii), there is a talent show for the whole school.

A recent appointment is the deputy head, who leads sport at the school. Lunchtime and after-school clubs include gymnastics, athletics, basketball, football, netball, judo and golf, as well as chess, Spanish and art. A private company (Fit for Sport) runs a breakfast club from 7.45am to 8.30am, and after-school care from 3.15pm to 6.00pm, both at extra cost.

Parents are drawn from across the social spectrum. Some children live in the huge mansions on Petersham Road while others are drawn from the council estate over towards Ham. The PTA organises social events and parents are encouraged to come into school for special assemblies. 'Since Mrs Leir took over we feel much more welcome at the school,' said one parent.

It feels like a village school and it's amazing to have such space on the outskirts of London. If you can turn a blind eye to the state of some of the buildings, then you'll feel very smug if you can manage to get a place for your child at Russell. Even more so when planned rebuild is completed.

St Elizabeth's Catholic Primary School

Queen's Road, Richmond, Surrey TW10 6HN

State • Pupils: 270 (plus 25 in nursery) • Ages: 3–11 • RC

Tel: 020 8940 3015

Email: info@st-elizabeths.richmond.sch.uk
Website: www.st-elizabeths.richmond.sch.uk

28

Headteacher: Since April 2014, Mrs Jane Hines BA PGCE CPD, previously deputy head.

Entrance: No point applying unless you are on first name terms with your Catholic priest. Serving four parishes covering Richmond, Kew, Ham and East Sheen, with a few from St Margaret's, the school is single form entry and heavily oversubscribed. More than 50 per cent of applicants fulfil the number one criteria of being a baptised, practising Catholic. After that priority goes to siblings (always lots) and then admission is based on proximity to the school. Nursery is separate unit on the same site in premises due for upgrading – same admissions criteria as school. Other feeder nurseries are Wyndham and The Barn. Ten classes from 2015.

St. Elizabeth's School agreed, at the request of the local authority, to raise its pupil allocated number (PAN) to 60 for entry into the academic year 2015-16 and again in 2016-17, enabling 60 children to enter reception.

Exit: To a wide range of schools, particularly new Catholic state secondary St Richard Reynolds; ones and twos to Gumley House Convent, Wimbledon College, the Ursuline Convent, the Sacred Heart School, Waldegrave, Cardinal Vaughan and the London Oratory. Some to Kingston schools, including two or three to Tiffin. Not many to other Richmond secondaries. A few to independent sector including St Benedict's in Ealing, Hampton School

and Lady Eleanor Holles in Hampton. 'Lots of doors open from here,' says school, though one ex-mother queried how much independent schools advice was on offer.

Remarks: Great Sats results, a clutch of glowing reports from Ofsted and the like, and a host of happy parents all pay tribute to this hugely popular school.

In ritzy residential Richmond, built to an unusual semi open plan arrangement which survives nearly 40 years on

Academically it certainly does the business, producing well above average results at key stage 2. Level 5s achieved by 70+ per cent of the pupils in English and maths, 90 per cent in science. A fairly stable, mostly female, small group of teaching staff, so everybody knows everybody – no hiding place for the feckless. It's a very expensive area of the country and high living costs mean there is some movement of staff; however, nearby are the well-respected teacher training facilities of St Mary's and Roehampton, so a good supply of fresh student blood is on hand.

A traditional place but the ICT is all there – whiteboards and wireless laptops mean the teacher is not stuck at the front of the class, but can be more flexible. Well-equipped ICT suite, large enough for whole-class teaching, just a few years old. More languages than many junior schools manage. Years 3, 4, and 5 learn Italian (courtesy of an arrangement with the Italian Embassy, which provides a teacher). Year 6 pupils learn French, visit France and study for the Lingua Bronze award – gives them a head start at their secondary school. There's also a Spanish club on the after-school activities programme which takes children from age 5.

Out year 6 guides were almost mobbed in an act of pure hero worship as we visited the class they monitored. Parents rave about the friendly atmosphere

Aesthetics not squeezed out by academia – music, art and drama all valued here. School views drama as a resource to be used whenever the opportunity arises. Every child in years 2 and 3 learns recorder and all year groups study singing. Most learn an additional instrument, typically cello, brass, flute, violin or guitar. All culminated in a highly praised production of Joseph and the Amazing Technicolour Dreamcoat for KS2.

Pupils do extremely well at swimming – all four junior classes swim every year, six weeks on, six weeks off – head believes no point in teaching them for one term and ticking the 'they can swim' box. Mixed-age team champions in Richmond Schools Swimming Gala. Other sports include netball, football, athletics, basketball and mixed tag rugby (Small School Champions).

Almost the only gripe from parents concerns the lack of space and facilities for sport on site. There's no playing field, only hard surface provision – basically the junior playground. 'It's a lovely place but I wish the children, particularly the boys, had more room to run around,' says one mother. Pupils do use the outdoor facilities of a nearby secondary school.

In ritzy residential Richmond, built to an unusual semi-open plan arrangement which survives nearly 40 years on. Staff and parents like it, feeling that it helps to promote an open atmosphere which pervades the whole institution. Don't worry; there are classrooms, but also lots of shared work and quiet areas. 'It has the advantage of helping to achieve consistency of teaching, as well as promoting openness of spirit and mind.' Light floods in through partially glazed ceilings giving a nice airy aspect to the place. Super security; gates are locked during the school day, entryphone access both at the gates and the main building.

Largely upmarket intake; some of these families could undoubtedly afford the private sector, but head describes intake as 'much more mixed than you might imagine for this area.' About nine per cent of the children qualify for free school meals, which is more than twice as many as at other schools round about. Mainly white British or Irish, but 25 per cent of the school has EAL. Lots of immigrant families tend to be Catholic – so there are Italian, Spanish, Polish, Filipino, Eritrean, Chinese and Indian children on the roll. About 18 per cent of pupils have some special need, most commonly specific learning difficulties around language acquisition, and some behavioural issues such as ADHD. No testing on entry, but school says it is happy to cater for all SEN and gifted and talented that fall within mainstream remit.

Children encouraged to take a real pride in their work; lovely displays and workbooks are the result. Perhaps it's the need to be considerate of others, necessitated by the open layout, which promotes the caring atmosphere in evidence. The older children take a fair degree of responsibility for helping their school mates in the lower years, lunch time monitoring, hearing them read and so on. Our year 6 tour guides were almost mobbed in an act of pure hero worship as we visited the class they monitored.

Parents rave about the friendly atmosphere between the children, transcending year groups, and bill and coo over the pastoral care. The religious ethos is strong – whole school assembly most days; mass celebrated periodically and on special occasions, prayers at beginning and end of day and grace before lunch; all on top of what's included in the syllabus, of course.

School is fairly demanding and standards are high, homework must be done on time, uniform absolutely on spec and so on – check that's you before signing up. Parents are a big part of the school: 'some parents get very involved in both daytime and after-school activities and without them it would not be, for example, the great swimming school that it is,' said one former mum. 'However, it is assumed that you want to give your time.' She felt that parental efforts were not always fully appreciated.

In a nutshell, the school ticks all the boxes for what parents would want from an ordered Catholic education – very strong spiritually, academically and pastorally. Not for the lackadaisical, nor for those hankering for informality and wide open spaces.

St Paul's School

Linked school: Colet Court, 186

Lonsdale Road, London SW13 9JT

Independent • Pupils: 1,378; 33 boarders • Ages: 13–18
• Sixth form pupils: 370 • Fees: Day £22,644; Boarding
£33,915 pa

Tel: 020 8748 9162

29

Email: admissions@stpaulsschool.org.uk
Website: www.stpaulsschool.org.uk

High Master: Since 2011, Professor Mark Bailey (50s). Married to an HR consultant, and with a teenage son and daughter. Career has included both academia and education: former head of The Grammar School at Leeds, he has also been a fellow at Cambridge and at All Souls, and professor of late medieval history at the University of East Anglia, with whom he continues to be involved. Found time to be a rugby international (1984 to 1990) and is now president of the Cambridge University Rugby Club. A thoroughly engaging, astute, relaxed and kindly man, the complete reverse of what one might expect of the high master of such a venerable institution as St Paul's. We meet many head teachers who are fonder of their school than of the pupils in it. Professor Bailey, extremely clever himself, still cherishes the achievements of others. A people-person through and through, who likes 'reading, walking and the wines of the Rhone Valley'. Talks with a refreshing lack of jargon.

Self-imposed mandate, on coming to St Paul's, was, 'Not to meddle with what this school does outstandingly well; leadership of exceptional institutions is as much about stewardship as change.' That said, he is skilfully overseeing a vast programme of refurbishment that is transforming the 1960s site into a school for the 21st century, and steering both school and students towards greater meritocracy and social responsibility.

Academic matters: The St Paul's recipe for academic stardom remains the same: cream off the very brightest, recruit the very best, light the blue touch paper and stand clear. The resulting sparks illuminate the sky. As one boy put it, 'The real pleasure about being here is going off-piste academically.' Another said, 'The quality of the teaching is beyond compare. It really pushes you further.' Parents agree. 'The teachers are brilliant at their subjects'; 'They're highly skilled at imparting their knowledge'; 'The teaching is simply superb'. A recent inspection report summed it up: 'The effectiveness of questioning in lessons, both from pupils and teachers, is outstanding.'

Broad and challenging curriculum includes ancient history, engineering and technology, and an excellent range of languages, Italian, Russian and Greek among them. Exam success is seen as a by-product of the boys' broader intellectual development, but it ain't a bad by-product: 97 per cent A*/A at GCSE in 2015 and 81 A*/A at A level. Amazing science building offers 18 laboratories, but such is the subject's popularity that, according to staff, 'space is still tight'. Beautiful library, silent and inviting, and facilities everywhere are excellent, although we were amused to see far fewer interactive whiteboards in the classrooms than we'd seen in a state primary school the week before. Interactivity here is still verbal and cerebral perhaps, rather than fibre-optical. Huzza! But we applauded the really intelligent decision to install air-conditioning in all teaching rooms, ensuring that minds stay alert in the muggiest of weather. (How many times have we seen pupils wilting in the heat of south-facing temporary classrooms?) Specialist support is given to those few students identified as having special needs, but this isn't the place for anything more than mild cases.

There are no plans to introduce the IB, which the high master describes as 'enforced breadth', adding that the Cambridge Pre-U is 'chunky and prescriptive'. A levels are preferred here, because 'they're the easiest of the post-16 qualifications; they enable the boys to matriculate, and this then leaves time to pursue other areas.'

You can feel the thinking going on here. Academically, a very special place.

Games, options, the arts: Superb facilities include six rugby pitches, six football pitches, five cricket pitches, swimming pool, courts for rackets, squash and fives, and its own boathouse stuffed with sophisticated rowing craft. The students wax lyrical about the sport on offer here – 'Sport for me has been the highlight here'; 'There is so much!'; 'It's a big part of my life at St Paul's'; 'Most of my friends have been the ones I play sport with' – and we saw dozens of boys throwing themselves about the playing fields in organised and impromptu games of just about everything.

'Paulines are lovely, decent boys, really articulate, fun, clever and very nice'

Music and drama are both extremely strong; concerts are held in the world-class Wathen Hall, and new Samuel Pepys Theatre was recently opened. Art is taught in a magnificent suite of rooms, and the engineering and technology room is surely every young boy's dream. Clubs cater for every taste, although oddly enough we didn't see any, despite having arrived at lunchtime; even the four lads we finally came across in the 3D Art room turned out to be revising their French ('I don't know why they're doing it here,' mused the art teacher). But the student-produced magazines we read were testament to the vibrancy of this community of thinkers: page after page of exceptionally mature, sparkily written articles on cinema, sport, current events, modern architecture; a real treasure trove of ideas.

Background and atmosphere: Founded in 1509 by Dean John Colet, and moved four times before arriving in 1968 at its present riverside home in leafy (and very wealthy) suburbia. A £77 million redevelopment has transformed much of the site. Visitors now are presented with an exceptionally elegant, blond, modern school campus; an architectural version of the Paulines we met, really, and with the same air of informality and purpose.

Having survived the Great Plague, the Fire of London, the Civil War and the 20th century, St Paul's can afford to relax and enjoy its own success. 'Academic rigour and loose ties' was how one parent described St Paul's today, and this was echoed by the high master: 'It has the feel of an über-grammar school. It's more like a university than any other school I've known.'

It's cool to be clever here, and so, inevitably, there is peer pressure to do well. This is mostly positive, say boys and parents, and drives everyone on, although one parent added, 'If you were at the bottom of the class, SPS would be a horrible place.' But high master denies this emphatically: 'More time than ever has been put into teaching underachieving boys and providing better support.' And another parent observed, 'The bottom of this particular pile still represents an extremely high level of achievement.' We saw boys working with good humoured focus for an eccentric and witty geographer who was padding around in Muppet-motif socks, interspersing teaching points with cheerful insults which the boys lapped up and batted back, in time-honoured boys' school way.

Indeed, SPS remains an extremely masculine community, where the testosterone coming out of the circuit-gym knocks you over at 20 paces; and perhaps this shows most in the school's being unaware of just how masculine it is. The sur master insisted that there was much 'mutuality' between the Boys' School and the Girls' School, but this was flatly contradicted by the Paulines we spoke to, and by one mother who felt that the school could do much more in this regard. We were ourselves surprised to find a large-scale female nude looking breastily down on us as we ascended the art department stairs, and more surprised to find another one as we went down a different way. There were no male nudes on display, and we couldn't help wondering why, out of all the subject matter that might have been on show, the school had chosen these particular canvasses. There are 'no plans whatsoever to admit girls at any stage of the school; no parents, boys or staff have ever suggested it' (high master). Which, if they want to go all Rubens-y about the stairwells, may be a good thing. But the Paulines we met were very personable young men, and the same mother who wanted more contact with SPGS also affirmed, 'Paulines are lovely, decent boys, really articulate, fun, clever and very nice.' Small community of boarders, a quarter of them from overseas. Many go home at weekends, often after Saturday morning sports matches.

Pastoral care and discipline: Vertical tutoring system, ie mixing the ages of form groups so that younger and older boys are together. The concept is simple: boys will listen to their peers sooner than their parents, so utilise the more experienced boys for pastoral care and to lead extracurricular activities. It's been in place for over 10 years, and is clearly popular. As one parent commented, 'From the moment they arrive, the 13 year olds meet boys in every other year and get a sense of what they might do.' Tutors stay with the boys throughout their time at the school, and, says school, often become family friends – the advisability of which the school may be reviewing, in the light of recent events (see below). The nature of this hand-picked community means that bad behaviour is rare:

'There's an intuitive understanding of where the boundaries are,' says high master. 'I've never seen any evidence of bullying here,' was a typical student comment, and sur master concurs: 'We have very, very few boys that would do what could be called bullying more than once, and if they do, we apply school sanctions quickly.'

The school, along with Colet Court, is currently under investigation following allegations of child abuse between the 1960s and 80s.

Pupils and parents: One of the most expensive day schools in the UK, and compared with similar institutions, financial support for poorer families is small – see Money Matters. The result is a community which is highly diverse religiously and culturally, but not socially. Parents mostly ambitious and successful professionals with sons to match, hard-working and free-thinking. Old boys list reads like a Who's Who of Influential Britons: a sample includes John Milton, Samuel Pepys, Field Marshal Montgomery, Isaiah Berlin, Oliver Sacks, George Osborne, Rory Kinnear – and Nicholas Parsons.

Entrance: State-educated parents who are starry-eyed for their children but don't know the entrance procedure should start reading it now. SPS takes about 180 13-year-old boys each year, but it's impossible to go there directly from a state school. The 13+ candidates apply either from Colet Court, whose 80-90 boys nearly all go on to the senior school, or from any other prep school – usually those in the London area. Colet Court has its own admission procedures at 7+, 8+ and 11+; see our separate entry, and don't leave it any later than September of your child's year 6 (be grateful, it used to be year 5). Prospective Paulines sit an online common entrance pre-test at their prep school, on the strength of which about 350 are invited for interview. The school then makes conditional offers: boys have to get at least 70 per cent at common entrance. The school is looking for 'intellectual curiosity and embracing of novelty'. About 20 more boys also join in the sixth form, which at SPS is called the Eighth.

Exit: In 2015, 56 Oxbridge places; the rest to Bristol, Durham, Imperial, Edinburgh, UCL and other top universities. An increasing number leave for USA Ivy League giants such as Harvard, Yale and Princeton.

Money matters: Only five per cent of students receive any form of means-tested bursary assistance (although for those few the assistance can be up to 100 per cent of the fees) and scholarships are honorifics only – £60 pa and a silver fish in memory of John Colet. Some remission for families who send three or more children to the school. High master's vision is to increase the amount of bursaries available, so that the school can become genuinely needs-blind.

Remarks: For very bright, confident, motivated boys who like to think for themselves, St Paul's provides a truly unrivalled education. A unique start in life.

Sheen Mount Primary School

West Temple Sheen, London SW14 7RT

State • Pupils: 475 • Ages: 4–11

Tel: 020 8876 8394

30

Email: info@sheenmount.richmond.sch.uk
Website: www.sheenmount.richmond.sch.uk

Headteacher: Since 2009, Mr Ian Hutchings BSc PGCE NPQH (30s). Previously deputy head here (since 2005) and before that at St John's Kingston and East Sheen Primary.

Having inherited an already successful and thriving school (he received huge backing from parents and staff to get the headship) the challenge has been to maintain and improve it. Parents seem happy with his progress, with one describing

'It's like having a very local private school on our doorstep,' said one mother. 'We do recognise how privileged we are'

him as 'a top man' and another as 'on the ball'. He's younger than some of his pupils' parents, but evidently a strong enough character to deal with a rather full-on cohort of mothers and fathers, locally famed for their hands-on involvement with the school. Operates an open-door policy and also usually around in the playground before and after school. He's 'fair, approachable and responsive,' say parents and any lack of experience is more than compensated for by his fresh approach and openness to new ideas.

He has a calm and considered demeanour, which seems to permeate the school. Focused and a little corporate on occasion – talks about 'free flow access to outside space' and 'delivery of ICT'. But behind the jargon one senses a caring man, very pleased to have this job and bursting with enthusiasm and ideas for primary education. Genuinely enjoys the company of the children – takes some cover lessons – and they like and respect him in return, although his dry sense of humour sometimes goes over their heads.

Married with a young daughter. Enjoys skiing in the holidays.

Entrance: Ridiculously small catchment area; you'll need to live very close to get a place at this oversubscribed school. Cut-off distance is normally between 300 and 500m and families moving to the area ask estate agents if houses are 'Sheen Mountable?'

In common with many schools Sheen Mount has added an extra reception class. With 90 in the year group, will mean larger than usual numbers of siblings taking priority in the next few years, accommodated in new building. School will slowly increase in size to around 600 by 2020, and says it's worth asking about occasional places higher up the school – but reality is hardly anyone leaves this place if they can avoid it.

Exit: Some 60 per cent hotfoot it to the independent sector, having used this place as a state 'prep'. Some 20 different schools feature on Sheen Mount's list of secondary destinations – literally one here, one there, from Colet Court to Wimbledon High, but always a contingent to Hampton Boys, Surbiton High (girls) and Ibstock (mixed). The other 40 per cent search for a state school to match their charmed primary experience at Sheen Mount

– parents openly yearn for a senior section to this school. Hardly any opt for the nearest secondary school option, Richmond Park Academy, although head commends its 'amazing resources' and says he tries to encourage the good state options available. Most popular local state choices are Grey Court and Christs, with Waldegrave Girls an option for those living that side of the borough. A few (again just one or two) to the Kingston grammars. School is alive to the requirement for information about independent schools and invites their representatives to its various 'future schools' information evenings.

Remarks: A super school, locally lauded as the best in the area, tucked away behind the stylish residential streets of up-market East Sheen. 'It's like having a very local private school on our doorstep,' said one mother. 'We do recognise how privileged we are.'

Underwhelming at first glance, hidden from view next door to a pub (but a gastro-pub of course and owned by a TV chef), the scale and scope of the school doesn't hit you until you get inside. The site is much larger than it first appears with buildings recently refurbished and seamlessly extended so that there are no obvious 'new' and 'old' parts to the school. Classrooms are big, bright and airy, first floor ones with a relaxing view of treetops. Playgrounds and playing fields have also been revamped so there is an outdoor classroom, a science garden, an allotment, lots of climbing equipment and overall a huge amount of greenery for an urban school.

But nice though it is to have everything ship shape, it would count for nothing were it not for the top-notch learning environment here.

School's strong teaching team is quite young, pleasingly includes some male teachers, and has developed its own curriculum. 'We are not constrained by the national curriculum requirements, but rather pick and choose what adds value; it's a really creative, cross-curricular offering,' says head. Seems to pay off big time – Ofsted rates the school outstanding, SATs results are sparkling and its value added score is 101.8 (particularly impressive when you consider the unremittingly middle class intake here means that Sheen Mount pupils are no slouches from the off).

There's a purposeful, industrious atmosphere in the classrooms. Children are really involved with the lessons and uber keen to share what they are doing – there was an audible groan from children not selected to answer a question or show some of their work. The vocabulary and empathy of even the youngest children as they answer questions about a piece of writing is startlingly impressive. Cursive handwriting similarly strong. The children do their work in a learning journal which moves with them through the school. This fits in with the cross-curricular approach to teaching and makes it easier to check progression; for example if a child's target is to improve use of punctuation, progress can be seen across all subject areas. The only subject not in the journal is maths, which is handled separately, but with equal focus. Mantra is 'excellence in all things' and to this end head has introduced more rigorous target setting and progress monitoring, all aimed at getting a better handle on each individual child. 'I believe that our high academic standards are almost a by-product of our efforts to make sure every child achieves their full potential, wherever that may lie,' he says. Special needs support is led by a full-time inclusion manager supported by a part-time teacher and a high proportion of teaching assistants throughout the school. Happy to take children with Downs and autism and most physical disabilities, as only one part of the building is not accessible by lift. School statistics show relatively high numbers of pupils with English as an additional language, but head says figures are misleading. Many children are automatically badged as EAL when in fact they may be newly arrived from Scandinavia with English a fluent second language and present no more of a teaching challenge than any native of East Sheen.

French is taught from year 1. There are weekly music lessons from a specialist teacher and a great dedicated music space, well-resourced with instruments. Head likes his technology and as well as an ICT suite children have use of netbooks and WiFi in their classrooms. Parents describe recent art and drama showcases as 'outstanding'. 'The children perform with huge confidence, and whether it's a big show or a class assembly, they all speak so clearly and every one of them is involved,' said one. Loads of artwork on display around the school.

Children consulted about new colour scheme (girls voted green and boys purple)

Quite a wide offering of sports for a state school with plenty of support from parents; for example, a qualified coach/mother runs the thriving netball club. A few moans about school's unwillingness to promote excellence and competition – 'those seem dirty words in a state school' said one parent. 'It's all about just taking part'. As well as its own grounds, including a smart open air, heated, swimming pool, the school uses nearby Richmond Park. School also takes full advantage of all the outreach opportunities offered by local clubs, such as Harlequins rugby coaching. Plenty of trips and lots of extracurricular, although one mother felt her

daughter was offered more opportunities than her son, who was not enticed by yoga, street dance and cheerleading clubs. Breakfast and after-school club provides care from 7.30am until 6pm, run by outside company, Fit for Sport. With no commitment required, parents who suddenly find themselves in need of help can book via website as late as the night before.

They all recognise it as a gem and are happy to give generously of their time and money

School describes its approach to behaviour management as 'positive'. There are five golden rules which are rarely broken. Every child starts with week with 20 minutes of golden time and will lose two minutes for every transgression, as well as a visit to head so that they can 'explain themselves'. But these children are polite and well-behaved for the most part and rarely take the walk of shame to his office. Parents very happy with pastoral care, describing it as 'excellent' and say home/school communication is good. 'I think parents will always be hungry for as much information as possible, but I think Sheen Mount does well enough', said one. Simple example of good school/pupil communications is the school toilets – children were consulted about the new colour scheme (girls voted green and boys purple if you were wondering), theory being they are more likely to value the space, and keep nice, something they've been involved in choosing. There's also a 'bubble box' in classrooms where children can post any concerns, which will be picked up by their class teacher.

Slight criticism of school dinners in our last review obviously stung. Head at pains to show off rebuilt school kitchen where all the food is prepared from fresh; not so much as a sauce or a pizza base bought in. We watched children tucking into a proper roast dinner, served on china plates rather than dreadful institutionalised plastic trays. Not masses of choice (though there was salad and fresh fruit) but actually nice that everyone was eating the same, sitting around in small groups rather than long benches. Children can bring in their own packed lunches and some do – but they are not segregated and can sit with friends who are eating school dinners. All very civilised.

About the only negative in the last Ofsted report was pupil attendance. Nothing to do with truanting here, but apparently caused by parents taking their children out for term time holidays. Some of the families have links overseas, or older siblings at private schools with longer holidays. These affluent types consider that the school's disapproval and only available sanction, the £50 (national figure) penalty, is a price worth paying for their convenience.

However that's not to say that parents are generally disdainful of this place – they all recognise it is a gem and are happy to give generously of their time and money to ensure the place is superbly resourced and has great facilities. Their support is a real USP of the school and goes above and beyond the norm. 'We are absolutely on board, there's no them and us,' said one. 'It's a bit full on,' ventured another. 'Because we all live locally and walk to school we all get to know each other and it's hard not to get drawn in.' Parents who prefer to keep their distance, beware.

Big wow to the PTA, which gets involved with major building projects and raises seriously impressive sums – typically £40,000 a year, but on occasion they have raised that through one big event alone. 'We raise so much money it is almost embarrassing,' said one mother. 'But there are also some purely fun events and I'm glad we now support outside charities as well'.

Definitely a cut above the (above) average state primary. Turns out confident, articulate pupils, who have enjoyed a really positive educational experience. Great sense of community. Fail to get involved at your peril.

Shrewsbury House School

107 Ditton Road, Surbiton, Surrey KT6 6RL

Tel: 020 8399 3066

Independent • Pupils: 320 • Ages: 7–13 • C of E • Fees: £16,665 pa

Email: office@shspost.co.uk
Website: www.shrewsburyhouse.net

11

Headmaster: Since 2010, Mr Kevin Doble BA (law and political sciences) PGCE (40s). Educated at St John's College, Johannesburg and has a postgrad degree in management. Previously second master and acting head at Edge Grove prep and before that head of English at Newlands School and Vinehall prep. This is his first experience of a day school, although he likens it to 'a boarding school with no beds' because of the breadth of opportunities

on offer to Shrewsbury House boys. 'I know that the move I made to Surrey was a crackingly good one,' he says.

Parents appreciate his softly softly approach. He's contained, but passionate about his work. Eloquent, focused and evidently relishes the vivacity of the school day. He's made a few changes (parents say largely logistic and for the better) and his staff appointments and promotions are popular. 'He's great,' said one parent.

Seemingly not enough hours in the day for the head – and the pupils he calls 'these little guys.' He cuts a rangy figure as he makes his presence felt around the place, at the gates morning and night and out on the touchline as often as possible. When he can be lured inside, he directs operations from his homely 'oval office' (named from its bay window looking out over the playground) and packed with books, art, sports memorabilia, and a big green leather sofa for his many visitors. Keen to keep up a continual dialogue with staff, parents, pupils and other heads, he's quickly gained a reputation as very approachable. Still fits in some teaching – takes each year 5 class for a lesson a week in English. 'My son is riveted by his lessons,' said one mother. 'He was telling ghost stories off the cuff the other day and evidently had them spellbound.'

Parents seem supportive and pupils evidently feel comfortable around him too. One mother told us that she overheard a boy asking why he had to have his hair cut short for school – 'and the head took him seriously and gave him a proper response, not just a "because we say so" answer.' Meanwhile another parent commented: 'It's rather a cliché, but he really does seem to combine youthful enthusiasm with respect for this school's reputation and heritage.'

He loves sport and has had great success managing the Saxon Tigers U15 and U17 squads for England hockey and in coaching cricket. Chairman

Fits in some teaching. 'My son is riveted by his lessons,' said one mother. 'He was telling ghost stories off the cuff the other day and evidently had them spellbound'

of IAPS committee for sports. Lists his recreations as (more) sport, drama, children's literature, opera, painting and drawing. Keen traveller, enjoys going out for meals and generally 'recharging' during weekends and holidays.

Entrance: At 7, there are up to 50 places available, with around four applications for each one. Currently receiving requests to register children at birth. Most come from pre-preps, including its own Shrewsbury Lodge (off-site, formerly Milbourne Lodge junior school, merged with Shrewsbury House in 2010), Weston Green, Wimbledon Common Prep, The Rowans, Park Hill, Linley House, Lion House School, The Merlin, Putney Park School and Athelstan House. Around 25 per cent come from the state system. While 20 years ago this was a very local school, now 50 per cent of pupils are bussed in from over five miles away.

The head believes that too often a school's admissions criteria will be overtly focused on one thing – 'usually a unilateral adhesion to academic demands' – and he personally eschews the notion of early assessment as 'ridiculous at that age.' But he acknowledges that the school has to ensure its boys are up to the above average requirements of coping with an intensive day. So Shrewsbury House does it slightly differently, with two types of entry – conditional (non-competitive, formerly called guaranteed) and competitive. But be warned, the 35 or so conditional places are snapped up sharpish and your son will still be gently assessed to ensure he'll be able to cope at the school. These tests are held in the autumn before anticipated entry and are for families for whom the school is first choice and are therefore happy to cough up half a term's fees as a deposit. Once these places are filled, then the remaining dozen or so competitive places are up for grabs by the boys who achieve the highest scores in non-verbal and verbal assessments. Some bursaries available.

This place is all about 13+ and there is no support or preparation for boys looking to move at 11+. Look elsewhere if you have your eye on other senior school destinations – it's not the path for you.

Exit: At 13, boys progress to an impressive range of some 15 senior schools, including King's College School (Wimbledon), Hampton School, St Paul's, St

John's, Epsom College, Wellington, Charterhouse, Tonbridge and The Royal Grammar School (Guildford). A few go to Eton and Harrow. The school's previous head (in post for 23 years) gave parents enormous confidence in this area, so the new head's challenge must be to forge strong links of his own. He's off to a good start. Parents describe him as 'very knowledgeable' when he discusses future schools for their sons, first of all in year 5, and he prides himself on his personal relationships with all the leading senior school heads. 'I know all these men and understand exactly how their schools are ticking on,' he says. Has just launched a scheme to send Shrewsbury House heads of department out to senior schools to improve their grasp of what's expected. Also talks of plans to track boys after they leave. 'I like his idea of making Shrewsbury House accountable,' said one mother. It's not just about getting them through CE and not caring past that – he seems to want to make sure the boys are equipped to thrive beyond this school.' Head particularly pleased to have enticed Anthony Seldon as a governor recently – 'it's not his usual thing at all.'

Remarks: This is a first class prep, where academic rigour is balanced by an equally strong offering in arts and sport. Although your son will need to be above average academically to cope here, with that proviso, the school says it takes a range of abilities. But be warned. As one mother advises: 'It's not intensely academic, but I wouldn't recommend it for a boy who just scrapes the test. It's quite full on.' Others agree it is not for the faint-hearted. 'You have to be quite committed to come here,' says a parent, 'and that includes parents as well as boys.' 'They are run ragged,' says another. 'But they come home happy.' Add to the academic and extensive extracurricular offering a packed sporting programme, rehearsals, performances, charity initiatives, competitions and trips and you'll get the picture – these are busy boys.

Shrewsbury House boys are set and streamed, tracked and given plenty of exam practice. 'I prefer to concentrate on performance, rather than results,' says head

Located on a quiet road in an up-market residential area of Surbiton, the school is one of the UK's oldest preps and celebrated its 150th anniversary in 2015. It is based around a Victorian house, but with additional purpose-built classrooms and impressive facilities, all on a six-acre site, including a playing field and a further seven acres at

Almshouse Lane, which includes all-weather pitches and pavilions.

Broad-based, eclectic curriculum is delivered by a talented teaching team, much praised by parents. 'They are inspiring,' one mother told us. Every teacher is a qualified subject specialist and sports coaches have all been outstanding in their fields – the promise here is that whatever his ability, every boy will be taught and/or coached by someone with real expertise. 'I can't praise the teachers enough', said a parent. 'They seem to be here morning, noon and night, and weekends, and even holiday time clubs are starting now. They go beyond just teaching them. I walk away from parent evenings thinking "wow, I wish I'd had teachers like that."'

It's a longish and busy school day, but the boys seem to rise to the challenge, arriving by 8.15am and staying until at least 4pm, and very often 5.15 or 6.15pm when involved in extracurricular clubs or sports matches. All the extracurricular you can shake a stick at – from cookery (very popular) to rifle-shooting – or they can just stay and do their prep. Homework is 30 minutes to one hour plus per night, right from the beginning. Quite concentrated in term time, but now none in the holidays. 'Work is pretty relentless and they have high expectations of the boys', a mother told us. 'The motto is "aim high" and they do.

Although the head believes there is generally too much testing, measuring and scoring in education these days, Shrewsbury House boys are set and streamed, comprehensively tracked and given plenty of exam practice. 'But I prefer to concentrate on performance, rather than results,' he says. 'If you get top performance, the results will come'.

Any special needs provision is given in the classroom setting, with staff supported by the special educational needs co-ordinator and a learning support teacher. Less than 10 per cent of boys have a learning difficulty or disability. All pupils have English as their first language or are fully bilingual.

Year 8s were getting on swimmingly with the Rime of the Ancient Mariner, having just finished some Dickens

Average class size is around 16 (fewer as boys move up the school and into sets), with an 8-1 pupil-teacher ratio overall. We saw some lively lessons, but always in a focused way, with all the boys on task. A French lesson, taught by a native speaker, with boys vying for an opportunity to speak was typical. Similarly, lots of fun and experiments in science. There's a particularly rich English timetable – year 8s were getting on swimmingly with The Rime of the Ancient Mariner, having just finished some Dickens. Asked if they found Dickens 'hard,' as per recent media coverage, they replied, 'no, because we had just done Othello and it was much easier than that.' Most classrooms are equipped with computer-integrated desks and the few without have Netbooks instead. Some great subject-specific classrooms, including a lively and bright maths room (50 boys won gold in the National Mathematics Challenge recently) and one of the best history rooms we've ever seen –a modern museum feel to the place with the teacher's own collection of helmets and weapons secured to the wall. Boys allowed to handle sometimes, which evidently helps bring the whole subject to life for them – a Shrewsbury House team has won the national Townsend Warner History Competition twice in the last four years. Even the Latin room, not traditionally a 'must-see' destination, was decorated with the teacher's own artefacts.

Music and sport are real strengths of this place. The school has an outstanding local reputation for sport, and several parents mention it as a deciding factor in their choice of Shrewsbury House. Major sports played are football, rugby and cricket, but, unsurprisingly following head's appointment, hockey is now writ large on the radar and other activities including fives and basketball have been introduced. School gives equal weight to the 'very good' and the 'not quite there yet' theory that many will get there in the end – as long as they are given the chance and not fobbed off with some French assistant keeping the fourth 11 busy. It's not unknown for boys to move from G team to A team during their time at the school. 'If you have a sporty son the school will embrace and develop that and take it to the max,' says one mother. 'But equally, my other son was not sporty at all, yet still received top-notch coaching and was proud to represent the G and H teams.' This expert coaching, coupled with the huge pride the boys have in representing their school, undoubtedly gives them the edge and makes them formidable opponents – they have a 70 per cent win rate across the board.

Despite this renown and head's own predilection for the sporting life, he seems almost irritated by the 'sporty place' label. 'We actually spend more time on music, but that's not as well known because sport is such an outward-facing part of the curriculum and tends to attract more attention,' he told us.

Music is the other stand-out subject here. Around 85 per cent of the boys take instrumental or singing lessons and they get plenty of chances to perform – there are 25 different musical groups and regular concerts, with jazz and brass band especially popular. 'The standard is incredible,' said one parent. The boys put on six plays a year and everyone is expected to get involved at some point, even if only as the back of a horse or with a single line – it's all about getting them out of their comfort zone sometimes. LAMDA examinations another recent innovation.

Lovely to see the splendid library heaving at break times. Total of 6,000 books, lots of magazines and good attendances for author visits (lately Josh Lacey, Robert Muchamore, Ali Sparkes and Charlie Higson). Reading club for lower years. Boys also sitting drawing, following how-to-draw guides or just copying pictures of tanks out of reference books – so they are evidently not all out on the sports field.

'We actually spend more time on music, but that's not as well known because sport is such an outward-facing part of the curriculum and attracts more attention'

Boys we saw were well-behaved – in fact an extremely courteous and friendly bunch. They won't get away with slacking, slouching or scruffiness as high standards prevail throughout, but overall the atmosphere is positive and they get plenty of praise where it's due. Healthy competition for 'plus points' – like house points except individual boys can win personal prizes, usually books, as well as credit for their house. Minus marks for minor misdemeanours, such as running in corridors or forgetting a book. Overall parents find school discipline is straightforward and consistent.

Some disquiet over variable school/home communications systems in the past – school says it has addressed this now and parents agree headway has been made. One big improvement is the instigation of a parent consultation evening, where the boys come with their parents to discuss their progress with teaching staff. This replaces a not very enticing invitation for parents to come in to discuss 'problems and difficulties.' Parents are also invited to head's biannual 'state of the nation'-type briefings and to a programme of lectures on subjects like happiness, self-esteem and revision technique. 'In the past the school gave you the feeling that they intended to get on with the job all by themselves and didn't welcome our input,' said one parent. 'But now it feels like more of a partnership.' Thriving parents' association does its bit too – organises lots of social dos alongside more heavyweight initiatives including £40,000+ project to refurbish the school's Irving room in celebration of its 150th anniversary.

A high achieving, all-round school, wonderfully purposeful and more inclusive than a first glance might suggest. Head seems to have parents and pupils on side and is making his presence felt.

The Study Preparatory School

Wilberforce House, Camp Road, London SW19 4UN

Independent • Pupils: 320 • Ages: 4–11 • Fees: £11,925 pa

Tel: 020 8947 6969

Email: admissions@thestudyprep.co.uk
Website: www.thestudyprep.co.uk

19

Headmistress: Since 2011, Mrs Susan Pepper MA PGCE NPQH (50s). Educated at Godolphin & Latymer School, read history at Somerville College, Oxford. Previously head of history and deputy head at Francis Holland. An interesting move/appointment for someone with previous experience only in girls' secondary schools, but it is generally felt she has found her niche. 'She is focused and dynamic but a softee at heart'. Determined to develop and

expand the school while maintaining its 'excellent ethos'. Has delighted parents by bringing in school lunches, with all food cooked on site. Has invested in ICT software and hardware and in-class staff training, and improved and streamlined communications. Parents say, 'very approachable, not at all forbidding', 'never hurries us in conversations', 'our children are in good hands', 'manages expectations well and gives good advice'. They feel that her knowledge of the senior school system has distinct advantages. She displays a commitment that should move the school from strength to strength. She will listen to others' points of view, but will always drive through what she sees as necessary change. Her mantra is 'do the best by every child'. One mother said, 'gives the girls lots of respect and makes it easy for them to talk to her'. Teaches RE to years 5 and 6; runs the debating club for the older girls and pony club for the younger ones. Definitely feels that the move was the right decision. We think she could be right. Married with one grown up son. Enjoys riding, keeping ex-battery hens, gardening, reading and cryptic crosswords in her spare time. When, we wonder, is that.

Entrance: Non-selective at 4+ by ballot and thereafter by assessment. Registration any time up to 18 months before entry. No point in rushing in at birth, it won't make any difference. Sibling priority. Mostly from local Wimbledon area but some from Kingston, Wandsworth and other surrounding areas. The usual cosmopolitan mix of nationalities and backgrounds found in London schools.

Exit: Mainly to local day schools, often with scholarships (17 in 2015), including academic, music, sport and drama. Wimbledon High is at the top, with, amongst others, Lady Eleanor Holles, St Paul's Girls, Putney High, Surbiton and Sutton High Schools, Kingston Grammar and Francis Holland following close behind. A few to boarding schools

All classrooms light and bright and busy. In year 1, we walked in just as a butterfly was emerging from a chrysalis – very exciting. Elsewhere, a show and tell session held everyone rapt. Basins with bear shaped taps

such as Frensham and Feltonfleet. Mrs Pepper really does try to make sure that the schools girls try for are the most appropriate. At the beginning of year 5 there is a general talk for all parents, after which she schedules individual sessions to talk them through their daughters' futures. 'She never hurries us and is so reassuring'.

Remarks: A happy school full of lively, enthusiastic girls. Parents love it and have nothing but praise. Couldn't find anyone with a serious criticism, but working parents would love a homework club. All feel that their daughters are nurtured from day one and are not overly pressurised. 'Huge strength is all are treated as individuals and their differences celebrated'.

Over 120 years old. The Study was originally just that, one room, three pupils, one governess. It soon grew and moved to 4, Peek Crescent, purpose built in 1905, now Spencer House accommodating the prep school girls. About 20 years ago another purpose-built school was bought and the pre-prep department moved to Wilberforce House, approximately 10 minutes walk away across Wimbledon Common. The result? One school, two buildings, great teaching and tip top facilities.

Two year 2 girls took us round Wilberforce House. Articulate and enthusiastic, they were keen to show us every nook and cranny. Remembering with joy. Colour coded classes for all levels. Reception now fully high tech: 'we never had computers like these!' But 'we've always had interactive whiteboards'. All classrooms light and bright and busy. In year 1, we walked in just as a butterfly was emerging from a chrysalis – very exciting. Elsewhere, a show and tell session held everyone rapt. Everything is done to provide a happy, relaxed learning environment. Plenty of art on display. Low level loos for the youngest and basins with bear shaped taps. Excellent library with ICT area. Fascinating DT projects. To help with transition, year 3 girls go to Spencer House for drama and art each week.

We were taken round Spencer House by two bright year 6 girls, eager to tell us what they liked best about their school. Seemed to be pretty well everything. Good-sized hall which doubles up as stage for plays and concerts and, on the day we visited, space for a charity fair. Very keen on their charity work: 'Year 6 choose the special ones for the summer term'. The whole school gathers there at least once a term and on special occasions as, for instance, harvest festival. One parent said, 'Spencer House seems a bit small', then went on to say 'facilities fabulous'.

Well-equipped library; excellent science room: 'we can use proper equipment'. High tech ICT room where all have a lesson once a week; as in the lower school, interactive whiteboards everywhere and computers abound. Art room under the eaves, with displays continuing on the walls along the corridor. Individual music rooms named after famous musicians, a wide range of instruments taught. Several choirs and a variety orchestras and groups. Raved about 'our amazing music teacher; really teaches in a fun way'. Music a great strength and leads to several scholarships to senior schools. Drama also huge. Props room known as Narnia; easy to see why. Our guides said, 'everyone does cooking' but we did not see where. A blip, we are assured: both sites have excellent kitchen facilities. (Certainly the 'snack lunch' we were given at the end of the tour was most impressive.) An exceptionally wide range of clubs before, after and during school. 'Latin club at 8am is great'. A parent said, 'something there for every girl, bright or not, will always find a way to shine'.

Teaching appears excellent. Relaxed for the younger children, form teachers covering most subjects; more specialists in the upper school. Those we met were friendly, welcoming and keen to inform. Girls like them all. Average age mid-40s, over a quarter having been there for more than 10 years. Sad lack of males, but head said good ones are hard to find. Average class size 22, never more than 24.

Weekly staff meeting for whole school when specific problems can be discussed. Up-to-date, well-informed learning support co-ordinator. Continuous assessment and plenty of help for those who need it, including the very able. One-to-one when necessary, charged as an extra. EAL lessons also provided, when needed, at extra cost. Comprehensive anti-bullying policy. Believe it is important to provide equal opportunity for all children and 'encourage them to think beyond the school gate'. Head feels they are particularly good at building up confidence. Apparently, teachers go out of their way to make sure that each child 'has a moment of glory'.

Good play areas outside both houses, with separate sections for the younger pupils. Sport and PE very important. They say it is all about 'enjoyment, opportunity, success and celebration'. Good variety, taught by specialist teachers. Competitive matches from year 3. National prize winners in netball, cross-country and athletics. Now have their own sports field. 'Head of sport has amazing drive and enthusiasm'.

Surbiton High Boys' Preparatory School

Linked schools: Surbiton High Junior Girls' School, 245; Surbiton High School, 246

3 Avenue Elmers, Surbiton, Surrey KT6 4SP

Independent · Pupils: 147 · Ages: 4–11 · Fees: Day: up to £12,543 pa

Tel: 020 8390 6640

Email: surbiton.prep@surbitonhigh.com
Website: www.surbitonhigh.com

Headteacher: Since September 2015, Mrs Sally Ralph, previously deputy head at both the Boys' Prep and Junior Girls schools. A mathematics specialist and formerly a head teacher, she has plenty of leadership experience in independent schools.

Entrance: At 4, by informal assessment in the previous November. Now two form entry. Occasional places in other year groups depending on availability. No need to register at birth, child's performance at the assessment is all that matters. 'We're looking for boys who engage with us, who try to answer questions with a thought process, and who can work with others.' Oversubscribed at all year groups, with at least two applicants for every place.

Exit: At 11, to a very good range of local schools – most to Hampton or Reed's, others to King's College Wimbledon, Kingston Grammar.

Remarks: Originally Arundel House Prep, the school has been part of Surbiton High ever since 1987, which, says Surbiton principal Ann Haydon, 'is a trinity of three schools in one' and very much operates as one school. The only difference between the girls' and boys' provision is that the boys have to leave at the age of 11. 'We'd love to have the boys in the senior school, but there's no space,' confirmed the principal.

Classes up to year 2 now based at newly acquired Charles Burney House. Lack of space in original site is evident in the boys' playgrounds, which are well-equipped but small. However, the boys don't seem to miss out. They have regular and frequent use of their sister school's facilities across the road and a coach service takes them to a variety of sporting facilities, where they play rugby, football, cricket, hockey, basketball and tennis. They can also do swimming, athletics and gymnastics. A splendid cabinet stuffed full of trophies attests to the seriousness with which sport is taken here.

Music also has a high profile, with choral singing a particular strength ('we're passionate about singing,' says the head of music). Boys regularly prepped for choral scholarships to Hampton and the like. Attractive new music room boasts an enticing array of instruments for the children to try and lots of boys take lessons on anything from guitar to trombone. Overall, the main school building – a typically elegant, old house in this affluent area – has great charm. The classrooms are colourful, inviting and all equipped with interactive whiteboards.

Broad curriculum, with particularly good opportunities for learning languages. French is taught from reception, and Spanish and Mandarin on offer as the boys go up the school. Cheerful and inviting learning support room is staffed by very friendly SENCo and caters for a variety of mild to moderate SENs, among them dyslexia, dyspraxia and Asperger's. Probably not the place for children with significant behavioural needs. 'We'd find that

Choral singing a particular strength ('we're passionate about singing,' says the head of music). Boys regularly prepped for choral scholarships

difficult with present staffing.' Two EAL teaching staff work across all three schools with children who need them.

Breakfast and after-school clubs are widely used by parents, who, says school, are usually both working; a network of coach routes helps with the journey to and from school.

The school prides itself on nurturing children's individual talents and strengths – this was confirmed by parents we spoke to, all of whom confirmed that the pastoral care was excellent and the staff both kind and supportive. 'The school is going from strength to strength,' said one very happy mother of two boys, 'and there's a lovely community spirit.' The classes we saw were purposeful and orderly, and the boys we talked to were likeable, articulate and personable young men, well-mannered, thoughtful and very smartly turned out in their bottle green and grey uniforms. They clearly had great affection for their school, and when asked what sort of boys would do well here, emphatically replied 'everyone!'

A happy school, where brisk kindness is part of the curriculum.

Surbiton High Junior Girls' School

Linked schools: Surbiton High Boys' Preparatory School, 243; Surbiton High School, 246

95–97 Surbiton Road, Kingston Upon Thames, Surrey
KT1 2HW

Independent • Pupils: 289 • Ages: 4–11 • Fees: Day: up to
£12,543 pa

Tel: 020 8439 1309

Email: surbiton.juniorgirls@surbitonhigh.com
Website: www.surbitonhigh.com

13

Head: Since September 2015, Clemmie Stewart, previously director of teaching and learning at Surbiton High; she continues to teach English at the junior school. She started her career at Farleigh Preparatory School in Andover, before moving to Talavera Junior School in Aldershot as a member of the senior leadership team.

Entrance: All girls are assessed prior to entry – an age-appropriate and child-friendly exercise. At 4+ the tests are based on cognitive and social development, with the girls doing simple tasks observed by teachers. At 7+ girls are tested in line with the national curriculum for English and maths and a school report is also requested. Most families come from immediate surrounding areas (11 school bus routes and 10 mins from BR station). Main feeders are Thames Ditton Infant School, Dicky Birds Nursery, Bushy Tails Nursery and Maple Road Infants School.

Exit: Some 90 per cent go to linked senior school as entry is now automatic (school prefers term

'natural progression'). Otherwise it's local grammars or other independents. Some parental moans that girls are not prepared for entry to other schools. The school counters that Surbiton is basically an all-through school, which parents know when they choose the junior section, and that girls leave the juniors with good results and are therefore quite capable of gaining a place elsewhere.

Remarks: Vibrant happy place, modern yet homely, with a good local reputation and turning out confident, articulate girls, largely for its own senior department.

Attainment is high. Teaching is rigorous and lessons move along at a brisk pace. Even the youngest quickly prove capable of working alone or in small groups for short periods. Teaching styles 'relaxed but productive – we don't mind a bit of noise as they process what they're learning and we want them to feel confident enough to take a risk, make a mistake, as they learn – it's the best way to learn.' Girls follow the national curriculum closely, but not exclusively, and take Sats in year 6, generally with great success. Pupils work hard and go home tired – so homework is scaled back accordingly to three 30 minute sessions a week and absolutely none during the holidays (though some will be provided at parents' request). Nice teacher/pupil relationships. Some girls from Korea and Indian sub-continent supported with EAL lessons. Learning support for mild difficulties such as dyslexia and dyspraxia, along with support and access improvements to help the physically disabled. Parents can pay extra for one-to-one SEN support. School has an SEN teacher who works three days a week. Enrichment groups in English, maths and science are laid on for the gifted and talented, in addition to in-class support through planned differentiation.

Outside pure academia there is lots going on. Plenty of clubs and outings, including residential trips from year 4. As with senior school, sport has been a concern here (small site militates against it) but generally seen as improving and the junior girls use the off-site extensive sports grounds at Hinchley Wood. Regular music and drama productions.

Lovely modern building was purpose-built – so no complaints there. Ten minutes from central Surbiton, it's a very urban space – local parking a nightmare so school has organised staggered start times to give all year groups a fair crack at the limited drop off area. Works well. Inside it's a bright and stimulating environment, a purposeful place with some outstanding specialist facilities – particularly art, music and science. Parents give special mention to the breadth of the curriculum and the child-centred approach – 'I like the ethos and the moral fabric of the school,' said one mother. The pupils are listened to and are happy that they have a voice – strong school council system.

Teaching styles 'relaxed but productive – we don't mind a bit of noise as they process what they're learning'

Real sense of pride in the place – very small girls who didn't realise they were being watched were seen holding doors open for each other, and one nonchalantly picked up an overturned waste paper bin as she passed without missing a beat. Lunchtimes have been much improved by a new system called 'family service' where, having previously chosen what to eat, the girls sit at the appropriate small table and are served by a member of staff or a year 6 pupil – changes the mix and fosters sense of community. Even the necessary but unappealing table-clearing duties carried out cheerfully afterwards. 'The whole lunchtime set up is lovely now – and the food's improved,' said one pleased mum. A kindly atmosphere pervades. 'There's no such thing as a perfect school – but what makes the difference is the way the school deals with any issues – here I always feel listened to and where it's been warranted, something has been done,' a mother said. A few gripes about home/school communication – claims that school is flaky over notifications of after-school clubs being cancelled and the like. However, with the linked boys' prep and seniors, there's a real family feel to the place, with many families having children at all three schools.

Surbiton High School

Linked schools: Surbiton High Boys' Preparatory School, 243; Surbiton High Junior Girls' School, 245

Surbiton Crescent, Kingston Upon Thames, Surrey KT1 2JT

Tel: 020 8439 1309

Independent • Pupils: 1,034 • Ages: 11–18 • Sixth form pupils: 235 • Fees: Day: up to £15,387 pa

Email: surbiton.high@surbitonhigh.com
Website: www.surbitonhigh.com

Principal: Since 2008, Ms Ann Haydon BSc (40s). Arrived with an excellent reputation from Guildford High (Surbiton's sister school) where she spent five years as deputy headmistress and therefore already au fait with school's owners UCST. Previously she was at Sutton High for seven years,

having joined as youngest-ever head of department (geography), and before that at Putney High.

Was quick to make her mark on the place, showing dynamism and commitment to change, but without making great waves. Homed in on music and sport – which our previous review identified as in need of some oomph – significantly

raising the profile of both. Has also expanded the extracurricular side. Girls like her, parents seem pleased and consensus is that she is good for the school. 'Supremely professional,' said one parent. 'She's very charming,' said another. 'Personable, but formal,' declared a third. Always around and has made great efforts to get to know the girls – teaches year 7 geography, holds form captain lunches, sees girls with especially good reports – which helps her put names to faces. She describes herself as 'passionate about the whole child – it may be a cliché but there really are only visible children as far as I'm concerned.' Hobbies include sport, theatre and music, while her real love is to travel – especially to Africa where she has set up, and continues to run, a children's charity.

Academic matters: Though not the crème de la crème, the girls are generally above average on entry and the school does well by them, delivering solid results with very good value-added. More nurturing than a power house. High quality teaching and learning – girls are pushed to their ability in appropriate sets for core subjects. In 2015 at GCSE (girls generally take nine or 10) over 70 per cent of the results were at A*-A grades, and 94 per cent were A*-B. Good place for linguists – wide breadth on offer at key stage 3 including French, Spanish, German and Latin – even Mandarin available through enrichment programme. Also separate sciences at KS3. At A level, nearly half of grades A or A*; 84 per cent A*-B in 2015. Less common offerings include Italian and Russian. Critical thinking and further maths also available. Most students get places at universities of their choice. Ms Haydon is

keen to increase Oxbridge candidates and has appointed a coordinator to promote the idea to the girls a bit more, with potential candidates identified in year 10 and supported with special lessons and master classes. Parental perception that Oxbridge places are coveted above all others has put a few noses out of joint.

Was quick to make her mark on the place, showing dynamism and commitment to change but without making great waves

Lessons are pacey, taking account of different learning styles, and the girls are well challenged. Excellent monitoring systems in place. Nice emphasis on encouraging pupils to organise themselves – good note-taking skills drilled into them from the off, so that by year 10 it is automatic. Well-resourced, the school makes excellent use of technology all round – one neat example is via Active Expression handsets, linked to software and interactive whiteboards, which the girls use to answer questions during lessons. Means that no-one can be anonymous and teachers can analyse the information later to identify anyone in need of support. The technology moves lessons along more quickly and is proving a powerful tool. School is in process of supplying iPads to every pupil.

Healthy mix of male/female, young/older teachers and pleasingly not much use of supply staff. No

SEN screening on entry but screening for literacy difficulties in year 7. Supported learning section provides individual and small group tuition as needed, literacy booster groups if required and EAL. Parents pay extra towards SEN but cost is subsidised by school – currently eight per cent of the girls receive such help. There is gifted and talented programme for the most academically able girls, involving masterclasses, mentoring and a range of challenging learning opportunities.

Games, options, the arts: Great tradition of high quality art – school has won 17 top candidate awards at GCSE – with girls flourishing in gorgeous open plan art studio. The artwork on display in reception is so good that a visitor might think it was professional. Budding thespians be aware that drama could be stronger – it's there but not as high profile as some places. Music is emerging from a bit of a dip and has been reinvigorated by a new director of music ('he's outstanding,' say parents). Although there appears to be lots going on and school points to a number of individual stand-out performances, parents generally don't recommend the place for a very sporty daughter. All could be about to change as Ms Haydon is determined to turn this around and wants all girls to have more opportunities to participate and perform. Initiatives include overseas hockey and netball tours, tennis development programme and a fitness suite for sixth form. In any event it's not at all bad – outstanding skiing (school produces champions on plastic and snow) with strong rowing (now has its own boat house) and gymnastics (one selected to compete at London 2012) and there's an existing gifted and talented programme for sport. School has also recently announced plans for a new sports hall with badminton and netball facilities. Strong

emphasis now on extracurricular clubs. There are over 70 options, from Bollywood films to word games – new ones include riding and astronomy – and breadth of interest is encouraged; girls are not encouraged to specialise academically or otherwise. Numerous examples of individual successes with girls winning places and competitions in all sorts of areas from music to design to literacy. Put some money aside for some enviable overseas trips – recently France, Spain, USA and Iceland.

Overseas hockey and netball tours, tennis development programme and fitness suite. Outstanding skiing (school produces champions on plastic and snow) with strong rowing (now has own boat house)

Background and atmosphere: School celebrated its 130th anniversary in 2014 – it opened at the same address in a large Victorian house in 1884. Still owned by the United Church Schools Trust, an independent Christian educational charity. But few other clues to such heritage these days. Newcomers searching for the place would easily mistake it for a corporate headquarters. School fills one suburban block, 10 minutes walk from main shops of suburban Surbiton, and is surrounded by assorted housing stock and wide, but car-choked, avenues. Recent years have seen tremendous investment and expansion – all good, but new buildings and layout involve girls in a fair bit of walking to different sites for different lessons – including crossing a main road, albeit with a permanent crossing warden. Refreshing exercise on a summer's day, more miserable in the winter, and it does put a few families off.

Classrooms are light and bright, and facilities first class. Only real minus is a lack of outdoor space on site. (Off site there are extensive sports grounds at Hinchley Wood.) Sixth form has its own building with good IT and private study facilities and a common room. Overall a purposeful, business-like atmosphere with pupils and parents alike raving about how friendly the school is. 'There's a lovely feel to the place,' sums up one.

Pastoral care and discipline: High praise for pastoral care. When talking to one prospective family visiting with their (generally) sweet 11 year old, school staff assured them that 'we'll still like her when she is 15!' 'And they do,' says that mother; 'the pastoral care is really very good.' Most parents report an immediate and effective response to any issues. Generally a well-behaved bunch – largely

complying with the zero tolerance policy on drugs, drink and cigarettes. Smokers hauled before Ms Haydon even if they were caught out of school hours and uniform. School nurse on site, doctor available weekly. Good induction routines for year 7s, followed up with 'big sister' mentoring programme. Healthy culture of 'telling' about problems and school quick to support anyone in difficulty and any of their friends who may have been involved. Not a bitch-fest – girls say their classmates are supportive of them. Parents pleased that school somehow manages to keep cliques and queen bees under control.

Pupils and parents: Townie mix – English middle-class predominate. Some families pay the fees without a thought, while other families work extra shifts to afford the place. 'We're a fairly down-to-earth bunch,' said one. Parents delighted when their unconfident 11 year olds emerge five years later completely self-assured. Several mention how their daughters have blossomed under the Surbiton High watch. Not the smartest set of girls and several parents said they'd like to see tighter monitoring and control of standards – usual problem of creeping hemlines. Sixth formers wear their own clothes – no 'business-dress' requirement. Street-wise, the girls are by and large dedicated and hardworking and can't get away with coasting as involved parents and caring school marshal them in an effective pincer movement.

Entrance: New initiative allows 'natural progression' from the junior to the senior school. 'We know our girls well and there is no need for them to have the stress of an exam,' says Ms Haydon. The 'handful' who may not make the grade are given fair (year 5) warning. Newcomers are assessed in English and maths and write a personal statement which they are encouraged to consider beforehand. Word on the street is that the exams are not as hard as others taken on the entry exam round. The

When one prospective family visited with their 11 year old, school staff assured them that 'we'll still like her when she's 15!' 'And they do,' said that mother

school says that 'interest in the school is such that we have become increasingly selective.' Six forms of 24 – though occasional one-off years of seven form entry. There are isolated parental moans that the school and classes are too big with such a substantial new intake every year – it is a large

school so make sure your shrinking violet would not feel lost in the crowd. Head says there is no such thing as a 'Surbiton girl,' but they are all 'interesting girls'. Intake from south-west London and north-east Surrey. Main feeder schools are Fern Hill Primary, Holy Cross Prep, Rowan Prep, St Michael's C of E, St Paul's C of E, Thames Ditton Junior and Twickenham Prep. For sixth form entry, offers are based on interview and GCSE predictions.

Exit: Some fall out at 16 (there's a good co-ed state sixth form nearby). Most of those who stay proceed to good universities – Bristol, Birmingham, Leeds. New emphasis on Oxbridge (one place in 2015).

Money matters: Parents happy they get value for money – it's not the dearest in the area. Some recent parental disquiet over reports that fees go towards subsidising other schools in UCST group – but the school says there is absolutely no truth in this statement. Help with fees available three ways: from scholarships – academic, music, art, sports; Church Schools Foundation Assisted places (dependent on family income) and bursaries for 'daughters of the clergy'.

Remarks: A large school with a good local reputation – it is not elitist nor a school that treats you as if you are lucky to be there. Head is forward-thinking and full of plans. Parents recommend heartily. Friendly place with happy girls who are achieving academically and progressing personally.

Sutton Grammar School

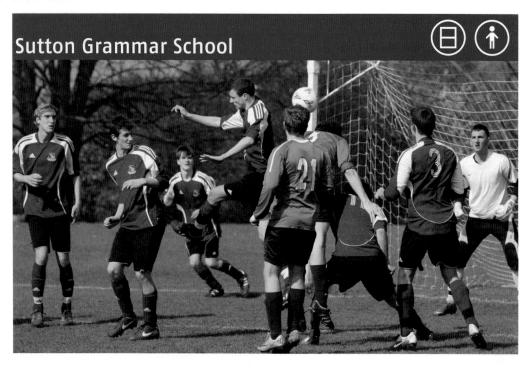

Manor Lane, Sutton, Surrey SM1 4AS

State • Pupils: 840 • Ages: 11–18 • Sixth form pupils: 240

Tel: 020 8642 3821

Email: sgs@suttonlea.org
Website: www.suttongrammar.sutton.sch.uk

34

Headmaster: Since 1990, Mr Gordon Ironside MA PGCE (50s). Read physics at Cambridge, then taught maths at Alleyn's and Sutton Grammar before becoming deputy head in 1987. Married to a fellow teacher, he has three grown-up children who all attended Sutton grammar schools. One son continues what has become a bit of a family tradition and teaches in another local grammar school. Head is involved in a lot of charity work; he is a governor of the local hospital school and adult education college. Affable, hard working and thoroughly dedicated to education all round. Parents say he is always on hand and has the confidence to allow his staff to run their own departments. They appreciate his experience and all the guidance he offers their sons. Head has many interests in the arts, sports and enjoys the occasional round of golf.

Academic matters: Highly selective and always in the top 10 per cent of the highest achieving schools. Needless to say, it delivers mostly excellent results: in 2015, 78 per cent of papers were graded A*/A at GCSE; 57 per cent A*/A at A level. The school specialism is science – all three sciences are very strong and many pupils opt for the science and maths route at GCSE and A level. Very inspiring large and

light labs, greenhouse on the roof and boys breed trout and salmon to release into the River Wandle. Two physics teachers run electronics project clubs and boys have won UK Engineer of the Year and Intech science awards.

Top performing pupils also excel in maths and physics Olympiads. Sixth formers help to teach science in primary schools, while some local schools visit Sutton Grammar to experience working in a lab. Early work experience is arranged in hospitals for those considering careers in medicine. Head stresses that staff work hard to make sure the curriculum is balanced with arts and humanities. Parents say the fairly dynamic English department really stretches boys, as well as organising fun activities with plays and poetry. No classics, modern languages only. Boys can choose from French, Spanish and German. Rigorous computing skills are taught – AIDA qualifications in year 9, leading to GCSE and A level computing. Good mix of male and female staff, most of them long serving. One boy told us 'it's great that the teachers guide the whole way through school'.

SENCo oversees SEN provision throughout the school for a small number of pupils with statements, SpLDs, sensory impairments or high functioning

ASD. Refreshingly honest approach from head, who says this is not school's area of expertise and stresses that pupils have to be able to cope and enjoy the fast moving and competitive environment.

Games, options, the arts: A fabulous 27-acre sports ground in Cheam, used by pupils, old boys and Surrey football clubs. PE staff make a tremendous effort to help boys find sporting pursuits they enjoy, from table tennis to county league cricket. Around 12 football teams and three rugby sides compete in fixtures list, along with a host of house sports competitions. The school also boasts its own largish heated open-air swimming pool. Standard D of E programme and well established CCF (run with Nonsuch Girls School). Parents say the sporting opportunities for all are a great credit to the school.

All three sciences are very strong. Very inspiring large and light labs, greenhouse on the roof, and boys breed trout and salmon to release into the River Wandle

Some impressive art displays around the school, although only a small number choose to take GCSE and A level art. Many more opt for the design and technology path, either in graphics or electronics.

Chamber groups, orchestras and choirs engage in a range of musical pursuits, including A Cappella singing. Tuition on any instrument of a boy's choice can be arranged. Composer in residence runs an annual composition festival. Music and drama departments team up with Sutton High School (neighbouring girls' school) for concerts and plays, including a biannual musical production. Both schools and parents pull together to produce fabulous productions. Drama on the curriculum: a reasonable number of boys go on to take GCSE and A level theatre studies. LAMDA courses and exams on offer too. The old gym has been converted into a drama studio (for which a talented pupil has designed a lighting system).

During the summer term there is an annual activities week; trips include foreign travel, adventure sports camps and a year 9 visit to the First World War battlefields. Others attend first aid training courses and some older pupils try their hand at teaching in local primary schools.

Background and atmosphere: The school has always been single sex. It opened as Sutton County Grammar in 1899, charging fees of two pounds and 10 shillings per term. More or less everything you could want is on site, so it's all fairly compact. New buildings are constantly popping up (the latest addition is a two-storey maths block).

Playground areas are small. Boys from year 10 upwards are allowed to go off site during the lunch hour. Sandwich bar in the playground (known as the Snack Shack) helps to relieve the lunchtime crush. Stylish but small newly designed canteen serves hot meals. Everything runs like clockwork in this traditional focused grammar school. Boys are well-behaved, motivated and articulate.

Pastoral care and discipline: Traditional house system and year group tutors look after pupils' welfare. One parent told us she felt confident that problems were dealt with 'very swiftly.' Boys taught to respect others and take responsibility for all aspects of the school and themselves. Everyone is expected to follow a strict but fair code on behaviour, hair and uniform.

The school has a no-nonsense approach to discipline and stresses to pupils that silly behaviour wastes valuable time. Parents' information evenings and discussion groups run on a wide range of topics, often led by outside speakers. Parents are canvassed on subjects they'd like to know more about each term and pupils are welcome to attend too if they wish.

Pupils and parents: Parents are mostly professionals from all kinds of backgrounds – wealthy Surrey and south Londoners along with those from less

affluent areas. Great mix of brains from all over the world, 30 to 40 per cent of the boys are from other cultures. PTA is an impressive group, raising around £60,000 each year for the benefit of pupils and for school developments.

School runs mock test days for around 2,000 children each year wanting to prepare for 11+ entry into selective grammar schools. When an application for a government grant to convert classrooms into a science lab was unsuccessful, PTA stepped in to help with the cost. The Suttonians have a very active old boys' network and a large number of them remain involved with the school. Famous alumni include Brian Paddick, Christopher Bigsby, David Bellamy and David Farrar.

Entrance: Places are highly sought after, with around 1,500 boys competing for 135 places at 11+ (includes extra 15 places added in 2015). School sets its own exam, reasoning paper, English and maths. Currently no catchment area, so highest scorers win the places. At 16+, approximately five competitive entry places are available for newcomers to the sixth form.

Exit: Almost all to university, although the occasional pupil takes up a specialist apprenticeship in the workplace. Eleven to Oxbridge in 2015 and good numbers to study veterinary sciences and medicine. Others to a range of top universities, with London colleges particularly popular.

Remarks: School offers fantastic opportunities for those who make the grade. A must for academically able and enthusiastic young men.

Sutton High Junior School

Linked school: Sutton High School, 253

55 Cheam Road, Sutton, Surrey SM1 2AX

Tel: 020 8225 3072

Independent · Pupils: 265 · Ages: 3–11 · Fees: up to £12,021 pa

Email: junioroffice@sut.gdst.net
Website: www.suttonhigh.gdst.net

Head of junior school: Since September 2015, Anne Musgrove. With a BA in education studies from the University of Warwick, she has over 20 years' experience of teaching in both the independent and maintained sectors including a number of years teaching in Australia. Formerly deputy head (academic) and acting head at Putney High Junior School, she joined Sutton High Junior School as

Well-stocked library has aptly been named the Discovery Zone. Colourful corridors lined with children's art, poetry and other achievements. Neat and amenable girls appear beautifully behaved, happy and involved

deputy head in 2014 and was promoted to head of junior school. She continues to pursue her interest in art and art history by visiting galleries and museums in the UK and overseas.

Entrance: Girls can join the nursery from their third birthday onwards and move onto reception at 4+. Younger children attend an informal play session before being offered a place; from 6+ girls sit assessment tests. For entry into other years telephone the school to enquire about occasional places.

Exit: At 11+ around three-quarters of the girls move to the senior school. Remainder move to co-ed or local grammar schools. Girls who are not suited to the senior school will be advised in year 5 to give them plenty of time to look for an alternative.

Remarks: Traditional junior school which aims to offer a broad and balanced curriculum to suit a range of tastes. Carefully structured early years stage focuses on instilling basic literacy and numeracy skills through structured play whilst also developing independence and confidence.

Moving up the school, everything appears to be well planned, with lots of music, drama and sport alongside traditional subjects. Setting for maths from year 4 and English from year 5. Impressive foreign languages programme: French starts in the nursery, years 3 and 4 are introduced to Spanish and years 5 and 6 start German and Latin. Teaching staff includes a few old girls; all are unanimous about aiming to pass on and develop a love of learning and natural curiosity in their young charges.

Well-stocked library has aptly been renamed the Discovery Zone. Colourful corridors lined with children's art, poetry and other achievements. Neat and amenable girls appear beautifully behaved, happy and involved in their work. Drama is incorporated into the English curriculum and taught by class teachers; girls are encouraged to take LAMDA grade exams, organised by visiting teachers. Dedicated music teacher works extremely hard and successfully, producing two big concerts each year, as well as regular musical assemblies. All pupils learn keyboard and recorder in class; individual tuition is available on any other instrument.

SENCo, and a part-time specialist teacher for small group work or one-to-one tuition, assist children with mild specific learning difficulties or differences. There is also an EAL coordinator. Tops and Tails provides an on-site wraparound care facility from 7:30am – 6:30pm. Everything from breakfast to homework club for 3 to 11-year-olds is available at a reasonable hourly rate. They also run a Thursday morning toddler group for boys and girls aged nought to three years.

Suits a wide range of enthusiastic little girls, and perhaps a good choice, with its complementary services, for working parents.

Sutton High School

Linked school: Sutton High Junior School, 252

55 Cheam Road, Sutton, Surrey SM1 2AX

Independent · Pupils: 368 · Ages: 11–18 · Sixth form pupils: 56 · Fees: £15,450 pa

Tel: 020 8642 0594

Email: office@sut.gdst.net
Website: www.suttonhigh.gdst.net

36

Headmistress: Since 2012, Mrs Katharine Crouch BSc NPQH. Joined Sutton High School in 2003 and has held many roles including head of biology, head of pastoral and deputy head.

Academic matters: Solid results across the board in academics and the arts; 62 per cent A*/A at GCSE

and 47 per cent at A level in 2015. Head is very aware that today's young people need a range of skills and accomplishments to succeed in the competitive 21st century world; provision throughout the school is being reviewed and updated. Teachers are currently trialling the best way to maximise each individual's potential; consequently, girls are set according to ability and their strongest learning style. School appreciates the importance of ICT skills, offering DiDA (Diploma in Digital Applications) and GCSE qualifications and an ICT club. Separate or dual award science. Maths fairly strong all round, although some parents feel that less confident mathematicians should be identified and assisted much earlier. Good, practical help is also available: everyone is taught about budgeting and money management. Very impressive results for Latin; French, Spanish, German and Latin are offered throughout the school, with Greek run as an after-school class. Decent number of trips both here and abroad. Lots of girl-power on the staff – female majority – who are all committed to ensuring there are no ceilings or barriers for any pupil. Small number of pupils with mild dyslexia are monitored and supported by the SENCo; provision for EAL.

Sixth formers undertake the Extended Project Qualification to help prepare them for university. Girls say it's quite a lot of extra work alongside A levels, but they generally consider it a good thing to do. Enrichment course enables sixth formers to look at a wider range of topics and skills from cookery to philosophy. Friday afternoons are set aside for community service and fundraising activities. Girls collaborate with Sutton Grammar boys for a number of activities, including the Challenge of Management conference, giving them the opportunity to gain an insight into the business world. Biannual careers fair invites representatives from many companies into the school to pitch career paths and ideas to the girls.

Gymnastics is popular and there is a beautiful new dance hall for budding ballerinas and dancing divas. Sporty girls do particularly well in athletics championships

Games, options, the arts: Fab facilities and very active and successful sports department. Enormous gym and 25m indoor pool, which is open to pupils and their families at weekends and in the holidays. Gymnastics is popular and there is a beautiful new dance hall for budding ballerinas and dancing divas. Sporty girls compete in house and in local competitions, and do particularly well in county athletics and cross country championships. Assortment of sports tours organised annually to all parts of the globe.

The arts fare well across the school, particularly music: dedicated music teachers, lots of practice rooms and music technology suite. Different choirs to choose from, traditional to gospel, depending on the girls' interests. Fine groups of young instrumentalists play in a range of ensembles; tuition can be arranged for any instrument, subsequently, dynamic and well-thought-of orchestras. All this considered, rather a low take-up of GCSE and A level music. In-house and joint music concerts and drama productions with Sutton Grammar. Largish hall for drama, department always welcomes volunteers who'd like to help with staging or learn to use

lighting equipment. Girls also have the opportunity to take the LAMDA acting and speaking exams.

Light, airy art rooms and a separate sculpture hut for pottery, an area where girls are particularly successful. Artistic types are offered the full range of art and design courses through to A level, being able to choose from painting and pottery, textiles, and resistant materials. More inventing and designing for all age groups goes on through the Young Enterprise Scheme. Some lovely creations, textiles, paintings and sculptures, are displayed around the school. Lunchtime and after-school clubs, for which an additional charge is made, offer further opportunities for sports and music. Most subject teachers run drop-in clinics to provide extra support for individuals and extension work.

Background and atmosphere: Founded in 1884 with just a handful of pupils. Over the years, as pupil numbers have grown, neighbouring buildings have been purchased alongside a rolling building programme to keep pace with modern demands. Latest additions include the sixth form centre and sports complex.

> *More inventing and designing for all age groups goes on through the Young Enterprise Scheme. Some lovely creations, textiles, paintings and sculptures, displayed*

In the midst of all the buildings, well-maintained gardens and sports areas create a cloistered look. Busy pupils move round the site in an orderly way. Girls have a good local reputation and the school is always interested in setting up community links, the most well known being their work and artistic pursuits with Sutton Boys Grammar. Old Girls' Association has a reunion at school every year.

Pastoral care and discipline: The headmistress is very keen to review and develop the pastoral care, so that she can build on the good foundations. All new entrants are allocated a buddy to chat to and to help them overcome any small problems. Professional counsellor visits weekly and there is also a school nurse. Head is clued up about the emotional needs and external pressures that affect young people. Form tutors and heads of year monitor academic progress, personal welfare and development. Student council helps compile the Code of Conduct in partnership with staff, giving everybody a chance to have their say.

Pupils and parents: Good mix, socially and ethnically; lots of local business families and City types. Others travel from the edges of south-west London and various parts of Surrey; school is conveniently located close to Sutton station so attracts a wide catchment. School bus services from Wimbledon and Croydon areas. The Parent-Staff Association works to arrange social events and to further sporting opportunities through the parent-run clubs Otter and Centipede. Staff and parents organise an annual multicultural evening. Interesting group of old girls include Dora Black (Lady Russell), Susan Howatch, novelist, and BBC correspondent Sue Littlemore.

Entrance: At 11+ examination in maths, English and online non-verbal reasoning tests plus an interview with a senior member of staff. At 16+ entrance test consisting of general papers, verbal reasoning and interview with the head of sixth form. At least eight GCSEs, grade A or above in subjects chosen for A level.

Exit: At 16+ some move to co-ed or grammar school sixth forms. At 18+ more or less everybody goes to a wide variety of mostly top universities or art colleges. One to Oxbridge in 2015.

Money matters: Academic scholarships at 11+ and 16+ based on top performance in entrance or public exams. Other small scholarships awarded for art, music, drama and PE. Means-tested GDST bursaries are also available.

Remarks: Would suit those who want a single sex education in a calm environment. Parents and friends are looking forward to the head bringing all the school's strengths out into the light. A school to watch?

The Tiffin Girls' School

Richmond Road, Kingston Upon Thames, Surrey KT2 5PL

State • Pupils: 965 • Ages: 11–18 • Sixth form pupils: 300

Tel: 020 8546 0773

Email: contact@tiffingirls.org
Website: www.tiffingirls.kingston.sch.uk

15

Head Teacher: From January 2016 Mr Ian Keary BA NPQH, currently head of Glyn School in Ewell. Before Glyn, was assistant head of the Tiffin School, the equally desirable boys' grammar for four years. Taught PE, worked in maths and IT department and was head of year. Sporty – PE, rugby, cricket, energetic skier. Despite being presented by pupils with model of Marvel character 'The Punisher', also has cracking sense of humour (say former colleagues).

Replaces Ms Amy Cavilla, who has held the fort since April 2015.

Academic matters: Outstanding results, of course, but how could they not be? If you get in here, you will be super-bright, be stimulated by your peers and superlatively taught and you will get the level of results that is normal and expected here. 2015 saw 92 per cent of GCSE grades at A*/A and at A level 93 per cent at A*-B and 75 per cent A*/A. Few GCSEs gain anything lower than B grades. Of the mainstream subjects, only the Englishes and sciences get a fair sprinkling of Bs – all the rest are largely A*/A.

Sciences are popular, languages less so. Latin survives and does well. Drama and art excel at GCSE. At A level, 19 subjects available plus general studies and enrichment programme – taken with

Tiffin Boys. Maths has by far the most takers with the majority achieving A*/A. Also popular are biology and chemistry, English and psychology. French and Spanish the only languages. Latin jointly with the boys' school and tiny numbers take music; few but increasing takers for DT. Lots of Oxbridge graduates on the staff and we heard nothing but praise for the teaching.

A ferocious fire demolished most of the teaching block and a lot of coursework. They talk about it still, down Kingston way

The stringently applied entrance criteria mean that few with learning difficulties clear the hurdle. However, the school is very accessible and would be a good option for your bright daughter with mobility or other physical difficulties.

Games, options, the arts: Rowing an increasing strength – very rare and pretty special for a girls'

state school and it's now on the KS3 carousel of sports – the J15 squad have won gold at the Kingston Small Boats Head; cross-country and volleyball similarly impressive and the school boasts a number of individual stars in various sports. Most games played on site though school also uses the Hawker Centre, a minute or two down the road. Six netball/tennis courts, small Astro for hockey, one field in front of school used when not muddy. Two adjoining gyms plus one small multigym. Sixth form required to do one hour's sport a week – but many do more outside school. Most take the CSLA award. Flourishing Duke of Edinburgh. Lots of trips – sensible, subject-based and not too exotic for most wallets though the US ski trip option seen as prohibitively expensive by many.

Witness the carousel in year 7 in which everyone has a chance to try out instruments; every girl in year 7 sings in the concert, and many join the choir

Art – judging from the massed and massive canvases that grace the corridor walls – is quite exceptional: figurative and topographical paintings which you want on your walls – brilliant use of mixed media and collage. The same applies to the ceramics and textiles. We loved the highly glazed ceramic shoes along one walkway – and art, though taken at A level by far fewer than the talent would suggest, is a key strength here. Music seen as very good if somewhat exclusive – this despite school's strenuous efforts to involve everyone: witness the carousel in year 7 in which everyone has a chance to try out instruments with the encouragement to learn one; and every girl in year 7 sings in the year 7 concert, after which many join whole school choir, for which there is no audition. In this, as in some other respects, the school's reputation seems to be lagging behind the reality. Drama clearly a major school occupation and great gusto expended on productions. Good programme of outside speakers and visits to museums etc. A great sense of the girls themselves using initiative to up their overall experience.

Background and atmosphere: In 1638, Thomas Tiffin, a prosperous brewer, left £50 so that the town clerk could choose a boy 'from ten years of Age, or there abouts' and educate him so that he might gain an apprenticeship and 'git his living'. His brother John left a further £100. There were further benefactors – eg Elizabeth Brown who wanted 'the Children of the poor inhabitants of the Town

of Kingston,... to read the English Tongue and learn some Godly Catechisme...' and Edward Belitha who, in 1717, left money specifically, and to his eternal credit, for the education of 'twenty poor Persons' Daughters'. However, no actual school was founded until 250 years later, after decades of local wrangling, when two 'lower middle class' schools – one for each sex – were established in the 1870s and named after the Tiffin brothers.

Initially, the boys and girls shared a school building – girls upstairs; the fees were modest and scholarships were offered. The schools blossomed and, in 1899, the girls moved to splendid new accommodation in St James's Road where they remained until a second move in 1937. Further expansion led to a another move to a former boys' secondary modern school building between Kingston and Ham. All went fine until 2003 when a ferocious fire demolished most of the teaching block and a lot of coursework. They talk of it still, down Kingston way. The final result of the fire was a terrific new building, at the centre of the present school, and which rescues the site from being sadly undistinguished to having a centre full of light and a sense of generous spaciousness.

The wide new corridors are hung with impressive canvases mentioned above and, in fact, the framing, glazing and hanging of the girls' art makes a major impression on any visitor. The hang is rejigged three or four times a year – we applaud. No classrooms seem crowded and we enjoyed the mix of layout – some are eyes forward to the teacher

behind her desk, others are arranged in tables for four and a wandering teacher. Whiteboards are everywhere and used imaginatively. Large school hall but also good drama studio with clever retractable seating. Good facilities for music, music tech and applied arts. Big project to refurbish and re-site the sixth form centre and the library recently completed – the girls involved in all aspects of the design. The result has been to put the sixth form back at the heart of the school and to give the library and other resources a new home. Girls greatly appreciate sensible central siting of all four IT rooms in the new main building – no hunting around for a free PC. New science labs and art room, plus refurb for Astroturf and netball courts. Security has been upgraded with keypad entry for students. Site is litter-free and functional and mostly in pretty fair nick, though some careful planting could humanise it considerably. Good food – really good – and on a cashless system.

Pastoral care and discipline: Some of the best-presented girls we've seen. Uniform was being reconsidered when we visited but all the girls we saw looked comfortable and tidy in mid-blue jumpers, knee-length grey skirts and, seemingly compulsory, long hair. Sixth formers just have to look respectable and they all do. Excellent new system of two head girls and seven deputies introduced by Mrs Ward. The deputies each have a 'job': environment, learning, integration, well-being, creativity, community, enterprise – and work to develop their area within the school. All girls in a house 'family' – one from each year – which strengthens relationships between the year groups and is a very good idea. The girls we met were adamant about not missing boys during their seven years. 'We see the Tiffin boys all the time,' we were

told. All those we asked said they would send their daughters to a girls' only school.

Praise for the head of pastoral care. The usual problems of highly motivated, clever girls, though no more here than anywhere. Some sense among some parents that not all staff have pastoral care as a priority. Mrs Ward stresses how much is done discreetly and behind the scenes and certainly we liked what we saw of girl-teacher relationships. Few transgressions of the drugs/drink/smokes kind.

A quite extraordinary sense of pride in the school pervades the place: 'We love singing the school song ... I wish we saw more of our Old Girls ... we could learn so much'

We have never met a more articulate, intelligent and thoughtful bunch of girls. They credit the school for giving them the confidence to hold their own in any context: 'They make you take an active role…. Everyone has to take an assembly at least once a year… You get very used to doing PowerPoint presentations, debating and we have masses of practice at presenting ourselves.' A quite extraordinary sense of pride in the school pervades the place: 'We love singing the school song… I wish we saw more of our Old Girls… we could learn so much from them.'

Pupils and parents: Pupils are the very bright daughters of highly organised and ambitious parents – historically not local, and there is some resentment amongst those who do live locally that this, the pre-eminent academic state school, has not until recently served their community. A knock-on is that, although tight friendship groups are formed inside the school, the demographic and logistics mean that socialising outside the school and in leisure time is less easy and some pupils and parents are saddened by the fact that girls live too far away or social life is not valued at home. One mother told us that only one girl in her daughter's class lived within walking distance, and others told us that developing a social life did not rank high in the priorities of many of the parents. This is something Mrs Ward and her team are very aware of and the school now prioritises applicants from local postcodes, which should in future build a more local school community. School also has clever ideas like getting year 10 parents to talk to the parents of girls in the year below and share experiences. Parents' evenings of all kinds – but there is a sense among some that once the big push to get a place at the school is over, too many parents sit back and don't involve themselves as they could.

Most parents voluble in their appreciation: 'they strive to bring out the best in the girls'... 'if ever we have a problem you can always talk to someone — they are good at getting back to you.' 'They are hot on time-keeping... and academically amazing'. Some parental scepticism too: 'It suits the academic, the focused, the conscientious. It wouldn't suit the erratic, the eccentric, those who are academically one-sided.' School strenuously refutes this and it is true that the range of opportunities and activities is impressive and the list of leavers' destinations is as varied as you could hope to find. It may just be that some pupils choose to focus exclusively on academic work and not take advantage of other opportunities.

Notable former pupils include Ritz muralist Helen McKie, actresses Jill Gascoigne and Katherine Parkinson, Lynne (Eats Shoots and Leaves) Truss and Olympian sculler, Sarah Winckless.

Entrance: This is probably the paragraph you are reading first. Some 1,600 applicants for the 180 available year 7 places. Worth noting is the fact that the selection dates are constantly changing and parents are advised to keep up to date with the school's website (currently, register by early September, first stage of test in early October and second in mid November).

Stage one is a 'sifting' test of English and maths multiple choice questions. Places allocated on the basis of results of stage two test, including written maths, reading and writing papers. Sixty places offered to girls living in the inner area, or being eligible for pupil premium funding and living in the inner or designated areas. Other 120 places to those living in designed area. Inner area based on local electoral wards, designated area on local postcodes.

In reality, the tests are sat by some of the brightest girls in the south east. A healthy tutoring industry thrives in the local boroughs, greatly boosted by introduction of maths and literacy tests.

Sixth form entry based on predicted GCSE grades and school report. Applicants must have at least two A*, four A and two B grades.

Exit: Very few depart after GCSE (under 10 per cent). Thereafter Tiffin girls leave for good courses everywhere. In 2015, 25 to Oxbridge and 80 per cent to Russell Group. Medicine and engineering, history and English predominate but really there's nothing they don't do – and do well.

Money matters: All families asked to contribute £30 per month to school funds.

Remarks: Don't apply if you live in an undesignated postcode or if your daughter is only average at school. If she is super-bright, loves to learn, to think and take part in everything, you could find no better school – anywhere.

Tiffin School

Queen Elizabeth Road, Kingston Upon Thames, Surrey KT2 6RL

State • Pupils: 1,109 • Ages: 11–18 • Sixth form pupils: 380 • C of E

Tel: 020 8546 4638

Email: admissions@tiffin.kingston.sch.uk
Website: www.tiffin.kingston.sch.uk

16

Headteacher: Since September 2015, Michael Gascoigne (40s). Deputy head since 2009, and previously head of history and head of sixth form. He is a history and politics graduate from Sheffield University and was educated at Whitgift School. Married with two children, enjoys politics, history, reading and sport.

Academic matters: Always among the highest performing grammars in the country. Results uniformly outstanding. Trad range of subjects – no business or psychology here – Latin sails on and the boys can take Greek. Maths popular as are the individual sciences followed by English, history and economics. Eighty-six per cent of all A level results in 2015 were A*-B, 60 per cent A*/A. GCSEs similarly – compulsory religion and philosophy much enjoyed and achieves sky-high results, as does maths. In 2015, 82 per cent of all grades were A*/A. Langs – never the top take in a boys' school – relatively strong and well-supported with visits and exchanges. Great common sense in allowing boys to take double or triple sciences – no regimentation means that natural artists or linguists do not feel squeezed out as in many more blinkered places.

It's not just results. Parents – and boys – praise the intellectually stimulating and challenging teaching styles – 'it's traditional and it's excellent,' we were told. 'The teachers don't feel they have to dumb down for these boys.' Learning platform – the VLE – enables rich interaction online between home and school.

Small number have SEN – mostly mild dyses – a few statemented pupils on the ASD spectrum ('we're used to dealing with bright Asperger's boys') and school accommodates with ease. Full-time SENCo plus full-time LSA and one part-time learning support teacher are 'there to support any boys with problems'.

Games, options, the arts: Huge sports hall incorporating dance studio on far side of field (very muddy when we visited). However, newish all-weather pitch and cricket nets. Most practices held 15 minutes' bus ride away on their extensive playing fields near Hampton Court. Sports engaged in as intensely as everything here and with proportionate results. Good showings in cross-country, badminton, sailing, tennis, rugby, cricket and rowing etc etc. For a school described by some as 'very male', the place has a tangible feminine side. A quarter of the staff are women and the arts life is remarkable in all areas. Music is massive. Around a quarter learn at least one instrument in school – many more learn outside. Deliciously refreshing to come to a school where music isn't all about 'tech' these days – blissfully, no music tech within these portals but real orchestras, choirs and bands and stunningly good performance values. Older boys tell us, 'it's brilliant if you hit the ground running but they won't give

Dance – uniquely in an all-boys' school – is hugely popular and seen as 'cool' by the coolest boys. It is compulsory for first three years under clearly terrific teacher

you the basics and help you up if you haven't,' – to which school's retort is a robust, 'the music staff is always on the look-out for potential' and, apparently, 'music is compulsory and every boy in years 7 and 8 performs at evening musical events'. And you can't quibble with the results and reputation – regular Oxbridge choral scholarships, legendary concerts, eg Mahler's 8th Symphony at the Royal Festival Hall, with a huge Philharmonia Orchestra, under the baton of leading international conductor Esa-Pekka Salonen – genuinely outstanding.

Dance – uniquely in an all-boys' school? – is hugely popular and seen as 'cool' by the coolest boys. Combining the physical with the aesthetic, it is compulsory for first three years under clearly terrific teacher and taken right through to GCSE, after which many boys continue to perform. Collaboration with Ballet Rambert. Good little drama studio but most productions take place in school hall – often including Tiffin Girls' girls who don't, seemingly, return the compliment. Great fun and energetic shows, we gather. Art is a delight. Three studios in various states of joyous, creative chaos full of things you want to stop and look, laugh and wonder at. We loved the tiles depicting

the Gujerati alphabet all made from lentils, the glorious fish mobiles, the totem poles made from 'kebabed' Greek pots, the witty, colourful textiles and the sense of discovery in boys who are allowed to explore rather than told what to do. Not that the basic skills are in any way neglected. Creativity notably encouraged in music, art and drama. Masses of achievements in every field. A 15-year-old Tiffinian won Countdown a few years ago! Boys regularly sing in the chorus at The Royal Opera House and one had just sung a solo the week before our visit. Several boys play games at national level.

Background and atmosphere: One of the few schools set up to educate the deserving – rather than the rich – which still fulfils its brief. Two local brewers, John and Thomas Tiffin, left money in 1638 to educate 'honest poor men's sons'. A convoluted history involving various other donors and institutions ultimately resulted in two new Tiffin schools in 1874 – one for boys, one for girls – this coinciding with the great surge in the movement to educate women. The boys' school moved to its present site in 1929, and became a grammar in 1943. 'Tradition and heritage is at the centre of school life for us,' an earnest sixth former confided. Tiffin has two official specialisms – in performing arts and languages – but it is hard to see that they excel any less in eg maths and the sciences.

The main building is attractive – especially the frontage which faces away from the street. Small, wonderfully old-fashioned school hall with glittery honours boards and stone tablets commemorating the dead of both wars. The additional buildings include Elmfield, a rather splendid, if somewhat obscured, building from the 1750s used as a classroom block but which also houses the school archives. Plans afoot to replace ghastly prefab that houses the canteen with dining hall-cum-conference centre. Surroundings notwithstanding, food is exemplary – eg scrummy marinated pork ribs plus trimmings and no junk on offer – and the neat sixth form café.

Three studios in various states of joyous, creative chaos full of things you want to stop and look, laugh and wonder at. We loved the tiles depicting the Gujerati alphabet

Newer blocks – easier on the eye than many school buildings – include the library, engagingly modelled on the British Museum Reading Room's wheel and spokes design – not that the pupils seem to know this – and it is well-used, well-stocked and cleverly enhanced with a circular gallery accommodating PCs. Super lecture theatre in which speakers – both teachers and external – give fortnightly lectures. It is only in the general internal maintenance of the buildings and, to some extent, the site as a whole that one is aware that this is not a privileged private school. The state of decoration could be better but the boys couldn't care less, for the most part, and why should they?

Pastoral care and discipline: Six houses of huge importance to the ethos, competitive spirit and much fun. Also good for mixing up the year groups – a real and valued feature here. System of prefects, head and deputy head boys with varying responsibilities greatly valued, especially on account of some of the choice in election being given to senior boys. 'It's a big honour,' said one modest – but ennobled – lad. 'I've been surprised by how non-corrupt it is.' Discipline, we're told, is 'firm but fair' – all concur. 'You don't accept a lack of respect or toleration,' affirms school and no incidents of on-site smoking, drinking, drugs recently. One exclusion for unacceptable behaviour. We saw only quiet, attentive classes. Few incidents of bullying dealt with robustly, parents agree. Lots of rewards – merits and demerits which matter. Uniform, which is really rather nice – stripey red and blue blazers for the younger boys and dark suits for the older ones with numerous different ties depending on your abilities and proclivities – is worn with more attention to smartness than we've seen in comparable schools. Blazer felt by some to incite aggression in local youths – 'this is not a fair statement on neighbouring young people in Kingston,' protests school – but accepted as an inevitable price for the privilege it brings. Remarkable latitude accorded to length and style of hair does much to soften any sense of over-uniformity.

Pupils and parents: Brains and aspiration the only common denominators. Most from local areas – 80 per cent come on public transport – though they commute from up to an hour away – into Surrey, up to Ealing, over to Wimbledon. School discourages longer journeys for good commonsensical reasons and now gives priority to those living reasonably locally. Some parental feeling that school-home communication could be better now countered by Parentmail – all can now email any teacher and response, in general, is good. Huge outreach programme and evening events. Parents and locals come in for everything from language classes to concerts to lectures. Ethnically as mixed as you'd expect – large Asian contingent from all over – most of the rest UK/European. And in the smart uniform they blend and mix perfectly. Around 30 per cent speak a language other than English at home though few require additional help. Socially equally diverse – plenty in this well-heeled area

This is a privileged education – available to all with the requisite brainpower, whatever their background; a great leveller

could afford to pay for education and very few of those offered places here still opt to shell out elsewhere. Hard to understand why they should. Others can't afford occasional extras – trips, music etc – and school fund helps out. This is privileged education – available to all with the requisite brainpower, whatever their background; a great leveller. Great for all who are open and eager to learn. Who would it not suit? Perhaps, say some, not so good for the shy and withdrawn – but school disagrees. Famous OBs include Jonny Lee Miller, Alec Stewart, John Bratby ARA.

Entrance: You may not want to read any further. Now 180 year 7 places. Some 1,800 applicants for these. Priority now given to those who live less than 14km from the school measured in a straight line; we suspect that there's no point in applying if you don't. New entrance tests are now conducted in two stages, both involving English and maths questions. Only those 'passing' the stage 1 tests will be invited to take the stage 2 tests.

If your lad is young for the year, you may cheer up a bit – the tests are weighted so as not to disadvantage younger candidates. Looked after children take precedence – so long as they make the grade. Very occasional places thereafter – apply to the local authority. For the sixth form, you will need at least four As and two Bs at GCSE and As in your A level choices – achieved with ease by most. NB The same criteria, in fact, are applied to internal candidates ie you don't progress to the sixth form if your GCSEs aren't good enough. Some 25 per cent of sixth form enter at this level.

Exit: As impressive as you'd expect. Most popular university destinations Oxbridge (20 in 2015), followed by Durham, the London colleges and Warwick. Subjects taken cover the range though science and related courses predominate.

Money matters: School asks for a contribution – £530 pa – and around 55 per cent of families give some or all of this. Funds used to widen opportunities for all, subsidise trips, IT or music equipment and help towards new facilities such as the all-weather pitch and cricket nets.

Remarks: If all state schools were as good as this the independent sector would die – fast.

Tower House Preparatory School

188 Sheen Lane, London SW14 8LF

Tel: 020 8876 3323

Independent • Pupils: 185 • Ages: 4–13 • Fees: up to £12,810 pa

Email: admissions@thsboys.org.uk
Website: www.thsboys.org.uk

31

Headmaster: Since 2009, Mr Gregory Evans MA BSc PGCE (40s). Arrived with an excellent reputation from Sussex House, where he was director of studies for five years. Previously he taught science at King's House School, Richmond and Twynham School, Christchurch. Lives locally and describes this appointment as his 'dream job'. Has been quick to put an Evans spin on the place, showing vim and vigour, but without upsetting the natives – just as well as he is quite likely (and perfectly happy) to bump into parents at the local Waitrose. Not at all remote and cerebral, think dedicated and willing to get stuck in instead. The boys like and respect him – he immediately made a positive impression by knowing most of their names by the end of his first day. By all accounts he is an excellent manager and administrator and has overseen significant new investment in IT and also expanded the extracurricular side. Calm and efficient, it's difficult to faze him. He is firm but lightens it with humour. Sets the pace and asks others to follow. Parents seem pleased and the consensus is that he is good for the school. 'He's great', says one, 'hardworking and conscientious – Tower House is lucky

to have him'. In another memory feat, he keeps up with news of all the boys' families and their out of school interests so that he can pass the time of day with anyone he comes across, parent or boy alike. He's a tremendous advocate for single-sex boys preparatory education and perfectly pitches the Tower House offering so that its small size becomes its greatest asset. Very sporty (well-used cricket ball on desk), he attends as many matches as his schedule will allow – at weekends too, often refereeing in his Tower House socks. Married, with young children of his own, he enjoys golf, fishing, reading and tending his allotment in his spare time. Has also recently completed an MA in educational management and research.

Entrance: Largely a local intake from south-west London. Non-selective, so no entrance test at 4+. The first 20 to register will be guaranteed places, although siblings of current pupils will be given priority. Occasionally names drop off the list, allowing some movement into the top 20. Some boys admitted to other years in the school where space allows – worth asking.

Exit: Boys generally get to their first choice school. At 13+ lots to Westminster, St Paul's and King's College Wimbledon. Others to Eton, Tonbridge, Hampton, Kingston Grammar, Bradfield, Wellington, Marlborough, The Harrodian, Stowe and Reeds. School works towards CE pre-tests, rather than 11+ and does not encourage leavers at 11. Not many want to anyway – the odd one to Latymer where it is felt it is sometimes easier to get in at 11+ before the clamour at 13. But those are the exceptions.

Remarks: This is a school in full swing. Unashamedly a traditional boys' prep school but with a modern twist. It's a good life for a boy here; he'll work and play hard. It has a great local reputation and as the only boys' prep in SW London with a single form entry, there's a homely, family feel throughout.

Academically strong but not a crammer. In fact, parents seem at a loss to explain how school does so well by their non-academically selected sons, who also find time for a full range of extracurricular activities. Good, dedicated and approachable teachers – many of them long-serving – obviously play a key part. Head describes his team as 'exceptional'. Parents agree, praising 'goddess of maths', 'Pied Piper' drama teacher and 'very capable' deputy among others – seems invidious to single anyone out as they all seem to be going the extra mile for the boys. Science and maths very strong.

There isn't a great deal of space, inside or out the late Victorian buildings. The newly built junior section is linked to the senior section by a

shared playground – it's a small site, but clever use of space helps. The playground is Astroturfed and surrounded by climbing walls so that literally not an inch is wasted. There's also a quieter area, with table football and ping pong and a cyber-café set up for the less sporty types. Pressure on space probably more of an issue for the junior boys still of an age to run everywhere, but they seem to cope. 'They move around calmly and respect their space – a bit like the Japanese,' joked one mother.

Terrific amounts of charity work, everything from fundraising (in startling amounts) to visiting the elderly and planting trees

In fact, throughout the school there is an air of decorum not always apparent in an all-male environment. It's not that the boys are under the cosh – rather that they seem to be made gently aware of what is expected of them, from behaviour and work ethic, down to neatness of uniform.

Classrooms are not hugely high-tech environments but there's good use of technology around the place, including 'voting pads', neat interactive handsets, which the boys use to answer questions during lessons. Means that no-one can hide and teachers can analyse the information during and after the lesson to identify anyone in need of support. Some interactive whiteboards, other classrooms use projectors.

On a more old-fashioned note, how nice to see handwriting practice going on. Little boys, tongues out in concentration, painstakingly perfecting their Ps and Qs, is a heart-warming sight. And said heart given a further boost by the (Mr Evans inspired) reading wall outside the library – essentially tapping into boys' competitive streak via a house competition for who can read the most books in a term. School makes no apology for encouraging frequent library lessons and ring-fencing reading time – 'it's essential'.

Light homework from year 2 (one subject, once a week) obviously hotting up to three 40 minute assignments by year 8, but apparently nothing more onerous than necessary for CE. French from day one, Latin from year 5. Average class size is 20.

SEN catered for via what Mr Evans describes as a 'Harley Street' approach – bespoke attention given either individually or sometimes in small booster groups, all overseen by a full-time learning support teacher. The school is not suited for boys far along the spectrum, but can happily cope with mild to moderate physical disabilities, dyslexia, dyspraxia and dyscalculia, with a small number of boys using laptops as their method of recording information. Can also cater for boys with mild speech and language difficulties. Special provision for gifted and talented boys at the end of key stage 1. Between 10 and 15 per cent of pupils receive such support.

Sport is enjoying its moment in the sun lately. Obviously this is traditionally difficult for a small school which will struggle to put up a second XV – but TH can punch above its weight on occasion. 'We are no longer the enthusiastic but polite losers,' says Mr Evans. 'These days we make a decent match of it and are more than capable of a win'. Tower House teams have indeed begun to beat larger local rivals and claimed third place in a recent IAPS Sailing Regatta. All sport takes place at the nearby Bank of England grounds – fabulous facilities used by lots of strapped-for-space London schools, but parents feel TH gets the best of it. 'We always seem to have the best, more convenient pitches, feels like it's ours really', said one.

A great tradition of drama here. 'It's weirdly good' said one mother. Production values are said to rival those at Eton and Harrow – it's apparently all seriously top class. Former pupils prove the point, including young actors Rory Kinnear, Robert Pattinson and Tom Hardy and comedian Jack Whitehall. Multi-purpose art and DT attic studio, complete with pottery wheel. Lots of 3D work on display during our visit and some good stuff on the walls which was done by their teacher – so good it could almost dishearten before it inspired. Lots of music, with something for everyone – a swing band, an orchestra, two choirs (including an adult choir for parents) and three rock bands. About 70 per cent of pupils learn a musical instrument up to grade 6.

An overarching attitude that everyone gets to 'have a go'. Had a flute lesson? Join the orchestra and we'll give you a note to play. Auditioning for a production? We'll make sure you get a part

Pastoral care and discipline is as you would hope in such a small school, and there was high praise in the most recent ISI inspection report, where boys' personal qualities were described as 'outstanding'. Boys encouraged to grow into their own skin and develop a great sense of self worth. Although undoubtedly a privileged bunch, they are encouraged to put something back into their community. Considering their age, the boys undertake terrific amounts of charity work, everything from fundraising (in startling amounts) to visiting the elderly or planting trees. 'The last thing we want is a generation of arrogant teenagers,' says Mr Evans. 'So we make sure they are aware of how they can help others less fortunate and so infuse them with a healthy dose of humility'. School runs its own Dan Phillips award, named for an old boy and similar to Duke of Edinburgh scheme, in that they gain awards for their efforts.

But it's not all work – boys go on a super range of trips from year 4 to year 8, culminating in the post-CE exam trip where boys will get to fly a helicopter ('super' science teacher takes them up individually) and to deep-sea dive. 'My son has had experiences here he would simply not have got anywhere else,' says one mother. Head prides himself on a policy of 'no extras', so that even the cost of these plentiful school trips are included in fees. 'Parents are working hard and we don't want to keep asking for more,' he says.

This head knows his local demographic. For East Sheen read Banker Valley – school has a very IT literate clientele who appreciate the top notch information systems Mr Evans has introduced. Homework, syllabuses, team sheets, maps for fixtures – it's all on-line and a click of an iPhone away for busy parents who no longer need to rely on 'boy mail'. Even the weekly newsletter (always at least three pages) is available as a pdf. 'We make sure parents get information quickly and clearly, says Mr Evans. 'Our intranet system is the envy of many senior schools'. Typically both parents of a TH boy will be working, so find systems like this a boon. 'We always know what is going on', said one mother. 'We can email and the Clarion text system is really useful too'.

An overarching attitude that everyone gets to 'have a go'. Had a flute lesson? Join the orchestra and we'll give you a note to play. Auditioning for a production? We'll make sure you get a part. Think you don't like sport? Try fencing.

Although there are definitely no plans to grow pupil numbers, there is some physical expansion to come, with a new pre-prep department built, and an art room extension and classroom improvements

among various projects on the cards. Mr Evans is not inclined to sit on his hands, so he has plenty to tell prospective parents, and always includes this promise in his patter; 'At 13, your son will be able to sit in any south-west London dinner party and entertain and inform the other guests, while also being the most polite person at the table.'

An unashamedly traditional place at heart (boys still sing Jerusalem in assembly) but it's not stultifying – staff are very much alive to the latest educational thinking. A boys' school, but not an aggressive, overly-masculine environment, rather a place where boys can express their gentler selves if they want to and where arts are valued as highly as sport.

Unicorn School (Richmond)

238 Kew Road, Richmond, Surrey TW9 3JX

Independent • Pupils: 171 • Ages: 3–11 • Fees: up to £11,400 pa

Tel: 020 8948 3926

Email: registrar@unicornschool.org.uk
Website: www.unicornschool.org.uk

32

Headmaster: Since September 2013, Mr Kit Thompson, previously deputy head (academic) of Twyford School in Hampshire. He will need to keep a tight hand on the tiller to maintain school's highly individual, non-pressurised yet astonishingly successful course – where else do pupils routinely turn down places at top London secondaries like Godolphin and Latymer or Lady Eleanor Holles? – whilst resisting undue interference from articulate, heavily involved parents who, as school owners, enjoy having their say. It's a big ask.

Entrance: Single form all the way through and non-selective for those who arrive in the nursery aged 3 – 'you can't measure intelligence by the way a child holds a pencil' – though arrivals in other years are assessed in English and, in juniors, maths and reasoning, too.

As for special needs, around 17 have some form of support, none statemented. 'We get what we get', though school stresses that long term, it 'can't cater for severe learning difficulties'. Success here, however, is much praised by parents. 'At my daughter's previous school, she was having issues with her reading, so she was in my mind a special needs child. When we moved her here she had so much encouragement she just blossomed – it was the best thing we ever did,' says one.

Clientele very local – you only have to watch traffic grinding along nearby South Circular Road

to see benefits – with few coming from further away than Chiswick or Barnes and 50 per cent or so within immediate Kew/Richmond vicinity. Most hear about school through word of mouth recommendation or personal experience – 'I am an old Unicorn and had always said that my experience was so good that if I were able to send my children there I would,' says one mother.

> 'At my daughter's previous school she was having issues with her reading, so she was in my mind a special needs child. When we moved her here she just blossomed'

Though horribly over-subscribed with many children registered at birth – would be even earlier if parents had their way – school is keen to point out that despite reputation of being 'impossible' to get into, there's a regular trickle of occasional places, often freed up when parents with mega-important jobs relocate. (Means-tested bursaries are available, too, covering up to 100 per cent of the fees and awarded at the discretion of the governors.) New arrivals include occasional prep school refugees in search of a less traditional mind set.

Colourful Jan Pienkowski–style murals, conceived by the children and realised to interior designer standards by a group of talented parents, add colour to the light wood

Conversely, there's also (very small) reverse migration. School's ethos, low on formal tests, high on parent involvement, ranging from reception swimming (prepare to get wet – no passive poolside role here) to ferrying children to activities (there's even a mum's choir that regularly wins first place at local music festival), isn't for everyone. 'The school operates so closely as a community that I think they'd feel outside if they weren't part of it,' though some frantic working mothers send nannies or fathers as proxies and 'it's really not that arduous,' emphasises one mother.

Exit: Nothing unconventional about secondary school destinations. You name it, they get in, with a spread that includes Tiffin Boys, West London Free School and Grey Court plus ultra-desirable top league independents: St Paul's Girls, Colet Court, Latymer, Ibstock Place and Hampton among them as well as occasional boarding places (Tudor Hall, Downe House). Some scholarships most years.

Children usually sit exams for three or four secondaries, one aspirational, one probable, one backup and almost invariably end up with several offers, usually including first choice schools. Some, particularly if in search of elusive place at one of 10 times oversubscribed Surrey grammars may take rather more (invariably at parent's behest).

Preparation is covered with subtlety, starting in earnest only in year 6 when weekly tests, including post-swimming maths on Friday (not much enjoyed, judging by slightest of grimaces) are introduced. School's approach can require a parental leap of faith, especially for those more used to all-through exam-driven atmosphere of traditional preps. But though government tests were dropped some years back after it was decided that vertigo-inducing league table heights didn't compensate for stress levels generated, school's in-house assessments ensure staff are on the button when it comes to pupils' progress (results invariably put them streets ahead of national or indeed independent sector averages), with small group teaching by maths and English specialists to speed up pace for most able (gifted and talented by any other measure) and slow it down for those needing a little extra help.

Commendably, setting by stealth approach is so low key that, unlikely though it sounds, children who mentioned it seem genuinely unaware of its purpose. 'You start doing tests to see what suits you,' says one. They also speak warmly of teachers' reassuring presence when 11 plus nerves strike. 'I trusted them and they made every school sound great. You felt you could talk about anything,' says one.

Remarks: With its lovely double-fronted Victorian villa home opposite Kew Gardens, the school radiates solid values and has a price on its head to match – similar pads up the road go for multi-millions, so current management team must bless prescient school founders for acquiring freehold 40-odd years ago.

Colourful Jan Pienkowski-style murals, conceived by the children and realised to interior designer standards by a group of talented parents, add colour to the light wood and pastel-shaded décor, as do the rainbow leitmotifs that permeate school like letters running through a stick of rock. Parents will need to cultivate familiarity with the spectrum as each class is named after a colour with the oldest (year 6 in old money) housed on top floor (the younger the class, the fewer the stairs) and known as ultra violets, a witty touch not so far extended to their form chairs which, though colour coded for other years, are an anti-climactic grey.

School's ethos low on formal tests, high on parental involvement, ranging from reception swimming (prepare to get wet – no passive poolside role here) to ferrying children to activities (even a mums' choir)

Uniquely (it's thought) school is run as a limited company with one share per family, governors fulfilling dual role as board directors and an annual general meeting with state-of-union presentation by the head. While parents occasionally exceed their brief – 'because it's a parent-owned school, they feel they have a say in everything,' says one – there's a real 'do as I do' top-down ethos which extends to pupils who can serve on school council from infants onwards, or, in the case of the oldest, read stories or play games with nursery children, greatly enjoyed even though they give up some of their break time in the process. 'We help calm them down,' says one.

All in all, it's a happy continuation of the ideals that prompted the school's foundation in 1970 by a group of parents and teachers disenchanted with the fun-free learning inflicted on children elsewhere and in search of education with a creative spark. Once routinely described as bohemian or alternative, that's not the case now, say staff and parents (with a mere hint of politely gritted teeth) and the school excels at providing a child-centred education that's the real deal – short on edu-babble and 'stand and deliver teaching,' long on intelligence, spontaneity and enjoyment.

Much praised by all are the Thursday afternoon clubs that replace lessons for juniors, with 20 options or so ranging from sailing in Slough to riding at Ham House – most covered by the fees with a contribution for the priciest. A similar number and range of after-school activities is also on offer. In other years, however, trips don't have to be big to be clever with a one-stop bus journey for reception, dressed as evacuees, proving a stand out success.

As you'd expect, high calibre teachers come as standard issue here, a notably bright bunch of buttons who are required, like parents, to '... enjoy [our] philosophy and be happy to blend with it. Choosing staff...is perhaps more tricky than in other schools. While they're looking for particular skills to fill a gap, we're looking for a match and fit to the ethos, too.' Most are skilled up to the eyeballs; one, home grown, is just finishing her degree, and Oxbridge 'though not the be all and end all,' is well represented as are sports, with several high level players helping to lead football, netball, hockey and rounders teams, amongst others, to success.

The care taken over recruitment pays off handsomely with high grade work the norm, ranging from art (credible Catherine of Aragon glove puppets with papier-mâché heads and fabric bodies made by year 5s) to science (8 and 9 year olds, all red-fingered after creating their own bicarb of soda and vinegar volcanoes).

Nature is a big thing – a consignment of eggs with pre-confirmed hatching date is bought in each spring from nearby ethically-sound farm

Bottom line is that teachers love to teach and give pupils access all areas passes in lessons, encouraging them to think for themselves. Three Men in a Boat and Chaucer are on the menu after the 11 plus is done and dusted (no post-exam torpor here) while popular philosophy lessons let children choose which big questions to discuss. (One boy's place at Colet Court was secured when he enthusiastically told interviewer he'd studied 'nothing').

And it's not just the top years that benefit, with reception children ditching Wheels on the Bus

for Maybe it's Because I'm a Londoner, delivered with tasteful guitar backing and full complement of aspirants rather than Chas 'n' Dave pub-side bellow. 'We were learning about London and some of the children started asking about the war so we ended up having a glorious week,' explains teaching assistant.

Recently installed kitchen means welcome addition of hot meals, though children still also have option of bringing in a packed lunch, if preferred.

Aspirations may be vast, space less so. What space there is, however, is worked hard outside with a newly refurbished greenery-rich main playground divided into an Astroturf netball/football/running around area (fore), an action-packed, vibrant area filled with new and exciting equipment (midship) and quiet zone (aft). The latter sensible, given proximity to gardens of the no doubt vociferous well-to-do burghers of Kew). Rejigged interiors with corridor-free airy hall and previously poky first floor of coach house annexe re-synced into natty class music area with matching practice room next door (much used, with 130 timetabled instrumental lessons each week). Similarly upgraded is the reception and nursery classrooms downstairs, both bright and cheerful with their own secluded and plant-filled mini walled garden. Nature is a big thing – a consignment of eggs with pre-confirmed hatching date is bought in each spring from nearby ethically-sound farm. Chicks are returned, hens to have fulfilled life as layers, cockerels to face somewhat curtailed future – best to draw veil.

Parents are unfussed by size. 'It's typical for London,' says one, who also points to proximity of both 'the' Gardens opposite and the Old Deer Park (home of London Welsh RFC), both extensively used by school, latter for games.

Pupils, a loyal, friendly and articulate bunch (predictably in an area stuffed to the gunnels with highly educated professionals) have few complaints, either. While there's the occasional bout of out-of-teacher's-hearing bullying disguised as friendly teasing (mainly girls), it's dealt with quickly and effectively once reported and backed by a carrot-heavy rewards system, with prize-giving every term and a roll of honour featuring pupils and, pleasingly, teachers too, who nominate each other for doing the right thing.

Small, but with learning presented as a huge à la carte menu and not just the assessment-driven prix fixe, this is a special place. 'I can't believe that sitting multiple exams instils a love of learning. If we can teach children to enjoy learning, that's a gift for life.' No wonder school is loved by parents who even apologise for non-stop praise. 'I feel like I'm blowing the school's trumpet,' says one. Not bohemian – easy to rhapsodise, though.

Wallington County Grammar School

Croydon Road, Wallington, Surrey SM6 7PH

Tel: 020 8647 2235

State • Pupils: 1,033 • Ages: 11–18 • Sixth form pupils: 330 (86 girls)

Email: wcgs@suttonlea.org
Website: www.wcgs.org.uk

Headteacher: Since September 2013, Mr Jonathan Wilden (30s). Educated at St Joseph's College, Ipswich; studied geography at University of Wales (Lampeter), postgraduate degree from Bath, NPQH. Mr Wilden has taught in a number of south London boroughs and was formerly deputy head at Evelyn Grace Academy, Brixton. He joined Wallington as deputy headteacher in 2010.

Academic matters: You'd assume top grades in everything, all the time, and for the most part you'd be right, with results that make for the world's most boring game of Scrabble (depending on interest levels in vintage Swedish pop groups). In 2015, more than 75 per cent A*/A grades at GCSE. At A level, more of the same with nearly 87 per cent of grades at A*/B, 62 per cent at A*/A.

Being bottom in a class of over-achievers can be a lonely place but here, stigma is neatly sidestepped – or at least addressed with humour. 'I know when x and y first met, but still I am in the bottom set,' says prizewinning poem in newsletter.

'I don't think you have to excel. They give their form order so everyone knows who's bottom but from what I can tell, nobody is given stick, or jeered or sneered at,' confirms one mother. All this despite

the fact that the cleverest are 'ridiculously clever', say boys, citing a sixth former, nickname King Language, who taught himself Ancient Greek to A level standard in three years.

'I know when x and y first met, but still I am in the bottom set,' says prizewinning poem

While it would be awfully easy to ramp up the pressure – 'you can just push them, there's no limit to what you can get out of them,' says a teacher – the school knows where to exercise restraint. 'Extremely tedious' ICT GCSE was axed, leaving pupils free to concentrate on achieving 10 or 11 cracking GCSEs – eight core subjects, economics and business studies amongst the options – and up to four A levels, though 'they suggest only doing three so we get good grades,' confirms sixth former.

Around 80 per cent opt to keep going with a non-related but much-loved subject post-16 – one boy, hoping to study economics at university, was sweetening the pill of straight sciences and maths with art – virtuoso timetable juggling ensuring that just about every sixth former, somewhat amazingly, is able to follow chosen subject blend.

There used to be occasional frustration over use of supply teachers to cover long-term staff absences but things have improved, think parents, and there's non-stop praise for staff, many seen as an inspirational force for good: '...the only reason my son wants to study classics at university,' says a parent. Another pupil, initially planning to be an architect, was ambushed by the fascination of psychology. 'It's the way it weaves its way through society.'

With everything from innovative blood points awarded in history and classics – the more the gore, the better the score (one boy even made a Medusa cake) – to year 9 English students filming themselves looking moody and disenfranchised in (sub)urban dystopia (a 'gritty portrayal of life' says one – or as close as you get in leafy Wallington) it's not hard to see why teachers and lessons are so highly rated.

Consistent overall quality makes the very occasional slippage round the edges that much more noticeable, with a few more C grades in A level biology and physics than you'd expect and a tiny number slipping into D and E hinterland. Home influence can be a factor, thinks head. 'Though we have the conversation each year about how the subjects should be what the pupil wants to do, there is parental pressure to do the sciences even if they're not their best or favourite subjects.'

School, though, is far from passive. Flair-filled initiatives include book clubs and mini-libraries dotted around classrooms to get non-readers hooked (a surprising number see the printed word as a duty not a pleasure), while learning support for the 20 or so pupils with dyspraxia, dyslexia, ADD and ASD/Asperger's ranges from buddies to lend a hand with organisation to morale-boosting

training as cyber mentors. Even parents are paired with others whose children have similar needs.

Add an extensive range catch up clubs and sixth form mentors who help year 7s in lessons and offer a listening ear outside and rigorous plotting of academic trajectories, and it's hard to slip through the cracks. 'We know pupils better than ever before,' reckons head.

Games, options, the arts: Sport is 'central to school life' says prospectus (music merely 'flourishes'). Lots of team finals (rugby particularly) and individual success (water polo gold at London Youth Games). Hockey is in decline; football, recently introduced to the relief of many, on the up – though relegated to the public park down the road. Only rugby and cricket grace the well-kept sports field.

Wonderfully waffle–free policies ('scorn cheating,' exhorts section on sporting aims in pleasingly Tom Brown tones)

While the talented are encourage to sign up, adulation for sporting legends is low key and there's plenty of kudos to spare if, as a fair few do, you direct your talents elsewhere.

Outside school, pupils regularly reach the finals of national maths, science and spelling. Inside, the arts are well represented with traditional ensembles and a popular Battle of the Bands, though eclipsed by 'Singstaff' – a teacher talent show. (Previous head's version of 'Man after midnight' complete with 80s big tie lives on in legend, so we're told, though sadly not on Youtube). Drama bristles with high quality productions running the gamut from mainstream (including a well-reviewed Oliver!) to the quirky – sixth formers were 're-imagining' classics, 'the more eccentric the better,' said one, who planned a new take on the Odyssey. Art also has its idiosyncrasies, highlights including a jolly slimline Michelin man lookalike crafted from cling-film wrapped wire.

Lots of charitable activity with sixth form boys about to embark on moustache growth – 'few have the manliness,' says one – to raise awareness of testicular cancer, with Wednesday afternoons for years 11 upwards dedicated to enrichment activity (facial hair nurturing presumably being a 24/7 preoccupation) and science-based links with local primary schools a speciality, with would-be medics passing on resuscitation techniques and future scientists launching rockets on the playing field (arts types, meanwhile, prudently watched the fun from indoors).

Around 80 per cent of pupils, it's estimated, attend at least one of the 50 plus clubs that plug any gaps in the timetable, most with a strong academic raison d'être (physics geek club about as frivolous as it gets) though D of E is also on offer. There's even the Hutchins über-club, the society's society, that monitors the rest and 'aims to push the academic boundaries,' says a pupil, by ensuring other clubs are delivering suitably nourishing intellectual fare to their members.

Background and atmosphere: 'The deputy head told us to practise personal humility and professional will,' says sixth former. 'You never get too big for your boots but you're committed to doing well and going about it in a nice way.' Judging by polite clouds of year 7s trailing grinning deputy school captain to plead for coveted school pins, awarded for participation, it's a lesson learned early on.

Not that an indomitable spirit is anything new, surfacing during world war II when the school, then fee paying (it became a grammar in 1944) stayed open during the Blitz, despite two direct hits and substantial damage,

School's homely feel is 'such a cliché,' says pupil, rather crossly – but inescapable, while the presence of girls – first two joining in 2000 though one only lasted a fortnight, today making up a fifth of sixth form numbers – brings 'a different dimension,' says the school.

Slightly battered charm, with some areas just for best (like green and pleasant quad) and lots of period details add to the charm. But behind all those curvy art deco brass-topped bannisters, the sixth form art room nicknamed Middle Earth (it's sandwiched between two others rather than home to a bunch of hobbits) and an abundance of gothic gilt lettering, there's a definite appetite for change.

Recent additions include funky new sports hall, twinkling away on the far side of playing field with wow factors a-plenty (automatic doors, which have reset to manual, are the only feature not playing ball) which has allowed large scale musical classrooms elsewhere. Sixth form study area replaces the library, which has taken over the gym.

Food technology classroom features chairs in a zinging green that almost matches the walls and banks of ovens. Popular with everyone (there's already a school recipe book). Has also wrought miraculous reduction in queuing times at popular fundraising lunchtime barbecues.

Only loser is the sixth form common room, now given over to classics, though pupils take this in good part – 'we've lost a common room but gained a subject,' says one. A small patio constructed, by way of compensation, for their exclusive benefit, is little used, pupils congregating instead by the front entrance, as if waiting for a school bus that never arrives, while girls use their loos

as a walk-in wardrobe, with a mish-mash of coats, books and make-up stashed under the washbasins. 'Surprising,' says sixth form boy, with masterly understatement.

Pastoral care and discipline: Things are back on an even keel after a period of what school terms 'low level misbehaviour' when pupil respect towards staff dipped. 'Towards the end, you felt [a previous head] was off the ball,' confirms a parent. 'I was surprised at the amount of latitude.'

No chance now, with a rigorously applied code of sanctions (with input from pupils) and (existing) practical measures including a separate, well-patrolled areas for each year group, (though sixth formers, rather hurt at implied lack of trust, would like more mixing of the age ranges).

Wonderfully waffle-free policies ('scorn cheating,' exhorts section on sporting aims in pleasingly Tom Brown tones) leave no doubts as to what will and won't be tolerated. Drugs won't, though offenders expressing suitable contrition may get a second chance thanks to an informal 'you take ours, we'll take yours' agreement with Sutton Boys and Wilson's. (No guarantees, however.)

Incentives to behave are thick on the ground, from the six houses which 'exert an emotional pull,' says a pupil (victors' flags in the hall provide at-a-glance summary of current success), to ties that bind, with a cornucopia of neckwear on offer for games, arts or brainpower-based accomplishments.

Family links have been strengthened, too, with work and well-being themed workshops for parents (who also get on-tap access to form tutors, front of house contacts for day to day issues), though attendance for those living or working some distance away can be tricky.

Proof that it's all working just fine is provided by parental endorsement and pupil approval of pastoral head – 'he's tops,' says one. Tiny numbers, usually three or four at most, stay after school for Friday detention. More serious Saturday version vanishingly rare, says school.

Pupils and parents: Chris Woodhead of Cognita and Crimewatch's Nick Ross are best known Old Boys (Douglas Allen, later civil service chief Lord Croham, was debut pupil in 1927). Others include Surrey cricketer David Gibson. List is currently all male – Old Girls are, presumably, still chipping away at the glass ceilings.

Pupils temper intelligence with humanity – a useful quality for tomorrow's top scientists, lawyers and medics. A trustworthy bunch, too – possessions can be left confidently in the open bag storage areas, widely used round the school instead of lockers, ditched after a pupil vote.

Sixty per cent come from ethnic minorities and approximately a quarter speak English as an additional language. 'Culturally very mixed, more so than a lot of schools, so that attracted me,' says a parent.

Entrance: Year 7 candidates sit the Sutton Grammar Schools Selective Eligibility Test (SET) in September. Several grammars then carry out additional tests but Wallington has decided that from 2015 there will be no additional testing of its candidates after the SET.

Parents are advised to pay close attention to the admission criteria which have been changed in order to promote social mobility for disadvantaged pupils. As part of this initiative from September 2016 there will be a further small intake at 13+.

There are around 50 sixth form places for external students (including girls), based upon GCSE results.

Exit: A few leave after GCSEs though for almost everyone else it's straight to university after A levels, with 70 per cent to Russell or 1994 group members and around eight or so off to study medicine, dentistry and veterinary science. Other popular subjects include maths (though numbers have declined over past four years), economics, history, engineering (all sorts), physics and biomedical science.

Dip in Oxbridge success rates seems to have been resolved and 10 pupils achieved places in 2015. School has taken advice from big hitters in other top schools to ensure that only hopefuls with a realistic chance of success are put forward. Head also plans subject-specific clubs (medicine, law, architecture) run by sixth formers, with eminent Old Boys invited in to offer advice and set work.

Remarks: 'Wants the results but isn't pushy in the way another school might be,' says a parent. Cleverness, even brilliance, is there in force but never in your face and tempered with good manners and charm. No wonder pupils are attached to their school and 'boys cry more than the girls,' says a (male) sixth former when it's time to leave.

Wallington High School for Girls

Woodcote Road, Wallington, Surrey SM6 0PH

Tel: 020 8647 2380

38

State • Pupils: 1,320 • Ages: 11–18 • Sixth form pupils: 365

Email: info@wallingtongirls.org.uk
Website: www.wallingtongirls.sutton.sch.uk

Joint acting heads: Since 2015, Ben Cloves and Rachel Gibb. Prior to this interim appointment they were both deputy heads at Wallington High School for Girls. Previous head Jane Burton now has the permanent position of executive head of the Nonsuch and Wallington Education Trust (NWET) with overall responsibility for both schools. Has young son educated in Sutton and has been through purgatory of admissions systems herself, so has first hand empathy with parental anxiety levels (many can do fraught to off-Richter within seconds).

Not wild on getting up close and personal with this reviewer without complete 'editorial control' afterwards, so we had to be content with an encounter which, though delightful, was of a more distant variety. We ended up viewing her from the balcony of the school hall where, a well-manicured presence in corporate monochrome, she stepped up to the podium and, accessorised with a posse of head girls (well, two, anyway), delivered an efficient speech with commendable energy (one of six appearances that afternoon), complete with matching body language – outwards-thrust arms emphasising key messages.

Her aim is to turn out girls who will 'seize everything life throws at them.' Vim and vigour of those we saw suggests they're up for it

Mind you, you can't blame her for wanting to put a bit of blue water between her and the audience, some of the 1,500 pantingly keen parents who would probably do anything (and that does, probably, mean anything) to obtain a place for their child in this thoroughly desirable establishment.

As a grammar school veteran, she runs her senior leadership team, you'd imagine, with a tight grip, though they appear to be thriving under her regime.

Littlies (year 7s) are a bit confused about what she does. They reckons she teaches (she doesn't, say older pupils) but no one has a bad word to say about her. Mind you, they don't have that many words full stop, largely down to the fact that with just a year under her belt, her presence was only just beginning to make itself felt. 'We don't really get to speak to her,' thought older pupil.

Parents likewise, particularly in younger years. 'Haven't seen her personally,' says one. Information, sparse though it is, was favourable, if largely because she appears to be employing an if it ain't broke, don't fix it approach. 'I've heard everything is quite positive,' thought a mum. 'Sometimes you see a big difference [when a head changes] but it's been a small transition.'

Making her mark, however. Sixth formers now 'follow smart dress code' instead of home clothes. Second time lucky: Nonsuch girls appear to have fought off similar proposals under her watch, though appears to have fallen short of the mini me ideal she'd envisaged in initial consultation letter where 'business-like skirt[s], tailored trousers...and smart jacket[s]' were the goal.

Speech, shorn of corporate trimmings ('identity', 'mission statement', 'positive experience' tend to get fair share of the word count) suggests heart is in the right place. 'Girls are proud of themselves,' school is proud of them (group hug, everyone) and it does, above all, superbly well, adding value to your child – 'sounds a bit clinical,' she apologised – as well as straight results which are, of course, superb.

Her aim is to turn out girls who will 'seize everything that life throws at them.' Vim and vigour of those we saw suggests they're up for it.

Academic matters: Expectations exactly as you'd expect and terrific results to match – 79 per cent of 2015 GCSE entries at A*/A, 47 per cent A*/A at A level. Head, however, reinforces message that it's 'not an exams factory' and there's no sense of undue pressure from girls we spoke to.

Subject choices surprisingly wide-ranging with media studies and DT four different ways at A level as well as a few GCSE rarities including photography (like Latin, offered as a twilight course) as well as business and psychology (rated by school for honing research skills).

Everyone must do separate sciences in decent, bright labs (juniors 'tend to have same teacher') and at least one language at GCSE (school specialism), and it's two for all from year 7 (choose from French, German and Spanish – school will do best to accommodate preferences though GCSE numbers roughly equal for all three).

Forms (each recruited en masse to one of seven houses) taught together in year 7 so can stick together – almost literally as 'so big that for the first few weeks you just tend to follow each other round,' said one.

Minor criticism of maths is that with sets kicking in only at the end of year 7, can be a drag for most able first years, who have sometimes covered the ground already. One pupil, clearly at top end of ability range, felt it could be a bit 'boring if you knew the subject already.' 'At my daughter's primary school, they started doing some year 7 work, so it depends if the teacher realises,' thought parent.

Current school preoccupation is need to upweight thinking skills. Manifested at GCSE in fusion of philosophy and ethics with RS (short course taken by most) and in the sixth form with philosophy of religion and ethics as one of go-ahead A level options (school doesn't do the IB) as well as an extended essay project that encourages independent research.

Lunch card also acts as library ticket – food for the soul and stomach in one magnetic stripe

Though there are masses of subject specific events, typical month including trips to Royal Observatory, Maritime Museum and War Horse for physics, history and drama students respectively, spanning the year groups and adding interest for all, teacher are real stars of the show.

Swapping round groups in years 7 and 8 sensible 'as it means you meet new people', thought pupils, who have nothing but praise for staff, echoed by parents who extolled staff emphasis on morale boosting rather than pressure – slow boil rather than pressure cooker. 'You pick it up when you have parent evenings. Even subjects you think your daughter's not very strong in, the teachers are very encouraging,' says one.

Day to day, however, plenty of evidence of varied teaching styles that put a premium on initiative. Most recent inspection report was critical of over use of chalk and talk – now pared back to a minimum and group work something of a feature – 'we get 20 minutes to collaborate,' said year 7 pupil – and choice offered wherever practical: menu of experiments adds interest to science.

Lunch swipe card also acts as library ticket – food for the soul and stomach in one magnetic stripe – and everyone is instructed to have live book and not be scared to use it when reading is called for, which it often is – though all the girls we spoke to were enthusiastic readers, school diligent about keeping the light burning. If book is missing 'you'll be in trouble,' said teacher, with ferocious smile – in practice, means 'you get moaned at,' said pupil.

Just about every core academic subject has own club, some involving older girls. Space also freed up wherever possible to assist with private study. Library open all hours (or a fair few of them) while sixth form have own small but nicely kitted out conference room which can be booked out for meetings and quiet work.

No doubt where interests lie, however, with massive 140 currently taking A level maths, and sciences fab, too – 100 each for biology and chemistry and respectable 80 for physics. Head dismissive of any suggestions elsewhere that girls can't and won't do sciences as here they can and will – in their droves.

One gloriously cuddly example (creature, not teacher) was felt to be a particularly accurate representation of staff member's 'wacky hair'

Their popularity, influenced by what can be 'lots' of parental pressure, thought teacher, inevitably puts many other departments in the shade, though 'we're winning' says English teacher, who has seen rising AS numbers for Eng lit (currently just over 50 in year 12) as well as Eng lang and combined.

It's helped, she thinks, by growing desire by would-be employers to see evidence of broader spread of interests. Slightly disappointed by attrition rate into year 13, though in part, she reckoned, down to misapprehension that A level is a breeze – GCSE with a few more complicated bits – when 'it isn't.'

One parent felt that, in common with other local grammars, 'you can tell from the mixture of girls that with some, their English may not be very strong,' which she thought might affect the popularity of the subject. That said, all-round

enthusiasm is inescapable. What are school's biggest things? 'Everything here is a big thing,' said year 8 pupil with just a hint of reproof.

Games, options, the arts: Lots love sport, some don't and academic thrust can divert some who might otherwise be doing great things on the pitch, thought girls. While school scoops gold Artsmark award amongst others, sports equivalent is the conspicuous absentee on website roll of honour, with PE just about sole area not raved about by inspectors. Enjoyed by pupils, however. 'They have fun and that's part of it,' thought mum. Its standing on the website, lumped together with art and design, drama and music, under 'expressive arts' with no accompanying blurb pretty much says it all, as does minimal timetable presence – two sports/PE lessons a week, dance and gym dominating in winter, great outdoors (including cricket, rounders and tennis) to the fore at other times.

Small and hardy bunch go on to take PE for A level (currently half a dozen) and winners, both team and individual, including two budding sixth form football stars, recently awarded vast sports scholarships by US universities. Add favourable feedback and rapidly improving facilities, and will to ensure higher profile – and results – seems to be there.

Vast field, all-weather pitches (no Astroturf as yet, though four new tennis and netball courts recently added to existing two) joined by magnificent sports hall, a yodeller's paradise, mirrored dance studio on top just as nice and no gizmo spared, including retractable goals, dividing net allowing two classes to have simultaneous lessons.

Building, shaped like flat-bottomed sausage roll with rounded corrugated metal top, so bizarre-looking that to start with 'everyone was against it,' says sixth former. Now assorted delights are clear, 'we love it'. 'Amazing,' agreed parent.

Anything in danger of despoiling pristine floor, such as trampolining, is relegated to old gym, which also incorporates very compact fitness suite, housed in section of main building beyond school hall and now largely disused or converted section (antediluvian-looking changing rooms now used for storage).

Art and drama very strong, quality excellent, visible manifestation of school's desire to encourage pupils 'to be who you are.' All, from year 7 girls to sixth form, praised teachers' desire not to impose but to guide, with thorough briefing and lots of encouragement to personalise tasks en route to completion.

Thus masses of faces in art room (less scary than amazing but rather terrifying giant masks in school hall) are hugely different in style and design. We also loved pictures of lamas bearing staff names and chosen to 'reflect personality'. One gorgeously cuddly example (creature, not teacher) with fetching

Winners, both team and individual, including two budding sixth form football stars, recently awarded vast sports scholarships by US universities

crop of fleece was felt to be particularly accurate representation of staff member's 'wacky hair'.

Painstaking creativity also a feature of relatively recent tech block, 'best in the country,' thought pupil and, according to recent school survey, achieves some of highest pupil and parent happiness ratings around. Spreads the joy with lots of outreach to local primaries, separate building worth clocking for extraordinary through corridor, narrow but incredibly high, like passage way for emaciated, super tall giraffes.

Teachers diligent in 'explaining techniques', most projects starting with short list of designs and questionnaires designed to canvass friends' views ('You can ignore them but you have to explain why.') Projects included one of the most sensible we've ever seen – year 7s making covers for school planners – practical, fun and gorgeous (owners had gone to town on personalisation – initials as well as frills and furbelows a real feature).

Those who stay the course end up with fab A level creations including terrific lamp complete with fronds of LEDs and mood lighting. 'Took three months to make.'

Lovely music – particularly strong on vocals (recent finalist on TV The Voice is former school pupil) with five choirs – Glee and 60-strong gospel choir both audition only (latter mostly seniors; year 7 girls delighted that one of their number had just won place), junior and senior versions open to all. Joint orchestra with Wilson's School down the road a happy union of brass and percussion (mainly boys) with strings (mostly girls).

Enthusiastic teaching team feel GCSE numbers (currently around 17) could be higher. Though accept the necessity, slightly miffed that small number of A level students are currently having lessons at Wilson's and are fighting good fight to boost numbers so pupils can be brought back into the fold.

Background and atmosphere: Founded 125 year ago. About six minutes by bus from Wallington station, it's a fairly easy trek compared with boys' equivalents (detailed knowledge of public transport essential for first timers, emergency rations desirable) and presents unthreatening face to the world, brickwork, if not mellow, certainly not likely to frighten the horses (not that you'd see that many on these crowded streets).

Has embraced cultural diversity (and won an award for it, too) with gusto, recent events ranging from Japanese drumming to fab-sounding international evening where girls and families ate, drank and danced way round the world, each table in school hall themed to a different country.

Warren-like corridors are brightened wherever possible with rows of pictures, space at a premium with seven year 7 forms feeding through. Generous-sized lockers, dotted round the place, a well-used necessity. 'I could get winter coat, all books and full PE kit in mine,' reckoned pupil. New teaching block also on the way. In the meantime, subjects are ranged together wherever possible, occasionally dual use (modern languages lesson might take over English room, 'though never a problem as teachers always bring all the resources with them,' says pupil).

Food was 'pretty good' except for the cheese, seemingly added to rather more dishes than you'd like. 'Texture a bit of a problem,' thought pupil. However, does offer much enjoyed freedom for déjeuner sur l'herbe, on outside tables and even in classrooms ('though not hot food,' thought year 7 pupils, as 'that would be a health and safety issue.'

Has now formed a multi academy trust with Nonsuch High.

Pastoral care and discipline: School excels here with common sense approach with earlier start and finish (8.25am to 2.50pm) and prompt close on Friday afternoons, packed programme of after-school clubs (sports, including badminton, football and hockey the most popular) mainly Mondays to Thursdays only, ensuring that everyone (including hard-pressed teachers) can start weekends promptly and with clean conscience, felt school.

In addition to form tutor and head of year, those with problems have access to what one girl described as 'superb' counsellor, accessible at all hours and 'like a second mum', as well as caring staff who have manifest understanding of pressures that go with life in top-achieving school and go out of their way to deal with them.

Sports staff on hand for one pupil who 'went to them when feeling low just to spend time there and kick a ball around.' A huge help, she reckoned. Younger girls seemed largely content with system and own company – they tend not to approach older girls, who don't seem to have troubleshooting role, and in any case could be 'hard to find,' thought one.

As to bullying – incidents rare: 'one a year, if that,' thought year 7 pupil, while older girls marvel at school's success in avoiding issues that friends and family elsewhere report as being routine. 'Younger sister has all sorts of problems at her school,' says sixth former. 'Here, even though it's such a big year group, there's not even one.'

School, also praised for approach to those at the bottom of the academic pecking order. Teachers' policy is, sensibly, to compare the potentially down-hearted with the rest of the country. 'Don't remind us of our grades. We might be at the bottom here but for a lot of schools, that would be right at the very top,' said sixth former.

Others praised teachers' way of dealing with those struggling with the pace. 'Will go on to the next pupil but then come back to you and often see you in private to sort things out,' reckoned year 8 pupil.

Though rule bending won't be allowed (range of sanctions in place, from confiscation of offending items to letters of apology through to exclusion), little more, thought pupils, is usually needed than quiet chat. Behaviour policy states that 'staff are expected to use praise and appreciation many more times than they use sanctions.' Feedback suggests it's highly effective.

Pupils and parents: A super bunch – parents as well as pupils. No-nonsense, lacking affectation, warm and, reckoned would-be mum, 'not too up them-selves.' Really appreciate school's many virtues – head girls who speak of seeking office 'because we want to give [something] back' coming across as genuine rather than CV glory chasers.

'I've seen a lot of friends and they're all very different. Some are laid back, some studious, some sporty. I think a mixture of girls seem to be able to fit in really well,' reckoned mum.

Pill sweetened by red-robed gospel choir blasting the hordes with high energy numbers

Arrogance definitely absent from this picture, good manners and charm still in evidence even under trying circumstances. On crowded open day when had been on duty for over four hours, enthu-siastic escorts (guided by presumably exhausted staff, pleasant to the end) were tireless in efforts to ensure nobody missed a thing, even after end of official visiting time.

Entrance: Popularity not hard to fathom given numbers who came to hear the head's talk on open day. Not so much standing as queuing room only, despite promise that on-line version of talk would be posted the next day. Pill sweetened by red-robed gospel choir blasting the hordes with high qual-ity, high energy numbers including (appropriately) 'Ain't no mountain high enough.'

Would that it were true. Even the best grap-pling irons in the business may not be enough to haul you up these particular slopes. Following early September deadline for applications, anything north of 1,300 hopefuls sit mid-month VR and maths papers. The 700 or so who pass will hear in sufficient time to include school on CAF (common application form), though with only 210 year 7 places to fill, majority will go away empty handed when formal offers are made in March.

Head, however, keen to inject a little hope into the process, points out that with sizeable numbers also doing the grammar school rounds (Nonsuch, Tiffin Girls and Bromley bunch) means that 'you could argue it's more like 1,300 for a total of 400 [year 7] places,' says head. Lots of locals, open day blazer brands representing seemingly every primary and prep in the area, extending out to Croydon and Tooting. Distant reaches of London and Surrey not much represented – doesn't appear to have huge geographic catchment (though if results go up much further, it probably will).

Cleverness, though essential, doesn't have to be extreme, is head's message (though in many cases you'd imagine it is). 'Overwhelmingly, come with at least a level 5 in Sats, and if likely to achieve this in year 6, would be of similar ability to pupils at the school,' she says.

Where other heads have firmly set faces against tutors (Canute-like, you'd think, given overwhelm-ing parental mood), pro, or at least resigned to the inevitable, Mrs Burton is rather more pragmatic about the realities. Tests are designed 'to be acces-sible to all, whether tutored or not,' with exam content 'based on ground covered to end of year 5.' However, if content, particularly when it comes to VR, hasn't been covered, brief trip to WH Smiths or similar for a bit of mugging up can provide useful familiarisation.

Exit: Destinations ooze academic credibility though there's a decently mixed bag: one girl we talked to was part of a select group contemplating career in sport. Picky might hope for a few more to Oxbridge (eight in 2015) but around a third make Russell Group, further 10 – 15 go to medical school each year with similar numbers off to art college. Around a fifth take a gap year.

Remarks: Thoroughly genuine. School speaks of warm, friendly and purposeful atmosphere. Yada, yada, we thought, another bland statement. Yet from the minute you meet teachers and staff, coping with crowds and doing with smiles what Jesus did with loaves and fishes, you have impres-sion of a school that's genuinely living the mission statement. Though equally desirable, not all gram-mars are the same. We loved this one.

Wilson's School

Mollison Drive, Wallington, Surrey SM6 9JW

State • Pupils: 1,100 • Ages: 11–18. • Sixth form pupils: 300

Tel: 020 8773 2931

Email: office@wilsonsschool.sutton.sch.uk
Website: www.wilsonsschool.sutton.sch.uk

39

Head: Since July 2014, Nathan Cole BA PGCE (30s), previously deputy head. Read history at Nottingham and was a postgrad at Cambridge. Began his teaching career at Saffron Walden County High and joined Wilson's in 2006, rising through the ranks to become deputy head in 2010. An expert on the history of Italian fascism, he is also a keen musician.

Academic matters: One of a handful of grammars in the area, all high achieving (comparing their results is like differentiating between shiny, perfect apples from M&S and Waitrose: look hard enough and you might find the very occasional blemish but it's scarcely worth the effort), and the natural home of the innately clever child who is 'looking at getting four A levels at A grade and going to a Russell Group university', says a mother.

It doesn't, however, always do quite so well by the merely bright, not through neglect but because 'only certain people can put up with being bottom of the pile', though that's a relative term. All achieve startlingly good results (so many finish with A*s in maths, taken in year 10 by most able, that it's practically de rigueur). Setting is fairly extensive, starting with maths in year 8, followed by sciences, English and all languages except

Latin in year 9. Eleven GCSEs are the norm – eight core, including separate sciences, and AS level ICT among the options for the remaining three. In 2015, 83 per cent A*/A grades at GCSE.

GCSEs are followed by four AS and A levels plus either a formal extended project qualification (EPQ) or an internally assessed project. Modest menu of carefully chosen subjects – there's no psychology, for example (the demand isn't there, says school), though the numbers taking business studies are growing fast and economics is something of a star performer – bad financial news apparently does wonders for recruitment. Latin, though compulsory in year 7, doesn't have such an obvious current appeal higher up the school and is a 'Marmite' subject, says a pupil – though the keen are very keen and currently around 50 continue in year 9, when it becomes optional.

You're left in little doubt as to the big hitter subjects. Maths, daddy of them all, is taken by over two-thirds of pupils at A level with 90 per cent of entries securing A*-A grades (how many other schools have to ponder the potential problem of overcrowding?). It accounts, together with the sciences and economics, for almost twice as many entries as all the remaining A level subjects put together. Boys work hard 'because they know they'll get good grades, they know it's useful and they enjoy it', says a maths teacher – and that seems to hold true across the range of subjects. Overall, nearly 94 per cent A*-B (74 per cent A*/A) at A level in 2015.

Like beady-eyed shoppers, pupils know how to choose a basket of carefully matched subject goodies and exactly what they're worth in enhancing career prospects. Teachers use this to their advantage. 'We tell them early on that if they want to work for companies like Siemens or Deutsche Bank, all the meetings are held in German', says one. Coincidentally, numbers taking German A level (in terminal decline elsewhere) have recently shot up from single figures to around 20.

Lots of help on offer, with academic review meetings with tutors to discuss progress, and valued catch-up clubs in just about every core subject, introduced originally for GCSE pupils but now, by popular demand, run from year 7. Support also for those with learning difficulties – some borderline Asperger's and dyslexia crop up now and then but you don't sense it's a big feature of school life. Generally, 'teachers know when to apply pressure and when to ease off – they're very good at reading the students', said one. Having said that, strength of character and robust self-confidence can be required if you're towards the bottom of the academic pack – occasional pupils suffering from sense of being 'at the bottom end of the academic scale,' as one mother puts it, leave early (school says this has not happened for some years), though it's felt that school is now far better at talent spotting and encouragement all the way through.

School has created a trio of hovercraft, as you do (though no plans as yet to bring back the much missed Folkestone/Bologne route)

Atmosphere, however, is generally friendly and remarked on by visitors. One philosophy boffin 'said he'd been to plenty of schools where it didn't happen,' says a teacher and indeed it's unmissable. 'Teachers are very open,' said year 7 boy. The trust between teachers and pupils, slightly jokey but respectful on both sides, is evident and staff are missed when they go – one department head has recently been poached by private school for double the salary, it's said. Given emphasis in the prospectus on financial investment in top notch teachers, you have to hope that other even better funded institutions don't come to see staff list as akin to a particularly moreish educational tasting menu.

They'd find ways of deriving nourishment from the most barren of intellectual landscapes

Games, options, the arts: Take a hobby or sport, preface with the words 'one of the top schools in...' and that's pretty much the gist. School boasts that 'boys are never bored' though to be honest, even if it laid on nothing, they'd undoubtedly find ways of deriving nourishment from the most barren of intellectual landscapes. As it is, activities ooze from every pore – 'So many, it's silly,' says sixth former – with the usual suspects, including tip-top CCF (now one of the largest in the country in conjunction with a local girls' school) and D of E to gold award; some, like ecology, Freethinkers and even Rubik's cube clubs, set up by boys themselves.

As a sports specialist, school excels here as elsewhere (though 'we'd choose this school every time even if they didn't own a tennis ball between them,' said a parent). 'Paradise for the sporting boy.' Certainly true if you're fiercely competitive. 'There's a sort of elitism and you do have to be pretty good to get into teams,' confirmed a mother (school says it now fields up to F teams on occasion). Lots of incentives, including medals for anyone taking three wickets out of five or scoring over 50 runs, and a range of sports tours, some more enticing than others, with list offering cricket in Barbados and badminton in Bulgaria. 'I know which I'd choose', said would-be parent. To prove the point, reception area is stuffed with glossy photographs of sports champions, including Olympic hopefuls. Badminton and judo are among notable high points for individual players, though school is no slouch at team sports either, specialising in football while nearby Wallington County Grammar went the rugby route. Both now do the duo, ensuring double the competitive fun.

The un-keen and non-sporty get by, however. 'Nobody hates anyone who's bad at football', said one pupil, while from year 9 the timetable is compassionately arranged to allow students to choose how to fill two compulsory sports periods a week. 'My son isn't sporty and that's ok', said mother, whose child has opted for martial arts over team games.

While it's easy to define school in terms of conventional subjects you'd see as shorthand for academic excellence, that's not to underestimate success elsewhere. DT, for example, is a popular AS option, not just because it's fun but because it's valued on 'serious' academic courses such as chemical engineering: 'admissions tutors say it's really useful because of all the planning and the way you have to take things apart and think them through', said successful student. Work on display routinely, as you'd expect, exceeds the brief (one particularly stunning electric guitar scored full marks at GCSE). School has also created a trio of hovercraft, as you do (though no plans as yet to bring back the much missed Folkestone/Bologne route).

Indeed, extension activity is way of life here. Students acquire European Computer Driving Licences – often a sixth form add on – in year 9, while ICT GCSE has been ditched as 'too boring' in favour of programming lessons. 'Celebrate your inner geek' cutting is pinned up on one of corridor walls.

Art, too, is excellent (staff blog, containing trenchant views on the Turner prize, amongst other topics, is well worth a read) and approached via snazzy light blue corridor and toning floor which serves as exhibition area. Unusually, life drawing classes are taken from GCSE up (and very good the results are, too).

Music, meanwhile, is one to watch, with a department head aged just 24 when appointed – very possibly, he thinks, the youngest in the country (this reviewer still not totally convinced it wasn't one of sixth formers putting on staff identity badge for a laugh – though school confirms that several years in he now looks less like a sixth former). Big competitor is his equivalent at Tiffin, where choir regularly records, but 'we haven't got the same choral tradition,' he says. Watch this space. Professional choir director now in post; with three orchestras and selective choirs already going great guns, plus open-to-all school productions – excellent Les Mis had cast of 200. All year 7s get specialist free instrumental or vocal tuition and there are plans for a parents' choir; you can't help feeling that school's professional debut is but a baton's downbeat away.

Background and atmosphere: Many grammars give the impression of being a throwback to the 1950s. This one doesn't – 'deliberately', says school. Just as well, though it'd be perfectly justified in slipping into something a lot more traditional, what with the impeccable credentials: founded in the 17th century in Camberwell and, with the exception of a 38-year closure in the 19th century after a financial scandal, going strong ever since and celebrates its 400th anniversary in 2015. In 1975, lured by the space and local council's pro-grammar stance, it moved to its current premises, once part of Croydon Airport, and commemorated in nearby street names like Dakota Close and Hurricane Road.

While it's not a looker from the outside, with square brown buildings set uncompromisingly in a large, plain playing field, like so many upturned cardboard boxes, the interiors aren't half bad. Corridors might be on the pre-loved side

('it's because the buildings have been here since 1666 that they want to keep the old look,' says a pupil, with great presence of mind, if not architectural accuracy) but the classrooms, full of lovingly tended displays, more than make up for it. Science labs, too, slightly dishevelled from the outside, are a hive of well-resourced activity within.

No shortage of impressive large scale areas, either, including the traditional main hall which harks back to a glorious academic past (with still better to come, naturally) and a vast sports hall and gym (replacing expensive to maintain swimming pool and available for hire). But there are also more intimate and surprisingly luscious touches. The south canteen – as distinct from north canteen – (they don't go a bundle on fancy names; library has resolutely not morphed into a learning resource centre, for example) has cutting edge lighting, unschool-like black and orange walls and doubles as an attractive additional concert venue. Years 7-8 now have own brand new lower school with dining hall and classrooms.

Pupils whizz purposefully round the site, assisted by traffic calming measures including one-way staircases (suggested by student council). Like the school itself, they look initially unremarkable (crests and striped ties are the only distinctive features). All in all, a lesson in not judging by appearances.

Pastoral care and discipline: Motto is 'Non sibi sed omnibus' (not for oneself but for all) and quite right

too, given the huge emphasis on belonging, with forms recruited wholesale into one of six not overly competitive houses, and 'nobody a guest or merely tolerated'. It's helped by approachable form tutors, first point of contact for pupils and parents, who stay with the same group for two to three years – 'easy to talk to when I had worries,' said a parent. Each form has two tutors throughout years 7-11, with pupils in years 9-11 registered and tutored in small groups of 15. First class settling-in arrangements. Year 7s take precedence in the lunch queue during their first term, though after Christmas it's every boy for himself (works well, say pupils, with 'delicious' meals on tap even for latecomers).

When problems crop up they're 'churned through until they're resolved, no matter how long it takes'. Anxiety can be a problem and school is doing its best to pinpoint early onset symptoms and treat them quickly. On-site counselling is available, together with a popular mentoring system which gives year 7s a sixth form buddy who reaches the worries that staff can't because they realise that 'we're going through hormones and can relate to us', explained one. Pupil support manager coordinates regular one-to-one meetings between teachers and pupils who may be liable to struggle to meet expectations.

School makes no bones about what constitutes unacceptable behaviour, though if there's bullying (it's rare, stressed one boy, who had suffered at his primary school), understanding of the bully as well as the victim is encouraged. 'They can't

One 11 year old was busily teaching himself to multi-task 'so I can be as good as my older sister – I don't like sexism'

help it because they have issues, we do it in PSHE', said saintly year 7 pupil. One parent felt tolerance might occasionally err too much in the offender's favour, making recidivism a distinct possibility.

Detentions are widely used, or at least threatened (and immediate for unauthorised movement of instruments, thunders sign outside music room) though there's some wiggle room – it's three strikes and you're out when it comes to late homework, for example, and even the penalty is a starter detention lasting 10 minutes. With plenty of chances to step back from the brink, pupils considered the system a fair one.

Pupils and parents: Pupils are an unbounded delight. Hugely focused (one 11-year old was busily teaching himself to multi-task, 'so I can be as good as my older sister – I don't like sexism') and, boy, do they talk, with an almost evangelical desire to draw you into their world, apparently without drawing breath, though the kinder ones do pause occasionally to allow dull-witted adults to catch up. Some have their lives sorted aged 11 – most lean towards the professions (research science, accountancy and law all featured on careers shopping list). Not too dissimilar, in fact, from many of the parents.

School proud of its diversity – families encompass every major culture and religion and, currently, speak 40 languages between them. As to parental involvement, the opportunities are there, but 'not handed to you on a plate. You have to search them out', says parent, who recommended a spell as a parent governor as the best way of seeing inside the works.

Alumni include actor Michael Caine, fashion designer John Galliano, opera singer Mark Stone, mountaineer Paul Deegan and aviator Sir Alan Cobham.

Entrance: 'Boys here are clever but not geniuses. If they're doing very well at school, with high level 5 English and maths Sats tests in year 6, then they are clever enough to get in.' Ignore the horror headlines that tell of 10 applicants per place, school stresses, as it's simply the same children sitting each exam and the reality is more like four to one. No advantage in having a brother here.

Parents need to keep an eye on the calendar to avoid missing late August/early September deadline to register with the school for the entrance exams.

There are two, English and maths, 'not Everest but Ben Nevis, with a brisk wind'. Nothing is officially harder than key stage 2 work, though the word on the street is that final maths question can be a twister designed to give the most able chance to show the innermost workings of their minds. The English paper is based on comprehension, 'something every child is doing in primary school', though parents can help by building child's vocabulary and knowledge of literary techniques.

School is grimly resigned to inevitability of widespread tutoring though strongly disapproves. Has ditched verbal reasoning paper because 'we know it can be coached for'. For the same reason, doesn't make past papers available. Parents also urge caution. 'I really don't think you want to tutor your child and get them there under false pretences because they won't be happy', says one.

Pass/fail results in early October tell you if child is still in the running, giving enough time to include the school (essential that it's your top preference – non-selective backup choice should come further down to avoid missing a place) on council-wide school application form, with 150 places offered following March to highest placed candidates. Where there's a tie break, Sutton children have preference with distance to school the final deciding factor. Some join in the sixth form. Again over-subscribed, with offers based on current school's report and places awarded to top GCSE performers.

Consulted on, but rejected, plans to go co-ed.

Exit: Very few leave post-GCSE. The rest – top subjects, top universities – all absolutely as you'd expect, and lots of it. A pretty healthy number to Oxbridge although one sixth former thought grammars, placed awkwardly between better funded, Oxbridge fixated independents and more socially acceptable comprehensives may be faring less well. It's the case especially with screening essays for subjects like humanities, here a by the book DIY effort, elsewhere, he reckoned, toned and honed with expert out of school help. 'We don't have the immense preparation independent schools get or the bias comprehensives enjoy.'

Money matters: 'We are very grateful for the voluntary funding we receive from parents; they are very generous', says school. 'May the money keep coming,' adds a parent. 'We are in an area where it is needed.'

Remarks: Bright, clever and funny, and that's just the staff. Hard not to warm to a school where a pupil, asked what he likes best, says, 'everything's my favourite subject,' though wicked sense of humour ensures it remains a Pollyanna-free zone. A wonderful place if you're effortlessly clever, terrific for robust characters who need to work at it. Parents of bright but sensitive stragglers, however, may care to do a bit of soul-searching before calling in the tutors.

Wimbledon Chase Primary School

Merton Hall Road, London SW19 3QB

Tel: 020 8542 1413

State • Pupils: 730 • Ages: 3–11

Email: wcps@wimbledonchase.merton.sch.uk
Website: www.wimbledonchaseschool.co.uk

20

Head Teacher: Since 2001, Mrs Sue Tomes (60s) BEd NPQH. She arrived at the school as a French teacher over 30 years ago, ascending through the ranks as head of French, senior mistress and deputy head, and finally took the helm. Parents can't praise her enough for her almost lifelong dedication to the school and its pupils. Considered hard working and cheerful, one of those rare characters who makes time for everybody and everything, say parents. Popular with her pupils too; 'She is a lovely person,' one small pupil informed us.

Mrs Tomes maintains her links with France and is an avid supporter of teaching primary school children modern foreign languages across Merton. Part of her philosophy is that the children should be exposed to many different opportunities and experiences to help them discover their talents and develop as interesting and fulfilled youngsters. She and her staff aim to deliver the highest quality, meaningful, relevant and memorable education to all.

Entrance: At 3+ to the nursery and 4+ into reception. Now expanded to three-form entry. Non-selective; applications must be made through Merton Council, usual admissions criteria. For occasional places in older age groups contact school or the council.

Exit: At 11+ majority of girls go to Ricards Lodge, good few to the Kingston and Surrey grammars and local independents. Majority of boys go to Rutlish School, some to local grammars.

Remarks: Continues its long-held reputation for being one of Wimbledon's favourite choices for primary education. Very well thought of all round; academic expectations and achievements are high. Pupils are set by ability in maths from year 4. Stunning Starts, Marvellous Middles and Fabulous Finishes are how staff capture the children's imaginations and talents through the creative curriculum. Pupils are taught via many different media: lessons can include acting, music, dancing, art, design and technology. History and geography topics come alive through a variety of exciting activities. Everyone feels the positive impact and thrill of the creative curriculum; most notably these exciting projects have helped the children develop their writing skills. The arts make up an important part of the curriculum; full-time music teacher and specialist teachers for choir and orchestra also run brass groups, recorder club, drumming club and boomwackers percussion group. Teachers from Merton Music Foundation visit the school every day to give individual instrumental lessons. Musical evenings, assemblies, plays and concerts provide plenty of occasions for everybody to show off their performing skills.

Sizeable premises for a primary school, originally built as the girls' County Grammar in 1924. Playing fields, cricket pitch, tennis courts, a lovely wildlife area and gardens provide numerous outdoor and sporting opportunities. The children grow fruit, vegetables and flowers and are taught about which plants will attract particular birds and

Specialist teachers for choir and orchestra also run brass groups, recorder club, drumming club and boomwackers percussion group

insects. Nursery and reception classes have their own specially-designed playgrounds attached to their classrooms, with new wing added to create space for expanded intake. Now space for 730 pupils. Stylishly-designed new building to accommodate classrooms, cookery room, specialist music rooms, an additional ICT suite, gymnasium and after-school care rooms. Some parents felt that the expansion and building would be disruptive for pupils, but now all appear to be in agreement that despite the odd hitch, the new space and facilities are an advantage for all.

Over 35 native languages are spoken by pupils; effective EAL programme; consequently nearly everyone does very well in Sats. Inclusion manager coordinates SEN, with two specialist teachers and a team of teaching assistants; also a visiting speech and language therapist and a play therapist. The school is fully wheelchair accessible and has a 16 place unit for children with speech, language and communication needs. Pupils attending the unit join with the main school in the afternoons for the creative curriculum, sports and music activities.

Exceptional range of clubs and activities. Friday film club run by a parent in conjunction with the British Film Institute has produced some successful

young film critics. Far-reaching pastoral care; older pupils can train as peer mediators and playground buddies; any child feeling unhappy or needing to talk to an adult can post a note in the worry box. Parent support adviser is available to any parent who might wish to discuss their concerns. The Wrap Around Centre enables the school to offer a breakfast club, full-time nursery places and after-school care.

Parents are very much partners at Wimbledon Chase, assisting with hearing children read, clubs, general maintenance and the upkeep of the extensive grounds. Fund-raising is also high on the strong PTA's agenda; dedicated parents' room, the nerve centre for meetings and a relaxing cuppa. Always keen to involve the wider community and improve their skills base: non-parent volunteers are welcome; a local volunteer has taken on responsibility for maintaining the wildlife garden.

An exceptional and innovative school and community with pupils, parents and staff all apparently delighted to play a part. Enthusiastic children bounce into school each morning eager to know what the day holds in store.

Wimbledon High School Junior School

Linked school: Wimbledon High School, 285

Mansel Road,, London SW19 4AB

Independent • Pupils: 323 • Ages: 4 – 10 • Fees: £12,843 pa

Tel: 020 8971 0902

Email: info.juniors@wim.gdst.net
Website: www.wimbledonhigh.gdst.net

21

Head: Since 2003, Miss Catherine (Kate) Mitchell BEd MA (40s). Formerly deputy head at Alleyn's Junior School, Dulwich; before that deputy head of junior school at Ashville College, Harrogate, and Stamford School, Lincolnshire. Highly rated by parents as professional, approachable and dedicated. 'I'd say it's her vocation,' says one mother. 'She's lovely,' chorus others. Hasn't rocked any boats, preferring to 'refine things here and there'. Teaches verbal reasoning in preparation for 11+ and hears the infant readers. Has super rapport with the girls, knows them all and even recognises matching parent. Out of school, Miss Mitchell enjoys playing bridge and going to the theatre.

Entrance: Selective, mainly at 4+ with a handful of places available at 7+. Occasional vacancies as they arise. Popular and over-subscribed – there's a one in three and a half chance of a place. 'It's hard to assess a child at 4,' says head, 'but we're looking for potential, rather than how much a child has learnt so far.' A series of short assessments covering everything from maths and language to social skills and understanding of the world, are held in a relaxed nursery-style environment. At 7+, English, maths and non-verbal reasoning tests are more formal. 'We're aiming to get a cross-section of children, not just to pick up the more extrovert types.' No priority for siblings – little sisters sometimes disappointed, so entrance procedure evidently more than a formality. Attracts a predominantly local intake from Wimbledon and environs.

Exit: Most to the linked senior school, where 98 per cent are offered places, some with academic and music scholarships. Parents are warned in good time (year 5 at the latest) if their daughter unlikely to make the grade. Some academic and music scholarships elsewhere, including St Paul's and Kingston Grammar. A few to local grammars.

Remarks: Fantastic reputation means locals flock, attracted by the school's well-rounded offering and a (virtually) guaranteed transition to the equally well-regarded senior school. Does the business academically, with excellent maths, science and literacy levels. A recent shift to a 'creative curriculum', where one theme links creative writing, history, geography, art, design technology and ICT, has been very successful. Girls here are high achieving but not pressured.

> *'Teachers make lessons fun,' said our accomplished year 6 guides, who also appear to believe the number one rule around the place is 'to smile'*

For a private school, class sizes are not small – 24 per class for years 3 to 6. Mix of class-based and specialist teaching keeps things lively and the pace picks up as the girls move up the school. There's a co-ordinator to mentor the gifted and talented and parents of these bright girls are delighted at how their daughters are motivated and extended in lots of subject areas. All pupils are screened for SEN in year 2, with up to five per cent receiving extra help – parents make an additional payment. SEN is not a big issue here – few need SEN help, probably because they are bright buttons to start with. Teachers work with a learning support co-ordinator to ensure SEN pupils are accommodated in lesson plans – typically for barriers to learning such as dyslexia and dyspraxia. Targets are drawn up with parents, with progress monitored.

Like many London schools, the site is relatively small, and further space was lost recently when the new performance centre was built. Head's office looks out on to the junior playground – rather a hard, grey site, but colour recently added and new trees planted. There are plenty of games and equipment to keep the girls busy and a wildlife garden is proving popular with young gardeners. Junior school is housed in bright and cheery accommodation, purpose-built, set back behind the senior school (building comes as a pleasant surprise to visitors who can't see it from the road).

School is keen on the creative stuff, IT and sport which all have specialist rooms and facilities, share senior school facilities including fab pool and shiny new Rutherford Centre for the Performing Arts – named after (very) old girl, actress Margaret Rutherford. (More recent OGs include children's author Michelle Paver and journalist Rosie Millard.) Playing fields, games pitches and courts are a few minutes walk away (at least no need for buses) on the site of the original All England Lawn Tennis Club. Though 'Sport for All' is one of the school's boasts, virtually the only parental disquiet about the place is that only the best players are chosen for the competition squads. More run-of-the-mill players have to make do with what's on the timetable. 'It's frustrating if your daughter just falls short,' says one mother. Lots of extracurricular clubs on offer – all sorts of music, languages, art and chess etc.

Happy and purposeful atmosphere. 'I like the way the girls are really supported but never mollycoddled,' said a mother. 'They are taught to be quite independent by the time they reach the top of the school, which is great for their move to the seniors. I'd say a real stand-out feature of this school is the way the girls develop confidence as they go through.' Although a real shrinking violet may initially be a little overwhelmed, the encouraging nature of the school means that even quieter types should thrive here. Since her arrival, the head has beefed up the previously low-key house system. There's also a weekly 'celebration' assembly where the girls can show and tell about any out-of-school achievements. Parental praise for accessibility of (staff and) the head – she runs regular 'open mornings' when parents can drop in on her. Pupils too seem to have good relationships with the staff. 'Teachers make the lessons fun,' said our accomplished year 6 guides, who also appear to believe the number one rule around the place is 'to smile'. An amused Miss Mitchell has issued no such edict – but was delighted to hear that was the only rule the girls could come up with. 'I'm very fortunate that the children behave beautifully and I can keep things fairly relaxed. It's certainly not a strict place,' she says. Discipline not really an issue with these keen and motivated young girls – worst sanction seems to be a missed playtime.

Run by the Girls' Day School Trust, the school celebrated its 130th anniversary in 2010. Knows exactly what it's about and parents perceive it as excellent value for money and appreciate that they are not preyed upon to write countless cheques for extras. Parents are a mixed bunch – not all from the multi-million pound houses on nearby swanky Wimbledon Hill – and they value the fact that the school has a community feel about it. Multicultural, with the emphasis on professional types from financial and legal world.

In a nutshell, it's not a hothouse but is academically pacey and does very well by its brightest girls. Highly recommended by parents who generally don't seem to have a bad word to say about the place.

Wimbledon High School

Linked school: Wimbledon High School Junior School, 283

Mansel Road, London SW19 4AB

Independent • Pupils: 574 • Ages: 11–18 • Sixth form pupils: 155 • Fees: £16,521 pa

Tel: 020 8971 0900

Email: info@wim.gdst.net
Website: www.wimbledonhigh.gdst.net

22

Headmistress: Since September 2014, Mrs Jane Lunnon, previously deputy head at Wellington College. English degree from Bristol; began her career in marketing before taking up teaching. Spent much of her teaching career at Wellington, rising from English teacher to assistant director of studies over 12 years there. Thence to Priors Field, as head of sixth form then deputy head, before returning to Wellington in 2010 as senior deputy.

One of what is probably the GSG's first set of identical twin heads: her sister, Jenny Brown, took over as head of St Albans High in September 2014.

Academic matters: An academic place – but not pressured. Each girl encouraged to reach her own potential, whatever her personal ambition. Encourages risk-taking in the classroom and ensures intellectual and emotional robustness. Good scope for this via a broad curriculum including Latin and Greek, design technology and textiles. Popular options at GCSE are history, geography and French. A record breaking 94 per cent A*/A grades (71 per cent A*) in 2015, most girls get a full set of A*-B – a C grade is rare. At A2 high take-up of maths, biology and chemistry, results good across the board, 88 per cent A*-B grades (64 per cent A*/A) in 2015. Nice to see history of art option here. Good preparation for Oxbridge, but thankfully not a feeling that candidates are better than the rest.

School is active in London Challenge, bringing together the gifted and talented from neighbouring schools to participate in special projects

Class sizes are initially large for a private school at an average 28 for years 7-9 (except for maths which is streamed, science, art and DT), but down to 22 for GCSE classes and 15 (or often fewer) at A level. In sixth form (years 12 and 13) pupils are in mixed tutor groups of about 14. Experienced staff have very high expectations.

'They are largely a most dedicated bunch,' said a parent. 'Great mentors.' All pupils are screened for SEN on entry and learning enrichment coordinator (SEN specialist) supports those with specified needs, advises girls and parents on study methods and offers timetabled 'Learning to Learn' lessons in year 7. Gifted children offered regular extension activities. Weekly enrichment afternoon for years 11, 12 and 13. School is active in London Challenge, bringing together the gifted and talented from neighbouring schools to participate in special projects.

Games, options, the arts: Lots going on both in the classroom and after hours. Doesn't attract the uber-sporty, one parent feeling strongly that expectations are not high enough in this area, but pupils have been junior national representatives in skiing, three-day eventing and gymnastics. Usual compulsory sports and from year 10 upwards girls can also select from further offerings including aerobics, circuit training, squash, horse-riding, badminton, football, rowing and basketball. Wow-factor pool and sports hall on site. Girls go off-site to playing fields, games pitches and courts a few minutes walk away on the site of the original All England Lawn Tennis Club. Year 9 and 10 girls do duty as ball girls during Wimbledon tennis championships.

Drama and music strong and enhanced further by the opening of very impressive Rutherford Centre for the performing arts, which is now at the heart of all performance work. (It's named after old girl, actress Margaret Rutherford.) About 80 per cent of the girls learn a musical instrument. Autumn and spring concerts are highlights

From year 10 upwards girls can also select from further offerings including aerobics, circuit training, squash, horse-riding, badminton, football, rowing and basketball

– fathers and staff join as tenors and baritones, while at the informal summer soirée the girls' own compositions are showcased. Drama department stages many productions over the year, culminating in a summer musical.

Former head believed that most pleasure in life comes from hobbies and passions, 'They need to learn to use a hobby to help them to unwind and relax without resorting to blobbing in front of the TV. They need good habits for life,' she said. To this end girls take their pick from a pleasingly long and varied list of clubs, which as well as the usual offerings includes niche interests eg music for shy performers, 'knit and natter', mah jong and cryptic crosswords (solving and compiling). School's aim is for every girl to find her niche, however unusual or unlikely it may be. A new longer lunch break gives more time for clubs during the school day.

Background and atmosphere: Owned by the Girls' Day School Trust, the school celebrated its 135th birthday in 2015 – so great heritage and knows exactly what it's about. Like many London schools the site is relatively small; on the plus side its urban

location has the benefit of excellent local transport links with tube, train, tram and bus terminals all within eight minutes' walk. Don't be put off by first impressions: Victorian red brick building fronts the place, surrounded by a rather grey site and unwelcoming (almost prison-like) entrance lobby. Inside there are some super-smart facilities, but these vie with some old-style labs, smallish classrooms, peeling radiators and a few grim corridors where a slick of gloss paint wouldn't go amiss. But more importantly the place is friendly, the girls very happy and free to play to their strengths. Sixth formers busy with 'Six is the Best' project, which includes new accommodation and furniture for their common room – working party of pupils was sent off to Ikea to choose it themselves.

Pastoral care and discipline: Happy, high achieving pupils in no great need of discipline, but for the five per cent or so who do require correction it is described as 'firm'. Teachers, though approachable, are strict and there is a head mistress's detention every Friday. Strong head of year system. Sixth formers very good at helping to run house system and peer counselling. From year 7, girls have 'behaving nicely' drummed into them, zero tolerance of bullying. Problems such as eating disorders taken very seriously. 'We don't hesitate or pussy-foot around. We are straight in once we come across anything like this to support the girl involved and all her friends who undoubtedly will have been worrying themselves.' Less serious issues, eg uniform niggles, nicely handled – girls have worked with staff to draw up acceptable guidelines including deciding the maximum permitted distance above the knee for skirts.

Pupils and parents: Exuberant live wires and timid flowers will all find a happy home here – the school is very tolerant, even encouraging, of individual types and unusual characters. Good sense of community from a diverse bunch. English middle classes, mixed with Korean and East European families joining the longer-established Indian and Chinese communities. OGs include children's author Michelle Pavers, journalist Rosie Millard, investment banker turned Hollywood actor Amara Karan and Professor of Experimental Pathology, Harvard University, Lynne Reid. A chunk of parents from financial and legal worlds. Thriving parents' association.

Entrance: Selective at 11+ – verbal and non-verbal reasoning tests plus creative writing task. Typically between 350-400 applications for 45 or so places, depending on exactly how many of the 48 possible arrive from juniors (only a handful don't make it). Extra form intake in year 7 every five years – last

was 2014. Register from Easter the year before entry, interview in autumn term and exams the following January. School references and interview notes decide borderline cases. Attracts families from Wimbledon and wide surrounding area. Feeder schools include The Study and Holy Cross Prep, with other applicants coming from various state and independent schools. At 16+ girls need GCSE grade A in subjects to be studied at AS level.

Exit: About 80 per cent move up to the sixth form and 15 per cent join from other schools. School will have to work hard to keep the percentage up – some pupils swayed as nearby King's College School for boys has opened its doors to sixth form to girls. At 18+ most to good universities of their choice – mainly Russell Group; nine to Oxbridge in 2015.

Money matters: Academic and music scholarships available at 11+ and academic, science, music, drama, art and PE scholarships at 16+. Hundred per cent bursaries on offer at 11+ and 16+.

Remarks: Terrifically purposeful place, with tons going on – think Richard Scarry's Busy Town. Suits bright, hard-working girls prepared to muck in and have a go. All the activity is underpinned by hefty academic foundations, so a girl who would just scrape in or who doesn't like to knuckle down may want to look elsewhere.

South East

Bexley
Bromley
Croydon
Greenwich
Lewisham

Stoke Newington

Holloway Road

Ilford

Becontree

Hornchurch

Elm Park

Camden Town

Stratford

Dagenham

Kings Cross

Barking

Shoreditch

Holborn

Rainham

Poplar

Thamesmead

Southwark

Isle of
Dogs

Lambeth

Plumstead

Belvedere

Charlton

Greenwich

GREENWICH

Deptford

Camberwell

26

21

Battersea

25

27

Blackheath

Welling

BEXLEY

Brixton

24

Lewisham

Bexleyheath

Crayford

Wandsworth

East Dulwich

28

22

Bexley

29

23

Dulwich

3

Forest Hill

4

New Eltham

LEWISHAM

Sidcup

30

Downham

West
Norwood

31

Penge

Chislehurst

Bromley

1

Thornton
Heath

9

5

2

Petts Wood

6

19

Hayes

BROMLEY

Orpington

Croydon

West Wickham

14

10

15

7

8

Sutton

20

16

CROYDON

Keston

17

13

12

11

New Addington

Purley

18

Sanderstead

Downe

SOUTH EAST

BROMLEY

1. Bromley High School (GDST) Junior Department 314
2. Bromley High School (GDST) 315
3. Eltham College Junior School 330
4. Eltham College 332
5. Langley Park School For Boys 340
6. Langley Park School For Girls 344
7. Newstead Wood School 349
8. St Olave's Grammar School 373

CROYDON

9. BRIT School For Performing Arts And Technology 308
10. Coloma Convent Girls' School 321
11. Croydon High School 323
12. Cumnor House School (Croydon) 325
13. Cumnor House School For Girls 328
14. Old Palace Of John Whitgift Preparatory School 351
15. Old Palace Of John Whitgift School 355
16. Royal Russell Junior School 364
17. Royal Russell School 365

18. St David's School 368
19. Trinity School 380
20. Whitgift School 384

GREENWICH

21. Blackheath High School GDST 303
22. Colfe's Preparatory School + Pre Prep and Nursery 317
23. Colfe's School 318

LEWISHAM

24. Blackheath High School (Junior Department) 301
25. Haberdasher's Aske's Hatcham College Primary Phase 335
26. Haberdasher's Aske's Hatcham College 336
27. Prendergast School 360
28. St Dunstan's College Junior School 369
29. St Dunstan's College 370
30. Sydenham High Junior School GDST 376
31. Sydenham High School GDST 377

An introduction to South East London and its state schools

Bexley

On the edge of open countryside but only 12 miles from central London and still within sight of the towers of Canary Wharf, Bexley was extensively developed between the two World Wars. An amalgamation of suburbs around the older Erith and Bexleyheath, the A2 Rochester Way streams through en route to Kent, and with golf courses and grammars it hardly feels like London at all.

There are no less than four grammars to 'choose' from: Bexley is the current favourite, but Chislehurst and Sidcup, Beth's (boys) and Townley (girls) are nudging ahead at GCSE. Children no longer automatically sit the test for these schools; candidates must opt in online to take it. Bexley is a specialist language college – all pupils take two – with a further specialism in science and maths. Beth's has an international dimension and is a hub school for Mandarin. Townley specialises in performing and visual arts, plus maths and computing.

Moving here for grammar entry alone would seem quite high stakes as, to our minds, good state plan B options are thin on the ground. It has been noted that many of those pupils who achieve well at 11 are not achieving at a similar level a few years later. More grammar school forms of entry at year 7 would assist, and Beth's has recently added one. Meanwhile, there is always further afield: many Bexley children also sit the Kent Test aiming for the North West Kent Grammars of Dartford and Wilmington.

Grammars aside, Catholic families have the option of St Catherine's for girls and St Colomba's for boys, the latter seems to have shed its poor image but results are under-whelming as yet. Non church-goers might consider Bexleyheath Academy or Blackfen School for girls, Sidcup. Harris Academy Falconwood recently found favour with Ofsted and GCSEs are improving nicely. Worth a visit is Leigh

Technology Academy, Dartford, notable both for innovative teaching and its eco building design – the college structure may make its size less daunting. A new all-through (3-18) contender is Haberdasher's Aske's Crayford Academy. The school, which has a music specialism, opened in 2009 and has proved a hit with families, resulting in a teeny-tiny catchment. Whichever option you favour, be prepared to dance the fandango through myriad admission criteria and supplementary forms pertinent to each type of school.

There are not as many enticing primaries here as there are in neighbouring boroughs. The stars of performance, rating and location rarely fall into alignment, so proximity to the various commuter stations may also come into play and open day visits are essential. Top of the faith schools are currently St John Fisher Catholic and St Paulinus C of E, closely followed by St Michael's East Wickham C of E, St Stephen's Catholic, St Joseph's Catholic, Our Lady of the Rosary, St Thomas More Catholic and Old Bexley C of E. For others Castilion, Jubilee and Parkway clustered around Thamesmead, or Birkbeck, Bursted Wood and Barnehurst are amongst the most popular. Notable academically are Dulverton, Eastcote, Danson and this year's star, Orchard school. Uptake has been cautious in Bexley's first free school, the Hope Community School in Sidcup, but headed up by a former staff member from Birkbeck Primary for the pioneering it has to be worth a look.

Bromley

One of the greenest boroughs, Bromley includes part of the Kent Downs and was home to Enid Blyton and WG Grace in its heyday. For some, Bromley is 'London without the horrible bits', while urbanites may feel it threatens the twin perils of both village and suburb. Bromley is made for commuting – fast, short journeys into central London one way and the M25 on the doorstep

Star of the secondary show is St Olave's grammar for boys qv in Orpington. It regularly features in top 10 UK state schools and sends 20+ to Oxbridge annually. Competition for places roughly eight to one and the catchment area is huge, extending to Southwark and Lambeth.

Otherwise it's academies as far as the eye can see. Newstead Wood for girls qv in Orpington is selective, has recently increased its intake and performs excellently. Alternatively, the Langley Park qv schools in Beckenham, one for each sex – the boys' school with a stunning new building – are often cited as reasons for moving to the area. Well-thought-of back-ups might be Bullers Wood (takes boys in the sixth form), Darrick or Hayes.

For those looking to begin their children's schooling here the picture is challenging: parents advise us it is unusual to be in the catchment for more than one of the popular primaries, nail-biting when some such as Perry Hall and Valley are over-subscribed to the tune of seven to one. Applications at Farnborough, Alexandra Infant, Crofton, Unicorn and Bickley are not far behind, so perhaps take a look at strong academic performers such as Burnt Ash, Highfield and Hawes Down. Help is at hand with several new primaries imminent or open for business. In the south, La Fontaine is a French/English primary with only 50 percent of admissions distance based. Sure to create something of a stampede, the Langley Park schools, will open a primary in 2016 specialising in maths, and providing a way in to the senior schools. Then, two new Harris primary academies, one in Shortlands and one in Kent House.

Church-going families get a good deal here since church schools, despite their often good results and ratings, are not attracting such fierce competition for places. Chislehurst C of E, St James' RC, St Vincent's Catholic, St George's Bickley C of E and St Mark's C of E all do extremely well.

Croydon

The stock seems to be rising in London's largest borough, with house price ripples pushed ever outwards, a new Westfield shopping centre arriving in 2018, and various schools at both secondary and primary performing pretty nicely.

The secondary scene is dominated by Harris Academies – Crystal Palace is over-subscribed to the tune of 11 to one and there are three more in Norwood and Purley. For budding dotcom entrepreneurs a new Harris Invictus with a specialism in e-business opened close to West Croydon station in 2014. Trailing somewhat behind the Harris Academies in terms of results, but highly regarded in science, the Oasis Shirley Park is on the up. Croydon is also home to the famous BRIT school qv, the only free performing arts and technology school in the country with much to sing and dance about.

West Croydon's Coloma Convent qv is one of a kind, frequently cited as the top girls' comprehensive in the country, with stunning results to rival local independents Whitgift qv, Trinity qv and Old Palace qv. It's worth noting that unusually generous bursaries make these three possible alternatives to state schools, for those willing to compete. Also popular is Archbishop Tennison's co-ed C of E High School.

Despite a few provocative headlines about failing primaries, it seems many are holding their own, if not dazzling and there are some appealing neighbourhood options. Around Sanderstead are Ridgeway (Kate Moss's alma mater), Atwood, and Gresham. Greenvale, despite its Ofsted halo slipping recently, Howard and Park Hill are also very popular. Further north places are very much in demand at White Horse Manor, Elmwood, Gonville and buzzy West Thornton – you still need to live within scooting distance despite its expansion. Chestnut Park, a widely advertised, brand new three form entry academy, may help.

With so many chasing places it's worth seeking schools

that are somewhat overlooked, despite their good results: Oasis Shirley Park Primary and Wolsey, possibly Courtwood and Keston, and definitely new kid 'outstanding' Chipstead Valley. At some point the baby bulge should be catered for as academy openings are all the rage: the new Harris primary academy in South Croydon and Paxton Academy in Thornton Heath are worth a look, admissions as yet less fought over.

Notable faith schools include: St Cyprian's Greek Orthodox, St John's C of E, and both St Aiden's and St Chad's, with Ofsted best including Parish Church C of E Infant/Juniors, Coulsdon C of E, St James the Great RC, St Thomas Becket and St Mary's Catholic Infants.

Greenwich

Centre of the universe for the past 200 years, the Royal Borough of Greenwich has the classic splendours of parkland, Sir Christopher Wren's naval college, and views of the river and the City at its heart. The east – Woolwich, Plumstead and Eltham – is more affordable than Blackheath to the west, and the area increasingly attracts young families who have outgrown Docklands flats. Commuters may choose from ferry, cable-car, or train and North Greenwich is only one stop to Canary Wharf on the Jubilee line.

When even the estate agents admit that state school choices are known to be poor, there really is a problem. For now tumbleweed blows through the top of the performance tables, leading many families to opt for south London's independents or try for neighbouring grammars. Cue the extreme excitement surrounding the launch of the Greenwich Free School founded by the former head of education of the prime minister's strategy unit, local parents and a serving south London head teacher and much embarrassment when Ofsted's first impressions were that it could do better! It will be interesting to see how quickly it can improve and how far maintain its popularity – 700 applications for 100 places, allocated via ability banding, based in a former nurses' home backing onto Woolwich Common. Rumours of the school's primary application have gone strangely quiet.

Other options might include the Harris Academy, which has some distinguished leaders and scores highly amongst similar schools. Also worth exploring is Woolwich Polytechnic School for boys in Thamesmead which was shortlisted by the TES for Secondary School of the Year and was the first school in the country to go beyond 'outstanding' and win the Exceptional Schools Award from Ofsted. Eltham Hill, for girls with a co-ed sixth form and Stationer's Crown Woods College co-ed are on the up. A new free school, the International Academy of Greenwich, specialising in languages, is struggling to confirm a site but looks set to open autumn 2016.

For the vocationally minded there is the rare opportunity to apply to the Greenwich University Technical College in years 10 and 12 via an all-ability entrance test. Specialising in engineering and construction with exciting facilities, it guarantees students a place at the University of Greenwich, other FE opportunity or employment.

Catholic girls are in luck – St Ursula's gets good results, offers Japanese and exceptional extracurricular opportunities.

Primaries here offer a rather exhilarating ride: seeming to plummet up and down in favour, but for now at least it's been a good year for self-improvement. Over-subscription is rife for the chosen few, with tiny catchments – several schools have recently expanded over two sites. Extremely popular is the excellent Brooklands in Blackheath, followed by Invicta, Sherington, Cherry Orchard, Halstow and Gordon. Their equals academically are Cardwell, Deansfield, Henwick,

Hawksmoor and Horn Park. Faith school chart-toppers include: St Patrick's Catholic, St Margaret Clitherow, Christ Church C of E and Eltham C of E.

Lewisham

Lewisham is undoubtedly 'inner city' with regards to crime headlines, but for those attracted to the environs of Blackheath or Dulwich but wanting more for their money, Telegraph Hill, Crofton Park, Ladywell, Hither Green and Brockley offer period properties and increasing numbers of lattés. The East London or 'ginger line' overground direct to fashionable Shoreditch and the City has invigorated Forest Hill and Honor Oak Park, to name but two.

Until recently, secondary schooling in Lewisham languished near the bottom of London league tables but better news is that some of the better performing schools are rapidly expanding. The popular Prendergast School qv for girls (co-ed sixth form) has specialisms in languages, music, mathematics and computing. It started a reception intake in September 2014, en route to becoming an all-through destination. Within the same federation is Prendergast Vale, a co-ed 3-18 school in central Lewisham. As we go to press the school is consulting on whether to become a multi academy trust.

Haberdashers' Aske's Hatcham College qv, 3-18, in New Cross is one of the most over-subscribed state schools in London, with applications standing at 11 to one. It specialises in music and ICT, but is known for strengths across arts, mathematics and science. The expansion news here is the recent opening of Hatcham Temple Grove Free School primary with the curriculum taught immersively in both English and German.

Due to the huge jump in birth rates since the turn of the millennium, bulge classes have been all the rage in Lewisham primaries, leading to permanent expansion at John Ball and

Holbeach. With some annual intakes a mere 30 it's easy to see why the most popular – Horniman, Grinling Gibbons and Ashmead - are so over-subscribed. Luckily there are plenty of great performing primaries, so those free to choose may want to aim for a 60 intake at least and consider Fairlawn, Eliot Bank, Kilmorie, Gordonbrock or the new Brindishe Green with an intake of 90. Set to be popular are Beecroft, Haseltine and Rangefield, newly designated 'outstanding'.

Strong contenders for Catholic families include (in order of attainment): St Mary Magdalen's, Holy Cross RC, St Winifred's, Good Shepherd RC and Our Lady and St Philip Neri RC. For Church of England followers and non-believers scrambling for 'open' places there are: St Michael's, St Bartholomew's, All Saint's, St Margaret's Lee and St John the Baptist Southend.

Blackheath High School (Junior Department)

Linked school: Blackheath High School GDST, 303

Wemyss Road, London SE3 oTF

Independent • Pupils: 323 (plus 48 in nursery)
• Ages: 3–11 • Fees: up to £12,150 pa

Tel: 020 8852 1537

Email: info@blj.gdst.net
Website: www.blackheathhighschool.gdst.net

Head of Juniors: Since, 2012, Mrs Sarah Skevington (early 50s), LLB Sheffield, PGCE, formerly head of the school's early years dept. She practised as a solicitor specialising in family law then retrained as a teacher. She has taught throughout the EYFS and key stages 1 and 2 at local state primaries including Brindishe Lee – 'outstanding' in every category – and Invicta, which she found both challenging and inspirational.

She went to school in Greenwich, at St Ursula's and has raised her family here. Her three grown-up children attended a co-ed school, but since teaching at a GDST school she really appreciates 'what single sex can do for girls', and as a working mother has 'sympathy for working parents'. In her spare time she likes walking in Greenwich Park and lots of trips to the cinema and theatre.

Mrs Skevington is calm, quietly spoken and welcoming. Her office is the home of Florence the labradoodle, who on the day of our visit had flopped silently beneath her desk, offering a tantalising glimpse of a grey furry foot. Children delight in walking Florence. A parent commented: 'Mrs Skevington is wonderful. She has grown into the

role since taking it over and we are very happy with the direction the school is taking under her leadership. She is very good with the girls who really like her.' Another, 'She is professional, personable, level-headed, I could go on…'

She pays tribute to her incredibly hard-working staff, saying this is very much a Blackheath community school, 'it's culturally diverse and all the better for it'.

Entrance: By interview with parents and child. Whilst the child plays, the head is looking for parents who 'understand our offer', in other words are not super-pushy or those who might baulk at no formal homework in reception. Parents who will be happy here are looking for somewhere for their child to grow as an individual.

Exit: Most will be offered a place at the senior school. If the head considers that it isn't the best place, will discuss with parents at an early point.

Remarks: The junior school building is the original first GDST building. Inside is a beautiful Victorian school hall, brought up to date with the insertion of coloured panels into the large lantern skylight. On the sunny day of our visit the hall was full of bright colours, while children below practised their circus skills. A grand, double stone staircase sweeps down from the entrance to the classrooms on the ground floor, also featured in a wonderful portrait of the very first pupils and staff of the school. The walls feature quotes from inspiring women of our times: Maya Angelou, Anita Roddick and Deborah Meaden.

Classrooms are large, bright and airy, with one teacher and one teaching assistant in every class of 16 in nursery and around 48 girls in every other year group. Classes vary between excited exuberance at year 1 to quietly attentive year 5s. The library, recently rescued from an ill-judged make-over, has had its wonderful parquet flooring revealed, with new freewheeling bookcases in spring colours. Some girls are library prefects and make book recommendations. Playground in full swing at lunchtime was quite a sight, with girls busily making the most of all the different levels: there is climbing equipment, space to run around on hard surfaces, a sandpit in a separate area for the nursery, a maths hut, sensible sun canopy provided by the PTA, and even a small forest school, which the head admits is more concept than actual woodland. The girls' stripy summer dresses are just right for running around on a hot day.

Asked for an example of good teaching, the head cites lessons where year 5s designed an app, then linked up (virtually) with the nursery children, who tried out the app, giving instant feedback. 'Simple stuff done well,' says the head. She observed the head of English teaching girls about persuasive writing styles, saying the girls were hanging onto her every word, and later tried

Playground in full swing at lunchtime was quite a sight, with girls busily making the most of all the different levels: there is climbing equipment and space to run around

out their new skills writing to ask her to do away with homework.

A parent agreed her daughter is taught 'without feeling she is under pressure. Subjects are taught in an engaging, fun way which increases her enthusiasm to learn and do well.' Another liked the fact that 'the teachers use innovative ways to get concepts across – for example using a "money week" to make the concept of money and savings so much more exciting, and asking parents who work in the financial services sector to come into class'. The French teacher is the best of both worlds, a native French speaker, trained as a teacher in England. Currently there are iPads in group sets, but the school is working towards one for every pupil.

The junior school has 72 girls on the SEND register with needs such as mild speech and language difficulties, dyslexia, dyspraxia and other mild learning difficulties. Needs are catered for within the classroom through differentiation and TA support as well as small group and one-to-one withdrawal. The head says that dyslexia is on the rise. One parent who was appreciative of the school's support nonetheless found the part-time SENCo to be 'extremely stretched'.

Sport is set to have a change of pace with the appointment of another specialist PE teacher. To date, not the sportiest. Head and parents wish the school playing field was closer – it is a bus-ride away. To allow girls as long as possible on the field they have recently introduced a club prior to PE, so that parents drop girls off at the field. Dance is offered as part of the curriculum. Swimming is at the local pool.

Music flourishes under the 'talented and energetic' head of music: there are 150 music lessons currently timetabled each week for instrumental or vocal lessons – from beginner to grade 6. From the youngest performers in year 1 through to year 6, every year group entertains parents at an annual tea-time concert, and the juniors recently joined the seniors for a beautiful performance of Noyes Fludde at the Royal Naval College. Year 2 girls can have a generous 10 lessons for free on a new stringed instrument to really test whether they like it. The chamber choir is award-winning – four times in a row at the Beckenham Festival.

Girls recently displayed clay busts made in DT at Ranger's House owned by English Heritage in the good company of European masterpieces. We enjoyed the display of a recent holiday project where girls chose any piece of art to recreate photographically at home, with staff joining in too: super renditions of The Girl with A Pearl Earring, Frida Kahlo self-portraits, and our favourite: Mrs Skevington, the school caretaker and Florence posed as Mr and Mrs Andrews by Gainsborough.

A Stone Age workshop stopped just short of making fire in the school hall with two twigs, and seemed to be delivered by an actual cave man. The school makes the most of London, with girls popping out to explore the Cutty Sark, the front row at Wimbledon and further afield. Boasts over 50 clubs and must be one of the few junior schools with own radio station. A GDST alumna, Rachel Joyce, author of The Unlikely Pilgrimage of Harold Fry, adjudicated the annual poetry competition. 'They really do a wonderful job of including all the girls in class plays, assemblies, nativity plays,' said a parent. The hall is large with retractable raked seating so that everyone and their iPad can get a good view.

The co-curricular and extracurricular programme not universally popular with more than one parent who wished for more focus on academics. One said, 'I am not convinced the school is capturing the academic potential of all the children', and another, 'may not be a bad thing to ramp up the academics a notch.' The head says children are learning a great deal through structured play and that they don't drop everything for Sats, but nonetheless girls gain a plethora of level 5s, including girls who are more than mildly dyslexic and some level 6s, with girls exiting at 11 'ready for anywhere'.

Transitions are managed thoughtfully. Year 5s feel much more grown-up with the provision of lockers in their classrooms, as they begin to move around to specialist teachers. Year 6 pupils are made to feel special with a prize-giving and lunch with their parents before they head off to senior schools.

We agree with a parent who said, 'The school is friendly and welcoming – it feels like a family.' And everyone, but everyone, agreed on fabulous pastoral care, with one saying: '[It] is exemplary – the main reason we chose the school above others. Not only do the staff look out for the girls, they are encouraged to look after each other, and the buddy group system works well to encourage that. My daughter is thrilled that she can call some of the big girls her friends'.

Parents say the happy pupils we saw at lunchtime cannot wait to get to school in the morning. They might be described as 'bright and sparky, polite and well mannered, kind and empathetic. It's not for kids who want to be pushed, graded or constantly winning.' And as for self-portraits, a parent obliged: 'A nice mixture from different backgrounds and cultures who all want their daughters to enjoy learning.' One parent with a talent for slogan writing summed it up: 'Childhood is not a race and at BHH they enjoy the journey.'

Blackheath High School GDST

Linked school: Blackheath High School (Junior Department), 301

27 Vanbrugh Park, London SE3 7AG

Independent • Pupils: 374 • Ages: 11 –18 • Sixth form pupils: 77 • Fees: £14,766 pa

Tel: 020 8853 2929

21

Email: info@bla.gdst.net
Website: www.blackheathhighschool.gdst.net

Headteacher: Since 2014, Mrs Carol Chandler-Thompson BA in History and PGCE both from Exeter (early 40s), formerly head of the Girls' School, North London Collegiate, Jeju, in the Republic of Korea. Prior to setting up NLCS in South Korea, she spent seven years as head of history and politics at NLCS. Before that, teacher of history and head of PSHE at Haberdashers' Aske's School for Girls, Elstree.

The move to Korea was not simply in search of a headship or an international move, but enabled her to continue to be part of NLCS with the remit of setting up a school from scratch with a focus on the importance of the quality of teaching. She was drawn to the GDST for its 'girls first' philosophy but also the sense of community where 'older girls don't feel too superior to talk to the younger ones'.

Youthful, open, highly articulate and full of energy for the transformations in hand, she lives in Woolwich with her partner, Emma, and although barely having time for sport these days (though something of a triathlete), she enjoys the downhill run home from Greenwich towards the river when possible, and being back in vibrant London, after the monoculture of Korea. Having said that, she misses Asia and we met her just prior to a holiday in Sri Lanka.

It's never easy following a longstanding head – her predecessor, Mrs Laws, was head of Blackheath High for 14 years – but girls and parents alike have quickly taken to Mrs C-T. She is getting to know each girl gradually, teaching the year 9s history, joining in on a D of E challenge, and inviting them in twos and threes to have lunch with her. A parent said, 'She is approachable, energetic, personable and committed and will clearly blend her own ideas and purpose to good effect within the school as her influence evolves. She has very quickly secured a place of affection and respect amongst the girls and staff.' A pupil: 'She's refreshing; different in such a good way'.

The ISI's verdict on the sixth form, 'good and sometimes excellent', is a somewhat lukewarm tribute amongst a sea of 'excellents' for all other aspects of the school. As well as reinvigorating staff and teaching, working hard to push back the administrative tsunami to protect space for 'thinking about teaching', so that they can rekindle their own subject passion, the head will be bringing her experiences from NLCS's highly successful sixth form.

And whilst she's very happy for the school to be known for the strength of its pastoral care, she will be focused on moving that reputation to highlight academics. Having heard her talk about her involvement in this year's 11+ selection process, we've rarely heard of such care and attention given to spotting potential beyond mere performance on the day. Every applicant is interviewed and given a chance to shine even if not the most polished at 11.

Also on the agenda is raising the profile of sport. Never known as a sporty school – amusingly illustrated by girls in the playground sitting chatting either side of the nets on the table tennis tables – the head has appointed a new director of sport.

Originality is the order of the day: one girl even grew her own skirt. A parent added: 'The school offers an excellent series of TED lectures'

She will be aiming to ensure no ceilings are put on the girls. 'Girls are stretched and pushed here but they don't succeed through the failure of others; it's about challenging themselves'. Whatever girls want to do, whether it's apply to Oxbridge or become a professional singer, the school will absolutely support them. The word 'aspiration' crops up a lot, and parents say, 'She was very quick to pick up areas which needed improvement and is addressing them eg widening the girls' aspirations... She is very thoughtful and passionate to further advance the school.'

Academic matters: Results impress – fifty-seven per cent A*/A at GCSE and 38 per cent A*/A at A level in 2015 – but don't dominate league tables or the GDST leader board. Head says it's about value-added.

No surprises curriculum-wise. GCSE science starts in year 9. Excitingly, as befits the Greenwich

location, a handful of the top physicists are invited to study astronomy GCSE, alongside similarly selected state school pupils. Most lessons taught in mixed ability groups apart from maths set from year 7. As many achieve A*/A in English literature as achieve A*-B in maths. Computing, not ICT, thankfully. School, and the whole GDST, is keen on STEM subjects and a recent look to the future event allowed girls to have their eyes opened by an engineer, a dentist and a computer programmer. Art and design flourishes and is as popular as the single sciences. Plenty of keen actors: drama is a likely choice.

Proud to be one of the first schools to offer Mandarin. All pupils take Latin from year 7 plus a choice of modern foreign languages from French, German, Spanish and Mandarin. Some leeway for girls with SpLDs. Carefully structured language trips and exchanges, gaining in adventurousness as girls go up the school, taking in Paris, Trier in Germany, Castellón in Spain. 'Exchange trips with a school in Germany from year 8 onwards fostered her interest in and ability with the language, as did the encouragement to do work experience in Germany in year 12,' said an approving parent.

Things get more varied at A level with the addition of economics/business, further maths, music technology, textiles, theatre studies, politics and psychology. Highest grades recently in art and design and English literature. Biology, chemistry, business and economics rather bring up the rear and none of the mathematicians reach the tip of the top.

A parent said, 'Every subject area has had at least one teacher who has been inspiring and is completely trusted by the girls'. Our guides went further, telling us how much they appreciated the excellent standard of teaching; they could only think of one instance when a maternity cover teacher had not been up to scratch, but they felt it was quickly dealt with, and convinced us they wouldn't hesitate to raise this with the head of year. Another parent said, 'As a result of the excellent and inspirational teaching, she has developed a passion for the subjects which she intends to study at university.'

Co-curricular flourishes: eco week saw year 6, from the junior school, and year 13 geographers working together to experience what life is like for slum dwellers. During the recent election, the politics society organised mock elections with some pretty impressive drop-in guests, including all of the local party candidates, and a trip to Parliament encountered Andrew Mitchell, giving the girls the inside scoop on 'plebgate'. The newly introduced Wollstonecraft Programme, far more vibrant and modern than it sounds, offers girls from years 7 to 11 a non-examined choice of courses including the creation of Girls' Hour for broadcast (think

R4 Woman's Hour), creating and marketing apps, global perspectives, and introduction to film analysis.

The clunkily titled Matrix of Knowledge course in year 11, subtitled A History of Western Civilisation in 23 Lessons, prepares girls for entry into the sixth form and Russell Group applications – it develops critical thinking, research and debating skills and culminates in explorations of the riches of London such as The Wellcome Collection and Sir John Soane's Museum. Theory of Knowledge takes this further in the sixth form. And whilst the school isn't considering IB, other elements from this such as the extended project are in place. Originality is the order of the day: one girl even grew her own skirt. A parent added: 'The school offers an excellent series of TED lectures'. The librarian said she's just had her book budget increased and girls say the selection is well-chosen and they can also request anything they want.

Plenty of praise for the school's career preparation. Girls are encouraged to start thinking of their aptitudes and possible options for their future from around year 9. There are trips to inspire. Girls in years 9 and 10 were given a behind the scenes tour of Microsoft by interns, who had each fought off 60 others – let's hope they are being paid. Sixth formers make use of online help from Unifrog. A parent told us: 'My daughter received excellent advice, encouragement and support from the careers teacher regarding a work placement in year 11, and an opportunity in year 12 to shadow an undergraduate at a Russell Group university.' Another, 'The quality of the guidance and the fact that it is offered early ensures that the girls can build a very strong application, when the time comes, for places in further education.'

The head speaks warmly of the SENCo, currently studying for a masters, who initiated the 'pupil passport', where each girl records what works for them and their particular learning style in the classroom. The senior school has 56 students with a form of SEN, including dyslexia, dyscalculia and dyspraxia, and currently one child with a statement. Girls receive in-class and out-of-class support, which incorporates differentiation or small group or one-to-one support, depending on need. The head has also appointed a separate EAL co-ordinator.

Games, options, the arts: Despite its location close to the edge of Blackheath and more or less alongside Greenwich Park, the school's five acre sports field with a pavilion and an all-weather pitch is a short bus-ride away. PE is compulsory for all and anyone can play on a team; in fact girls are horrified to hear of friends who never get to play for their schools. Winter sports are netball, hockey and cross-country. Summer sports are rounders, athletics and tennis. Girls benefit from the wider GDST network for competitions as well as local tournaments. Our guides felt whatever your sporting interest, it would be made available. They try fencing, trampolining, gymnastics, table tennis, football and dance. The annual Iron House race sees 40 athletes from across the school, including staff, showing their stamina in Greenwich Park, including the gruelling near-vertical climb to the top. It's a breeding ground for competitive runners.

Who is this school for? According to parents it's for 'Children who are keen to try new things and get involved – the more you put in, the more you get out'

Girls with a love of the wider outdoors enjoy D of E – everyone does bronze, with just a hard-core few making it to gold. Also on offer is an international three week World Challenge – previous trips have been to Namibia, this year to Peru. The cost is steep but girls raise the money themselves, rather than digging into the bank of mum and dad. There are also taster sessions in canoeing, sailing and horse-riding, and girls get a chance to go on PGL adventures to challenge any fear of heights and brave the English weather.

The school makes the very most of its situation in Greenwich, recently putting on a stunning production, Noyes Fludde, at the Old Royal Naval College, featuring singing, dance and musicians from across the school together with a professional

Without boys to impress, there were none of the false eyelashes or make-up we've seen at co-eds recently. Girls between lessons were exuberant, loud, even

tenor. The new head of music, a former professional drummer, has shaken things up. There are over 200 music lessons a week and extracurricular is chock full of music: orchestra, chamber choirs, samba band, rock band, ukulele orchestra, glee club and a number of percussion ensembles aptly named Beat It!, Percussionistas and Mini-mallets. There are bi-annual international music tours, and many pupils study at junior conservatoires. Everyone arriving in year 7 can take part in a taster scheme where they have the opportunity to learn an instrument free of charge.

There are clubs timetabled for each year group from Viking and Anglo-Saxon club in year 7 to Iron Woman, self-defence, debating club, crochet collective – who meet in the outdoor classroom – and an F1 club. Any sixth former can start a society.

The Theatre is a purpose-built performance space on campus, but pupils also put on plays at Greenwich Theatre. A parent enthused, 'The drama was outstanding...always thoroughly engaging and bursting with energy and enthusiasm.' A competitive audition recently resulted in the world premiere of creepy Coraline, complete with button eyes: an ambitious adaptation scripted by the drama teacher. Plenty of rehearsal spaces and professional equipment

High quality art is displayed around the school. We were lucky enough to see the GCSE and A level examination pieces, including dresses one might covet, much in demand for the end of school ball. The art teacher welcomes all into the studio, even if just to do their homework in inspiring surroundings.

Background and atmosphere: The first purpose built GDST school, opened in 1880, it maintains the tradition of a thorough academic education for girls for highly competitive fees. The school is situated on one of Blackheath's fine Georgian streets, although now very busy with traffic. A tall, red-brick building with stone dressings, with the somewhat odd addition of a 1960s church, currently used as a dance studio. Some of the fine archival history of the GDST is here, but hidden away.

Development plans are in progress, first phase opening in 2016, with everything complete by 2018. The old building will be refurbished, whilst an entire wing is replacd, and an impressive, glassy entrance hall is added, with the library and resource centre heading below ground. Old will meet new, with one of the school's original stained glass windows dramatically incorporated into the new building.

Parents enthuse about the school's warm atmosphere, saying: 'By the time my daughter reached the GCSE years, the teachers knew her as an individual rather than as a number'; 'very positive atmosphere, friendly, supportive, collaborative'; 'everyone is enthusiastic about learning and has an open mind to new ideas incorporating very well the different cultural backgrounds the girls are coming from.'

Old girls include talents in all areas, particularly the media, perhaps most notably: Mary Quant; Baroness Jay of Paddington, Labour politician; Helen Lederer, comedian, and cookery writer, Katie Stewart.

Pastoral care and discipline: The head has split the roles of deputy into academic deputy and pastoral deputy, and there is a new part-time school counsellor. Pupils who volunteer are given training in peer mentoring by Childline. Mentors are assigned a year group and available at lunchtime, before and after school. One we spoke to clearly enjoyed it.

Parents praise the emotional support given to the girls: 'The teachers frequently remind the girls of the importance of finding time for rest and relaxation in their busy schedule to safeguard their well-being in what will be a very challenging world.' The head, too, is keen to help ensure girls develop healthy mental habits.

The head girl team takes the pressure off one individual and shares around the privilege. They clearly feel listened to and that this is their school. They've initiated eating with the lower school girls once a week, like kindly big sisters.

Good links with the local community including an outreach programme. Pupils from a local primary recently visited for a Shakespeare workshop, where year 10 girls entertained with Horrible Histories style dramas. The transition to year 7 is thoughtfully handled – new girls take part in a summer school, more for fun than anything else, with cake-making and a picnic in Greenwich park, making sure no-one gets lost on day one.

Pupils and parents: Pupils come from a diverse range of backgrounds. Nearly one third are bilingual.

Who is this school for? Parents say: 'For children who are keen to try new things and get involved – the more you put in, the more you get out' or 'girls who do not fit into a stereotype but have their own thoughts and opinions'. The sixth formers we met seemed confident, sincere, happy and very mature: a delight. Without boys to impress, there were none of the false eyelashes or make-up we've seen at co-eds recently. Girls between lessons were exuberant, loud, even.

A mother with two daughters at the school enthused: 'My children are ready for anything; they have been prepared step by step from juniors onwards to become increasingly independent. They are totally trustworthy and sensible. They can cope with minor emergencies and they look after one another. They support one another emotionally and practically.'

One parent without a typical home situation told us how supportive pupils had been of her daughters and others told us delightedly of making new friends themselves. The PTA is active and seem a relatively down to earth lot, organising car boot sales with bacon butties.

Parents feel in touch with the school. They receive grade cards or full reports twice a term with detailed information about a girl's progress, as well as strategies and suggestions for improvement. School days are long, cue a sigh of relief from

working parents: pupils can arrive at 7.30am and stay until 6pm. There are also minibus routes ferrying girls from all across Greenwich, Rotherhithe and Lewisham.

Entrance: There are 60 places at the 11+ stage and most recently there were around 190 applications. No guaranteed place for junior school pupils, but all year 6 girls take the entrance exam in maths, English and non-verbal reasoning. Senior staff interviews all candidates. Best performing girls attend an academic scholarship interview with the head. For casual places beyond year 7 applicants sit papers in English and maths. Given the proximity to Canary Wharf, families do move about. Will need a good reference from current school and finally, if all goes well, an interview for both pupil and parents with the head. Any SEN students with an ed psych report are granted extra time.

Girls come from a variety of primary schools, most commonly Blackheath Nursery and Prep, The Gatehouse, The Pointer, Halstow, All Saints C of E, John Ball and Brooklands. Pupils generally come from Blackheath, Greenwich, Charlton, Lee, Lewisham, Brockley, Eltham, Canary Wharf, Hackney and Rotherhithe. A few from as far away as Dartford and Chislehurst in Kent and Leyton, East London.

Into the sixth form, there are 60 places available, currently undersubscribed. The girls we met described lots of their peers being attracted elsewhere simply to try something new – and by 'boys'.

The school's redevelopment and new sixth form building is adding 100 new places. You'll need a good range of GCSE results with A*/As in the subjects that you wish to study, plus an excellent school reference.

Exit: Between a third and a half leave post-GCSE. Around half of sixth formers to Russell Group destinations eg Warwick. Three to Oxbridge in 2015. Few linguists. It's a very arty list of leavers, heading off for art foundations, even a famous shoe design course, but balanced with plenty of scientists, medics, a medical geneticist and dentist. These girls have found their passions and are not afraid to specialise.

Money matters: Scholarships and bursaries for girls entering years 7 and year 12 only. Scholarships based on entrance test results to a maximum value of 50 per cent of fees. In addition, scholarships are awarded for art, music and sport at 11+. A bursary takes into account means, plus academic merit. The maximum value of the bursary can be the full fees. There are a variety of sixth form scholarships including four provided by HSBC.

Remarks: The girls may not be super sporty, but they certainly seem super happy, comfortable in their own skin and a great recommendation for the school. One to watch under the dynamic new head with academic ambition and transformative building works soon to be unveiled.

BRIT School for Performing Arts and Technology

60 The Crescent, Croydon, Surrey CR0 2HN

State · Pupils: 1,190 · Ages: 14–19 · Sixth form pupils: 800

Tel: 020 8665 5242

Email: admin@brit.croydon.sch.uk
Website: www.brit.croydon.sch.uk

9

Principal: Since June 2012, Mr Stuart Worden BA MA GTP (40s). Previously school's director of theatre, though involvement stretches back, one way or another, almost to its foundation in 1991. Before that, was all over the place (literally, not metaphorically – he's highly organised) as, like so many of school's staff, has combined education, education, education with production, production, production. Though past isn't yet mythologised, may yet happen, given that when whistles through key moments of his career, 'the years change each time,' says affable minder.

First act of our (possibly world exclusive) version opens in Chichester, where the 'first and only' theatrical type in his family (brother, also in education, got there by more conventional means), he was taken on regular trips to the theatre – 'virtually at the end of my road' by 'lovely' mother. Was hooked, particularly by the language, leading to writing/producer roles with everyone from the National Theatre to the Royal Exchange Manchester, Playwrights' Co-operative and Working Title Films.

Teaching cropped up early on, too, with FE/HE posts on the film writing MA course at Sheffield

University in 1990 as well as a spell as drama teacher at Lansdowne College in Kensington, reprised during two years at the Chichester College of Technology in 1991-1993.

May not look like conventional head (he's creative industries smart, down to intelligent glasses) but is meticulous when it comes to rock solid efficiency of school administration. His ethos is creativity within a framework, from the details (photographic ID for visitors, lessons that run to time or he'll want to know why) to the big things – buildings, new and refurbished, that are no architectural folly but really work.

Wants students to leave not just with creative potential on the way to being realised but equipped with hard-headed entrepreneurial nous to back it up (there's praise in literature for a student's massive on-line following).

His long term involvement in community arts – helped create Steam Industry, a theatre for all initiative – has also led to blossoming of school's outreach programme which is increasingly varied and demanding, though also, he stresses, 'purposeful and long term.' Virtuous circle, too, as those seeking to make career in the area can opt for community arts practice BTec qualification – developed by school and so far unique in the UK.

Pupils work with hospice patients, asylum seekers and rape victims and also act as talented big brothers and sisters to pupils in new, much-needed primary that Mr Worden helped get off the ground – projects naturally including a home-grown musical. BRIT Kids, for local 8-15 year olds, includes community classes and free performances at local Ashcroft Theatre, themed day for tinies, too.

He attracts huge praise from staff. 'He's professional, a good leader, very polite, expects high standards and is very positive,' thought one, speaking for everyone else.

Pupils, too, like his friendly, hands-on approach. 'When I needed help with recording for radio, he was like, "give me a minute and I'll do it",' said one. As a result, takes a while for everyone to work out who he is, particularly those whose previous experiences with authority figures were of a bruising nature. 'He doesn't give out a principal vibe,' says year 11 pupil who had only recently clocked who he was.

An educational showstopper you definitely won't want to walk out of, which tempers sprinklings of stardust with nuts and bolts reality checks

Older pupils, though, had no problems with identification. 'Love the way he comes round, sits with us and chats,' said sixth former. 'Not like any principal I've met,' reckoned another. 'He makes an effort to talk.'

Perk of job is 'daily' feedback about pupil success (during GSG visit, it was smash hit involvement in London Fashion Week). As to qualities required by prospective students, he's 'not sure' where talent features in the equation or passion, either, come to that. Instead, stresses importance of being 'nice and kind. Creativity and the arts need you to be open and then you should be willing to share your skill with others. I think that's a special quality.'

Is regularly asked whether school might extend to cover wider age range or sprout satellite versions in the regions. Likely to remain a one-off, he thinks, an 'extraordinary' place that does far more than equip pupils for careers. 'Parallel with that is the sense that the school goes to so many people and uses the arts to enrich their lives.'

Academic matters: Wouldn't be hard to see school as a giant performing arts centre with added class-rooms. Not that 'straight' academic teachers would thank you for the description, or principal, come to that. ('Not a Fame Academy' a recurring leitmo-tif in literature).

Staff are either traditional types who 'come here because they think it's the right school to teach at and want to be part of what we're doing here' or creative industry professionals who want to teach 'in a place that specialises in what I'm skilled at,' thought principal. No passengers: cho-reographers, film makers, playwrights, composers all welcomed but need to commit to training: on the job GTP programme is particularly popular.

Academic staples are bunched together, with sociology, humanities, science and musical thea-tre in East Wing (actually the main building of Old Grammar school – pay attention at the back). While inevitable focus on performance can make it seem as if you're never more than two minutes from a rehearsal, rooms are well-soundproofed to avoid stardust leakage into classes.

Staff work hard to harness pupils' energy, GCSE groups enjoying animated discussions on causes of youth crime in lively sociology lessons, maths teacher moving us along from fidgety class, dis-tracted by visitor. 'This is a creative enterprise,' says young, happy-looking teacher.

Driving everything is all-round enthusiasm, fuelled by wide range of specialisms and staff contacts – brilliant, of course

Once here, it's a hard place to leave. Teachers, like pupils, praised 'inspirational' atmosphere – latest arrivals include new head of costumes, fresh from Eastenders – and warmth that 'sucks you in'. Though no coloured hair (something of a pupil spe-ciality, though 'they get over it after the first year'), they span the gamut from blouse and skirt to finest beard, bomber jacket 'n' red trainers combo.

Star quality tends to reside in BTec results. Full-on approach makes results extra impressive.

In years 10 and 11, pupils take BTec level 2 diplomas (counting as four GCSEs) as well as following well-equipped and solidly taught GCSE classes in core subjects – some streamed, if ability range demands it, subjects broadly EBacc-themed.

Staff work hard to harness pupils' energy, GCSE groups enjoying animated discussions on causes of youth crime

Given intake at year 10 – nerve-wracking stand-ing start for any teacher – results are spectacularly good when it comes to performance-related topics such as dance and drama, and pretty respectable in the must-do areas, too. In 2015 at GCSE or equiva-lent, 68 per cent gained five A*- C grades including English and maths (31 per cent A*/A).

Inevitably, still greater pressure for sixth form, with BTec diploma (choice of broadcast and digital communication, community arts practice, dance, interactive media, music, musical theatre, techni-cal theatre, theatre and visual arts and design) the starting point with rich rewards.

Everyone also takes additional AS or A level(s) (15 subject choices) or additional BTec qualifica-tion. Results largely respectable – 51 per cent A*/B (19 per cent A*/A) in 2015.

Welcome flexibility allows teachers to devote whole days to some post-16 BTec modules. 'Means you really get to learn,' thought one, approvingly. Course options can lead to slight difficulties: not everyone, for example, is drawn to the sewing that's currently a must-do part of the visual arts and design and technical theatre arts courses – though discussions are currently under way on possibility of evolving a stitching-light option.

For those needing extra help – there's screening for all during May induction day – terrific SEN is a huge strength, generously accommodated, includ-ing cosy, cushioned area and Smartboard-equipped classroom – 'keeps sense of routine' – where strug-gling pupils (SpLD biggest need, also some ASD and ADHD) get parallel lessons at slower speed, mul-tisensory approaches added 'until it works'. Most staff 'very supportive and recognise that approach builds self-esteem'. Doubters (and there are a small number) are won over by success stories, including pupil who went from U to A* in English GCSE.

Whatever the choice, it's a full-on commit-ment, eminently do-able for the already organised, efficiency step-change required for those who aren't, and a tough old regime for all which can come as shock to anyone expecting straight drudge for drama swap.

'Same as any old school but one where there's less time for academic subjects,' thought slightly jaded year 11 boy. Even with sensible timetable structuring separating academic and performing arts days, extra workload means 'you need to push yourself and get ready to learn.'

Games, options, the arts: Stuffed with opportunities for performance and just about everything that goes with it, arts naturally the main drain on space, from eight music rooms, all sound-proofed (plus innumerable additional rooms for individual lessons – drums, vocal, keyboard, bass all popular) to two theatres – one, Obi (as in benefactor Sir Maurice Oberstein rather than Kenobi) complete with two storey barn doors to make scenery shifts from adjoining scenic workshop easy peasy.

Textiles/costume design space in main building a pleasure to experience, too, recently remade with retractable door splitting teaching space, allowing GCSE students to spark off older pupils.

Hands-on stuff rules, however. Literally so in case of portable appliance test, pupils shinning impressively up ladders to check the lights. 'Need to understand what's dangerous,' said teacher (and a useful all-purpose teenage rule, too).

With students billed by specialism, (dancer x and musician y) in school literature and so much going on, can sometimes be hard to know where lessons end and the extracurricular begins. Even college awards nights become performances, most recent complete with Great Gatsby staging and X Factor style audience votes (which would brighten up more conventional speech days elsewhere no end).

Driving everything is all-round enthusiasm, fuelled by wide range of sixth form specialisms and staff contacts – brilliant, of course – with some interactive media students, for example, getting chance to work with Aardman studios.

Sixth former taking BTec in technical theatre had had a ball working on Tim Burton-inspired costumes for Hamlyn, put on in local theatre and one of 40 productions through the year ranging from Artaud and Brook to Brecht, Caryl Churchill and much in the way of full-blown Shakespeare, many others with words and scores written by the staff and/or pupils.

Traditional educational add ons far from absent, however. Duke of Edinburgh runs conventional course (though Jack Petchey awards – imaginatively awarded for academic rather than community service excellence in years 10 and 11 – do not). Sport isn't neglected either. School has own Olympian to its name, and while council has hung on to school's (small) sports field, necessitating relocation of sports day (and other fixtures) to nearby Norwood Lakes, the keen have school gym – somewhat battered but serviceable – for basketball (popular girls' team, which meets on Mondays, 'vicious', thought year 13 boys, admiringly).

Background and atmosphere: Patriotic acronym is down to British Record Industry Trust – great and good still feature on governors' list – whose funding and influence led to school's foundation in 1991 (after Mrs Thatcher, fearing creation of home for resting thesps, had been won round – or so the legend goes).

They're hugely proud of what they've created, says principal, and with good reason. Despite growth of vocational training colleges covering the 14-19 age range, school remains a one-off, the only free (prospectus uses capitals to emphasis) performing arts and technology school in the country, state funded but outside LA control.

Set within easy walk from Selhurst Station – not likely to become new Hoxton any time soon – school, though not an obvious looker from the outside, is full of thought, care and taste when it comes to the interiors. Inevitable tired corners mainly in vintage old school building (site originally housed Selhurst Grammar), one of three of varying styles and vintage. Newest, light and bright, is very plush indeed though smart rooms and corridors largely rule throughout the site, with plenty of tarting up (paint 'n' porthole doors even in otherwise non-refurbished areas, for example).

Feel is urban grit, rather than Surrey Downs (even feels like a long way to leafy South Croydon) with undeniable pressure on space. No pupil common rooms, for example (one year 11 girl had asked teacher to keep an eye on possessions during the day – gladly done, too) – immaculate carpeting in many corridors provides comfortable sitting space for the needy (speckly stone finish remains in original school building) with one student sitting by banked lockers busily sorting out vast pile of music.

Little in the way of school jargon, bar slightly confusing names. (Blue Block, though lovely, isn't blue). Main (and alias-free) building, built new for school's opening, has been substantially refreshed. Features include internal windows opening out on to corridors (principal's office too, at his request, providing a window on to the world), walls liberally decorated with high quality art (everything from Aboriginal-motifs to Banksy lookalike and delicate Japanese figures disporting themselves against parchment backdrop).

Academic year, too, is unusual with five eight-week terms, interspersed with fortnight breaks. Officially 'best supports delivery of the curriculum and ensures students return refreshed', though according to one teacher, production demands mean 'you'll often find students coming in over the holidays'.

With the exception of occasional overt whackiness – bins spray painted in wild array of colours following theatre teacher's guerrilla decoration initiative over the summer holidays – what dominates is sense of all-through professionalism.

Walls liberally decorated with high quality art (everything from Aboriginal-motifs to Banksy lookalike and delicate Japanese figures on parchment)

And while absence of uniform, bells (and whistles, at least off stage) may not tend towards the norm, expectations certainly do, with teachers unlikely to indulge in too much time-drift as 'students will tell you when break is,' reckoned one.

Pastoral care and discipline: It's a busy old day; lights up 7am, not dimmed until 12 hours later. Though 'no-one will be here all that time,' says principal, some will operate in unconventional hours – drama and dance students, for example, warming up in the early hours before auditions or classes, studios booked up way in advance so pupils can edit their films.

Outstanding attendance, particularly at sixth form level, testament to commitment but also in stark contrast, in some cases, to pupils' unhappy educational experiences elsewhere. Several talked about feeling 'like outsiders' in other schools. Here, blend of rigour and tolerance seems to suit everyone. 'I felt I'd found people like me,' reckoned one sixth former.

'We think it's a good place to be looked after,' says principal, who is particularly proud of large scale speed meet and greet induction where grizzled year 11 veterans help newly arrived year 10s to settle in.

Body image can (predictably) be an issue, countered by strong message highlighting the glory of the individual, school stressing its more unconventional successes such as Adele to ensure that identikit size nothings aren't touted as the only aspiration worth pursuing.

On-site counsellors, presence discreetly advertised to students via form tutors, provide additional back up, while healthy eating (just about the only niggle otherwise superlative inspection report could find) is now a major school focus, with year 10 science pupils reporting on savoury snack fat content to year 13 dancers, canteen staff challenging pupils 'in a friendly way' if appear to be opting for unhealthy/minimalistic lunch (those on free school meals compelled to have healthy meal, though 'it's not about being a dictator but guiding and supporting,' thought staff member).

Staff enforce gentle discipline – students in library, verging on slight chattiness in quiet zone, were instantly quelled by (silent) entrance of smiley but no-nonsense librarians. Creativity within a framework something of a necessity, especially with school jam-packed, recent BTec additions adding another 200 to sixth form so 'as much as can take without bursting,' says school.

May be a timetable but there's 'no "you will do this number of hours" – it's their school,' says principal. Adds up to atmosphere that engenders sense of independence combined with professionalism – a lesson for the future, as with sixth form pupils given permission to leave lesson to conduct library research, but with return time and teacher expectations clearly outlined.

Pupil voice is heard loud and clear, too, in everything from 'almost daily' cake sales to fundraising for forthcoming productions to active student council which recently voted to ban environment-unfriendly disposable cups at lunchtime, 'commit to bringing in refillable bottles'. No wonder giant painted portrait of the blessed Jamie on wall of bigger canteen dispenses saint-like smile like a South American folk hero by way of inspiration.

Pupils and parents: Education should be accomplished without removing innocence along the way, thinks the principal. 'Friends assume it's going to be like Fame, but it's really down to earth,' felt sixth former, though performers in particular exhibit healthy dose of chutzpah and aren't backwards in coming forwards, adding in a couple of pirouettes and a solo on the way in. We enjoyed early morning dancing huddles outside (professional-looking gurning, too, in one case) – and tales of close harmony rivalry in the canteen.

Though unified by drive – 'at an ordinary school she'd be the leader of the pack, here, she's in a class with 30 of them,' reckoned mother of aspiring dancer – school community otherwise diverse. Families range from chimney sweeps to the loaded, many drawn from immediate area, which is 'socially complicated,' says principal, characterised by side-by-side pockets of affluence and deprivation – eligibility for free school meals is above the national average, and school also runs 'BRIT loves Selhurst' campaign, offering free tickets to locals.

Entrance: Not for everyone. One talented singer-songwriter had opted instead for Guildford ACM. 'They advertise it as once you go there, 75 per cent of your future career is done, but I know it's hard work.' Some find the place for themselves – press coverage is pretty much non-stop. One girl, now in sixth form, paid first visit to keep friend company and ended up the one with the place.

A minority very local (15 per cent from Croydon), though vast majority (75 per cent) from South London, remaining 10 per cent, selected on raw talent, not postcode, can come from anywhere in UK. (School stresses desire to avoid impossibly long journeys, somewhat spoiling effect with X-Factor winner Leona Lewis, quoted as describing two-hour round trip as 'so worth it'.)

Oversubscribed all the way through, less so for those entering in year 10, massively for sixth form. For 14 year olds seeking place in year 10, process less daunting, though useful to muster clear ideas on what pupils would gain from coming here.

Technical courses based on portfolios followed by workshops the norm. Inevitably stressful for would-be performers. 'She got recalled, she cried, she stuffed up in her first audition and thought "that's it" – but got in,' said parent who felt school wasn't looking for fully formed talent (there are rumours of already successful child stars being turned away) but 'something in kids that they can bring out – they don't necessarily want someone who's completely polished and finished and looking for it as a way into the next big thing'. A fair comment, thought school. 'It's about unlocking potential rather than a finished product.'

Exit: In a handful of cases, some year 11 pupils may not make the sixth form, most after discovering that love for performing arts has worn off. 'Might get to age 16 and think, I don't want to be a dancer – I want to do something else with my life,' says principal. 'They might just change and that's a good thing.'

There's 'no "you will do this number of hours" – it's their school,' says principal. Adds up to atmosphere that engenders sense of independence combined with professionalism

At least 90 per cent, sometimes more, do carry on into sixth form, and almost everyone, even those who leave post-16, go on to further and higher education elsewhere – most recent extreme example swapping bright lights for animal husbandry.

Principal stresses proof that employability issues amongst the young can be triumphantly overcome. According to school survey, 70 per cent of past pupils end up working in creative industries. A few are household names but this is definitely not yardstick of measurement. All, says principal firmly, are superstars even if not household names because 'are the best box office manager or record label executive.'

School's well-designed vocational courses, with an eye and a half on the future, help speed the process along. Community-related courses, for example, lead to a virtuous circle, helping local bodies and in the process raising future trained community facilitators – a growing area for well-regarded HE courses such as Royal Central School's applied theatre and education BA degree. Others end up at RADA, Rose Bruford, Drama Centre, East 15, Bristol Old Vic and LAMDA, or head off to university – Leeds, York, Sheffield and Birmingham amongst them.

Once through, you'll find their words, music, performance, directorial and backstage talents just about everywhere you look, from fashion shows to musicals, national theatre to community arts, in the UK and internationally.

Remarks: Vocational dazzler with some academic bright lights as well. An educational showstopper, and one you definitely won't want to walk out of half way through, which tempers sprinklings of stardust with lashings of nuts and bolts reality checks. That's what they say. We secretly think it's like collecting every school's coolest kids and putting them in one place. If we could set this review to music, we probably would.

Bromley High School (GDST) Junior Department

Linked school: Bromley High School (GDST), 315

Blackbrook Lane, Bickley, Bromley, Kent BR1 2TW

Tel: 020 8781 7001

Independent • Pupils: 310 • Ages: 4–11 • Fees: £12,423 pa

Email: admissions@bro.gdst.net
Website: www.bromleyhigh.gdst.net

Head of Junior School: Since 2012, Ms Claire Dickerson BA. Has been at Bromley High for 12 years, starting in year 4 and then moving to become a reception teacher. Promoted to head of prep in 2008. Outside interests are skiing, swimming and theatre.

Entrance: At 4+ and 7+ competitive entry assessment, always oversubscribed, thereafter waiting list for occasional vacancies.

Exit: Around two-thirds to senior school.

Remarks: Strong academics, arts and sport; the junior school benefits from being able to share a fantastic range of sporting and musical facilities at the senior school, as well as own music wing. Year 5 and 6 pupils are able to link with subject specialist teachers in the senior school. Tuition is available on any instrument. Wind and string ensembles and training orchestra prepare pupils for the variety of orchestras that the music department run. Drama and dance also play an important role in the curriculum. New outside areas including learning area

with mini stage; there is also an outside stage and work table so lessons and performances can take place al fresco. Purpose-built site is rather utilitarian, softened by numerous imaginative art and project displays which offer an insight into the broad curriculum.

Dedicated, mostly long serving class teachers run a full range of extracurricular clubs and activities. Latest initiative is Forest School – offers lots of opportunities for outdoor learning. Lots of hard work going on, crisp orderly little girls present as purposeful and happily engaged.

Bromley High School (GDST)

Linked school: Bromley High School (GDST) Junior Department, 314

Blackbrook Lane, Bickley, Bromley, Kent BR1 2TW

Independent • Pupils: 580 • Ages: 11–18 • Sixth form pupils: 125 • Fees: £15, 405 pa

Tel: 020 8781 7000

Email: admissions@bro.gdst.net
Website: www.bromleyhigh.gdst.net

Headmistress: Since September 2014, Angela Drew BA PGCE MBA (50s). Read English at Durham and spent a year post university working for L'Arche, a community for mentally disabled adults. Previously deputy head (academic) at Epsom College and has also taught at Whitgift School, Prior Park College, The Mary Erskine School and George Watson's College. Has a passion for theatre, debating, public speaking, books and France. Genuine interest in education – including previously shadowing headteachers in Swedish and Finnish schools. Married with two children.

Academic matters: Academic results consistently high – 73 per cent A*/A at GCSE 2015 and 54 per cent at A level. Science and modern foreign languages remain particularly strong and a number of girls go on to study these at top universities. Modern foreign languages department has links with France, Germany and Spain and arranges much better than average exchanges, visits and work experience placements. Recently awarded the British Council's full International School Award. All subject areas have dedicated heads of department who ensure high standards and excellent results. Parents say the teaching is solid and fairly traditional, maths teaching is especially impressive and a top subject choice in the sixth form; school adds that staff changes have led to more diverse teaching styles.

The head and her senior management team work extremely hard to make sure that the curriculum is really flexible, so girls can have as much choice as possible in all the age groups and fit in extra GCSE subjects if they want. Smart modern classrooms and sparkling labs inspire the girls to work hard and care for their environment. All pupils have a personal tutor who tracks their progress and sets targets with them for their academic and personal development on a regular basis. Well-stocked library looking out onto woodland provides an inspiring place to work before and after school.

Cool, calm atmosphere pervades the corridors, which are lined with notice boards announcing forthcoming events and successes

Two part-time SENCos provide additional support on a one-to-one basis for pupils with specific learning differences and run study skills programmes for all pupils. EAL is available as required.

Games, options, the arts: Great opportunities for the sportswoman here – acres of space, indoor swimming pool and gym, athletics track, three hockey pitches, including an Astroturf which can be hired by local clubs. Pupils frequently win awards at national, county and borough level across athletics, gymnastics, hockey and netball, tennis and swimming; cricket enjoying great success. A number of specialist coaches are employed to enhance sporting opportunities via school clubs. Duke of Edinburgh scheme rapidly expanding (more than 150 pupils involved), annual World Challenge expeditions, and international cultural exchanges to Asia and China for sixth formers.

Performing arts and dance studios recently updated to create an incredibly clever and versatile performance space. Dance is a full academic subject (school offers dance GCSE). Regular in-house drama and music festivals and pupils achieve distinctions in LAMDA and ABRSM exams, including musical theatre. Music department to be enjoyed, producing a lovely range of concerts; everyone is encouraged to learn an instrument or join a choir. International tours for the various choirs and orchestras and a yearly middle school music tour to Paris. Artwork is of a very high standard, some talented GCSE students do really well, textiles and photography recently introduced as A level choices for budding artists.

Background and atmosphere: Originally founded in 1883. In 1982 moved to its present 25-acre site, complete with woodland and a lake. Cool, calm atmosphere pervades the corridors, which are lined with noticeboards announcing forthcoming events and successes. One area is dedicated to the school's

Well-stocked library looking out onto woodland provides an inspiring place to work before and after school

history and a gallery of portraits.

General impression is of a busy and active school. School tells us the uniform is 'not dreary and maroon any more – we have a smart new grey blazer and maroon/grey check pleated skirt for the seniors and a pretty maroon/grey check tunic for the juniors – the girls and parents love this new uniform'.

Recent £1m refurbishments include sixth form common room, dining room and two Apple Mac music technology suites.

Pastoral care and discipline: All pupils have a personal tutor whom parents can contact at any time to discuss pastoral or academic matters. Democratic elections run for the selection of a head girl, two deputies and senior prefects. Sixth form girls can train as peer counsellors and access to a professional counsellor on a drop in basis or by appointment. Older girls are encouraged to mentor younger pupils and gain work and life experience by helping in the junior school. Paperless home-school communications – a boon for busy parents.

Pupils and parents: Predominantly local families, however some travel from all over Kent and south London. Parents mainly hard-working types from the professional classes, small social and ethnic mix. Dedicated parents organise the active PTA, running fundraising events and the school book-shop. Parents' forum discusses school issues and aims foster good working relationship between staff and parents.

Old girls include Margaret Hodge, Prof Joan Walsh; Richmal Compton was once a member of the teaching staff.

Entrance: At 11+ competitive entrance exams involving creative writing, non-verbal and verbal reasoning, an interview and reference from junior school. Sixth form entrance requirement is a minimum of six GCSEs A*-B grade. Scholarships and bursaries available in the senior school

Exit: Some 30 per cent leave at 16+ to attend co-ed sixth forms or local grammars. Most sixth formers

go on to higher education, mainly good universities; five Oxbridge offers in 2015, and one to Princeton; others to a range to study eg medicine, maths, music, art, ancient history and architecture.

Money matters: Everyone sitting the 11+ entrance exam is automatically entered for academic scholarships – music and sports scholarships also available in year 7 and year 12. Sixth form scholarships for art, music, sport and academics. Means-tested bursaries, Founders awards, are available up to 100 per cent of fees in the senior school.

Remarks: A selective school, offering a wonderful range of opportunities to widen horizons and develop new interests. Suits academically able girls with lots of drive.

Colfe's Preparatory School + Pre-prep and Nursery

Linked school: Colfe's School, 318

Horn Park Lane, London SE12 8AW

Independent · Pupils: 417 · Ages: 3–11 · C of E · Fees: up to £12,555 pa

Tel: 020 8463 8240

Email: prep@colfes.com
Website: www.colfes.com

22

Head: Since April 2013, Mrs Sarah Marsh (40s) BEd, previously deputy head of St Andrew's prep school in Woking. She started her teaching career

as a PE specialist, followed by director of studies at Guildford High School. Currently she is completing a masters in education leadership. She is very enthusiastic about the expansion of the junior school and is looking forward to building on all the good practices she has inherited. She enjoys going to the gym, jazz dance and skiing holidays.

Head of pre-prep since January 2013 is Sarah Redman (50s) BEd. Mrs Redman was deputy head of the nursery and pre-prep school for some years before becoming head teacher. Parents comment on her warmth and friendliness, 'exactly the sort of person you can entrust your small child to'. Married to a fellow teacher, who is head of a local state primary, with three grown-up children, one of whom is an actress. She enjoys gardening, theatre, arts and crafts, the influence of which can be spotted around the pre-prep.

Specialist art teacher organises end of year exhibition. Six-year-olds upwards learn French and Spanish. Musical education starts early with recorder

Entrance: Most join at 3+ into the nursery or 4+ into the pre-prep via information observation morning. Year 3 no longer a main point of entry; assessment for occasional places further up the school.

Exit: At 11+ about 80 per cent move into the senior school; a few opt for local state grammars.

Remarks: Green and tranquil setting on the edge of the main school; new buildings are shooting up so the school can now accommodate three classes across the age groups. Well-planned academic curriculum runs alongside inspirational sport and arts

options. Mixed ability classes of around 18; each child is monitored regularly to check progress. Lively pupils perform well in both national and house competitions; particularly successful teams for maths and chess. 'A very caring school, where the teachers recognise every child as an individual.'

Art is incorporated into much of the curriculum and classrooms are bursting with interesting displays, models and sculptures. Specialist art teacher organises a big end of year exhibition. Six-year-olds upwards learn French and Spanish in alternating years. Musical education starts early with recorder in year 1 and ukulele in year 2. With around 80 per cent taking instrumental lessons, the school boasts choirs, orchestras, chamber groups, rock band and specialist brass programme. Creative drama, regular plays and lots of opportunities for performers in musical and dramatic assemblies. Dance workshops are popular and include everything and anything from flamenco to African dancing. Annual Ugly Bug Ball celebrates pre-prep children moving to the junior school, and into school houses.

On-site sports facilities are shared with the seniors, including a swimming pool for weekly lessons. More or less everything on offer on the sporting front, with lots of house competitions. Junior girls' netball team are national prep school champions. Help is on hand via learning support teachers for pupils with mild difficulties, dyslexia, dyspraxia and dyscalculia. Active PTA, parent volunteers assist with all sorts of activities including fundraising, costume making and art and design. Fantastic choice of lunchtime and after-school clubs; also a breakfast club from 7:30am and after school care until 6pm.

Sound all-round education, well tried and tested teaching methods mixed with a great range of arts and sports, produces happy pupils and contented parents.

Colfe's School

Linked school: Colfe's Preparatory School + Pre prep and Nursery, 317

Horn Park Lane, London SE12 8AW

Tel: 020 8852 2283

23

Independent • Pupils: 645 • Ages: 11–18 • Sixth form pupils: 200 • C of E • Fees: £15,489 pa

Email: admissions@colfes.com
Website: www.colfes.com

Headmaster: Since 2005, Richard Russell (50s), previously deputy warden of Forest School. Educated in Ireland and went on to read classics at Cambridge. He started his career as a Latin teacher; teaching initially attracted him as it would allow him to

pursue his interest in archaeology and attend digs during the long summer holidays. Knows everybody and what they're up to, teaches Latin to year 7. He spent 15 years at Sevenoaks coordinating the IB programme; however, he has never thought it

particularly suitable for Colfe's and is a great fan of A levels. A professional and pleasant person, say parents, easy to get on with and ambitious for his pupils. He lives in Blackheath with his wife, who works in the City. Nowadays holiday times see them heading for their house in Sicily, where they make their own olive oil.

Academic matters: Exam results heading upwards every year – 51 per cent A*/A at GCSE in 2015, with particularly strong showing in maths and science and 48 per cent A*/A, 84 per cent A*-B at A level. Maths, English and the sciences are popular closely followed by economics and history. Most take nine or 10 GCSEs including a language, choice of German, French, Spanish or Latin. Whole school aim is to make classes active and stimulating; everything is in place for high flyers who might be heading for Oxbridge but also for those who might need to go more gently. Setting for maths, sciences and languages. History and maths departments are particularly strong performers; provision for accelerated learning groups for additional maths qualifications. Sixth formers can take Extended Project Qualification. Students with mild specific learning difficulties are supported by specialist staff. The library is a well-used resource, full-time librarian who also doubles up as head of careers, open until 6pm, during Easter holidays and to students on study leave. Outstanding advice and guidance on selecting courses and universities. The school recently ran a conference to introduce the option of going to university in the Netherlands.

Games, options, the arts: Arts and sports are strong all round, structured to suit all tastes and talents. 'Sport for all' policy means there is something for everyone, be it dance or being a member of one of the successful rugby teams. On-site facilities including a gym and 25m swimming pool, which hosts swimming galas, kayaking, water polo and lifesaving courses for year 10s. Additional large playing fields at Leathersellers' sports grounds a few minutes away by minibus on the Sidcup Road. Former Surrey and Kent opening batsman coaches cricket, and athletes often selected to represent Greenwich in the London School Championships. CCF with its unique Army Air Corps unit popular, as is D of E, with many progressing to gold award.

Aim is to make classes active and stimulating; everything is in place for high flyers who might be heading for Oxbridge but also for those who might need to go more gently

Large art department includes printmaking equipment, a kiln for ceramics and a dark room. Parents comment on the energetic drama department; pupils encouraged to write and produce their own plays. LAMDA classes, stage management and technical theatre skills all on offer; impressive variety and number of productions. Up-to-date music rooms and individual soundproof practice studios; swing bands, orchestras, and choirs galore. Huge range of clubs and societies to join: particularly popular are maths, chess and debating along with many inter-house competitions, quizzes, drama, sports and concerts. Regular outings, theatre visits and trips abroad; sixth formers visit the Gambia annually to help build and maintain a school. Good participation in the arts, but relatively small numbers go on to take these subjects at A level, drama and media studies taking the lead over art, design and music.

Background and atmosphere: Founded in 1652, to educate 'the poor boys of Blackheath' by the Rev Abraham Colfe of Lewisham. Later the school was left in the trust of the Leathersellers' Company, whose livery members make up a majority of today's governing body. Leathersellers have recently pledged an additional £1 million in bursaries. Was a state boys' grammar school for some years before opting to go independent in the 1970s rather than become a comprehensive school. Went fully co-ed in 1999. Strong links with six state schools, five local, one in the Gambia.

Corridors adorned with pupils' work and achievements; atmosphere is positive and busy with smartly dressed, friendly pupils and helpful staff. Bleak, utilitarian brick buildings softened by shrubs and trees. Large building programme providing pre-prep extension and sixth form centre now completed.

Pastoral care and discipline: Pastoral care continues to be excellent and very much part of the school's ethos. Well-established house system; everyone attends regular house tutor meetings; years 8-11 are in vertical age groups, sixth formers and year 7s in separate groups. There are lots of opportunities for leadership and mentoring within the house system to help pupils develop maturity, gain

confidence and a range of life skills. Frequent house activities and competitions ensure everybody is involved in the school community. School nurse and independent counsellor. Parents say home-school links are encouraged and the head of pastoral care is always available to speak with them. One commented that pastoral staff have done well in creating a supportive and caring atmosphere. Pupils seem thoughtful and considerate to others, older pupils particularly good at mentoring younger ones.

Regular outings, theatre visits and trips abroad; sixth formers visit the Gambia annually to help build and maintain a school. Good participation in the arts

Pupils and parents: Mainly professional types from Blackheath, Lewisham, Lee and more recently other areas accessible via train links. Head is keen to recruit from as varied a pool as possible, so a lot of effort is made to encourage children from state primaries as well as independents to apply. Big old boys' and girls' society runs a number of activities and fundraising events. Everyone is invited to the annual service in memory of the founder Rev Colfe. A good all-rounder school producing an interesting range of pupils going into many different careers. Alumni list reflects the school's diverse range: Eric Ambler, author, Lord Vaizey, economist Kenneth Grayson, first professor of theology at Bristol University, to name but a few; also actors, musicians, politicians and sportspeople.

Entrance: At 11+ interview, reference from current school and exams in maths and English. Sixth formers are offered places on the basis of an interview, reference and predicted GCSE grades.

Exit: Around 20 per cent leaves at 16+ for sixth form colleges. At 18+ to huge a range of different universities (majority Russell Group), including four to Oxbridge in 2015.

Money matters: At 11+ and 16+ scholarships and means-tested bursaries are available for drama, art, sports, music and academics. Around 20 to 30 per cent of pupils receive some form of fee subsidy.

Remarks: Pleasant, relaxed atmosphere. Provides a high standard of education without being overly competitive. Its focus on individual successes and promoting a balanced approach to life and learning is not to be underestimated in today's hectic world.

Coloma Convent Girls' School

Upper Shirley Road, Croydon, Surrey CR9 5AS

Tel: 020 8654 6228

State • Pupils: 1,075 • Ages: 11–18 • Sixth form pupils: 340 • RC

Email: webadmin@coloma.croydon.sch.uk
Website: www.coloma.croydon.sch.uk

10

Headteacher: Since 1995, Maureen Martin (50s), BA economics and history, then additional RE and education management qualifications. Whilst on foreign postings with her family had a varied teaching career in international schools, including deputy headships at Alice Smith International School, Kuala Lumpur and El Collegio Britannico, Mexico. Grew up locally and attended Coloma as a child.

Bounding with energy and ideas, deeply committed to educating all young people to the highest possible level, equally committed to ensuring the staff access additional qualifications and attend continuous training programmes. Much-admired by the local and school community, she will make time for you, but she can be hard to catch as she is so very busy. Alongside all her sterling work at Coloma, she is executive principal at The Quest Academy – Coloma Trust, a non-denominational, co-ed secondary school in Croydon. She has also been involved in transforming the lives and education of primary school pupils by taking their school out of special measures.

Academic matters: In 2015, 90 per cent 5+ GCSEs at grades A*-C including English and maths. At A level, 62 per cent A*-B – consistently in the top 30 comprehensive schools; specialist status for music and science. Every pupil is tracked and monitored throughout their school career to ensure that they are taught and learn properly and achieve their potential. Subject teaching across the curriculum is considered to be very strong; where weaknesses are identified they are dealt with swiftly.

Years 7 to 9 are mixed ability, with setting from year 8 for maths and sciences. Staff continually research and develop ways to assist pupils' learning and much time is given to researching work-related courses and activities. Head of economics has recently introduced personal finance GCSE to ensure the girls understand how to manage money as well as the consequences of redundancy, unemployment and recessions. Language choices are French, German, Spanish, Latin club and Italian in sixth form; annual European trips and homestays are arranged. Further developments include establishing a modern foreign languages network so good practice can be shared. Dual award or three separate sciences as well as food and nutrition can be studied in well-resourced labs.

Full-time learning support coordinator oversees additional support in maths, English and study skills, including organisational and life skills. Specialist staff visit the school to provide one-to-one tuition as required. Reading ages of new entrants are assessed as part of tracking and monitoring scheme for each individual pupil. Those identified as struggling to make progress, regardless of ability, are offered support.

Inclusive sixth form centre aims to suit many, offering 28 A level choices; development plans include introducing some further BTec/diploma courses. Sixth formers gain experiences and skills from an extensive range of extracurricular and enrichment opportunities on-site and in partnership with other schools. Well-established tradition of public speaking, debating, musicianship and business enterprise; the girls scoop countless prizes at competitions and national events.

Whole school benefits from a managed learning environment – web tools are used to enrich learning, access homework and help home-school communications. Good mixture of male and female staff, a number of whom have dual roles; scholarly and generous types who are willing to share their skills and talents throughout the school.

Games, options, the arts: Exceptional and active music department: about 400 pupils learn an instrument; two orchestras, several choirs, including gospel choirs, and large instrumental ensembles. Regular winners of awards at the National Festival of Music; around half the pupils belong to one of the choirs, which tour and perform all over the world. As a specialist music college the school has developed additional recording, composing, and performance facilities and provides courses in music technology and performing arts. Over 40 musical and dramatic events are organised every year in-house, at the Fairfield Halls and beyond.

As a Roman Catholic foundation, has special ethos: 'Every member of the school community is motivated to see that they can make a positive difference through love, commitment and service'

Recent performing arts centre means whole school play reinstated, aiming to include all ages and talents, staff welcome too.

Range of sporting options; standards are high, netball, lacrosse and tennis admired and a number of girls go on to play for local and national teams. Indoor and outdoor facilities for all weathers, football and cricket clubs increasingly popular, 3G floodlit pitch. Dancers were recently invited to perform at Sadler's Wells. Duke of Edinburgh Award scheme runs and CCF is available as a joint venture with neighbouring Royal Russell School. Year 9s go on very popular annual trip to a trust house in Austria, where pupils can ski and spend time in an Austrian school.

Background and atmosphere: Founded in West Croydon in 1869 by a Belgian order, the Congregation of the Daughters of Mary and Joseph, led by Reverend Canon Van Crombrugghe. Opened with three nuns and one pupil; after a couple of years they moved to a larger house. 1965 saw the move to the present large, leafy site on the edge of Shirley Hills, and in 1978 the convent became an RC comprehensive. Ever developing and striving for excellence by keeping in step with modern educational demands, has high performing specialist status and science specialism. A bright, clean, hard-working environment, highly structured but also welcoming and inclusive.

Celebrated its 140th birthday with a huge party in the Royal Festival Hall, music specially composed by Howard Goodall. The celebrations were widely attended by members of the convent, school, friends and old girls, who are also active in helping to fundraise for school enterprises. As a Roman Catholic foundation, has special ethos: 'Every member of the school community is motivated to see that they can make a positive difference through love, commitment and service. Prayer, respect for one another, integrity, kindness and compassion are greatly valued'.

Pastoral care and discipline: Some girls feel the school rules are a bit strict, but most parents and pupils feel pastoral care is thoughtfully planned and helps to ensure everyone feels equally valued.

Home-school contact is thought to be very good, with most documentation provided in 'read friendly' format. Full-time pastoral manager supports staff, ensuring the daily well-being, behaviour and progress of each pupil. Hand-picked counsellors visit the school and referrals can be made to other agencies. The PSHE programme is boosted by outside organisations and special issue days. Girls learn to be considerate, reflect on others' feelings and the possible consequences of thoughtless actions. Staff and pupils join disabled children on the annual Easter pilgrimage to Lourdes.

Pupils and parents: No particular catchment area or feeder primary schools. Girls come from all over south London, Kent and Surrey. Hard-working, motivated and committed Catholic families who wish to support their daughter's education, along with all the charitable projects Coloma is involved in. Champions of fundraising, staff, pupils and parents organise a magnificent number of events for school buildings, equipment and numerous charitable projects. Events manager assists the charity committee coordinating events from concerts, fetes, readathons and quizzes to the annual rag week, which alone can raise as much as £28,000. Helps to fund a school in Uganda, in addition to supporting other charities at home and abroad. Pupils very proactive in creating new ideas and opportunities to fundraise – Christmas fête has included an ice rink. Unsurprisingly, many ex-pupils choose to work in education, social and caring professions.

Entrance: At 11+ non-selective; statemented and looked-after children and then a points system to assess practising Catholic credentials. Entry into the sixth form includes students of other denominations and faiths who are in sympathy with the ethos of school.

Exit: Around 35 per cent leave post-GCSE for local colleges or co-ed schools. About 85 per cent of sixth formers to university or art foundation courses: three to Oxbridge in 2015, others to eg Leeds, Sussex, Loughborough, King's College London and Bournemouth.

Money matters: Parents encouraged to donate monthly via school's Pass the Baton scheme, and most do.

Remarks: Truly remarkable school for its vision, academic achievements, charitable activities and contribution to society. Considering it operates on a budget less than 40 per cent of an independent school, must also be commended for economic genius. Produces well-rounded, articulate and innovative young women.

Croydon High School

Old Farleigh Road, South Croydon, Surrey CR2 8YB

Independent · Pupils: 400 · Ages: 11–18 · Sixth form pupils: 100 · Fees: up to £14,994 pa

Tel: 020 8260 7500

Email: admissions@cry.gdst.net
Website: www.croydonhigh.gdst.net

11

Head: Since May 2010, Mrs Deborah Leonard MEd BEd (40s). Deputy head of Nottingham GHS, arrived towards the end of the academic year as acting head for the following year after only brief tenure of predecessor. Previously deputy head of Thetford Grammar and head of PE and school development at King Edward's Birmingham. Her masters is in management and learning and she is passionate about girls' education. A very keen sportswoman, she has been a national league hockey coach and plays golf. She grew up in the Lake District and enjoys climbing and walking.

Academic matters: GCSE results excellent – 71 per cent A*/A grades in 2015. Good all-round education with a strong performance from the science, maths, English and modern foreign languages depts. French, German, Spanish and Latin offered; talented linguists can take up to three options at GCSE, putting linguists on a par with the scientists. Newly-decorated, bright, clean science and language labs, with recently updated resources. Parents report very solid teaching in maths; quite a few go on to take maths and further maths at A level. A tracking and monitoring system recently introduced to help move towards more individualised learning, the aim being to ensure everyone meets their potential. Year 9 girls encouraged to try out subjects and choose a balanced mixture of GCSEs before making A level choices – always guided towards their strengths.

Subject choices at A level now expanded; 71 per cent A*/A grades in 2015. Sixth formers link with Whitgift and benefit from a good range of sporting, artistic and practical enrichment activities. Accessible careers centre which maintains links with outside agencies; girls also encouraged to get involved in voluntary work, help run school clubs and with the younger children.

ICT centre and library stay open until 5pm; library is run by a much-appreciated and knowledgeable librarian, who facilitates book groups and a number of other literary related activities. Pupils volunteer to assist in the library, designing information posters and leaflets. Girls say library comfortable to work in, with desks overlooking attractive grounds, a popular place to be – good stock of books, audios, periodicals and DVDs.

A few wobbles recently on the staff front but we hope now settled down. Reasonable mix of long-serving and new, younger staff. Part-time SENCo organises additional support which includes screening and study skills for all age groups.

Games, options, the arts: Something for everyone – energetic sporting calendar: hockey, netball, tennis, cross-country, rounders and gymnastics. School has won the netball national finals 14 times in the last three decades and is successful in many other national events. Large sports centre, which doubles as a private club, houses gym, sports hall, dance studios and pool, where the highly successful swimming teams train. Recreational sports include badminton, self-defence, table tennis, aerobics and salsa. D of E award scheme thrives, also regular field trips as well as adventure holidays, music tours and skiing. Year 7s go to an activity centre in Devon for a week of outdoor activities.

Comfortable atmosphere pervades, possibly influenced by the many links encouraged between older and younger girls. All appears to be quiet and purposeful

Traditionally strong music, say parents – instrumental tuition available on most instruments including tuba and harpsichord. Wonderful choirs, orchestras and bands in-house and Fairfield Hall concerts are always a sell out, musicians are involved at local and national levels. Own annual chamber music composition competition judged by an external adjudicator. Music and drama departments work together to produce spectacular musicals each year. Surprisingly few choose to take music GCSE or A level, a shame for such an innovative group of musicians. Art teachers continue the open-door policy so pupils can use facilities – which include pottery studio and dark room – outside timetable classes.

Girls also get out and about and take part in national and local competitions; enthusiastic debating groups and year 7 recently made finals of a national spelling bee.

Background and atmosphere: Founded in 1874, the school moved in 1966 to its present purpose-built site, which accommodates the junior and senior schools. The buildings, which are rather utilitarian from the outside, provide excellent, well-proportioned rooms. Lots of refurbishment under way.

Spacious landscaped grounds supply superb sporting and recreational space for both juniors and seniors. A few well-loved school pets enjoy the grounds too. Comfortable atmosphere pervades, possibly influenced by the many links encouraged between older and younger girls. All appears to be quiet and purposeful.

Pastoral care and discipline: School code of conduct is included in pupils' yearly planners; school rules are mostly common sense or based on health and safety requirements. Sixth formers train as peer listeners to befriend younger pupils. No outside counsellor, however referrals can be made through the school nurse. All girls are encouraged to look out for each other and respect each other as individuals. Teachers are available to pupils on a drop-in basis first thing in the morning.

Pupils and parents: From around 70 feeder independent and state primaries. Catchment area stretches from south London to rural Surrey, although the majority lives within a five-mile radius of the school. Pupils come from a range of backgrounds, mostly professional; proportionate racial mix with around a dozen different nationalities attending. Link with Shenzhen in China, so a small number of Chinese students are able to live locally to attend the sixth form. PTA runs fundraising events and sixth form fashion show often raises around £4000 for charity.

Alumnae: Jacqueline du Pré, Helen Chadwick, Elizabeth Laird, Jane Warr and Marilyn Cutts etc etc.

Entrance: At 11+ annual entrance test in November and informal interview with the head or deputy. All those offered places attend a special induction day during the summer term before entry. At 16+, interview, report from the previous school and seven GCSEs, B grade for subjects to be studied at A level,

A grade for mathematics, chemistry, physics and modern languages.

Exit: Around 30 per cent leave at 16+, mostly for co-ed schools or state sixth form centres and colleges. Great majority to university, a handful a year to Oxbridge (one in 2015); Nottingham, Durham and Manchester popular, otherwise anywhere from London to Edinburgh. Combined degrees becoming particularly popular, eg engineering or law with a modern language.

Money matters: Standard GDST scholarships and bursaries are available. Music, art, drama and sports scholarships for year 7 entrants. Jacqueline du Pré music scholarship and sixth form scholarships.

Remarks: Consistently good results, pupils motivated and accomplished. Maybe too rigorous for a sensitive soul.

Cumnor House School (Croydon)

Linked school: Cumnor House School For Girls, 328

168 Pampisford Road, South Croydon, Surrey CR2 6DA

Tel: 020 8660 3445

Independent • Pupils: 420 (200 in co-ed nursery) • Ages: 2–13 • Fees: up to £11,640 pa

Email: registrar@cumnorhouse.com
Website: www.cumnorhouse.com

12

Headmaster: Since 1999, Mr Peter Clare-Hunt MA (Ed) Cert Ed (50s). Came into education after ending up as a construction worker on the A23 and feeling

there had to be more to life. He must have been quite something even then, because St Dunstan's College welcomed him with open arms and kept him for 18 years. He then did four years at Northcote Lodge, fulfilling a number of roles including deputy head, director of studies and head of sport before taking the post of assistant headmaster at Cumnor House in 1998. A year later, he became head, and is still brimful of energy and showing no signs of wear. Married with two young daughters, mad about cricket and hugely admired by parents, the female half of whom all appear to be in love. 'He's a guide, not a principal!' 'He's adorable!' 'You won't find a better headteacher!' were typical comments.

In calmer language, Mr Clare-Hunt is a man who knows how to talk to boys, and how to motivate and challenge them. He genuinely likes them, and they like him back. To talk to him is rather like reading a Jennings story, but one relocated to a school that's bang-up-to-date and highly efficient. He comes across as honest, open and refreshingly funny. And of how many headteachers can we say that?

Entrance: Three form intake with 20 boys maximum in a class. Automatic entry from the school's Treetops Nursery, which parents told us they found a very attractive feature of the school. Otherwise, boys come in at 4+ for a taster day, which for most is nothing to worry about. 'First and foremost, I find out if he's a nice young man,' says head. 'If he is, that's good enough for me.' Maths and English are checked to ascertain if the child will cope at Cumnor, but not formally assessed. Other entry points at 7+ and 11+. School aims to be as inclusive as possible, and all kinds of families pay the (very competitive) fees to send their boys here.

> *'It's a lovely, brilliant school. I would recommend it to anyone!' cried one mother. 'The boys are lovely young men, and the teachers are amazing, they always want to go the extra mile'*

Exit: Given the school's non-academically-selective admissions process, Cumnor's exit record is truly remarkable. Students can be prepped for either 11+ or 13+ depending on parents' and boys' wishes, which, families affirm, the head is always careful to consult. Those who opt for 11+ are put in a dedicated class, and win places either at local grammars (Wilson's and Wallington's), or at independents such as Trinity and Whitgift, often with scholarships. Those who've chosen to stay until 13 also go on to a whole range of top-brass schools including Westminster, Eton, City of London and Tonbridge. Such is the school's success that refugees who come to Cumnor at 11 often pass at 13 with scholarships into schools which turned them down two years previously. 'I've been in the game long enough to know what the senior schools are looking for,' says head, simply. And year on year, the results prove him right.

Remarks: After years in the schools' reviewing business, we were nonetheless surprised by the fervour with which parents talked to us about Cumnor

House. 'It's a lovely, brilliant school. I would recommend it to anyone and everyone!' cried one mother. 'The boys there are lovely young men, and the teachers are amazing, they always want to go the extra mile,' said another. 'It's been a really positive experience for our son,' said a third. 'We couldn't fault it.' 'No negatives, and nothing to regret. It's fantastic!' said a fourth. And this is just a sample.

Cumnor House is surely triumphant proof that single sex education from an early age can really work. If a How-I-Hope-My-Son-Will-Turn-Out contest existed, the boys we met here would all be candidates to win. Their manners are astonishingly good. Everywhere we were greeted with courteous smiles and handshakes; in one instance, even with a bow! Whilst they hurled themselves around the playgrounds at break-time, they were nonetheless well-behaved and considerate, both to each other and to us. 'You might want to walk quickly, 'cause it's raining,' urged one of our tour guides with anxious politeness.

Everywhere we saw evidence of lively and careful teaching, and the boys were vociferous about how much they enjoyed lessons. 'History is my favourite, because it's all about old things, and did you know that Henry VIII died because his bottom exploded on the toilet!' cried a year 2 lad enthusiastically. The older boys were more conservative in their praise, but no less warm. 'The teachers are very kind', 'They're inspirational!' 'Lessons are always fun', 'Because of my science teacher, I want to be a scientist,' we were told. Work on the walls was imaginative and of a consistently high standard. Strong SEN team supports boys in need of extra help; the school welcomes all learners, although the head acknowledged that boys with more than moderate learning difficulties would struggle at Cumnor, and we ourselves felt that this wouldn't be the right place for them.

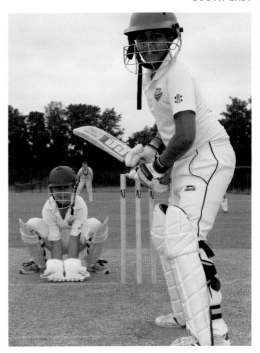

Cumnor House is triumphant proof that single sex education from an early age can really work. If a How-I-Hope-My-Son-Will-Turn-Out contest existed, the boys here would all be candidates to win

Parents in search of flashy facilities might initially be nonplussed by Cumnor's honeycomb, let's-patch-on-another-annexe-here school campus. The main site used to be residential, and the impression is still of a large, rambling house full of staircases and inglenooks. Decor-wise, it would be fair to say that it lacks the feminine touch: somehow, despite the displays and children's books lining the walls, there isn't much colour in the place. Desks are endearingly old-fashioned, and occasionally downright scruffy. But honestly, who cares? The classrooms are all well-resourced, there's an excellent ICT suite, the boys radiate contentment and their achievements speak for themselves. And there's nothing scruffy about the sports facilities: the huge sports ground boasts £50k's worth of new cricket nets and a new clubhouse, the sports hall is adequate and the swimming pool block was warm, light and inviting, which may be why the reception teachers were all in the water with their young charges when we visited. Cumnor's swimming is very successful (the swim squad practises from 7am), and the school has won national as well as local competitions. Football, rugby, cricket and athletics are likewise strong, nurtured by a team of very dedicated PE teachers. Old boys include Mark Butcher, Alistair Brown, David Sales, Chris Robshaw and Elliot Daly.

For the non-sportsmen, however, there is plenty of other fare on offer. Music is flourishing, with over half the boys learning at least one musical instrument, and a pleasing variety of bands and ensembles to join. The school's choral singing is particularly impressive: previous fixtures include Salzburg Cathedral and the Barnardo's National Choir Competition (which they won). Drama is also lively, and the school puts on at least two productions a year. There are lots of clubs and societies, and the boys are encouraged to try new things. 'I don't want boys who are in at 8.30am and out at 3.30pm,' says head. 'I want them to take risks. I tell them, if you haven't auditioned for the school play, why not? If you aren't learning an instrument, why not?'

A few years ago Cumnor joined the Cognita schools group (the brainchild of Chris Woodhead), thereby increasing its financial clout in a very competitive locality. The Lodge Schools on the other side of the Purley Way declined and fell during the financial crisis, whereupon Cognita bought up most of the site and asked Cumnor to open a girls' school (see our separate entry) and expand Treetops, their excellent nursery provision. Reception boys are also housed on this site in Woodcote Lane, and we wondered if that didn't provoke grumbles from parents dropping off more than one child. But no: the school runs a shuttle service between the two sites,

and parents can choose to which one they deliver both sons and daughters, knowing that the school will safely ferry their children to where they need to be. (And this, frankly, is more than can be said for some of the parents; the thoroughfare outside the Pampisford Road site gets very exciting at drop-off time, as local residents will feelingly confirm.)

The Croydon area is multi-cultural, and one of Cumnor's greatest successes is the way that it takes a highly diverse group of boys – every colour and creed is represented on the school roll – and helps them all become polished and likeable English gentlemen, in the best possible sense of the phrase. It may not be the place for the kind of child who just isn't into school no matter how good it is; incurable mavericks would be exhausted by the ebullient enthusiasm and team spirit here. But make no mistake, this is boys' education at its best.

Cumnor House School For Girls

Linked school: Cumnor House School (Croydon), 325

1 Woodcote Lane, Purley, Surrey CR8 3HB

Independent • Pupils: 180 • Ages: 2–11 • Fees: up to £11,640 pa

Tel: 020 8660 3445

Email: admin.purley@cumnorhouse.com
Website: www.cumnorhouse.com

13

Head: From January 2016, Mrs Dina Mallett BA Ed (Reading), currently deputy head at City of London School for Girls Prep School. She replaces Mr Peter Kelly Dip Ed MEd, popular head since school came

into being in 2010, who taught at Cumnor House Boys before becoming head of West Dene Preparatory School, a co-ed prep school which in turn merged with Downside Lodge in 2008. When all the Lodge schools got into financial hock in 2010, the site was bought by Cognita Schools who turned it into Cumnor House Girls, to the delight of many local parents.

The standard of work here is high, all the more creditably given the school's non-selective intake. Literacy and numeracy are very strong, and the work on the walls bore testimony to imaginative and effective teaching

The hapless Lodge schools may have been swept away, but Cumnor House Girls has been popular from the outset. Numbers expanded from 60 to 100 before they even opened their doors, and have almost doubled since. 'We've a clear vision,' is school's explanation. 'Our aim is to offer girls choice at 11. That's what we're good at.' Are they academically aspirational? 'Without question. Girls cover the curriculum more quickly, so we're able to really push them on academically.'

Entrance: Two-form entry with up to 20 per class. Automatic admission for girls at Treetops, Cumnor's excellent and increasingly sought-after nursery. Otherwise, entry is 'mostly non-selective', and at 4+ consists of a taster day where the girls' literacy and numeracy is checked 'to see where they're at', but not formally assessed. 'Very rarely say no,' says school. But with a growing reputation in the neighbourhood, we suspect that will change. Register early to be sure of a place. Apparently there's means-tested assistance plus the odd scholarship available at 7+, but we couldn't find any mention of this on the website.

Exit: To an impressive range of local selective schools, often with scholarships. Recent destinations include Wallington, Nonsuch, JAGS, Caterham, Croydon High, Lady Eleanor Holles and City of London Freemen's.

Remarks: Poor Commonweal Lodge School, now being busily converted into flats (it was the bit that Cognita didn't want), broods mournfully from afar over this happy and flourishing newish venture on the leafy Webb Estate, but c'est la vie. We don't think Cumnor House Girls will go the same way; the signs are too promising.

There are girls here who joined the school when it was Downside Lodge co-ed, and as far as they're concerned, things just keep getting better. 'This is the best school anyone could ever choose',

'It's amazing here', 'I'd give the school five stars', we were told. Did they miss having boys around? 'Well, they were loud,' commented one girl cheerfully, 'so it's good that they're not here, really, and it's nice to have smaller classes.'

Whatever its secret, the standard of work here is high, all the more creditably given the school's non-selective intake. Literacy and numeracy are very strong, and the work on the walls bore testimony to imaginative and effective teaching. A girl who'd transferred to Cumnor from another independent school told us, 'I feel here they're pushing me a bit more.' But this clearly isn't at anyone's expense. The same girl added, 'There wasn't as much learning support at my old school, and Cumnor has a nicer atmosphere.' And indeed, we thought the learning support room was particularly welcoming. The SEN team is strong and vigilant, and difficulties are picked up early. The head meets with the SENCo every week, and 'dynamic support' is offered quickly to those who need it. We were impressed by the Games Club, a nurture group for girls with social difficulties, but also by the Quest Club for the gifted and talented students. We certainly saw some lovely examples of the latter.

Sport at Cumnor House Girls is 'MASSIVE!' and 'VERY, VERY important!' according to its young devotees. Rounders, netball, gymnastics, athletics

and tennis are all on offer (but no football, which the girls said they would have liked; school please note), and all girls from reception upwards have weekly swimming lessons at Cumnor House Boys. 'They include everyone in the sports here and it's great fun,' insisted a self-confessed non-sporty type.

There was some gorgeous artwork on display, including a wonderful Olympic themed sculpture in the foyer; the art teacher, we were told, 'has many different ideas, she's amazing!' The head is also a firm believer in music and drama, with both integrated into the curriculum. Free instrumental lessons are offered to all girls in year 3, many choose to continue them afterwards, and the school fields two choirs and an orchestra. Wherever possible, they team up with the boys' school for drama productions; previous shows include Bugsy Malone and Aladdin. The hall struck us as rather old-fashioned, but the girls adored it, and told us, 'This is a very, very exciting stage!' Lots of clubs, including dance, chess, judo and sewing, and Business Club ('so we get confident in speaking') – though none of the debating, science and electronics clubs offered at the boys' school. Food technology is on the timetable (unlike at the boys' school, which seems to give rather more emphasis to the sciences in lessons too) and is very popular, and the school has a lovely garden which provides the vegetables for lessons – we were proudly shown shallots, parsley and runner beans. (On the subject of actual school lunches the girls were

diplomatically loyal, which, after the stone-cold and unappetizing fare we'd been offered, we thought very praiseworthy of them.)

They team up with the boys' school for drama productions such as Bugsy Malone and Aladdin. The hall struck us as rather old-fashioned, but the girls adored it, 'This is a very, very exciting stage!'

The girls themselves, smartly attired in a sensible and well-cut uniform, are the surest proof that this is a school doing well by its students. Lively, happy, enthusiastic, well-mannered and articulate, they were a pleasure to meet. Parents agree. 'It's a very child-orientated school; the girls are allowed to have fun,' said one. Other comments include: 'The teachers are very caring', 'My daughter loved it from the beginning', 'The academic provision is very good, and my daughter's become very confident', 'It's a lovely old-fashioned village-y atmosphere, and she's made some great friends', 'It's a fantastic school; I have no issues at all.' Our verdict: a blossoming school with much to offer; the clever choice for Croydon daughters.

Eltham College Junior School

Linked school: Eltham College, 332

Mottingham Lane, London SE9 4RW

Independent • Pupils: 210 • Ages: 7–11 • Fees: £13,671 pa

Tel: 020 8857 3457

Email: juniors@eltham-college.org.uk
Website: www.eltham-college.org.uk

3

Master: Since 2010, Mr Edmund Cavendish, previously deputy head of the senior school.

Entrance: Selective and competitive. Approximately 80 boys at 7+, trying for around 40 places. Saturday activity morning in school followed by assessment by master and testing of reading, maths and language skills, in small groups. A few more spaces at 8+, so always worth retrying if 7+ doesn't work.

Exit: About 75 per cent to the senior school, usually around a quarter with scholarships. Others to mainly local schools.

Remarks: Situated in its own corner of the main school grounds, with own entrance and playing fields, here is a mini version of the senior school. Redeveloped a few years ago – when we visited then, we got the impression of lots of light, glass and bang up-to-date facilities. Great glass-roofed art and DT room, science lab with a particularly lively teacher, ICT suite where other subject lessons can also take place, well-stocked library, bright interesting-looking classrooms. Assemblies held every day in main hall – our youthful guide pointed out with glee the fact that hymn books are no longer necessary, as the words descend on a special screen.

Use is also made of senior school facilities, particularly the sports hall and swimming pool, the chapel, the dining room (where the food is apparently 'yummy') and the theatre.

The usual broad curriculum with one unusual innovation: Mandarin Chinese is now taught from day one instead of French. They believe this is the way forward and that it has many, much wider, educational benefits and cross-curricular links. Certainly when we visited, the school was right into the Chinese theme. But then it was not long after the annual China Now! day. Parents seem to have mixed views: some think it is an excellent idea and that it is what the future is about, others feel it is gimmicky and they would rather stick to European languages for now. We think it could be very good move, but only time will tell.

> *If a boy is not particularly good at one thing, they encourage him to shine somewhere else – 'All children have something and will find their niche somewhere'*

All boys screened for dyslexia in year 3. Class teachers and tutors are constantly on the watch for any other learning problems that might develop. Sympathetic and knowledgeable learning support co-ordinator, who parents say is 'wonderful', 'easy to talk to' and 'always available'. If a boy is not particularly good at one thing, they encourage him to shine somewhere else – 'All children have something and will find their niche somewhere'.

> *The usual broad curriculum with one unusual innovation: Mandarin is now taught from day one instead of French*

High quality music. Every child in years 3 and 4 learns an individual instrument, initially free of charge. Three choirs, an orchestra and several specialist groups – the variety is huge. Masses of sport, extracurricular activities, internal and external competitions. An impressive number of trophies on display. In fencing, have been épée British School team champions and foil runners up. Two boys selected for the England under-11 chess squad and two more played for Kent in the victorious under-9 team. Concerts, plays and lots of outings home and abroad – really should be something for everyone here. Only possible niggle is that it tends to be always the same children selected to lead and star – does this totally fit into 'giving everyone a chance to shine'?

Ease of contact seems very much the culture of both halves of the school. Good pastoral care – peer mentoring certainly helps and form teachers and tutors are always there to talk to. Any problem is usually dealt with quickly and sensibly. Boys are 'treated as individuals for both strengths and weaknesses'; 'We try to look after all the boys and give them the best experience we can'.

Eltham College

Linked school: Eltham College Junior School, 330

Grove Park Road, London SE9 4QF

Independent · Pupils: 640 · Ages: 11–18 · Sixth form
pupils: 210 (60 girls) · Fees: £15,486 pa

Tel: 020 8857 1455

Email: mail@eltham–college.org.uk
Website: www.eltham–college.org.uk

Headmaster: Since September 2014, Guy Sanderson, previously deputy head of Reigate Grammar. Read PPE and modern history at Oxford, began his career in the City, then trained as a teacher at St Paul's Boys' School. Has also taught at Whitgift and City of London schools. A keen open water swimmer, skier, and church elder in Sussex. Married to Laura, a headhunter; they have three children.

Academic matters: Though 2015 A level results, 54 per cent A*/A and 85 per cent A*-B, were somewhat lower than previous years, results generally reflect a highly academic approach where pupils are stretched to the limits of their abilities. Yet, parents tell us, this academia is nurtured into them and they are taught to be well-organised and to want to succeed. The teaching is, parents say, 90 per cent excellent – teachers are always prepared to give extra help and support if a pupil asks for it. Teacher/pupil relationships appear relaxed and respectful.

Broad curriculum and the school works hard to identify the particular strength(s) of each child and build on them. Languages very strong, many taking two or three at GCSE. French and Mandarin

compulsory in year 7, German in year 8 and Spanish can be taken up in year 9. Latin also compulsory in years 7 and 8 and all do short course GCSE RS. The three sciences studied separately unless circumstances exceptional. 'Science is fun,' we were told by a boy. 'All theory is backed up by experiments.' Maths and science are taken as IGCSEs. Three streams in each subject, according to parents – 'top, middle and could-be-better': no-one here is 'bad' at anything. In 2015, 72 per cent A*/A at GCSE.

Support and encouragement is part of the school ethos and, according to parents, communication is easy and as frequent as necessary

Full-time learning support teacher. All new pupils screened on entry for possible difficulties and, if anything arises, parents immediately involved and a programme devised. Support and encouragement is part of the school ethos and, according to parents, communication is easy and as frequent as necessary. When we asked about G and T, we were told that really every child in the school is gifted or talented and that, because of the huge range of activities in the school, everyone should be properly stretched. Also that teaching is always done to the top level, on the assumption that all are perfectly able – we're not sure that parents of middle-of-the-road, less motivated boys agree or are happy with this.

Games, options, the arts: Sport is considered an essential part of school life and everyone is encouraged to participate. With 60 acres of playing fields and an all singing, all dancing sports centre, something for everyone. In the sixth form it could be just table tennis, but before that rugby, hockey and cricket are tops and played competitively at all levels internally, against other schools and nationally. Also regular overseas tours. Plenty of other options as well; the girls have a couple of strong

> *This school really does believe in getting out and exploring the world. Some of the sixth form went cycling in China and younger pupils take part in exchanges with schools in Beijing*

netball teams; foil and épée fencers recently qualified for the British Championships and even a golf team. Swimming also popular. Duke of Edinburgh Award scheme followed to gold level, though parents said the expedition costs seemed rather high. The less sporty can still find their niches and are encouraged to excel in their individual talents.

Plenty for budding thespians. Drama is on the curriculum for all in years 7-9 and can be taken at GCSE and A level. Productions range from Shakespeare to blockbuster musicals, so something for everyone and a great theatre in which to perform. Pupils thrilled with the experience of taking shows to the Edinburgh Festival.

Music very impressive. Chances for everyone to join in – the school thinks it is good for teamwork. Lots of choirs, orchestras and jazz bands. About 65 per cent learn an instrument. A parent said she makes a point of going to every musical occasion and is in total awe of their capabilities. Apparently choral singing an exceptional strength; several pupils also members of local and national youth choirs. The trebles have international engagements and performed with Sir Simon Rattle and the Berlin Philharmonic, also at the BBC Proms. On the last night of the Proms, music and picnicking in the grounds – a popular end of year event.

Great art on display in the main entrance hall and elsewhere – lots of talent here. On average a dozen take art A level, all getting A*, A or B, mostly As. Sculpture displayed outside along route to junior school. The Gerald Moore Gallery for modern and contemporary art is a new centre for learning used by the school and wider community through exhibitions and an outreach programme.

A multitude of trips or, as they call them, journeys every year: art galleries and museums at home and abroad, adventure courses for younger pupils and advanced D of E, languages in their countries of origin, geography, biology, history, theatre, music – any excuse for adventure. This school really does believe in breadth, encouraging research and getting out and about and exploring the world. Some of the sixth form even went cycling in China and younger pupils are scheduled to take part in exchanges with schools in Beijing. Parents praised this cultural aspect and are exceptionally happy with the organisation of language exchanges.

Background and atmosphere: Originally started as a small boarding school for the sons of missionaries – still a strong Christian foundation, with the importance of caring for the community and travelling far and wide part of its ethos. Since moving, in 1912, to this elegant 18th century mansion surrounded by green fields, it has grown in size, stopped taking boarders, introduced girls into the sixth form and become thoroughly part of the 21st century, opening up great opportunities for today's youth. Yet its aims are still very much the same: to produce polite, caring, focused young people ready to go out into the world knowing what they want and where they are going.

Buildings very much the usual mixture of old and new. The central hall and the chapel, where

pupils attend a service every morning, could not be more traditional, but the surrounding class-rooms and buildings are bright, up to date and contain every modern technological element. Good resource centre for languages, excellent science labs, computers everywhere. Several exciting projects, particularly perhaps the 'green car challenge', voluntary at any age, where, every other year, students design and build an electric car to run at Goodwood. Wow!

Hard-working atmosphere prevails. Reasonably turned out, well-mannered pupils smiled at us wherever we went and looked thoroughly involved in their lessons, whether mechanical or creative. Excellent library, the use of which is built into the curriculum, with quiet areas for study and where prep can be done before going home. A green oasis in the middle of busy, bustling SE London that still has a bit of a boarding school feel about it. A warm welcome greets anyone walking across the threshold, and the enormous statues in the central courtyard, representing power and speed (they came from the old Tricity Building in the Aldwych and were donated by, amongst others, old boy Dr Gerald Moore), illustrate the sense of purpose that exists equally amongst pupils and staff.

A green oasis in the middle of busy, bustling S E London that still has a bit of a boarding school feel about it. A warm welcome greets anyone walking across the threshold

Pastoral care and discipline: Comprehensive anti-bullying policy and zero drug tolerance. Parents sign contract outlining, amongst other things, acceptable behaviour in school. Fairly strict, disciplined environment. Tutors expected to know everything about the children in their care. Pastoral team meets weekly to discuss potential or ongoing problems. Popular school nurse always available for chat. Head of girls for those in sixth form. Communication lines between school and parents excellent, problems answered promptly. House system also enables peer mentoring.

Pupils and parents: Solid SE London, mainly from within five-mile radius. Good social mix with a wide range of backgrounds, all keen to ensure good education for their children. Lots of working mums – pupils can be dropped off at 8.00am if necessary. Several school buses ferrying backwards and forwards. Lots of social occasions for parents to meet and mingle.

For children with enquiring minds, adventures to be had, chances to learn, to give to others and to grow. Those who are kind, considerate and passionate about something will flourish

Ex-pupils include early sons of missionaries, Eric Liddell, Olympic runner, after whom the sports hall is named, and Mervyn Peake, author of fantastic Gormenghast trilogy. More recently, Major Phil Packer, military hero, and former MP Jim Knight, now Baron Knight of Weymouth.

Entrance: Seventy-five places at 11+, of which about 50 per cent come from the junior school, the rest from about 60 local primary and private schools. Occasional spaces at 13+. Girls included in 16+ entry which increases the sixth form by about a third. School insists no specific quota. Head interviews all candidates, looking for those that 'want to have a go'. Says 'sponges' would not do well here – pupils need to have drive and really want to do well. Regards interview as most important part of entry process.

Exit: Up to 20 per cent leave after GCSEs. Pretty well all sixth formers to top universities. Ten to Oxbridge in 2015: Exeter, Leeds, Warwick, Southampton and Loughborough all popular.

Money matters: Up to 20 academic scholarships available at 11+ and 15 more at sixth form level for art and drama. Also several for music and sports. Bursaries available for the needy. Apparently fundraising in last few years has been very effective, so the money is there – five to six per cent currently benefiting from bursaries. The school would like this to continue and grow.

Remarks: An academic arena for those who know what they want and are willing to give anything a go. For children with enquiring minds, adventures to be had, the world to understand, chances to learn, to give to others and to grow. Those who are kind, considerate and passionate about something will flourish here, but the insecure, and those who need more than a gentle nudge, may not get as much out of it. Fantastic opportunities here for grabbing; boys and girls emerge with a well-rounded, worldly education, ready to take whatever chances life may give them.

Haberdashers' Aske's Hatcham College Primary Phase

Linked school: Haberdashers' Aske's Hatcham College, 336

Hunsdon Road, , New Cross, London SE14 5RD

Tel: 020 7652 9510

State • Pupils: 415 • Ages: 3–11

Email: hreception@haaf.org.uk
Website: www.haaf.org.uk/Hatcham-College

Headteacher: Since September 2015, Emily Gyimah, previously deputy head at Hatcham Temple Grove. Degree in primary education from Brunel; spent two years as a KS1/KS2 class teacher at Monson primary school and then taught for five years as a KS1 and literacy leader at Hatcham Temple Grove. She was then promoted to Haberdashers' Aske's Federation phonics consultant, a position she held for three successful years before returning to HTG in 2014 as deputy head.

Entrance: Two form entry. Sixty places in reception, with four more available further up the school. Usual state school admissions criteria apply: looked after children, medical needs, siblings, proximity. Oversubscribed. About 25 children come up from the school's own nursery, but parents should be aware that a place at the nursery does not guarantee a place in reception.

Exit: Almost all pupils transfer to HAHC secondary phase, to which they have automatic right of entry.

Remarks: Originally Monson Primary School, which was failing. HAHC took it on in 2008 and turned it around in three years. It is now rated outstanding.

The school was being extensively refurbished when in 2010 a builder managed to cause a fire that gutted the place. The primary children and staff camped on various floors before moving into the new building in 2015.

The school's unique selling points are its music (check out our entry for the secondary school) and its German immersion programme, which has been running for three years and which pupils begin in year 1. According to the school, the children are taught for half a day, every day, in German, and staff with ability to speak German are actively recruited. It's had a big impact on the children's academic performance. 'Our phonics results went through the roof, because German is very phonic in the way it's spoken' with 'skilled and fluent German speakers coming up through the school ranks.' This is all excellent stuff, and we were thrilled to have 'Heads, shoulders, knees and toes' sung to us in German by a flaxen-haired child of 6 who could have stepped straight out of Hamlyn. Every primary parent we spoke to, however, told us a different story. 'My son's been doing it for two years now, and he can only tell me the nouns. He doesn't have any better grasp of German than if he'd been taught it in the usual way,' said one parent. Another said: 'It was sold to us as an German immersion programme, that they'd be taught in German every afternoon, but in reality, it's turned out to be a couple of afternoons a week and it's teaching things like colours and days of the week. It isn't immersion.' Even the most enthusiastic of school supporters said: 'I don't really know if they teach the German – just once in a while, maybe.' Quite a mismatch. School please note.

The music was uniformly praised. Class music begins in reception, everyone learns recorder in year 3, and in year 4 those who are progressing well – generally around half of the class – are invited to learn violin, cello or clarinet. 'It's the discipline and the dexterity; and it's much easier in year 4 than when you're an older child.' The lessons are free and all children are allowed to carry on in year 5 if they want to, which at least a third of the year group always do. Those who don't want to continue can still be involved with the junior choir, and the Haberdashers' Livery Company and Temple Grove Trust can award bursaries to parents whose children want to learn other musical instruments outside school. Lots of concerts and the choir busks in Lewisham Shopping Centre to raise money for the 999 Club.

Sport plays an active part in the curriculum, with basketball, athletics, swimming and football on offer and funding awarded for Saturday and after-school provision. School adroitly links this

Plenty of trips: river walks, London Eye, museums, visits to the theatre, all helped by an active parent body. Good programme of drama

with academic achievement – 'you have to be in the reading group to be in Saturday football.' The Little Leaders Group offers leadership exercises for children who don't get out much at home. Plenty of trips: river walks, London Eye, museums, visits to the theatre, all helped by an active parent body. Good programme of drama, and children are encouraged to do public speaking in assemblies etc.

Reflecting the area, this is a very diverse community both socially and culturally, with about 50 per cent of pupils coming from ethnic minorities. As we walked about, this impressed us as a lively, happy and well-behaved community of children. There were a couple of dissenting voices, including one who claimed that if it hadn't been for the automatic entry to HAHC's hugely-oversubscribed secondary phase she would have moved her child to a different school. The majority of parents, however, told us they were very happy with both the academic standards and the pastoral care. 'My daughter loves it – she wants to go even when she's sick,' said one mother, and others agreed. Comments included: 'The teachers are always helpful'; 'well done to all the teachers keeping standards up during all the moving about'; 'the encouragement and welcome my daughter receives has made her time at the school a pleasure,' and, from a mother without much English, 'I think it's a good school, really, really good.'

Haberdashers' Aske's Hatcham College

Linked school: Haberdashers' Aske's Hatcham College Primary Phase, 335

Pepys Road, London SE14 5SF

Tel: 020 7652 9510

State • Pupils: 1,370 • Ages: 11–18 • Sixth form pupils: 350

Email: hreception@haaf.org.uk
Website: www.haaf.org.uk

26

Principal: Since 2008, Mr Declan Jones LLB PGCE NPQH (50s). A man totally in love with, and at ease with, his chosen sphere – 'this is an exceptionally exciting time to be in education,' he says. Grew up in Ireland, read law at Birmingham, then travelled the world for three years teaching English as a for-

eign language. Settled into a PGCE on his return and taught at various London comprehensives before coming to Hatcham in 1999 as curriculum manager. Became deputy head in due course, and was instrumental in expanding 'The Hatcham Brand' across Lewisham. Became acting head, then head in 2008,

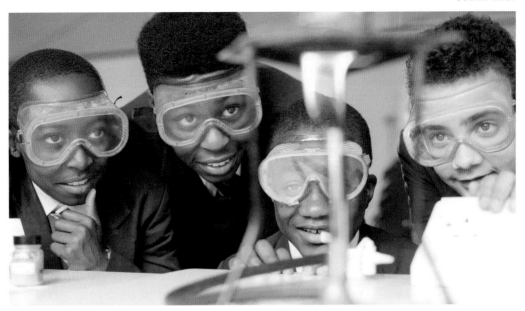

leading the school to its first outstanding Ofsted. Married with two teenage daughters.

A music lover, who is, in his words, 'very privileged to be principal here.' Extremely proud of the way the school has invested in children's musical ability. Particularly enthusiastic about the school's choirs: 'it pulls people together, because you're participating in a sound you can't make on your own.' A particular interest in 'growing your own' led to Hatcham becoming an all-through school in 2008 by taking on the then failing Monson Primary and turning it into an outstanding school in three years.

It's impossible not to be enthused by his passion for the school and his pride in its achievements. A number of parents, however, commented that he was rather remote from their day-to-day experience of the school, and that they saw more of the vice principal.

Academic matters: In 2015, 70 per cent of students got 5+ A*-C grades at GCSE, including maths and English, and 25 per cent of grades were A*/A. Very good results, although oddly, they seem to have mostly got incrementally lower year-on-year since 2009. At A level, 45 per cent A*-B.

Parents are generally satisfied, with most reporting that academic standards are good. 'Homework is prolific,' said one parent, adding, 'but it's mostly well thought through, well explained and supports classwork.' One parent was unhappy, reporting that their very bright child was 'constantly bored during lessons' and that 'the curriculum, especially in science and maths, is very basic, and the teachers, with a few exceptions, are not willing to take pupils beyond it.' The school contests this: 'We

have the experience to help G&T children to get on,' and the leavers' destinations are certainly good. Principal adds: 'We run The Brilliant Club for our academically able students. You join in year 9, and you're assigned a PhD student [from Goldsmith's over the road] and given a task to do.'

Wide range of languages – year 7s get to choose two from German, French, Spanish, Mandarin and Latin, and higher up the school there are opportunities to learn classical Greek. Sixth form courses are 'strongly academic' – no BTecs offered, only A levels; the IB was explored but rejected as not inclusive enough for HAHC students.

> *The music at HAHC is astonishing. No other word for it. We see many schools which claim to have marvellous music, but they really do have it here*

Our impression was that the academic performance is very creditable given the non-academically selective intake, and that the school is both enriched and held up to critical scrutiny by a highly articulate parent body who expect the best and give no quarter when they don't get it.

Games, options, the arts: The school has its own sports centre in Nunhead, and students can do cricket, basketball, volleyball, football, netball and rugby (when we visited, the rugby team were about to head off to play another Haberdashers' school in Monmouth).

The music at HAHC is astonishing. No other word for it. We see many schools which claim to have marvellous music, but they really do have it here. We sat, open-mouthed, through student performances of Soave il Vento from Cosi Fan Tutte (sung in Italian), Mozart's Divertimento No 1 scored for two clarinets and a bassoon, Bartok's Mikrokosmos on the piano – all of it delivered with exquisite taste, sensitivity, musicality and technique. Then, just as we were preparing to move on, the choir started a ravishing rendition of Lotti's Crucifixus and we sat back down again. 'It's like being at a professional concert,' said the vice principal, with pardonable pride.

Unusually for a state school, classical music takes centre stage here, but it's for the many, not the few. Virtually all the children learn at least one instrument, and the lessons are free. The school abounds with orchestras, chamber music, and choirs of every kind, and there are jazz bands too. Parents were uniformly delighted with this aspect of the school. We heard comments like 'all the music groups are fantastic,' 'there are concerts all the year round, musicals and even a school opera,' 'the music staff teach with ambition, enthusiasm and humour, and my children love it' and 'HAHC is a vibrant place where you are encouraged to fulfil

your artistic potential.' We heard a murmur that rock music doesn't get quite the same encouragement, and the school admitted that this might be so. But what is on offer is so amazing, that it's hard to grumble. HAHC choirs provide the music for City Hall's annual Remembrance service as well as carols for Southwark Cathedral. The Haberdashers Company regularly asks school to provide chamber ensembles for events. As the vice principal put it: 'A very good part of this school is that the students gain the cultural capital to function beyond it.'

On a different note, the CCF also flourishes at HAHC, attracting some 160 students, and with a Corps of Drums that is, according to a visiting instructor, 'better than Eton's.'

'The children respect the staff and the staff are interested in the children themselves, what their interests are and what makes them tick'

HAHC is proud of all aspects of its enrichment programme. The school is 'thronged' with students after lessons finish, says vice principal – but parental feedback we received about it was mixed (music excepted). A common complaint was that it was hard to get information about the various clubs and activities and that a number of initiatives, such as Artsmark and D of E, had unravelled due to poor organisation or lack of assessors. 'All a bit half-hearted,' was how one parent described the netball, and another said that her children felt that 'a huge opportunity is being missed in terms of sport... things just don't get organised.' These concerns were at odds with the school's excellent facilities and range of provision offered, and we asked the principal to comment. He agreed about the D of E – 'the member of staff responsible has left and we have a six-month plan to right that issue' – but robustly defended the school's record on Artsmark ('I've handed out the certificates in assembly') as well as on sport, and the students we spoke to seemed happy.

Everyone agrees that debating is strong. Sixth formers have started a tutoring cooperative, coaching students from lower down the school and getting paid for it too. In general, HAHC students seem to gain confidence and skills from what is an unusually broad and intellectually stimulating extracurricular programme.

Background and atmosphere: One of the Haberdashers' 'family' of schools, both state and independent, and one of three schools in the Haberdashers' Aske's Federation, the others being

Knight's Academy in Bromley and Crayford Academy in Bexley.

Hatcham itself is divided between three sites. Jerningham Road, built in 1889 as a girls' school, now houses years 7 to 9 and is a very pleasing old Victorian red-brick, although some parents were critical of the state of the classrooms and toilets. We weren't shown these areas and can't comment. The older students study at the Pepys Road site, a rather gruelling 15-minute walk up Telegraph Hill. Minibuses shuttle pupils and staff between the various school buildings, all of which appeared well kept, blending tradition (stained glass, honours boards) with bang-up-to-date innovation and décor; in the parts we were shown, at any rate. School is co-educational, but in years 7 to 11 teaching is in single-sex groups wherever possible.

School-home communication much criticised by parents and we ourselves found this a difficult school to make contact with. (New direct lines for each school may help: until recently, all calls to any of the Federation schools had to be routed through the Haberdashers' Aske's Federation office, a system which parents loathed.) School counters that it has a policy that all emails must be replied to within 48 hours, that its communication is 'pretty good and pretty effective' and that all parents receive a handbook at the start of each year. But, acknowledges principal, 'these days there's a need for real-time information.'

Pastoral care and discipline: Behaviour at HAHC reflects the school's large and diverse intake, but is perfectly fine, and all pupils we spoke to reported feeling safe here. The uniform is smart and smartly worn.

Many people commented on the school's 'good and healthy' atmosphere. 'The children respect the staff and the staff are interested in the children themselves, what their interests are and what makes them tick,' said one mother. Another wrote: 'The atmosphere is friendly and good pastoral care is provided.' The young people we met were courteous, assured and proud of their school. 'It's very welcoming here, I've made a large group of friends,' said one. 'The music department is great at involving everyone'; 'there's a really nice community feel here and the older and younger students talk to each other' were typical comments. Parents report that SEN provision is much improved and HAHC is the borough's school of choice for wheelchair-bound students.

Pupils and parents: An extremely diverse community, both culturally and socially. As one member of staff dryly observed, at the end of the school day equal numbers turn either right into the Telegraph Hill conservation area, where a five-bedroom house might go for £1.3m, or left towards New Cross and

some of the worst social deprivation in London. A number of professional musicians send their children here for the music provision. The school appears genuinely to integrate all its various members successfully. Ofsted recently wrote: 'The promotion of racial harmony within the college's richly diverse community is exemplary.'

Entrance: Massively over-subscribed, with at least 10 applications for every place. HAHC has its own primary school and 64 pupils from its year 6 have automatic entry. Ten per cent of places allocated on musical aptitude – these pupils are selected by aural test. Otherwise, standard local authority criteria apply: looked-after children, siblings, proximity etc, and the school aims to recruit a broad spread of academic ability. 'Admissions is a hot potato for this school,' admitted the vice principal. Appeals by parents are in excess of 100 each year, but be warned – the school's decisions are almost always upheld, 'because we're exceptionally compliant with the rules.'

About 60 to 100 sixth form places available to external students – no admissions tests, but a minimum of five A*-C grades required at GCSE, the same as for internal students.

Exit: After year 11 about 60 per cent progress to the school's sixth form, the rest to a variety of post-16 provision. Some don't get the grades necessary to move up to year 12 at HAHC and go to other local schools and colleges; a tiny number opt for Dartford Grammar and the IB. Careers officer follows the progress of all leavers, and the school is proud of having had no NEETS (young people not in education, employment or training) for five years.

Around 10 per cent of AS students don't achieve the minimum grade Cs required to move up to year 13. At 18, about 80 per cent to university, including 50 per cent to Russell Group. In 2015, four students to Oxbridge. Of the remainder, nearly a quarter take a gap year, often applying to university through HAHC once they've got their A levels.

Money matters: State-funded academy. Parents not asked to pay voluntary contributions, and vice principal looked astonished when we asked if they were. Unusual and generous provision of scholarships to the 10 per cent selected on musical aptitude – the school will partially fund them to train at the Saturday junior departments of the main London music colleges, the Royal Academy of Music, Royal College of Music, Guildhall and Trinity. In addition, instrumental lessons offered at HAHC are free to all students, regardless of ability or level.

Remarks: A large and flourishing comprehensive that's lifted above the crowd by its results and amazing music and attracts many aspirational families into the area. Plan early if you want your child to go.

Langley Park School for Boys

South Eden Park Road, Beckenham, Kent BR3 3BP

State • Pupils: 1,690 • Ages: 11–18 • Sixth form pupils: 625 (230 girls)

Tel: 020 8639 4700

Email: office@lpbs.org.uk
Website: www.lpbs.org.uk

5

Headteacher: Since September 2013, Mr Steve Parsons (40s); has BA in history from King's College, MA in school effectiveness and improvement from the Institute of Education and the professional headship qualification, NPQH. He has lived nearby in Beckenham for many years with his wife Ruth, also a senior school headteacher, and could not quite believe the fortuitousness of the top job arising at Langley Park at just the moment he felt ready to take on a headship.

Having come straight from Dunraven School, the highly sought after south London co-educational state secondary in Streatham, where he spent seven years as deputy head, he would seem to be a very good fit. As Dunraven too underwent lengthy transition to new buildings, he is relieved to find himself in Langley Park's stunning new quarters post the spade-work. Prior to Dunraven he was assistant head at Crown Woods College.

The previous head was at the school for 15 years, and Mr Parsons is aware he has a lot to live up to, speaks highly of the past head's vision for the school and says it will be 'evolution, not revolution', confirmed by parents: 'the transition from the previous head seems to have been very smooth: we have not noticed any major changes'.

Parents told us: 'I find him inspiring and a great leader for the boys' and 'he seems a committed, positive and hardworking head'. We found him to be very approachable, focused, modest, extremely tall and not lacking in courage, not only in taking over from a much-loved predecessor but in resolutely describing himself as a fan of football – more armchair than playing these days – in a school where rugby is the sporting religion.

Academic matters: Thrillingly good results given the non-selective in-take. In 2015, 76 per cent of boys achieved 5 A*-Cs at GCSE including English and maths, 33 per cent A*/A grades; a strong showing of A*/As in Spanish, music, statistics, physics, IT, computer studies and chemistry. English language GCSE is so good the school is in the top five per cent of results nationally. At A level 26 per cent A*/A, 61 per cent A*-B in 2015.

Everyone can find their level, with the seven entry forms at 11+ divided into eight ability-based learning groups at key stage 3, 10 at key stage 4 for English and maths. There is definitely no resting on laurels in sight: the head has ambitions for academic improvement, introducing the new year 7s recently to Dr Carol Dweck's Growth Mindset, inspiring them to believe they can do better and that everyone has the potential for success, a philosophy which will be taken up by the whole school. He's also aware of the need to future-proof students by teaching flexibility and adaptability to meet a barely imagined future job market.

Students we saw during our visit were working diligently and told us, 'If you say to others, "I need to work," they respect that'

Curriculum wise, at GCSE there is science at every level – so triple or general science and three art and design choices. Some creative options rarely on offer elsewhere at 16+, such as film studies, media studies, drama and dance, point the way to this being an amazingly artistic school. The idea behind the Langley Baccalaureate, promoted by the school instead of the EBACC, is that pupils are encouraged to retain an arts or creative subject when they're making their exam choices.

Pupils are also advised to study a modern foreign language, but it is not compulsory. German is twice as popular as Spanish and even more popular than French – more by tradition than design. The school has no plans to switch the emphasis at the moment. Special status in maths and computing with links to other schools to offer masterclasses. And the school is one of the few state schools offering engineering.

An exceptional example of comprehensive education with a sporting and artistic offer to match many an independent in smart new facilities

Apart from English and maths, the three sciences, particularly biology, are the most popular A level choices. There are also higher education oriented subjects on offer such as law, philosophy, psychology, economics, politics and further refined arts subjects – fine art and music technology.

On our visit the staff room was buzzing with a vibrant mix of grey haired and younger teachers including several former pupils. More than 20 per cent have been at the school over 10 years.

Parents see staff as hard-working and committed, enthusing: 'teaching staff are inspirational, very knowledgeable about their subjects and keen to stretch the students', 'the teaching is inclusive and of a high quality,' and 'assessment and feedback is thorough.' There is particular praise for English teaching, and the inspired geography teacher with packed classes who uses angel cake to explain coastal erosion – delicious! Pupils give rave reviews, mentioning teachers plugged into the wider world, bringing the latest research back into the classroom, and nothing being too much trouble.

Several parents we spoke to were in agreement regarding the relative lack of intense pressure and level of homework – very little or no homework during holidays – from lower school to sixth form. Whilst this could be good news for some, one, not alone, says: 'We live in such competitive times and I personally think my boys could be pushed harder'. The head disagrees, believing many feel the pressure on their sons is quite high.

Sixth formers are entrusted with independent study, nine free periods a week, and have several light and airy spaces, plus the café, around the school to work in, only lightly supervised by teachers based in semicircular goldfish bowl-like hubs. Pupils see the advantage of having their teachers close to hand – they always know where to find them when they need help. Students we saw were working diligently and told us, 'If you say to others "I need to work" they respect that'. The library with full-time librarian is open every day until 7pm.

The sixth formers we met impressed us with their drive and focus – they were determined on their university applications; one to Cambridge – and saw the school as doing everything to prepare them for their final exams: 'We work backwards from the final exam from week one'. Parents have confidence in the school's preparation for the next stage. Students speak of help with UCAS forms by a specialist, and joining with pupils from other south London schools in preparation for Oxbridge assessments.

With more than 30 learning support staff – visible in every class we visited assisting pupils – the needs of those with learning differences, particularly those with autism, are exceptionally well catered for here, attracting more than the average numbers to the school. The Sunil Centre, the base for learning support activities, is a discrete part of the school with its own courtyard garden and even magazine. Some 76 pupils are currently offered support and specialist input. Much is done in the classroom through differentiated learning, but the Sunil centre also provides quiet, smaller spaces and a separate exam room.

Four per cent of students have EAL requirements. The second most prevalent home language, after English, is French, followed by Lithuanian.

Games, options, the arts: A very sporty school – seven pupils currently play at national levels in sports from cycling to squash. Almost the only 'old school' features of the modern building are the traditional wooden boards in reception honouring sporting heroes.

A minimum of two hours sport a week is compulsory until the sixth form, and each Saturday one quarter of every year group represents the school in matches. 'We play the best of the best: all the independents', says the sports director of the fixture

list. He commands an accomplished coaching staff, including former national league coaches, and 27 of the entire school staff are involved in extracurricular sport too.

No football; rugby takes centre stage in every way, not least the newly-seeded pitch in front of both the main school and sports building. On our visit it was still being cossetted behind fences, tantalising our guide who wondered if he'd ever get to play on it. The trophy cabinets bulge with local and national trophies for rugby, hockey, cricket and athletics. In the spirit of inclusivity, parents would like to see more matches for the lower ranked teams. New million pound hockey pitch. The under 16s were recently national champions, the first state school to make it to the top.

The school has held the Artsmark gold award for well over 10 years. The art department flourishes at an exceptionally high standard. Five students were recently chosen to have their work displayed in The Mall galleries at a Royal Society of British Artists exhibition, with two students being honoured as RBA scholars, a first for the school. The department holds an annual summer show where A level final work is hung for friends' and families' enjoyment in a local church. For those wishing to pursue the subject, a former pupil fresh from the cool of Shoreditch had recently returned to inspire budding graphic designers. The sixth form magazine was recently the winner of three national awards.

The 600 seat performance hall, also the home of the Bromley Symphony Orchestra, is rarely out of use. Dance is exhilaratingly popular here. Recent collaborations saw the PE department taking to the stage, whilst pupils provided an inspired interpretation of a WW1 love story as part of the school's commemorations. The riches of London's dance scene are mined, such as during a recent trip to see Matthew Bourne's Swan Lake at Sadler's Wells. A level dance is a new option. One parent: 'Our boys are not particularly interested in dance or drama; however, our eldest recently took part in a short dance performance during a show and loved it.'

A busy music department with dedicated practice rooms, large teaching spaces and a technology suite. Around 400 pupils learn an instrument, either during school or through private lessons mostly facilitated through a link with the Bromley Youth Music Trust. A dozen or so have reached the pinnacle of grade 8 and beyond, with some students performing in the National Youth Orchestra, the London School Symphony Orchestra and the London Jazz Festival. There are Christmas and summer Showcases, an annual music tour and gala concerts.

Several by invitation lunchtime and after-school music clubs such as wood and string quartets or, for something a bit different, cantabile, or Cuban band.

A society or club for most academic subjects each week plus a few extras such as Jaguar cars, GCSE dance, Christian union and scrum half clinic, which sounds as if it mends broken noses, but apparently is more about technique.

Pupils give teaching rave reviews, mentioning teachers plugged into the wider world, bringing the latest research back into the classroom, and nothing being too much trouble

Enrichment really comes into its own in the sixth form, with everyone taking on a couple of new things as well as their A levels, which can be either a sport or arts subject. Most popular are rugby, football and table tennis, but almost a third of students are trying out Japanese, with others learning Dutch, counselling or taking part in the Duke of Edinburgh Award or a current affairs group, Think Tank. If performing arts is more their thing, students can experiment with dance, taiko drumming, creative composition or world music.

Background and atmosphere: The school has been through a number of metamorphoses in terms of buildings, names and indeed locations since its first incarnation in 1901: at one point a technical college, then a grammar school. Having settled on its current location in Eden Park, Beckenham, it eventually outgrew its buildings, leading to a huge development project to create the site we see today. Pupils moved in during 2012, whilst the old school was entirely demolished.

Appropriately enough, given the sporty nature of the school, on first sight the whole complex appears like a smart new sports centre with ample parking. The red-brick main building with curved roof and exterior walls appears hardly large enough to house over 1,600 pupils, but inside the design functions brilliantly, with large classrooms, mezzanine levels, spacious corridors hardly appearing to be corridors because of light from above and large break-out study areas for sixth formers. Everywhere are dazzling white walls and carefully hung student artwork.

Each of the lower years has its own small playground. During our visit, seagulls swooped down trying to snatch snacks from the boys – 'time to get the hawks out,' said a passing teacher, not joking apparently.

Pupils in the lower school wear maroon blazers, graduating to less eye-catching black ones. Then sixth form boys may wear a suit of their choice and girls have recently adopted a jacket of their own choosing – all look very smart.

Perhaps it was our exuberant guides, but as we walked the school we felt palpable excitement and energy amidst hard work. Everyone is agreed on the inclusive ethos of the school. One parent told us, 'The school is competitive but it seems to us that every aspect is valued at the same level. This is great as the boys always seem to be able to feel proud of some achievement: receiving a good grade, being in a team for rugby, being identified for great effort in art, having the opportunity to dance on a stage, working on a science project.'

Works collaboratively with new multi-academy trust formed by Langley Park Girls, Hawes Down junior school and Hawes Down infant school. Mr Parsons is a firm believer in the benefits of through schools, enabling a seamless curriculum, with benefits for teachers as well as pupils, enabling them to understand more closely the skills pupils arrive with. The trust has permission for the 'pre-opening phase' of a new primary school, due to open in September 2016.

Pastoral care and discipline: School rules are traditional – no earrings for boys. Pupils need a cycling proficiency certificate to bring a bicycle to school. Respect, calm and litter picking mandatory. Mobile phones are allowed for sixth formers, but must be handed in lower down the school. The head says that exclusion figures are 'very, very low' and that 98 per cent of parents recently surveyed were very happy with the pastoral care and discipline at the school.

Form tutors are the linchpin of pastoral care. Several parents mentioned talking to staff on behalf of their child, but also reported problems being swiftly dealt with to their satisfaction.

There is deliberately no separate sixth form building, so that the younger years have role models around the school. The appointment of prefects by the head is like a mini job application – those putting themselves forward must each gather four or five recommendations from teachers.

Some thought might be given to the external sixth form candidates, who seem forever after to go by the unfortunate label of 'externals'. Our two tour guides both bore the label resolutely, but thought it unlikely their fellow externals, or indeed girls, would ever be school captain.

Pupils and parents: Parents as well as pupils are proud to belong to the school. We're told 'the term Langley Boy is one that is highly regarded and proudly stated.'

One parent explained: 'The school attracts gifted boys and later girls for the sixth form, who work in an educational environment that expects a lot of them. This high expectation draws parents that would normally be looking at independent schools.'

By far the majority of pupils are white British, with other white, black Caribbean and black African larger ethnic groups. The head describes his pupils as: 'confident, hard-working, proud of their school, articulate, supportive and active.'

Who will thrive here? Clearly the sporty, arty and academic, but parents add: a child who is 'well mannered, respectful, takes pride in their school's reputation, is a team player and competitive'; 'this school will allow your child to achieve their academic dreams and to bring out talents they never knew they had.' We'd only add the school seems to support and nurture ambitions and interests wherever they lie.

Communication with parents has been a weak spot and parents still shared a few niggles with us, but the head cites recent surveys of parental satisfaction.

Entrance: There are 210 places annually at 11+. With applications at just under three to one, chances of getting in could be far worse, but you will need to live within one mile of the school. Local estate agents say many move nearby simply for the school, creating something of a squeeze on prices. There are 45 local feeder primaries including: Balgowan, Clare House, Hawes Down, Highfield, Marian Vian, Oaklodge, Pickhurst Junior and Unicorn.

It's far harder to get into the sixth form: most recently 850 candidates fought tooth and nail for 150 places. Girls from Langley Park Girls School next door are subject to the same admission criteria as others.

Exit: Over 80 per cent stay on to the sixth form, with those leaving mostly going on to do vocational qualifications. The same proportion then head to university, very slightly more girls than boys.

Most popular recent destinations were Portsmouth, Brighton, Sussex and Bournemouth, with 25 per cent of those taking university places heading to Russell Group destinations such as Birmingham and Southampton. One to Oxbridge in 2015.

Most popular subjects seem to be English, history, law, accountancy, engineering, physics and business with quite a few medically related, plus some budding pharmacists and psychologists. One lone actor, an aerospace engineer and a couple of architects.

Remarks: An exceptional example of comprehensive education with a sporting and artistic offer to match many an independent in smart new facilities. Easier to enter at 11+ (boys) than battle into the sixth form with increased competition from all around including girls.

Langley Park School for Girls

Hawksbrook Lane, Beckenham, Kent BR3 3BE

State • Pupils: 1,690 • Ages: 11–18 • Sixth form pupils: 500 (20 boys)

Tel: 020 8663 4199

Email: info@lpgs.bromley.sch.uk
Website: www.lpgs.bromley.sch.uk

6

Headteacher: Since 2011, Dr Anne Hudson, MA BA PGCE PhD, (50s). Though local – lives in nearby Beckenham with husband Stuart, a retired teacher (no children) hence appeal of current job – this is her first professional move into suburbia. Was previously head of Central Foundation Girls' School in Tower Hamlets, her fifth inner-city comprehensive, the other four co-ed and all universally on the up, with one (Dunraven School in Lambeth, where she was deputy head) teetering on cusp of outstanding inspection score.

Precise (always a pleasure to encounter 'syllabi' in briefing notes), energetic (a keen cyclist who misses 'therapeutic' 24-mile round trip commute to last school) and articulate (diction so crisp you could serve it with dips at a cocktail party), she's

notable for a jaw-dropping back story that's more Cry the Beloved Country than Être et Avoir.

Raised in Southern Africa, put aside early dreams of being a teacher when was sent to boarding school in 1970s segregated Zimbabwe – 'if we went to town, my best friend and I weren't allowed to sit at the same table' – and was confounded by 'boring history lessons' about Tudor and Stuart goings-on in distant England while civil war, raging on doorstep, was completely ignored. After dropping out of English and French degree at University of Cape Town, signed up for 'voluntary work' with Namibian resistance until deported to UK by South African-controlled government. You hope for tales of derring-do with bandolier over shoulder and grenade clenched between teeth but 'not heroic,' she insists, as 'they deported lots of bishops too.'

While working at Namibians' London HQ by day, took BA in economics by night followed by an MA in history and, teaching aspirations rekindled, a PGCE at Institute of Education (and has since been awarded a PhD in education by Leeds University). Started career as history teacher in Enfield with 'rusty' French on the side, criss-crossing London's eastern reaches to take up ever more senior posts. Spent seven years as assistant head at Deptford Green School in Lewisham, famed for transformation from near write-off to teacher's pet under headship of establishment darling Sir Keith Ajegbo, who also nudged Dr Hudson into studying for a doctorate ('an accident,' she says modestly) after she had accumulated a thesis's worth of raw data on whether citizenship can be a whole-school specialism. (Apparently it can.)

Teaches some PSHE and GCSE history lessons and is a highly visible and hands on presence – 'my sister saw her clearing rubbish round the garden,' said awed year 7 girl. Parents, who don't know her that well, equally don't see this as a problem. She gives out direct email address and is a reliable presence at school events – 'walks round saying "hello" at parents' evening,' says year 7 mother.

Desire for headship born not so much from personal ambition as clear-sighted grasp of its benefits – 'I could see that having power in the school could help you shape things.' Style is going down a storm with the pupils, who without exception cite reinstatement of own clothes day, banned for five years after bullying incident, as biggest achievement to date (Dr Hudson, you'd imagine, would hope for a legacy with a little more gravitas). Many (unprompted) praised her cheerful, high-profile presence round school. 'I've spoken to Dr Hudson

at least three times,' marvelled year 11 girl. 'I didn't talk to the old head once.' 'She's far more relaxed,' confirmed a parent.

Academic matters: The reason parents send their daughters here. 'It was the academic side that appealed,' said one, who moved house specifically to secure a place. Plenty to shout about, too, with GCSE 5+ A*-C pass rate including English and maths 83 per cent in 2015 (head's publicly declared goal is five good GCSE passes for all by 2020) and 40 per cent A*/A grades – particularly high percentages in single subject GCSE sciences and fast track languages, both reserved for most able.

Style is going down a storm with the pupils, who without exception cite reinstatement of own clothes day as biggest achievement to date

Good news continues in sixth form. While new vocational courses are being added to roster that currently includes business, travel, health and social care with aim of broadening appeal (almost the only 'could do better' in otherwise glowing inspection report), the emphasis, says head emphatically, is unapologetically skewed 'towards the more able students'. Results – 42 per cent A*/B grades in 2015.

Success doesn't, however, come at expense of the 200 or so pupils with special needs, many speech and language related (about 20 have statements). Good-sized and centre stage learning support unit, home to two key workers under direction of deputy head with SEN background, is widely appreciated as a whole school safety valve offering help for anyone under pressure.

Add enthusiastic teachers, including one working her socks off to spark discussion on ethics of designer babies amongst slightly somnolent GCSE biology class, and the technology head extolling the wonders of the computer programmed laser saw that cuts anything (Goldfinger would be envious, though less fussed by its ability to add detailed floral motifs) and it sounds like roses all the way.

Well, up to a point, Lord Copper. There's the odd wilting bloom. Success in some small but perfectly formed subjects (GCSE music, growing fast, consistently secures 100 per cent Bs or higher) is balanced by occasional whole-subject wobble (applied science a case in point). And despite GCSE success in languages, one of school specialisms (others are technology and sport) numbers die away post-16, with totals for German, French and Spanish scarcely into double figures (reflection, sadly, of national malaise). It's not for want of trying, what with Mandarin and Latin both available as popular lunchtime and after-school clubs, and the 150 EAL students, many bilingual, able to take community languages as additional GCSE. Currently, advanced linguists who take French GCSE early follow a slightly waffly culture-related programme with some cake-making but little academic bite in year 11. Head's plan to move them on to AS level work may help though, judging by less than encouraging results in other schools, it may not.

Pupils from year 9 onwards lend a hand at local primaries while year 12s, who have Wednesday afternoons free, can fill them with voluntary work, part of thriving D of E programme

Then there's the little matter of boys' school next door which clocks near identical GCSE results to its neighbour – 'girls should do at least six per cent better,' says Dr Hudson – and is also seen as the place to go for sixth form sciences. Resulting mini brain drain especially in chemistry and physics is cause for concern but could soon be reversed with appointment of whizzy new head of science who comes with tried and tested Pied Piper-like A level recruitment skills. Shouldn't be rocket science – sixth formers who ignore hype and stay on for science are glad they did. 'Class sizes are very big in the boys' school – I knew the school and the teachers and the course seems to suit me,' said one.

Head wants everyone, including staff, to up their game, crunching primary school data so hard you can almost hear it squeak in effort to identify budding talent from arrival in year 7 and laying down the law with clear minimum academic goals for pupils (with hope, of course, that these will be routinely exceeded). 'Boys are often deluded about their own potential, whereas girls tend to underestimate themselves,' says head, crisply. If she has her way, however, certainly won't be the case for much longer.

Games, options, the arts: Sport highly rated. 'Amazing,' says one pupil. Lots to do and places to do it in – large if slightly sombre sports hall and gym inside and five tennis courts and an all-weather pitch in addition to five acres of green space outside. Old Girls include Ellen Gandy, 2012 Olympic 100m butterfly finalist, and with current pupils making literal waves in diving and even water polo, and figuratively in squash, could be first of many.

Favours the competitive (lots of wins for netball and hockey squads in local championships) so 'you need to push yourself,' says parent. Theoretically, however, something for everyone and if the timetabled sport doesn't do it for you there's probably a club that will, from yoga to fencing. 'They really shine. You name it and they'll have it,' says pupil.

Robust though sport is, tends to be swamped by performing arts which have pirouetted across website and ousted match results from shared online notice board, replacing them with close-ups of recent and seemingly non-stop round of acclaimed productions. Frequent high-quality, whole-school collaborations between dance, drama and music include large cast versions of Annie and Alice in Wonderland, which have gone down a storm, while with around 300 students learning instruments, there's a decent range of ensembles, too, including 50-strong jazz orchestra which recently toured China.

Mini BRIT academy feel never stronger than with dance: tap and street offered, but classical ballet a particular strength, masterminded (and frequently choreographed) by three dance teachers whose remit covers everything from hit versions of Twilight and Beauty and the Beast to GCSE, A level and, coming soon, BTec courses complete with glamorous overseas revision courses, all apparently done without drawing breath. Indeed, a new dance studio was recently opened by Deborah Bull of King's College London. Motto, unsurprisingly, is 'anyone can dance,' though, as sixth form boys as yet unconvinced, male performers are currently imported from next door.

In addition to 'look at me' events, lots of looking after others, with pupils from year 9 onwards lending a hand at local primaries while year 12s, who have Wednesday afternoons free thanks to miracle of timetable coordination, can opt to fill them with voluntary work, often as part of thriving D of E programme, open to all though you'll only get the go ahead if you're doing 'what your predicted grades say you should be,' said one. You can't keep staff away either: science teacher – a 'bundle of energy,' says head – awarded MBE for educational work in community.

Background and atmosphere: In its 90-year history (last 50 on current leafy site), school has had several Time Lord-like incarnations, beginning as a county girls' school, becoming a grammar in 1945, a comprehensive in the 1970s and achieving the full collector's set with academy status in 2011. Connections with the past haven't been sloughed off, however, with original society for Old Girls (known as Adremians) still going strong. There's also traditional, ultra-smart uniform much cooed over by outsiders, less so by current parents faced with dry-clean-only blue piped blazer and hard-to-press pleated tartan skirt. 'I get granny to iron it,' confesses one.

School design, mid-20th century standard issue, features two-storey main building with separate blocks for drama/sport, science (11 perfectly decent labs), sixth form and technology (newest and nicest of the lot with six well-equipped workshops), together roughly framing three sides of large and

picnic table studded if slightly bleak courtyard (the main R&R outside area until student council secured leave to use 'head's own garden', a green and pleasant space round the corner). Effect is pleasant and unintimidating. New girls get maps and are quickly at home – in some schools you feel satellite tracking and emergency rations wouldn't come amiss.

Everyone now very nice about multi-million pound newly rebuilt boys' school (similar name, no relation). Wasn't always thus. Dr Hudson's predecessor fought plans all the way to Supreme Court and won what turned out to be pyrrhic victory as second application was nodded through shortly afterwards. Bridges now mended, cordial relationships re-established and girls offered use of new facilities, notably the hear-every-bat-squeak acoustically advanced auditorium – 'when boys aren't using it,' says head, without apparent irony. Big brother (though a benevolent one) rules.

Make do and mend philosophy only goes so far, however. An additional floor on top of sixth form building (including café and social facilities) has just opened, likewise a new dance studio. Head has planning permission for new music block.

Surprisingly little sense of overcrowding, and there's even a whole school assembly once a term or thereabouts – though 'if it were all boys, there would be accidents,' says head. (One pupil confessed to eating outside 'even when it's raining' just to get away from it all). Children seem to move in mysterious ways (possibly by converting themselves to compressed data format at busy times, more likely by learning to keep elbows in when using corridors). It's particularly noticeable at break, when what should be a scrum for the food and drink somehow isn't.

Something for everyone and if the timetabled sport doesn't do it for you there's probably a club that will, from yoga to fencing. 'You name it and they'll have it'

Mood is welcoming, helped by delightful, off-beat art displays (ceramic artichokes on sticks, anyone?) partial door 'n' floor refurbishment (light wood/portholes combo gives vaguely Nordic/nautical feel depending on preference), and homely areas including large, book-lined library, well used in and out of school hours, which hosts termly themed parties complete with cakes to keep reading top of mind when 'other things step in,' says librarian, diplomatically.

Pastoral care and discipline: Four houses; Lambda (yellow), Kappa (blue), Sigma (red), and Gamma (green) – fortunately no Brave New World Epsilon – as much an admin tool as a motivational one, used for imposing a little organisational clarity on eight-form entry. It's two forms to a house (block booking, no arguments) and little sense of feverish competition 'except on sports day,' say girls.

Friendship issues inevitably the biggest problem cited by parents, especially lower down the school. 'They look so grown up,' says worried mother who mentions daughter's need to apply defensive make-up following pressure to fit in.

If there is a problem, overwhelming pupil consensus is that there's always somebody to talk to – 'even the canteen people are friendly,' says one. Staff are often very popular, with tears on departure, though 'a few scare me, and I'm the parent,' said one mother.

Relationships improve the further up the school you go. 'Students do have problems with teachers – no school's perfect but mostly they're great and there if you want them,' added another. Discipline, though firm, is considered: if there's out of character bad behaviour, staff will 'try to find out where you're coming from first,' said year 11 pupil, with exclusion very much a last resort and help provided, wherever possible, in situ.

Officially, form tutors are first point of contact, often staying with same group for several years.

Parents praise ease of communication – teachers are listed in pupil planners and there are individual email addresses for all, up to and including head. 'If you expect other members of staff to give out their contact details you should be willing to do the same thing,' she says.

Highly effective school council, a model of its kind, 'lets teachers know what students are thinking, rather than what they assume they are,' said pupil, and gets things done – broken soap dispenser that had languished for weeks in one of toilets was 'fixed within days' after complaints. It's helped by involvement of sympathetic teacher who 'is on our side but is honest and will say if we're asking for outrageous things.' Youngest girls have as much of a voice as senior pupils and an equal chance of being chosen from full meeting to present ideas to head. 'You even hear what sixth form are doing,' says one.

Pupils and parents: Tight catchment area means many new pupils arrive with others they know. While behaviour is 'fairly standard for teenagers these days; you stop for 10 minutes to let them cross and nobody says thank you,' harrumphs slightly gloomy local, her experience seems exception rather than rule: on morning of our visit no sign of anything other than almost universal good manners. Lots of hands raised in salute to waiting cars as girls (boys, too – a symphony in blue and burgundy respectively) arrived in their hundreds.

In school, too, doors are routinely held open and there's general sense of courtesy towards others (helped, quite possibly, by numbers of teachers in corridors, though a benevolent rather than sentry-like presence).

Parents are necessarily local, many the hard-working exemplars praised by politicians of every hue. As a fair percentage commute to jobs in London, don't necessarily see much of each other, although with quite a few events (first class fireworks display, for example) 'opportunities to socialise are there if you want them,' said one.

Entrance: Large school, tiny catchment area (has shrunk to under a mile before now though normally hovers just over). Means that despite size of intake (240 places in year 7) it's routinely oversubscribed and there's always a waiting list.

Pupils come from nine or so local primaries (Oak Lodge, Marian Vian, Highfield Junior, Pickhurst, Unicorn, Balgowan, Clare House, Hawes Down and St Marys Catholic Primary) though feeders in name only as attendance is no guarantee of place and distance (barring standard priority given to looked after children) is king.

Estate agents testify to school's popularity. Parents vote with their square feet. 'We specifically moved to get a place,' says one (though other more dubious practices aren't unknown either).

Three-quarters stay into sixth form, again oversubscribed (minimum of 10 places available to external candidates, usually more in practice) and, like majority of local schools, co-educational, though boys so thin on the ground (around 20 a year) that spotting them not unlike real life version of 'Where's Wally?'

A level places dependent on securing minimum of seven GCSE passes (about 50 turned away at application stage) with minimum B grades in four including chosen AS/A level subjects, A*/As preferred for toughies like chemistry and teacher recommendations for languages. Anyone opting for performing arts will also need to pass audition.

Exit: A third or so who leave post-GCSE stay close, some moving to boys' school next door (with a few, who don't care for the size, moving back) while a very few opt for selective grammars like St Olave's and Newstead Wood or independent schools like Trinity School in neighbouring Croydon. A few head off to larger colleges to study work-related courses, though head keen to slow exodus of less academic – should have 'right to continue here even if not high flyers,' she feels.

No compromises when it comes to onwards academic journey. Almost all make it into higher education, nearly all first or second choice universities with Bristol, Leeds, Warwick, Southampton 'all popular,' says head of sixth form, and the most able encouraged to try for Oxbridge – normally a couple of places each year and the same again for medicine. Law, business and administration, biological sciences and creative arts and design (including music and drama) head the list of subject choices, with social services, maths and English not far behind and a light dusting of languages and engineering.

Brand new careers academy 'will provide specific advice and guidance backed up with seminars, careers days, contact with employers and practice at interviews and skills'. School 'has been commended for its outstanding preparation of UCAS applications.'

Remarks: Short on square feet but, remarkably, feels as if has enough breathing space for everyone, helped by honest, intelligent leadership, enthusiastic staff and pupils who seem happy to be here and for the most part do well. A real breath of fresh air.

Newstead Wood School

Avebury Road, Orpington, Kent BR6 9SA

State • Pupils: 1,049 • Ages: 11–18 • Sixth form pupils: 340 (41 boys)

Tel: 01689 853626

Email: office@newsteadwood.bromley.sch.uk
Website: www.newsteadwood.bromley.sch.uk

Head: Since April 2014, Alison Ross BA MA AdDip Ed, who took charge when previous head Liz Allen stood down in December 2013. She has worked in a range of schools and previously headed a girls' grammar in Lincolnshire for 15 years and, briefly, an academy in Peterborough.

Academic matters: Not so much an academic hothouse as the sort of place where if you don't work reasonably hard you're the odd one out. School places great emphasis on staff and pupils 'co-constructing' the learning experience and on staff leadership and development – they should be critical questioners and facilitate, rather than direct, learning. An active school parliament and students lead the review and revision of the school's mission statement. In addition to termly reports and annual parent teacher meetings, an academic tutoring day each term includes individual interviews to discuss achievements and set targets for improving learning.

Building learning and thinking skills starts early. Year 7 Journeys of a Lifetime programme encourages pupils to articulate how they learn and where they need to focus and is allied to lots of opportunities to expand and get beneath curriculum subjects. Further up the school, the engineering diploma (years 10-13), IB and extended project in the sixth form are designed to promote independent study and breadth of learning. Exam results are consistently impressive, with popular subjects being biology, chemistry, maths, English lit and psychology. In 2015, 81 per cent A*/A grades at GCSE. A level results no less creditable: 80 per cent A*-B grades and 46 per cent A*/A grades. Average IB point score of 35.

Strong enrichment programme – the usual timetable is effectively suspended for three weeks each year. Specialist engineering and languages status provides opportunities to extend the scope of study (eg engineering diploma and Mandarin Chinese and Japanese from year 8). Also a designated gifted and talented lead school – these pupils aren't noticeably singled out for special treatment but staff ensure lots to stimulate and push them. Dyspraxic and dyslexic pupils' coping strategies often uncovered during GCSEs. Individual education plans then agreed between pupils, parents and staff to overcome any difficulties.

Games, options, the arts: 'Whatever they do, they do well,' says one parent and the evidence seems to support this. Good performances in hockey, netball and gymnastics and, though the school has no pool, it tops the results tables in national and county swimming events. Older girls help the youngsters.

The year 7 and 8 vocal ensemble was conceived and is run by sixth formers, one of several choirs and orchestras which perform regularly. Music is a real strength and taken seriously and at tempo here (better make sure you rehearse!) Vox CC, its senior choir, has performed at the Royal Albert Hall and in Prague. Drama is popular; 20+ student societies in anything from debating, politics, history, the environment, medicine to law, all run by year 12 pupils. Leadership and participation is very much what this school is all about and it's rare to find a sixth former who doesn't voluntarily take on extra responsibilities. For others, too, judging by the somewhat overwhelming stream of calendar reminders on the electronic board in reception, little excuse to be idle. Lots of after-school and lunchtime activities, as well as positions as sports ambassadors, Arkwright scholars to promote engineering in schools, language teaching in local primary schools, maths and debating competitions, Dragon's Den workshops and charity events – plenty going on.

Background and atmosphere: Set in a quiet residential area, has wonderful views across the playing fields towards the Downs, but the school buildings, though quite spacious, are unremarkable and jumbled – the 1950s, when it was established, not perhaps the best architectural era. Inside, the walls are brightened with artwork and a lick of paint from the girls over the holidays. Additions and upgrades include new suite of maths rooms and sixth form block, improvements to staff areas and lab refurbishment. Already has wonderful indoor tennis courts open to the public.

Pastoral care and discipline: Ongoing and slightly half-hearted battles regarding sixth form dress code but in the school's view it's churlish to make too big a fuss when most girls behave and perform well. In an all-female environment they are generally not interested in acting beyond their years and the school encourages them to assess for themselves what's appropriate in different circumstances.

Travel buddy scheme combines environmental targets to reduce car use with accompanying year 7 pupils on public transport for their first weeks

More commonly issues arise through poor organisation or conflicting priorities, typical amongst bright, enthusiastic pupils.

As long as you are willing to work with the school, issues are normally swiftly resolved in liaison with staff, the emphasis being very much on motivation rather than chastisement. Parents cite examples of a generally good response to concerns voiced, whether individual (friendship) or more general (chain emails). The school is also alert to mixed expectations relating to academic and home life. In such cases, a counsellor and family worker are available to provide guidance and support. A strong PSHE programme, which, eg, incorporates financial literacy, in which pupils can gain accreditation. Careers support very good with lots of individual advice, a calendar of related events, a well-stocked library and lots of exposure to different areas of work through placements and contact with professionals.

Occasional incidents of bullying are addressed, with the girls themselves tending to side with the victim. Informal vertical contact is encouraged through extracurricular clubs and older pupils acting as mentors. The travel buddy scheme is a nice example, combining as it does environmental targets to reduce car use with accompanying year 7 pupils on public transport for their first few weeks. Occasionally girls are to be seen eating and smoking outside the school grounds, but few complaints from local businesses and residents, who seem grateful to have such a well-thought of school in their midst – 'we'd all like our kids to go there'.

Pupils and parents: Says one parent, 'If they're really not up to and up for it, they won't enjoy it' – ie you need to be self-motivated rather than coached to get here. From a range of socio-economic and ethnic backgrounds. 'They stand out for being bright, self-confident and just getting on with it,' says one business regularly offering work experience to pupils from local schools. PA is active and effective, holding a variety of social and fundraising events over the year, as well as organising regular fairs through its careers sub-committee. Notable former pupils include Christine Hancock, Emma Johnson (clarinettist who came back to hold a masterclass at the school), Josie Long and Kim Medcalf.

Entrance: Most from local state primary schools. For year 7, entrance tests in verbal and non-verbal reasoning in November. Standards high, but the test experience 'more friendly' than for other local schools. Around 650-700 applications for 130 places. When, very occasionally, places come available further up the school, those on the waiting list are invited to take an age-appropriate test and the highest scorers offered a place. Additional places are available for sixth form entry – including boys. A minimum of six GCSE grades A*-C with A* or A in the subjects for further study needed.

Exit: Those entering at 11 are expected to stay the course and only a few leave at 16, mostly to pursue specialist studies, eg performing arts or media studies. In 2015, nine to Oxbridge.

Other popular destinations are London, Leeds, Nottingham, Bristol, Birmingham, Exeter, York and Durham as well as art, drama, music, veterinary and medical colleges.

Money matters: Dedicated and enthusiastic PTA raises £30,000 to £50,000 annually, which funds the artists in residence each year and extra teaching resources. A covenant scheme and continuous fundraising events and activities to support the ongoing developments. Girls raise money for charities during house charity week.

Remarks: Capable and committed girls do really well here, most setting out on their future studies and careers well-qualified and equipped for the challenges ahead.

Old Palace of John Whitgift Preparatory School

Linked school: Old Palace of John Whitgift School, 355

2, Melville Avenue, South Croydon, Surrey CR2 7YN

Independent · Pupils: 150 (150 in nursery) · Ages: 3 m–10 · C of E · Fees: up to £10,383 pa

Tel: 020 8686 7347

Email: schooloffice@oldpalace.croydon.sch.uk
Website: www.oldpalace.croydon.sch.uk

14

Head of Preparatory: Since September 2015, Tim Horton, who has 23 years' experience of teaching in the independent sector. Previously at The Hall, Hampstead but has also held posts at Abbots Bromley School and Birkdale School, Sheffield. He graduated from Jesus College Cambridge. Married with four children. Interests include cricket, reading and cooking.

Head of nursery is Miss Jacqui Hines, NNEB (40s), two teenage girls, one a gold-medal gymnast. Formal title, day care manager. Feisty, fast-talking with supportive, calm deputy – 'I run around like a loon, she's yin to my yang' – and runs a tight-knit team of 35 full and part-timers. Started as second in command, promoted to current post three months in.

Can't imagine doing anything else. 'Children are so lovely and innocent and speak their mind. Whatever you're pouring into them, you're shaping their lives.'

Entrance: First come, first served into often over-subscribed reception, with many girls moving up from separate and flourishing Old Palace co-ed nursery located on the far side of school playing field, and which expanded three years ago to offer full child care from three months upwards. Individual age and development determines speed of progression through well-equipped baby, toddler, kinder, transition and finally pre-school rooms, with a gradual induction into school ways (school tracksuit is worn by the oldest, for example).

A fair few newcomers join the prep in other years and are quickly absorbed, with firm friendships quickly established, say pupils. Assessments, from reception onwards, are on the rigorous side,

Plenty to gladden the heart – a library with splendid tables fringed with solid, comfortable chairs (each one donated by a former grateful pupil some 60 years ago)

including tests in English, maths and reasoning as well as observation of their social interaction. Parents are also asked how they will support their daughter (some don't, hence early flagging up).

There's a fairly intense focus on exam preparation all through, intensifying in the run up to 11 plus (school runs workshops on the topic, open to pupils elsewhere). Aim is for year 5s to be working a year ahead with entrance exam success the acid test – school doesn't take Sats.

Nursery open 51 weeks of the year, highly in demand and with waiting lists to match (though most are eventually accommodated). For the baby room, early registration essential. 'We get women phoning us the day the baby's born.' No formal entrance tests though mobility is pre-requisite for toddler room (most start aged 12 to 15 months); freedom from nappies or close for kinder room (around 2). Followed by transition room, while a fair few join in final pre-school year, the biggest group with 40 places and the only one with a minimum attendance requirement of three days a week (Tuesdays to Thursdays are the most popular). Elsewhere, it's down to parental needs (many work) and availability. Some children will do full 7.30am to 6pm days from the start, others attend just a few mornings or afternoons a week.

Exit: Nearly 90 per cent progress to the senior school, often with scholarships. NB Year 6 is part of the senior school. Vast majority of leavers do so for 'nice' reasons, securing places at one of the highly desirable local grammars (Wallington High School and Newstead Woods head the list). A few others are helped to the realisation that senior school is not for them, 'though we would never ask anyone to leave,' says school. Perhaps not, though one parent was fairly devastated to be told bluntly by another member of staff during a meeting that her child was 'unlikely' to make the senior school (though this was followed by some fairly nifty backtracking).

For girls at the nursery, assumption (by parents and school) is that they'll go on into Old Palace reception. Though their passage there isn't automatic (there's an assessment), in practice 'all our girls get places,' says head of nursery. Boys tend to stay in independent sector, with Cumnor House and Elmhurst the most popular destinations, Park Hill Infants for those going on to state schools.

Remarks: Originally just across the road from the senior school, prep school was re-homed on Croham Hurst's leafy south Croydon site, just a short tram ride away.

Year 6s stayed behind in central Croydon as 'baby seniors', a move that brings structure into line with Trinity and Whitgift, the other two schools (both for boys) in the Whitgift Foundation's educational trio.

With a whole senior school to themselves, the 160 reception to year 5 pupils have oodles of space to play with and in, and all the trimmings, including vast spaces for DT and ICT. The separate nursery takes children from 3 months and is housed in its own building on the far side of the playing field.

Year 5s, as top dogs, acquire the trappings of seniority a year early. All can be prefects and have their own centre, located opposite reception classes 'so you see how our school goes round in circles,' says typically bright, eloquent and eager-to-please pupil. The most coveted perk, however, is sitting on benches rather than joining the hoi polloi on the floor for daily assembly, one of the many small formalities which, like grace said at the end of every meal, add a pleasantly traditional punctuation to the school day.

The range of architectural styles allows you to channel Malory Towers, complete with enticing attic rooms one moment, up to the minute modernity the next. Fresh-looking, white-walled dining hall with jolly pictures adding a splash of colour is particularly nice. Heart of the original building, facing on to the Croham Road, is Small Hall, an unromantic title for what's effectively a mini-mausoleum to Croham Hurst's founders – galleried, beamed and stuffed to the gunnels with ancient honour boards and a sketch of the second Croham head, Theodora E Clark, looking wistfully into the middle distance. Visitors of a gothic disposition could have a ball.

Plenty to gladden the heart – a library with splendid tables fringed with solid, comfortable chairs (each one donated by a former grateful pupil some 60 years ago) that should entice the most reluctant of readers (and there are a few). Palatial size creates a few technical difficulties. All roads tend to lead to back of the school, a sort of nesting place for the many fire escapes, while enthusiastic guides initially struggle to find any other pupils, making school's assertion that 'one of the few things you'll see is teachers at standing at the front and just spouting,' literally true, if not quite in the sense intended.

Parents have had their ups and downs with staff here and in senior school, not helped by uncertainty caused by some (expected) post-merger redundancies. Once found, however, lessons here don't disappoint, with a jolly English teacher surrounded by chatty, cheerful year 5s attempting a modern take on John Keats' Ode to Autumn.

Technical glitch resulting in a temporary computer failure could have been the reason for all the smiles and interaction. Though you hope not, slight sense of apology when noise reached a smidge over conversational levels did suggest otherwise.

Would parents mind if teachers' voices remained the dominant sound? Debatable. There's good, solid curriculum, taught in classes of around 15, with pretty much everything for all, French from reception and a modern foreign languages 'experience' designed to fill a few cultural gaps on the way. Much is made of use of topics to link subjects with a unified theme, as well as learning for life (reasoning and evaluation as well as fact collection, carried on into seniors).

For most parents, preparatory is the key word, exam success its most obvious manifestation and a place either at the senior school or one of the local grammars the desired goal. Major focus, consequently, is on doing well. 'It is an academic school,' confirms a mother. 'They've never tried to hide it.' Study the prospectus, with plentiful references to academic excellence and you can't say you haven't been warned.

Most coveted reward for success is a highly desirable celebration tea with head. It's within everyone's reach, school insists, based on the completion of 10 extension tasks designed to recognise 'all girls who rise to a challenge and are putting in lots of effort.' Not all parents are convinced. 'My daughter said "I'll never go to one of those tea parties, will I?"' says one.

Success-driven outlook could perhaps account for what some parents see as slight ambiguity towards learning needs. Though mild difficulties, headed by dyslexia, are officially something the school takes in its stride (even offering in-house consultancy), parents report mixed messages, in particular when it comes to all-important, high pressure exams. School seems to be trying harder to get it right.

Everyone plays in a netball or rounders team 'even if you're useless'. Big on inclusivity, low on wins. 'I like it but we always lose,' says one pupil resignedly

Outside lessons, masses going on. Clubs are blossoming, from sewing to ballet, even including Japanese as a one-year wonder. Activities start young and increase fast – begins and ends with Indian Dance for reception but by year 1, there's a choice of seven. Popular lunchtime Christian Union club (Little Wigs) attracts a range of different faiths and delivers fun, un-preachy messages – on day of visit, pupils were busily decorating their faces with sticky spots as the prelude to a discussion about leprosy. Teacher in charge, enjoying it as much as pupils, was unfussed about missing lunch break. 'Who would miss the chance to do this?' she asked with evident sincerity.

Sport comes with different aspirations. Super facilities include use of senior school swimming pool and their own large playing field 'for best', say girls, featuring splendid coronation oak planted in 1953, and stretching away across to the nursery wing (their gym doubles as prep school dance studio). Miniature pavilion, aching to be used for classic mid-match teas, currently houses spare minibus seats.

Lots to do – girls were particularly keen on weekly lunchtime table-tennis session. Everyone plays in a netball or rounders team 'even if you're useless'. Big on inclusivity, low on wins. 'I like it but we always lose,' says one pupil resignedly. However, school says there are now more fixtures – and successes.

Reception pupils have a nicely kitted out separate play area as a gentle introduction to the rough and tumble of 'big' school, with a soft surface, sheltered spot for wet weather play and even a tiny adventure playground, grassed area with tree and three side-by-side Wendy houses, a mini estate in the making.

Music also flourishes, with a good range of free taster sessions in year 3 and many learning instruments, excellent facilities (a big, terraced room, piled high with xylophones and five practice rooms dotted round the place) and a decent range of groups, instrumental and vocal, headed by the audition-only Junior Polyphonic, which performs with seniors in Croydon Minster (high on parental frisson-factor).

As to the future? Mood in school is upbeat. One parent, also a teacher, praises 'careful engineering' that helped girls to feel part of a 'new and evolving thing'. Though most parents seem minded to agree, a few, particularly those whose offspring are still at subsonic speed compared with high flyers, or need a bit more support, view the Darwinian model with some reservations.

Nursery occupies former Croham Hurst Junior School, acquired in 2008 by the Whitgift Foundation, with former senior school on the other side of the playing field now housing Old Palace Prep. While 'we never used to feel part of the Old Palace structure', the nursery has now, under senior school headship of Mrs Jewell, been brought fully into the fold, getting the full corporate branding to the point where prospective parents, confused by location, occasionally get lost en route.

Though exterior gives the impression of rolling square feet upwards and outwards, it's a slight Tardis in reverse as top two floors are unoccupied and will remain so, if Miss Hines has her way. While success of nursery, which has grown from 26 to 104 in just three years, has Old Palace management gleefully rubbing hands at thoughts of future money-making potential, she is adamant that predominantly single floor layout and instant access to outdoors space is a non-negotiable.

Even the pre-school children, the only ones based on the first rather than ground floor, take turns to spend full days in recently built outdoor classroom so they can have free access to real if diddy tree for climbing (staff stand underneath just in case) and other outdoor highlights including fence strung with assortment of pots, pans and hooters, though high-decibel wind up fire bell acquired at a car boot sale by bargain hunting deputy has, unfortunately, gone missing. (Silence-loving local residents are chief suspects). Veg is enthusiastically grown, recently scooping three prizes in local produce show.

Head of nursery is particularly keen on directed play and staff are encouraged to watch out for and gently discourage aimless wandering: one pupil was enthusiastically helping to rake up leaves, the rest seemed happily occupied.

Lots to do inside, too (we loved the small staircase/ramp that permits endless up and down games – Escher minus the impossibility) and attention to detail is jaw-dropping. Every parent is presented with a daily record of child's achievements complete with photograph, while there are regular diplomatically phrased parenting tips covering everything from reading to cookery.

There's an equally thorough approach to everything from stopping pupils' work being over-prettified by staff ('if they draw a dog with three legs, that's what we'll display,') to discipline. With no refuge in naughty steps (or indeed, use of the word 'naughty' which is banned) anyone being unkind is talked to about their behaviour and the need for 'kind hands' repeated ad nauseam until the message gets through (time-consuming but effective, say staff).

No chocolate or crisps (and of course no nuts) rules firmly enforced with children bringing in fruit on birthdays, rather than cakes or sweets. School chef rustles up appetising breakfasts, lunches and dinners, all included in the fees, catering with aplomb for every dietary requirement, with meals served to older children in pocket-sized, delightful dining hall and to babies and toddlers in their own rooms.

Staffing is thoughtfully planned, with at least one experienced mum 'who has seen everything'

in each of the bright, light and appealing rooms as instant source of wit and wisdom. Once in place, each room tends to keep the same staff group – children and parents appreciate continuity. Currently just one man on the team (hugely popular with all) though diversity is the name of the game elsewhere, with staff (like pupils) spanning vast range of backgrounds and cultures. Huge range of activities and events makes the most of this, from songs and counting in Italian to a recent visit by Rastamouse.

For pre-school group, ICT room, whiteboards, (optional) homework and uniform (trackies and sweatshirts) gently introduces some 'big school' elements. However, 'we're not a Montessori,' says head of nursery and parents expecting everyone to be reading by the time they leave are gently disabused of the notion: emphasis is on cultivating desire to learn so children are raring to go when they start in reception. Feedback suggests it works.

Old Palace of John Whitgift School

Linked school: Old Palace of John Whitgift Preparatory School, 351

Old Palace Road, Croydon, Surrey CR0 1AX

Tel: 020 8688 2027

Independent · Pupils: 510 · Ages: 10–18 · Sixth form pupils: 120 · Fees: up to £13,497 pa

Email: admissions@oldpalace.croydon.sch.uk
Website: www.oldpalace.croydon.sch.uk

15

Headmistress: Since 2011, Mrs Carol Jewell, MA PGCE DipEd NPQH CSBM (50s). Preceded by a brief spell as acting head and a longish one as deputy, a role she took on in 2005, having originally joined the school in 1997 as director of music. Before that, had assorted teaching roles in a 'tiny' London sixth form college, a Banbury comprehensive and then (after a spell in Wales) at top-rated St George's School back home in Edinburgh (she's Scottish born and bred) where she achieved first senior management role, before heading south again. Rambling cross-country route (even Virgin Trains would shun the franchise) was dictated by husband's burgeoning career, first in further education, then IT. 'I was always following on – it's one of those inevitable things,' she says, matter of factly.

Though a musician by training (at St Andrew's, where she studied with Cedric Thorpe Davie), a head by inclination and posture. Nobody with such an immaculately straight back could, you feel, be anything else. Melodious voice helps, and is also useful cover for wry wit that's probably kept largely under wraps in school hours.

Her office, formal but friendly, sets her off to a tee. Only drawback is its slightly thin, no doubt listed, walls that render conversations in adjoining office intermittently audible, though visitors distracted by outlook from study windows – delightful medieval garden with (in season) suitably onomatopoeic bees – may not notice. (General gorgeousness means ever-present danger of 'oohs' and 'ahs' overload).

She's out and about a lot, running regular surgeries for parents, taking weekly assemblies at the prep school

Her appointment followed a turbulent time for the school, which in 2008 acquired nearby Croham Hurst, a failing and less academic secondary. Parents on both sides greeted the news with fury.

Matters weren't helped by parental concerns about Dr Judith Harris, Mrs Jewell's predecessor.

Though well-intentioned, was considered to be dangerously progressive. 'The girls liked her but the discipline wasn't very good, or the finances,' said a mother.

Parent body, the Whitgift Foundation, issued masterpiece of corporate understatement, with Dr Harris agreeing that 'the situation presented her with a unique opportunity to pursue her career aspirations in education,' and exiting.

Enter Mrs Jewell, radiating copious amounts of 'all's well' reassurance and felt to be a safe pair of hands. Expressive ones, too, says an old girl, who admired conducting technique. Mrs Jewell is now definitely the Sir Simon Rattle of the show, in overall charge of the whole kit and caboodle, prep and nursery too, with section leaders responsible for the day-to-day nitty gritty. School is now, think most, back to the road more travelled, bounded by the familiar trappings and traditions that were its pre-Dr Harris hallmark. 'Very committed to the school,' says one. 'She's bringing up the standards, getting it back to what it was. It had lost its way.'

Liked by many. 'Gorgeous,' was one verdict. Her emphasis on courtesy and manners is just the sort of thing parents want to hear. Naturally good, you feel, at rising above problems, though not remote, thanks to a strong dose of gentle self-deprecation. 'As a Scot, I probably have some very traditional and quaint ideas,' she says. Parents, confounded by her suggestion for rustic game at school fair ('it wasn't turnip throwing, but it was close,' says one), wouldn't disagree. Phrasing, too, can be a charming blast from the past. 'We don't need to have a fit of the vapours because we're expected to put out cups and saucers,' she says, explaining importance of hands-on role.

She's out and about a lot, running regular surgeries for parents, taking weekly assemblies at the prep school ('She's joyful,' was one pupil's verdict). Thanks to marvels of rigorous Scottish four-year degree, also teaches Latin to pupils in years 7 and 9.

Though parents understand her need to stick to the official script, some feel she can over-adhere to the party line, giving impression that their concerns aren't being registered. One mother felt she was treated as 'a child (rather than) an intelligent professional'.

'I've always thought of her as a softish music mistress and very quiet, but I think behind the façade is a robust personality,' says an insider. With some aftershocks from the merger still to be negotiated, it's probably just as well.

Academic matters: The long-drawn out nature of the merger, with juniors and some staff settling into Croham Hurst site in South Croydon (everyone was previously at Old Palace) perhaps accounts for varying shades of parental opinion that cover the pantone range.

'A Marmite school,' said one old girl of her time here, and little seems to have changed, with everything from effusion ('I wanted the best education my daughter could get and I've been really pleased,' said one) to praise with reservations. 'I have mixed views,' said another.

Specific concerns include quality of maths teaching, felt to be variable, while loss of other talented specialists, notably art teacher, was also keenly felt. However, there's a sense that the worst is past. 'They've sorted the problems of transferring staff and children and it seems to have settled down now.'

Entertainment value (much appreciated in sea of tranquility) came in the form of lively A level biology lesson led by an amiable teacher and involving a great deal of yeast

Results bear this out, ranging from good to vintage: in 2015, A*/A grades in 53 per cent of GCSEs and 44 per cent of A levels, where 81 per cent were A*-B. Plenty of choice post-16, with a good range of two-year AS subjects (including dance, critical thinking, DT, philosophy and PE) plus normal A2 selection (nice to see both Latin and Greek offered).

Given aspirations of pupils and parents, you'd expect maths and sciences to lead the popularity pack, as indeed they do, with twice as many taking biology and chemistry as physics (and psychology). Predictably good showing for English literature (less rigorous English language not offered), French and RS, with history the aberration.

Good range of languages offered, modern and otherwise, with GCSE French (taught in sets, as is maths) way ahead on numbers, as is Latin. Some pupils also take Gujarati (Chinese and modern Greek pop up in other years) while Russian is available as a sixth form option.

Parents who, like particularly discriminating sundials, tend only to record the top results are, in general, satisfied with how their 'good, good girls who want to please their parents,' as one put it, are doing. Mention of occasional 'over-exuberant' behaviour in recent inspection report causes head to bristle slightly – it's not a picture she recognises and tour of school elicits absolutely no signs of roaring, gorging or indeed anything untoward.

Not that we were encouraged to get too close. One drama teacher was notably unkeen on our presence. Elsewhere, we were ushered away from classroom doors if heads started to turn, for fear (presumably) of providing an alternative source of interest. Entertainment value (much appreciated in sea of tranquility) came in the form of really lively A level biology lesson led by an amiable teacher and involving a great deal of yeast. 'Smell this!' said animated student, thrusting a steaming, strongly scented beaker in our direction.

The overwhelming impression, based on brief glimpses of heads bent conscientiously over books, was of orderly, efficient learning in classes that average around 20 up to GCSE, dropping to far fewer at A level (three isn't uncommon) and where motivated, bright girls do their utmost to get their grades. Learning support, as with the juniors, is in place, with range of needs catered for, says head, including ADHD, though emphasis on pace and focus would indicate compatibility with mild difficulties only (and 'we're not equipped to take on children with serious SpLDs.'). With parents' experience in some cases at odds with official line, dyslexia in particular, it would be worth, if possible, asking to speak to parents who know the ropes.

In contrast, there's excellent joined up academic support. Stunning library, far more than a pretty face, features syllabus-linked book displays helping the focused to plan their own 'now read on' programmes: one conscientious modern language specialist was ploughing her way through Gabriel García Márquez's oeuvre to complement modern language studies. Key subjects also have timetabled clinics run by staff and older pupils, more informal help on tap, willingly given by tutors. 'You don't feel as if it's a hassle,' said pupil. 'They'll say "Come and find me".'

School is currently trying to up parental involvement, which doesn't come naturally to all. Website goes back to basics, highlighting (startlingly for some) importance of eye contact, praise and even turning up at child's concerts. Message reinforced in workshops. Head herself addresses parents on need to 'read aloud to your child every night, ideally into their early teens,' getting a fair few abashed looks in the process. 'I said "Come now, there's no need to look down and be apologetic",' she says.

A few idiosyncrasies to get used to, headed by two-weekly timetable – a breeze once acclimatised, apparently, allowing longer, more productive lessons – and separate though apart presence of year 6s. From the security of own 'little empire' as head puts it (two bright classrooms and pleasant courtyard garden), they make controlled forays into main school, while imaginative 'expanding horizons' curriculum knits humanities together, with Victorian life and times, for example, covered by church visit (RS) and river trip (geography). It all adds a dash of va va voom to what can, post 11 plus, be a fallow year.

As to the future? You could be picky and argue that an all girls' selective school should regularly trounce the equivalent boys' version. No chance thus far, with Whitgift the outlier, streets ahead especially at A levels. Trinity (co-ed at sixth form) does better too.

There is, though, potential to be stronger still, especially given head's uncompromising focus on quality over quantity. Though school isn't at capacity (it's down 20 in current year 7) she won't 'bring in girls to be miserable' to make up numbers. 'We allow a bit of scope but it's an academic setting.'

Games, options, the arts: Hockey sticks not really jolly, with parent mood neutral to apathetic. 'She doesn't like group sport,' said one father, while another confirmed that 'If your girl's sporty, you're not going to go to Old Palace.' Prospectus, by way of corroboration, doesn't go a bundle on action shots (girls raising hands in class is about as energetic as it gets) though fab new pool (devoid of pupils) does feature and is extremely popular, with plans to increase squad training for the best and lunchtime clubs for the rest soon. Recent introduction of football could also prove a popular move, bumping up the number of sports, dance and fitness-related extracurricular activities – which also includes Duke of Edinburgh – to a round half dozen.

Arts and DT include lively pieces, nicely displayed. Biggest buzz, however, comes from performance side, admirably embracing school's history and culture. Drama department plans to 'develop work that explores the theme of pilgrimage to Canterbury' (school was on the route). For the musically inclined, the take is topical rather than Chaucerian. While three smaller music rooms are used for teaching (with as much fabulous classic choral singing as you'd hope for, including monthly evensong in the Minster), biggest is dominated by thriving steel bands, one per year group, with many pupils playing in highly-regarded external ensembles like Croydon steel orchestra and heading off to Notting Hill Carnival.

Background and atmosphere: Some of the oldest buildings in use as a school within the M25. Site of Croydon Minster, dating back to the ninth century and long-time summer palace for assorted Archbishops of Canterbury, who abandoned it in the 18th century for a drier new build. Somehow

escaped demolition, though endured a century's rough treatment as, amongst other things, a calico bleaching factory, before being given to the Sisters of the Church, who founded a school here in 1899. Visitors flock (by pre-arrangement) to gawp at early brick guardroom (now library), medieval great hall (one of south England's finest) and 15th century chapel.

The site, in current scholastic incarnation, works perhaps unexpectedly well, though with some of the more idiosyncratic uses of space, such as IT support housed in gallery pew off the chapel, an effort of will can be required to banish Hogwarts-related thoughts.

Though there's a bit of a sub fusc feel on the cathedral side (and little in the way of outside space) the school modernises where it can. However, those in search of light-flooded rooms are best served by the attractive Shah building across the road. Housing a large sports hall, attractive language and performing arts rooms together with super dining hall, where girls linger at the long, attractive dining tables complete with fresh flowers, it is also home to comfortable sixth form common room. 'They know how to live,' says teacher, surveying end of day overflowing bins.

With such an array of goodies to enjoy, it's unsurprisingly easy to forget the contemporary world outside, though total escape from Croydon's signature tower blocks is impossible – a prize-winning specimen rears up across the road.

Contemporary life does have its uses, however, what with the handy tram stop located a stone's throw away from the front door, though many parents prefer to drive. You sense slight disapproval from Mrs Jewell, who feels parents worry unnecessarily about the area. Even the 2011 riots, though not exactly the publicity you'd seek, left the school completely untouched. 'Parents are more edgy. The girls are fine,' she says.

However, while we're told that for hungry sixth formers, the main city centre feature of note is the nearby McDonalds' lunch menu, location is an issue for a minority of families. 'Mrs Jewell won't have it but the middle of Croydon isn't what it used to be,' says a grandparent. 'If the girls are coming out of school late, you have to pick them up.'

For majority of parents, though, the charm of the school trumps the area. Variations of 'girls are so privileged to be here and they just don't appreciate it,' were heard more than once.

Pastoral care and discipline: These are, you feel, girls with high energy levels, carefully checked by fairly heavy staff presence in the corridors and on surging staircases: one pupil departs for the day trailing slipstream of bubbles aft, wand and detergent to the fore. Ban on mobile phones up to sixth form helps create calm atmosphere, thinks head, though wonders how long technological tide can be resisted. Outside, there's the wonderful Michael who mans the street crossing and is renowned for impeccably good humoured early morning banter and 100 per cent recall of every pupil, parent and sibling.

Recent introduction of football could also prove a popular move, bumping up the number of sports, dance and fitness-related extracurricular activities – which also includes Duke of Edinburgh

House system is the glue that creates the unifying bond between youngest and oldest pupils. Even year 6s elect officers, take an active part in meetings and 'may find themselves planning and speaking in assembly,' says head. Strong ceremonial aspect includes regular house assemblies in the delightful chapel as well as an end of term church service, with bannered-up procession down the aisle.

Pupils praise what one describes as a 'big support network with a form tutor and deputy form tutor'. Essential for girls expected to care for younger children where, says Mrs Jewell, 'life is not always easy,' and also the key to swift resolution of bullying ('friendship issues' as ever the biggest cause). 'My daughter had a problem with a friend but the class teacher called us and it was quickly sorted out,' said father.

Pupils and parents: Splendidly multi-cultural, spanning the gamut of faiths, cultures and backgrounds and seemingly an accurate reflection of the local area rather than gated ghetto for privileged Caucasians. Old Girls (strong, loyal network – hugely active) approve. 'I go down for founders' day and it's lovely to see the church full of every colour and race under the sun, all wearing the Old Palace uniform. Very moving,' said one.

Families praise the sense of community while not necessarily playing much part in it. While there's equal involvement of both parents in their daughters' education (and fathers dominate at drop off and pick up), interest tails off when it comes to socialising with other parents, and the PTA survives, but sometimes only by a thread. 'It's something I can take or leave,' said one mother we spoke to. She wasn't alone. 'A very mixed crowd,' said another parent. 'Some are lovely individuals, trying to work very hard to pay the fees and keep their jobs so they genuinely can't get involved. With others, the idea of paying for an event is ridiculous because what are the fees for?'

Entrance: Like Whitgift boys' schools Trinity and Whitgift, has prep year within the senior school. Unlike them, also has prep school, making for slightly clunky structure with junior school ending in year 5, year 6 pupils moving across to senior school. Anyone arriving in year 6 from outside and passing assessment (English, maths, reasoning, social interaction and parental support) will gain automatic entry to year 7. Everyone else sits 11+ exams (similar content) though 90 per cent make it through. Those who need it will be allowed extra time (this wasn't, thought parents, the case until very recently).

Occasional places on offer up to year 10 – same subjects again but minus social interaction, plus satisfactory school report. School reporting some readmissions when girls who secure grammar school place find it not to their liking. 'We don't crow,' says head. 'It takes courage to retrace your steps.'

Catchment area largely but not exclusively local, with increasing levels of interest from Wandsworth and Clapham fringes as London day school bunfight for places continues to superheat, and bus routes to all points on the compass.

At sixth form level, you're not left in any doubt as to what the school wants. 'Is Old Palace right for your daughter?' thunders large font heading, warning of the dangers of poor choices that could leave students to 'flounder' and feel 'unstretched, lost and overwhelmed.' The bottom line: don't leave home without a goodly number of B grades at GCSE as bottom line minimum and preferably better.

Exit: Almost everyone to well regarded universities including Imperial, Warwick and Durham. One to Oxbridge in 2015. Favourites are headed by science, chemistry and biomedics in particular. Law also popular, ditto psychology, otherwise broad range of subjects and destinations.

Money matters: Whitgift Foundation does what it says in the prospectus – some families suffer real hardship after losing jobs (and in case of one parent we spoke to, home as well) yet manage to keep daughters at the school, thanks to the near 100 per cent bursaries it can provide. Scholarships for academics, music and sport.

Remarks: It's a question of Annie, get your grades. Having had a period of thinking outside the box, this school seems to have hopped back in to give parents what they want – a decent, solid education in beautiful surroundings with few surprises. Message to outside world is just want you'd want to hear (unless sports success is the deal breaker). How well it matches up to the reality of life on the inside remains an evolving story.

Prendergast School

Hilly Fields, Adelaide Avenue, , London SE4 1LE

Tel: 020 8690 3710

State · Pupils: 882 · Ages: 11–18 · Sixth form pupils: 300 (91 boys)

Email: admin@hillyfieldscollege.lewisham.sch.uk
Website: www.prendergast-school.com

27

Head Teacher: Since 2008, Sue Roberts (50s) BEd from Goldsmiths College; says her first love has always been education itself. Her first post fresh from training was at a state senior school in Tower Hamlets, thence a promotion to a nearby Hackney state senior. Following a four year stint in Papua New Guinea at a state boarding school, she returned to London and Prendergast School, where she has remained for the past 27 years, the last six as head.

She is married to a retired London headmaster, with twin boys just through university and now 'gainfully employed'. In her spare time she likes to travel as much as possible, read and visit the theatre. Having kept her maiden name, she notes wryly she is rarely afforded the opportunity to use the title she acquired when her husband was awarded a knighthood. Keenly aware of the perils of the 'informal' GSG style review, which her governors would have preferred to avoid altogether, we found her to be understandably wary.

Open day attendees cannot miss her natural satisfaction in three consecutive Ofsted 'outstandings' in all four categories, but dig a little deeper and subtler satisfactions emerge: the school is recognised nationally for its value-added with pupil

premium students. She's proud of how hard they have been working to close the gap, taking an evidence-based approach on what really works, just one of those being residential trips or school journeys. The results are, as she says, 'life-changing', and highly commendable. She ensures the school is highly focused on pathways and progression routes from entry to exit point.

The Head has no doubt that girls will leave with strong results and social skills, but sees a real challenge in having the confidence to prove themselves in the workplace: 'It's about being strong, confident and articulate young women.' She sees the role of the school as very much about inspiring ambition. As an illustration, she related her delight in a group of year 12 and 13 girls who had set up a mechanical engineering society and booked one of the last remaining tours of the Large Hadron Collider, and are now preparing to pitch to her to secure funds for the trip.

We found her to be a pragmatic subscriber to the school of relatively tough love, telling us that she was unlikely to say 'there, there', but more likely to look at what she and her staff could do in educational terms to help a pupil with difficulties.

Parents describe her as: 'down to earth, extremely dedicated and full of common sense and good values'; 'a good leader'; 'she relates well to the students'; 'she helps students progress academically and cope with social and developmental changes in adolescence'. A newbie year 7 we talked to clearly, overwhelmed by the very idea of a head, said, 'She's not really scary once you get to know her'.

Academic matters: In 2015 at GCSE, 56 per cent A*-B grades (37 per cent A*/A). Pupils join with only just above average profiles and achieve well, particularly in English, placing the school amongst the top 100 state comprehensive schools for progress at GCSE English, maths and three others.

The school's specialisms may not mean too much on the ground, but music and languages continue to be a focus. Students study French and Spanish, with Japanese and Latin offered as clubs, whilst native speakers may add a qualification in their own language.

Whilst there are certainly stars, with pupils from years 7 and 8 bringing home gold and silver medals in the recent UK junior maths challenge, maths GCSE is not so golden, but steadily improving. Strongest performing subjects most recently: all three sciences, textiles, product design, art, French and PE.

School trips which caught our eye include a visit to Greenwich ecology park to hold slugs and newts and a more appetising day trip to a French chocolate factory, whilst an amusing time was had at the Tintin museum in Brussels. Sixth form journeys alternate between Barcelona and Rome.

A third of teachers have been at the school for over 10 years. Several former Prendergast students and several staff have daughters at the school. Parents say: 'My daughter is really enthused by the teachers'; 'interesting projects in maths and languages (subjects that can often be dry to learn).' The average class sizes vary considerably between 12 and 30 with relatively minimal streaming.

One parent noted, 'The lessons have led to many fascinating debates around feminism/young women today', and as if on cue, we observed a memorable history class where the teacher led the girls in a discussion of an original illustration depicting a hunger striking suffragette being force-fed.

Unusually, everyone in agreement that the level of homework and holiday project work is well managed, and not overwhelming: 'The school seems to understand that learning requires periods to rest and recuperate' and 'There is not a lot of pressure, instead girls seem self-motivated'.

Careers preparation starts at year 7 with a Dragon's Den style business enterprise day, with traditional work experience placements in years 10 and 12 and subject specific careers weeks. A new speed networking event for years 9 and 10 makes the most of the professional experience of the whole school community.

Two per cent with statements and 10 per cent school action plus. The head of learning support is full-time and also teaches English. There is an intensive phonics course in year 7 for those with reading difficulties, otherwise some individual support and in class support in the main. Head: 'We try to keep students in their classes wherever possible'. Praise for teaching staff from a parent of a dyslexic pupil: 'They seem to be able to balance the needs of individuals in the class and motivate across the board.'

The head bangs the drum in terms of the expectation that every pupil entering the school at year 7 will stay on to the sixth form and most do, with the addition of boys. There is a dedicated sixth form study centre. Every pupil has use of his or her own laptop for just a nominal cost.

Sixth formers don't wear uniform, although almost all wear comfortable leggings or jeans and sweatshirts, a uniform of sorts. The head defends the lack of business suits, saying they have enough transitions to make at university.

'My daughter is really enthused by the teachers'; 'interesting projects in maths and languages (subjects that can often be dry)'

Ofsted says 'good and improving' at sixth form, but results are a key focus. In 2015, at A Level 51 per cent A*- B and 25 per cent A*/A. Mostly B grades and above in English, geography, textiles, art and sciences, with ICT currently weak.

Figures show the sixth form is strong in terms of valued added – the head points out that with pupils entering from over 40 local senior schools, there is a lot of 'training' to do, and as she says: 'Maybe they've done really well to get their C'.

School aims to give a wide choice of A level combinations, with an eye to what works for progression to university – nothing either too avant garde or soft an option. Drama and theatre studies now replaces performing arts, indicating something of a statement of intent to raise the bar academically.

Solid preparation for university applications including mock interviews with staff and industry experts and sensible advice on how to manage financially at university. For some, eyes are opened with summer schools and shadowing former pupils at Oxford and Cambridge, and 45 year 10 students each year attend a residential course at the University of East Anglia.

Possibly room for growth in leadership opportunities which currently include mentoring younger students, leading the school council, organising the year 13 summer ball, D of E and 'homework club'.

Games, options, the arts: Pupils may not be competing at national level for mainstream sports, but the school works hard to get them involved and active. Pupils in the lower years describe their peers as 'sporty', and 72 per cent take part in out of school sporting activities: pupils say 'it's a good way to make friends'. A shuttle bus takes girls to a sports field at nearby Bellingham.

Girls can continue their netball, hockey, athletics and rounders or try their hand at something new: the school is now embarking on touch rugby and girls can row at the London Regatta Centre. They've also invested in cycling and make use of Herne Hill velodrome. One surprised parent: 'I love the fact that my non-sporty daughter now loves football. No boys: she can get stuck in.' Girls are also clearly good with a pom-pom as the school team is ranked third in the British schools cheerleading championships.

A new purpose-built music block, with practice rooms, a recording studio and teaching spaces open all hours for practising is a real strength of the school. Around 40 per cent study an instrument at some time during their school career, from beginners to grade 8. The school has an orchestra, chamber choir, its own recording label, Hill Sound and a biannual music tour. Musicians are carefully showcased at assemblies and prizegivings.

Strong art offer includes variants such as product design, textiles and photography. Thought-provoking work of a high standard is on display throughout the school, such as a dress made of the traces left behind by animals, dog-hair and glue in this instance – the student collected hairs from her

Airedale until she had enough to make a dress – dedication indeed. Teaching has good links with appropriate courses such as Saturday clubs with University of the Arts. We suspect more could be made of drama with pupils, parents and head struggling to cite much except a large scale Shakespeare production.

'All children are individuals and the school allows for that. Diversity is celebrated.' Parents speak of the value of the social mix

After school and lunchtimes are busy with a wide range of clubs – cycling, walking, creative writing, gardening, debating, trampolining, medical society, chamber choir, orchestra and gospel choir appreciated by pupils and parents: 'The staff show a lot of dedication and commitment to making the clubs such a success'. D of E at bronze, silver and gold is small but thriving. A homework club where kindly sixth formers offer assistance every day after school until 4.30pm seems particularly valued by the keen students we met.

Background and atmosphere: Turn the corner from a promising but still rather gritty south east London high street where betting shops and secondhand white goods crowd the pavements, and one seems to have fallen down a rabbit hole to somewhere altogether more delightful. Hilly Fields, saved from urban sprawl in the 19th century by high profile campaigners including Octavia Hill and William Morris, sweeps up steeply surrounded by fine examples of Victoriana, circled by an avenue at the foot of the hill – a leafy and highly desirable conservation area in the midst of urban Lewisham.

Originally founded in 1890 as West Kent Grammar School, Prendergast School now occupies two sites, a short, energising walk apart, at the top and bottom of the hill. The original Queen Anne style red-brick building perches atop the hill, reaching dizzying heights by the time one has climbed the numerous stairs to the maths floor and sixth form common room near the roof. The listed assembly hall is show-stopping. First discovered by this editor in a World of Interiors spread, it was decorated in the 1930s with pastoral murals loosely based on Aesop's fables by four RCA artists, including the only official female war artist of World War 2.

Both the original building and the remodelled building at the foot of the hill – all angles, glass, sharp graphite bricks and splashes of bright colour – make the very most of the situation. Baroness

Beeban Kidron opened the newly completed arts, English and science blocks. The classrooms have something of a wipe-clean look and can seem a bit gloomy due to dark blue paint, but corridors are wide and windows cleverly oriented to capture views over the sedum roof to the tree-tops of Ladywell, Brockley and beyond to Kent.

In its long history the school has changed its name more than most. As Prendergast School. it is part of a growing federation of four local schools – Prendergast Vale, Prendergast Ladywell and the new Prendergast Primary – with some governance and funding provided by the Leathersellers' Federation.

The atmosphere seems to be that of a relatively small community school where many of the parents know each other well from their primaries. One tells us: 'It's a very friendly environment', another 'feels part of a family'.

Parents say: 'The school is very inclusive. It never lifts the top students at the expense of the average or lower but tries to bring everyone up together'; 'The school feels encouraging and supportive, strict but fair'; 'The girls are allowed to perform, experiment and make mistakes in a safe, nurturing environment.'

Pastoral care and discipline: There are clear rules, everyone knows what is expected of them and parents say they are enforced. As she walks the school, the head insists pupils have a note to leave their classrooms. No visible mobile phones, but nose-studs may be worn. One pupil tells us that teachers carry make-up and nail polish wipes and aren't afraid to dish them out. 'No time in school is wasted managing behaviour,' says the head. Pupils seem mostly keen and studious, borne out by higher than average attendance, although not without a few grumblers in a couple of the classes we visited. A mother told us: 'My daughter wanted to go to a school where she wouldn't feel out of place for being competitive and clever'; another agreed: 'There is a great work ethic which encourages the girls to try their best.'

Form tutors are the key liaison with parents and are considered sufficiently on the ball to pick up any concerns quickly and report back to parents. Bullying is not unheard of, but parents say the school is quick to step in: 'very caring and intervenes when needed.' One concerned parent noted: 'The school does not have a counsellor and there is not one within the federation'. A deliberate choice: the head points out that pupils will be advised to access counselling through their GPs if necessary, preferring to reserve her budget for education.

Pupils and parents: Students hail from ethnically diverse backgrounds with 68 per cent from a black or minority ethnic background – the largest groups being white British, African and Caribbean. Some

22 per cent speak a language other than English at home but there are no early English speakers here. A parent said: 'All children are individuals and the school allows for that. Diversity is celebrated.' Parents speak of the value of the social mix to their children's empathy and awareness. We were particularly impressed by the school's efforts to support the significant number of students who are young carers.

What kinds of pupils would thrive here? A parent: 'A child who enjoys working within clear structures and guidelines'. Girls we spoke to seemed a little bemused to find themselves at a single-sex school, the older ones rather looking forward to the co-ed sixth form. A parent chimed in: 'This school may not work for a girl who is desperate to grow up or wants the whole boy thing to happen soon. This school is about really close female bonding.'

A parent described her peers approvingly as 'laid back and not the type to hire tutors.' Friends of Prendergast School Association does much valued work, this year raising money for a journey to France, a dissection club and the purchase of iPads for use in geography.

Entrance: There are only four forms of entry, co-ordinated by Lewisham using the fair banding system. Skewed by the numbers in each ability band, the distance criteria can be as wide as 2km or a little as under 700m, barely stretching to the fringes of Forest Hill, Honor Oak or Blackheath. Ten per cent of places are music places for which applicants can sit an aptitude test, and which trump distance criteria. The majority come from nearby primaries with Gordonbrock, a few streets away, the biggest feeder.

Entrance to sixth form requires five GCSE passes at grades A*-C, with a B required in the subjects of advanced study. Sibling on the roll trumps distance at application stage. Progression to year 13 is dependent on attaining at least a D at AS level.

Exit: Every student who wants to go on to higher education attains a place. One to Oxbridge in 2015. Some 30 per cent to the Russell Group including Exeter, King's College London, LSE, Warwick and York. The breadth of course destinations is a testament to interests nurtured and inspired: law, English with creative writing, biomedical science,

pharmacy, archaeology, architecture, drama, sports psychology, and script-writing. In previous years: zoology, medieval languages, history of art, graphic design, midwifery and American studies as well as places at leading art colleges including Central St Martins, Camberwell and Chelsea.

Money matters: Support given to some students in the sixth form – 50 bursaries given this year. Three Leathersellers' Federation bursaries awarded each year to students about to go to university, comprising £700 towards each year of study.

Remarks: Girls who arrive here often feel very lucky; we can see why. There is space to breathe in this leafy spot, where girls can be and find themselves.

Royal Russell Junior School

Linked school: Royal Russell School, 365

Coombe Lane, Croydon, Surrey CR9 5BX

Independent • Pupils: 310 • Ages: 3–11 • Fees: up to £12,750 pa

Tel: 020 8651 5884

Email: juniorschool@royalrussell.co.uk
Website: www.royalrussell.co.uk/Juniorindex.php

16

Junior school headmaster: Since 2009, Mr James Thompson BA QTS (30s). Previously director of studies at Kingswood Prep, Bath, and then deputy head at Ardingly College Prep School. Married to Viv,

head of a nursery school in Notting Hill Gate; prior to that she ran the marketing for the junior school. They have two young daughters who both attend the junior school. Mr Thompson initially trained as a PE teacher; his other specialist subjects are mathematics and geography. His passion for sports rubs off on the school – a keen skier, he has introduced an annual family skiing trip. He is also involved with a large charity assisting them in running sporting events and umpires for premier league hockey.

Entrance: At 3 and 4+: Selective (informal teacher observational assessment) entry to the nursery and early years classes.

At 7+: Children are invited to spend a day at the school for an entry assessment to gauge their potential.

Exit: At 11+ most (nearly 90 per cent in 2015) continue through to the senior school. A few leave for local grammars – Wallington, Wilsons or Archbishop Tenison, Bromley.

Remarks: Accommodated in its own buildings, on a lovely rural site opposite the senior school. Classrooms are bright and spacious, along with three well planned playground areas including an adventure playground set into the woodland.

A strong tradition for music, art, drama and sports and an extremely active extracurricular programme. Exceptional music for a junior school, 70 per cent of children learning an instrument, in addition to class music. Year 1s learn the recorder and the following year everybody learns keyboard and a string instrument. An orchestra, rock group, jazz and choirs all perform regularly at school and local events.

Small classes of around 18, mixed ability, with setting for mathematics from year 3; staff aware of the need to include differentiation in all the

Lovely child-friendly library – each class has allotted library periods and storytelling sessions. Classrooms are well resourced

lessons. Additional support is arranged as required in small groups or one-to-one lessons. ICT is used across the curriculum to enrich lessons, everyone is taught to touch type on specially designed colour-coded keyboards. Head keen to involve parents in their children's education – runs regular workshops to give parents a good understanding of subjects children are studying and encourages them to come in and work with reading groups. Once a term homework is suspended for a week for a creative home/school project, the idea being to get the children thinking and investigating different topics and ideas, then creating a piece of artwork. Children learn Spanish in years 3 and 4 and French in years 5 and 6, so they have a good grounding in two foreign languages ready for senior school.

Lovely child-friendly library – each class has allotted library periods and storytelling sessions. Classrooms are well resourced, the juniors have their own science lab and pupils enjoy the senior school facilities increasingly as they go through the age groups, including the performing arts centre, indoor pool and other extensive on site sports facilities (including new all-weather pitch).

Similarly to the senior school, staff are dedicated to aiming high whilst developing well rounded and confident children.

Royal Russell School

Linked school: Royal Russell Junior School, 364

Coombe Lane, Croydon, Surrey CR9 5BX

Independent • Pupils: 605 (135 boarders) • Ages: 11–18 • Sixth form pupils: 180 • Fees: Day £16,560; Boarding up to £32,745 pa

Tel: 020 8657 4433

Email: admissions@royalrussell.co.uk
Website: www.royalrussell.co.uk

17

Headmaster: Since September 2011, Mr Christopher Hutchinson BMet Sheffield, PGCE Cambridge FRSA (40s). He started his teaching career at Clifton College in Bristol, where he was head of physics and a housemaster. Thence to Wellington College as head of science and assistant director of studies, before taking over the headship of Newcastle School

for Boys. Married to Alex, a fellow science teacher, he enjoys singing, squash, tennis and gardening. Committed to providing a stimulating classroom education alongside a robust co-curricular programme. He has been officer commanding the CCF and also master in charge of rowing.

Academic matters: Exam pass rates generally improving - 42 per cent A*/A grades at A level and 38 per cent A*/A at GCSE in 2015. Mathematics is one of the school's strengths with a number of pupils taking GCSE a year early and AS in year 11, carrying on to A level and further mathematics and the sixth form. A flexible approach is taken to setting; most classes are mixed ability and pupils move into sets for maths, English, science, and modern languages for GCSE. Good choice of GCSEs offered. Pupils can study dual award or three separate sciences, although only two languages – French and Spanish – available.

Recently upgraded ICT – everything is interactive with a parent/pupil portal which enables school computer system to be accessed from home. According to parents, good team of male and female teachers from the more mature to young sporty and artistic types. Healthy turnover sees new blood and new ideas coming in each year. Refreshingly unfazed by the league tables, staff are committed to ensuring every pupil reaches their potential. Whilst the school is academically rigorous, a focus on producing broad, well rounded young people.

ESOL tuition is included in the fees and is available for pupils whose first language is not English. Strong learning support department, a charge is made for one-to-one lessons. All departments run lunchtime and after school clinics offering additional support to those who require it. Beautiful library and sixth form centre with small classes and individual attention. Added value is outstanding; sixth formers feed back very positively.

Games, options, the arts: Arts strong all round. Flourishing music department has earned an

Just about everything is on offer from traditional sports to archery and windsurfing. Eager representatives at local, regional and national level sports teams

international reputation, orchestras and choirs travel far and wide to perform. Over 200 ABRSM exams taken by pupils each year – needless to say, pass rate is 100 per cent. Musical experiences are enhanced by workshops, excursions and working with professional musicians. Enviable suite of rooms, including a recording studio, lovely light practice rooms and a 200 seat concert venue.

Lively drama department teaches all age groups, giving pupils the opportunity to try their hand at acting, directing and being light and sound technicians, whilst developing public speaking skills and learning to work cooperatively. Theatre history is also taught and pupils can become involved in helping to make costumes and set designing. Theatre groups visit the school to perform and run workshops, also after-school drama classes and trips to local and West End performances. Pupils benefitting from the recently opened superb performing arts centre. Martin Clunes and Naoko Mori are former pupils. Inspiring light airy art studios where students benefit from expert teaching and a great range of resources.

Just about everything is on offer from traditional sports to archery and windsurfing. Eager

representatives at local, regional and national level sports teams and events, school and house matches – being physically active and enjoying sport considered part of pupil well-being. Lots of fun and successes. Teams are coached by outside specialists as well as in-house PE teachers. Extensive playing fields and courts of every shape and size, cross-country course through their own woodland, indoor swimming pool and sports complex, where £2m refurbishment was recently completed. All sporting facilities are well utilised and operate as a local sports centre for the public, parents and local clubs, adding to the community feel of the school. Community link with Coloma Convent for CCF. The range of clubs, societies and activities is almost unlimited. Large number of senior pupils participate in the Modern United Nations programme and the school hosts one of the biggest UK conferences.

Background and atmosphere: Hidden from the public eye beyond a long driveway lies a great school for the 21st century offering a remarkable number of opportunities for all tastes and talents. Once thought rather down in the doldrums, now offers stiff competition to other south London and Surrey schools. Open-minded and flexible in its general approach, the atmosphere is vibrant and purposeful, a very busy place. The senior management are thought to be caring and in touch with the requirements of today's parents and pupils. An optional extended school day.

Small tutor groups also ensure parents and pupils are kept well informed about academic and personal development

Established in 1853 at New Cross for the sons and daughters of textile workers – one of the earliest co-ed schools. In 1924 purchased the Ballard's estate, an extensive, wooded, 110-acre site, which now houses both the junior and senior schools. Long history of royal patronage – the present queen has visited the school four times since the 1950s and the Earl of Wessex opened the performing arts centre. Lots of new buildings have popped up recently: a rolling rebuilding programme to upgrade and redevelop is underway and some rather unattractive 1960s buildings have been pulled down and replaced. Christian based, now multi-faith and boasts its own recently restored chapel – much of the original stonework carved by Eric Gill in the 1920s.

Pastoral care and discipline: House system, nine houses, three of which are boarding houses. Approximately 130 pupils board. Boarding houses have been refurbished and a full programme of activities runs at weekends. Day pupils enjoy the luxury of having their own houses, with sitting rooms for each year group to relax and socialise in during breaktimes and after school. Supervised homework sessions run each evening and day pupils can stay at school until 9pm (evening meals are included in the fees). Prefect system with head and deputy head boy and girl; each house has its own head of house and sports captains, so a large number of pupils are involved with aiding the day to day running and school functions.

Pastoral staff pride themselves on their knowledge of the needs of young people and understanding the whole child. Housemasters and mistresses together with the chaplain are always available to talk, pupils are treated as individuals and staff go out of their way to help sort out any problems. Small tutor groups also ensure parents and pupils are kept well informed about academic and personal development. School rules regularly reviewed, predominantly in place for everybody's security and safety. Quite strict uniform code and tip top behaviour expected at all times. Pupils tell us the food is delicious, plenty of choices and everybody eats together – the sizable dining hall provides the perfect place to enjoy the company of others.

Pupils and parents: From around 20-mile radius between Clapham Junction and the M25, Bromley, Dulwich, Wimbledon and Croydon. Fortuitously, the tramstop is opposite the entrance, making it an easy journey for many. Folk from all walks of life – many different types and characters, first-time buyers to children of old Russellians. Interesting mix of nationalities, the sixth form being particularly popular with foreign students. Very active PTA helps to organise the numerous social activities, car boot sales and fundraising for charity.

Entrance: At 11+: exam (English, maths and computer based verbal reasoning or cognitive abilities test), interview and reference from previous school. Small number of places are usually available at 13+ and 16+ for sixth form.

Exit: At 16+, a few to local colleges to study vocational courses. At 18+, all to university or art colleges, an increasing number of students choosing law, economics and veterinary sciences; Exeter, Imperial, Durham, Birmingham and Southampton all popular.

Money matters: All applicants for year 7 and year 9 are considered for academic scholarships via their performance in the entrance exam. Further scholarships are available for year 12 on the basis of GCSE results. Also junior, senior and sixth form art, music and drama scholarships. A limited number of means-tested bursaries. Five per cent discount for siblings.

Remarks: Confident and socially accomplished pupils, proud of their increasing successes across the curriculum. Solid reputation for producing cheerful young people, well-prepared for successful futures at university and in the workplace.

St David's School

23/25 Woodcote Valley Road, Purley, Surrey CR8 3AL

Tel: 020 8660 0723

Independent · Pupils: 152 · Ages: 3 – 11 · C of E
· Fees: up to £9,150 pa

Email: office@stdavidsschool.co.uk
Website: www.stdavidsschool.co.uk

18

Head: Since May 2011 Miss Cressida Mardell (40s) a classicist, BA PGCE. Before joining St David's in 2007 she was a senior teacher at St Christopher's School, Epsom. Parents appreciate her positive approach, hard work and sound judgement, alongside a jolly personality and a good sense of humour. She lives locally and enjoys holidaying in France and walking with her two lively Border collie rescue dogs.

Entrance: Most join the nursery at 3+ (18 places); another four places in reception. Non-selective at this stage; occasional places in year 1 upwards subject to 'satisfactory assessment'.

Exit: At 11+ most popular choices are the local grammar schools Sutton, Wilson's Wallington, Nonsuch and Tiffin's. Others to Royal Russell, Whitgift, Trinity, Old Palace, Greenacre and Woldingham.

Remarks: Mixed ability school, which skilfully blends academic excellence alongside a good range of musical, creative and sporting opportunities. Founded in 1912 with just five pupils, by Welsh (hence school's name) sisters Margery and Mary Talfourd Jones. The school has thrived through the decades and today's multicultural clientèle is still proud of its founders' Welsh connections. Pupils join in the Eisteddfod Festival and fly the flag on St David's Day.

Dedicated class teachers run maths and English lessons mostly in the mornings and then teach specialist subjects in the afternoons. There is an ICT room and a room for arts, science and technology; pupils often split for these subjects so class sizes are around 10, optimising opportunities for individual attention and development. French is taught throughout the school and year 6 learn Latin. Specialist teacher visits three days a week to assist children with any special educational needs. Additional support is provided in small groups, one-to-one or in class at no extra charge. ESOL can be arranged.

Very busy music department has a gifted and talented choir, brass ensemble, string ensemble and rhythm group. Most pupils play at least one instrument; older pupils are introduced to filming and music composition with the occasional commission, most recently a jingle for Halfords. Some great achievements on the sporting front; St David's has its own large playing fields a few minutes' walk from the school building complete with tennis and netball courts. Gymnastics is particularly strong; the school has won the ISA competition on several occasions. Swimming is another area where pupils

Most pupils play at least one instrument; older pupils are introduced to filming and music composition

excel, with eight children being selected to train as divers at Crystal Palace for the next Olympics programme. Parents felt clubs had been rather limited; this is now an expanding area, and the aim is now to offer a much wider choice of activities, after-school and at lunchtimes. Chess team have made it into Champion League finals for primary schools and the maths team recently came third in the Sutton Maths Challenge. After-school care (at extra cost) is provided by the Jancett Nursery Group until 6.30pm.

Refreshingly, St David's has retained its independence and remains a small charity with a non-selective intake, so far avoiding being swept up by one of the large education businesses. Very successful results at 11 into the local grammar and independent schools, especially considering the non-selective intake and inclusive approach. Terrific value for money.

St Dunstan's College Junior School

Linked school: St Dunstan's College, 370

Stanstead Road, London SE6 4TY

Independent • Pupils: 290 • Ages: 3–11 • C of E • Fees: up to £14,604 pa

Tel: 020 8516 7225

Email: rscard@sdmail.org.uk
Website: www.stdunstans.org.uk

28

Head: From September 2015, Mr Paul Cozens. Mr Cozens was educated at Millfield School and graduated from Exeter University with a BA in educational studies with music and French. He was previously deputy head of St Paul's Cathedral School. Mr Cozens began his teaching career at South Hampstead Junior School and the Beacon School before being appointed as director of studies at Newton Preparatory School. Mr Cozens is an experienced ISI inspector and he is very involved in music and drama, both in and out of school.

Entrance: At 3+ informal assessment and interview with parents for nursery places. At 4+ competitive assessments held in November each year. At 7+ competitive assessments, which focus on numeracy, literacy and social skills. For entry into other year groups contact the school for occasional vacancies.

Exit: At 11+ the majority move to the senior school, others mostly to selective maintained sector or specialist music and sports schools.

Remarks: A medium-sized, spritely school. Traditional academic curriculum jazzed up with lots of outings and visitors. Living history days, visiting authors and investigative workshops. Lots of creative thinking going on for the children and teachers.

Music, drama and sport all have an important place: many children learn instruments and the school boasts wind, strings and brass bands along with two choirs. Pupils regularly put on musical and dramatic performances so everyone gets a chance to be involved, in addition to the extensive range of after-school clubs and activities.

Pupils regularly put on musical and dramatic performances so everyone gets a chance to be involved, in addition to the extensive range of after-school clubs and activities

All the superb senior school sports facilities including the swimming pool are available to younger pupils. Food freshly cooked on the premises.

St Dunstan's is keen for the older children to prepare early for moving to the senior school – their staff teach older prep pupils and run specialist activity days with this in mind.

Pastoral care is carefully monitored and parents meet regularly with teachers to discuss their child's all-round progress. Split into two departments, prep 8 to 11 years and the pre-prep, 3 to 7-year-olds, which is housed in its own building, formerly a headmaster's house. Before and after school care runs from 7.45am – 6pm throughout the week.

A friendly school with a good community feel, focusing on developing each child's aptitude and interests.

St Dunstan's College

Linked school: St Dunstan's College Junior School, 369

Stanstead Road, London SE6 4TY

Independent · Pupils: 562 · Ages: 11–18 · Sixth form pupils: 130 · C of E · Fees: £15,438 pa

Tel: 020 8516 7200

Email: Info@sdmail.org.uk
Website: www.stdunstans.org.uk

29

Headmaster: Since July 2014, Nicholas Hewlett. Formerly head of Boys' School, North London Collegiate School Jeju, South Korea. First in geography from King's College London; has also been head of geography and housemaster at Magdalen College School, Oxford.

Academic matters: Not the top of the South London heap, but ability to breathe no longer the only entry criterion. School now more sought after and the proportion of SEN children has fallen, but it cherishes those that remain, and the old, good habits that came from a focus on SEN – teachers taking an interest in individuals, picking up problems fast – are still encouraged.

Splendid results considering the still broad intake. In 2015, 50 per cent A*/A grades at GCSE; 47 per cent A*/A grades at A level. Class sizes average at around 20, dropping to 14 or so at GCSE.

An arty school in overall feel, but maths is a strong subject (good results in competitions and exams) and, with the more academic intake, the sciences have been given a boost. Available as three separate subjects, though most do dual award, and much lab refurbishment. French, Spanish and Latin at year 7 – 9 with older pupils being offered German and Italian. Classics department continues to thrive with around a third of pupils taking Latin GCSE; ancient Greek is offered as a club.

Lively sixth form, was the only one in south-east London to offer the choice of A levels or IB but IB no longer offered after 2016. School says the A level only curriculum will retain some elements of the IB, in particular the extended essay.

Pupils setted for most subjects. All screened for specific learning difficulties in year 7, those identified given an individual Pupil Profile which sets out strategies and support needed. SENCo works with teachers to assist them in developing inclusive and multisensory teaching within the classrooms. Extension classes are run for more able pupils in a range of subjects and those who are ready can sit maths, languages or science GCSEs early. New skills for life course with emphasis on health, wellbeing and employment skills for years 7, 8 and 9.

Friendly staff work hard to make their teaching exciting and inspirational. Lots of creative activities in all the academic subjects; trips, workshops and competitions back up solid teaching.

Games, options, the arts: Sporty school with great on-site facilities considering its inner city location. Everyone, including the juniors, has a full afternoon's sport each week – part of the 'fitted to do well in life' business.

All trad sports on offer, plus rugby fives, golf and sailing. Very active D of E and CCF, which is increasingly popular and operates in partnership with St Matthew's Academy. Links with the Worshipful Company of Marketors, who installed Mrs Davies, the previous head, on a float for the Lord Mayor's show.

Drama and music very strong, again with a wide range of opportunities. Drama department puts on several performances each year from traditional Shakespearean plays to modern musicals. For those not so keen on acting there are many other technical and design areas to be involved in. Choirs, bands, orchestras and ensembles of almost every style run with the options growing each year depending on pupil's interests and talents.

An arty school in overall feel, but maths is a strong subject (good results in competitions and exams) and, with the more academic intake, the sciences have been given a boost

Two lovely light art studios, where a very high standard of work is produced. Countless clubs and societies at lunchtime and after school. Hamster club is popular with younger pupils who learn how to look after small animals whilst making new friends. Inter-house mastermind and drama competitions run alongside electronics, modern language society, drawing, sewing and debating. In conjunction with all the sports, arts and clubs are a fabulous selection of annual expeditions to join from singing in Estonia to diving in Egypt.

Background and atmosphere: Busy inner-city site next to a road junction is not enviable, nor is tangling with the South Circular a joyful way to spend your mornings. The original school was a 15th century foundation in the City of London; hence the continuing links with livery companies. St Dunstan's was refounded and relocated in the 1880s to the current site in Catford.

Striking in appearance – some would say ugly – the main Victorian buildings are aptly described by the children as 'very Hogwarts'. The interior is a warren of corridors, lunatic-asylum style, but with some effective efforts to soften the look and an attractive enclosed garden. Great Hall for assemblies, performances and other gatherings, recently restored Victorian stained-glass windows tell the story of the school.

Dining room, purpose-built in the '50s, has plate glass windows with a curved roof (like a Pringle crisp) and no pillars – an amazing space. Doubles up as the ideal spot for school discos and other social events.

Pastoral care and discipline: Pastoral care excellent, continues to be hymned by parents. Pupils, parents and staff encouraged to contact each other whenever they need. The school expects everyone to be supportive and helpful to each other; relationships between sexes are exactly what you would hope for from a co-educational school – realistic and not primarily hormone fuelled. House and prefect system. Bullying is not tolerated and is dealt with swiftly when it occurs. A strong and successful drugs education policy – the school takes a harder line than the rest of society on misdemeanours.

Pupils and parents: Largish multicultural mix reflecting the local area. Hard-working and aspirational parents, many of whom are first-time buyers in the independent sector. Mostly professional, down-to-earth types, who might consider the

Dulwich foundation schools rather too pushy or even aloof. Huge catchment area from Kent and all over south east and south west London; coaches run from Blackheath, New Cross, Clapham, Streatham, Farnborough and Bromley. Catford stations are a few minutes' walk away bringing children from central London. The continuing success of the IB attracts new groups of parents and young people to the school each year. Notably enthusiastic and active 'family society' runs fêtes, social and fundraising events throughout the year.

Hamster club is popular with younger pupils who learn how to look after small animals whilst making new friends. Inter-house mastermind and drama competitions popular

A friendly school that appeals to, and produces, interesting people across the disciplines. Old Dunstonians are musicians, politicians, businesspeople, sportspeople and scientists. Professor Sir Martin Evans, Nobel Prize winner for genetics, the very Rev Dr John Hall, Dean of Westminster, and Lord Grade of Yarmouth, former ITV chairman, are among them.

Entrance: Harder than it was, but gentle by London standards. 11+ competitive entrance exam with papers in maths, English and reasoning. Children registered to sit the exam can opt to attend 11+ preparation classes held shortly before. Fifty per cent of the intake comes from the prep school. Common entrance at 13+, entry to the sixth form at least seven GCSEs grade B and above with A grades in the subjects to be studied at AS or higher level IB.

Exit: University, and a good one, is the object of most – ambitions have risen along with the entry hurdle. Between five and 10 to medical schools, veterinary colleges and Oxbridge each year (four in 2015). At 16+ a few leave for local sixth form colleges or specialist arts courses.

Money matters: Full fees bursaries from age 11. Art and design, music, drama, sports and academic scholarships at 11, and for sixth formers at the discretion of the head.

Remarks: A place with a good strong heartbeat taking care of individuals and considering what is best for each. Turns out well-prepared, mindful citizens.

St Olave's Grammar School

Goddington Lane, Orpington, Kent BR6 9SH

Tel: 01689 820101

State · Pupils: 1,011 · Ages: 11–18 · Sixth form pupils: 365 (145 girls) · C of E

Email: office@saintolaves.net
Website: www.saintolaves.net

8

Headmaster: Since 2010 Mr Aydin Önaç (50s) BMus BSc ARCM FRSA. A grammar school boy himself, who grew up on a council estate in Derby. Trained at the Royal College of Music as a pianist and still devotes several hours each week to the piano, but found it impossible to make a living as a musician and took a maths degree at UCL instead. After a short spell in the City, he found his vocation as a maths teacher, got a job at Hemel Hempstead, and began a rapid rise to the top. St Olave's is his third headship, after Tewkesbury School in Gloucestershire and Fortismere in north London. Two grown up children from his first marriage, and two teenage step-children in his second; his wife also works in education.

Ambitious and energetic, Mr Önaç has also been something of a controversial figure during his career. After reputedly receiving a 'golden handshake' of £40k to take on Fortismere School, where he introduced 10 per cent selection for musical pupils, he left after only four years for St Olave's, where he has driven already-impressive results still higher and made Cambridge the school's most common university destination, with an average of 30 leavers a year gaining places there. 'The challenge for me was keeping the school at the top,'

he told us, 'A lot of heads tend to duck that challenge, but I revel in it.' Parental enthusiasm for the school's performance is universal, but the feedback we received about the head suggested that parents feel kept at a distance by him. Comments included, 'Not enough interaction on a personal level,' and 'Not really a people person.' Mr Önaç's response to these observations was surprised and robust: 'I attend every single school function, and I try to be very visible. I have an open door policy, and I welcome people coming in to talk to me.'

Academic matters: By any measure, St Olave's results are top-notch. In 2015, 84 per cent of GCSE results were at A*/A, with maths particularly strong. At A level, 77 per cent of grades were at A*/A and over 94 per cent were at A*-B. 'We have the very highest aspirations for all our students, and that translates into having the highest expectations. It's a given at St Olave's, as far as I'm concerned,' says head. Parents and boys alike describe the staff as 'dedicated', 'professional' and 'enthusiastic'. Students are encouraged to go well beyond the demands of the syllabus. 'There's a focus here on going further than the curriculum, on exploring and expanding your knowledge,' said a very personable sixth form girl. Boys from years 7-11 confirmed that the teachers were 'really good at spotting where you might need help.' 'St Olave's promotes independent learning, it has done from the beginning,' reported a satisfied parent. 'Our son can structure his own time without needing any input from us.' 'The academic rigour of lessons is great: our son is challenged, and he has the opportunity to share his ideas in a supportive atmosphere,' said another. 'High-achieving in a relaxed learning environment,' said a third. 'Our approach can be summed up in one word: scholarship,' affirmed the head.

Very broad curriculum, encompassing everything you'd expect, and a few things you wouldn't: we were particularly pleased to see the new food technology room, and to hear that cookery was a popular part of the lower school curriculum. Lots of emphasis on computing, and robotics has taken off in a big way. Latin is compulsory in year 7, and Greek, Japanese and Mandarin are all offered as extracurricular options, but a recent decision to axe (school prefers the phrase 'phase out') Spanish and drama from the curriculum has ruffled the waters somewhat. The head urged us not to dwell on the matter, but parents and pupils alike told us they were disappointed about it (or, in the words of one, 'annoyed and angry'). We put these concerns to the head, who responded that the school had had to cut its cloth because of forthcoming government cuts, 'and we just haven't the numbers to fill a GCSE set.' According to the website, both subjects were popular and successful, so this struck us as a little odd.

School has now moved to a three-year KS4, so that students will choose their GCSEs in year 8 and begin their courses in year 9. At sixth form level, the school remains wholly committed to A levels (as opposed to the IB or Cambridge Pre-U). 'We prefer

Lots of wonderfully cerebral stuff going on in clubs: we saw a superb English version of a German children's classic, translated and published by the students

the depth,' said the director of studies, 'and complemented by a vibrant extracurricular provision, they suit our students best.'

Games, options, the arts: There can't be many state schools where rugby and Eton fives are the main sports. Fives is hugely popular, with many boys playing it every day ('It's quick and easy, and you can play it in your uniform!'), and the school's rugby teams regularly win success at both local and national level. Cricket is also big here – the school toured recently to South Africa. Broad range of other sports, including tennis, hockey, football, swimming, basketball, squash, badminton and athletics. The arts are also strong. 'The music is fabulous here,' said the head fondly. 'The jazz band is terrific,' agreed one parent, remembering a recent concert in Croydon's Fairfield Halls. Lots of choral singing, with all tastes catered for – 'I sing in six choirs!' one boy told us, proudly – and the school supplies all the choristers for the Queen's Chapel of the Savoy (one of them recently won BBC Radio 2's Chorister of the Year). Children can learn almost any instrument here, including the organ in the school hall, and take their skills into the school's many orchestras and bands. We're pleased to report that drama is also strong. A few years ago, there was just one annual production, and that was for sixth formers; now there are plenty for everyone, several of them directed by the students themselves. Lots of wonderfully cerebral stuff going on in clubs: we saw a superb English version of a German children's classic, translated and published by the students themselves, plus erudite student-produced journals for the Law Society, the History Society, the Medics' Society, and more. Boys report being made to feel welcome in all the activities they tried. Ambitious and enticing programme of trips and excursions: in recent months, students have had the opportunity to visit Iceland, New York, Paris, Greece, South America, central Africa – the list goes on.

Background and atmosphere: Originally located in Tooley Street, Southwark, St Olave's received its royal charter in 1571: display cases in the corridors show treasures from its archive collection, and watercolours show the school at its various stages. It moved to its present spacious site, complete with beautiful modern chapel, in leafy

Orpington in 1968, in quest of more space and its own playing fields – also, perhaps, to get away from the threat of being turned comprehensive. Long and proud history of being academically selective, with which the present head is completely in tune: 'I believe this country neglects its brightest youngsters at its peril. They are the wealth creators and the job creators of the future. I spent 22 years in the comprehensive sector and I remain dedicated to its aims, but I'm also completely committed to giving these students the education they deserve.'

And yet, with all that was going on, and every reason for the Olave's air to be full of buzz and liveliness, we can only comment on what we found, which was a curious guardedness whenever we hove into view, not least in a reluctance to let us talk to the students without a member of SMT present; although, on our pressing the matter, they did agree. All staff, from the head downwards, reacted with surprise and displeasure when we passed on parental criticisms (perhaps, like some other high-achieving and over-subscribed schools, they don't often hear them), and a couple of the older staff simply refused to talk to us, actually getting up and walking away when we tried to ask them questions. One parent, whose son is doing very well at St Olave's, described the school as 'incredibly defensive', to which the head's response was, 'We don't have anything to be defensive about!' Others, however, have described a very different experience. 'On the few occasions I have needed to contact staff by email, their response has been prompt and helpful,' wrote one mother. 'Our sons have been incredibly happy at the school and we cannot fault it,' wrote another.

Pastoral care and discipline: Mixed responses from parents, with some praising the school's 'very caring ethos', and others saying that bullying issues took too long to be resolved. Strong prefect system ensures older boys take responsibility for leading and mentoring the younger ones, and highly selective intake plays its part in developing the very strong work ethic apparent in lessons. 'It's almost unheard of for behaviour to be poor here,' says the head.

Pupils and parents: From all over the borough and beyond; nearly 50 per cent from ethnic minorities. Less diverse socially, with only two per cent of students on free school meals. Extremely supportive and active parents' association, which works tirelessly to raise funds for equipment, facilities and travel opportunities.

Entrance: Roughly 1,000 boys apply for 124 places, and an additional four places are offered to choral scholars who must pass the same stringent entrance tests.

New admissions policy for 2016/17 entry into year 7. First stage is logic, maths and English test in September. Those who pass invited to sit second stage English and maths test later in the autumn. First and second stage marks combined to give final score and the first 124 applicants in rank order offered places.

Around 500 boys and girls apply each year for the 110 sixth form places on offer to students from other schools. Those candidates whose predicted grades meet the school's requirements (minimum six As and three Bs at GCSE) will be asked to take written tests in their four chosen AS subjects.

Exit: At 16, the great majority to St Olave's sixth form, although between four and eight per cent of Y11 students don't get the grades needed and have to leave. A few also eased out at 17 (school prefers the phrase 'fail to meet the published criteria') if they haven't got the AS grades required (three Bs) to progress to Y13. At 18, everyone goes to university. Majority to Russell Group destinations; 53 places for Oxbridge/medicine in 2015.

Money matters: State-funded grammar school, supported by Bromley education authority and the Diocese of Rochester. Parents invited to pay around £500 pa in voluntary contributions to help fund facilities, etc.

Remarks: For the bright, motivated boy who is prepared to knuckle down, St Olave's is an excellent fit. As one parent put it, 'Very good, very impressive, very supportive. And we haven't had to pay for it.'

Sydenham High Junior School GDST

Linked school: Sydenham High School GDST, 377

15 Westwood Hill, London SE26 6BL

Independent · Pupils: 220 · Ages: 4–11 · Fees: £11,991 pa

Tel: 020 8557 7000

Email: admissions@syd.gdst.net
Website: www.sydenhamhighschool.gdst.net

Head: Since September 2014, Ms Claire Boyd, previously head of lower school and on the senior leadership team of Ravenscourt Park Prep. She has a politics degree from Royal Holloway College and a PGCE from Roehampton.

Entrance: Informal entry assessment at 3+ – 'gives us an edge over some of our competitors who do formal assessment – children skip out of here, find experience enjoyable, even fun.' 'Weed out the stroppy and difficult' so hope it doesn't fall on a day when your child's in a bad mood!

Exit: Around three quarters to senior school. Rest to a range of schools, both state and private, including other GDST schools. Progression to senior school expected but not automatic.

Remarks: Good facilities, new library and IT suite, classrooms brimming with lively displays. New playgrounds, additional classrooms and specialist science, art and ICT facilities were all recently added. Close links with senior school – head spends an afternoon a week in the junior school, takes

assembly, which girls love and say is a very special time. Year 6 girls permitted to wear senior uniform. Masterclasses at senior school for years 5 and 6 (most recently in maths, science, history and Spanish); sixth formers run clubs and activities.

New playgrounds, additional classrooms and specialist science, art and ICT facilities were all recently added

French for all from 4, Latin is taught to the top two years; emphasis on music, sport and drama. Currently caters for range of mild SEN: dyspraxia, dyslexia, dyscalculia, Asperger's, autism, ADD, ADHD and EBD, but all must be able to manage the curriculum. Some specialist support available.

A very welcoming environment.

Sydenham High School GDST

Linked school: Sydenham High Junior School GDST, 376

19 Westwood Hill, London SE26 6BL

Tel: 020 8557 7000

Independent • Pupils: 420 • Ages: 11–18 • Sixth form
pupils: 70 • Fees: £15,246 pa

Email: info@syd.gdst.net
Website: www.sydenhamhighschool.gdst.net

Headteacher: Since 2002, Mrs Kathryn Pullen BA MA PGCE (50s). Studied English and American studies at Warwick, later completing a PGCE in drama. Began her teaching career as head of English at St Saviours and St Olave's before moving on for a brief period at Glenthorne High School. Despite more than 20 years at Sydenham, first as deputy head, she shows no signs of getting stale. Quite the reverse. She oozes enthusiasm for the girls and clearly works hard at creating a dynamic environment to match their diverse backgrounds and interests. She counts amongst her main achievements giving them a voice in shaping the school and building a senior management team excited by and responsive to change. 'I've got no magic wand, but the eager and intellectually curious will find plenty to stimulate them here.'

Academic matters: Of course the school has an eye to results and, given its broad intake, achieves well. In 2015, 63 per cent A*/A at GCSE and 72 per cent A*-B (disappointing 28 per cent A*/A) at A level. But it hasn't lost sight of the need to relieve the pressure and inject fun into, in particular, years 9-11.

Many activities designed to develop personal learning and thinking skills and break the routine. A parent attendee at the year 7 study skills workshop throws up her arms: 'Why oh why didn't schools teach me good habits so early on?' Year 12 has a busy schedule of outside speakers to help pupils make decisions about their future. In younger years an annual off-timetable day encourages them to reflect on themselves as learners using anything from Dragon's Den workshops to mixed discussion groups.

Staff clearly recognise technology's potential to engage pupils. In its first year, the maths blog with lesson podcasts received over 37,000 hits in the run-up to GCSE, indicating the high standard of teaching in this area. Other web-based tools are available and staff welcome email contact, particularly during study leave and from parents with concerns. Pupils can take some GCSEs early to free up time for other interests and areas of study. Science is an area of strength – two year 10 and sixth form pupils recently won national awards and another sixth former a Nuffield bursary to study cancer treatments at King's College. Getting science GCSE out of the way in year 10 doesn't deter pupils from taking it up again in sixth form and beyond. Care is taken to highlight the relevance to different careers, leading to a high proportion taking science-based degree subjects. Their flying in the face of gender stereotyping is a source of great pride at the school.

Standards are high, but above all girls seem to relish the freedom of being able to join up with friends and enjoy themselves

As you move around the school, there's a real feeling that pupils and staff feed off each other's enthusiasm. The teacher looking on almost smugly, they positively fall over themselves to show off their geography presentations. The GDST network also provides a wider forum for experience and idea exchange, impressing many parents. 'Staff are endlessly inventive and flexible in meeting different pupils' needs.' It helps being relatively small. 'Many pupils leaving after GCSEs are surprised how much they miss being known to staff and the reassurance that familiarity provides,' says one parent and, as many others, identifies it as a real asset which the school often doesn't do enough to promote. SEN pupils are well-catered for too. There is

dyslexia screening and other testing in year 7 and the Learning Strategy Team provides by all accounts excellent tailored support with a clear focus on inclusivity. Says the head, 'We know girls don't want to feel different, and if printing exam papers on yellow paper helps some of them, then why not do it for all?'

Games, options, the arts: Stalwart and welcome efforts from newer staff to raise interest and standards in sports are reaping rewards. Regular netball and hockey clubs are well attended and successes against local schools are notching up. Rugby, football and cricket also have a keen following – they are not girly-girls. Trampolining is popular and, to encourage the less sporty, the school has recently introduced fencing, golf and scuba diving. Even so, most parents agree that this is not the best place for the more competitive, 'never happier than when on a games pitch' girl. The separation by a short bus ride of the main school site from the major eight-acre sporting facilities is probably a deterrent, but also the distraction of other strong departments, most notably music and drama. However, recent initiative, the SydElite programme, gives monitoring, mentoring and workshop support to talented athletes balancing high level sport with academic and social life.

Supervised and informal music and drama rehearsals are very much in evidence around the school, with girls so absorbed that they barely seem to register your passing. Even those not opting to take exams get involved and opportunities abound. In addition to two junior and two senior drama productions each year; a variety of choirs and orchestras, ranging from wind, guitar, string and jazz, perform regularly with an expanded schedule of diverse concerts in the school's new 90-seater recital hall, complete with music technology department. A number of girls have auditioned successfully to appear in West End shows and the school choir has been invited back time and again to appear at the Royal Albert Hall at Christmas. Standards are high, but above all girls seem to relish the freedom of being able to join up with friends and enjoy themselves. The slightly chaotic art room is overflowing with talent and more and more are going on to study art-related subjects at university. Usual range of extracurricular clubs, including D of E and some, such as ICT, maths and DT, designed to bolster academic progress. More unusual tastes – code-breaking, Japanese and fashion – are catered for too. Recent additions to enrichment activities include cookery for years 7 and 12 and first aid, photography and indoor rock climbing for year 12.

Background and atmosphere: The original Victorian buildings where the school opened in 1887 are across the road. In 1934 the school transferred to its current main building which is slightly set back and surrounded by a jumble of more recent additions, most prominently the music block and sports hall. While they provide welcome facilities they, and the sixth form block, rather detract from its overall elegance. Away from the busy road with buses struggling up the hill, you can imagine girls sunning themselves on the terrace overlooking the large Astroturf pitch bordered by mature trees. Inside, a relaxed, friendly and purposeful air with girls unselfconsciously running from one lesson to the next. 'So nice that they don't seem to feel the need to have the latest phone or bag.' Intimate feel in the sixth form block. 'Some felt uncomfortable being in a small independent girls' school but those of us left behind really appreciate it.'

Pastoral care and discipline: Parents praise staff for understanding girls' different character traits and identifying individual strengths, focusing on those in order to develop all-round confidence. Nice touches such as cards of congratulation posted home and the odd hug in the younger years. They also sense a 'spirit of sisterhood' and 'moral strength' amongst the girls, which prompts them to be mutually supportive and keep each other in line, generally without disciplinary measures from staff. The school prides itself on understanding girls; the needs of each year group are carefully considered and programmes developed to support them. A full-day of PSHCE each term often involves outside speakers and is designed to engage pupils fully. There is a clear underlying message. If they are to succeed, they must take the initiative and think for themselves.

Nice touches such as cards of congratulation posted home and the odd hug in the younger years

Pupils and parents: Tends to attract creative parents – less from established professions – of varied social, cultural and racial backgrounds who don't feel their girls would completely fit the mould elsewhere. They and staff tend to think of the girls as 'edgy, quirky and boundary-pushers' though they don't overtly appear so (little evidence of uniform rules being stretched). They want their uniqueness to be celebrated and for them to have the freedom to be themselves. For most it is a careful investment calculated to bring maximum return – many first time buyers. Old girls include actress Margaret Lockwood, Philippa Darbre (scientist), Sophie McKenzie (author), Sandy Powell (Oscar winning costume designer), Claire Bennett (fencing champion) and Winifred Gerin (writer).

Entrance: Of around 200 applicants, 40-50 girls join the 30-plus coming up from the junior school. Most are from local preps and state primaries, although also from Wandsworth, Bromley and, since the opening of the East London overground, from north of the river. Many have brothers at Dulwich College. The head and senior teaching staff interview all girls, inviting them to talk about something they are proud of. They also take an entrance exam in English and maths in which they are expected to attain equivalent to level 4 or 5 in national curriculum KS2. Occasionally places come up in other year groups and the school is keen to expand its sixth form. Overall there's been a drop in numbers in recent years, which the head attributes to the effects of the economic downturn and more boys' schools opening up to girls.

Exit: After GCSEs some feel they have outgrown the school. Cost-saving, convenience and co-education are also factors and about 50 per cent leave; some to go to local state schools or co-ed independents and some to board outside London. Of those who stay, occasional Oxbridge places, with others going to eg Edinburgh, Manchester, Leeds and Cardiff.

Remarks: The school doesn't have an instant wow factor but there's a palpable, almost defiant, energy running through the place. It seems to say, 'I will be who I want to be'. Girls emerge independent thinkers and confident communicators. All credit to the school that they become so in a happy, mostly settled environment.

Trinity School

Shirley Park, Croydon, Surrey CR9 7AT

Tel: 020 8656 9541

Independent • Pupils: 980 • Ages: 10–18 • Sixth form
pupils: 280 (60 girls) • Fees: £15,147 pa

Email: admissions@trinity.croydon.sch.uk
Website: www.trinity-school.org

Headmaster: Since 2006, Mr Mark Bishop MA MBA PGCE (40s). Educated at Charterhouse and Oxford. Prior to Trinity, spent a decade apiece at Caterham as deputy head and the Royal Grammar School Guildford, where was head of department, then head of year.

Blessedly normal, the sort of head you could imagine in the pub with colleagues at the end of the week rather than at the top of ivory tower buffing up his ego. Might attempt to learn saxophone – 'I'm a frustrated musician' – but research would exercise greater lure, you'd imagine, given relish for recent term-long sabbatical, where combined bursary-funded research into causes of Afro-Caribbean boys' educational under-achievement with spell in City quizzing CEOs about how to stand out at interview.

'A wonderful head – and attractive, which helps,' one mother told us (we couldn't possibly comment). Ambitious and personable, radiating effective blend of charm and chutzpah, which goes a very long way with parents. He's highly able, an excellent businessman who is first rate at adding ingredient X to school mix to maximise appeal.

Has pushed up academic side, retaining outstanding music. School rising under his leadership to top of the school shopping list for many. Aiming high is an essential given excellence of local competition from Dulwich College, Whitgift and several top grammars on doorstep. 'Schools have to be exceptional at everything,' he says.

Firmly believes that 'teaching, teaching, teaching' is what schools should be about. May not be realistic to want every lesson to be outstanding, but a goal worth pursuing. Words matched by actions. Will be one of few schools to opt for deliberate downsizing, reducing numbers to 950 over next five years – desire to fit whole school in the hall for weekly assembly a priority.

No shirker when it comes to corridor presence and manages first week word-perfect recall of new boys, something that contributes to 360-degree good vibes and is a major factor in parental gushing. 'He's very much there, welcoming the boys – speaks volumes.' Success down to memorising photographs over summer hols, brave given 'very funny looks on a plane,' he says. Particularly good with the high performers, though adamant that spends

more time with those experiencing problems. One parent queried commitment to supporting pupils with learning needs, robustly defended by head, who points to expansion of SEN team and recent praise from inspectors. 'Something we do better now than we used to,' he says.

Aim is to produce pupils who can eyeball CEOs with same confidence and sense of enquiry as shop floor workers. 'I want them to leave with a genuine sense of compassion for others, fulfil their potential, not [just] try to emulate someone else's achievements,' he says.

Standing down in July 2016.

Academic matters: Results particularly good at GCSE with steady rise in top grades (78 per cent A*/A in 2015). At A level, 88 per cent A*-B and 65 per cent A*/A in 2015. Business studies, chemistry and economics down over previous years, though head 'expects the new head of department to swiftly turn this round...' Lots of stars, however, with biology, Eng lit, maths (far and away the single biggest subject) and further maths amongst the large-entry subjects regularly achieving 90 per cent at A*/B or above. School trawls in the prizes, too, awarded for everything from investment to science plus Maths Olympiad gold medals. Finalists in international safe-cracking competition (success determined by physics know-how, not gelignite).

Universal appreciation by pupils and parents for staff attitude that blends amiability with professionalism. 'Friendly but with a distance, which I liked'

The head is open-minded to range of teaching techniques, from whizzy interactive lessons to more conventional didactic ones. Plenty of both going on as far as we could see. Best, certainly as a spectator sport, are those that spill out into the corridors – we enjoyed watching group of boys whizz humming tops down long lengths of rope to demonstrate Doppler effect. 'Sums up boys' education, boys who are doing boys' things but with real enthusiasm – that's how lessons should be,' says the head.

Admirable get-ahead approach sees early start made in key subjects. Some of maths GCSE basics, for example, covered in year 8, reckoned a parent. Helped, too, by enthusiastic teachers managing largish groups (20 average class size, maximum 24) with aplomb, considerable stock rotation seeing oldies replaced with a fair few first jobbers (also cheaper, pointed out parental cynic). Includes some former City bods who have made their money – and enjoyed spending it, too – see staff car park for details. 'Proof that they are doing the job because they really want to,' thought a sixth former who had seen teaching standards rise during his time at the school, Another praised 'great young teachers' with inspirational lessons notable for minimum of note-taking drudgery.

When worst anyone can say of teaching is that it can be 'a tad bloodless,' there's not much to worry about. Some inevitable variance – a literature-averse child encountered English teacher who interrogated parents on son's interests so could 'get him reading' and hasn't stopped since. Another, less fortunate, '...arrived not liking reading and left feeling just the same,' said a mother, who felt a few more initiatives based in large, well-lit library – book clubs and the like – wouldn't come amiss. Individual subject libraries come in for particular praise from older pupils.

Universal appreciation by pupils and parents for staff attitude that blends amiability with professionalism. 'Friendly but with a distance, which I liked,' thought a mother. Tolerant of parent visits, too, in contrast with other schools where, said a parent, 'you feel that you're totally unwanted and you shouldn't go past the gate.' We even heard of a dedicated mother sitting at the back during maths lessons. Parents feel confident that on the very rare occasions that issues with teachers crop up they will be listened to and the problem quickly resolved. Pupil absences well handled, knowledge gaps quickly filled.

Homework, too, normally well managed. 'Not excessive and if there's occasional congestion, will get in touch,' thought a parent who, like others, rated home school communications highly. 'Teachers will always email back and apologise if they haven't done so immediately' – though felt that occasionally had to nudge the school a bit to get different departments to communicate with each other if, for example, sports or music looked in danger of overwhelming academic commitments.

Only unspoken issue is dreaded letters home, sent to around 20 boys underperforming in year 10 exams and unlikely to make the grade at GCSE. Rumours abound. Felt by one mother to be an anomaly in an otherwise compassionate environment. 'School takes them in, then they're thrown back,' thought a mother. Head stresses that letters are invariably the last stage in a programme of interventions which work in almost every case, all but three from latest batch making it through to sixth form. 'Our intention is that everyone will stay on,' he says. Points out, however, that for pupils struggling at the bottom in high-achieving school, it may be better to move to different school where confidence and performance are often transformed.

Head is understandably wary (and weary) of changes to A levels and GCSEs. Fine for school, but pupils only travel this way once, so important that 'not in the vanguard of untested novelty.' What matters above all, he says, is 'the quality of the people standing in front of children day in and day out.' On the basis of results, it's in plentiful supply.

Games, options, the arts: Super at sport, stunning at music and while not exactly hiding its light under a bushel – 'exceptional' is school's own verdict – you'd be hard pressed to find much to carp at, bar occasional organisational blips. 'Gave up asking which kit to pack years ago as never heard back,' sighs a parent.

Show enthusiasm here and you'll be encouraged to find your niche, with fair share of trophies making their way to display shelves by way of proof. Team sports are rugby, hockey, swimming, golf,

cricket, tennis, with many a final reached but perhaps slightly fewer of the top prizes scooped than a few years back. Head thinks that while those in search of year in, year out national trophy glory would probably still head for Dulwich or Whitgift, it depends 'how you measure sporting success.' If formal premiership existed, school would score a top 10 place.

Several parents described some under the surface frustration that needs excising. 'There's so much talent that could be converted into success,' said one, who thought more input from talented individuals – there are currently 40 regional and county players doing wonders in everything from triathlon to high and triple jump – might nudge teams to greater efforts.

Pupils clearly enjoy what's on offer – pressure of a low key nature, enjoyment pretty much guaranteed, inclusiveness stressed. Some of lower teams named after colours rather than letters, a disguise presumably aimed at avoiding discouragement.

DT is a wealth of traditional skills delivered with novelty, with bells, whistles (and entrancing flashing lights)

High tolerance for the less keen who are just 'happy to tick along.' Some pupils, according to parents, see relegation to alternative indoors activity as a positive perk, particularly on chilly afternoons.

School principally known, however, for its music, which is so good – drama almost equally so – that parents mention school in same breath as top specialist music colleges. Music is everywhere, strains of flute and keyboard piercing the air like shafts of sunlight, dedicated staff teaching 500 individual lessons a week and top quality instruments as standard (school first in London to boast all-Steinway line up, though arguably trumped by recent chance for top string players to play a real Stradivarius). Around 100 pupils a year are involved in professional productions, appearing everywhere from national radio and TV to Ronnie Scott's, Glyndebourne and Royal Opera House. Six on tour in US on day of visit.

Musicians and singers are 'picked up, nurtured, taken off and encouraged,' says a parent. With the exception of bit of below the barline muttering about recent departmental changes, nothing but praise. No wonder some of the most talented pupils even turn down grammar school places to take advantage of seemingly endless opportunities. Choice of 50 ensembles caters for super-talented and less so, with enthusiastic beginners getting as much of a kick out of performing as gifted peers.

Even school mag describes arrival of girls as 'adding a different octave' (on a more prosaic note, their presence means boys smell better too, according to school nurse).

Stunning and sometimes unsettling art that, in the case of naked (female) mannequin, arms outstretched against cross, part Borg, part Passion, haunts the brain for hours afterwards. DT is a similar wealth of traditional skills delivered with novelty, with bells, whistles (and entrancing flashing lights). Extracurricular programme is rich, particularly in first three years, with 150 lunchtime clubs and much in the way of community work. 'My son's passions are covered 100 per cent,' said a mother. Another said 'everything' is on offer, from foreign trips (Spanish students to Salamanca, photographers to Florence) to domestic outings (sixth form psychologists to London Zoo to study spider and other phobias).

Icing on the cake would be for DT (popular GCSE and A level choice) to be joined on the timetable by cookery. Particularly galling, felt mother, as at least one of local state schools now has boys arriving home with gourmet dishes on regular basis. 'It just doesn't get on private boys' schools' radar, but who is going to cook for these boys when they grow up? The world has changed.' More cookery coming soon in Portakabins freed up by soon to be renovated pavilion (no exam though).

Background and atmosphere: Pupils, staff and even head don't beat about the bush when describing school. Comments include 'ugly' and 'like a 1960s conference centre,' but as they point out, 'what matters is what goes on inside.' There's no getting away from it, though. Acres don't roll so much as jut, grey building block frontage effectively though bizarrely concealing considerable greenery at the back.

Choice of 50 ensembles caters for super-talented and less so, with enthusiastic beginners getting as much of a kick out of performing as gifted peers

Even so, immediate vibe is welcoming and slightly quirky, from multitude of well-lit spaces (many accessorised with pianos), cheerful staff and clear affection for surroundings, to pleas to 'visit us' prominently displayed on website. School essence summed up by picture of animated science lesson, pupil on what looks like giant vacuum cleaner (actually a hovercraft) being chased by laughing teacher, other boys cheering them on from the side. Certainly looks like fun, though tolerant, grown

up feel makes school far more than cheeky young whippersnapper to staid sister and brother schools (Whitgift and Old Palace respectively) that make up the Whitgift Foundation. Baffled by the relationship between them? 'You're not the only one,' says the head (joking, we're sure).

Extent of what a parent describes as 'sibling rivalry' between the two (mainly) boys' schools can only be guessed at (heads are coy about this). Parental rumour mill has it that decision to have girls in sixth form here – popular with all, though fairly low vis for youngest pupils – went to the wire because of fears that popularity, already at a high, would impact on application numbers at other Whitgift schools. Alarm understandable given school's many natural advantages. May not have quite the same presence as more historic establishments but then nor is it on quite the same scale, with smaller roll and more personable feel that has even parents with children elsewhere sounding slightly wistful when they talk about it.

Pastoral care and discipline: Taken very seriously. Sixth formers trained as mentors. Issues, including bullying, appear rarely but are swiftly and effectively sorted when they do. 'When another kid picked on my son it was dealt with sensibly,' thought a mother.

Year 6 juniors, known universally as J-bugs on account of 'being a bit annoying' in addition to short stature and giant backpacks – 'you get used to it,' thought one, with slight weariness – go straight into the mix with minimal cossetting and equanimity, furnished with map and high expectations. 'Teachers expect you to be on time from the second week,' said one, who clearly didn't see it as a problem.

Plenty of rewards, ranging from post-duty free lunches for prefects (who can recommend other pupils for commendations but don't wield much in the way of sticks) to teachers' end of term treats, including whole class outing to Nando's (dream choice). Conventional sanctions through system of 'signings' in homework diaries. Three strikes and it's a Saturday detention (chief crime usually not handing in homework on time). Lots of nurture on site, including school nurse, sympathy on tap (first visit goes unremarked, second in a term flagged up with phone call home).

Pupils and parents: Parents approve of the mix. 'A real balance in the classes, ages and races,' thought one. State primaries (some local, many further afield) field just over half of the pupils and around 45 per cent come from preps. Good bus services – mainly within a 10-mile radius (Oxted, Wandsworth, Dulwich, Farnborough and the like).

One parent thought addition of girls in sixth form was great for boys but 'wouldn't send my own daughter.' Head disagrees – the ebullient and confident may flourish here but so, equally, do 'the more reserved. In the same way, we have bright, strong, talented and shyer boys.' Girls themselves, including one who visited out of curiosity but signed up on strength of head's presentation, felt that a range of characters is catered for, though sufficient confidence to voice views in male-dominated classes was a character essential. Much pride that current girl physicists, though a minority, outshining the boys, who are 'a bit annoyed that we're better.'

Amongst the parents, little one-upmanship. Fewer feverishly competitive types than elsewhere and socialising so much fun that events attract complete outsiders. No pressure to attend events but the many who do tend to stay late. 'Have left car outside school overnight...' said one.

Entrance: In some cases, actually preferred over local grammars, particularly for super-talented musicians if fees can be found. Praise doesn't come much higher.

Biggest intake (70) is in year 7. Also takes around 42 boys in year 6 and a further 20 in year 9. All sit papers in English (comprehension and essay) plus maths and VR, shortlisted candidates attending interview. While desire to boost results has pushed up entry standards (papers broadly the same, pass mark higher), won't turn away those who need support as long as they can cope academically, range of difficulties happily accommodated. Another 30 are added in the sixth form.

Exit: Some to specialist music schools including Yehudi Menuhin, testimony to lure of music

excellence here (generous scholarships too). Others, occasionally ('handful in eight years,' says head) for less happy reasons (London exposure to drink and drugs the inevitable issues) are eased out but with discreet generosity that usually guarantees a second chance elsewhere. 'They don't blank them out but leave it open to go to another place,' said a parent.

After A levels, vast majority head to university; thirteen to Oxbridge in 2015. Other top destinations include Bristol, Southampton, York, Edinburgh and Manchester, plus normal London suspects (King's, Imperial, UCL, LSE). Huge range of courses taken, music and sciences of all descriptions well represented, from bioveterinary sciences to mechanical engineering.

Money matters: Exceptionally good for support. Scholarships worth between 10 and 50 per cent of the fees awarded for academics performance, plus music, sport, drama, art and (less common) design technology. Supplemented by excellent range of bursaries from Whitgift Foundation, which ensure that the gifted but less affluent won't miss out on a place.

Remarks: Grey outside, bursting with colour within. 'The school of the moment,' says a parent. Top sporting talent may haver slightly but if academic strength, music and general joie de vivre are your bag, practically perfect in every way. Forget the slightly unpromising surroundings. When the atmosphere is so buzzy that one parent said she even looked forward to the school run, you know you're on to a winner.

Whitgift School

Haling Park, South Croydon, Surrey CR2 6YT

Independent • Pupils: 1,455; 58 full, 54 weekly/flexi boarders • Ages: 10–18 • Sixth form pupils: 339 • C of E • Fees: Day £17,988 pa; Boarding up to £34,656 pa

Tel: 020 8688 9222

20

Email: admissions@whitgift.co.uk
Website: www.whitgift.co.uk

Head: Since 1991, Christopher A Barnett BA MA DPhil (60s). Previously second master, Dauntsey's School and before that head of history at Bradfield. Married to Laura, psychotherapist and author, four grown up children, one daughter, three sons who all came here, all scaling assorted dizzying career heights from bloodstock agent to Twitter supremo.

First post was in higher education as economics lecturer at Brunel in the 70s, combined with political research for MP. Logical, given impressive

string of qualifications to his name, Oxford and history-based for the initial bunch, including doctorate; extras from – amongst others – Downing, Cambridge where he's a fellow commoner (more important than a college lecturer; less than a bye-fellow, apparently) and French government (who wouldn't want luscious-sounding Chevalier dans L'Ordre des Palmes Académiques?).

Switched from higher to secondary education because of power of education to 'impact on the

whole child'. Also, you suspect, to provide suitable canvas for his innovations. 'A minefield of ideas,' as colleague put it.

Supremely confident (quality shared by pupils). Rather than endure months of time-sapping debate on funding decent grand piano when first arrived here, simply went out and bought one. Can even stop rain and replace with sunshine – we saw; we believe. Performed similar trick when Patron Duke of York visited. Father shared knack, so 'everyone booked their holiday when he did.'

Unsurprisingly, shuns dead hand of risk-averse culture, leading decisively from the front and exuding vim and vigour, even more energised now, he says, in contrast to other heads who 'fade away' in final years.

'Building a country,' reckoned one parent. Thinks massive, from annual replacement of framed photographs of school achievements lining corridors to big-canvas projects, borrowing £8 million at commercial interest rates to fund sports facilities paid for by rising pupil numbers – now 1,370 from 875 when arrived, could rise another 100 (but no higher) and greater economies of scale.

Probably best known for love of natural world, from dog inclusion policy, horses ditto – school racing syndicate is about to be reinstated, equine visitors not unknown – to assorted wildlife, particularly exotic birds. 'A bit like Dr Doolittle,' thought mother. 'He feels that it gives boys a sense of calmness', reckoned another (boys say they quickly get used to peacocks' shrieks at exam time).

Though pushmi-pullyu yet to make an appearance, other treats include wallabies, turacos and, our favourite, photogenic cranes waiting

(unsuccessfully) by back door to be let in (backstage team 'specially trained' in deep-cleaning the mats).

With so much on the go, Dr Barnett delegates 'hugely. If I can engage every one of my 200 staff, then that's 200 times the power of me.' Unsurprising that for some parents he is a slightly distant figure 'pulled out for public occasions,' though agreed that deputy heads and heads of year are able day-to-day managers.

Probably best known for love of natural world, from dog inclusion policy, horses ditto – school racing syndicate is about to be reinstated

Supporters praised individual take on the role. 'I suppose you've got to have someone a little bit off centre, not toeing the academic line too much,' thought mother. 'A lovely man, very approachable – not completely aloof,' said another. One member of staff expressed fervent hope that, paraphrasing Ramsbottoms, she would have many sons to her name so could send them there.

Emphatically not a timeserver, Dr Barnett is a man who relishes ability to make things happen, sparking like a Catherine wheel (favourite description of his hero, Disraeli). Style may not please all – but then, nor did Disraeli's. Has announced that he will be retiring in July 2017.

Academic matters: The full English but with continental option – A Levels, IB (bilingual option for most advanced French speakers), BTecs and even the occasional Pre-U (occasional top ups for those requiring extra stretch). Extended essay qualifications and the like just about the only no-goes – IB covers the ground, feels head.

Results consistently good. In 2015, 88 per cent of A levels graded A*-B, 70 per cent A*/A. IB marks healthy at average 38. Maths leads subject popularity by a mile, sciences follow, English and humanities put in good showing. Rest – PE, computing and music among them, lag in single figures at the rear.

GCSEs (IGCSEs in English, maths, science, languages) similarly healthy with 83.5 per cent graded A*/A in 2014. Ten sat by most. Options chosen from relatively compact range bar terrific languages (three rather than two studied) with Japanese and Mandarin already on offer and Arabic and Sanskrit possible future additions. DT hugely popular (we were shown wide range of delightful projects ranging from solar-powered beeswax storage unit to hockey stick unit).

One outsider wondered how staff can cover the range effectively, especially with same teachers for A levels and IB. Their idea, says head. Teachers, a level-headed bunch, averaging late 30s with a quarter into second decade, agree. Benefits of pupil choice outweigh double preparation time, said dedicated scientist, while some subjects with low A level numbers (such as DT) positively gagging to have a second go at IB now previously dreary syllabus is getting a makeover.

No shortage of teacher talent – former senior bods have gone on to headships everywhere from Magdalen College School to RGS Worcester. School has been academic non pareil in the area and 'the crème de la crème in every respect,' says local and could 'be in the top 10 [nationally] again,' says head, though not a fan of league table glory however.

Classrooms have trad feel (admittedly hard to compete with new build excitement elsewhere), pupil numbers around 18 per class, 10 in sixth form. Behaviour immaculate – all rise for adults. Fun year 7 maths class working out probability by throwing dice, sixth form biologists fighting coursework deadline (easy listening music in background to counter tension).

No shortage of teacher talent – former senior bods have gone on to headships everywhere from Magdalen College School to RGS Worcester

Well on the way to building an education that ensures those focused on academic excellence get their fill, but will customise for those with exceptional sports, musical or other talents – fistful of scholars desirable but making A*s the priority for exceptionally gifted violinist headed for music college is pointless, thinks head.

Good reports for most subjects. More experienced teachers tend to be kept for best, thought a parent, focused on GCSE years and above, though any problems raised (including those with individual teachers) are quickly sorted at whatever stage. Increasing provision for the 10 per cent of pupils with SEN (largely dyslexia though also ADHD, ASD, three statemented), team about to increase to six, including two full time teachers. Currently around 30 EAL pupils from 20 different nationalities.

Homework sensibly organised and, though workload is ramped up from around year 8, staff stick to allocated days and good at helping absentees catch up on missed sessions while 'emails fly back all the time for boys who can't quite manage it.' Felt that would be useful to have drop in clinics and clubs in key subjects focusing more on lesson content exam technique – and we heard of parent being 'actively encouraged' to seek private tuition when child fell behind. Summer school opening for first time in 2015.

Head librarian in senior library (cosier separate version for juniors – some subjects also have their own areas) talked enthusiastically of ways and means to boost reading interest, from book clubs to brunch events. With many boys glued to laptops at break, blind to lure of enticingly packed shelves, looked like an heroic endeavour.

While the academically capable flourish, parents warn that while school 'does what it says on

the tin,' pays to be on the ball, proactive parents getting in touch the second a report shows unexpected (downwards) grade movement. Former coasters are in for a shock. 'They do expect you to work to your optimum and you always need to be performing.'

Practical teacher input praised – one boy, struggling with twin demands of homework and role in musical, had rehearsal time halved so able to catch up. 'We can't speak highly enough [of the school],' said mother. 'Their expectations of the boys really surprised us, that everything was possible.'

Games, options, the arts: 'We allow pupils to follow their passion,' feels head. 'I'm only really interested on what we can do for the individual child.' Means pupils don't have to go to university to find out who they are, he reckons (though we worry about all that existential angst forced to find other outlets...). Finding niche can require strong-mindedness, however. One up-and-coming rugby star – Harlequins hopeful – had given it all up for love of singing.

For the natural joiner, undoubtedly paradise, and starts early with all new pupils getting free golf and instrumental lessons (though not simultaneously). Much of massive co-curricular programme included in the fees (100 or so options, from animal to Islamic club). 'So many activities that by the time you leave, you'll have other interests,' thought sixth former.

One mother felt that sporty, academic or artistic groups of boys tend to follow separate paths. Once, perhaps, said pupils, but no longer the case. 'Have friends with very different interests,' said one.

Head librarian in senior library (cosier separate version for juniors – some subjects also have their own areas) talked enthusiastically of ways to boost reading interest

Sports facilities terrific, luring in outsiders from Surrey cricketers to Olympic hopefuls – approving quotes dot prospectus. Goodies include assorted pitches where seriously rugged hone skills to sports centre with squash courts, fencing salle and fitness suite, as well as swimming pool (different depths fit all, from armband armies to water polo teams). There's even a Transformers-style sports hall (now you see it, now it's a 1800-seat conference centre).

While talent levels mean pupils who would have made top teams elsewhere may not do so here, even C and D teams often win against other schools' As and Bs, while starry coaches including

Colin Pates (Chelsea) and Steve Kember (Crystal Palace) are doing for football what is already the norm for rugby, hockey and the rest. Almost easier, in fact, to list sports that don't feature amongst over 100 national titles secured in past five years.

Performing arts also getting substantial injection of resources with International Music Competition for string players, inaugurated 2013, soloist opportunities and fees the prize, and attracting talent from Eastern Europe. Six full scholarship boarders now in residence with more to follow; all potential soloists, reckons head.

With sell-out musicals, some outstanding actors (one has already written and starred in own play) and 380 learning an instrument, some to diploma level, performing arts already in good shape, spaces indoors and out, from Founder's Garden to old swimming pool, all imaginatively used for everything from Shakespeare to sell-out musicals (West Side Story was in rehearsal when we visited), concerts ranging from beginner strings to Mahler at Royal Festival Hall.

If there's a corporate refrain, it's 'best anywhere'. Only parental niggle would be more access to facilities. Pool, for example, is 'amazing' but opportunities to use it outside the timetabled six weeks a year would be appreciated – tricky, admittedly, given extensive use by outside groups. Bottom line, though, is that 'if you're good at something, they've got all the facilities in the world,' thought mother.

Background and atmosphere: Ancient name, lovely and unusual site – cross between wildlife park and landscaped RHS outpost. Whipsley, perhaps? Don't expect acres of Tudor panelling, however. Though school was founded in 1600 and current site was owned by Henry VIII (and home to Lord Howard of Effingham, son a very early Old Boy) most is vintage 20th rather than 17th century (well worth seeing fascinating archive) and pleasant rather than grand in feel, despite commanding hilltop view over south Croydon.

Deep community roots, however, not only endure but extend each year, involvement ranging from extensive financial help for families of pupils in need to vast year-round outreach programme costing around £100,000 and involving 55 local schools, each spending a week at the school with dedicated classrooms and seconded staff with sessions covering sport, arts, science and languages.

Next step will be audition-entry weekend arts academy, free to local children as well as school's pupils, currently in trial phase, major beta problem the clash with Saturday sports fixtures.

Numbers standing up well to scrutiny and, as the biggest leading independent boys only in the area, as well as highly academically successful, so you'd hope. Theoretically a matching pair with Old Palace, the girls only school also in the Whitgift Foundation, though not an exclusive relationship – joint drama and music productions with Croydon High and St Andrew's C of E High School, too.

Trinity the big rival – 'You have to say "T" word,' counsels pupil, though others would like more contact. Head says tricky logistically and for now, schools likely to keep dancing to individual tunes. While Trinity has co-ed sixth as a USP, here they've upped ante with boarding (new house catering for 100 13-18 year olds opened 2013). Bright and beautiful, partially powered by solar (though water 'too grey' to recycle, says new boarding housemaster – one of the many staff with rugby-fuelled handshake).

'We were blown away when we saw it,' says mother. Doesn't stop, either, planned science biodomes each featuring slice of life (flora and fauna)

Features super common rooms, welcoming but airy, uncluttered feel, upmarketing furnishing (new Yamaha piano) and Subbuteo for juniors, snooker (and superior view over greenery) for seniors next door. Beds specially ordered for seven footers and, amazingly, every fragile-looking wall-mounted loo so far intact (must be made from same makers as indestructible cushions).

Highly successful, it's reckoned and, with 40 full boarders at weekends, no forlorn few testing the echoes. While activities generally good they sounded a little low-key when majority are off on voluntary exeats. Actively not trying to create

traditions (can be where problems begin, is view of school, which numbers consecutive year groups 1, 3 and 5...).

In unlikely event that new buildings don't deliver wow factor, outside loveliness certainly will, from Founder's Garden, created for 400th anniversary and graced with very own new rose, to Whitgift water gardens, tape cut by Sir David Attenborough, who was bowled over by visions of loveliness before him, rare emerald starling adding final touch of enchantment.

'We were blown away when we saw it,' says mother. Doesn't stop, either, planned science biodomes each featuring slice of life (flora and fauna) from round the world. Like the Eden Project, says head, only better (from educational perspective at least – though does win on location). Butterflies soon on order. Giant tortoise being debated.

Pastoral care and discipline: Big on nurturing from day one with older boys mentoring younger ones (a few blank looks from mentorees-in-waiting) on top of formal tutor system. Older pupils often turn to subject teachers for 'excellent' ad hoc support.

Fab induction trip to Lake Garda for year 6s (heavily subsidised) within first few weeks works wonders even for the very shy. Great care taken to create school within a school, 10+ and 11+ intake in own very pleasant building and, with the obvious exceptions such as art, music, games, form-based for lessons, and even a separate house system.

Only question mark was over slightly bleak asphalt-covered junior playground, bins the only ornament. When quizzed, pupils and head unanimous in stressing year-round use for ball games (surrounding windows correspondingly battle-weary), rendering any embellishment undesirable.

Masses of boys can mean occasional testosterone overload, though any low level disruptive behaviour is effectively sorted out as pupils move up through the school. Fisticuffs rare but not unheard of, though parents tend to take this calmly. 'Typical of boys' schools,' said a mother. Ditto pupils. 'It happens. It's better just to deal with it,' said pupil.

Though corridor supervision appeared low key, boys reckoned teachers were never far away – even super sixth form common room has head of year's office in corner, though clearly gaze is benign, judging by relaxed crowd sprawled on easy chairs, one minus shoes.

Hot on effective sanctions, too, reckoned a parent, with school services – times spent doing something useful, such as lunchtime litter clearance or cloakroom tidying, cordially loathed and thus highly effective deterrents.

Head plans mass pupil engagement programme – will see around 700 over next year in small groups for elevenses, lunch and tea. Though mainly for success stories, is also asking for teachers to refer boys who may need little extra pepping up to join them.

May answer plea by one parent for more sugar to help medicine go down. 'I think I'd like it to be a little less pressurised and use more carrots rather than sticks.'

Pupils and parents: Many Croydon-based, or close; nearby grammars and Trinity the main alternative senior schools, with around 60 per cent of intake from state primaries (preps were in majority when head first joined school, but feels that links with community have boosted appeal to first time buyers). Increasingly attracts those from further afield – into deeper Surrey and even north London with boarding opening it up to the world (Taiwan the latest country expressing desire to forge links).

Fab induction trip to Lake Garda for year 6s (heavily subsidised) within first few weeks works wonders even for the very shy

With Old Boys numbering TV illusionist Derren Brown, actor Martin Jarvis and Premier League star Victor Moses amongst ranks, average career hard to define, though being a reasonably tough personality to make a success of life here and later on probably helps. 'I think if you can't hold your own then you're going to sink,' felt mum.

For the right child, however, approach works wonders. 'If he'd gone to one of the state schools I don't think he'd be the confident young man he is now,' reckoned mother. 'He's much more able to walk into a room full of strangers and hold a conversation.'

Easy-going parents can come as a relief to newcomers. 'Thought they would be very highbrow and stuffy but not at all.' Terrific socialising, too. 'We have the best time...we went to a quiz night, there's a summer ball, it's everyone mucking in,' says one.

Entrance: Entrance exam early Jan, day at school. Majority sit 10+, 11+ or 13+ exams (maths, English, VR). Fewer at 12+ and 14+ (maths, English and science). Likelies invited back to interview. Sixth form candidates need seven GCSE passes with A/A*s in A level subjects (similar for IB), though possible to enter to take BTec sport, in which case five A*/C passes will suffice. Interesting advent of dual sixth form streams, second for less academic but highly sporty. Head talks with winning enthusiasm for need to educate nation's footballers post-16...

Exit: Little fall-out – 20 per cent left after GCSEs in 2014; those with below par AS results often redoing a year or retaking modules. Occasionally pupils 'advised' to look elsewhere. 'Nobody is ever directly asked to leave,' said senior pupil. Vast majority who sail on reach splendid destinations. Offers from all the big beasts (Warwick, Southampton, Bristol, UCL, Edinburgh etc) and pupils clearly well thought of – one had received Oxford IB offer of 38, high but not stratospheric. Big range of subjects from geography to performing arts and professional sport. Twenty-four to Oxbridge in 2015 – 'What you're paying for,' said parent. 'What you're paying for,' said parent.

Money matters: Scholarships are one of Whitgift's huge strengths, the number of bursaries and amount of financial help makes school a possibility for those from most deprived of backgrounds. Sensitively handled, too, with those in need of extra funding for school trips given subtle means of applying so need never miss out. Aim is for one in three boarders (mainly music but possibly sports as well) to be on full scholarships.

Remarks: 'Happy and high achieving,' thought a parent, with traditional virtues pushed but never, under sparky headship of Dr Barnett, a dull place to be, even though Zoological Society of London has declined request for elephant. Natural home for academically inclined, sportsmen and performers and ideal not just for wallabies and flamingos but also for confident joiners who may not yet have settled on their passion in life but relish process of discovery.

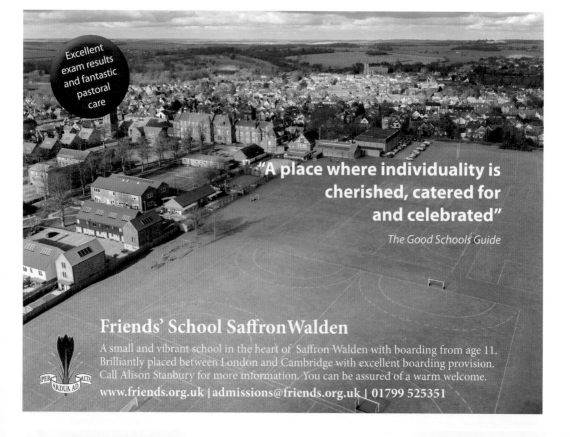

Children with special educational needs

Whether you are moving to London or already live here, the process of choosing a school is fraught with difficulties; throw into the mix a child with special needs and the challenges increase. You want your child to have an unparalleled education, but what are your options, and how do you work out what really is best?

What counts as a special need?
If your child has a difficulty that makes learning harder for them than for most children of the same age – whether the difficulty is social, emotional, intellectual, behavioural, physical, sensory or a mixture – then they may well have a special need. The most complex needs are generally diagnosed at birth or soon after, but other conditions, such as mild autistic spectrum disorders or specific learning difficulties such as dyslexia, may not be identified until well into their schooling. Indeed, you may well have to work hard to have your child's need recognised as 'special'. These needs may be transitory or permanent, but what matters is getting good help and support as soon as possible.

State schools – your choices
All state schools are in theory open to children with special needs – though for grammar schools they will need to pass the entrance exams. If your child has a Statement or, since September 2014, an Education Health and Social Care plan (EHC plan – next page) then it may be possible to add special schools to the list.

Independent schools – their choice
Independent schools choose the pupils they want to teach – if they don't want your child there is not a lot you can do about it. Some, such as Finton House in Wandsworth, keep a handful of places especially for children with special needs,

others have a healthy, helpful attitude and will look at each child on merit.

London is blessed with some very good SEN specialist schools but the number and type of places available are limited. They tend to be expensive, too. Occasionally, an LA may agree to fund a place at an independent school (even if it is not in their own borough) but such places and funding are increasingly rare.

If a special or specialist school catches your eye, approach the school and ask them if they think your child might fit. They are likely to ask you to send reports, visit, even pay for an assessment. If they subsequently think they can help, they may offer assistance with the knotty process of securing LA funding, but be prepared for a long, fraught, frustrating fight with no guarantees.

SEN: a state of flux

Since September 2014 any new assessment for the two per cent or so of children with greatest needs is via an EHC plan rather than a Statement. Many of the finer details of EHC plans have yet to be worked out, but they are intended to cover both education and health needs, giving greater flexibility and greater autonomy for the child and their family. The picture is less clear for those whose needs are less severe, but most likely schools will have to provide help for them with no extra funding.

School admissions

If your child has an EHC plan or Statement you can, with the help of your LA, name the school you would like them to attend. Mainstream or special state schools, and independent special schools, must in theory admit your child unless the governing body thinks doing so would be 'unsuitable for the age, ability, aptitude or SEN of the child or young person;

or the attendance of the child or young person there would be incompatible with the efficient education of others; or the efficient use of resources'. If the school says no, you can appeal to the SEND tribunal.

Evaluating schools for children with SEN

Before signing on the dotted line, check out inspection reports, school policies, school websites and any independent reviews such as those by The Good Schools Guide – do they reflect a positive approach to SEN?

Once you've done the virtual work, arrange to visit schools, request a tour and ask to meet with the head and SENCo. Do they have a flexible and positive approach to SEN? Is support an integral part of school life? How is individual progress monitored? Is there a widespread celebration of achievement? Is the school generally geared up for diverse needs?

Try to visit two or more schools so you can compare them and make the best choice possible. Keep an eye on entry requirements and deadlines; rules and timings can and do change. Finally, remember to look beyond your child's special needs to ensure their strengths, talents and interests will be well catered for too.

For more information, visit www.goodschoolsguide.co.uk/sen

SEN schools in South London

The following schools offer specialist, targeted help for specific learning difficulties such as dyslexia, dyspraxia and ADHD. Some of their pupils may be able to return to mainstream school after a period of specialist teaching, but all will benefit from teaching methods and therapies specifically designed for these difficulties.

Blossom House

Station Road, Motspur Park, New Malden KT3 6JJ
020 8946 7348
www.blossomhouseschool.co.uk

Head: Since its founding in 1983, Mrs Joanna (Joey) Burgess (60s) DipCST MRCSLT Dip RSA SpLD PGCE. Enchanting, with a wicked sense of humour, the diminutive Mrs B is described by parents as elegant, petite, beautiful and kind, with a steely will. 'Joey doesn't just light up the room – she lights up lives,' said one grateful parent. 'We have the most wonderful dos – it is a very sociable school. Joey wouldn't have it any other way – she loves a party'.

Entry: Most have additional needs including ASD, dyspraxia, sensory integration difficulties (can cater for the 'fizzy, whizzy' child but not the aggressive or violent), dyslexia (school is CReSTeD registered) and ADHD, occasional selective mute. It is not unusual for youngsters to exhibit a deal of frustration and anxiety as a result of their language disorders, but the school would not suit those whose primary needs are either ASD or behavioural.

Entry: Via a detailed three-day assessment followed, for some, by a trial six week period to ensure the child will benefit from a Blossom education. On entry, approximately one third of the nursery children have very limited speech, but thanks to timely, expertly delivered interventions, this reduces significantly as youngsters progress through the school. Quite a few come from mainstream. 'Some cope there initially – they don't look any different to their peers – but as they get older, their difficulties become apparent and frustrations are compounded. It takes a deal of time and devotion for us to get them back on track'.

From a wide area of London, Surrey and Kent. Fees reflect the high level of support, but 90 per cent of pupils funded by their local authority.

Exit: Majority stay at 11+, others to specialist schools: More House (Farnham), Moor House (Oxted), The Moat, St Dominic's Godalming, Sibford, St Catherine's. A few to (supported) mainstream state schools: Wimbledon College, Ursuline Convent etc. Recently started 16+ provision – no leavers as yet.

Remarks: All have an Individual Education Programme (IEP) based on personal learning styles, combined with visual communication aids, such as timetables of the day. Offers a relatively rare, educational-health-emotional package of teaching, speech and language therapy, occupational and physiotherapy, art, music and drama therapy.

Teaching is multi-sensory, with 'over-teaching', and is linked to an innovative sensory integration programme which helps children regulate and focus: 'It is possibly the most important thing we have introduced'. All follow the national curriculum, adapted as necessary. Touch typing from age 7. All work towards GCSEs and/or entry level exams, vocational qualifications and practical courses in a range of subjects including art and design, science, maths, English, DT (food or graphic products), media and ICT.

All youngsters have group music and art lessons – teachers aim to develop creativity, build self-esteem and encourage interaction and communication. Variety of sports on offer and older pupils are encouraged to work towards Duke of Edinburgh and sports leader awards. Tends to play inter-house sport rather than inter-school, as early outings resulted in crushing defeats and squashed esteems.

Many older children arrive feeling angry, let down, stupid and unworthy, so staff unapologetically focus on the individual and work to reduce anxiety and stress. 'We do what is needed – if that is a Theraband on a chair or bluetac to squash, that's fine,' said one therapist, adding, 'Tinies arrive surrounded by chaos and mess. It is our job to untangle. We help them make the links, so they understand their significance to themselves and others.'

For the right child with speech, language and communication issues few rosier places to develop, mature and bloom.

Centre Academy

92 St John's Hill, London SW11 1SH
020 7738 2344
www.centreacademy.net

Principal of the Centre Academy Schools: Since 2007, Dr Duncan Rollo BA MA PHD (60s), born in Scotland, raised in the USA. Popular with parents; personable and empathic with a can-do approach that, say parents, has made a real difference. Knowledgeable and charming, an expert on SEN matters, he is also refreshingly honest – if mistakes are made or something needs improving he takes it on board.

Entry: Admission from 9+ years, then as places become available; caters for a range of needs including milder autistic spectrum disorders, dyslexia/ADD/dyspraxia and complex processing difficulties. Eccentricities can be managed but not aggressive or violent behaviour. Officially, first step is to have a conversation with Dr Rollo to check the school is what you are looking for. If all agree it may be suitable, the next stage is to send in the relevant documentation, eg medical and psychological reports. The family will then meet with Dr Rollo, and the child will be invited to spend two or three assessment days. Assessment is two-way, to see how the child copes and to ensure the school will be able to meet particular needs.

Exit: A few return to mainstream schooling before the end of key stage 3. At 18+ mostly to university, odd one to FE college; UK universities have been happy to accept the four-year USA high school diploma as an equivalent to GCSE and A level.

Remarks: Small classes averaging five or six pupils enable group work as well as individual teaching. Every effort is made to adapt the curriculum to the needs of the individual with timetables monitored daily by tutors. Broadly follows the national curriculum to year 9 (age 13), thereafter GCSE, USA high school diploma or vocational courses – whatever suits; the continuously assessed American system works particularly well.

Own in-house language and occupational therapists and all staff attend regular specialist training sessions. Pupils are confident about their learning – in recent years almost all have achieved some A*-Cs in GCSE English.

Annual trips to adventure camps, places of interest and, for older students, overseas. No on-site sports facilities, so pupils make full use of the local sports centre and nearby playing fields. Drama important, not just for fun but for supporting language and communication skills too, with the neighbouring church hall providing much-needed space for the expressive arts. Art studio is a hive of activity – traditional drawing, painting and sculpture offered alongside weaving and embroidery; plenty of opportunities to develop fine motor skills and concentration. Regular clubs include arts, sports and community service offerings.

Many of the pupils have not fared well in other schools and so clearly appreciate the friendly staff; one boy confided, 'This is the first school where I have felt confident enough to ask the staff questions without fear of getting into trouble'. Life skills are an integral part of the curriculum, with pupils encouraged to use their initiative and get involved, hence the recently-opened pupil-run tuckshop for break times. A highly experienced counsellor runs an impressive support team.

A unique school that recognises one size definitely does not fit all.

The Dominie

55 Warriner Gardens, London SW11 4DX
020 7720 8783
www.thedominie.co.uk

Head: Since 2007, Miss Anne O'Doherty BA Dip Spld (Barts) Dip Montessori (50s). Miss O'Doherty has been at the cutting edge of researching and teaching children with specific learning difficulties for over 30 years and has a wealth of knowledge and experience working in both mainstream and specialist schools. Was co-director of the Kensington Dyslexia Teaching Centre, where she worked for 14 years.

Miss O'Doherty, accompanied by Maisie the school terrier, leads a dedicated team at The Dominie. The common aim is to restore pupils' confidence and help them discover the joys of learning and succeeding.

Entry: Any time from 6+ as places become available. Parents need to provide the school with as much information as possible about their child along with the educational psychologist reports. Prospective pupils are invited for a three-day trial to enable staff to assess individual needs and ensure that the school is going to be a suitable placement.

Exit: To a mixture of day and boarding schools. London day schools include The Harrodian, More House and Broomwood. Boarding and outside London: Bethany, Tudor Hall and Dunhurst.

Remarks: A small specialist school providing education for children affected by dyslexia, dyspraxia, dyscalculia and related conditions. The whole school approach is multi-sensory and multi-disciplinary, each child's developmental needs are considered and addressed. One-to-one sessions with physiotherapists, occupational therapists and speech therapists are arranged as required.

Mornings are dedicated to English and mathematics. In the afternoons, the children have topic lessons in history, geography and science as well as art, drama, music and sport. Pupils can enjoy individual instrumental tuition and everyone looks forward to the annual autumn term school play. All of the children are entered for the English Speaking Board certificates. The children enjoy after-school clubs as well as visits to places of interest. Years 5 and 6 go on a residential trip to PGL each summer term.

The Dominie is situated in converted premises on a residential road in Battersea, a stone's throw from the park where the children have their playtime and PE lessons. A carefully planned sports curriculum helps the children develop manual dexterity and physical confidence. They also enjoy weekly swimming lessons.

The school's particular strength is its ability to differentiate the curriculum and tailor it to individual requirements. The success of its carefully structured programmes is evidenced in that the majority of pupils, in their own time, will return to mainstream schools.

"If everyone is thinking alike, then no one is thinking."
Benjamin Franklin

At Frensham Heights, we are proud to think differently. We know every child is an individual and we treat them as such. That's why you'll continue to find Old Frenshamians leading in everything from medicine to opera and from the boardroom to the stage.

Come and see for yourself what makes Frensham so successfully individual. Visit www.frensham.org or call 01252 792561 to order a prospectus or arrange a visit.

Frensham Heights | Think, Create, Explore

Frensham Heights, Rowledge, Farnham, Surrey GU10 4EA Tel. 01252 792561 Charity No. 31205.

Are two languages better than one?

Bilingualism remains, for monolingual parents, an impossibly glamorous idea. One language is good, two languages even better. Three languages? Why, the world's your oyster, huître or – depending, of course, on what those languages are.

London's linguistic make-up is becoming increasingly complex. Almost eight in 10 pupils in Newham primary schools, for example, speak English as an additional language. And as the capital becomes ever more culturally diverse, the number of schools offering a bilingual education is also increasing.

The French have been particularly energetic in working with local authorities to offer a small (very small) number of children a bilingual, French and English education in state schools. Danish and Italian bilingual schools, amongst others, are cropping up too. Given that the French make up one of the largest expat groups in the country, their enthusiasm is understandable. But if you're a really ambitious family, French may not be enough.

Bilingual nurseries

A new nursery in east London is tapping into the growing demand for families convinced that early exposure to Mandarin is a sure fire path to academic career success. Their statistics are an exercise in appetite whetting and there are plenty more out there, showing how a bilingual education can contribute to everything from improved concentration to better exam results.

Bringing up baby in more than one language isn't, however, always problem-free. Nor is it an easy way of guaranteeing top results. As one international school expert points out, it's not bilingual crèches that put Singapore at the top of the education achievement tables.

Exposure to a language and immersion are two very different things, while the simultaneous bilingualism that can occur naturally when the family is bilingual is a far cry from the bilingual crèche approach. Regardless of how many languages parents would like their child to speak, it is crucial that they develop a firm foundation in at least one to get the most out of their education.

The reason? It can take between five and seven years to develop the full literacy in a second language necessary to be a fully functioning bilingual. To be truly successful at school, children need fluent academic English. Being able to chat just isn't enough.

Lacking foundations

Too many students speak and function in two, three or more languages without having developed full literacy skills in any single one, something that is particularly likely to happen if they have not had proper EAL foundations provided in primary school.

If this doesn't happen, problems may not show up until children start to fail at Common Entrance or the 11+, missing out on offers for selective independent secondary schools because their higher-level cognitive thinking skills have not developed. For other students, the crunch point comes at 16, when IB diploma choices loom, with the need to be able to write critical literary analyses in their first language whilst also studying a second. It becomes clear that they do not have sufficient proficiency in any language to cope with this demanding course.

'Behind closed doors, we refer to these children as the 'bi-illiterates' – illiterate in two languages,' says one international schools expert.

In addition to ensuring children become truly proficient in at least one language, it is also important to understand that some children with learning needs will be worse off with a multilingual education. Speech and language processing problems, for example, can be magnified. A child struggling in one language can find it doubly hard to cope with two.

Mandarin or Martian

Any language, French, Mandarin or Martian, could end up holding back your child unless their school is also able to ensure that they acquire full literacy skills in the mother tongue or first language.

That said, pupils who achieve a good fluency and form a strong foundation in a first language can successfully go on to learn many more. But the bottom line is that parents who want their children to be educated in an English-speaking school need to ensure that their children have a sound foundation in their first language, otherwise the subtleties and complexities of higher order language processing will always elude them.

Wonderful though it is to be able to converse in and understand other languages, children need at least one they can learn in – and this generally means the one they think in. Speaking one language at home and another at school must therefore always be carefully thought through so children do not feel excluded or become disenfranchised.

City slippers – boarding for Londoners

Boarding, like sheep herding, polytunnelling and plume scrumpling, is something many Londoners assume to be an exclusively rural activity. Not too rural, of course. These days, families are increasingly selective about just how countrified they want the boarding experience to be. Greenery, yes. Day-long hikes to sports day, on the whole, not.

It's no coincidence that boarding schools whose yield per hectare, if not quite a match for top cash crops, comes close, hit greatest density levels within easy reach of London's top postcodes – no more than a sonic boom's echo from Heathrow or Gatwick.

Most famous of the lot are Eton and Harrow. While other schools have not just rolled over in response to parental requests for part-time boarding but also offered to juggle a couple of hoops with their front paws, there are no such concessions here. When boys' only full boarding for all has worked for centuries, you can't really blame them.

It's the same story for the girls at St Mary's Ascot, which held its nerve through the dark days of the recession and has been rewarded with record demand. Parents who don't buy in to the idea of boarding the traditional way are gently – but firmly – urged to look elsewhere.

Some city slickers don't buy into boarding, full stop. Others start to wonder whether the bracing two hour trek across London to and from that excellent day school and in the dark both ways during winter really is as character-forming as they'd hoped.

For these families, boarding can seem life-enhancing, making it possible to start early and stay late with food and friends provided – and without a punitive journey at the beginning and end of the day.

B&B

Many schools make a virtue – and success – of combining education with what can feel like a large-scale bed and breakfast operation: some pupils day only, some there pretty much full time, others opting for in-school sleepovers because of parental commitments, exam revision, late night games or early morning training.

Girls'-only establishments offering boarding and day places within or close to M25 range from Woldingham in Surrey, Marymount in Kingston-upon-Thames and St George's Ascot to the south and south west, while the Royal Masonic School for Girls and St Margaret's fill a similar niche north of the river. Boy boarders, meanwhile, can opt for Reed's School in Cobham, Surrey (girls are admitted in the sixth form) or Dulwich College, though day pupils dominate at both.

Those in search of a co-ed environment are, if not spoiled for choice close to London, far from being deprived, with Epsom College in Surrey and LVS in Ascot among those giving their accommodation eye-popping makeovers, from colour-coordinated furnishings (it's hard to spot a cushion that isn't tonally related to the curtains) to unlimited fresh fruit to snack on. Further north, there's Mill Hill School, with 150 weekly and full boarders.

Boarding, like every other aspect of education, has its fair share of curiosities. Like the ravens at the Tower of London, boarders at the City of Freemen's School in Ashtead, Surrey, specified by statute, must always be part of the community (though, unlike the ravens, wing-clipping isn't required to keep them there).

Schools for skills

Then there are the specialists – such as the Yehudi Menuhin School (music) and Tring Park (performing arts) – where boarding helps the super talented to hone their skills in and out of hours, free from tube strike blues and similar aesthetic lows; the different (eg St Christopher in Letchworth, set up by the Theosophists) and the new (flushed with the success of its first boarding house, Whitgift School, in the non-plush territory of South Croydon, is already mulling over a second).

Even costs don't necessarily need to be sky high if you opt for a state boarding school such as Cranbook (selective) and Gordon's (all-comers) where parents pay for accommodation while teaching comes courtesy of the ever-generous taxpayer.

For any dyed in the wool Londoners who come over all faint at the prospect of breathing air outside the congestion zone, no longer enhanced with flavoursome carcinogens, it's hard to beat boarding, literally, on your doorstep.

Westminster School, with 185 or so boarders (including girls, admitted in the sixth form), is pretty much as close as you can get to total immersion in the beating heart of the city without squatting in Big Ben. 'You get that sense of community,' says a former Westminster parent. 'You have more time to get involved and people tend to stay late anyway.'

For some London parents, day places will always be the educational black, the only goal worth pursuing, with boarding the reserve choice when all other options have been exhausted. Others, relishing the out of hours opportunities, from extra tuition to drama, debate, music and sport, feel very differently. Costs permitting (and boarding is, undeniably, costly) it could well be worth taking a look at both.

HURTWOOD HOUSE

THE BOARDING SCHOOL FOR THE CREATIVE & PERFORMING ARTS

www.hurtwoodhouse.com

Gumley House School FCJ

Gumley House School FCJ provides a Catholic Education for girls, including boys in the sixth form. (Open policy with no faith requirement for sixth form)

The Gumley Journey: Our students benefit from a strong academic learning environment, whole person development, extensive extracurricular provision, pastoral support, diverse international opportunities and abundant grounds and green spaces.

Top Performing State School: Academic results reflect our tradition of achievement; the students' high levels of ambition and expectation and the teaching and dedication of our staff.

Latest results:

- A Level: Continued success with 100% pass rate and Oxbridge entrance. Results exceed by far the national average. Our A* results of 15% are the highest in the borough.
- From Year 7, students can study Mandarin, one of 4 languages taught. Almost 90% of GCSE students taking a language regularly achieve A*- C grades.
  (Gumley is one of only 8% of state schools teaching Mandarin)

Sixth form results

Please do contact us anytime directly on
general@gumley.hounslow.sch.uk

Shower Gel to Start Up Business! Imperial College Science & Enterprise project.

THE GOOD SCHOOLS GUIDE

For our review visit
www.goodschoolsguide.co.uk/schools/100540/gumley-house-school-fcj

www.gumley.hounslow.sch.uk

Get set for the school run

Between 6.45am and 8.00am every day in term time, a rash of buses appears on London's streets. Some are vast coaches, school destination announced in flashing letters; others smaller, anonymous white minibuses. Big or small, their purpose is the same – to ferry hundreds of children, some as young as 4 and 5, to and from school each day.

As the race for places at desirable schools, both state and independent, hots up, a longer home to school commute seems to be an additional price that increasing numbers of desperate families are willing for their child to pay to secure the best possible education.

While some parents would prefer not to buy in to transport arrangements that segregate their children from others and make their educational experience even more rarified, for others, it's a lifesaver. International school ACS Cobham, for example, offers a door-to-door service covering swathes of Surrey, from Guildford up to Teddington and Woking to Thames Ditton – a godsend for anyone finding relocation to the UK complex enough without adding the stress of a beat-the-clock school run.

And catching a daily bus certainly isn't all bad. One leading headmaster even praised its – admittedly subtle – benefits. Pupils look forward to their daily commute, he said, because in such a pressurised environment, it's just about the only chance they have to relax.

There are other factors, too. Traffic and children aren't a natural mix. For the truly worried, there's even a website that lets you search accidents by postcode. Though overall figures are down, injuries or worse for the young would give even well-adjusted parents the jitters, with a third of incidents involving 11 and 12-year-olds, coinciding with a longer commute to senior school and possibly not unconnected with a rise in smart phone ownership.

Then there's crime. One leading boys' school has become

notably relaxed about its pupils shedding uniform for their homeward journey after its distinctive blazers – as good an indication of quality merchandise as a Harrod's label – made them easy pickings for muggers. Instead, pupils are advised to don hoodies (sensible) or 'overcoats' (a Crombie a day keeps the robbers away? Well, perhaps).

All in all, it's not hard to see why a DIY approach to transport, however well-intentioned, can have limited appeal.

Smooth operators

Whatever the reasons, the number of school bus routes has climbed. Some schools even attract more than one operator. One leading girls' school, for example, has two, serving broadly similar routes, though there's no sign so far (fun though it would be to witness) of punch ups between rival firms at going home time.

Around the capital, the route permutations are sufficiently varied to keep an anoraks' convention happy for days. Hampton Court House, a co-ed, all-through school in a picturesque south of the river location, brings in pupils from Chelsea, Twickenham and Esher, while Dulwich College buses track through the southern hinterlands of Clapham, and Streatham, Upper Norwood and Raynes Park.

Rules of the road

It's worth noting that, unlike formal school trips, morning and afternoon bus commutes are less regulated. Nor is the age your child can travel to and from school fixed in stone. At one leading girls' school, pupils are welcomed on board from reception age onwards but others have higher age limits.

Operating companies, too, vary in what they can and can't do. Routes shouldn't generally be than 15 miles in London to avoid going above a maximum journey length of around 75 minutes for older children and 45 minutes for little ones.

The strictest rules apply to firms registered as licensed operators, where drivers and the buses themselves are allowed on the road only after they've shown themselves to be fit for purpose and even non-driving directors have to pass exams to show they know what they're doing.

But when it comes to the increasing numbers of minicab firms offering door to door school pickups round London in smaller vehicles – up to eight passengers, plus the driver – there's rather less officialdom. It's worth checking who your driver will be, whether you'll have the same one each day and their experience, background and checks.

Best of both worlds?

Finally, for families who have had enough of the whole London education experience, several schools offer what they (inevitably) describe as the best of both worlds – home in the big smoke, education in green home counties acres.

Some (such as Woldingham) meet, greet and sweep up from the local station – handily it's on a direct route from Clapham Junction, and just happens to border their extensive grounds. Others like Caldicott and Papplewick (boys' prep schools near Ascot) run their own daily return bus service from assorted West London destinations (Brook Green, twixt Hammersmith and Shepherd's Bush, is the minibus equivalent of platform 9¾ at King's Cross).

Routes can, of course, change, as families' postcodes differ and bus services that were over-booked one year empty out in the next. But whether through the school itself, parent-organised services or independent companies, it's more than likely that however esoteric the journey your child needs to take, from the shortest cross-borough hop to a cross-Capital marathon, someone will be able to help. And if all else fails, there's always London Transport. We've heard it's quite good these days...

Tutors and tutoring in London

Tutoring is endemic in the UK these days, and nowhere more so than in the capital, where top agencies have parents queueing to pay £70+ an hour to buy 3 year olds an advantage in the selection stakes. But keep your head, even if your child's already turned 2. Remember, an anxious mother and her money are soon parted, and the race has only just begun.

Two is too early

Seriously, there are folks out there offering to tutor children as young as 2, but it's all snake oil. Don't be taken in. Spend the money at one of London's wonderful bookshops and read to your child instead. What pre-school-age children need is not tutoring and angst, but time and love from the grown-ups who care for them. If you're reading this article, you are by default an educated, thinking parent who wants the best for your child, so give her the treasures of your mind, your vocabulary, your tastes; they will far out-class anything a paid charlatan can provide.

When do you need a tutor?

Put simply, when there is a clear and specific reason for using one. Your child may need help with the 11+ or 13+ entry to an academically selective senior school. Or perhaps he's struggling with a particular GCSE/A level subject. Or she may be falling behind at school. Or he may have missed school through illness or some other crisis. Where there is a known goal to work towards, or a genuine problem to address, tutoring comes into its own.

For a shy child who's under-performing, a friendly tutor can be a godsend. Free from the distractions of the classroom and other pupils, he or she can sit quietly with your child and concentrate solely on whatever's confusing her, filling in gaps in her knowledge and building up her confidence. Grades start to improve, and the child becomes a happier learner, keener to put her hand up in class and more relaxed about going to school. For a teenager who's struggling with maths, demoralised by always coming last in his set and stressed about approaching exams, quality one-to-one teaching from someone with no preconceptions about him can make the difference between failure and success; between giving up and keeping on.

It could be that you're putting your child through the state system to begin with while you save up for the independent senior school you hope he'll attend. If this is the case, he will need help with exam preparation. You may feel confident going through maths and English 11+ preparation books and past papers with him, but if not, tutoring is pretty much essential. No matter how bright your child, he'll be up against other children who have been intensively coached. If he's to stay in the game, you'll have to do likewise.

But tutoring is one of those things parents usually do in secret, either because they don't choose to tell it around that their child struggles at school, or because they've no wish to increase the opposition's chances in the race for places. Perhaps you feel your child needs a tutor even though he's already at a good preparatory school. Well, maybe. Be very sure, though, that the need is real. Depending on where he is, a year's tutoring in the run-up to common entrance may make sense, if only because it'll bring you peace of mind. But to have your tutored 7-year-old win a place at a high-achieving prep and then immediately start having him tutored some more just because everyone else is doing it, will only exhaust him and your bank account. Wave him off to St Brainiac's with a proud smile, and let the school do its work.

No matter now bright your child, he'll be up against other children who have been intensively coached. If he's to stay in the game, you'll have to do likewise

On the other hand, if you've just relocated to the UK from overseas, using a tutor is an excellent way to get your kids up to speed with the English system and help them to feel more assured and comfortable in lessons. This in turn will help them to make friends, and the whole settling-in process will be smoother. For a child in a new country, confidence is key.

If a person's replies to your messages are semi-literate, don't engage them as an English tutor

If you want a tutor for your child, how do you find one? The best way should be word of mouth, of course. But tutoring is one of those things parents usually do in secret, either because they don't choose to tell it around that their child struggles at school, or because they've no wish to increase the opposition's chances in the race for places. Try asking a friend with an older child, who won't begrudge your using what they no longer need. If this doesn't bring results, don't worry. This is London, and you have plenty of options.

Tutor companies

We review many of the best tutor companies on the Good Schools Guide website, and using them has a number of benefits. They'll be skilled at matching your child to the right person, and will give you redress if you're not happy. This is the most expensive way of employing a tutor, however. Almost all companies charge a registration fee, anything from a few quid to a hair-raising £180, and the hourly rate for tuition is high (be prepared for at least £45), because the company takes a cut before paying the teacher. Some of the really big tutorial companies cover too wide a geographical area to interview all their tutors in person, but they will have interviewed them by phone, and checked their references and DBS record.

Tutor websites

A cheaper option is finding a tutor online. There are a number of websites on which tutors can advertise, and whose contact details you buy, usually for around £20, after you've had an exchange of messages with your selected tutor to see if they're the right fit. Tuition rates vary from £16 ph – probably an undergraduate trying to earn a bit of extra cash – to £45+ ph for an experienced and qualified teacher. The website companies run checks to ascertain whether the tutor advertising is who they claim to be, but otherwise it's down to you to judge people's suitability. Websites like these can be very useful and we regularly hear reports from satisfied parents, ourselves included. Again, use your common sense. If a person's replies to your messages are semi-literate, don't engage them as an English tutor.

Don't believe them when they say they can get from Wood Green to Putney in half an hour, they absolutely can't

Do your homework

Self-employed individuals are unlikely to be DBS-checked, because the law prevents them from running a check on themselves, so ask to see references or to speak to previous clients. In fact, do this even if they are DBS-checked. Interview the tutor on the phone before fixing a first date, and don't feel pressured into accepting someone who doesn't sound right. Don't be afraid to sit in on the first lesson, and afterwards ask your child what she thought. If the tutor is travelling to you, check that they can get there easily. Don't believe them when they say they can get from Wood Green to Putney in half an hour, they absolutely can't. Lastly – and this wisdom comes from years of weary experience – insist on punctuality. A tutor who is routinely late will soon drive you up the wall.

With careful preparation, your child's tutoring experiences should be happy, productive and affordable. Good luck.

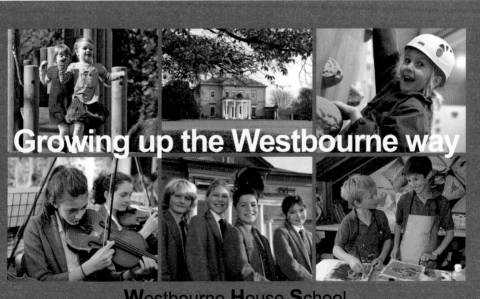

Child protection

If you are preparing to entrust your child to a school –
whether day or boarding – you will most likely assume that
your child will be safe and that all members of the school's
staff will take the greatest care to ensure that this is always
the case. The chances are that your expectations will be
fulfilled. Unfortunately, in a sad minority of cases that is not
what happens.

What can you do?

Parents can warn their children – gently but seriously – of
the dangers, however remote these may be, so they feel that
it is easy to speak to you should they meet them. It is worth
pointing out that abuse can come from anyone – including a
teacher or an adult they know well.

At any school you may be considering, inquire about the
steps taken to safeguard children in the same way you might
ask about bullying or learning support. As always, much can be
gleaned from the head's attitude when questions about child
protection are asked. Openness is what you're looking for.

For those who want to probe further:

Where can I find the school's child protection policy?
Every school is required to have a child protection policy that
is made available to staff, volunteers and parents on request.

*Where can I and my children find out who the child protection
officers are?*
Ideally, a school should have more than one designated
person and they should be named on a public notice board,
so that everyone knows who to talk to.

What training do staff receive in child protection?
Training is mandatory every two years for designated officers,
and every three years for all staff who work with children.

Is it the school's written policy to report child protection allegations to the Local Authority Designated Officer ('LADO')?

A good head will have a good working relationship with their LADO, so that both can have confidence that incidents will be well managed.

How many 'referrals' have been made to the Department of Education in the past three years and for what reasons?

A referral means a member of staff has left the school in circumstances which indicate they were unfit to work with children. Do not rule out a school because a case of abuse has been brought to light there. Tabloid coverage can be the price the school has to pay for handling a case of abuse or bullying openly.

Further reading

The Good Schools Guide 20th edition
Features independent and unbiased views of over 1,200 state and independent schools throughout Britain, written by parents for parents.

The Good Schools Guide online subscription
Read all our reviews plus exam data, catchment maps, university entrance information, and advice on choosing a school, tutors, SEN, talented children and much more.

Uni in the USA
Written by students who have been through the US system, features in-depth descriptions of 65 US universities, plus the inside track on getting in and preparing for life across the pond.

Uni in the USA and Beyond online subscription and ebook
Also includes unis in Europe and the East, from Alberta to Abu Dhabi, and advice from SATS to visas.

The Good Schools Guide International online subscription
The one-stop educational shop for ex-pats, it reviews the best state and independent schools round the globe, plus insider knowledge on life overseas.

All available via www.goodschoolsguide.co.uk/shop-online

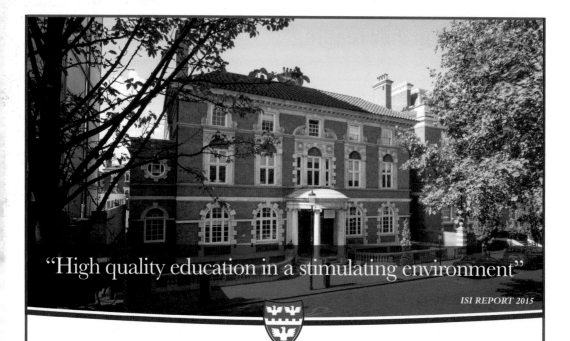

Educating mind, body, heart & soul

Open Mornings: Friday 20 November 2015, Thursday 10 March, Tuesday 19 April 2016

To see first hand how we can help your daughter to flourish academically, to develop her talents – wherever they lie – and discover hidden ones, join us for an open morning or personal visit.

- **New Sixth Form Centre**
- **Oxbridge Success**
- **Full & Weekly Boarding**
- **Creative Thinking**

01435 874642
admissions@mayfieldgirls.org
The Old Palace, Mayfield, East Sussex TN20 6PH
www.mayfieldgirls.org

Mayfield

An independent Catholic boarding
and day school for girls aged 11 to 18

BERKHAMSTED

The School that grows with you

BERKHAMSTED day nursery

BERKHAMSTED
PRE-PREP

BERKHAMSTED
PREP

BERKHAMSTED
GIRLS

BERKHAMSTED
BOYS

BERKHAMSTED
SIXTH

- 30 minutes direct by train from Euston
- Situated in an historic market town with easy links to Heathrow
- Consistently high academic results, achieved alongside a broad co-curricular timetable
- Diamond School, Co-education (3-11) (16-18) and Single Sex (11-16)
- Supporting working parents through extended hours and holiday care

For more information on admissions and scholarships call
01442 358001 or visit our website www.berkhamstedschool.org

London South school index

School	Region	Page

London South districts index

List of advertisers

Notes

Notes

Notes